For the Parish

For the Parish

A Critique of Fresh Expressions

Andrew Davison
and Alison Milbank

scm press

© Andrew Davison and Alison Milbank 2010

Published in 2010 by SCM Press
Editorial office
13–17 Long Lane,
London, EC1A 9PN, UK

SCM Press is an imprint of Hymns Ancient and Modern Ltd
(a registered charity)
13A Hellesdon Park Road
Norwich, NR6 5DR
www.scm-canterburypress.co.uk

Second impression 2011

Scripture quotations are from the New Revised Standard Version of the
Bible, copyright © 1989 by the Division of Christian Education of the
National Council of the Churches of Christ in the USA.

Extracts from *Common Worship: Services and Prayers for the Church of
England* are copyright © The Archbishops' Council 2000 and reproduced
by permission.

British Library Cataloguing in Publication data

A catalogue record for this book is available
from the British Library

978-0-334-04365-2

Originated by The Manila Typesetting Company
Printed and bound by
CPI Antony Rowe, Chippenham SN14 6LH

Contents

Introduction

This book is written in the belief that an important choice is offered to the Church of England: to embrace her historic mission
to evangelize and serve the whole people of this country, or to
decline into a sect. We are responding to the most significant development in the Church of England in recent years: the 2004
report, *Mission-shaped Church*, and the subsequent encouragement of extra-parochial congregations, called 'Fresh Expressions
of Church'.[1] The report and the initiatives launched at its prompting are an attempt to respond to what is perceived to be the near-
complete secularization of Britain and the hegemony of market
values. While the aim of engaging with our contemporary context is admirable, it is done, we argue, on the basis of a defective
methodology, an inadequate theology, and by accepting the very
choice-led individualism from which Christianity should seek to
liberate us. It is a capitulation to market values rather than a critique where it is most needed or a counter-cultural vision of the
kingdom.

What is new about these Fresh Expressions initiatives as of-
ficially conceived is that they are not intended to be out-workings
of the mission of the local church but independent entities without
any relation to the parish in which they operate. They are not the
sorts of Christian communities modelled by the parish, open to all.
They are special interest groups: 'church' whether of bikers, book-
group members or participants in any other leisure activity or de-
mographic that defines the consumerist criterion for membership.

---

1 *Mission-shaped Church: Church Planting and Fresh Expressions of Church in
a Changing Context*, 2004, London: Church House Publishing. All other references
are to this edition and are noted in the text.

For the Parish

On the frail foundation of only nineteen pages devoted to theology in the *Mission-shaped Church* report, a massive redirection of mission and ecclesiology has been effected. A new orthodoxy, with cultural, financial and legal implications for the whole Church, has taken hold, but with little ·discussion about the biblical and theological foundations on which it is based. On the surface, it may appear that the inherited parochial system can carry on as before, but if it does, the older understanding no longer defines the Church of England's ecclesiology. If Fresh Expressions is as equally valid a form of life for the Anglican Church as the parish, then what is common to both forms, the defining minimum of our identity, is greatly contracted. Since one is forbidden from suggesting that there is anything lacking from the vision of the Church embodied in Fresh Expressions, its attenuated ecclesiology thereby becomes the new contracted norm. This has implications not only for the Church's self-understanding but also our conception of salvation, as we explore in Chapter 3 of the present volume.

In what follows, we offer a thoroughgoing critique of Fresh Expressions on theological and philosophical grounds. In particular, we deprecate the way in which the movement seeks to separate form and content, with the assumption that the essence of the Church exists separately from its living forms of expression. On the basis of this assumption: adherents of Fresh Expressions believe that the Church can be divested of her inherited practices, structures and disciplines and go on to be 're-expressed' in new ways, with little or no sense of loss. In Chapter 1 we draw upon a wide range of theological and philosophical sources to argue for the inextricability of form and content, Wittgenstein among them–for whom values, meanings and convictions do not so much lie *beneath* our communal behaviour and 'forms of life' as *in* them. The separation of form and content is one aspect of a further theological error: a profound unease with mediation. Chapter 2 demonstrates the centrality of mediation to any Christian account of redemption, and Chapter 3 uses St Paul's Epistles to show how unbiblical the *Mission-shaped Church* account of the Church has become in its desire to underplay the corporeal and participatory aspects of ecclesiology.

Introduction

The Fresh Expressions model of the sector, choice-led worshipping group represents a flight away from the mixed community of the parish and towards segregation, as we argue in Chapter 4. The network of consumer choice is privileged over the parish as a site of difference and reconciliation, following the 'Homogeneous Unit Principle' of American Protestantism. It is also a flight from the value of tradition, common worship and the embodied self. The abandonment of stability for novelty and given liturgy for 'choice', results in banality and pastiche, as well as a frail and atomized subjectivity, as we demonstrate in Chapter 5.

In Chapters 6–9, we turn to a defence of the inherited parish system, which is routinely belittled and cast as unhelpful and irrelevant in Fresh Expressions writing. We argue the opposite: that the parish, nested in deanery and diocese, is poised to be a vital resource for mission in the future. We begin by sketching the theology of mission implicit in the parish vision of salvation in Chapter 6, with an examination of the value of locality, placement and inclusiveness represented by the parish church in Chapter 7. In Chapter 8 the task of rebuilding the Christian imaginary of time, place and narrative is described in detail, while Chapter 9 shows how our engagement in liturgy as a form of life develops the Christian virtues as much by gesture, space and movement as by what we say. These practical chapters aim to show how form and content work together to our human flourishing within the mediating structure of the local church.

This book is the fruit of a conference, 'Returning to the Church', held by St Stephen's House in Oxford in collaboration with the Centre of Theology and Philosophy at the University of Nottingham in January 2009, at which a fruitful mixture of lay people, students, bishops, curates and academics came together to explore the traditions and future mission of the Church of England. Our two papers, on the importance of the parish and on the value of mediation struck such a chord with the delegates that we were commissioned to go away and unite them into a pamphlet, which has become this book. The conference was energetic and positive, and people visibly unfurled as we were able to speak about and value the ordinary practices, disciplines and ministries of Anglican life.

There was also, however, a strong feeling of disenfranchisement, of a disconnect between classic Anglicanism and the growing orthodoxy of Fresh Expressions, and, in particular, of the way in which the 'mixed economy' idea sanctions part of the Church floating free from Anglican norms.

In what follows, we have no desire to criticize the valuable work of reaching out to the unchurched in mission and service. As priests ourselves, we see this as part of our own vocation and the natural outflowing of the parochial system's cure of souls. Lynda Barley reported to the General Synod in 2007 that over 50 percent of parishes had launched or were about to embark on a Fresh Expression.[2] Where we take issue is the way in which first, the group centred around the extra-liturgical activity of football or the book-group is to stand on its own as a church, and second, in the marketing model of the Faith as a commodity, which is cheerfully embraced by synod members such as Michael Streeter, for whom the church 'is a consumer product', and which is implicit in the terminology of Fresh Expressions (which as we discovered, is already a commodity in the American supermarket: a brand of scented cat litter)[3].

This is unapologetically a work of theology, which is the subject least valued in recent reallocation of resources and in the literature surrounding the Fresh Expressions developments. It is wholly Anglican in seeing a direct link between the *lex orandi* and the *lex credendi*: how we pray expresses the manner in which we conceive God and the world. We wish to offer a theology that will restore the flagging morale of parish clergy, who often feel undervalued and unresourced, and that will allow us confidently to re-engage with our own tradition in the broadest sense of the term. We also hope that our critique might change the hearts of those who still seek the separation of what are often highly estimable outreach initiatives from the parishes in which they are based, and signal the end of the segregation of the 'mixed economy' approach to ecclesiology. Our

---

2 Report to General Synod, February 2007, p. 43.
3 'Fresh Expressions Lavender Valley Scoopable Cat Litter' is available at www. petco.com.

country is crying out for a rebirth of locality, of counter-cultural values that resist the market, and for the restoration of social bonds. We know that these goods are only fully realized 'in Christ', through his body the Church, into which we were baptized. Let us then pursue all that makes for peace and builds up our *common* life.

The Union of Form and Content

Mission-shaped Church is a flawed document. Yet, at present, it determines the shape of ecclesiology in the Church of England. The flaws of the report are both theological and philosophical. We will highlight some of the theological concerns. Behind many of them lies a philosophical mistake that is too significant to pass over. Theology is the fulfilment of philosophy. All the same, theology needs philosophy if it is to expound the Christian revelation with clarity and consistency. The underlying philosophical mistake is that the forms of the Church are one thing and its inner reality is another. This is the mistake of attempting to disentangle 'form' from 'content'.

As the report sees it, the Church can take an endless number of forms. In each case it is the same Church, but expressed in different ways. We can change the practices of the Church, her forms of life, as and when we like, to fit in with the surrounding culture. This treats the disciplines and practices of the Church as so much outward clothing.

The argument of Fresh Expressions would make no sense unless the 'outward forms' of the Church were one thing and the inner message or essence of the Church another. It allows for radical changes in the way the Church lives without – as they assure us – reinventing the Church of England in the process. We argue that this is a mistake. Form and content are much more closely bound up with one another. The theoretical basis for Fresh Expressions rests on a mistake about 'expression'.

It is certainly possible to make a distinction between form and content. The distinction is a useful one. By 'content' we mean what the Church is about: its message, purpose and identity. By 'form' we mean the way this is lived and embodied. Form relates to what we call practices and disciplines of the Church. It is obvious that we can *distinguish* these two ideas; the mistake is to suppose that we can *separate* them. They are bound together: the content is in the form; the meaning is in the practices. Change the form and we change how we understand the content; change the practices and we at least risk changing the meaning. That is what we argue in this chapter.

For an excellent example of the interweaving of inward 'meaning' (or message) and outward 'form' (or practice), we have only to turn to *Mission-shaped Church* itself. The authors describe the pioneering work of Vincent Donovan among the Masai in East Africa:

> Significant cultural challenges arose. A notable example was that Masai men and women do not eat meals together. Communion then raised very basic issues. But the converted Masai understood that the change of their beliefs included that Christ made different kinds of people one, because they were equally loved, and this pattern would have to change. So men and women of the Masai 'brotherhood of God' (their name for church) ate together for the first time – ever. (pp. 92–3)

The association of Christians across old divisions and differences is an important way in which the forms of the Church embody its Faith. This example is all the more striking since the report itself endorses segregated communities and the idea of the 'homogeneous unit principle', as we will discuss in Chapter 4.

The language of fashion and fusion

To see the extent to which form and content are dissociated in Fresh Expressions we need only notice how fond these authors are of metaphors of fabric, fashion and clothing. 'The gospel', they say, 'may have many clothes, but there is only one gospel' (p. 97). According to our analysis in terms of form and content,

The Union of Form and Content

the gospel here is the content; its 'clothes' are the forms. In another passage the report describes the attitude of young people towards 'denominations'[1] in terms of shopping for clothes. The various traditions of the Churches amount to no more than 'different types of clothing, most of which are not thought "cool"' (p. 25). Whether or not this is what young people think about the Church, the report does nothing to challenge it. The authors might wish that the denominations were held in higher esteem than they are, but they do not fault the terms of the analysis. For them, as for the putative 'young people', the forms of the Church really are so many fashion options. Our inherited ways of 'being church' are simply outward forms that clothe, this way or that, some inner essence of the Church.

The clothing metaphor comes into its own towards the end of the report, in a headline recommendation: 'there is a fabric of the old way of being society and being church. We are not about patching the fabric of that old garment but seeking to set up a new loom to weave the new fabric for tomorrow's society of the kingdom' (p. 126). The authors leave us in no doubt. They want a radical upheaval, a disjunction between the old garment and the new, between old ways of 'being church' and new ones. This disjunction works only on the basis of the prior conceptual disjunction: between body and clothes, form and content.

Alongside fabric metaphors, the authors also write a great deal about 'style'. On the one hand, there is the underlying essence of the Church and the simple message of the gospel. On the other hand, there is the outward 'style' taken by any particular 'expression of church'. For *Mission-shaped Church* the practices and disciplines of the inherited church are just one of many potential 'styles of doing and being church' (p. 80). In this world of 'style', everything is up for change. The authors are quite clear that we must welcome any number of new styles into the Church of England. They are also quite clear that there is no reason why these new

---

1 It is already to yield a great deal of ground to think of the Church of England as simply one denomination among many in this country. Historically, this is not how we have seen ourselves, nor does it reflect our legal position.

3

styles should bear any resemblance to what has gone before. Even more than that, it would be *wrong* to expect that sort of resemblance. The inner meaning of the church and its outward forms are so entirely separable that when a group 'plants' a new church it cannot possibly 'begin with a clear understanding of what form of expression the resultant church may take' (p. 30). The shape or form of the church floats free, this time from anything that has gone before.

The theory behind all of this comes to the surface in words that the authors borrow[2] from the Lausanne Haslev Consultation.[3] 'There are many', they lament, 'who still fuse the meaning and forms of the gospel' (p. 91).[4] We should note the tone of exasperation at this point: some people fuse meaning and forms; how foolish they are! The enlightened reader is supposed to recognize that the 'meaning' and 'forms' of the gospel are very different things. Upon this everything else rests.

The two authors of this book are among those who still 'fuse the meaning and forms of the gospel', and with them, the meaning and forms of the Church. We are supposed to be on the back foot here. With this book we wish to prove that we are not. The

---

2 It is a feature of Church of England reports in recent years that they make some of their most significant points by means of quotations from other authors. In earlier decades each point was argued in full rather than resting on such (often relatively minor) authorities. This trend towards using the words of others may represent a lack of confidence in the teaching office of the contemporary Church of England. Alternatively, it may suggest confusion as to the purpose of these documents and, in particular, whether they speak for the Church of England in any official sense. Once, Church reports laid out the content of the Faith; now they function as 'discussion documents'. Consequently, the style has shifted away from argument and the integration of points within a narrative under the control of the author or authors towards the presentation of a pot-pourri of ideas and citations for the purposes of subsequent discussion and consultation. The question then arises whether acceptance of such a 'discussion document' by General Synod constitutes an authority for root and branch reconfiguration of the Church.

3 In its own words, the Lausanne Movement is 'a worldwide movement that mobilizes evangelical leaders to collaborate for world evangelization' (www.lausanne. org).

4 Quoting *Report of the Lausanne Haslev Consultation: Contextualization Revisited*, 1997. No page number given.

mistake is not associating the form and content of the Church, but rather to disassociate them. The message and purpose of the Church are to be found *in* the way she lives and worship. When it comes to the union of form and content, it is the Fresh Expressions writers who are out of date. It is difficult to imagine that a philosophically informed writer of any age would prise form and content apart so glibly. It is all the more remarkable for *Mission-shaped Church* to argue in these terms in 2004, coming after a century when Western thought became all the more aware how closely form and content are entwined. In this chapter we will establish this point from a number of philosophical sources. First, however, for an exercise in common sense.

The meaning is in the form

Imagine I tell you that my best feature is my boundless hospitality. I want to be like nothing so much as a Benedictine monk, giving food and shelter to all who come my way. Imagine also that my house is surrounded by a tall fence, with barbed wire and a guard-dog. You would not believe my claims. The form of my life would belie my message. As another example, think how much we say about ourselves by the way we dress. It would be incongruous for a headmistress famed for her strictness to wear a tracksuit to school. It would be incongruous for a headmaster known for his low-key approach to discipline to wear a three-piece suit. We would expect them to dress in a way that lines up with the way they exercise their authority. The image they create for themselves is an important part of how they get their job done. We make use of these 'cultural symbolics' all the time: those complex cultural codes to which we are all finely attuned.

The best example that Christian theology provides of the relation of form and content is in the theology of the sacraments. Here there is the most intimate link between the outward elements and the inner reality, between bread, wine and water on the one hand and the grace they convey on the other. The Church is herself a kind of sacrament – an outward sign of an inward and invisible grace. Many of the principles that apply to the sacraments also apply to the Church.

It is no quirk that we use bread and wine for Holy Communion or that we use water for baptism. The sign used in the sacrament is consistent with what the sacrament promises and bestows. Here form and content belong together, for all the 'form' is natural and the 'content' is supernatural. For instance, when Christ chose bread and wine, he identified himself with both the ordinary and the joyful. Bread shows that the life we receive from God is not a supplement or luxury. Without it, we cannot properly live. Christ is not a gourmet dish but our 'daily bread'. At the same time, the life of Christ is 'abundant life', not just more of the humdrum same. Because of that, he offers himself to us in wine, not water. None of this is captured by pizza and a Coca-Cola. That is why the Church of England insists that we celebrate Holy Communion with bread and wine: 'the bread, whether leavened or unleavened, shall be of the best and purest wheat flour that conveniently may be gotten, and the wine the fermented juice of the grape, good and wholesome.'[5] Similarly, the material element for baptism is water. As the common practice from the earliest times it is 'living' or flowing water. This is because baptism washes away sin and brings eternal life.

The sacraments were instituted wisely. In each one many different aspects of symbolism come together. The water of baptism, for instance, is primarily an indication of washing, but it also evokes refreshment and sustenance. For that reason we could not baptize someone in detergent. It would express only one part of what baptism is. Baptism is washing but not only washing. Water, and baptism, has nothing of the harshness of soap. The Church has a sacramental function. In her 'outward and visible' life we encounter the 'inward and invisible' grace of the life of Christ. That invites us to show a little more caution in changing those outward forms – a little more caution than the Church of England has, of late, been willing to admit.

---

5 Canon B 17.2, available at www.cofe.anglican.org/about/churchlawlegis/canons/sacraments.pdf.

The Union of Form and Content
Lessons from aesthetics: what is lost in translation?

Fresh Expressions are presented to us as a sort of translation. They take the Christian tradition, supposedly encumbered by the practices of the inherited church (as the parishes are now often called), and present it in the language of our times. They translate the Church into expressions fit for the twenty-first century. Invocation of translation brings us to the area of philosophy known as aesthetics, which is a good place to examine in relation of form and content.[6]

Roger Scruton covers this ground in his recent book entitled *Beauty*.[7] He argues that form and content are so closely bound together in a work of art that the content is precisely *in* the form. This accounts for one of the more uncanny features of art: we know that a particular work of art means something but we cannot say what it is. This is because the meaning is in the form of the work itself. Any translation of that meaning into another form would be a loss. We cannot describe in words what we encounter with our eyes. This also means that whatever a particular painting communicates or 'has to say' cannot be represented by another painting or photograph of the same subject.[8] As Scruton puts it, 'the real meaning of the painting is *bound up with, inseparable from*, the image . . . and cannot be translated completely into another idiom.'[9]

Over the second half of the twentieth century, this language and these ideas have found currency in Christian theology, not least because of the pioneering work of the Swiss theologian Hans Urs von Balthasar and his seven-volume work *The Glory of the*

---

6 We do not intend to subjugate theology to philosophy. It is simply that no one can undertake the work of theology without making use of the tools of thought. These are what philosophy can provide. We are willing to make use of any discipline, albeit critically, which seeks to make clear the nature of things or provide us with the means to think clearly and incisively. Our principle is that of 1 Thessalonians 5.21: 'test everything; hold fast to what is good.'

7 Roger Scruton, 2009, *Beauty*, Oxford: Oxford University Press.

8 The meaning of the work of art cannot be translated into words because 'it is a particular content *as presented* – seen, in other words, as inseparable from form and style' (Scruton, *Beauty*, p. 111). The emphasis is in the original.

9 Scruton, *Beauty*, p. 110. The emphasis is in the original.

Lord. Here, among many other ideas of great value, we find an exploration of Christology in terms of the inseparability of form and content.[10] In Christ, all the elements of his life and person come together in his *form*. His person, actions and preaching are inseparable within this whole, as are his divinity and his humanity.[11] Here the Church imitates the Head of which she is the Body. For her also, her identity and her forms of life, her actions and her message are all of a piece.

Returning to aesthetics, the same dynamic that we noticed in the visual arts is at work in poetry. We know that we are dealing with a *poem* when what we have in front of us could not be paraphrased without missing the point. Any attempt to extract the meaning and express it prosaically would do violence to the poem. Scruton makes this point in *Beauty*.[12] The poet Robert Frost had already said the same thing: 'poetry is what is lost in translation. It is also what is lost in interpretation.'[13] The Italians have a pleasing and accurate proverb, *tradurre e tradire*: translation is treason.[14]

---

10 See, for instance, Hans Urs von Balthasar, 1982, *The Glory of the Lord: A Theological Aesthetics, Volume 1: Seeing the Form*, Part 3, 'The Objective Evidence', Edinburgh: T&T Clark.

11 Balthasar's work helped to precipitate a widespread revival in theological work on beauty and aesthetics ('theological aesthetics'). A good introduction is the anthology edited by Gesa Thiessen, 2004, *Theological Aesthetics: A Reader*, London: SCM Press.

12 Scruton, *Beauty*, pp. 108–13, 140.

13 Edward Lathem, 1966, *Interviews with Robert Frost*, New York: Holt, Rinehart and Winston, p. 203.

14 For an exploration of philosophical writing on this theme see John Sallis, 2002, *On Translation*, Indiana University Press, pp. 72 and 104. See also George Steiner, 1998, *After Babel: Aspects of Language and Translation*, New York: Oxford University Press. This proverb can be seen to apply all the more generally after work in the twentieth century showed that the metaphorical way of writing we associate with poetry is not confined to poetry. It is the rule for all of language. For the definitive statement see George Johnson and Mark Lakoff, 2003, *Metaphors We Live By*, Chicago: University of Chicago Press. Metaphors allow us to build up meaningful sentences by bleeding one set of references into another. Since metaphor goes all the way down, so does this colouration. There is no style-less, analytic and non-poetic speech that dispenses with metaphor. Consequently, all re-expression involves using another frame of reference and, ultimately, replacing one set of metaphors with another. To change the metaphor is, at least subtly, to change the content.

The Union of Form and Content

We do not mean to suggest that the form of the Church has not evolved, slowly and over time. Nor are we saying that all 'translation' of the Church into new situations is wrong or futile. We *are* saying, throughout the first half of this book, that form and content are more closely bound together than the Fresh Expressions writers suppose or are willing to admit.

In the Church as in the poem, the message is in the form. In neither case can we simply extract the meaning and rearticulate it in a new form without loss. One reason for this is that so many things count – in both the life of the Church and in the poem – and in so many ways. The traditional patterns and disciplines of the life in the Church embody the Faith and they do so on many different levels. To extend our literary parallel, this is like the levels of meaning and invocation in a poem. To use a word of Scruton's, the potential meanings of the poem are 'polysemous'[15] (meaning many things), and so are the multifaceted practices of the Church.

This suggests a fruitful line of analysis when it comes to Fresh Expressions. Any particular Fresh Expression may well embody one aspect of the Church's life and mission extremely well. It is unlikely that it will embody them all, or even very many of them. It may be that a Fresh Expression lives out one element of the Church's life *more clearly* than the forms of the inherited church were able. It might embody accessibility, or creativity, or work with the old, or the young. This has its advantages, but it also has its disadvantages.

For one thing, a Fresh Expression is tailored to one situation, so when the situation changes it will lack wider resources. In contrast, the deeply layered life of the inherited church allows it to face the widest variety of situations. In this way, parish churches maintain their witness over centuries. It is the parish church, in the end, that is able to change and adapt. The Fresh Expression will simply fold when it has run its relatively brief course – or turn into something much more like a parish church.

In contrast to the Fresh Expression, the parish church is committed to the longest possible time-scale. It intends to be in the community

---

15 Scruton, *Beauty*, p. 112.

9

For the Parish

as long as the community exists. In this way, parish churches can gain enormous standing in a community. Through their deep-rooted commitment to people and place, they have the resources to minister in good times and in bad, in war and peace, prosperity and adversity, and to adapt as the locality changes. During his curacy, one of us was profoundly aware that the warmth of the community towards the parish church and its priests was the fruit of eighty years of faithful ministry by those who had been there before: 'others have laboured, and you have entered into their labour' (John 4.38).[16] Our purpose with this book is to call for a reflection upon dynamics at work here, and a greater degree of awareness that there are losses when old forms are lightly discarded.

Ludwig Wittgenstein

The most significant consideration of form and content in the last century came from the Austrian philosopher Ludwig Wittgenstein. Born in Vienna in 1889, he spent much of his adult life in England. His work could not be more pertinent for understanding the systematic error that lies at the heart of *Mission-shaped Church*.

A great many theologians have recognized the significance of Wittgenstein for Christian thought. We are particularly in debt to the Dominican Fergus Kerr and his *Theology after Wittgenstein*.[17] When the history of theology in the late-twentieth century is written, his book will be seen to have caused a minor sea change all of its own.

Wittgenstein's work falls into two halves. We will be concerned with the latter portion.[18] It represents one of the most revolutionary, white-hot outpourings of ideas in the history of philosophy. It is summed up in the *Philosophical Investigations*, published

---

16 All biblical references unless specified are to *The Holy Bible containing the Old and New Testaments with the Apocryphal/Deuterocanonical Books: New Revised Standard Version*, 1995, Oxford, Oxford University Press.

17 Fergus Kerr, 1986 (2nd edn, 1997), *Theology after Wittgenstein*, Oxford: Blackwell.

18 The first period culminated in his *Tractatus Logico-Philosophicus*.

The Union of Form and Content

only after his death.[19] The principle insight we will take from Wittgenstein is that we cannot understand how language works without recognizing just how much speaking is bound up with acting and belonging together to a community. In particular, for Wittgenstein, we have a common understanding of what words mean – which is what language is about – because we also share common practices.

Wittgenstein insisted that language is a thoroughly communal affair. So is everything that flows from it, such as identity, conviction and meaning. In this 'communitarian turn', Wittgenstein had certain excesses of Enlightenment thought in his sights. The tendency had been to treat human beings as autonomous and isolated thinkers. Each of us, on this account, is supremely self-assured in the solitude of his or her own mind.[20] It is in this mental isolation that we are supposed to be most ourselves. We sally forth into the realm of communal relations only when we need to, in search of some particular goal: to work, eat or reproduce. Wittgenstein denied this. He rejected the priority of the individual over the social and cast things the other way round. In many ways, the communal comes first. It is obvious that we owe our natural life to others, to our parents and those who nurtured us. In just that sort of way, we also 'come to birth' as thinking, self-aware people within the human community – again thanks to others.[21]

The key to appreciating this is to consider the role of language. Without language we cannot grow into what it means to be a human being. Crucially, we only learn language thorough contact within the human community. Equally crucially, for Wittgenstein,

---

19 Ludwig Wittgenstein, 1953, *Philosophical Investigations*, ed. G. E. M. Anscombe, Oxford: Blackwell.

20 As modern people we tend to think that a person understands the world in the 'epistemological solitude of the individual consciousness', as Kerr puts it. In the words of Wittgenstein, 'Nothing is more wrong-headed than calling meaning a mental activity,' *Philosophical Investigations*, §693, quoted in Kerr, *Theology after Wittgenstein*, p. 42.

21 For a discussion of the priority of the communal in Christian ecclesiology, see Chapter 3.

For the Parish

we learn language as part of our gradual induction into practices of common life.[22] Kerr summarizes this clearly:

It is established practices, customary reactions and interactions, and so on, that constitute the element in which one's consciousness is created and sustained: my sense of myself, not to mention the contents of my mind and memory, depend essentially on my being with others, my being in touch with others, of my physical and psychological kind . . . Nothing is more foundational to the whole human enterprise than the community that we create in our natural reactions to one another.[23]

Even in something as seemingly inward and individual as my 'consciousness' and 'sense of self' emerges only out of a shared life, with its 'established practices, customary reactions and interactions'. Our existence is a shared existence and it becomes intelligible only through distinctive, shared ways of life. Language allows us to understand ourselves, and our practices, but it also works the other way round. Language gets its intelligibility from the shared practices in which it is embodied.[24] Wittgenstein called these 'forms of life', or *Lebensform* in German.[25]

---

22 Ludwig Wittgenstein, *Philosophical Investigations*, §19.

23 Kerr, *Theology after Wittgenstein*, p. 76.

24 For Kerr, Wittgenstein's insight is that our sense of the meaning of things is worked out and taken on board at the level of 'the practical exchanges that constitute the public world which we inhabit together', *Theology after Wittgenstein*, p. 45. As an illustration of this, we need only think of the debt we owe to others for having been taught a language.

25 David Tracy makes a link between Wittgenstein's 'forms of life' and the 'mode of being in the world', associated principally with Martin Heidegger (David Tracy, 1996, *Blessed Rage for Order: The New Pluralism*, Chicago: University of Chicago Press, p. 101 and associated footnotes). As Tracy puts it, for both moral and religious language there are 'forms of life which each discloses'. As Tracy comments, this is something that even the secular world recognizes about 'religion'. The prevailing culture, even if it does not believe what the Church believes, sees that the Church is potent in its 'paradigms, parables, stories, and rituals' (that is to say, what we are calling the practices, disciplines and patterns of the inherited church). Even the atheist sees that these communal stories and practices are 'reasonably useful' for 'being moral'. They are still celebrated by many outside the Church as able to stimulate us, or at least our children, 'to perform the right, the ethical action'.

The Union of Form and Content

Towards the beginning of the *Investigations*, Wittgenstein puts this idea succinctly: 'to imagine a language means to imagine a form of life'.[26] A community is bound together by its language on the one hand and by its forms of life on the other – and the two are not really such different things. Some examples might be helpful. Our parents did not teach us the definition of a fork in abstract isolation. We learned what a fork is by seeing forks in use, and by learning to use them ourselves. The same principle applies to cups, books and magnetic resonance spectrometers. It is also by induction into practices and through communal interactions that we learn what it means to be a friend or an outsider, or what it means to forgive or to pray. In summary, words can only mean something to us because they relate to certain ways of life: 'words have meaning only in the stream of life',[27] as Wittgenstein put it. Language is a 'practice', in the sense of there being *practices* that 'gives words their sense'.[28]

It follows from these ideas that knowing, believing and meaning demand to be understood within a distinctively communal sense and setting. Our beliefs and understandings are not the labour of the isolated mind. The work of understanding the world is something we do together. Our identity is fashioned in the ordinary to and fro of our communal habits and disciplines. In the words of Fergus Kerr, 'what constitutes us as human beings is the regular and patterned reactions that we have to one another. It is in our dealings with each other – in how we *act* – that human life is founded.'[29]

---

26 Wittgenstein, *Philosophical Investigations*, § 19, quoted in Kerr, *Theology after Wittgenstein*, p. 29.

27 Ludwig Wittgenstein, 1980, *Remarks on the Philosophy of Psychology*, ed. G. E. M. Anscombe, G. H. von Wright and Heikki Nyman, trans. G. E. M. Anscombe, C. G. Luckhardt and M. A. E. Aue, 2 vols, Oxford: Blackwell, 1980, vol. 2, p. 687. Quoted in Kerr, *Theology after Wittgenstein*, p. 134.

28 Ludwig Wittgenstein, 1980, *Culture and Value*, ed. G. H. von Wright with Heikki Nyma, trans. Peter Winch, Oxford: Blackwell, 1980, p. 85. Quoted in Kerr, *Theology after Wittgenstein*, p. 152. As Terry Eagleton puts it, 'a word for Wittgenstein acquires meaning through its use; and this involves it entering into rule-governed relations with other signs in a specific form of life' (Terry Eagleton, 2008, *Trouble with Strangers*, Oxford: Wiley-Blackwell, p. 6).

29 Kerr, *Theology after Wittgenstein*, p. 65. Kerr is commenting on Ludwig Wittgenstein, 1967, *Zettel*, ed. G. E. M. Anscombe and G. H. von Wright, trans. G. E. M. Anscombe, Oxford: Blackwell, pp. 567–9.

For the Parish

As a consequence, it is usually quite obvious what a group of people hold to be true and significant: you see it in the way they behave. Our convictions are not *beneath* the actions somewhere; they are *in* the actions. To see what matters most for a group or for a person, we need only look at what is *ordinary* for them: what is regular, habitual and conventional. It is there, in the practical, commonplace features of our everyday lives that our basic, governing convictions are to be found.

Wittgenstein offers a startling new perspective. If we follow him, we will no longer think of human identity as something ethereally 'spiritual', abstract or internal. It is found in our actions. It is something that we grow into together. Similarly, Christian identity is formed and matures in the context of a common life of Christian practices. Redemption and transformation are not 'merely spiritual', not something abstract and inward. They are worked out in our relationships and forms of life. The church is the place where new ways of living and relating take shape. That is why the shape that the life of the Church takes matters so much. It is in the practices and disciplines of the Church that our faith is embodied. It is through them that our identity and convictions are refashioned. The form of the Church is the mould; by it the life of the Christian is re-patterned.[30]

This suggests certain consequences for Christian discipleship, most of all that it is a matter of practical initiation. The Church has usually approached discipleship in this way. It has long been aware that common practices shape our identity. Wittgenstein denied 'that one is able to get hold of anything independently of one's being initiated into certain common practices'.[31] The Church has known this from the beginning. In the Early Church, conversion was profoundly bound up with joining the Christian community and adopting its way of life. This dimension of conversion was as important as learning and assenting to ideas. This explains the emphasis given to *mystagogy*: the convert had to

---

30 As Kerr puts it, 'I discover myself, not in some pre-linguistic inner space of self-presence, but in the network of multifarious social and historical relationships in which I am willy-nilly involved.' Kerr, *Theology After Wittgenstein*, p. 69.

31 Kerr, *Theology after Wittgenstein*, p. 104.

be instructed and inducted into the liturgical disciplines of the Church in order to be formed as a Christian. In contrast, Fresh Expressions stand for undoing any sense of a 'church culture' and minimizing any sense that the convert need change her forms of life.

Wittgenstein did not particularly have the Church in mind when he wrote any of this. His attitude towards Christianity was by turns dismissive and respectful. It bemused even his closest friends and most perceptive commentators.[32] He was not concerned with Christian redemption, but he was certainly interested in sanity and wholeness. And here he saw the importance of ways of life and communal practices: 'the sickness of a time is cured by a change in a people's way of life.'[33]

Forms of Life and *Mission-shaped Church*

Wittgenstein led a sea change in contemporary thought: there are no disembodied ideas; convictions are not separate from ways of life. Nobody contests that the Church expresses her beliefs in words. We need to appreciate that her beliefs are also to be found in her disciplines and the ways in which she orders her common life. Our practices are not so much window dressing. They are the arena in which our convictions are learned and held. It is precisely these disciplines and forms of life that are being re-written in *Mission-shaped Church* and re-invented in Fresh Expressions.

The practical changes that *Mission-shaped Church* invites are not at all minor. There is a far greater contrast between the inherited church and Fresh Expressions than might appear at first

---

32 Kerr points us to the comment of Elizabeth Anscombe, recorded by Norman Malcolm, that nobody understood where Wittgenstein stood in relation to religion. Norman Malcolm, 1984, *Ludwig Wittgenstein: A Memoir*, Oxford: Oxford University Press, p. 18.

33 Ludwig Wittgenstein, 1978, *Remarks on the Foundations of Mathematics*, ed. G. H. von Wright, R. Rhees and G. E. M. Anscombe, trans. G. E. M. Anscombe, 3rd edn rev. and reset, Oxford: Blackwell, p. 23. Quoted in Kerr, *Theology after Wittgenstein*, p. 169.

sight. The Fresh Expressions theorists reassure us that we are dealing with changes only at the level of 'style'. They protest that their movement is no siege upon Anglican belief or identity, that they are concerned merely with changes in outward forms. We reply that there is nothing 'mere' about outward forms. These writers do not appreciate just how much the Faith is embodied *in* those forms, just as it is also embodied in the words of our theology. Those who follow *Mission-shaped Church* are turning their back on traditional 'ways of being Church'. This is to turn one's back on the theology and identity that those forms of life embody. A change in our practical forms of life means a change in the theology that goes along with it. We offer some practical examples.

Until now, the average Fresh Expression has had little or nothing to do with its parish, deanery or diocese. This stands in contrast to the average parish in the 'inherited church'. A Christian who makes her home in the Fresh Expression will find that her week-by-week experience expresses a very different doctrine of the Church and its interrelations than if she belonged to a parish church.

As another example, the inherited church embodies the Anglican vision that wherever someone lives, he or she already has as place in the Christian community. Everyone lives in a parish; they are always already members. Our fellow Christians are our family. Just like our biological family, we do not choose them. In contrast, the Fresh Expressions movement sets out a very different vision in its practical forms. The emphasis is on choosing the 'expression' of Church that suits you. Consequently, a very different set of values looms large, centred around freedom and choice. The same contrast could be made over the way in which the community worships: is there a liturgy, which is received as a 'given', or is the emphasis on 'devising' worship differently from week to week?

As a final example, consider what the contrasting forms of life of the parish and the Fresh Expressions say about their attitude towards time and space. Do they celebrate novelty or enduring presence? Is the network central, or is place? What is more real, the virtual or the concrete?

Those who separate form and content usually do not appreciate the significance of form. When form is treated as separate from content, it is rendered marginal. If we do not appreciate just how much theology comes wrapped up in practices then we will treat those practices lightly and not fully appreciate their usefulness. This is exactly what we see with Fresh Expressions. By and large, the people who write this literature do not appreciate how much the practices of the inherited church offer for mission and discipleship. They discount the forms of the inherited church without appreciating their potency for bringing the Faith to bear upon our time and space. They neglect the potential of these ways of worship and forms of relation to reorder our lives. To throw over the practices of the inherited church is both to weaken our grasp of the Faith, and also to weaken its grasp on us. It is also to neglect opportunities for mission. The traditions of the inherited church are living parables for the Faith and have great potential for witness. We take these ideas up in Chapter 8.

Any form of Christianity that can dissociate form and content to the extent of *Mission-shaped Church* is really very different from Christianity as the Church of England has known and practiced it. The communitarian vision of identity and rationality held out by Wittgenstein in the twentieth century, and by many others, is of a piece with the approach of the English Church down the centuries. All of a sudden, we are now presented with radically novel forms of association, and ways to live the Christian life. The practical proposals of Fresh Expressions show that their theorists have come up with some very different answers to certain searching and foundational questions: are knowing and believing something that the individual does by herself or are they something communal? Is Christian belief mainly a matter of ideas and words, or is it something that involves shared activities and forms of life? Do we accept that human beings are now basically atomized individuals or do we hold on to a more communal setting for human identity? Is choice the ultimate human good? Is freedom everything? How deeply entrenched in our theology is the idea of gift? Are we consumers or producers, or both and more than either? How do we stand in relation to time and history, or to the body and place?

Ignoring post-liberal theology and the communal turn: the danger of intellectualism

Fresh Expressions literature has hardly engaged with contemporary theology beyond the popular paperback. This is as true of the *Mission-shaped Church* report and of almost everything that has come it its wake. The Church of England has never dispensed with scholarly theology to this extent before. Even the doctrinal crises of the 1960s and '70s were carried out in dialogue with academic theology – albeit of an anguished variety. Today, the Church is being redirected on the basis of writing that draws upon a list of sources so unimpressive that it would perform poorly if it were submitted as written work for a master's degree.

It is impossible from this literature to tell that we are in the middle of a renaissance in English-speaking Anglican theology. There is no reference here to Oliver O'Donovan, John Milbank or N. T. Wright. The commission that wrote *Mission-shaped Church* contained no theologians of the stature of Sarah Coakley, Graham Ward or Michael Northcott. Many wholesale developments in contemporary theology are not represented at all.

One important landmark on the terrain of twentieth-century theology, ignored by the report, is 'post-liberalism'. Just as the middle of the twentieth century belongs to 'neo-orthodoxy' and the pre-eminent figure of Karl Barth, the closing decades deserve to be called the era of post-liberalism. This is more of a trend than a tightly defined school, but it is possible to identify common themes. It represents a new interest in methodology, asking just what it is that we are doing when we think theologically. It represented a renewed conviction that the Bible must shape our understanding of the world at the deepest, conceptual level. One consequence of this was the birth of 'narrative theology', which

The Union of Form and Content

belongs as an important strand of post-liberalism. This movement also has a strongly communitarian sense of how theology is carried out and what it is for. Part of this involves a new awareness of how the Faith is embodied in the way the Christian community lives. This is obviously of interest to us here. Finally, post-liberalism stands as a return to tradition, but not as if the liberal crisis of the middle of the twentieth century (and before) had not happened.[34]

In the brief discussion that follows, we will take George Lindbeck as a representative of the post-liberal approach, not least because he was one of its instigators.[35] His most significant book is *The Nature of Doctrine: Religion and Theology in a Postliberal Age*.[36] Here he takes up a central methodological question: what are we doing when we express what he calls a 'religious conviction'. For Lindbeck, we might be doing one of three different things. To start, there is the 'experiential-expressive' approach. This is primarily a matter of feeling. Taken this way, our theological statements try to turn religious experiences into words. Another approach is what Lindbeck calls the 'ontological' understanding. People who understand religious convictions this way take them to be objective claims about the nature of reality – what is *out there*. The third alternative is what Lindbeck calls the 'cultural–linguistic

---

34 For an introduction to some of the earlier theologians in this trajectory, see John Webster's 2000 anthology, *Theology after Liberalism: A Reader*, Oxford: Blackwell. For an introductory study, see George Hunsinger, 2003, 'Postliberal Theology' in *The Cambridge Companion to Postmodern Theology*, ed. Kevin Vanhoozer, Cambridge: Cambridge University Press, pp. 42–57, and for a good recent discussion of where postliberal theology may lead see C. C. Pecknold, 2005, *Transforming Postliberal Theology: George Lindbeck, Pragmatism and Scripture*, Edinburgh: T&T Clark.

35 Some followers claim his work as the next stage of a basically liberal project. Others see his work as a return to more traditional and conservative methods and concerns. For the first group, his work appears to be an exercise in non-realism. Seen this way, it would not matter so much for Lindbeck whether religious beliefs are ultimately *true* in a traditional sense – indeed, that may be an outdated notion – but rather that they work for me, or rather, for Lindbeck, *for us*. Although we can see why this concern arises, ultimately we would not lay the charge of non-realism at Lindbeck's door.

36 Philadelphia: Westminster Press, 1984.

19

dimension'. This is his particular insight. It stresses the link between theology and the way we live the religious life together. Seen this third way, religious convictions express how a community lives. A religious statement is true when it lines up with the way of life of the community that makes it. An 'utterance' is true when it agrees with what Lindbeck calls 'the total relevant contexts'. It makes sense not only in concert with the other ideas we believed but also in relation to the community's 'forms of life'.[37]

This 'cultural-linguistic dimension' might be clearer if we turn to an example. Lindbeck chooses one relating to the sovereignty of Christ: 'for a Christian . . . "Christ is Lord" [is] true only as [part] of a total pattern of speaking, thinking, feeling and acting.' It is false when '[its] use in any given instance is inconsistent with what the pattern as a whole affirms of God's being and will.'[38] This is important for our purposes. It means that we cannot know what even this seemingly basic affirmation – 'Jesus is Lord' – means without reference to the way of life of the community that makes the claim.[39]

Lindbeck's point is similar to Wittgenstein's. The meaning of our words is not separate from the context in which we use them, or from the actions with which they are associated. Lindbeck extends his example: 'the crusader's battle cry "*Christus est Dominus*," [Christ is Lord] for example, is false when used to authorize cleaving the skull of the infidel (even though the same words in other contexts may be a true utterance).'[40] For Lindbeck, what the warrior means by 'Christ is Lord' it is not what the Church *really* means by it, since the Church is a community of peace. For Lindbeck, 'Christ is Lord' is simply *not true* in the way that the crusader means it. On that occasion it means something

---

37 Lindbeck, *Nature of Doctrine*, p. 64.

38 Lindbeck, *Nature of Doctrine*, p. 64.

39 To return to our example, Lindbeck draws on both Paul and Luther and suggests that they had a similar view to him of what it would mean for us to say 'Jesus is Lord' and for it to make sense: 'What they were concerned to assert is that the only way to assert this truth is to do something about it, i.e., to commit oneself to a way of life.' Lindbeck, *Nature of Doctrine*, p. 66.

40 Lindbeck, *Nature of Doctrine*, p. 64.

like 'Christ is Warlord', and this is not true. More generally, we could only say 'Christ is Lord', and mean it, if it is consistent with the form of our common life. This does not leave truth at the whim of the community, as if hatred of women would be 'true' if that was how the group happened to behave. There is also what Lindbeck calls the 'ontological' dimension to truth. This asks whether the shape, stories and sayings of the community line up with 'God's being and will'.[41] Another way Lindbeck puts this is to contrast 'intersystematic' truth with ontological truth. Something is intersystematically true when the meaning of the words and the accompanying actions line up. This can then be true in the objective, 'ontological' sense – it can 'correspond to God's being and will' – or not, as the case may be.[42]

In saying all this, Lindbeck wants to draw our attention back to practices and church life, and to insist that they must enter into any proper understanding of theology. Consistency of life and thought is not everything; our words and our patterns of life can be consistent but still erroneous. All the same, it is a basic precondition for truth of the deeper sort. That 'ontological' truth requires 'intersytematic' consistency.[43] For Lindbeck, our theology cannot even begin to be true in the more usual sense of the word unless it lines up with the form of the Church's life: 'content' and 'form' coinhere.

Lindbeck's most significant contribution is to point us back to the communal and practice-bound nature of theology. His work is not without problems. Sometimes he seems to subjugate doctrine too completely to an ethical standard of judgement. For our purposes, however, his insight stands. He reminds us that there is more to theology than propositional statements. Truth is also embodied in forms of life.

---

41 'If the form of life and understanding of the world shaped by an authentic use of the Christian stories does in fact correspond to God's being and will, then the proper use of *Christus est Dominus* is not only intersystematically but also ontologically true.' Lindbeck, *Nature of Doctrine*, p. 65.

42 This is why Lindbeck is not a non-realist. He does not make intersystematic or 'cultural–linguistic' truth the only standard.

43 Lindbeck, *Nature of Doctrine*, p. 65.

Without the sort of contribution made by post-liberalism there is a danger that our understanding of the faith will be located too much in ideas and not enough in practices. There is a danger that our approach will be purely 'intellectual'. *Mission-shaped Church* ignores trends like post-liberalism and, sure enough, it is thoroughly 'intellectualist'. That might sound like a very bizarre claim. After all, the report hardly looks like an 'intellectual' document. Its theology is thin and its philosophy is lightweight. It is intellectualist all the same, in the sense that it gives the upper hand to ideas and runs practices down.

Mission-shaped Church is intellectualist because it treats the Faith as a set of ideas we can understand. Christian belief comes down to so many propositions. These authors might admit that the Faith is also bound up with practices, structures of relation and forms of life, but these are strictly secondary. They must be, or the practices of the Church could not be swapped so lightly and often. It is not that the authors of *Mission-shaped Church* deny these other means of signifying, what we might call the cultural means of meaning. Expression in culture (or 'enculturation') is paramount for them. Taken so far, however, this undermines itself. The more fluid the cultural expressions are, the more need there is for a set of stable concepts behind them. The more mutable the cultural forms, the more thoroughly *non-cultural* the underlying concepts have to be. Fresh Expressions writers can only insist that we must not 'fuse the meaning and forms of the gospel' on the assumption that there is an abstract, non-cultural 'meaning of the gospel', which can be reduced to so many propositions. In their language of fashion, these ideas are the 'body' of the faith, which is wrapped in the clothing of this or that particular culture. An example of this kernel might be the *Universities and Colleges Christian Fellowship* (UCCF) 'Declaration of Faith'. In any particular new culture, this is then clothed in culturally appropriate garments.

Against this, set post-liberalism. Approached that way, the Faith cannot be reduced to a string of propositions (the 'meaning of the gospel', as the Lausanne Haslev Consultation had it), which can float freely in relation to our practices (the 'form' of the gospel,

The Union of Form and Content

in the Haslev terminology). We can only know what statements mean in relation to the practices that go along with them. The practices are fundamental to understanding the ideas. These practices constitute 'a form of life, a way of being in the world'.[44]

For the Fresh Expressions thinkers the relation between 'meaning' and 'form' is far looser than this. This leaves 'meaning' as far *more* abstract and cultureless than in the inherited church, for all this might seem paradoxical. Fresh Expressions writers may seem attached to culture, but their logic appeals to an abstract and cultureless deposit of the Faith that is to be enculturated here and there. In its pristine form (as so many statements, no doubt largely to do with the atonement), the Faith is cultureless in itself. We see this worked out, for example, when the report insists that a 'church plant' grows out of only one culture: that of the people to whom the planters are witnessing. The Church grows out of that culture, on the one hand, and the 'faith uniquely revealed in the Scriptures' on the other (p. 105). The reference back to the Scriptures here is significant. It allows the writers, and the putative church planters with them, to bypass the culture of the Church. We are not supposed to need the tradition – which is to say, the cultures of thought and practice through which the Faith has been mediated down the centuries. We have the pure word of the Bible, and have no need of the practices of interpretation – either practical or intellectual – that the inherited church has to offer. Only something impeccably abstract and conceptual could so readily be clothed in this or that 'cultural expression'.

The alternative for which we have been arguing says something like this: the forms of the 'inherited church' are not so many husks to be thrown away once we have extracted the kernel of the gospel message. The meaning of the Christian faith is found *in* the forms of the Christian Church. It is *in* the practices and discipline that are its 'form of life', not behind them or beyond them. Different Christian traditions have different forms of life – but that is because they do not believe exactly the same thing. Put another way, any root and branch 're-expression'

---

44 Lindbeck, *Nature of Doctrine*, p. 65.

23

of the Church, in new practices and forms of life, involves an equally thoroughgoing re-configuration of what the Church believes. At the very least, Fresh Expressions shift the balance of what the Church of England holds to be true. They redefine what it means to be an Anglican. We explore some practical examples in later chapters.

Negative theology and the virtue of reticence

The current militancy of atheism in the English-speaking world has produced some significant responses.[45] One of the more perceptive observations is of a lack of theological humility: in both New Atheist writing and in the unreflective Christianity they attack. In a word – albeit an unfamiliar Greek word – there is too little *apophaticism* in public Christian thought and in public atheist rebuttal. The word comes from the Greek for 'negative'. In the words of Karen Armstrong, it refers to 'the breakdown of speech, which cracks and disintegrates before the absolute unknowability of what we call God'.[46] This strand of theology stresses how little we can know about God in his transcendence. For this reason it is sometimes called 'negative theology'.[47] Its more moderate advocates say that we *can* speak truly of God, not least because of God's revelation of himself, but that we cannot *comprehend* him with our speech nor enclose him with our minds. Descartes

---

45 These include David Bentley Hart, 2009, *Atheist Delusions: The Christian Revolution and its Fashionable Enemies*, New Haven: Yale University Press, Karen Armstrong, 2009, *The Case for God: What Religion Really Means*, London: Bodley Head, and Terry Eagleton, 2009, *Reason, Faith, and Revolution: Reflections on the God Debate*, New Haven, NY: Yale University Press. See also Eagleton's review of Richard Dawkins, *The God Delusion* in the *London Review of Books* (available at www.lrb.co.uk/v28/n20/terry-eagleton/lunging-flailing-mispunching).

46 Armstrong, *The Case for God*, p. 126.

47 For a detailed treatment see Denys Turner, 1998, *The Darkness of God*, Cambridge: Cambridge University Press. For a more popular introduction see Melvyn Matthews, 2000, *Both Alike to Thee*, London: SPCK. One of the greatest works of English spiritual writing explores this idea at length: the anonymous *Cloud of Unknowing*.

provides us with a useful image: we can touch a mountain but we cannot get our hands all the way round it. In this sort of way, we can know something of God but we cannot comprehend him in this sense of enclosing.[48] The incomprehensibility of God was particularly stressed by the Cappodocian Fathers – three saints, and their associates, who did a great deal to formulate the doctrine of the Trinity as we have it today.

Recently, Karen Armstrong has remarked that a rejection of the apophatic tradition is characteristic of both fundamentalist Christians and of hard-line atheists. It is one of several ways in which the two schools of thought are the mirror image of each other. The believers imagine that they understand God. They have him pinned down in their theology. They believe in God and they know exactly what this God is like. The same goes for atheists: they know exactly what the God is like in whom they do not believe.

Fundamentalism and much contemporary atheism are the self-reinforcing offshoots of an intellectualist approach to theology and religion. The fundamentalist talks about God with a glibness that denies all mystery. The atheist finds this God unbelievable. Both perpetuate the same mistake, but in different ways.

All of this rests on a thoroughly modern error. It takes belief and theological knowledge as separate from religious practices and shared forms of life. Previously, Armstrong writes, 'people believed that God exceeded our thoughts and concepts and could only be known by dedicated practice'. Now, however, 'we have lost sight of this important insight' and, she adds, 'this is one of the reasons why so many Western people find the concept of God so difficult today.'[49]

Neither fundamentalists nor the New Atheists properly consider that God might be beyond human knowledge. There is little sense, on either side, that God is not like any other object of belief or knowledge – indeed, that he is not an 'object' at all. God, for

---

48 Letter to Marsenne, 27 May 1630 in *Œuvres de Descartes*, ed. Charles Adam and Paul Tannery, 11 vols. (Paris: Librairie Philosophique J. Vrin, 1983), vol. 1, p. 152.
49 Armstrong, *The Case for God*, p. 9.

fundamentalists and New Atheists alike is a big thing, if invisible; he is knowable, if a little strange. Over the course of history, Christian theologians have been far more circumspect – as have Jewish and Muslim thinkers. Theologians have put a great deal of thought into how religious language works. The consensus is that we *can* talk of God – as just, living and good, for instance. We must, however, admit that we do not know quite what these words mean when applied to God.[50] We do not grasp exactly what it means for God to be just, living or good. He is each of these things in a more excellent manner than we could imagine. In fact, even to say that 'God exists' is problematic – not because God does not 'exist' but because God's mode of existence is something that surpasses our ability to know. We might say that God 'super-exists', and super-existence is beyond our comprehension.

Karen Armstrong stresses just the point that we have been making in this chapter. Precisely because our conceptual knowledge of God is so limited, we must also stress another sort of knowledge through art and ritual, shared stories and shared forms of life. These are what she calls the 'mythos' of our religious traditions. Religious knowledge resides here as well as in analytical thinking, or what she calls 'logos'.[51] 'Religion is a practical discipline', writes Armstrong, 'and its insights are not derived from abstract speculation but from spiritual exercises and a dedicated lifestyle. Without such practice, it is impossible to understand the truth of its doctrines.'[52]

---

50 There is a middle way between extreme apophaticism (equivocity) and a naïve sense that we know exactly what words mean when applied to God (univocity). This is the doctrine of analogy. This allows for a more positive sense of how much we can say and know about God than that given by Armstrong. According to analogy, what a word means applies in fullest degree to God and only in a derived sense to creatures. God is truly good; things partake of God's goodness in a limited fashion. Our grasp of the way the words work, however, applies first of all to things in the world and only by analogy to God. For instance, we get our sense of what 'good' means from the goodness of creatures and we are stretching our sense of what goodness means when we apply it to God. For the best presentation of analogy see Thomas Aquinas, *Summa Theologiae*, I.13.

51 Armstrong, *The Case for God*, p. 3.

52 Armstrong, *The Case for God*, p. 305.

The Union of Form and Content

The fundamentalists and the New Atheists fall into a characteristically modern trap and so do the Fresh Expressions theorists. The authors of *Mission-shaped Church* think of a 'kernel' of the Faith in largely abstract and propositional terms. This lies behind any particular embodied form, and can be translated from one to another very easily. They dismiss lightly the wise 'mythos' of the inherited church – those 'insights' from 'spiritual exercises' and ways of life, without which 'it is impossible to understand the truth' of doctrine.

As Armstrong suggests, Christians who think that they can dispense very lightly with the traditional practices and forms of the Church will have little time for apophaticism. They imagine that we have direct and simple access to the nature of God and the content of the Faith. Here the Fresh Expressions writers belong with the New Atheists and the rather shrill Christians that the New Atheists attack. In contrast, those who deny that we can pin God down in our thoughts are more likely to value disciplines and traditions. These then emerge as an indispensable part of how we know what we know about God. This is the orthodox, traditional and historical approach.

2

Theology and Mediation

The interweaving of form and content is not the preserve of philosophy. We have already seen the principle at work in talking about the sacraments or in George Lindbeck's analysis of what Christians mean when they talk about God. The union of form and content is a matter of mediation, and mediation is a defining feature of Christian theology.

We know that we are in the territory of mediation whenever one thing is encountered in another, or through another, or by means of another. There is mediation when God is revealed through the Bible, for instance, or is served when we care for the poor. Mediation is at play whenever one agent works through another: for instance when Theresa of Avila says 'Christ has no body now on earth but yours, no hands but yours, no feet but yours.'[1] Patterns like these are woven into the Christian vision of the world and its relation to God. Mediation is particularly integral to the Christian doctrines of creation and the Incarnation.

The doctrine of creation teaches that God acts in all action; he is encountered in every good that creatures possess; he is present at all times and in all places. There is no goodness that does not come from God, including the good of existence. The doctrine of revelation is also full of mediation. God reveals himself in a way appropriate to our status as creatures. He speaks *through* human words and historical actions. He appeared *in* place and time. We know him, most perfectly, *in* and *through* a person, Jesus Christ. In accounts of salvation we also come across mediation.

---

1 Quoted in Monica Furlong, 2004, *Women Pray: Voices through the Ages from Many Faiths, Cultures and Traditions*, Woodstock, VT: Skylight Paths Press, p. 136.

Theology and Mediation

God saves us *by* and *through* means that are suited to our status as material creatures. He saves us *through* the human being who is God incarnate, *through* human birth and death, and *through* the Resurrection of that human body.

This is a book about the Church, and the doctrine of the Church – ecclesiology – is a branch of theology shot through with mediation. The benefits that Christ won for us are brought to us *through* the Church. Salvation comes to us as material, speaking and communal beings: *in* the matter of the sacraments, *through* water, bread and wine, *in* the deposit of the faith handed on in human words and human cultures, and *through* the mission of a visible body of people, the Church. In this book we argue that the Faith is to be found in the practices of the Church and the forms of her common life. This is also a matter of mediation, and mediation therefore lies as the heart of his book. Similarly, much of what is at stake in Fresh Expressions writing involves the denial of mediation. For this reason, it is worth taking a little time to consider the subject of mediation here.

Definitions of mediation

Mediation has many dimensions and all of them bear upon theology one way or another. The *Concise Oxford Dictionary* gives several definitions for the word 'mediate'.[2] The first is the most common usage today and it relates to reconciliation. Mediation in this sense is work to 'intervene (between parties in a dispute) to produce agreement or reconciliation'. This is not the principal meaning of mediation encountered in this book. It is significant, all the same, that when the dictionary introduces us to mediation, it takes us to reconciliation straight away – something integral to the Christian understanding of salvation.

---

2 *The Concise Oxford English Dictionary*, 1990, Oxford: Oxford University Press. For a thorough discussion of the history of the word 'mediation' and of the ideas associated with it, see also the entry in Raymond Williams, 1988, *Keywords*, London: Fontana Press.

For the Parish

The second meaning of 'mediate' is to 'be a medium for bringing about (a result) or for conveying (a gift etc.)'. Here we get closer to the theological heart of mediation. This sense of mediation is close at hand whenever we use prepositions such as 'by', 'with', 'in', 'through' or 'by means of'. God acts through his creatures. In this, he does not rob them of their own identity or agency. On the contrary, he is the one who bestows both. In the next chapter we will comes across an argument that the Church cannot be the agent of salvation, because God is that agent. A properly Christian account of mediation will not stand for this sense of competition. God's work does not inhibit ours; it is the precondition for our work. Similarly, the work we do in fulfilment of God's will does not detract from God, since all our powers, and our very existence, comes only from God.

If we approach things with a Christian sense of mediation, God's agents are not inert or arbitrary bearers of what they convey, whether that is a message or, as the dictionary definition has it, 'a gift'. They are changed by what they bear. In fact, they often *become* what they bear. The messenger becomes the message; we receive the gift of being gifts ourselves.

Christian ideas of mediation see creatures elevated above the status of instruments. Again, this will bear upon our discussions in the next chapter. Mediation in Christian theology is about more than being a go-between or an imperfect likeness of something else. Instead, Christian mediation turns on notions of co-operation, overlap and participation: the quality of one thing is made present in another. God acts through the creature and in the process the creature is transformed, redeemed and ennobled.

Theology works with common notions of mediation but changes them in the process. Theological mediation is not unconnected to mediation discernable in the common features of human society, but neither is it a carbon copy. Theological notions of mediation are more interesting and more paradoxical than those in the world. This becomes clear when we turn to the primary and foundational case of mediation, which is the person and work of Christ.

To illustrate this we need only consider the third dictionary definition for 'mediate', which is to 'form a connecting link between'. This sense is often invoked in Christian accounts, but again with a difference. A link sounds as if it were a third thing, coming between two others but not itself either of them.[3] The mediation of Jesus subverts this. He is the mediator between God and human beings, but he is this precisely as both God and a human being. He is both of these fully, without one eclipsing the other. As an example of this, think of the Christ Child in the manger: he is divine, and not *in spite of* his humanity. He is revelation itself, the divine Word, and not in spite of his inability to speak. God's love for us is proclaimed eloquently in his infancy.[4] The divine condescension is there for all to see. The union of natures in the human infant *is* the revelation of God. Christ is the ultimate expression of God's love for his creation and the ultimate expression of mediation in Christian theology. Here we find overlap, union and exaltation without abolition, conflict or competition.

Dignifying all created things

This pattern of union, overlap and distinction is replicated in the sacraments. This is not surprising, since they are the chief material means by which we are united to Christ. With the kind of overlap we grow accustomed to in a Christian account of mediation, the sacraments are symbolic but also convey that which they symbolize. They are redeeming, but in a sense they are also redeemed. In the sacraments, matter, words and gestures take on a new and elevated significance. Bread, wine and water come into their fullest dignity when they are used at the altar and the font. This dynamic is found first of all in Christ. He is both redeemer and the first

---

3 For a discussion of this dynamic in the works of the Jewish philosopher Simone Weil, see Andrew Davison, 'The mediating possibilities of absence in the thought of Simone Weil', *Theology*, 111 (2009), pp. 3–13.

4 He 'cried in the manger in wordless infancy, He the Word, without Whom all human eloquence is mute.' Augustine of Hippo, *Sermon* 199, ii, 2, ed. Erich Przywara, 1945, *An Augustine Synthesis*, London: Sheed & Ward, p. 182.

fruits of that redemption. As the Son of God he has come to re-store us; as the Son of Man he is the human being perfectly united to God. He is both the God who is worshipped and also the high priest who worships God. The magi from the East presented their offerings to Christ as oblations before a god; they also present Christ with the instruments of his priesthood. He is both adored saviour and adoring saviour, as patristic readings of the Epiphany Gospel sometimes stress.

Mediation by Christ sets the tone for mediation in the Christian life. Mediation from the perspective of Christian theology is not simply traffic across a distance bridged in such a way as to leave the distance unchanged. The distance is simultaneously preserved and abolished. It is preserved, in that things are honoured for what they are: they are not hybridized, they are not smudged. At the same time, the distance *is* abolished, in the sense that a perfect union is created. These two elements are found in what the Chalcedonian Definition says of Christ. He is

> one and the same Christ . . . acknowledged in two natures which undergo no confusion, no change, no division, no separation; at no point was the difference between the natures taken away through the union, but rather the property of both natures is preserved [the dynamics of distinction] and comes together into a single person and a single subsistent being; he is not parted or divided into two persons, but is one and the same only-begotten Son, God, Word, Lord Jesus Christ [the dynamics of union][5]

There is no more able exploration of the interpenetration of our action and God's than in the works of Thomas Aquinas. He is the supreme theorist of mediation. As an example, take this passage from the *Summa Contra Gentiles*:

> even if God can by himself produce all natural effects, it is not superfluous for them to be produced by other causes. This

---

5 Norman P. Tanner (ed.), 1990, *Decrees of the Ecumenical Councils*, vol. 1, London: Sheed & Ward, p. 86.

is not a result of the inadequacy of divine power, but rather of the immensity of his goodness, whereby he has willed to communicate his likeness to things, not only so that they might exist, but also that they might be causes for other things. Indeed, all creatures generally attain the divine likeness in each of these two ways . . . By this, in fact, the beauty of order in created things is evident.[6]

God's means are lavish but not wasteful. There is no pointless superfluity, and yet in a sense there is something about God's works that are fully superfluous: the superfluity which characterizes grace – 'from his fullness have we all received grace upon grace' (John 1.16). What God could do without us, he nonetheless does with us.

At the heart of the account of mediation given by Aquinas is a vision of the human being in the image of God *twice over*: first in creation ('by giving them existence') and second in action ('in making them the causes of other things'). This makes sense. We are created in the image of God. Even to speak of God as creator is to point to him as being creative. The image in which we are made is that of the creative God. We therefore bear the imprint of the creator in our own creativity. This is one key to understanding the place of mediation in Christian life and thought. God works through our actions, words and communities because he is the active, speaking, communal God, whose image we bear.

Nowhere does Aquinas spell out this dynamic with such eloquence as in relation to goodness:

The creature is made like God in two ways; first, in that God is good; and so the creature becomes like Him by being good; and secondly, in that God is the cause of goodness in others; and so the creature becomes like God by moving others towards goodness.[7]

---

6 *Summa Contra Gentiles* 3.70.7. Translation based on Vernon J. Bourke, 1956, University of Notre Dame Press.

7 *Summa Theologiae* I.103.4. Translated by the Fathers of the English Dominican Province. 1920.

For the Parish

A lesser theologian would stop at the first point: God is good and we grow into God's likeness through goodness. However, even in saying this Aquinas discerns a second point. The image we bear is that of One who communicates and provokes goodness.[8] We bear a likeness to a goodness that is diffusive. We can express that goodness by leading and provoking others to goodness ourselves.[9]

God works this way, involving us where we did not need to be involved. He takes what we might call the long route to reach us, the messy route of flesh and blood, of history, and of human language and culture. This is what John Henry Newman called God's 'wisest love',[10] a love that chose to draw human beings into the work of their own salvation. What the first Adam had lost, God restores through a second Adam (Christ).[11] As sin entered the world through the disobedience of the first Eve, the saviour enters the world through the obedience of the second Eve (Mary).[12] As

---

8 It is of the essence of goodness, according to Pseudo-Dionysius, that it is diffusive of itself. See *The Divine Names*, 712B in *Pseudo-Dionysius: The Complete Works*, 1987, trans. Colm Luibheid, ed. Paul Rorem, *Classics of Christian Spirituality*, London: SPCK, p. 82.

9 The theme recurs throughout his writings. To give two further examples: 'What comes from God is well ordered. Now the order of things consists in this, that they are led to God each one by the others.' (*Summa Theologiae* I–II.111.1) and 'All creatures participate in the divine goodness, with the result that they pour forth to others the goodness that they themselves possess. For it belongs to the nature of goodness to communicate itself to others. (*Summa Theologiae* I.106.4)

10 From the hymn 'Praise to the Holiest in the Height': 'O wisest love! that flesh and blood,/ Which did in Adam fail,/ Should strive afresh against the foe,/ Should strive and should prevail.' The hymn is marked by the twists and turns of mediation. We see this in the interweaving of prepositions: 'that He, who smote,/ In Man *for* man the foe,/ The double agony *in* Man/ *For* man should undergo.'

11 For instance, Romans 5.9; 1 Corinthians 15.21–2. Some commentators see a parallel between the first Adam, created 'in the image and likeness of God' and Paul's description of Christ as the 'Image of God' (2 Cor. 4.4, Col. 1.15 and perhaps Phil. 2.6 – see also Hebr. 1.3). For a fuller discussion see Herman N. Ridderbos, 1977, *Paul*, trans. John Richard de Witt, London: SPCK, pp. 68–78.

12 See, for instance, Irenaeus of Lyons, *Against Heresies* III.22.4, which concludes 'the knot of Eve's disobedience was loosed by the obedience of Mary. For what the virgin Eve had bound fast through unbelief, this did the virgin Mary set free through faith.' (Translated by Alexander Roberts and James Donaldson, *The Ante-Nicene Fathers*, vol. 1. Reprinted by Hendrickson Publishers. 1995.)

the Fall involved a tree, so wood is given a place in the work of redemption, in the form of the cross.[13] This is a distinctive aspect of a Christian account of salvation: human beings are elevated and ennobled by being given a part in the scheme that achieves their salvation. As a further example of this, we will consider how God's dealings with us take up human language and culture.

Mediation, language and culture

The gospel comes to us by cultural and linguistic mediation. God addresses each of us individually but by communal means. The Faith is saving knowledge, which comes to us through history. It was copied for most of its transit by hand, from manuscript to manuscript. It has been probed and elucidated by human thought, a flame passed from mind to mind, from life to life. Our encounter is a mediated encounter. The revelation of God comes to us through human links stretching back to the coming of Christ. In fact, even to talk of the passage from 'mind to mind' underplays mediation. That transition is itself mediated by physical things: by objects and the body, by book and pen, by mouth and ear, by drama and liturgy, by imitating our parents and grandparents.

God entrusts the message, work and legacy of salvation to the human community of the Church, to human language and to human culture.[14] In this, God extends the logic of the Incarnation, of handing himself over to the world. The poet David Jones wrote that with the Last Supper, 'he [Christ] placed himself in the order of signs'.[15] God has chosen to communicate himself to us in the

---

13 See the Preface for the second part of Lent in *Common Worship*: 'the tree of shame was made the tree of glory; and where life was lost, there life has been restored', or the Passiontide hymn '*Pange, lingua, gloriosi*' by Venantius Fortunatus (530–609): when we 'fell on death, by tasting/ Fruit of the forbidden tree' God had pity and 'another Tree was chosen/ Which the world from death should free.' *Common Worship: Services and Prayers for the Church of England*, 2000, London: Church House Publishing.

14 The faith, says Jude, 'was once for all entrusted to the saints' (Jude 3).

15 Epigram to *Epoch and Artist*, 1959, London: Faber. In 'Art and Sacrament', within that volume, he attributes the quotation to Maurice de la Taille.

way human beings communicate. As the poet Elizabeth Bishop had it, our knowledge is historical and 'flowing': it is 'dark, salt, clear, moving, utterly free, drawn from the cold hard mouth/ of the world, derived from the rocky breasts/ forever, flowing and drawn, and since/ our knowledge is historical, flowing and flown'.[16] With the Incarnation, supremely, but also through the prophets, God has entered into this stream. Not, of course, that communication is some human thing to which God is accommodated. Rather, 'in the beginning was the Word'. It is our relations and our communication that join what God already and always is. It is not God who joined our conversation but we who have joined his. In Christ as God Incarnate, God then participates in our participation in his life.

If it were not God of whom we spoke here, we might say that this was a risky endeavour. Certainly it is an endeavour not without the possibility of loss, as meaning can be tarnished as well as polished. Handing on is handing over. As we may know from generations of Holy Week sermons, *traditio* is both 'tradition', that which preserves the faith, but also 'betrayal'.

To put it another way, God undertakes to place the supernatural into the hands of the natural. Daniel Dennett, a vehement critic of religion, speaks legitimately when he describes religion as a 'natural phenomenon'.[17] Except, of course, that it is not *only* a natural phenomenon, and in the providence of God the natural comes to be the bearer of the supernatural, without being itself undone.

By revealing himself in language God places himself under the mediation of language. In giving himself to be understood by us in the way we understand – with language – he also gives himself over to being misunderstood. His revelation of himself in language opens the possibility that the revelation could be tainted by its mediation. If we look at the history of the Church, and even at the Church in our own day, it is clear that this is the case. God hands himself over into language and can be misunderstood

---

16 Elizabeth Bishop, 'At the Fishhouses', quoted in Paul Muldoon, 2006, *The End of the Poem*, London: Faber, p. 97.

17 This comes in the title of a recent book against religion: Daniel Dennett, 2006, *Breaking the Spell: Religion as a Natural Phenomenon*, London: Viking.

– even if we would not all agree where the misunderstandings lie. The message of the gospel can be corrupted, by associated actions as well as by word, and it can be appropriated and put to misuse, whether in simony or in conquest. There is the risk of misuse and betrayal, but there are also the glorious embellishments of distinct cultures upon the message of redemption – whether in the B Minor Mass or in the icons of Russia. They become themselves part of the fruits of redemption.

The revelation of God is not something inert or static. We are justified in talking about a 'deposit of the Faith', that Faith 'once for all entrusted to the saints'. Nevertheless, the communication about God is in some sense the communication of the ever-living God himself. It is not something that can be frittered away, or diluted, or gradually lost without the hope of renewal. If God is given to be misunderstood then he is also given to be re-understood. The Holy Spirit guides the Church so that the Church is indefectible in the end.[18]

It is the culture bearing the gospel that is caught up and affected by God, and not the other way round. God gives himself over into language and culture so as to redeem language and culture. Our sinful use of language means that we can betray this revelation. But then, the giving of God into language also means that our sinful use of language can be redeemed. God is mediated to us through culture, and the culture is patterned by the transmission. We can defame God by associating him with base and ignoble culture. We are warlike and we can co-opt God in the blessing of bombs and tanks. We are slothful and can make of religion a drab thing, which commands only indifference. Mediation here is the basis of a betrayal. Always working against this, however, the mediation of God in culture can effect the gradual redemption of culture. In mediating God to us, our cul-

---

18 'In the process of testing such [new] formulations [for the Christian Faith], the Church has moved cautiously, but with confidence in the promise of Christ that it will persevere and be maintained in the truth (cf. Matt. 16.18; John 16.13). This is what is meant by the indefectibility of the Church (cf. *Authority in the Church* I, 18; *Authority in the Church* II, 23). Anglican–Roman Catholic International Commission, 1999, *The Gift of Authority*, London: Catholic Truth Society, § 41.

ture is also redeemed. We can invoke God to bless tanks, but we can also learn by our God-bearing cultural practices not to glory in tanks and bombs at all.

We are, if anything, too used to this Christian 'stain' upon our culture to notice it. Take the example of forgiveness. Hardly anything similar exists in the traditions of the ancient world. We take the acceptability of forgiveness for granted but, historically speaking, we should not. When we see forgiveness depicted in our culture, we think nothing of it, but we should. Take the conclusion of Rossini's seemingly frivolous opera *La Cenerentola* as an example. In this version of the Cinderella story, forgiveness has a prominent place at the end of the story. Even such a light-hearted work as this is therefore *profoundly* Christian. It is intelligible for us to encounter forgiveness at the end of the story only because of the centuries over which our culture has mediated ideas of forgiveness, and been transformed in the process.

Here we return to the same dynamic that we saw played out with men and women, trees and wood: that which needs to be redeemed becomes, under the grace of God, a means in the work of redemption. God draws culture and language into the redeeming work, elevating and redeeming them.[19]

We have been able to consider only a few of the avenues down which the imagination of the Church has run in expounding God's dealings with the world. It is this order of mediation that *Mission-shaped Church* so signally passes over, plays down and denies. In the next chapter we will see how ill at ease the report is with the involvement of the Church in salvation – either as part of the means or as part of the goal. More than that, the movement seems ill at ease with the Church, full stop. Martyn Percy has expressed this well:

'church' – as an institution – emerges as the problem . . . For it is the church . . . that is held to have masked or corrupted an arrangement of people and ideas that should be fairly simple,

---

19 This takes in not only words, but also gestures and the principles of movement and transmission, and of imitation and mimesis themselves.

and in some ways quite virginal. For this reason, I note with interest that very few participating within the fresh expressions movement add the rider 'of church'. The second part of the phrase has been quietly, innocently and unconsciously parked by most adherents.[20]

The impulse is to clear away all that is complicated or messy, to open up a space for a direct encounter with God. This represents a classic Protestant unease with mediation.

Fresh Expressions can do away with mediation because, for these writers, culture is so inherently neutral that it is merely clothing for the Church, of one fabric or another. Culture is like the transparent air through which the message of the gospel is projected, not like the flesh and sinews, the places and history where it is incarnated in the inherited church.

A theology comfortable with mediation rejoices in the overlaps and interweavings of mediation, in the co-operation of human beings and God. A theology ill at ease with mediation chooses to separate them and see them as in competition. It ensures that the Church is extrinsic to salvation, as we will see in the next chapter. This is a supreme loss, for mediation is not accidental to mission. We cannot understand mission properly without elaborating it in mediatory terms. In mission we share God's work; in mission we pass on the saving message through human words and communities, through human words, drama and music. Supremely, what we draw people into though mission is the life of Christ lived out – and thereby mediated – in the community of his Body, the Church.

It was with ideas such as these that the Swiss theologian Hans Urs von Balthasar – a pre-eminent theoretician of God's mission – closed his *Epilogue*, itself the coping stone laid upon his three multi-part works stretching across sixteen volumes:

---

20 Martyn Percy, 2008, 'Old Tricks for New Dogs?' in Louise Nelstrop and Martyn Percy, *Evaluating Fresh Expressions*, Norwich: Canterbury Press, pp. 27–39 (28–9).

As a fellow human being with us, Jesus can do no other than draw other human beings into his unique and incomparable work. And so he calls others to join with him in the special task of continuing his work. From the very beginning, in the call of the Twelve, Jesus gave a share in his authority both before the Passion ('Do this') and after it ('Whose sins you shall forgive . . .'), drawing them ever more deeply into his own mission. In this way he made them capable as well of drawing others into his special mission. We must see all these aspects together, as intimately bound up with each other, if we want to perceive, at least to some extent, the mystery of the fruitfulness of the continued life of the incarnate Word – called the Church – without abridgment.[21]

21 Hans Urs von Balthasar, 2005, *Epilogue*, trans. Edward T. Oakes, San Francisco: Ignatius Press, p. 113.

3

The Church in Fresh Expressions: Mistakes in Soteriology and Ecclesiology

Mission-shaped Church is a turning point in the self-understanding of the Church of England. With it, our doctrine of the Church has leapt, not drifted, in the direction of Free Church Protestantism. It marks a wholesale reconfiguration of the identity of the Church of England: partly because our theology is changed significantly and partly because our theology is set aside and trumped by pragmatic considerations. The theological departures and dismissals of *Mission-shaped Church* then lead to parallel departures and dismissals in Anglican law and culture on the ground. The majority of English churchgoers are quite unaware of what is going on, but these changes need not go unchallenged.

At stake are not simply our ideas about the Church but also our understanding of salvation. The Church announces redemption and is the company of the redeemed. Our sense of the Church goes hand-in-hand with our sense of salvation. This chapter explores that relation.

Fresh Expressions work with an attenuated and insecure doctrine of the Church.[1] This is all the more striking when we consider there was a remarkable rediscovery of the Church and her significance in the theology of the twentieth century. Theologians

---

1 As Martyn Percy notes, 'the official fresh expressions website is rather coy about ecclesiology. It acknowledges that definitions of the church are "difficult", and that fresh expressions are therefore not easy to define.' (Martyn Percy, 'Old Tricks for New Dogs?' in *Evaluating Fresh Expressions*, ed. Louise Nelstrop and Martyn Percy (Norwich: Canterbury Press, 2008), pp. 27–39 (p. 36).

of all traditions returned to the place of the Church in God's work of salvation. One of us has elsewhere called this the 'Return to the Church' in both doctrinal and biblical theology.[2] In this chapter we will consider the relation of Church and salvation under two broad headings. First there is the idea that the Church is the goal of salvation, second the role of the Church in the process of salvation. Fresh Expression thinking typically ignores the Church as part of the goal of salvation and marginalizes the Church as part of the means.

After a century when the ecclesial dimension of salvation came to new prominence, Fresh Expressions writing is a retreat. This is most clear when it comes to biblical theology. Twentieth-century theology returned to the Church, most of all, because of a careful attention to the Pauline Epistles. It is thoroughly biblical to give a central place to the Church in the plan of salvation. In contrast, *Mission-shaped Church* and subsequent writing is embarrassed by the Church. It can only play the Church down by ignoring some of the New Testament's most significant ways of talking about the Church.

The Church as the goal of salvation

Most of the main images of the Church given in the New Testament present a vision of what salvation looks like in its final achievement. The ecclesial shape of salvation is made clear in images of the Church as Body, Bride, Temple, People of God, New Israel and New Jerusalem.[3] Each of these images describes the Church and also what salvation looks like when it is realized. In each case, salvation is a communal union with God through Christ. These ideas are found throughout the New Testament, but most of all in the writings associated with St Paul. He is the first ecclesiologist of the Church, and in his thought salvation and the Church are closely interwoven.

---

2 For a fuller discussion, see Andrew Davison, 2010, 'Theology and the Future of the Church' in *Hope of Things to Come: Anglicanism and the Future*, ed. Mark Chapman, London: T&T Clark/Continuum, pp. 69–87.

3 For biblical references, see p. 44.

The Church in Fresh Expressions

In contrast, the Fresh Expressions literature has almost no sense that the goal of salvation is an ecclesial one. *Mission-shaped Church* rejects 'church-shaped salvation'. This leaves a hole at the heart of the report.

Although Paul describes the Church as the Bride of Christ and the Temple of God, his pre-eminent image is of the Church as the Body of Christ. In the middle of the twentieth century, John Robinson argued that the Church-as-Body-of-Christ is the central motif of Paul's entire theology, not only for his ecclesiology.[4] Robinson's study, *The Body: A Study in Pauline Theology*, remains a classic of New Testament scholarship. It is an important corrective to *Mission-shaped Church*.

Paul's description of the Church as Christ's body cannot be dismissed as a poetic metaphor, as Robinson shows. This is not picturesque language for Paul; it is not dispensable, or hyperbolic. The Church-as-Body is too closely woven into the texture of his theological vision for that. Robinson's point has been confirmed by subsequent Pauline scholarship. Particularly important is the recent attention paid to Paul's motif of being 'in Christ', which has emerged as central to his thought.[5]

Union with God 'in Christ' is not an individualistic matter, but corporate and ecclesial.[6] The idea that the Church is the Body of

---

4 'The concept of the body forms the keystone of Paul's theology', John Robinson, 1952, *The Body: A Study in Pauline Theology*, London: SCM Press, p. 9. The book is still in print. This early work by Robinson represents his work as one of the greatest English biblical scholars of his generation. It is in a different world from the later, iconoclastic writing of the Robinson of *Honest to God*.

5 See James Dunn, 2006, *The Theology of Paul the Apostle*, Grand Rapids, MI: Eerdmans, p. 319, Morna Hooker, 2003, *Paul*, Oxford: Oneworld, p. 84, N. T. Wright, 2005, *Paul: Fresh Perspectives*, London: SPCK, p. 46 and N. T. Wright, 1991, 'ΧΡΙΣΤΟΣ as "Messiah" in Paul: Philemon 6' in *The Climax of the Covenant: Christ and the Law in Pauline Theology*, Edinburgh: T&T Clark, pp. 41–55; E. P. Sanders, 1977, *Paul and Palestinian Judaism*, London: SCM Press, pp. 455–6. For some additional comments, see Andrew Davison, 'Theology and the Future of the Church'.

6 See, for instance, E. P. Sanders, 1991, *Paul*, Oxford: Oxford University Press, J. A. Ziesler, 1990, *Pauline Christianity*, Oxford: Oxford University Press, p. 72, Jouette M. Bassler, 2007, *Navigating Paul: An Introduction to Key Theological Concepts*, Louisville, KY: Westminster John Knox Press, especially Chapter 4, James Dunn, *Theology of Paul*, p. 411, Morna Hooker, *Paul*, p. 86 and Michael

Christ and the idea that salvation is a matter of being 'in Christ' are two sides of the same coin. Salvation is a matter of incorporation into Christ through incorporation into the Church, which is his body.[7] We have only to turn to the treatments of baptism in the Epistles to see how Paul works out two ideas in tandem.

The image of the Body is Paul's great ecclesiological insight and is found almost exclusively in his writings. Many of his other images of the Church are to be found elsewhere in the New Testament. The Church is a Temple in the Pauline corpus[8] and also in the 1 Peter 2 and the Revelation 3.12. Paul's image of the Church as the Bride of Christ is echoed in the Book of Revelation (Rev. 19). The same description is there in the teaching of Jesus as preserved in the Johannine tradition, where Christ describes his relationship to the community of his disciples as that of a bridegroom to a bride.[9] Similarly, in both Paul and John we find the Church described in the botanical imagery of communal grafting, whether into the vine that is Christ (John 15.1–11) or into the olive tree of the People of Israel (Rom. 11). Paul's description of the Church as the People of God (or instance, Rom. 9.22–26; 2 Cor. 9.12; Eph. 2.19; Col. 3.12) is found elsewhere in the New Testament (Heb. 13.24; 1 Peter 2.9,10). The Book of Revelation offers us another description of the communal and ecclesial goal of salvation in its description of the Heavenly Jerusalem (Rev. 21.2).

These thoroughly communal images present us with a vision of Christian destiny: the Church as the Body of Christ, the temple of the Holy Spirit, the bride of Christ, the vine grafted into Christ, or the People of God. Although they are everywhere in the New

---

J. Gorman, 2004, *Apostle of the Crucified Lord: A Theological Introduction to Paul and His Letters*, Grand Rapids, MI: Eerdmans, pp. 126–7.

7 As James Dunn puts it, the 'study of participation in Christ leads more directly into the rest of Paul's theology than justification [does].' *Theology of Paul*, p. 395. For a short discussion of the history of this idea in the twentieth century, see Andrew Davison, 'Theology and the Future of the Church'.

8 As well as numerous references where the temple might be the individual Christian or the Church, we have a clearly ecclesial references in Ephesians 2.21.

9 In his saying about fasting (Mark 2.19–20, Matt. 9.15, Luke 5.34–45), in the saying about the friend of the bridegroom (John 3.29) and in the imagery of the parable of the wise and foolish virgins (Matt. 25.1–10).

Testament, they hardly receive a mention in *Mission-shaped Church*. The Bible presents us with salvation realized in corporate, ecclesial terms. Fresh Expressions writers rarely acknowledge this, and they play it down when they do. For them, the Church does not figure as part of the goal of salvation. At best, the Church is simply part of the means.

Salvation as reconciliation

The images of the Church just listed underline her place in the plan of salvation. Salvation is corporate and 'Church-shaped': it is membership of the Body, the bride, the new people.[10] Thinking about the corporate dimension of human life is what we call ethics and politics. If salvation and church life are thoroughly corporate then it follows that there must be to them an ethical and political dimension.[11] This is evident throughout Paul's writings, as N. T. Wright, for instance, has recently made clear. In this chapter we will concentrate on two Pauline letters where the ethical–political freight of salvation and church life are particularly close to the surface: the Letter to the Ephesians and the Letter to the Colossians.

In these letters, salvation is described as the reordering of the world by Christ, bringing harmony and peace. This salvation undoes enmities and heals divisions. It comes about because Christ unites all things to himself in his body. This is done first in his body on the cross and then his body the Church (Eph. 1.22–23).

Salvation and the Church belong together in Ephesians and Colossians. The Church is where reconciliation appears in the

---

10 The Presbyterian theologian John Baillie put this succinctly in the mid-twentieth century: 'Just, then, as in ancient Hebrew times religion meant membership in the Israelite community, so now Christian religion means membership in the Church of Christ. Unless we understand this, we understand nothing about Christianity – or nothing as it ought to be understood. Christianity is essentially a community affair.' John Baillie, 1942, *Invitation to Pilgrimage*, London: Oxford University Press, p. 118.

11 Throughout this book we use the word 'political' in the sense in which Aristotle first developed the idea, as 'communal ethics', rather than in the sense of 'party politics'.

world and where it is worked out in strikingly tangible terms. The Church is the place where disunity and enmity are overcome. None of this is incidental to salvation. Peace in the Church is not a happy by-product of salvation, or simply its sign. Reconciliation of enmity and difference within the Church is the advent of salvation among us here and now. These are the terms in which the Letter to the Ephesians describes Christ's redeeming work:

[Christ] is our peace; in his flesh he has made both groups into one and has broken down the dividing wall, that is, the hostility between us. He has abolished the law with its commandments and ordinances, so that he might create in himself one new humanity in place of the two, thus making peace, and might reconcile both groups to God in one body through the cross, thus putting to death that hostility through it. (Eph. 2.14–16)

He achieved this reconciliation in his body on the cross and it is now to be found in his body the Church. She is the new 'household of God' (Eph. 2.19) and the new commonwealth (Eph. 2.12ff.). Here, the reconciliation most in view is between Jews and Gentiles. Together, they are now 'citizens with the saints' (Eph. 2.19). The Church is a new temple and 'dwelling-place for God' (Eph. 2.21–22). In the Church, salvation is displayed for the entire world to see.[12]

To see the scope of this reconciliation played out to its fullest extent, we should turn to the Letter to the Colossians. Here, it takes in the whole cosmos. The dynamics of reconciliation parallel those in Ephesians, but in Colossians Christ overcomes every enmity in heaven and earth. In Christ, God 'was pleased to reconcile to himself all things, whether on earth or in heaven, by making peace through the blood of his cross' (Col. 1.20). The Church is in the forefront here: this reconciliation is described in explicitly

---

12 Cf. Ephesians 3.9–10: 'to make everyone see what is the plan of the mystery hidden for ages in God who created all things; so that through the church the wisdom of God in its rich variety might now be made known to the rulers and authorities in the heavenly places.'

ecclesial terms. Christ brings it about as 'the head of the body, the church' (Col. 1.18).

Christ is the reconciler. If we step back for a moment from these two letters to take in the whole Pauline corpus, we see that Christ reconciles Jew and Gentile, men and women, slave and free, heaven and earth. There is nothing intangible or ethereal about this. He does it in and through the Church. In the Church it becomes visible. In the Church it comes to be.

The Church is the corporate and tangible outworking of a salvation that was won in the concrete events of the Incarnation. One way the theological tradition has expressed this is to say that the life of the Church 'continues' the Incarnation. The idea is there throughout those twentieth-century authors whose 'Return to the Church' we have already mentioned. 'We do not know the whole fact of Christ incarnate', wrote Michael Ramsey, 'unless we know His Church and its life as part of His own life.' We cannot, certainly, identify head and body: 'to know the Church is not to know the inexhaustible truth of the Christ who has ever more to give to men.' Nonetheless, as he goes on, 'the Body is the fullness of Christ, and the history of the Church and the lives of the saints are the acts of the biography of the Messiah.'[13] Eric Mascall's discussion of the Church bears a telling subtitle: 'A Study of the Incarnation and its Consequences'.[14] The Eastern Orthodox theologian Sergei Bulgakov opened his book on the Church with the boldest formulation of this idea: 'the Church is the work of the Incarnation of Christ, it is the Incarnation itself.'[15] Each of these writers, and many more besides, is simply elaborating upon a biblical theme. From the beginning, the Church was carrying forward the work of the Incarnation. So profound is this identification that Christ asks Saul – who is persecuting *the Church* – 'why are you persecuting *me*?' (Acts 26.14).

---

13 Michael Ramsey, 1956, *The Gospel and the Catholic Church*, London: Longmans, Green and Co., p. 35.

14 Eric Mascall, 1946, *Christ, the Christian and the Church*, London: Longmans, Green and Co.

15 Sergei Bulgakov, 1988, *The Orthodox Church*, Crestwood, NY: St Vladimir's Seminary Press, p. 2.

For the Parish

We cannot separate the Church from who Christ is and what he does. As Ephesians puts it, Christ's reconciling work has made him 'the head over all things for the church, which is his body, the fullness of him who fills all in all' (Eph. 1.2). This makes it all the more strange that writing about Fresh Expressions *of Church* has so little place for the Church in what it says about salvation. As often as not, when the Church features among the *dramatis personae* of salvation's story, it is as a hindering force or as a merely human construction.

This will not do. The Church is not simply part of the order of this age, destined to pass away with the coming of something else (frequently identified with the Kingdom). For Ephesians, the consummation of all things involves *more* Church, and not less Church, as Fresh Expressions writing would have it. The goal of salvation for that Epistle might even be said to be *all* Church. The report *Doctrine in the Church of England* put it like this: 'we see in the Church in its consummation the vision of "the goal of perfected unity", which is the bride made glorious, the body, the sphere of the Spirit and the *pleroma* or "fullness" of the Christ who is at last to be "all in all".'[16]

Christians await a Church-shaped salvation. As a corollary of this, the outworking of salvation in our own time is found, first and foremost, in the life of the Church. The consequences are demanding. The quality and shape of community in the Church should already prefigure the final results of grace. Henri de Lubac put it like this: 'between the means and the end there is not merely an extrinsic relationship'.[17] '*Gratia inchoatio gloriae*', as he reminds us, 'grace is the beginning of glory'.[18] This old theological adage is taken up by writers as diverse as Thomas Aquinas ('grace is nothing else than a beginning of glory in us'[19]) and the English

---

16 *Doctrine in the Church of England* (1938, London: SPCK), p. 104 (quoting Eph. 1.22–23; 4.4,15, 13; 5.27; Rev. 21.9ff; 1 Cor. 12.12–27; Col. 1.18; 3.11).

17 Henri de Lubac, 1988, *Catholicism*, trans. Lancelot C. Sheppard and Elizabeth Englund, San Francisco: Ignatius Press, p. 73. This bears the shape of Christian theology of mediation discussed in Chapter 2.

18 De Lubac, *Catholicism*, p. 73.

19 *Summa Theologiae* II–II.24.3, reply to objection 2.

The Church in Fresh Expressions

puritan Richard Sibbes ('grace is glory begun, and glory is grace perfected'[20]). In contrast, this connection between grace and glory is missed in the *Mission-shaped Church* literature. For them, the Church is not part of the goal of salvation but rather some extraneous means.

As we have already pointed out, the Church and salvation are communal, and communal life is the arena of corporate ethics, or politics. Fresh Expressions writing overlooks this in the Bible and in the theological tradition. As we might expect, the practical consequences are far-reaching. If we deny that salvation is 'Church-shaped' in its fulfilment, then we will deny that the Church must be 'salvation-shaped' in the days of her pilgrimage on earth. For the Pauline Epistles, salvation is reconciliation within the Body of Christ. This means that the Church, here and now, should be reconciled and reconciling. As the House of Bishops have recently put it in their theological statement *Eucharistic Presidency*, in this sacrament 'the Church is granted an anticipation of the final fulfilment of the divine purposes for the entire creation.'[21] Because of 'our regular celebration of the Eucharist, the future is no stranger to us'.[22]

When salvation loses this ecclesial dimension, it is a very different thing. It is no longer so imperative for the Church to embody, here and now, the redeemed community it is destined eventually to be. This contrast is pivotal to what we will discuss in later chapters. As an example, the Pauline vision of a salvation-shaped Church requires that the local church should be mixed and harmonious in the face of difference and enmity. In contrast, Fresh Expression thinkers are comfortable with homogeneous and segregated congregations. This is the subject of the next chapter.

---

20 Richard Sibbes, 1863, 'The Excellency of the Gospel above the Law' in *Complete Works*, 7 vols, Edinburgh: James Nichol, 1, p. 288.

21 *Eucharistic Presidency: A Theological Statement by the House of Bishops of the General Synod*, 1997, London: Church House Publishing, pp. 35–6.

22 Paul McPartlan, 1993, *The Eucharist Makes the Church: Henri de Lubac and John Zizioulas in Dialogue*, Edinburgh: T&T Clark, p. 6, quoted in *Eucharistic Presidency*, p. 36.

For the Parish
Church, Kingdom and mission

Mission-shaped ecclesiology is a departure from the theological centre of gravity of the mainstream churches and from the explicit teaching of the Church of England. It is such a marked deviation as would take some pulling off. One method that *Mission-shaped Church* uses is a sharp distinction between the Church and the Kingdom of God. With this binary division in place, it can cast the Church as 'human' and the Kingdom as 'divine'.[23] It can characterize the Church as an instrument for salvation and the Kingdom is the goal of salvation. It can present the Church as a sign, and the Kingdom as that to which the sign points. As a characteristic statement of this manoeuvre, consider the following quotation: 'the Son of God expressed this mission in terms of the kingdom of God. The kingdom is a divine activity whereas the Church is a human community' (p. 86).[24]

This sort of Church/Kingdom distinction is fundamental to much of what follows in the report. It is also something that subsequent literature takes for granted: we should speak only of the *Kingdom* as goal and of the *Church* only as a helper in the process (and this at best). Even authors who find fault with the report, such as John Hull, uphold the distinction. Hull, in fact, urges us to press it further, to focus on the Kingdom[25] and to be forgetful

---

23 In the words of Rowan Williams, 'In many of our current debates in the Church the underlying issue is often whether or not we believe the Church is a supernatural reality.' Rowan Williams, 2006, 'To What End Are We Made?' in *Who Is This Man?: Christ in the Renewal of the Church*, ed. Jonathan Baker and William Davage, London: Continuum, pp. 1–12 (p. 10).

24 The idea that Jesus concerned himself with the Kingdom and not the Church further illustrates the tendency of this report to preferring words and ideas over actions and forms of life. It is true that in his words Jesus favoured the language of the Kingdom – but by his actions he built the Church. He gathered a group of disciples around him. He chose leaders, in the form of the twelve, training and commissioning them. For a detailed study of how intimately the Church features in the life, teaching and legacy of Jesus see Gerhard Lohfink, 1985, *Jesus and Community: Social Dimension of Christian Faith*, trans. John P. Galvin, Minneapolis, MN: Augsberg Fortress Press.

25 So that 'the focus of the Church's activity . . . is . . . not upon itself but upon the coming of the kingdom of God,' John Hull, 2008, 'Mission-shaped and Kingdom Focused?' in *Mission-shaped Questions: Defining Questions for Today's Church*, ed. Steven Croft, London: Church House Publishing, p. 114.

of the Church.[26] Hull is often considered as critic of *Mission-shaped Church*, but on this point he has captured the spirit of the Fresh Expressions movement very well. For him, as for Fresh Expressions writers, we must embrace (as he puts it) a 'mission-shaped Church' and that requires us to turn our backs on 'a Church-shaped mission'.[27]

With the Kingdom as the goal, the Church is left simply as the means. In fact, for Hull the Church is turned into an instrument at a double remove. The 'Christian faith', he writes, is 'an agent of the now and future kingdom' and the Church is simply 'an agent of Christian faith for the same ultimate purpose'. Only the Kingdom is the 'object of mission' (and therefore, as he puts it, 'self-authenticating'), whereas 'both Christian faith and church are instrumental to kingdom'.[28]

Hull's essay is starkly representative of the Fresh Expressions approach because it asks us to be forgetful of the Church for the sake of mission.[29] This takes it for granted that the Church cannot be part of what we announce in the gospel. As Hull puts it, mission that pays attention to the Church is 'a mission that is essentially shaped by the interests and concerns of the Christian Churches' – and consequently weakened and inauthentic. This is a typical Fresh Expressions concern. The assumption is that the business of being the Church – our 'concerns and interests' – is incidental to the coming of the Kingdom, and most likely harmful. Against this we want to set what we consider to be the New Testament's message: the Church is the principal form that the coming Kingdom takes.

For further example of pushing the Church to the margins of thinking about mission, we can consider an essay by Martyn Atkins, then President of the Methodist Church of Great Britain.

---

26 To become 'a Church that, forgetful of itself, is ready to perceive and respond to the mission of God'. John Hull, 2008, 'Mission-shaped and Kingdom Focused?' p. 114.

27 John Hull, 'Mission-shaped and Kingdom Focused?', p. 114.

28 John Hull, 'Mission-shaped and Kingdom Focused?', p. 114.

29 John Hull, 'Mission-shaped and Kingdom Focused?', p. 114.

Like other writers, Atkins sees the Church–Kingdom division as a natural and helpful one. Once again, the Kingdom is the goal and the Church is the instrument. The Church works with God in his mission, 'the goal of which is the coming of the kingdom'.[30] For Atkins, the Church is secondary not only to the Kingdom but also to mission: 'being mission minded is the highest and proper calling of the church, and through it the Church finds its best reason for being'.[31] This is classic Fresh Expressions thinking: the Church is for the sake of mission, not mission for the Church. As the initial report puts it 'church planting should not, therefore, be church centred. It should not be another device to perpetuate an institution for that institution's own sake' (p. 85). This stands at some distance from the Pauline idea that in Christ the Church grows to 'fill all things'. Here, in contrast, the Church is simply 'an institution' – not the Body of Christ, not part of the Good News.[32]

All of this reflects the ultimacy that *Mission-shaped Church* accords to mission. Mission is the goal, and the Church is only for the sake of mission.[33] Even worship is sometimes said to be for the sake of mission.[34] When we take a step back, it becomes clear

---

30 Martyn Atkins, 2008, 'What is the Essence of the Church?' in *Mission-shaped Questions: Defining Questions for Today's Church*, ed. by Steven Croft, London: Church House Publishing, pp. 16–28 (p. 19).

31 Martyn Atkins, 'Essence?', p. 22.

32 As a further example, consider the following passage from *Mission-shaped Spirituality*: '[the] Christian community . . . points towards the kingdom of which it is a sign – in fact, not simply a sign, but *the* sign . . . People can get healed through being accepted in the community of Christ. Local communities can be changed through the activity of the local church.' Susan Hope, 2006, *Mission-shaped Spirituality*, London: Church House Publishing, p. 50. Here, Susan Hope expresses a larger vision for the Church than simply as a sign – here the Church begins to accomplish what it signifies. Nonetheless, such mission-shaped writing fights shy of developing such interweaving of mediation, and will not generally advance beyond the idea of the Church as the 'sign' that 'points to' the kingdom.

33 The primacy of mission over the Church is picked out in bold as one of the principles of the report: 'it is not the Church of God that has a mission in the world, but the God of mission who has a Church in the world' (p. 85). On the same page we read that church planning should be for the sake of mission and not for the sake of extending (or 'perpetuating') the Church, which is here described as a mere 'institution'.

34 The report is clear that worship is not secondary to mission (p. 85). This is not necessarily carried through in the Fresh Expressions movement, where worship is

that this is a strange position to hold. If everything is for the sake of mission – even worship and the Church – then what is *mission* for? The adoration of the Trinity would be a sensible answer, as would the creation of a new community, but we are not allowed to say this. In the contemporary Church of England it will not do to orientate mission towards anything outside itself. Secretly, mission becomes about nothing but itself. In this literature, mission is a self-justifying good. This explains much of the rest of the report and what it recommends.

The nihilism of mission-as-an-end-in-itself finds no more forceful an expression than in *Mission-shaped and Rural*, written by Sally Gaze, one of the authors of the *Mission-shaped Church*. The experience of working on the report shifted her outlook profoundly, she writes:

> Being on the working group which wrote *Mission-shaped Church* brought it home to me again and again how easily I slip into thinking of mission and the Church the wrong way round. Even now, I still find myself talking of mission in Church-centered ways, as if the point of mission were merely to make the Church grow or at least keep the Church alive . . . However, my priorities have changed. The mission of God is not only a higher calling than the maintenance of the Church. It is the very reason for which God brought the Church into being.[35]

This is an instructive passage. Mission is exalted so far above the Church that even to seek for church growth ('to make the Church grow') or vigour (here degraded to nothing more than a wish 'to

---

often seen in more pragmatic terms as an instrument for mission. Elsewhere the idea that the Church exists primarily for worship is played down (for instance, 'those expressions of church seeking to connect with people from post-Christian cultures would say that the *provision of worship* is not the right starting point', p. 23). It would be less of a concern that these 'expressions' put a reduced emphasis on worship if they were to be seen as mission initiatives. It becomes far more problematic given that we are told that they must be seen as fully-fledged churches, not as stages on the way.

35 Sally Gaze, 2006, *Mission-shaped and Rural*, London: Church House Publishing, p. 3.

keep the Church alive') is seen as an unworthy desire.[36] Concern with the Church is cast as obsession with mere 'maintenance'.[37] All the same, the nagging question comes back: if the Church is for mission, then what is mission for? It seems that mission is an ultimate goal, complete in itself.

In sharp distinction, we wish to argue that mission cannot be a proper ultimate goal, or even a sensible one. To suggest this is the ultimate heresy within the contemporary Church of England. At the moment, the simple mention of the word 'mission' trumps every other consideration. Any attempt to assign to mission a place alongside other aims is unthinkable. Any attempt to subjugate it to a higher end is a scandal. All the same, this is what we must do. When mission becomes everything, it becomes empty; it becomes something sinister.

When mission is cast in these terms, it becomes an idol. When it is an end in itself, much will be sacrificed for its sake. There is something of this sacrificial zeal in *Mission-shaped Church* and Fresh Expressions literature. Fresh Expressions writers have the fervour of devotees casting around for increasingly precious things to offer up to mission. The favoured sacrifices are the practices and traditions of the inherited church. To mission, every and any treasure must be sacrificed. The demand is not so difficult for these authors to make, since it is others in the Church of England, and not them who value what is to be given up.

We have no desire to play down the mission of the Church. Christians should be missionary with all their strength and imagination. It is just that they should be missionary for ends that lie beyond mission. This should be obvious. There will come a time when the mission of the Church will be over: there will be no missionary work in the life of the world to come. The goal of mission is the company of the redeemed, adoring the Lamb for ever. As the *Westminster Shorter Catechism* puts it, the Christian's destiny is

---

36 We should note that the Church is presented as sick thing: it is something that we might toil 'to keep alive'.

37 See also *Mission-shaped Church*, p. 85. To look down on 'maintenance' is to ignore the strong tradition in Christian spirituality of valuing quiet and unshowy faithfulness – with 'keeping on' to the end with diligence and dignity.

worship: 'man's chief end is to glorify God, and to enjoy him for ever'. Far from the Church and worship being for the sake of mission, it is mission that is for the sake of the worship and the Church.

The Church as means

Fresh Expressions literature writes the Church-as-goal out of theology. This leaves us with the Church as 'means'. Even this reduced sense of the place of the Church in salvation is often worked out in anaemic terms. When these authors talk about the Church as part of God's means in bringing people to salvation, her role is usually passive. As an example, the report tells us that the human communities of the Church are 'not to be seen as agents of the kingdom, for that is one role of the Spirit' (p. 43).[38] This is a perfect example of the Protestant tendency to deny mediation on the grounds of competition: something cannot be the work of the Church because it is the work of God. There is no sense that something can be simultaneously God's work and, in a delegated sense, ours also.

Consequently, in this writing the Church is less of an *agent* and more of an *instrument*. What is particularly missing is the sense of salvation as incorporation into the Church. Typically, for Fresh Expressions writers, the Church points people to God but once the sinner stands before God, the Church fades into the background. A direct, unmediated and individual encounter can then take place. If salvation is not seen as ecclesial – if membership of the Church is not part of what salvation looks like in the end – then it is no surprise that the work of the Church is strictly preparatory for something that goes on between the sinner and God, in the isolation of the sinner's heart. This fits with the individualistic account of our relation to God found in the conservative American Protestantism that influences this movement.[39]

---

38 The report claims here to be endorsing and quoting the work of Lesslie Newbigin: a reference is given to Lesslie Newbigin, 1989, *Gospel in a Pluralist Society*, London: SPCK, but with no exact citation.

39 See Chapter 4.

If, on the other hand, we take the Church seriously as the Body of Christ, this account will no longer be satisfactory. The Church is the means to salvation in more than this strictly extrinsic way. Membership of the Church is far more closely bound up with salvation than that. We are saved by incorporation into the Body of Christ, which is the Church. The rite of regeneration – baptism – is central in the Scriptural and theological accounts of salvation. It is not that baptism saves us and incidentally also makes us members of the Body of Christ. Church membership is not simply a pleasant or useful side benefit. We are saved by being taken into the Body of Christ, the Church.[40]

Our incorporation does not unite us to some vague entity. It is not simply a matter of taking on board an *idea* of the Church (or, worse still, of 'church'[41]). It is union with the visible Church, historical and tangible. The questions addressed to parents and godparents at the baptism of children in the Church of England stress this: 'will you draw them by your example into the community of faith?' and 'will you help them to take their place within the life and worship of Christ's Church?'[42] The prayer that accompanies anointing at baptism refers to membership of 'the company of Christ's pilgrim people'.[43] This is not left in abstract terms. The prayer defines this 'pilgrim people' as the community where the Spirit renews us in our *day-to-day existence*. It is the tangible, local, historical community of the Church.

On this point, the twentieth-century 'Return to the Church'[44] was anticipated by the Anglican 'Catholic socialists' of the nineteenth

---

40 The other Dominical sacrament, the Eucharist, extends this point. Holy Communion is the means by which our identity as the Body of Christ is expressed and strengthened. In the words of St Augustine, it is the sacrament by which we receive what we already are – the Body of Christ. *Sermon* 272.

41 See Chapter 5.

42 *Common Worship: Services and Prayers for the Church of England*, 2000, London: Church House Publishing, p. 352.

43 *Common Worship*, p. 357.

44 Eric Mascall, among these writers, puts this well: 'incorporation into Christ is incorporation into the Church, since the Church is in its essence simply the human nature of Christ made appropriable by men', *Christ, the Christian and the Church*. p. v.

century. They foreshadowed the insights of the biblical critics of the later-twentieth century. They recognized that being 'in Christ' is everything for St Paul, and that this involves the visible Church. They argued this well before Bulgakov or de Lubac had stressed again the ecclesial location of salvation. We find Charles Gore, for instance, insisting that Paul's account of justification is through and through about membership of the Body of the Church.[45] Similarly, Gore's associate, the preacher and social activist Henry Scott Holland, wrote that 'to be saved is, of its own inherent nature, if only we understood it, to be saved into a church; to be saved into an assembly of the firstborn – a city of God'.[46]

So surely is the Christian account of salvation a communal one that the isolated and autonomous Christian would make no sense to a member of Early Church. The New Testament writers make this clear.[47] Across his letters, Paul addresses a wide range of errors and dangers facing the churches. Individualism seems too outrageous a deviation for even the Corinthians or Galatians to have contemplated. As Gore has it, 'the idea of a faith in Jesus which does not seek admission into "the body" or disparages it even while it accepts it, does not even present itself to St Paul's mind.'[48]

On the contrary, enforced individualism – excommunication – was the ultimate penalty and remedy for offenders. Turning someone into a cut-off Christian was the most severe corrective the

---

45 See, for instance, Charles Gore, 1899, *St Paul's Epistle to the Romans*, London: John Murray.

46 Henry Scott Holland, 1897, *God's City and the Coming of the Kingdom*, London: Longmans, Green and Co., p. 25, quoted (without citation) in W. C. E. Newbolt, 1899, *Religion*, London: Longmans, Green and Co., p. 229.

47 This is further underlined by the extent to which ethics for St Paul are community ethics, not individual ethics. J. Louis Martyn makes the point that the vices and virtues that Paul lists in Galatians are thoroughly communal: 'The effects of the Flesh are developments that destroy community – outbursts of rage, etc. – and the fruit of the Spirit consists of characteristics that build and support community – love, joy, peace, etc. Thus, in the apocalyptic war of the end-time, vices and virtues attributable to individuals have lost both their individualistic nature . . . They have become marks of community character, so that if one speaks of "character formation", one adds that it is the community's character that is being formed by the Spirit (cf. Gal. 4.19).' Louis J. Martyn, 2005, *Theological Issues in the Letters of Paul*, Edinburgh: T&T Clark, p. 261.

48 Gore, *St Paul's Epistle to the Romans*, p. 34.

Apostle Paul had at his disposal, and was reserved for cases of intractable immorality, as in 1 Corinthians 5. Even in these cases, excommunication was envisaged as lasting for only a period. It was a sanction so severe that it could only be contemplated as a short, sharp shock.

In contrast, the autonomous Christian is never far away in Fresh Expressions writing, not least because choice is paramount. The congregations of Fresh Expressions are assembled on an opt-in basis. Logically, the atomized individual comes first and the community second. We notice this, for instance, in the discussion of Sunday worship in *Mission-shaped Church*. According to the report, Sunday is no longer convenient or 'feasible' for many Christians.[49] This does not worry the authors, who add in a cheerful tone that 'some people may be keen to meet with other Christians regularly' even if not on a Sunday (p. 12). Even to speak in these terms is to misrepresent Christian identity or, at least, to condone and continue its misrepresentation. The Church is not a group of separate saved individuals, who happen 'to be keen to meet . . . regularly', either for encouragement or for the pragmatic reason that mission is more easily undertaken together. As W. C. E. Newbolt warned in 1899, if we see the Church as simply a 'combination of those who think alike on the same subject, united by a common purpose in the furtherance of a common design',[50] then we miss the intrinsically social nature of Christian identity.

This tendency to see the Church as an elective gathering of autonomous Christians recalls Immanuel Kant's attempt to recast Christianity in isolated, cold, rationalist terms.[51] Kant's vision in *Religion within the Bounds of Mere Religion* is exactly what *Mission-shaped Church* edges towards: primarily, there are individual Christians; thankfully, some are still 'keen' to meet together. Against this we may set the words of Archbishop Frederick Temple in a sermon preached at the consecration of Truro cathedral:

---

49 Note that it is Christians for whom finding time to worship on Sunday is 'inconvenient', not the as-yet unconverted person.

50 W. C. E. Newbolt, 1899, *Religion*, London: Longmans, Green and Co., p. 231.

51 *Religion within the Boundaries of Mere Reason*, part III, division one.

The Church in Fresh Expressions

We are sometimes asked to think that the Church only exists in the union of believers, and has not a reality of its own. Now it is perfectly clear that in the New Testament the idea of the Church is not that. Men talk sometimes as if a Church could be constituted simply by Christians coming together and uniting themselves into one body for the purpose. Men speak as if . . . the origin of the Church was in the wills of individual Christians who composed it.

This is something that the teaching of the apostles specifically denies:

Men were not brought to Christ to believe in Him and His Cross, and to recognize the duty of worshipping the Heavenly Father in His Name and then decided that it would be a great help to their religion that they should join one another in that worship, and should be united in the bonds of fellowship for that purpose. [On the contrary] Everywhere men are called in; they do not come in and make the Church by coming.[52]

Salvation is no abstract, rarefied, or purely spiritual matter.[53] In two related ways it is concrete and worked out in flesh and blood: it meets us in corporeal and social ways and then it reorders our patterns of life and relations in the world.[54]

---

52 Frederick Temple, 1888, *Twelve Sermons Preached at the Consecration of Truro Cathedral,* Truro: no publisher given, pp. 17–20, quoted by W. C. E Newbolt, *Religion.* pp. 231–2.

53 See Chapter 5 for a discussion of the 'virtualizing' tendencies in Fresh Expressions writing, not least in the reduction of '*the* Faith' to 'faith' and '*the* Church' to 'church'.

54 François Amiot describes this as an idea entirely fundamental for St Paul: just as we were 'interdependent with the first man in sin', even so, and much more, are we 'interdependent with Christ for salvation'. In both of these ways our fate is bound up with a community. In Christ 'the search for salvation cannot be an individual matter (1 Cor. 15.45–9; Rom. 5.12–21). In the same way that the human race is affected by the fall both collectively and individually, those who are saved make up a new humanity of which all the members are henceforth one in Christ (Gal. 3.28)'. François Amiot, 1962, *The Key Concepts of St Paul,* Edinburgh: Nelson, p. 171. The Church of England has been quite clear about this in earlier days: 'the

The overlap of means and ends

Salvation is an ecclesial matter. It is ecclesial in its goal and ecclesial in its means. In Fresh Expressions literature, the former is denied and the later played down. In both ways, an attack is made upon the mediatory role of the Church in salvation. As we saw in Chapter 2, Christian accounts of mediation are marked a sense of co-operation. It is precisely this sort of vision that is missing in the writing under discussion here. Separation is the watchword, not overlap. As an example, the Fresh Expressions theorists call us to separate the Church and her mission – to downplay the first and concentrate on the second. This is a false distinction, not least because the Church is central to what she proclaims in her mission. We cannot write the Church out of the gospel. Nor can we legitimately sideline the Church by using the language of the Kingdom instead. This would be to ignore the Creeds, which proclaim the Church. The Church is part of the gospel because – as the Doctrine Commission of the Church of England has put it – 'the Church is part of its own creed'.[55]

The Church is part of the goal and also part of the means. Whenever theology takes mediation seriously we encounter this sort of theologically charged connection between means and ends, an overlap between signs and that which is signified, an intermingling of agencies. Conversely, any theology that denies or avoids mediation will tend to make sharp distinctions between these things, and not allow that one can bleed into the other.

We can see just such an analytic separation of the means and ends in the essay by John Hull that we have already considered.

---

essentially social nature of Man and of the sin of Man calls for a social redemption, constituting a fellowship of those who have laid hold of the redemption wrought and offered by God in Christ', *Doctrine in the Church of England*, p. 100. We are human beings, and our salvation comes through a human being who is also divine. We are material beings: our salvation was accomplished in flesh and blood, with the wood of the cross and the iron of the nails, and we enter into it through the materiality of the sacraments. We fell though a human fault, so we are redeemed by the merit of a human being, Christ.

55 *Doctrine in the Church of England*, p. 99. 'I believe in . . . the holy catholic Church' (Apostles' Creed) and 'We believe in one holy catholic and apostolic Church' (Nicene Creed), *Common Worship*, pp. 35, 173.

The Church in Fresh Expressions

As he puts it: 'the mission of God [is] distorted when its agent becomes its objective.'[56] To see the inadequacies of this statement, we need only consider the role of Christ. In him we find that the agent is precisely the objective. Christ is both the agent of mission and the end to which mission leads. He is 'the beginning and the end'.[57] He is the initiator and the goal. In the majestic language of the Letter to the Colossians, '*by* him all things in heaven and on earth were created . . . all things have been created through him and *for* him'.[58] Christ is the beginning ('by him') and the end ('for him').

The characteristic overlaps of mediation found in the Church are founded upon Christ because the Church is his Body. From the union of the Church with Christ all the entanglements of mediation follow. In the Church, as in Christ, we encounter interweaving of ends and agency, of means and goals. John Hull represents the Fresh Expressions school of thought when he urges us to keep agent and objective separate, but we cannot. The Church is precisely both agent and objective. Few have expressed this with as much poetic vigour as Henri de Lubac. The Church is simultaneously both the recipient and bestower of redemption:

> She is the Church that gives . . . Baptism . . . and the Church that receives it . . . She is a reconciling power and the family of all the reconciled; a double mystery of communication and communion . . . She is shepherd and flock, mother and people . . .[59]

As bride she is both 'the wretched being on whom the Word took pity' and 'the new Jerusalem, the bride of the Lamb "coming down out of heaven from God". She is both *Corpus Christi mixtum* [the

---

56 John Hull, 'Mission-shaped and Kingdom Focused?' p. 127.

57 'I am the Alpha and the Omega, the beginning and the end' (Rev. 21.6). To adopt Aristotle's perennially helpful terminology for causation, Christ is both the efficient and the final cause – the one who acts, and reason for which there is action.

58 Col. 1.16. Or from Rom. 11.36: 'For from him and through him and to him are all things.'

59 Henri de Lubac, 1956, *The Splendour of the Church*, trans. Michael Mason, London: Sheed and Ward, p. 106. See also his *Catholicism*, p. 68.

mixed body of Christ] and *Ecclesia in sanctis, virgo mater* [the Church in holiness, virgin mother].'[60]

De Lubac establishes these points on the basis of Christology and the union of the Head and Body, as they should be:

> since the Bride is henceforward but one with the Bridegroom . . . no longer is she a means to unite humanity in God, but she is herself the end, that is to say, that union in its consummation. *Christus propter ecclesiam venit.* [Christ came for the sake of the Church.][61]

De Lubac's quotation here comes from the Irish theologian and mystic John Scotus Erigena.[62] Alongside it de Lubac places the words of the early Father, Clement of Alexandria: 'in the same way that the will of God is an act and it is called the world, so his intention is the salvation of men and it is called the Church.'[63]

Searching questions and practical demands

We should not close this chapter without admitting that the vision of the Church presented in this chapter sets enormously high standards. The role that is given to the Church within salvation, according to the Epistles and the Christian tradition, demands a great deal. It asks nothing less than that the quality and form of our common life in the Church should anticipate the reconciled community of the life of the world to come. These points pose

---

60 *The Splendour of the Church*, pp. 68–69. De Lubac draws attention to Rev. 21.9 and 3.12, and to Gal. 4.26.

61 De Lubac, *Catholicism*, p. 70.

62 *In Johannem*, ed. Migne, 1853, *Patrologia Latina*, vol. 122, p. 326.

63 *Paedagog*, Lib. 1, c. 6. Quoted in de Lubac, *Catholicism*, p. 70. Such claims about the Church are ancient. For instance, in the *Shepherd of Hermas*: 'she [the Church] was created first of all . . . and for her sake was the world made,' Alexander Roberts and James Donaldson (eds), 2001, *Fathers of the Second Century, The Ante-Nicene Fathers*, vol. 2, Grand Rapids and Edinburgh: Eerdmans and T & T Clark, p. 12.

vitally important challenges for all our churches, both old and new, both inherited and 'fresh'.

As the current Archbishop of Canterbury has put it, the Church exists to embody and to witness to the new humanity given in Christ.[64] Or, as Henri de Lubac would have it, the Church is to be 'the true universal community in embryo'.[65] As we have seen from the Apostle Paul, the Church does this most of all by being a community of reconciliation. As Paul writes in 2 Corinthians, the Church is the community of the reconciled, and to have been reconciled is to be commissioned as a reconciler.[66] This makes us 'Christ's ambassadors', with a clear and simple message: 'be reconciled to God'. The Church, as she exists here and now, is to be both an agent of forgiveness and the 'site' or place where it can happen. We are to do this by being a community that transcends divisions and hostilities. In the Church we begin the 'recovery of lost unity'[67] in a divided world. The Church must be 'a foreshadowing, dim but certain, of a new paradise . . . "Through the communion of grace truly the communion of nature begins to be restored."'[68]

The form of the Church here and now begins to live out the reconciliation that she promises in her message of salvation. It is to this that we turn in the next chapter, and to the Church as a mixed community in particular.

---

64 Williams, 'To What End Are We Made?', pp. 1–23 (p. 10).

65 The phrase is John Milbank's summary of de Lubac on this theme, see John Milbank, 2005, *The Suspended Middle: Henri de Lubac and the Debate Concerning the Supernatural*, London: SCM Press, p. 2.

66 'All this is from God, who reconciled us to himself through Christ, and has given us the ministry of reconciliation; that is, in Christ God was reconciling the world to himself, not counting their trespasses against them, and entrusting the message of reconciliation to us. So we are ambassadors for Christ, since God is making his appeal through us; we entreat you on behalf of Christ, be reconciled to God' (2 Cor. 5.18–20).

67 De Lubac, *Catholicism*, pp. 35, 80.

68 Baldwin of Canterbury, *Tractatus de Vita Conenobitica*, ed. Migne, 1853, *Patrologia Latina*, vol. 206, p. 562. Quoted by de Lubac, *Catholicism*, p. 80.

4

Fresh Expressions: The Flight to Segregation

The argument of this book is that the form of the Church embodies her Faith. The willingness of Fresh Expressions thinkers to jettison classic Anglican forms of life suggests that they do not appreciate the extent to which our Faith is bound up with these practices. We should not divest ourselves of them so easily. In this chapter we consider one particular facet of the communal life of the parish, namely that it is a mixed community. This is reflects our belief in the gospel as a message of reconciliation, forgiveness and peace. The parishes of the inherited church are heterogeneous communities (and all the more so compared with Fresh Expressions). The parishes demonstrate the belief of the inherited church that the work of redemption is one of reconciliation in the face of difference and enmity.

The local church should be a 'mixed community'. Both aspects are important. They are *communities* because the goal of salvation is the reconciliation of a community to God, and of its members to one another. We have considered this in the previous chapter. Our communities are also *mixed*, because our gospel is one of reconciliation – reconciliation with God and with one another. The work of Christ overcomes old enmities and makes peace. Christ overcame divisions on the cross. We have already seen this in a passage from Ephesians 2.14–16:

For he is our peace; in his flesh he has made both groups into one and has broken down the dividing wall, that is, the hostility between us [Jew and Gentile] . . . so that he might create in himself one new humanity in place of the two, thus making peace, and might reconcile both groups to God in one body through the cross.

We have chosen to take the mixed community as our extended example that the Church embodies the gospel in her common life for two reasons: it is one of the most important ways in which this happens; it is also one of the patterns most thoroughly discounted by the Fresh Expressions project. *Mission-shaped Church* is a recipe for segregated Christian congregations, and that is what it has produced in Fresh Expressions. Far from breaking down 'the dividing wall' (Eph. 2.14) the network model of Fresh Expressions is one that builds walls up.

At the roots of this movement is a shift in how we understand what unites members of a congregation. It is a move from geographical locality to membership of a particular 'network'. It is this feature that makes Fresh Expressions communities uniform. Networks are predicated upon similarity of occupation, outlook or interest even more than locality is. Networks are often 'membership societies'. They are unified, for instance, by 'leisure interest, music preference, or disability', to use the examples given in the report (p. 63).[1] The result is churches for skateboarding teenagers,[2] for women who enjoy making greetings cards, or in the form of a sewing circle.[3]

The motivations behind these homogeneous congregations are noble. Fresh Expressions pioneers want to attract people to church and introduce them to Christ. They assume that people will come more readily if only the 'church experience' could be made

---

1 One additional kind of network is listed: one based on 'common work'. We can see that this might be the basis for a mixed community. If, in a factory, workers from the shop floor belonged to the same Fresh Expressions community as the clerical staff and managers, then a mixed and reconciling community would be in view. It is clear from the invocation of the 'homogeneous unit principle' (see below) that this is not what the report has in mind. Instead, it imagines something like a church for barristers or for shop assistants at a particular supermarket.

2 'Legacy XS' in Benfleet, Essex at www.legacyxs.com.

3 The two last examples are mentioned on the webpage 'The OUT dimension of church' at www.sharetheguide.org/section1/4/out.

comfortable enough. In particular, this means setting aside the expectation that converts will have to meet and mix with people different from themselves. The motive is commendable, but segregation is segregation and it is in conflict with the Christian gospel. Stanley Hauerwas has addressed this theme in relation to the separation of churches along racial lines in North Carolina. 'Eleven o'clock on Sunday morning', as he puts it, 'remains the most segregated hour in North Carolina.' This is highly problematic, not 'because it offends democratic egalitarian presumptions' but rather 'because a church so constituted is not gathered and therefore not able to properly worship God'.[4] With *Common Worship* in 2000, the Church of England put new emphasis on the 'gathering' at the beginning of a service as a significant part of the liturgy. For Stanley Hauerwas, and for us, homogeneous congregations are inadequate as gatherings of Christians, and they are inadequate as communities into which to gather those currently outside the Church.

The example of the early Church

The Fresh Expressions ideal is for a mixture of network communities. In contrast, the inherited church is a network of mixed communities. This is a pattern that the inherited church really has *inherited*. This commitment to mixed communities is something that has been passed down from the earliest days of the Church. From the very beginning, the Church stood against the segregation and stratification of society in the ancient world. The Church was perhaps the only place in the Roman Empire where slaves mixed equally with the freeborn, men with women, the old with the young, the educated with the uneducated, the poor with the rich. This breaking down of barriers is something demanded by the inner logic of the gospel. The Church took a stand against divisions by race, religious background, gender, age, education and status

---

4 Stanley Hauerwas, 1996, 'The Liturgical Shape of the Christian Life' in *Essentials of Christian Community*, ed. D. F. Ford and D. L. Stamps, Edinburgh: T&T Clark, pp. 153–68 (p. 41).

Fresh Expressions: The Flight to Segregation

as slave or free.[5] This took concrete form in the life and order of the Early Church. Admittedly even then the Church did not always live up to this ideal[6] – although she did to a remarkable degree. What is important is that the New Testament teaches a Gospel of reconciliation and that it expects this reconciliation to

---

5 1 Cor. 12.13 (Jew and Gentile, slave and free); Gal. 3.28 (Jew and Greek, slave and free, male and female); Col. 1.22 (Greek and Jew, circumcised and uncircumcised, barbarian, Scythian, slave and free). Consider also 1 Corinthians 1.26: 'Not *many*' were 'wise by human standards . . . powerful . . . [or] of noble birth' (emphasis added). This entails that some were. We therefore have reference here to a community that is mixed in three additional ways: there are the learned and the unlearned, the powerful and those lacking power, those of noble and those of humble birth.

6 There is emerging archaeological evidence that some early church communities gathered in household groups, at least for some of their meetings. These meetings of 'cell' churches may have taken in the whole of a household, including slaves, and a household may have invited neighbouring Christian households to join with them. This already undermines the sense that these communities represent Early Church segregation. All the same, it is conceivable that in a Jewish neighbourhood these small Christian communities were largely of Jewish background, and in a gentile neighbourhood, largely gentile. Even if this was so, the evidence is that the church as a whole, in a given city, met together often, cutting against all divisions. There is, however, a deeper methodological point here. If a tendency of affluent households to meet together in rather a sealed off manner were to be shown in the Early Church, this does not provide either a blueprint or a licence. It is the scriptural writings of the Early Church that carry the primary authority. The Church of England has historically taken a particularly strong stand against Christians sequestering themselves into chapels in wealthy family homes, away from the diversity of the parish church. In the words of canon B 41.1, 'no chaplain, ministering in any house where there is a chapel dedicated and allowed by the ecclesiastical laws of this realm, shall celebrate the Holy Communion in any other part of the house but in such chapel, and shall do the same seldom upon Sunday and other greater Feast Days, so that the residents in the said house may resort to their parish church and there attend divine service,' www.cofe.anglican.org/about/churchlawlegis/canons/sacraments.pdf. There is a tendency for Fresh Expressions writers to place such emphasis on the practices of the earliest Church that even their mistakes (according to biblical measures) are to be emulated. For instance, in Steven Croft's essay 'Transforming Evangelism' he takes the animosity of Hebrew and Gentile Christians in the earliest days of the Church as a template for homogeneous congregations: 'it is clear from the early chapters of Acts that there was some kind of cultural divide even in the Jerusalem church between those of Greek background and Jews from Jerusalem itself. They are called in Acts 6 the Hellenists and the Hebrews. They clearly exist as separate but related communities within Jerusalem in the years immediately following Pentecost. In time they needed their own indigenous leadership to flourish fully.', Steven Croft, 2005, *Evangelism in a Spiritual Age*, ed. Steven Croft, Rob Frost, Yvonne Richmond and Nick Spencer, London: Church House Publishing, pp. 126–47 (p. 146).

take concrete form in a mixed and reconciled community. To take the example of economic status, the argument begins that none of us are rich before God without grace. We are, all alike, saved by God's mercy. There is therefore no place for hierarchies based on wealth. This is not simply an inspiring idea; it is to be worked out in the life and practices of the church. It is as concrete a matter as who sits where, as the Letter of James explains:

> My brothers and sisters, do you with your acts of favouritism really believe in our glorious Lord Jesus Christ? For if a person with gold rings and in fine clothes comes into your assembly, and if a poor person in dirty clothes also comes in, and if you take notice of the one wearing the fine clothes and say, 'Have a seat here, please,' while to the one who is poor you say, 'Stand there,' or, 'Sit at my feet,' have you not made distinctions among yourselves, and become judges with evil thoughts? (James 2.1–4)

Time and time again the Church has been tested over the principle of heterogeneity. In the twentieth century the challenge was often whether practical forms of church life would withstand the onslaught of prejudice over race. Would churches be segregated in North America or South Africa? Where would they stand in Germany towards Christians of Jewish descent? How would the parish churches of the Church of England behave in face of immigration after the Second World War?

Fresh Expressions tend towards homogeneity because they are detached from locality. On the other hand, the openness of the parish follows from its rootedness in a place. The parish churches of the Church of England are there for everyone, as we shall discuss in more detail in Chapter 6. Were Fresh Expressions linked more closely to the parishes in which they find themselves, they too would be more open to the community as a whole. This is not the path the proponents of this movement have chosen in writing *Mission-shaped Church*. Instead, they urge us away from mixed communities into homogeneous units. We will return to this below.

Fresh Expressions: The Flight to Segregation
Deferral to concept and future

Fresh Expressions writers argue that the Church of England should move away from its commitment to congregations that cater for 'all sorts and conditions of men [and women]'. As we have seen, they look for 'new ways of being church' that will cater for people separated by age group, 'leisure interest' or 'musical preference'. Segregation by class, economic status and educational background follows from this, although this is far less often discussed.

Mission-shaped Church justifies these homogeneous congregations in three ways. One is deferral. It acknowledges the importance of unity across difference but defers it either to the future or to the realm of ideas. The second angle is to mask segregation with the language of a 'mixed economy church'. The third approach acknowledges Fresh Expressions homogeneity as the innovation it is, and mounts a direct defence.[7]

The first approach might be called eschatological deferral. We are told to expect the reconciliation of all difference within the body of the Church, but only at some future time, or at the end of the world. There is also a conceptual version of deferral. Here, the unity of the Church across all difference is celebrated, but left in the realm of ideas.[8] There are points when *Mission-shaped*

---

7 We also encounter a fourth justification in this literature, namely an appeal to the prompting of the Holy Spirit in such a way as to close down argument and discussion. As an example, in *Mission-shaped Spirituality* Susan Hope begins with a comment that all Christians have a general call to mission. She goes on 'but, increasingly, clusters of Christians from all traditions are discovering a "specific missionary call": a call to go to specific people-groups, or age groups. It is impossible to categorize this kind of call, for the way it comes and its outworkings are as diverse as the number of people who are hearing it and responding' (p. 9). It is a general feature of this literature that the work and calling of the Holy Spirit are invoked in such as way as to render what is said unassailable and to prohibit discussion or contradiction. This is to be seen, for instance, in the frequent boxes with 'reports from the front line' that pepper many of these books.

8 As an example, consider the discussion of 'network churches' and universality in *Mission-shaped Church*. These churches sit outside of parish structures; in practice, if not in theory, they also sit lightly to deanery and diocesan structures. All the same, we are told that 'they have chosen to be more directly and closely accountable to the church-catholic than have perhaps most parishes' (p. 65). This is a topsy-turvy use of the word 'accountable'. Can one be 'accountable' to the 'universal' if that

Church talks about universality and reconciliation: they are acknowledged in passing but undermined at length. (This dynamic is a general feature of the report: it will acknowledge that a theological point is important on one occasion but stand against it with the rest of what it argues and recommends.)

The reconciling universality of the Church – or at least of the Kingdom – is acknowledged, but is left as a beautiful *hope*: 'God's kingdom . . . is a future in which . . . all visions of race, culture and national identity disappear as we discover we are all family together and we worship our God for ever' (p. 89). This sentence is the high point of the report on this question, but we should notice that even here it is something for the future, or for the life of the world to come. Fresh Expressions authors often say, quite explicitly, that they are committed to gathering people of every nation, identity and culture into the community of the redeemed. It is not this that we fault,[9] but rather that they are so often content to leave the fulfilment of this vision in the future or at a conceptual level. As this writing has it, we will have to see one another face to face after the General Resurrection, but for now we can keep to ourselves, filtered into groups according to interest and social

---

relationship is entirely on one's own terms? In contrast, the parish church is precisely *accountable*. It is joined to the universal Church in mediated terms, through deanery, archdeaconry and diocese, in such a way that they demand something of the parish. Here really is mutual *accountability*, with the catholic encountered in the local. This is precisely what is missing from these network churches.

9 This sense of the erasure of difference may in fact be taken too far here. We agree that the future promised by God is one where we 'discover we are all family together and we worship our God for ever'. This does not necessarily mean that 'all visions of race, culture and national identity disappear'. Harmony across difference is one thing, but the *disappearance* of difference is another. Here we are in one of the more speculative realms of eschatology but the questions are not unimportant. In Revelation, the lamb ransoms 'people from every tribe and language and people and nation' (Rev. 5.9; see also 7.9). This does not entail that these strands of identity disappear. We would rather say that grace perfects all of these aspects of human identity and individuality – and others – rather than that it abolishes them. This is illustrated beautifully in the paintings of Blessed Fra Angelico, where his saints burst with a character and particularity only made the more substantial by redemption. See, for example, the throngs of saints in the side panels of 'Christ Glorified in the Court of Heaven' from the Fiesole San Domenico Altarpiece in the National Gallery in London.

background. Or, taking the conceptual tack, we simply celebrate that we already belong together, side by side, in the universal Church, but leave this as an idea without physical embodiment. Pushed to the future or left as a pleasing idea, none of this makes any difference to the everyday existence of Christians because it is not expressed in the form of the local church.

For another mission-shaped discussion of these ideas we can turn to Sally Gaze's book *Mission-shaped and Rural*. There she argues for congregations and Fresh Expressions separated according to interests and demographics. The justification is that 'there is more than one way of being a heterogeneous body of Christ'.[10] What this seems to mean, in particular, is that the Church need not be heterogeneous *in particular*. We can be heterogeneous in theory without ever having to be particularly heterogeneous in actuality. We do not need to be heterogeneous in any practical way, precisely because heterogeneity is impractical. As Gaze puts it, achieving the unity-in-difference of a properly mixed Christian community is extremely difficult and naively optimistic. To have different sorts of people meeting together, actually in the same place at the same time, 'might be the least helpful way in which to demonstrate our unity, resulting in culture wars or the pressure of constant compromise'.[11]

We warm to the sense in her book that individual congregations and Fresh Expressions should have a lively interrelation, for instance in 'shared meals or shared social action'.[12] Nonetheless, the vision elaborated there is still too willing to reduce commitment to unity-in-diversity to an idea. We wish to push further in saying that the reconciled and reconciling identity of the Church should be worked out in ongoing concrete forms of life on the ground. Gaze fears that mixed worship must inevitably fall prey to 'culture wars'. It is surely the calling of the Church to rise above such secular futilities. Referring to her comment, this may well mean that Christians have to 'compromise', and even to do so 'constantly'. This is an avenue that Gaze dislikes, whereas we take such

10 *Mission-shaped and Rural*, p. 48.
11 *Mission-shaped and Rural*, p. 48.
12 *Mission-shaped and Rural*, p. 48.

compromise to be part of the virtue of charity: love 'does not insist on its own way; it is not irritable or resentful' (1 Cor. 13.5). This is precisely what Samuel Wells sees the liturgy as teaching and enacting Sunday by Sunday. We will turn to his analysis in Chapter 9.

In short, there is a choice to be made here over how to respond to the New Testament's injunction against divisions, as for instance we find in 1 Corinthians: 'I appeal to you, brothers and sisters, by the name of our Lord Jesus Christ, that all of you should be in agreement and that there should be no divisions among you, but that you should be united in the same mind and the same purpose' (1 Cor. 1.10). Does this call for divisions to be overcome within a particular community of faith that embraces difference? Or, is that so far from possible that we must attempt the next best thing, which is have separate communities, based on likeness, where unity is easier to achieve?

Behind the willingness of *Mission-shaped Church* to reduce reconciliation to something virtual – either by reducing it to an idea or deferring it to a distant future – lies a failure to see that salvation is corporate and that this dimension must to be worked out in the particular. Christian redemption is more than the sum of a billion separate and independent reconciliations with God. Reconciliation with God is also reconciliation with one another. Most properly, this should be expressed in the form of the local church. The Church bears witness to unity at the local level as well as at the universal. If we remain with notional unity only at the universal level, then unity remains an idea. This allows us to sit easily to the divisions of the Church and to be comfortable with homogeneity and segregation. This has not sufficed for Anglicans. The universal and the particular have always to intersect. More than that, their intersection is an intersection of particulars. As Bishop John Inge has written, this intersection happens in a place – in the crossing of ways that is the parish.[13] It also happens in the person of the bishop, who is at once both the shepherd of

---

13 Paper at the conference *Christian Social Teaching and the Politics of Money: An International Conference on Religion and the Recession* held at the University of Nottingham, 9 and 10 July 2009.

the particular locality and joined by bonds of collegiality with his brother (and sister) bishops throughout the world.[14]

The mixed economy

This is to say something about the first of the justifications for segregation given in *Mission-shaped Church*. The second justification for homogeneous congregations shifts our gaze from individual churches to an ensemble of churches. The crucial idea here is that the reconciled breadth of the church need not be reflected in any one 'expression'. Looked at this way, even segregated Fresh Expressions embrace the full breadth of diversity found inside the church, so long as we consider many of them together. The favourite formulation of this principle is that Fresh Expressions are legitimate in a 'mixed economy' church. There is room in such a mixed economy, they say, for many 'different ways to be church'. This idea is at the forefront of Fresh Expressions thinking at present. The annual journal is called *Mixed Economy*.[15]

The phrase 'mixed economy' was put forward by Rowan Williams when he was Archbishop of Wales.[16] Despite its distinguished

---

14 The episcopacy a definitive feature of Anglican ecclesiology, we should therefore consider what the authors of *Mission-shaped Church* had in mind in saying that non-parochial network churches commonly seek for an 'ongoing relationship with the wider Church' in a way that makes them even more 'directly and closely accountable to the church-catholic than have perhaps most parishes'. The argument is that 'many have steering groups drawn from within and even beyond the diocese'. This choosing of their own overseers, some from outside diocesan structures, is uncharacteristic of the Church of England, and yet we are told that this represents an 'Anglican desire to express an identity that is equally local and diocesan'. They circumvent the authority of the bishop and diocese, but this is said to represent 'working with the synodical and the episcopal'. In particular, what does it mean for them to be more 'directly and closely accountable to the church-catholic' than the parishes? There is little sense here of the Anglican vision of accountability to the universal through the local, in the form of the diocesan bishop and canon law. The parish is 'accountable' through the very structure of visitations, licensing, declarations of assent and synodical processes from which they are exempt, or to which they sit lightly.

15 Available from www.freshexpressions.org.uk/mixedeconomy.

16 'We may discern signs of hope. These may be found particularly in the development of a mixed economy of Church life . . . there are ways of being church

provenance, the idea must to be criticized. At least as it is now used, it allows for both too much diversity and too little. When it comes to Anglican identity, it allows for too much diversity. A 'mixed economy' is attractive to the Fresh Expressions world because it licences deviation from Anglican norms. 'It takes all sorts,' the argument goes, 'so let a thousand flowers bloom. As long as we don't prevent you from doing what you like to do, please don't stop us from doing what we want.' Deployed in this way, the 'mixed economy' gives permission to ignore church structures and depart from the liturgical norms required by the canons. This is not benign toleration. If almost anything goes, then our Anglican sense of the identity of the Church is reduced to almost nothing. The essence of the Church becomes a list of bare minima.[17] This will bear little relation to the previous, 'reformed Catholic' self-understanding of Church of England, which is something deeper, more historical and more theological than what is now on offer. The invitation to a mixed economy must not allow Anglican congregations and their leaders to behave in ignorance, contempt or apathy towards Anglican law, liturgy, spirituality, history and theological traditions.

---

alongside the inherited parochial pattern.' Forward to the Evangelism Research Group of the Church in Wales' Board of Mission's document *Good News in Wales*, p. 3, quoted in *Mission-shaped Church*, p. 26.

17 We find an example of this in Steven Croft's argument that we should shift our sense of the defining marks of the Church of England towards 'values' (and away from the canons, liturgy and history of the church.) His proposed 'five values' for tying us together are a commitment to 'Scripture; the sacraments of baptism and Holy Communion; listening to the whole Christian tradition and seeing that tradition expressed in the historic creeds; the ministry and mission of the whole people of God and to the ordering of ministry through the threefold order of deacons, priests and bishops; the mission of God to the whole of creation and to the whole of our society as defined and described in the Anglican Communion's five marks of mission.', Steven Croft, 2006, 'Conclusion', *The Future of the Parish System*, London: Church House Publishing, pp. 178–82 (pp. 181–2). These are all commendable, but it is difficult to see what is distinctively Anglican about them. With the exception of the reference to the threefold ministry, they could apply to the Methodist Church; with the additional exception of the mention of the creeds, they would apply to Baptists – and even then, Baptists might not be too put off by the idea of 'listening' to the tradition or acknowledging that it is 'expressed' in the historic creed. The move from the defining marks of the Church of England to 'values' is a move into a barely differentiated pan-Protestantism.

The 'mixed economy' can justify too much diversity. Paradoxically, however, it also allows for *too little* diversity. As we have said, from her beginnings, the Church was committed to mixed communities. The reconciling work entrusted to her is seen and accomplished in her particular, local existence. As we have noticed, a 'mixed economy' church turns out to be one with segregated church communities, constituted by interest group and personal preference. The 'mixed economy' tag turns out to signal no more than a vague commitment to the sort of idealized, and eschatological, mixing and diversity we have considered above. The 'mixed economy' label is a fig leaf to cover the exact opposite of what it suggests. The 'mixed economy' is a blueprint for an unmixed economy. In the words of Philip Lee, a North American Presbyterian minister:

> No self-justifying declarations about the need for homogeneity will work: [arguments that] doctors, lawyers, [and] professional people are simply more at home in their own sort of church; whereas working people are more at home in their sort. Whether the appeal for homogeneity comes from the market-oriented Growth movement or from more sophisticated circles, it is always an excuse, an excuse for an inexcusable affront to Jesus Christ![18]

The homogeneous unit principle

The third and final justification for segregated congregations is the highly contentious 'homogeneous unit principle' (HUP). This was first formulated by the missiologist Donald McGavran in his 1955 book, *Bridges to God.*[19] His argument was that people convert to Christianity more readily if they are able to stay within the same closely defined social boundaries that they occupied before. As *Mission-shaped Church* puts it, quoting McGavran, 'people

---

18 Philip Lee, 1992, *Against the Protestant Gnostics*, New York: Oxford University Press, p. 265.
19 Donald McGavran, 1955, *Bridges to God*, London: World Dominion Press.

like to become Christians without crossing racial/linguistic/class/ cultural barriers . . . Culturally they remain the same, and tend to gather with others from the same culture who share the faith' (p. 108). McGavran formulated the HUP having observed missionary work in India. He noticed that Christianity became less attractive to potential converts if missionaries insisted that Christian commitment required them to reject the caste system and to associate with 'inferiors'. The authors of *Mission-shaped Church* acknowledge that McGavran's idea is 'one of the most contentious issues that arise in connection with church planting' (p. 108).[20] This does not stop them from endorsing it with enthusiasm. It is the foundation for many of the report's proposals.

Ever since it was proposed, the HUP has provoked controversy. *Mission-shaped Church* gives half a paragraph to these objections. That is fifty-eight words for fifty years of principled theological opposition. Only one charge against the HUP is discussed. It is close to what we have argued here. Salvation involves reconciliation: 'the New Testament sees Jesus as a reconciler, breaking down barriers between God and human beings, and between human person and human person' (p. 108). A quotation is given from Galatians in support: 'there is no longer Jew or Greek, there is no longer slave or free, there is no longer male and female' (Gal. 3.28). Following this half paragraph of objection, the report devotes four paragraphs to a defence of the HUP: four hundred and thirty-seven words in reply to fifty-eight words of opposition. The report offers three justifications, which we will consider in a little detail. The first involves an appeal to the doctrine of creation. The second justification points to the Incarnation. The third argues that when people from different social and economic backgrounds mix, the more powerful inevitably dominate the weaker. On this basis, it is better for the poor and disadvantaged to be given churches of their own.

---

20 As Martyn Percy puts it, McGavran's homogeneous unit principle 'was subsequently widely discredited by theologians, and also widely condemned by missiologists for its focus on pragmatism, and its willingness to sanction narrowly constituted groups (on the basis of age, gender, race, class, wealth, etc.) as "church", which of course legitimizes ageism, sexism, racism, classism and economic divisiveness'. 'Old Tricks for New Dogs?' in *Evaluating Fresh Expressions*, p. 38.

The first reply to criticism of the HUP amounts to an argument for the good of human culture. It takes as its premise that 'specific and diverse cultures' are part of God's creation. Although 'damaged' by the Fall, they are to be valued nonetheless. This is a somewhat tangential defence of the HUP. As an argument, it rests upon much that is left unsaid. The goodness of human cultures does not stand against heterogeneous congregations – not unless it can be shown that heterogeneity necessarily stifles culture. It is not obvious why this should be so. It is possible to be in full agreement with the report at this point over the goodness of cultures, and to agree with the report that these cultures should be brought into the worship and social life of the church, and remain opposed to the HUP.

The inherited church already values and embraces culture. In most parish churches, for instance, the musical and culinary traditions of its members are taken up as part of parish life. The point is that the cultural interests of church members can be valued without having to structure an entire church around them. A Christian's cultural associations are not stifled just because they are not made central to the identity of the local church. It may be helpful here to return to some of the examples of identity- and interest-based Fresh Expressions given above: the greetings–card makers and the sewing circle. An expert maker of greetings cards should be able to belong to a community where this is not the focus of shared life without feeling stifled – at least if he or she is a well-adjusted adult. Similarly, the seamstress or tailor is not belittled because his or her church is not a sewing-themed congregation. If there are a good many sewers, they can form a church sewing circle if they want to. It can take on a missionary dimension. There is no reason why we should make this into a 'church' all of its own. We could multiply examples: the ballet-lover can organize church trips; he can lead study groups on dance and theology. He does not need his own 'ballet church'. The birdwatcher can channel her passion into a parish 'green concerns' group. She does not need a church only for birdwatchers. This is one of the several levels at which the proposals of Fresh Expressions are basically infantilizing or adolescent.

To look at this from a more theoretical perspective, this first justification of the HUP in *Mission-shaped Church* implies that the traditional Church undervalues culture as a category. This is quite wrong. The theoretical stance we propose in this book shows that the inherited church attributes to culture a role and significance far in excess of anything to be found in *Mission-shaped Church*. For the report, culture is simply clothing for the gospel or the Church. For us, culture is far more constitutive. The Christian Faith is bound up with Christian practices. The task of redeeming culture is also far more important and extensive than the report will allow. Largely absent from the report is any sense that the Church directs and sanctifies our individual and group cultures through a culture, practices and disciplines of her own. We agree that the 'style' or colouring of the Church's culture in any given place will be flexible, but the basic norms of her culture as a whole are far less dispensable than the authors of *Mission-shaped Church* imagine. They are the embodiment of the Christian Faith and the stuff of Christian discipleship.

This brings us to the second justification for the HUP, that we should value individual cultures on the basis of the 'incarnational principle'.[21] It is certainly true that the gospel is to take root in

---

21 Even the phrase 'incarnational principle' should give us cause for concern. The Incarnation is the central, distinctive Christian belief and must be brought to bear upon all that we do or think. A phrase such as the 'incarnational principle', however, can serve as a short cut, deflecting us from more careful and involved theological thinking. The 'incarnational principle' can serve a similar purpose for catholic Anglicans as a pre-packaged invocation of the 'cross' does for evangelicals. N. T. Wright describes the dynamics at work here as like folding up theological arguments and biblical interpretations and locking them away in suitcases bearing certain labels. N. T. Wright, 2005, *Scripture and the Authority of God*, London: SPCK Publishing, pp. 17–18. Suitcases are useful for summarizing or 'carrying around' a great deal of material, but their purpose is only fulfilled when we open the cases, take out the arguments and engage in the hard work of theological analysis. Too often, as Wright puts it, we leave the ideas stored away and simply wield the suitcases as offensive weapons. We trade blows with the 'incarnational principle' or the 'cross'. The 'suitcase' of the 'incarnational principle' needs to be opened and the doctrine of the Incarnation put to work on the question of cultures and their individuality in a far more serious way than we find in *Mission-shaped Church*. Not least, we have to ask in what way the Incarnation can serve as a *general* principle at all. It is a supremely specific event, which stands outside any general pattern. In any case, the

particular cultures. This does not stand against the parish church. Parishes are a forceful example of the Church rooting down and engaging with concrete particularity. Just as much as the Fresh Expressions writers, we want every culture to be Christianised. It does not follow from this that every sub-sub-culture ought to have its own specialist church. Throughout Christian history, the Church has struck a balance between being enculturated and being mixed. The local church must embrace cultural specificity, but there are reasonable limits to how far that specificity should go. If it is taken too far, the Church will fragment and segregate on the basis of micro-cultures: skateboarders, affluent young accountants, Goths of a particular variety in their twenties, the long-term unemployed and so on. Quite apart from anything else, such a degree of segregation and homogeneity is psychologically unhealthy. Unwillingness or inability to integrate within a wider community is a mark of insecurity or of psychological disturbance. The Church is committed to the health and development of the whole person. If, for whatever reason, people cannot move beyond such isolation, the Church will want to remain with them as they are. It will explore ways to draw alongside them in the only form their life can, for the moment, take. This an extreme reaction to an extreme situation, and it always has reconciling goals in mind. It cannot be taken as a general endorsement of settled interest-group churches. It is an argument, once again, for Fresh Expressions as

---

Incarnation cannot be left to stand alone. Severed from the cross and Resurrection, and turned into a 'principle', it becomes a blessing for vague 'inclusiveness'. The Incarnation never served this purpose in full-blooded Catholic or Protestant theology. The irony is that evangelicals of the Fresh Expressions school are in danger of taking over a supposedly 'Catholic' notion at its weakest and most liberal. As de Lubac comments, we should not put forward the Incarnation without the cross or Resurrection: that is, without judgement and transformation. 'If Christ were not truly man, conceived and born of a woman, He would not truly be our Savior. But if He had not also really died and been resurrected, then our faith in Him would be vain and we would not be saved. Death and resurrection do not destroy the work of incarnation; they consummate it . . . a spiritual Christianity, a Christianity which puts the sign of the cross on everything and which accepts no human value without taking care to transform it, is not a disincarnated Christianity; it is the only authentic Christianity, the only one in which the "incarnation" is not a snare.' Henri de Lubac, 2000, *Paradoxes of Faith*, San Francisco: Ignatius Press, p. 67.

mission initiatives, which are linked to parish churches and feed into them.

The third justification for the HUP in *Mission-shaped Church* is put forward in the name of 'Good News for the Oppressed' (p. 104). As the report has it:

> Sociological study shows that, when two cultures are together in a social context, a healthy heterogeneous mixture does not result – one tends to dominate the other. The culture of those with the educational and economic power tends to come out on top. An attempt at diversity becomes dominance. (p. 109)

This passage is an extraordinary abdication of any sense that the Church has a supernatural identity and mission. Sociology is allowed to triumph over theology. Sociological studies may well show that dynamics such as these characterise our fallen world. This does not doom everyone to reproduce these patterns. There is hope of something better when any group of people seek, carefully and deliberately, to rise above this and to build a community committed to reconciliation rather than dominance. This general dynamic certainly does not damn the Church to such futility – not, at least, if we believe that the Church and her members are temples of the Holy Spirit. As the First Letter of St John has it, 'the one who is in you is greater than the one who is in the world' (1 John 4.4). The Church is not one more voluntary association alongside others, to be analysed on secular sociological principles. She is not even one more group of people of good will.[22] The 'law

---

22 We encounter this tendency to see the Church as one more human institution in other places, coupled with the same reluctance to view the Church as marked out by the supernatural life of the Spirit. One example is the discussion of church planting in terms of the 'analogy of seeds and plants' in *Mission-shaped Church* (p. 31). We are given a list of 'basic genetic factors' that describe the dynamics of church planting and growth. The features are entirely generic and could apply equally well to any pastoral-minded organization, and with a little modification to any voluntary society with local groups. (What it calls the 'relationship to the wider Church' refers simply to a generic relation of the parts to the whole.) Having discussed this in general terms, the report adds that 'the list ought now also to include reference to Christ, worship and discipleship, in order to be more fully rounded and specifically

of sin and death' may be at work in the world but the Church is the realm of the Spirit of life (Rom. 8.2). The Church is the Body of Christ and the bearer of his mission in the world. St Paul did not give up on the hope of reconciliation between Jew and Gentile on the grounds that it was not sociologically feasible. James insisted on a new set of economic relations within the Church, unperturbed by any sense that it was psychologically unrealistic.

The passage from the report under discussion here illustrates a feature we frequently encounter in Fresh Expressions writing: again and again they take their lead from the social sciences and not from the theological tradition of the Church. In this case, the authors ask us to give up on mixed communities because of some sociologically inevitable dominance of the educated and economically powerful. This is an extraordinary failure of confidence, a denial of responsibility and a thoroughgoing underestimation of the revolutionary nature of the Church. It is one more expression of the chronic lack of theological confidence in *Mission-shaped Church*, put most clearly of all in its shameful endorsement of the suggestion that someone can 'ignore God and the Church and yet be none the worse for it'.[23]

The market approach

Behind the HUP lies another important influence on Fresh Expressions: the American 'Church Growth Movement'. For this movement, 'if local churches want to grow, they must find out

---

Christian.' In other words, the Church and its mission can be analysed from the beginning in terms applicable to any organization and then, only at the end, receive a supplement of Christ-specific themes. There is no sense here that the Church is unique, that she is the Body of Christ. There is no sense that her nature is supernatural or that the dynamics of her life can only properly be understood when they are understood theologically.

23 David Bosch, 1995, *Believing in the Future: Towards a Missiology of Western Culture*, London: Continuum, 1995, p. 15. Quoted in *Mission-shaped Church*, p. 23. As a further example of this lack of confidence, consider Steven Croft's unease with the idea that the Church represents something better than the world. Steve Croft, 'Transforming Evangelism' in *Evangelism in a Spiritual Age*, p. 134.

what the people want and then give it to them'.[24] Something like the homogeneous unit principle naturally follows: 'surveys have consistently shown, for example, that "a church usually grows among one kind of person".'[25] According to the Church Growth Movement, the Church is most attractive when it offers the world something recognisable and familiar. Mission is most successful when a church offers a version of the prevailing culture, but in a religious mood. We see this in the 'mega churches' of the United States, which provide a complete American lifestyle, dressed up with a mixture of Protestant theology and self-help training. The same ideas are at work in Fresh Expressions.

That 'giving people what they want' should be the lodestone of the Church is wrong twice over. First, it is the primary duty of the Church *to be the Church*, whether that makes her popular or unpopular. Second, all theological arguments aside, we are not convinced that the Church *does* make herself more attractive when she back-pedals on what makes her most distinctive. To develop this last point first, it is our experience that people find the Church appealing, when she is most the Church, not least.[26] Merton College chapel is very well attended, and it does not go in for religion-lite. Highlights of the year are the solemn Requiem on All Souls' Day and the High Mass for Candlemas, when the congregation can flow over into the ante-chapel. The thoroughly traditional Advent carol service is repeated across two evenings, because even the

---

24 Philip Lee, *Against the Protestant Gnostics*, p. 210. Lee's work has influenced our discussion here. The quotation is from C. Peter Wagner, 1975, 'Confused about Church Growth?', *Church Growth Canada*, 2, Regina, Saskatchewan, p. 3. Lee goes on to quote Wagner further: 'I remain convinced that without faith, it is impossible for churches to grow. *Empirical evidence* also validates the absolute necessity of faith *or whatever else you want to call it* – possibility thinking or goal setting – as a prerequisite for church growth.' C. Peter Wagner, 1976, *Your Church Can Grow*, Glendale, CA: Regal Books, p. 55, emphasis added. As Lee comments, the roots of this movement lie in the 'positive thinking' of Norman Vincent Peale. In this quotation it is particularly clear.

25 Wagner, 'Confused about Church Growth?', p. 3.

26 On this see pp. 111-13 and the comment that Fresh Expressions run the risk of offering the world an imitation of the world's own imitation of our traditions and liturgy, rather than the real thing.

ante-chapel could not hold the over-spill otherwise. Many cathedrals tell a similar story. Characterful Christianity is appealing.

The other point is also important: it is the primary task of the Church to be faithful rather than popular. In a world of sin the Church should be marked by a certain 'Christian difference', to use an eloquent phrase from Stanley Hauerwas.[27] The Church is an agent of conversion and stands for something different from this and every age. The Fresh Expressions theorists appeal for a church 'in the world' but not 'of it'. Their willingness to replace the patterns of the inherited church with the patterns of the world tells a different story. We find little sense in this literature that Christians are called to be 'outside the camp' with Jesus, as the Letter to the Hebrews has it: 'for here we have no lasting city, but we are looking for the city that is to come (Heb. 13.13–14).'

'Church growth thinking' proposes to run the church along the lines of free market capitalism. People make choices about what to do with their time and money. The aim is to attract them to church as one more option. If they are already minded to go to church, then churches can compete for them in free market terms. This is capitulation to the spirit of our age. In contrast, Hauerwas argues for a church that resists the market in its very constitution. In fact, he holds that Christians can only do this in an ecclesial way.[28]

---

27 Stanley Hauerwas, 2005, 'The Christian Difference, or Surviving Postmodernism' in *The Blackwell Companion to Postmodern Theology*, ed. Graham Ward, Oxford: Blackwell, pp. 144–61.

28 'Any response Christians have to the challenge of the global market will be ecclesial.' ('The Christian Difference', p. 153). In writing about the Christian difference here, Hauerwas draws upon the work of Nicholas Boyle. The opposition to overweening capitalism will come not by rejecting its supposed universality but by living the true universality of the Church in a distinctive way. For the Church, universality is expressed at the level of locality. Hauerwas follows Boyle in arguing that the Church will 'need to draw its moral strength not from its international presence but from its claim to represent people as they are locally and distinct from the worldwide ramifications of their existence as participants in the global market'. Nicholas Boyle, 1998, *Who Are We Now: Christian Humanism and the Global Market from Hegel to Heaney*, Notre Dame, IN: University of Notre Dame Press, pp. 91–92, quoted by Hauerwas, 'Christian Difference', p. 145. The universality of capitalism and globalisation is a 'grand process' with no regard for 'the small scale [which is] . . . full of details which the new world will dismiss as superficial and inessential'. Boyle, *Who Are We Now*, p. 92, quoted by Hauerwas on p. 154. The Church, however,

It may be that fallen human beings are more comfortable going to church with other people that they can accept as 'people like us'. It may be that Gentiles are comfortable with Gentiles, Barbarians with Barbarians, Scythians with Scythians, men with men, women with women, the rich with the rich (Gal. 3.28; Col. 3.11). It may be so, but the Christian is called to something higher. Redemption is transformation; salvation is recreation. The Church is a new, reconciled, truly mixed community. 'Church Growth Thinking' seeks to attract as many people as possible but it risks adapting the church to such a degree that it is diminished in the process. What would it profit the Church to gain the whole world but to lose her own soul? In any case, as we have already asked, is a worldly church really an attractive one? More appealing is the distinctiveness of the Church, presented with vigour and charity. The Christian difference is the basis of our appeal to a lost world, not studied similarity.

Ecclesial segregation and political conformity

Lying close to the heart of these discussions is the question as to whether our contemporary society and culture are really so bad. Are they so confused and off the rails? The authors of *Mission-shaped Church* are quite clear that they wish 'to close the divide between the experience of church and the rest of life' (pp. 44–5). They cannot, then, agree with us in finding the contemporary milieu – by and large – to be vacuous, selfish and lost.[29] Terry Eagle-

---

has an entirely different universality, which is small, particular, *local*, and in every place. It is a matter of worship and centred around the Resurrection (p. 154). It pays particular attention to the poor and those so disenfranchised that capitalism considers them as 'non persons' – the elderly poor, the sick and long-term unemployed (p. 154). These are the very groups that even the Fresh Expressions movement agrees are better served by the parochial system.

29 In short, the world is fallen. Expressions of the Fall in late modernity are particularly nasty – unless one is rich and comfortable, in which case they are simply empty. To point to four examples, we have the triumph of soulless capitalism, to the extent that every conceivable human good is measured in monetary terms; the triumph of vague spirituality over religion, of a sort that is careful not to interfere with the practical details of everyday conduct and is inherently individualist rather

ton has described the cultural and intellectual environment of the contemporary Western world as one with

> an atomistic notion of the self, a bloodlessly contractual view of human relations, a meagrely utilitarian version of ethics, a crudely instrumental idea of reason, a doctrinal suspicion of doctrine, an impoverished sense of human communality, a self-satisfied faith in progress and civility, a purblindness to the more malign aspects of human nature, and a witheringly negative view of power, the state, freedom and tradition.[30]

This is the legacy of modernism turned post-modern. The inherited church resists it, not only by her teaching but also by the forms of her life. In contrast, almost every one of these features is accepted and exemplified by *Mission-shaped Church* and Fresh Expressions.[31] Their attitude to the world around us is one of acceptance. There are occasional comments about the need for the correction and redemption of culture.[32] Given that they are not worked out in terms of practical suggestions, it is difficult to see them as more than a smoke screen.

---

than communitarian; ignorance of the teaching Christian religion, which would direct the individual and the society as a whole towards salvation in this life and in the life to come; the widespread breakdown of communal bonds, as is exemplified in the collapse of membership societies and the unwillingness of many to participate in voluntary groups.

30 Eagleton, *Reason, Faith, and Revolution*, p. 94.

31 To go through them in order: the individual comes first and contracts into the church of his or her choice; the report represents the low-point in the use of reason in a Church of England report, both theologically and philosophically; doctrine is noticeably absent, not least in the propensity to jump straight from biblical texts to applications with no reference to centuries of interpretation; the vision of 'human communality' presented is thoroughly impoverished; anything that is traditional and 'old-fashioned' is to be put behind us and transcended; the world is to be embraced, with its many streaks of darkness passed over (not least in the new enthusiasm for engaging sinister spiritualities); finally, the form of Christianity behind these initiatives is vigorously individualist and opposed to structure and hierarchy.

32 For instance, in the introduction to *Mission-shaped Church*: 'any principle based on Christ's incarnation is inherently counter-cultural, in that it aims at faithful Christian discipleship within the new context, rather than cultural conformity' pp. xii–xiii.

Fresh Expressions writers are horrified by the idea of any divide between the culture of the Church and the culture of the world. Noticing that the Church and Western culture have 'drifted apart', they call upon *the Church* to 'repent': 'this is also a moment for repentance. We have allowed our culture and the Church to drift apart, without our noticing' (p. 13). In contrast, it seems to us that such a distinction between the Church and 'Western culture' is more necessary than ever. For the Fresh Expressions community the problem is that the church – as they put it – is 'churchy'.[33] They clearly mean something pejorative by this, although it is not usually spelt out quite what. Certainly, we join them in not wanting a church full of people obsessed only with church detail ('obtrusively or intolerantly devoted to the Church'[34]). We *do*, however, want the church to be 'churchy' in the most basic sense of that word: 'like a church'.[35] We need communities that exemplify the character of the Church, strikingly themselves, in sharp contradistinction to the world, founded upon charity in an uncharitable world: a witness, a counter-culture and a refuge. We need churches 'blameless and innocent . . . in the midst of a crooked and perverse generation, in which [they] shine like stars in the world' (Phil. 2.15).

How radical is conversion?

If the sinfulness of the world is under dispute, then so is the nature of conversion. Is conversion simply a matter of stepping over a threshold when I 'ask Jesus to come to live in my heart', or is it a longer haul? We do not want to play down the importance of the moment of conversion. We believe in once-for-all regeneration (which, it is clear from the New Testament, comes at baptism). All the same, after this there remains a whole life of conversion to Christ. Conversion is rebirth, but it is also the reformation of

---

33 Throughout this literature: see for instance Susan Hope, *Mission-shaped Spirituality*, p. 26.

34 *Concise Oxford Dictionary*.

35 *Concise Oxford Dictionary*.

prejudices and the growth of Christian character. Conversion is the reordering of the way we think, live and associate. These themes will be developed in Chapter 9, where we consider the role of the liturgical practices of the inherited church in Christian discipleship.

It is part of the Fresh Expressions vision that people should be able to convert to Christianity without having to change their 'culture'. The ideal is for converts 'to remain who they are culturally while changing to being Christian' (p. 108). From one angle, this is reasonable. Although conversion re-orientates everything, there is a valid sense that we can 'remain who we are' culturally – at least if we take culture to mean no more than matters of 'leisure interest [or] music preference'. This is indeed what these writers principally mean by 'culture' – but it is a very thin account indeed. In contrast, we take culture to mean the vast web of ways of life, individual and communal, that embody our fundamental outlooks and convictions. Culture is more than so many basically value-neutral preferences; it is the ways in which our forms of association, our instinctive reactions, our uses of time, our passions and our habits embody what we hold most fundamentally to be true. All this *does* need conversion, and it is achieved by the submission of our way of life to the way of life of the Christian community.

To become a Christian must be to convert one's way of life, even if that is the work of a lifetime. The practices and disciplines of the inherited church embody the truths of the Christian Faith. They do so far more than Fresh Expressions literature will allow. Part of what it means to take these truths on board is to allow them to subdue our own personal 'culture' to Christ: to subdue our time by Sunday worship and observance of the calendar, to subdue our forms of association as part of a mixed-community, and to subdue our self-understanding in the transformation offered by participation in the liturgy.

In contrast, Fresh Expressions writing urges us to relate 'to society as it is and to people as they are, rather than expecting people to conform themselves to "our" way of operating or structuring our church life' (pp. 18–19). The inference is clear: we want to change people's ideas (to 'believe the gospel') and allegiance (to belong on our church register) without necessarily changing their actions (here merely 'ways of operating') or patterns of life (dismissed here as merely the 'structuring' of church life).[36] This is a mistake. The principle of 'giving people what makes them comfortable' might make 'conversion' a little easier, if by conversion we mean some one-off moment, the recitation of the sinner's prayer, and little else. This is an impoverished account of conversion, which we should instead understand as the turning the whole of life to God.

The principle of 'giving people what they want' distorts the life and witness of the Church. As one obvious consequence, the Church loses her critical function and her political voice. When churches are competing with one another to make their message palatable there is little room for judgement and the uncomfortable call for reformation. Certain moral bugbears may remain. As likely as not, they will simply reproduce the knee-jerk disapprovals of the particular social bloc for which the congregation or denomination is angling. A church for 'people like us' will disapprove of the values of 'people who are not like us' but turn a blind eye to the particular sins of its constituency. We see this, for instance, in the obsession of wealthy middle-class churches with sexual sins while at the same time ignoring the evils of an economic system that leaves one billion people in the most abject poverty – with which the wealth of these very Christians leaves them complicit.

Churches that seek to give people what they want are unlikely to be politically outspoken or subversive. If the governing principle is to make church life comfortable, what follows is political quietism. The Presbyterian writer Philip Lee traces just such a trajectory in the United States over the second half of the twentieth century. He locates the roots of the Church Growth Movement with two 'very different Protestants', Billy Graham and Norman

---

36 We should note the 'intellectualist' paradigm at work here: mission is about changing people's ideas rather than changing their practices and ways of life. On the attachment of this literature to a fundamentally abstract notion of the Faith, see Chapter 1.

Fresh Expressions: The Flight to Segregation

Vincent Peale. 'Faith for them', according to Lee, 'has to do with the relationship between the individual and God, one to one.' Political quietism is what these otherwise incongruous figures have in common. 'For both Graham and Peale, the world itself and its various communities are, at best, neutral. The real world with which religion has to do is the world within.'[37] The consequence is to shift the judgement of the Church away from economics and social justice, which they dismiss as *merely external*: 'along with the great majority of popular religious leaders, both Graham and Peale would uphold the status quo.'[38] Martyn Percy suggests that these features are clearly in evidence among Fresh Expressions:

Fresh expressions do not gather individuals around overt campaigning or left-wing agendas. They are not like the base communities of South and Central America . . . rather, fresh expressions are mainly right-of-centre and bourgeois, or individualistic and apolitical – which is, of course, anti-political.[39]

These American trends are increasingly mirrored in the Church of England, for all we occasionally read of Fresh Expressions congregations that want the Church to be an activist force in the world. Even then, they operate within the general Fresh Expressions assumption that the Church is most effective when it adopts the cultures of the world. We argue the opposite. The Church is

---

37 Lee, *Against the Protestant Gnostics*, p. 199.

38 Lee, *Against the Protestant Gnostics*, p. 199. Lee adds that they both also 'strongly support the entrenched American way of life, because any progressive social program would indicate that human welfare could be improved on a corporate, non-spiritual level . . . Such preaching has accomplished nothing in terms of gathering a Christian consensus for social justice or for international understanding.' Susan Hope comments in *Mission-shaped Spirituality* that 'the local Christian community has often felt detached, helpless, uncertain about whether or not to respond to local need. It has even meant, at times, a kind of passive acceptance of the status quo' (p. 89). This strikes us as a description of the attitude of Fresh Expressions writing, not of the inherited church. The parish priest is often the principal social commentator and activist, not least because he or she necessarily lives in the place, rather than travelling in to 'do good' from the outside.

39 'Old Tricks for New Dogs?' footnote 9, p. 205. See Percy's examples on pp. 205–6.

a unique and potent force in our society precisely because of its difference. The identity of the Church and of the Christian comes from beyond the order of this world: 'our citizenship is in heaven' (Phil. 3.20; cf. Heb. 13.14; 1 Peter 1.17). Far from hindering our witness, it is because of this difference that the Church can take her stand in the world for the sake of the world.[40] This difference allows the Church to make a unique and radically practical commitment. In the words of Henri de Lubac, 'belief in eternity does not tear us away from the present, as we are sometimes told, to make us lost in dreams; it works just the other way. It is rather by disregarding eternity that Christians have disregarded their times.'[41] Graham Ward has called this the unique and potent 'exteriority' that the Church brings to politics and ethics. It derives from having a theological view founded on revelation.[42]

The writers of *Mission-shaped Church* and of more recent literature wish to celebrate contemporary culture. They concentrate on what they find convivial there and less on its highly undesirable features. Even when these aspects are noted, they are usually

---

40 As the second-century *Epistle to Diognetus* has it, Christians adopt the customs of their locality (as much as they are compatible with the Faith) but do so from the perspective of strangers and aliens. It is this that allows them to live and associate in a radically different way. This, we might add, constitutes their judgement upon the place and time where they live: 'they take their full part as citizens, but they also submit to anything and everything as if they were aliens. For them . . . any motherland is a foreign country. Like other men, they marry and beget children, though they do not expose their infants. Any Christian is free to share his neighbour's table, but never his marriage bed . . . their days are passed on the earth, but their citizenship is above the heavens.' Maxwell Staniforth (trans.), 1968, *Early Christian Writings: The Apostolic Fathers*, Harmondsworth: Penguin, pp. 137–52 (p. 145).

41 De Lubac, *Paradoxes of the Faith*, p. 93. Later in the same collection, de Lubac adds 'It might be thought that by establishing the distinction between the spiritual and the temporal, between religion and politics, between the salvation of the soul and the interests of the city, the Gospel provided a principle that led away from social action. It is the contrary that has happened and logically so . . . The Gospel had to make us, as it were, come unstuck from the earth, to make something emerge in us which escapes the earth, so that interest in the social problem might itself break free from that interest in the city and its cohesion which led sway in the ancient world' (p. 114).

42 Graham Ward, 2005, 'Introduction: "Where We Stand"' in *The Blackwell Companion to Postmodern Theology*, Oxford: Blackwell, pp. xii–xxvii (p. xviii and throughout).

accepted in quietist form: passively, as brute facts.[43] There is almost no sense that the Church might take a political stand against the errors and tragedies of contemporary society, not least in offering practical resistance through its forms of life. As an example, the authors of the report simply note rising rates of divorce and increasing social fragmentation. They offer no protest; they refrain from labelling them as examples of the lostness of contemporary society.[44] This fits in with the triumph of empirical sociology over theology that we have already noted in this literature. There are certain immutable facts to which theology must bend or accept as given, and these include the ills of our age. Similarly, and in typically quietist fashion, secularisation and the eclipse of the Church are taken as an inevitable feature of the contemporary landscape: 'what is taking place is not merely the continued decline of organized Christianity, but the death of the culture that formerly conferred Christian identity upon the British people as a whole.'[45] There is not a little of the sense of 'good riddance' to such a culture in this writing.

Occasionally, these theorists admit that there are casualties from the processes they otherwise embrace as inevitabilities.[46] On the subject of network cultures, for instance, Sally Gaze asks whether Fresh Expressions enthusiasm 'constitutes embracing a cultural

---

43 Consider Graham Cray, who now leads the Fresh Expressions initiative, in his forward to *Evangelism in a Spiritual Age*: 'our consumer culture puts huge pressures on individuals to navigate their own way through life, offering an apparently limitless range of options, but implying that there are no longer any overall or universal answers' (p. ix). As they are presented, Fresh Expressions simply accept and reinforce this governing dynamic of 'consumer culture', choice and self-determination.

44 For instance, *Mission-shaped Church*, pp. 3–4.

45 *Mission-shaped Church*, p. 11, quoting Callum Brown, *The Death of Christian Britain* (London: Routledge, 2000), pp. 193, 198.

46 The report argues for our embrace of contemporary cultures and it does so in the name of the Incarnation. Here an aphorism from Henri de Lubac is useful, to the effect that there is more to the Christian Faith than Incarnation (or embrace), it must be accompanied by the cross and Resurrection: 'Incarnation, death, and resurrection: that is, taking root, detachment, and transfiguration. No Christian spirituality is without this rhythm in triple time' (*Paradoxes*, p. 66). The embracive gesture of 'Incarnation' is incomplete without an expectation of judgement and the hope of supernatural resurrection. See footnote 22 above.

reality, which ought rather to be resisted'.[47] As she confesses, 'the network society has many casualties'. As she says, 'those people who are unable to be mobile will find themselves in no community at all due to the weakening of the neighbourhood as a friendship base . . . [e.g.] elderly people, those without jobs or cars, those suffering from long-term illness.'[48] Even this writer, having recognized that there is a problem, urges the Church no further than that she should 'mourn' this suffering and loss.[49] At least Gaze offers some moral perspective upon the features of the current social landscape. Mourning is not enough, but it is further than most of these writers will go. All the same, should there not be a wide-ranging and more practical response? Might the response of the Church be a call to repentance and a commitment to defend that which is under threat and to rebuild what has been lost?

In contrast to the Fresh Expression, the parish church is not constituted for political quietism. Its historic commitment to mixed communities prevents it from turning the universality promised in the gospel into simply a good or rousing idea. In the local community the reconciling force of the gospel is mediated and realised, represented and worked out. It is precisely this commitment to see the reconciling identity of the Church expressed in each place in concrete terms that is passed over by *Mission-shaped Church* and by later books and essays. Over and against this, the mixed community of the parish church is our local witness to the Church as mixed, universal and all embracing. It is a politically charged act of resistance to the forces of the age.

---

47 Gaze, *Mission-shaped and Rural*, p. 47.
48 Gaze, *Mission-shaped and Rural*, p. 47.
49 Gaze, *Mission-shaped and Rural*, p. 48.

5

Fresh Expressions: The Flight from Tradition

The Fresh Expressions movement is at the forefront of the Church of England's response to contemporary culture. With it, the Church of England embraces post-modernity (just as, perhaps, it has reached its sell-by date). In this chapter we argue that much about this choice to throw our lot in with contemporary trends is mistaken. It represents a failure to judge what is valuable and what is corrosive about contemporary trends. The Church is worried to find itself at a distance from the world. The danger is that it will join the world in its flight from geography, history and tradition into the virtuality of choice, network and an atomized individualism. In later chapters we will hold up the parish as a practical form of resistance to these trends.

The new over the established

Mission-shaped Church is a call for radical reinvention. On almost every page we read that we need *new* forms of 'being church'. The newer these are, the better. Each Fresh Expression is to be a unique exercise in recreating the Church, since each Fresh Expression is to be shaped only by the context in which it is planted.[1] Even a family resemblance to what has gone before is seen to be too restrictive. This may sound like an exaggeration, as if all the authors really ask for is a little more sensitivity to local needs. Here we should let the report speak for itself: it does not so much call for

---

1 *Mission-shaped Church*, pp. 20ff.

us to *adapt* the distinctive forms and identity of the Church of England from one situation to another; it calls for those forms to be cast off, and for new ones to be invented.

The word the authors use to describe the impact of the context upon a Fresh Expression is not *influence*. Nor do they suggest that the new Christian community should be *shaped* by its context. The word they use is 'determine': the form of the church is to be *determined* by the surrounding culture (pp. 20–1).[2] They occasionally concede that 'listening to both contemporary culture and to church tradition is vital' (p. 105). We soon find just how little that 'tradition' counts. We are told to clear our minds of any notion of 'how the inherited Christian tradition works' and attend solely to 'the mission context' (p. 105). Only later can we bring the tradition to bear – and the rest of the report shows what a circumscribed notion of the tradition that is.

For these writers, we cannot know in advance what a new Fresh Expression of the Church will look like. As *Mission-shaped Church* has it:

> the discovery since [the publication of *Breaking New Ground* in 1994] has been that church planting that sets out to serve an "identifiable group, culture or neighbourhood" cannot begin with a clear understanding of what form or expression the resultant church may take (p. 30).[3]

---

2 In *Mission-shaped Spirituality* Susan Hope defends this idea that 'the shape of the Christian community that may result from the missionary journey must not be predetermined' on the basis of a gloss on Luke 9.3: 'take nothing for your journey, no staff, nor bag, nor bread, nor money – not even an extra tunic' (*Mission-shaped Spirituality*, p. 35). As she puts it, 'the "nothing" that we are to take as apostolic people might include, then, the "nothing" of presuppositions, or preconceptions, of prejudging what shape the church will take. It is the refusal to engage in a kind of cultural imperialism, the refusal to impose a vision of how church life and worship should be expressed' (p. 45). Quite apart from the unsophisticated and rather-too-easily-made charge of 'cultural imperialism', this is a novel reading of this verse, new to the tradition of exegesis and calling for a far more careful treatment than it is given there.

3 See also *Mission-shaped Church*, p. 31.

Fresh Expressions: The Flight from Tradition

Here the authors follow the lead of the Anabaptist writer Stuart Murray Williams. They throw in their lot with someone they admit to be 'the most trenchant critic' of the assumption that a new Church might reproduce the forms of life that have gone before (p. 20). The authors betray no sense here there might be something problematic about this from an Anglican perspective. They give no sense that Anglicans are more deeply invested than Anabaptists in traditions of ecclesial form and structure, ritual and liturgy, canon law and attachment to place. So weak is the authors' grasp of Anglican ecclesiology that the Church of England may as well be another radical Protestant movement.

Fresh Expressions writers want to wean us from the 'particular cultural patterns' of the Church of England.[4] We must face the possibility that this is because some of these writers have little historic attachment to the Church of England in the first place. Over the past few decades many who would previously have worshipped in non-conformist churches have found some sort of home within the Church of England, even if theirs is a loose attachment. It is reasonable to ask whether a portion of the church leaders driving Fresh Expressions, although by no means all, are not relatively new to the Church of England and not entirely comfortable with what it means to be an Anglican. With Fresh Expressions they are attempting to find legislative freedom from the determinative historical and cultural identity of the Church of England. Might they not be doing so, largely, because they have never become comfortable with it in the first place?

More significant than the influence of unconvinced newcomers to the Church of England – if this is indeed a factor – is the influence of ideas from outside the Anglican fold. If such ideas are unwelcome, it is not simply because they did not spring up within our Church. We are not an insular body and it is part of our identity to be open to ideas from beyond our ranks. Nonetheless,

---

4 For Steven Croft's comment that we should follow the populous in their 'growing interest in spirituality' and unease with 'conformity to particular cultural patterns', see Steven Croft, 2005, 'Transforming Evangelism' in *Evangelism in a Spiritual Age*, pp. 126–47 (pp. 128–9).

there must be a proper sense of weighing and checking. This is precisely what is lacking, and what is urgently needed. One only has to read an analysis of the American situation, as given for instance in Philip Lee's *Against the Protestant Gnostics*, to see how many of the ideas behind *Mission-shaped Church* come from across the Atlantic. An even simpler way to assess the influences on these writers is to read the list of references at the end of the report. Most come from Protestant sources, with very little from either Orthodoxy or Roman Catholic writers, except for a few liberation theologians. As one of us has written elsewhere, the list of citations reads like the inventory of the second-hand paperback section of an evangelical bookshop.[5] These sources are deployed with no obvious discernment as to how these traditions might be different from our own. There no sense, for instance, that Anabaptist ecclesiology might not be entirely compatible with Anglican ecclesiology.

Innovation over common worship

When deacons, priests or bishops take up a new appointment, they are required by law to make the Declaration of Assent.[6] They swear that 'in public prayer and in the administration of the sacraments, I will use only the forms of service which are authorised by Canon'.[7] A common liturgy is central to the identity of the Church of England, as this oath makes clear. For the purposes of this chapter, we will take the liturgy as our primary example for the dynamics of novelty and tradition. 'Liturgy' here takes in both the common prayers of the Church, and the calendar and lectionary. Together, they represent, embody and strengthen the unity of the Church.

Anglicans have a liturgy because they acknowledge that they belong to a tradition that is larger than they are, and because they

---

5 Andrew Davison, 2009, 'The C of E should nurture theology', *Church Times*, issue 7612, 6 February 2009. Available at www.churchtimes.co.uk/content.asp?id=70053.

6 Canon C 15, available at www.cofe.anglican.org/about/churchlawlegis/canons/ministers.pdf.

7 Readers and Lay Workers make the declaration but without the words 'and administration of the sacraments'.

wish their community to be one bound together by worship. Until the liturgical reforms of the past few decades, the Church of England had a truly universal liturgy in the Book of Common Prayer. This universality spoke eloquently of the fundamental unity of the Church, whether it was celebrated with high-church ceremony or with low-church simplicity. It was the basis of a profound commonality and this was no accident. The Elizabethan settlement insisted upon a common liturgy for the sake of the unity of the English people. The alternative service provisions of the 1970s and '80s somewhat softened this commonality. Parishes now had two rites from which to choose, and a widened range of choices within these newer services. *Common Worship* extended this further in 2000. Even now, however, the Church of England retains a tradition of worship that possesses a common structure and common texts, even if there is significant choice between variants.

If anything, the new degree of legitimate variety within *Common Worship* ought to should make it a more potent force for cohesion than previous twentieth-century rites have been. Before 2000, some parishes deviated from the Book of Common Prayer or the Alternative Service Book (albeit illegally) because they saw them as representing something distant from their own particular parish tradition. They avoided the liturgy of the Church of England as either too catholic or not catholic enough. With *Common Worship*, we have a liturgy that is malleable to the use of both Protestant-minded and Catholic-minded parishes. *Common Worship* gives us a legal provision that ought to be palatable to all Anglicans. There is less reason than ever for members of the Church of England to deviate from the liturgy that they are obliged by law to use, and which binds them together as a single Church.

We are told in Fresh Expressions writing that a sense of belonging to the wider Church is important and should be cultivated. Loyalty to the authorized liturgy is the principal way this is shown in the Church of England. It is not a Church that relishes doctrinal definitions. In that sense it differs, for instance, from the Roman Catholic Church. The common faith of the Church of England is expressed most of all in common liturgy. In as much as Thomas Cranmer was the architect of a new identity at the Reformation, he did it by producing a prayer book for all to use, not through a common confession. In this respect, as in many others, the Church of England is different from Zwinglianism, Calvinism and Lutheranism.

This approach, which makes liturgy the focus of unity, illustrates the continuity of the Church of England with its past. It is a link with an ancient way of conceiving of doctrinal identity: the Church of England is supremely a church of *lex orandi, lex credendi* (the law, or pattern, of our praying is the law, or pattern, of our belief). Recently, this has been underlined by the Church's renewed commitment to 'liturgical formation'. This is the idea that the Faith can and should be taught through attention to liturgical texts and practices. In the years since the completion of the main body of *Common Worship*, this has become the principle work of the Liturgical Commission: 'the present Commission is focusing not on liturgical texts but on liturgical formation. The Church of England has always maintained that it is in worship that we express our theology and define our identity.'[8]

The *Mission-shaped Church* report acknowledges that if Fresh Expressions are to bear a 'family likeness' to the rest of the Church, that likeness must be found in their corporate worship (p. 117). On this point many Fresh Expressions are even less Anglican than the report envisages. They neglect to observe even the bare legal requirements of the Church when it comes to forms of worship. Here, however, they are only fulfilling a logic that has been present from the beginning. From *Mission-shaped Church* onwards there have been calls to do away with the requirement for anything distinctively Anglican to their worship. Two paragraphs after the comments about 'family likeness' just quoted, the report suggests that even the newly extended provision of alternative forms and texts authorised in *Common Worship* 'may not prove sufficient' (p. 117). They call for 'church planters' to be given a free hand. As far as these authors are concerned, as long as these people are 'trained in the overall structure and patterns of Christian worship', the individual minister should be 'trusted with the freedom, together with their congregations, to develop culturally appropriate

---

8 www.transformingworship.org.uk/TransformingWorship/?page_id=4.

liturgy from below' (p. 117). In other words, they should be allowed to do as they wish, even when it comes to the core agreed parts of the liturgy such as the Eucharistic prayers. The alternative is pilloried as 'the cloning of patterns of liturgy' (p. 117).

It is clear that some Fresh Expressions writers are aware of the value of a common liturgical tradition. When commending this tradition to their constituency, they have to do so at an extraordinarily basic level. This shows just how far from agreed liturgy many Fresh Expressions are. As an example, the *Share the Guide* website – the official site for discussion and teaching on Fresh Expressions matters – ventures 'one suggestion' to those planning worship. It is the idea that 'those responsible for worship within a fresh expression might find it helpful to look at some orders of worship in a church prayer book, such as *Common Worship* in the Church of England'.[9] Using authorized liturgy is such an innovation that it has to be floated as a 'suggestion' that readers 'might find . . . helpful'.

We are arguing for a sense of commonality across the Church. All theological reasons aside, it is also important for an extremely practical reason: people move house. Because of this, some degree of coherence across the congregations of the Church of England is terribly important, especially for Christians who are reasonably new to the Faith. The question is as basic as this: will people find a worshipping community in their new home that bears some likeness to the one they are used to? A move to a new area is an occasion when church-going can slip. This is all the more likely when there is a strong dissonance between what went before and what is now available. There are disparities between varieties of Anglican churchmanship in the parishes, but these are as nothing compared with the disparity of worship, style and structure in Fresh Expressions, standing as they do outside the framework of common liturgy and practice. Fresh Expressions are almost each one of a kind. The person who has come to faith through a 'skateboarding church' or a 'greetings-card-making church' is very unlikely to find anything on offer in a new locality that even approaches what

---

9 www.sharetheguide.org/section1/4/up.

will have been his or her only experience of church life up to now. This is a further reason for insisting that Christian maturity ought to bring involvement with something like a parish church. (And, we would add, maturity is likely to be brought about by involvement with the inherited church.)

Novelty over stability

Character is formed by repetition and routine. This is the way in which things become habitual. By this route, we are formed in good habits. In the words of Sam Wells, liturgy does its work through repetition in its 'very ordinariness'. It forms character and 'helps Christians take the right things for granted'.[10] As Stanley Hauerwas has it, repetition fits us for the Christian life in much the same way that the repetition of practising a musical instrument makes for effortless skill in musical performance.[11] These ideas are discussed in more detail in Chapter 9.

None of this is palatable to postmodernity, which adheres to a cult of novelty – and Fresh Expressions are nothing if not postmodern. There is also something firmly middle class about this sort of preference for novelty. Again, this is not surprising – postmodernity is nothing if not middle class. Postmodernity's restless desire for change floats on the comfortable and undisciplined affluence of the middle class. The lightweight character of this novelty is desirable for people who devote immoderate numbers of hours to work, which cramps cultural and creative interests. As a darker example of the link between middle-class affluence and the cult of novelty, consider how firmly the phenomenon of 'swinging' belongs within a middle-class milieu of fitful boredom.

There is something ironic about the association of this cluster of middle-class concerns (novelty, boredom, postmodernity) with Fresh Expressions. It is a favourite accusation from Fresh Expressions

---

10 Samuel Wells, 2002, 'How Common Worship Helps Form Local Character', *Studies in Christian Ethics.* 15, p. 66.

11 Stanley Hauerwas, 2004, *Performing the Faith: Bonhoeffer and the Practice of Nonviolence*, London: SPCK.

writers that the parish church is inexorably middle class.[12] On
the contrary, it is the Fresh Expression and not the parish church
which is most constitutively middle class. As Martyn Percy has
observed:

the fresh expressions movement is a curiously bourgeois phenomenon . . . There are meals, walks in the park, holidays, days out,
art galleries, exploration and journeys. The imagery is telling –
stones, rivers, sunsets, sky; children, young people and families.
No old people, death, images of decay or hardship. The language
is born out of a middle-class thirty–forty something age-group
beholden to 'fresh' and 'organic' concepts . . . a God of the Gap,
or Habitat consumer.[13]

As the comfortable middle-class people that they are, the fram-
ers of Fresh Expressions praise novelty and all that is freely chosen. They then wish to extend this novelty across the Church.
They assume that it will be welcomed as enthusiastically as they
have welcomed it themselves. As a middle-class project, however,
it is framed against a background where money makes choice possible, and were money grants the security that prevents 'the new'
from being too destabilizing or confusing. In contrast, the poor,
the elderly and the perplexed recognize that the familiar and the
trusted have their own merits. Choice is the preoccupation of the
rich, not the poor. It is the desire of the powerful, not of the dis-
possessed. For those without stability – which might be geographical or domestic, economic or emotional – the vagaries of choice
and novelty can be terrifying. We should not expect ecclesiastical
novelty to be welcomed across the Church to the extent that the
Fresh Expressions writers hope.

As a counterbalance to the writings of this movement, it should
be said that stability and familiarity are also good things. As Terry
Eagleton has often noted, the tenured professor is in a position
to extol the virtues of flux and change with a post-structuralist

---

12 For instance, see *Mission-shaped Church*, pp. 49, 55, 56.
13 Percy, 'Old Tricks for New Dogs?', p. 34.

flourish; the migrant worker is likely to recognize the value of stability. Only those who are rich in this world's goods are likely to side with Eagleton's fictional but representative postmodern thinker, who looks forward to a future that is like the present 'only with more options'.[14] For many people it is this dynamic of breaking apart and opening up that is the problem. Time and again, *Mission-shaped Church* and its accompanying literature treats the fragmentation in the culture around us as both inevitable and innocuous. Their response is never to suggest that the Church of England could hope to offer something stable and secure (and yet, paradoxically, ever new).

The chosen over the given

According to *Mission-shaped Church*, 'the core value of society has moved from "progress" to "choice"' (p. 9). There is plenty of both—progress and choice—in the report. The attachment of Fresh Expressions writers to the cult of the new displays a thoroughly Whiggish belief in the onward march of progress. In the style of New Labour, or of Richard Dawkins for that matter, things can only get better. They present the growth of Fresh Expressions and the eclipse of the parish as part of this inevitable journey along the path of progress. As an example, *Mission-shaped Church* asserts that the Church of England's previous report on church planting, *Breaking New Ground*, 'moves on our thinking' (p. 18).[15] Shortly afterwards, we find a section in *Mission-shaped Church* entitled 'thinking moves on' (p. 22). Fresh Expressions writing may represent the triumph of choice but this does not stop it from also exhibiting a thoroughgoing belief in progress.

It is with choice, however, that we will concern ourselves here. It is notable that every Fresh Expressions starts with what is *chosen*, whereas the inherited church is more likely to start with what is

---

14 Eagleton, *Reason, Faith, and Revolution*, p. 45.

15 'Without destroying former ways of working,' they claim. We see it otherwise: even to see the parish as simply one 'way of working' among various 'equally Anglican' alternatives is already destructive of what they are about.

given. In the traditional liturgy, for instance, we do things because we have received them as things to be done, as ways to express praise, and to allow the Faith to pattern our lives. For instance, we have reached this section of the Creed ('and was incarnate . . .') so we *do this* (we bow). This is what we are 'given' to do by the tradition. Or, it is Maundy Thursday, therefore we *do this*: we travel to the Cathedral; we participate in the blessing of the oils; we meet in the evening to wash feet, break bread and share wine; we watch with Christ, on our knees, into the night.

Notice that the given goes along with the physical: the practices described above are all bodily affairs. Even when the 'given' element is a matter of words, they are particular words, given to us and not under our control. This is significant. Like the grace they describe, and indeed mediate, the traditions of the inherited church are not primarily our work; they come from us from beyond ourselves. This also means that they have the necessary 'exteriority' to be able to judge us and to change our perspective.[16] We will return to this point later. In contrast, Fresh Expressions revel in the chosen. Each Fresh Expression begins with the black slate of the possible. In the words of *Mission-shaped Church*, any attempt to form a new congregation can only be 'serious' if it refuses to 'begin with a fixed view of the outward form of the local church' (p. 91). Any initiative to serve an 'identifiable group, culture or neighbourhood' – which between them cover almost every conceivable case – 'cannot begin with a clear understanding of what form or expression the resultant church may take' (p. 30).[17]

This commitment that we must begin, completely undermined by whatever has gone before or by what we share as Anglicans, is difficult to conceive within the polity of the Church of England. It begins to make sense if we see that that the 'sending' or 'planting'

---

16 The 'theological project . . . can radically challenge the system from elsewhere, from an exteriority, or what Ernesto Laclau calls a "constitutive outside". Challenged from outside, a transformation of the cultural . . . become possible,' Graham Ward, 2005, 'Introduction: "Where We Stand"', pp. xii–xxvii (p. xviii).

17 The report justifies this by invoking the principle of 'dying to live' from 1 Corinthians 15.37–8 and John 1.23ff. This is theologically, and morally, the most dubious train of theological exegesis (or arm-twisting) in the entire report.

congregation may already see itself as outside the structures, traditions and laws of the Church of England. If the planting congregation is hardly Anglican in any functional sense, it is no surprise that there is almost no expectation that the planted congregation should be either. The most they will have is a local 'style', determined largely by the personalities involved.

Once a church group has put itself beyond traditional forms, anything and everything is possible. To put this in philosophical terms, the virtual and potential reign, not the actual and particular. Fresh Expressions pioneers are faced with an untold variety of options. They fish around for the great *idea*, snatched from the boundless virtual world of possibility. We should contrast this with the inherited church, which asks what the tradition has given us. Above all this tradition comes to us in the structure of the church's life and in the liturgy as it unfolds week by week. These are accepted as the gifts they are. The question is not so much what we will make of the tradition, as what the tradition will make of us. In contrast, Fresh Expressions start with questions such as 'what do we choose to be?' and 'what will we make of ourselves?' These questions are there at the beginning of their life. Likely as not, they persist afterwards, since novelty continues to be valued highly. We see this demonstrated in the language that Fresh Expressions writers use to discuss the liturgy. It is almost always that of 'designing' or 'constructing'.[18] This is one more way in which this movement represents the embrace of postmodernity by the Church: there is a fascination with construction and self-invention. It ties in with the language of consumer choice that is endorsed and used by the movement.

---

18 Beyond *Mission-shaped Church*, see for instance Pete Ward, 2008, *Participation and Mediation: A Practical Theology for the Liquid Church*, London: SCM Press: 'ministers preach sermons, *design* liturgies, *choose* hymns, make pastoral *decisions*, plan programmes of mission, and so on' (p. 48). There are strands in the emerging church movement for which the work of devising worship is thought to be at least as important as the act of worship itself. We find this perverse and self-centred. Need we impose meaning on the Eucharist, for instance, which is already 'about' many things, and superabundantly so: life and death, creation and redemption, past and future, and every other Christian concept and hope?

For a portrait of this tendency to exalt choice above all else we have only to turn to the writings of Pete Ward, a prominent contributor to the thinking of Fresh Expressions and the 'emerging church' movement. In his book *Liquid Church*[19] he sketches a picture of the church of the future, where choice has been taken to the furthest degree. Ward's proposed church would be a centre run along what amount to free-market lines. People would travel to a location that suits them, when it suits them. There they would find a 'church' to be used as a resource for developing their spirituality. Ideally this building would have a number of separate rooms. In each one some spiritual technique would be on offer. The user would choose what he or she wanted and stay with it for as many weeks as it seemed useful. After that, he or she would choose something else from the options on offer. When a particular spiritual skill was no longer in demand, the church centre would close that programme down and bid for the interest of the spiritual consumer with another option.

The inherited church values the given over the chosen because what the tradition gives us is wise. Our own personal resources are not nearly so broad or deep. The liturgy we have inherited is both wide-ranging and specific. It is a tradition both steady and surprising. The language of 'freshness' in Fresh Expressions can imply that there is something inevitably 'stale' about the parish tradition. In fact, nothing is quite as stale as a fad fifteen years on, or as the products of ephemeral human creativity after the first flush of excitement has worn off. The liturgical tradition is the work of a million minds over two thousand years. In contrast, the range we encounter in the liturgical innovations of Fresh Expressions is narrow and predictable.

The lectionary provides the perfect example of the freshness of the inherited approach. It leads us into unexpected places and presents us with the whole of the Scriptures. As we follow it week by week, it represents the Church as the master of a household, who 'brings out of his treasure what is new and what is old' (Matt. 13.52). In contrast, the 'innovative' world of congregations

---

19 Pete Ward, 2002, *Liquid Church*, Carlisle: Paternoster Press, 2002, p. 76–7.

that ignore the lectionary presents us with something very different. There we find far fewer readings in any given service – perhaps only one, when the inherited church is told to have three or four, and does. The readings in churches that do not use the lectionary are also likely to be drawn from a far narrower range of biblical sources. Preachers can stick to their favourite passages and theological hobbyhorses.

On occasions, Fresh Expressions writers recognize that the practices of the church can mediate the message and values of the Church.[20] The attachment to novelty and choice, however, undermines their potential for long-term formational influence. In contrast, the features of the inherited church are a constant feature on the landscape, there when we like them and when we do not. Because of this, that they are particularly able to judge us.[21] Each of us has blind spots when it comes to our own particular weaknesses and besetting sins. This is as true of groups as of individuals: each particular age and culture has its own particular shortcomings, which it is unable to see. As Karl Marx is said to have put it, each age asks only such questions as it is prepared to answer. All of us, together, are heirs to these common misconceptions.

Exposure to the wisdom of the past is especially able to draw attention to the wrongdoings and mistakes that we take for granted. The past gives us a perspective from outside our own time. C. S.

---

20 For instance in Steven Croft, 'today, much of the British population knows less and less about Christianity . . . Signs, symbols and traditions which mean a lot within the Church are very hard for an outsider to understand. We need fresh expressions to church for those who need to begin at the very beginning,' Steven Croft, 2005, *Moving on in a Mission-shaped Church*, London: Church House Publishing, p. 2.

21 In the words of the Archbishop of Canterbury at the recent Catholic Fresh Expressions Conference held at Coventry Cathedral, 'The temptation is to think you can always reinvent yourself and that you are what you say you are or what you'd like to be at any moment . . . Here the catholic insight is counter-cultural. We have, it says, a story, a drama to show you . . . Every year, the process is re-enacted,' Rowan Williams, 2009, 'Address to the Fresh Expressions National Pilgrimage, Coventry Cathedral, December 2008' in Steven Croft and Ian Mobsy (eds), *Ancient Faith Future Mission: Fresh Expressions in the Sacramental Tradition*, Norwich: Canterbury Press, p. 5.

Fresh Expressions: The Flight from Tradition

Lewis made a strong case for this in his essay 'On the Reading of Old Books':

> Every age has its own outlook. It is specially good at seeing certain truths and specially liable to make certain mistakes. We all, therefore, need the books that will correct the characteristic mistakes of our own period. And that means old books. All contemporary writers share to some extent in the contemporary outlook – even those, like myself, who seem most opposed to it. [22]

In old controversies, even opposite sides hold many of their assumptions in common:

> We may be sure that the characteristic blindness of the twentieth century – the blindness about which posterity will ask, 'But how *could* they have thought that?' – lies where we have never suspected it, and concerns something about which there is untroubled agreement . . . [Old books] will not flatter us in the errors we are already committing; and their own errors being now open and palpable, will not endanger us. [23]

It is not that previous ages were without blind spots and errors of their own. It is just that they are unlikely to be the same as our own. Contact with the past opens our eyes to things that we cannot see because of their very proximity. The inherited church lives this way. It is afforded the perspective of the ancients, when it likes it and when it does not. There cannot be this perspective when everything is freely chosen. Nor, if the emphasis is on choice, change and variety, does anything last long enough to have an effect on us. Even when something wise is lighted upon, and begins to mould us, it is not given time to sink in before we move on to the next novelty.

---

22 C. S. Lewis, 2000, 'On the Reading of Old Books' in *C. S. Lewis: Essay Collection and Other Short Pieces*, ed. Walter Hooper, London: Fount, pp. 438–43 (p. 439).
23 Lewis, 'On the Reading of Old Books', p. 439.

Pastiche over authenticity

In our experience, much of what is offered liturgically in the world of Fresh Expressions is somewhat lacklustre and inept. It has an air of syncretism and pastiche. Others writers have already commented on this.[24] There are philosophical matters at stake here. We have already considered the significance of Ludwig Wittgenstein. Perhaps the other greatest contributor to the philosophy of language in the last century was Ferdinand de Saussure.[25] His insights were not so dissimilar to Wittgenstein's. He turned our eyes away from isolated elements in language to a wider system. In Saussure's case, this was the interlocking system of a language as a whole. In particular, he showed that the meaning of any part of a system (for instance, the meaning of words in a language) arises out of its relations to other parts of the system.[26] Saussure's 'structuralism' makes us aware of the vast web of interrelations and distinctions that together allow us to use words meaningfully. The ability of language to mediate meaning emerges from the structure of the language as a whole and from the patterns for relations within it. The liturgy is also a system of meaning, and the same principles apply.

---

24 Angela Tilby puts this particularly well: 'Most Catholics would distance themselves from one contemporary view (shared by some Anglicans) that history is like a theme park or antiques shop. You wander round, pick and choose the pieces that attract; a bit of Celtic here, a bit of Syrian Orthodox there; *ancient is awesome*.' Angela Tilby, 2008, 'What questions does Catholic ecclesiology pose for contemporary mission and fresh expressions' in *Mission-shaped Questions*, ed. Steven Croft, London: Church House Publishing, pp. 78–89 (pp. 78–9).

25 Saussure stands at the wellspring of a revolution in thought known as 'structuralism'. His own work transformed the discipline of linguistics; within a generation his ideas influenced many other disciplines, not least sociology and anthropology. For an introduction see Jonathan Culler, 1976, *Saussure*, Glasgow: Fontana Press, and essays in Carol Sanders (ed.), 2004, *The Cambridge Companion to Saussure*, Cambridge: Cambridge University Press. Saussure's monumental work is his 1974 *Course in General Linguistics*, trans. Wade Baskin, Glasgow: Fontana.

26 Saussure showed that a language is a structure of relations. A structure can convey meaning because of the relations and oppositions between its elements. Gone was the emphasis on a neat one-to-one relation between a word and a meaning. Saussure saw that these relations rest on a more fundamental set of relations: the relations of word to word. Particularly important are relations of opposition: things are defined by what they are not.

Fresh Expressions: The Flight from Tradition

Fresh Expressions typically display a piecemeal approach to the traditions of the past: a bit of this from here, a little of that from there. Saussure's structuralism helps us to understand what is lacking in this 'pick and mix' attitude toward liturgical tradition. It passes over the fact that meaning and significance arises from interrelations within the liturgical tradition as a whole. From a structuralist perspective, the significance of any particular liturgical element unfolds in terms of its relation to other elements. In contrast, Fresh Expressions are liable to extract isolated elements. Any church congregation or mission initiative can certainly benefit from the treasures of the 'catholic and contemplative' traditions, whether ritual or textual, visual or musical. All the same, the greatest benefits of this tradition come when it is experienced as it co-inheres in the whole, in the fullness of its own integrity.

Take, as an example, the service of compline. It is one thing when it is part of a richer whole, and another if it were all that was on offer. Compline makes sense as part of the wider cycle of worship and community life. Imagine, however, the as-yet-imaginary 'Complinist Fresh Expression', where 'church' consists of nothing more than plainsong compline every Saturday evening. No matter how beautifully this was done, it would be sorely deficient. More than that, the service would not have the same meaning and significance as in a wider parish setting – even if the Fresh Expressions service were to be 'identical' in every respect. The addition of Saturday night compline to the liturgical round of a parish church is a worthwhile 'parish Fresh Expression'. On the other hand as *all* that a particular community had to offer – as an 'autonomous Fresh Expression' of the sort that *Mission-shaped Church* prefers – it would fall severely short of what the Church should be.

The risk for 'Catholic' Fresh Expressions is that 'Catholic practice' is seen as a box of odds and ends. We pull out elements as we please and assemble them as we wish: some incense, but in a bowl; an icon, but no kissing; sprinkling with holy water, but no confession beforehand. In our experience this usually results in thin fare. The elements do not have the same embedded meanings as they had in their original settings and feel flat as a result. The liturgies and forms of life that result lack cohesion or inner logic.

All too easily they have the feel of syncretism and the appearance of pastiche.

By all means let such elements be disseminated, but they will lack much of their power in isolation from where they came. In order to appreciate them for what they really are, they should be encountered in their original setting. Rather than rearranging them, we should allow them to rearrange us: our priorities and our understanding of ourselves, of the world and of God.

It is the vast web of relations between elements that gives meaning to any particular element in such as system. This is how aspects of the liturgical tradition work in the inherited church. There is an almost unfathomable depth to any given element. In contrast, in a Fresh Expression, elements are more likely to be laid on for a narrow range of reasons. It is often simply that they are evocative of the past or appealing to the senses. Incense, for instance, lends an air of historic exoticism and engages the sense of smell. In one way, there is nothing wrong with either of these reasons. Incense *is* evocative. It does places us in a line of ritual practice that stretches back to the Early Church, and before that into Judaism and the other religions of the ancient world. Catholic worship *is* indeed multi-sensory, and incense is part of this. It is part of the way in which the liturgy of the inherited church draws the whole person into worship.

This is not the full story, however. There is more to it than this for the inherited church. Her practices pick up layer upon layer of meaning from the web of uses with which they are associated. Incense, for instance, is burnt at evening prayer, following the Jewish offering of incense at the evening sacrifice. It is used to prepare people and things for holy use, such as the bread, wine and worshippers at the Eucharistic offertory. It is used to honour holy things, such as the consecrated elements of the Eucharist or the images of the saints. That then allows for an extraordinary and moving association: the censing of the body at a funeral, as a holy thing. The web of associations extends further still. This is the incense that was bought, perhaps, by a member of the congregation as a gift for the church at Epiphany. This was in honour of the incense presented to the infant Christ by the

Magi. Incense just like it is pressed into the Paschal candle at the Easter Vigil: five grains for the five wounds – 'by his holy and glorious wounds may Christ our Lord guard us and keep us'.

When incense, to continue our example, is taken out of this web of practices and their interrelations, its use comes closer to ritualism and mere effect. The charge is sometimes levelled against the inherited church that her practices are empty, they take pleasure in purely outward things. This is an unfair accusation, for there are many layers of meaning for each element of her liturgical life. The accusation could apply to a more substantial degree to experimental liturgy in these Fresh Expressions. Paradoxically, it is there that we encounter an interest in ritual for its own sake, rather than as something with an embedded and established meaning. It is in piecemeal, concocted liturgy that the driving principle is pleasure in outward things.

This tendency to ignore the interrelation of meanings within the liturgical tradition as whole is one way to appreciate what is missing in the Fresh Expressions approach to liturgy. Another follows directly from Church Growth Movement, and the idea that we should simply observe what people want and give it to them in church. The Fresh Expressions liturgist observes how 'unchurched' people express their latent religious desires and then uses that as the pattern for 'new forms' of worship. He or she notices the fondness of the populous at large for New Age folly and the spray-on faux-Celtic mood. This is brought into church. The Fresh Expressions liturgist recognizes that the presentation of flowers at the site of a road accident is an act of remembrance and inchoate reaching out for the transcendent. This becomes the template for liturgy within the church. The results are not attractive. We find the church filled with improvised candle-lighting rituals, shading into aromatherapy.[27] This is domestic religious life for many

---

27 Such a vision of a patched together religious life outside the Church finds its most scathing expression in David Bentley Hart's recent book *Atheist Delusions: The Christian Revolution and its Fashionable Enemies*. Here he talks about 'modern Western religion's pastel-tinged margins, in those realms of the New Age where the gods of the boutique hold uncontested sway. Here one may cultivate a private atmosphere of 'spirituality' as undemanding and therapeutically comforting as one

people outside the Church. It is a tragedy that the Church herself should sink to this level rather than offering something better and more profound.

When we copy the world's pseudo-religious rites, the Church is often simply mimicking the world mimicking us. The danger is that much of what is billed as 'catholic and contemplative' in Fresh Expressions is a matter of holding out to the world an imitation of its own imitation of the services of the Church. It is a copy of a copy of what we really ought to be offering. We give people an inoffensive version of the bowdlerized rites that are their attempt to do what the Church does, only without coming to church. Rather than striving to move people on, from the copy to the reality, we are in danger of producing a copy at a still further remove.

All this is done in the name of reading the signs and of giving people what they want. It may be inept even in those terms. The principle of 'giving people what they want' is a questionable one at best. Even so, we may not even be fulfilling its potential, such as it is. Consider for instance how the church is presented in contemporary film. It is never shown as a Fresh Expression; it is always recognizable as the inherited church. Indeed, when the church is presented on screen it is almost always in the throes of fully fledged liturgy. There are choirs, altars and vestments; there may well be incense.[28] The world outside the church wants us to

---

likes simply by purchasing a dream catcher, a few pretty crystals, some books on the goddess, a Tibetan prayer wheel, a volume of Joseph Campbell or Carl Jung or Robert Graves, a Nataraja figurine, a purse of tiles engraved with runes, a scattering of Pre-Raphaelite prints drenched in Celtic twilight, an Andean flute, and so forth, until this mounting congeries of string, worthless quartz, cheap joss sticks, baked clay, kitsch, borrowed iconography, and fraudulent scholarship reaches that mysterious point of saturation at which religion has become indistinguishable from interior decorating. Then one may either abandon one's gods for something new or bide with them for a time, but in either case without any real reverence, love, or dread. There could scarcely be a more thoroughly modern form of religion than this' (pp. 23–4). Fresh Expressions writers have of late been celebrating the triumph of the 'spiritual' over the 'religious'. As Bentley Hart comments, the problem is knowing where spirituality (in this mood) ends and where interior decoration begins. Each seems to be about the expert placing of candles. We are grateful to Justin Lewis-Anthony for bringing this quotation to our attention.

28 It is unlikely, even, to be shown in the minimalist style of the post-Vatican II settlement, but rather in the exuberant style of the 'British Museum religion' such as

be ourselves and to be authentic. As film demonstrates, this is how people desire the church to be.

The virtual (or general) over the actual (or particular)

Language gives us a valuable insight into the spirit of a movement. This is certainly true of *Mission-shaped Church*. From even a cursory reading, the casual Anglican reader may well recognize that there is something about the report alien to the Anglican spirit. 'The Church of England does not talk like this,' he may exclaim as he reads about 'birthings' (p. 48) and 'giftings' (pp. 13, 54, 133, 147).

The language of the report is particularly telling in its tendency to omit the definite article. The trend is perpetuated in later Fresh Expressions writing. It shows quite clearly how the architects of this movement prefer the virtual and potential over the actual and given. For instance, strictly speaking, they are not writing about 'Fresh Expressions of *the* Church' but 'Fresh Expressions of *church*'. There is no definite article.[29] In a similar way, though a little less often, Fresh Expressions writers talk about 'faith' and not 'the Faith'.

What significance lies in dropping the short word 'the'? The answer is a great deal. The emphasis on 'church' over 'the Church' shows a preference for an idea over an actuality, for the virtual over the particular. It is one thing to say that we believe in 'the Church' and to belong to it. '*The* Church' is there in front of us; it is visible, tangible and obstinately not of our making. In contrast, to say that we believe in 'church' is far more vague. This suits the purposes of Fresh Expressions. 'Church' is considerably less demanding, either in terms of theology or of belonging. In fact, it is difficult to know what it would mean to belong to 'church'. This usage leaves the

---

would warm the heart of Percy Dearmer and other early twentieth-century Catholic Socialists.

29 The definite article is also dropped before 'church' outside of this particular phrase. For instance, on page xii we read that 'Church has to be planted, not cloned.'

definition of 'church' up for grabs. It can be accommodated easily to our notions and desires; 'church' can be re-imagined and newly expressed as we fancy. Not so with 'the Church'. It was around before we got there. Its practices and its disciplines loom large. They are more likely to change us than we are to change them.

The preference among Fresh Expressions writers for 'church' over 'the Church' is of a piece with their celebration of fluidity and plasticity, of change and choice, of novelty and experimentation. Dropping the definite article also renders the Church less historical. 'Church' is something dissociated from a past; 'the Church' is an entity existing through time. 'The Church' is what it is now to a large degree because of the inheritance of the past. 'Church', however, is an idea, abstracted from particularity, history and tradition. To drop the definite article is also to play down any sense that there is an entity, a community, *a body* (the Body of Christ) towards which I stand in a particular relation. I can say that I joined 'the Church' at baptism and was joined – for my salvation – to the Body of Christ. It is difficult to see what is salvific about the something as vague as 'church'.

Even by its own standards, this distaste for the definite article in Fresh Expressions writing is problematic. The movement is notably weak on ecclesiology. Even its strongest advocates admit this from time to time.[30] Such discussions of ecclesiology as there

---

30 For instance, the authors of *Mission-shaped Church* offer their sketch of ecclesiological principles in chapter five of that report against the background of a comment that 'the time has come to ensure that any fresh expressions of church that emerge within the Church of England, or are granted a home within it, are undergirded by an adequate ecclesiology' (p. 84) – in other words, there is very little ecclesiology as it stands and even what they offer is only a start. Later, the team leader of Fresh Expressions, Steven Croft, wrote an article on the Fresh Expressions website in which he commented that the 'task of re-imagining the Church is at the heart of encouraging fresh expressions . . . But the task of re-imagining the Church is . . . difficult. Like taking up a new form of exercise, it stretches muscles that haven't been used for some time. We need to learn again to use the e-word: ecclesiology . . . In my experience, ecclesiology is a word which stops conversations more than it starts them. Some people are afraid of it and don't dare to drop it into the conversation. Many evangelicals fall into this category. We are comfortable with technical theological language about (say) the atonement but not with the same level of language about the church . . . for those who know this task is important but who, like me, are trying to learn a new subject, here is a sketch map of the territory . . . We need to be

have been have often focused on the 'four marks of the Church': that it is One, Holy, Catholic and Apostolic. Attention to the first of these marks suggests that we are not as free to drop the definite article as these writers would like. We say that we believe in '*One*, Holy, Catholic and Apostolic Church'. The word 'One' stresses concreteness. We believe in only one Church – which is to say, in *the* Church and not simply in 'Church'. 'Church' falls foul of the criterion that there is 'one Church' twice over. It is too amorphous to be 'one' and at the same time far more than one. On the one hand, 'church' is so virtual that it is not *even* 'one'. It is an idea that fails to reach particularity. On the other hand, 'church' multiplies beyond the 'one Church' into a radical plurality of instantiations of church. In contrast, the creedal Churches, of which the Church of England is one, affirm their belief in 'One . . . Church'. We believe in '*the* Church' and not in 'church'.

A little less common, but still noticeable, is the tendency among these writers to refer to 'faith' rather than 'the Faith'. It is there, for instance, in the subtitle of Steven Croft's Fresh Expressions collection, *Evangelism in a Spiritual Age: Communicating Faith in a Changing Culture*.[31] As with 'church', dropping the definite article here is a virtualizing move. It shifts the emphasis away from the historical and very particular deposit of the Christian Faith (for which we reserve a capital letter). The 'faith' that they talk about instead has none of this specificity. It shifts us from the objective to the subjective. It puts the emphasis not so much on what we believe ('the Faith') but on the act of believing ('faith'). The stress is on some quality belonging to the believer, rather than on the qualities of God.[32]

---

an ecclesiologically literate church. More work is needed' (www.freshexpressions. org.uk/section.asp?id=2477).

31 Steven Croft, Rob Frost, Yvonne Richmond, Nick Spencer, 2005, *Evangelism in a Spiritual Age: Communicating Faith in a Changing Culture*, London: Church House Publishing.

32 The Presbyterian James B. Torrance captures this tension perfectly in his rejection of 'the existential, present-day experience model' of salvation where the emphasis is on '*our* faith, *our* decision, *our* experience' in favour of an 'incarnational Trinitarian model': 'at the centre of the New Testament stands, not our religious

Faith certainly has a subjective element in traditional Christian theology. It is a matter of assent as well as understanding, of trust as well as sight. However, even the subjective element ('having faith') is a matter of informed rather than uninformed will. The Faith celebrated by Christianity is not some generic human capacity ('faith'). It is faith in the God who is taught in the Christian Faith. More specifically, it is faith grounded upon the faithfulness of God. One way to put this is to say that we are saved not by our human 'faith' but by God.[33] Faith serves to apprehend the salvation offered by grace. The danger is that our faith becomes some activity of our own: it is turned into a work. This is the very thing that Christian theology has wished to avoid, ever since the days of the Apostle Paul. It lurks at the door as soon as we reduce 'the Faith' to 'faith'. There is a clear example of this in *Mission-shaped Spirituality*:

[our announcement of the gospel] – in word or deed – has within it the power to make present the future. It can do this because it *draws on, utilizes,* faith. In fact, faith is the beginning, middle and end of the whole endeavour. It is by faith that we announce, herald, introduce, the reign of God into the 'now'.[34]

In contrast, it is not so much our faith that matters as the object of our faith, which is God.

---

experiences, not our faith or repentance or decision, however important these are, but a unique relationship . . . between Jesus and the Father . . . But it is not my faith or my decision and conversion, my dying and rising which washes away my sins. It is Christ's vicarious Baptism for us in blood on the cross, his death in which we, by grace, participate through water and the Spirit'. James B. Torrance, 1996, *Worship, Community, and the Triune God of Grace*, Carlisle: Paternoster Press, pp. 18–29 (p. 22).

33 Notice that in the classic Pauline formulation of Ephesians 2.8, we are saved *by* grace (through faith) and not *by* faith: 'for by grace you have been saved through faith, and this is not your own doing; it is the gift of God'.

34 *Mission-shaped Spirituality*, pp. 77–8.

Fresh Expressions: The Flight from Tradition

Particularity, postmodernity and postmodernism

In giving priority to 'church' over 'the Church' and to 'faith' over 'the Faith' the virtualizing tendency of Fresh Expressions we have noted before is confirmed all the more. We see yet more clearly that the movement is a thoroughgoing embrace of postmodernity. It prefers the virtual over the particular, the dispersed interest group over the geographical neighbourhood, the new over the time-honed. It is a flight from locality, temporality and particularity. In that it eschews these, and also the corporeal practices and disciplines of the inherited church, it is also a flight from the body.

In his introduction to *The Blackwell Companion to Postmodern Theology*, Graham Ward makes a helpful distinction between postmodernism and postmodernity. Postmodernism is a way of thinking or a spectrum of philosophical positions. Postmodernity is the present cultural situation of the West, and increasingly of the whole world. It is the triumph of capitalism, freedom, and, as Ward puts it, 'the commodification of all values (moral, aesthetic, and spiritual)'.[35] We are cautiously enthusiastic about some postmodern thought but hostile to the cultural condition of postmodernity. We warm to the work of some recent Continental philosophers, which in any case chime with the theological legacy of the Church, but lament the current moral, cultural and economic climate. Postmodernism has insights from which we can benefit; the condition of postmodernity is largely something deplorable. It is shallow, callous, selfish and hollow.

Mission-shaped Church and Fresh Expressions take exactly the opposite view from us. They embrace postmodernity but reject the insights of postmodernism. Their project rests on an attempt to separate form and content, kernel and husk. Innumerable philosophers have disabused us of this idea in the twentieth century, as we discussed in Chapter 1. Here, the Fresh Expressions literature ignores one of the more valuable insights of postmodern thought. At the same time, it accepts and even celebrates so many

---

35 Ward, 'Introduction: "Where We Stand"', p. xiv.

of the mistakes of postmodernity: fragmentation, consumer culture, the primacy of choice, the slow triumph of the virtual and the eclipse of the local and particular. It does this just as the world may be waking up to the need for something better, for the sake of our communities, for the sake of our planet and for the sake of our own souls.

6

Recovering a Theology of Mission and Mediation

In this chapter, we begin to move away from critique towards a positive vision of mission, beginning, as does the *Mission-shaped Church* report, with mission as describing the action of God himself. Our positive valuing of mediation, however, will produce a more generous, cosmic and material understanding of the Trinitarian life into which we are all caught up.

Mission as the overflow of God's triune life

The central doctrine of God as Creator understands his action as totally free and generous. God does not need to create the world, but does so out of his overflowing love. He creates difference itself: a world which can then respond in loving freedom to its origin. In God there is no lack; he is complete in himself: God lacks nothing, not even his own worship, as John of Damascus reminds us.[1] Our own worship is through Christ, in the Spirit as we participate in this divine liturgy. The same is true of our sharing in God's mission. *Mission-shaped Church* is right to state that our mission is actually God's; this is also the position of classic Christian theology. If God is without lack, however, then so also is his mission. While the whole creation may groan in the birth pangs of the Kingdom, God's mission is expressed as a serene outpouring of creative love that sustains the world and holds it in being. If we

---

1 John of Damascus, 2003, *Three Treatises on the Divine Images*, trans. Andrew Louth, Crestwood NY: St Vladimir's Seminary Press, p. 105.

are to share in his mission, we too must confess out of our own love for the world in Christ. As God sees us, so we must see others. Mission therefore is not primarily an instrument of Church growth or a perception of paucity, or any other end apart from that generous outflowing of creative love that seeks to draw others into the divine liturgy. The best evangelism, whether Protestant or Catholic, has always had this completely positive character, following in the footsteps of Christ himself. In the farewell discourse of John 17, Christ says to his Father, 'I glorified you on earth by finishing the work you gave me to do' (John 17.4). Those who believe share this glory, reflecting back the glory of the Godhead, and in this way evangelism reflects the scintillation of the Divine glory into the world. As Pseudo-Dionysius so eloquently puts it, God's radiance 'like a light . . . flashes onto everything the beauty-causing importations of its own well-spring ray'.[2]

The outpouring of the Holy Spirit at Pentecost as described in Acts 2 furnishes an example of this positive conception of mission. It is the ecstatic nature of the event itself and the sudden noise of the disciples speaking in other languages within the room that draw the crowd to find out what is going on. The Spirit's arrival is excessive; through the sound of wind and tongues of fire the creative generosity of the Divine life is made manifest. Peter and the eleven come to address the crowd, who are composed of devout Jews from every nation of the diaspora, but that is in response to, and an effect of, the Spirit's outpouring. One cannot reduce the coming of the Spirit to the function of evangelism, as the uncontrollable modes of fire and wind themselves witness: 'the wind bloweth where it listeth' in the evocative sibilants of the King James version of John 3.8.

The Jewish men are all gathered for the feast of Pentecost in the Temple. What had formerly been an early harvest festival had in New Testament times become an ingathering of God's people as the bearers of his law. In the Acts Pentecost festival we see the action of the Spirit effecting a new human unity, and superseding the limitation and duality of the Law as defining and embodying

---

2 Pseudo-Dionysius, *Complete Works*, p. 76.

human relation to God. The inclusive generosity of the Divine reconstitutes the human family as one through excessive wind and fire, and then through the incorporation of baptism, 'devotion to the apostles' teaching and fellowship, to the breaking of bread and the prayers' (Acts 2.42).

The sending of the Spirit effects all this in one great movement of Divine cascading of creative life, drenching the Early Church, and taking all those who join the apostles into that same life of transformative love. It is a crucial, foundational moment in the Christian story of entire positivity, for not only are the believers so united with each other that they share their possessions, but also they 'have the goodwill of all the people' (Acts 2.47). There is no negativity in the whole story. And although those called to the Jewish festival of Pentecost are adult males, Acts 1.14 makes it clear that Mary, the mother of Jesus, and other women are also present in the room with the apostles, and Peter's quotation of Joel in his address to the crowd specifically includes women and people of all ages as recipients of the Spirit:

'In the last days it will be, God declares,
that I will pour out my Spirit upon all flesh,
    and your sons and your daughters shall prophesy,
and your young men shall see visions,
    and your old men shall dream dreams.
Even upon my slaves, both men and women,
    in those days I will pour out my Spirit;
        and they shall prophesy.' (Acts 2.17–18)

Thus, with the creative action of the Spirit, God renews the Jewish covenant as he does at every Pentecost festival, but now those present as witnesses are of both genders and both old and young. The 'last days' of Joel have also become a renewal of the beginning: of creation itself. The Church is both an anticipation of the cosmic marriage at the end of time, signalled in the reference to 'the last days' but equally a new entity, a Divine cosmic covenant of renewal. Both beginning and end are marked by the fullness of the Divine action and its excessive overflow.

Henri de Lubac speaks eloquently of the link between the Church and the first creation:

> Before the law of Moses, the Church existed under the 'law of nature'; she exists *ab exordio saeculi*. There has always been a people of God and a vine that the Father tends unceasingly; the union of Christ and his Church is prefigured in the union of Adam and Eve. Here, says St Paul, is a 'high mystery'.[3]

The Church therefore is a Divine creation, and a sign of the unity of humanity in God. It is not, as *Mission-shaped Church* has it, that 'the Kingdom is a divine activity whereas the Church is a human community' (p. 86). Rather, as at the harvest festival Pentecost in Acts, the Church *is* the first fruits of the Kingdom. The frequent unripeness or sinfulness of the Church's members is itself a sign of the Kingdom, showing that God loves and saves sinners. As W. H. Auden puts it in *For the Time Being: A Christmas Oratorio*:

> Though written by Thy children with
> A smudged and crooked line
> The Word is ever legible
> Thy Meaning unequivocal
> And for Thy Goodness even sin
> Is valid as a sign.[4]

We have moved from God to the Church, because the Church is the mystery of God's redemptive work in the world. As we have already argued in Chapter 3, the Church is neither a pure instrumentality, nor disposable. She is not confined to this world whether in the form of her living members on earth or those in eternity. Indeed, as de Lubac goes on to write after his remarks on her Adamic prehistory, the Church is already present in the mind

---

3 De Lubac, *The Splendour of the Church*, trans. Michael Mason, pp. 61–2.

4 W. H. Auden, 1991, *For the Time Being: A Christmas Oratorio* in *Collected Poems*, ed. Edward Mendelson, New York: Vintage, p. 374.

of God, where she finds herself flowering 'with Christ by the will of the Father, the Son and the Holy Ghost and recognised in the mysterious Wisdom that, with the Creator, presides over the first creation itself'.[5] Such a high view is not an aggrandisement of the Church as an earthly institution but a revelation of her heavenly origin, destiny and role as House of Wisdom:

Wisdom has built her house,
    she has hewn her seven pillars.
She has slaughtered her animals, she has mixed her wine,
    she has also set her table.
She has sent out her servant-girls, she calls
    from the highest places in the town,
'You that are simple, turn in here!'
    To those without sense she says,
'Come, eat of my bread
    and drink of the wine I have mixed.' (Prov. 9.1–5)

Through the Blessed Virgin Mary, God in Christ takes on human flesh, so that humanity in its physicality forms the 'house' of Wisdom, and from that house Christ, the Divine Wisdom, calls all people to eat and drink of himself.

John's Gospel is the fruit of this wisdom tradition, in which Christ declares himself 'the bread of life' (John 6.35), which gives life to the whole world. His whole mission – and this most theological of Gospels is also completely missionary in character – is eucharistic, transfiguring the stuff of earthly life into spiritual food. To see Christ, in John, is to know him and to know him is also to 'eat this bread'. Mission is wholly aimed at participation. As Christ knows the Father, so are his friends to know the Father through him. Every one of the great signs of the first half of John's Gospel has this element of participation: the water of purification becomes the wine drunk by everyone at the wedding; branches are part of the vine; water is drunk; entering the kingdom requires

---

5 De Lubac, *Splendour of the Church*, pp. 62–3.

'being born of water and Spirit' (John 3.5). Light is by its very nature shared; the shepherd guards the sheep safe in the fold.

Mission is the eschatological unveiling of the Church

If Wisdom is the forming and formed indwelling of God in creation, then the action of God in history, through his Spirit, is to make her known and through her, the Divine Wisdom whose house she is. For God's creative activity is not some anterior Paleyite clock-winding, after which the machine is left to tick, but an ever-present holding us in being, infused by the breath of the Spirit and formed by the Word. Humanity as the stuff of the earth is only given life by God acting within and beyond nature and her processes. Too much mission theology ignores all this presence of God, preferring to see mission as implantation rather than revelation. The real human tragedy, as G. K. Chesterton sees it, is that 'we are all under the same mental calamity; we have all forgotten our names. We have all forgotten what we really are.'[6] Mission therefore is the restoration of a ruin, and an uncovering of the glory of humanity in Christ. We cannot know ourselves at all – our self, as Chesterton says, is as distant as any star – unless we know our self in the Body. As we have already demonstrated, mediation is necessary for any knowledge at all. We cannot know ourselves, unless as known by God. The incarnation of Christ is itself an uncovering, both of God at work in creation but also of our own humanity. What the Incarnation reveals is that Wisdom has been from the beginning – 'In the beginning was the Word' (John 1.1). This is particularly the insight in John's Gospel, with its paradoxical metaphoric structure of sending and abiding. 'He was *in* the world, and the world came into being through him; yet the world did not know him. He *came* to what was his own, and his own people did not accept him' (John 1.10–11, my italics). The Son as Word is the formative principle in all life from the

---

6 G. K. Chesterton, 1957 [1908], 'The Ethics of Elfland' in *Orthodoxy*, London: Bodley Head, p. 81.

beginning: he abides. As incarnate he is sent to his own world. Yves Congar shows the relation of this to mission:

> Mission presupposes a connection with the one who sends – the Father, who is the Principle without a beginning, sends, but cannot be sent – and a connection with those to whom the one sent is sent. This is so whether the one sent begins to be near or with those to whom he is sent, not having been there originally, or whether he comes there in an entirely new way, being already there. The Word, then, was already in the world from the beginning (John 1:10), but he also came into the world (1.11,14). The Spirit was also already there (see Gen. 1.2) and he also came.
>
> The fact that the Word and the Spirit *come* does not mean that they move. It means that they make a creature exist in a new relationship with them. This means that the procession that situates them in the eternity of the Uni-Trinity culminates freely and effectively in a created effect.[7]

In the same way as the Incarnation is an unveiling of an already-present reality, so also is the mission of the Church. In uncovering and restoring the persons loved by God, we assert both their status as human creatures while drawing that creaturehood into relation with Christ and his body the Church. If the Church is anything, she is the mode of relationality itself whereby *koinonia* (inter-communion) is expressed. She is that mode of life in which, to quote Auden again, 'everything be[comes] a You, and nothing [is] an It.'[8] For this mission does not stop at humanity but involves the whole created order: the transformation of the material world into the Divine life of relationality. In this re-creative activity, the mission of the Church is to be 'sent' as a pledge, an engagement ring for the eschatological cosmic marriage.

---

7 Yves Congar, 1999, *I Believe in the Holy Spirit*, trans. David Smith, New York: Crossroad, 2, p. 8.

8 Auden, *For the Time Being, Collected Poems*, p. 399.

Such a bridal theology as this enables us to detect the Church *in potentia* in just and loving practices, and in men and women of all faiths and none. Our role as Christians is to witness to the 'matter' of human sacramentality, while acting to bring it to 'Youness' through Baptism and the Eucharist. In this unveiling the world perceived as atomized, dead and cut off in its secularity is reborn; it is recreated as participating in the Divine life. Mission is primarily baptismal in returning to the moment of creation when the Spirit brooded over the waters and the earth was formed. The Church, like God's playful daughter, the Wisdom of Proverbs 8, is there co-operating, 'like a master-worker': 'When he established the heavens, I was there, when he drew a circle on the face of the deep' (Prov. 8.30, 27). Drawing humanity from the waters of chaos into connected life, it is then ready for the life of relation in which 'matter' – bread, wine, the self – are given and received, and we are constantly remade. In this sense, the dictum of the Orthodox theologian, Nicholas Afanasiev, that 'the eucharist makes the church' is true.[9] In acts of loving self-giving we give ourselves and the world back to our Creator to be reconnected, shaped and divinized.

Mission and Culture: unveiling not implanting

We have come a long way from *Mission-shaped Church*'s view of the Church as a human institution and a purely utile instrument that could even, potentially, be discarded. It may seem, however, that we have come closer to their view of enculturation, since Fresh Expressions attempts to bring the gospel to contemporary culture and to view that culture positively. However, since *Mission-shaped Church* theology lacks, as we have demonstrated, any conception of mediation, it is unable to articulate a theology of culture at all. This is evident in the way in which the interpretation of the parable of the sower is applied in its language of church planting, whereby the 'seed' is 'sown' or 'inserted' into the inert soil, and separates gospel and culture in the same action that seeks to bring them

---

9 Nicholas Afanasiev, 2007, *The Church of the Holy Spirit*, Notre Dame, IL: Notre Dame University Press.

Recovering a Theology of Mission and Mediation

together (pp. 18, 157, n. 24). One clear example of this is in the way in which *Mission-shaped Church* speaks of Christ 'identifying' with Jewish culture, as if from outside it, whereas, of course, he *was* his culture (pp. 87–8). As incarnate, Christ was a first-century Jew: he did not hover over his culture from outside.

This interpretation of the parable of the sower as pure implantation is not actually biblical. As Matthew's version of the parable makes clear, the word/seed is offered to 'the heart' (Matt. 13.19). This rich Hebrew word, *leb*, or *kardia* in Greek, encompasses affective and mental interiority and is central to Jewish anthropology.[10] In the Old Testament it is the temple where God may be known, and the place where the law is written (Jer. 31.33). In the parable, the good soil is necessary for the word to take effect. It never enters a neutral, inert medium. So Fr V. Potapov writes that 'the word of God, that is, the seed, is not at all something alien to us . . . The Gospel is life in God, to which we are introduced already from our very conception by the power of the Holy Spirit, the power which makes us conformable to God, Godlike . . . the Word of God is immanent in us.'[11]

Similarly, our contemporary culture is already potentially divinizable. That is, it is soil in the sense of being God's creation, and as a human construct the Spirit is naturally at work within it, albeit in ways that need discerning. For the *Mission-shaped Church* approach, however, social and cultural expressions are regarded as fixed givens, with which the gospel must 'identify' (p. 87). This wooden conception of 'culture' is oddly monolithic for the pluralism of our own day, and it leads to some unfortunate usages of language, already discussed in Chapter 5. *Mission-shaped Church* assumes the solidity and ubiquity of commodity capitalism, and therefore privileges its debased and dehumanized discourse. The term, 'Fresh Expressions', itself is taken directly from the discourse of food advertising, in which the word, 'fresh' is particularly

---

10 See, F. H. Von Meyenfeldt, 1950, *Het Hart (Leb, Lebab) in Het Oude Testament*, Leiden: Brill and Timothy Terrance O'Donnell, 1992, *The Heart of the Redeemer*, San Francisco: Ignatius Press, pp. 23–36.

11 V. Potapov, 'The Parable of the Sower' at www.stjohndc.org/Russian/parables/e_Par_1_01.htm.

useful because of its ability to suggest novelty without any specific content. We have already drawn attention to the fact that 'Fresh Expressions' is a market commodity: a lavender-scented cat-litter. The reason for such naivety is that secular culture and particularly, consumerism, is a given and discrete fact into which one inserts the gospel. Hence, the gospel necessarily becomes a 'brand'. The use of marketing and capitalist language has another unfortunate element in that it is so tied to the market that like the other commodities, it quickly loses allure and is obsolescent. For example, the term, 'brokers in mission', to describe the role of bishops, looks immediately tawdry and actively off-putting in the context of a recession caused in great part by the banking system and its questionable ethical practices.

The adoption of the 'pastoral cycle' in much theological training for the ministry is another practice that is responsible for much unfortunate thinking about the mission of Christianity to culture. This model, which originated in Marxist 'consciousness-building' and reached the Church via Liberation Theology, assumes, in its 'pastoral cycle' progression, that contemporary human experience in Britain is wholly secular.[12] The pastor works with this fact as he or she accepts the already-givenness of experience, and then employs theological tools to 'reflect' upon this situation. Not only does this model imply the separation of sacred and secular realities, and denies the complexity of present-day experience, but it also assumes that the pastor herself can bracket off her own religious reading of experience. Self-enclosed secularity is tragically assumed, at the same time as a Christian perspective is 'applied' to it and one gets the worst of both worlds.

The model of mission as unveiling what is truly real avoids these pitfalls in both searching experience, people and events for signs of the infusion of the Spirit and the shaping of the Word, while seeing equally clearly through the illumination of that same Word

---

12 See Gustavo Gutiérrez, 1988, *A Theology of Liberation: History, Politics and Salvation*, trans. Caridad Inda and John Eagleson, Maryknoll, NY: Orbis, and James Woodward, Stephen Pattison and John Batton (eds), 2000, *The Blackwell Reader in Pastoral and Practical Theology*, Oxford: Blackwell.

and Wisdom the need for revivification and justice. As Augustine of Hippo puts it in the *Soliloquies*:

> God is to the soul what the sun is to the eye. God is not only the truth in, by, and through whom all truths are true. He is not only the wisdom in, by and through whom all humans are made wise. He is also the light in, by and through whom all intelligible things are illumined.[13]

In mission, cultural expressions of all sorts from art and music to politics and transport are attended to and in every case illumined by the light of Wisdom to discern a Divine formation. We judge also by our own ecclesial culture, which is the outworking of the Holy Spirit in the Church, formed by the treasures of tradition in scriptures and sacraments, which have been tested over generations. This does not mean that new songs or ways of expressing our faith may not be added but they have to be judged by the scriptures and traditions of our common faith. Wesleyan hymns made their way eventually into hymnbooks of every denomination because their use of scripture and their theology was so rich, and their poetry so beautiful. They are complex, sustaining works of art that enable us to articulate our common faith. A hymn such as 'Love divine, all loves excelling', for example, narrates the whole drama of salvation, its Trinitarian action, and culminates in cosmic restoration and participation in God.[14] African-American spirituals similarly are wholly liturgical in developing and enabling movement and liberation within pattern and repetition. 'An' He never said a mumblin' word', the refrain to a passion hymn, grows in strength and irony as each painful event of the crucifixion succeeds another.[15] Every song, prayer and image used in any church

---

13 *Soliloquies* 1, 1, 3 quoted in Allan Fitzgerald (ed.), 1999, *Augustine through the Ages: An Encyclopedia*, Grand Rapids, MI: Eerdmans, p. 438.

14 Charles Wesley, 'Love divine, all loves excelling', in Percy Dearmer and Ralph Vaughan Williams (eds), 1906, *The English Hymnal*, London: Oxford University Press, p. 282.

15 Silvestre Cornelius Watkins (ed.), 1944, *Anthology of American Negro Literature*, New York: The Modern Library, p. 145.

context needs to be tough enough to match up to the depths and breadth of Christian experience. We use the whole scripture as seen through Christ as our mode of interpretation. Similarly, we need the whole of Christian tradition in the widest sense to judge the cultural productions of our own day. Do they exhibit the Christian virtues? Do they seek the common good? Do they tell the Christian story? Are they faithful to the creeds? Do they embody a full vision of the human person? And crucially, following our discussion in Chapter 1, does the form match the content?

The model of implantation in *Mission-shaped Church* is used to describe the missionary activity of the apostle Paul, who is used to justify the Fresh Expressions approach to missionary inculturation. He is described as making himself a Jew to win Jews and a gentile to win them also for Christ (1 Cor. 9.19–27). The implication is that the Church should 'shed' her historical embodiment for a new situation. We have already shown the theological incoherence of treating the material expression of the Church as so many outer garments, separate from the 'essence' of the Faith. Here we have an odd view of what it means to be a person, as if we could separate ourselves from our embodiment. The reason for this lies in the way in which *Mission-shaped Church* interprets the self-emptying of Christ, referred to as *kenosis* by the apostle Paul in Philippians 2.5–7.

> Let the same mind be in you that was in Christ Jesus,
> Who, though he was in the form of God,
> Did not regard equality with God
> As something to be exploited,
> But emptied himself,
> Taking the form of a slave,
> Being born in human likeness.

In the report, the Church is asked to die so that contemporary culture may be saved. The idea is that we are like Christ, and need to empty ourselves. The problem is that we are *not* Christ in this sense to begin with, not being Divine. Paul uses this hymn to suggest that Christians should be humble and serve each other. There cannot be an exact analogy between our humanity and Christ. Our only 'descent' is as a race, from our original closeness to God into sin. To suggest that our present character is one of Divinity, which must be 'exchanged' is blasphemous (pp. 88–9). The exchange of which the early Fathers speak is one of *theosis*, whereby we die to *sin* and live in Christ, participating through him in the Divine life. As Christ takes humanity into the Godhead he takes us with him, as it were. To suggest that we should shed our whole tradition and practices to take on the values of modern consumerism and individualism as a kenotic exchange is truly bizarre. It is, however, typical of a report which lacks an entry for 'sin' in its index and lacks the confidence in the power of the Christian gospel to challenge and convert. Moreover, 'self-emptying' does not mean an evacuation of a God content or power, so much as an outpouring of the self, very much in the manner in which we have described mission in this chapter.

Here also we can see a misunderstanding of Paul's missionary strategy. For this section of 1 Corinthians 9, in which he speaks of becoming all things to all people, is a complex, paradoxical passage that relates ironically throughout to the 'right' of freedom that the lawless Corinthians were seeking to claim for themselves. Paul shows his authority as an apostle precisely because he gives up that freedom. But what he does adapt here is his own belief in Christ's superseding of the Jewish law: he re-enters the world of Jewish exclusivism to win them for a wider vision. So it is hard to see this passage as a justification for the Church 'dying' in its present form to be reborn as consumer-friendly, Christianity-lite religion. Rather, it is an example of Paul voluntarily bearing the burden of the Jewish law.

Indeed, Christianity spread like wildfire through the Eastern Mediterranean precisely because the area had a *common* Greek culture. Judaism itself had spread there and was already highly Hellenized. Paul, like us all, had a mixed identity: he was a Hellenized Jew and Roman citizen who could make the most of this common culture. He did not, however, pander to his hearers' culture and beliefs. When he addressed the Areopagus in Athens, for example, he spoke in highly critical terms of idolatry. Where he was positive was in demonstrating a possibility even in the Greek polytheistic tradition of the 'unknown God' (Acts 17.23). Paul therefore brought the whole Judaic–Christian faith to bear upon Greek culture but discerned within it a true wisdom in the possibility of a God the Greeks did not own. There is no evidence that he accommodated in any way Christian faith to say, Epicureanism or any other Greek fashionable belief or practice.

Our own culture is indeed full of 'seeds of life', but they are not to be found in consumerism that destroys families, communities and gives young people such an impoverished conception of success. Nor are they to be found in much so-called 'popular' culture, which has become in many areas the cynical manipulation of markets by recording-companies. It is not popular in the sense of produced by the people but in being marketed to them. Market forces, moreover, aim at diversifying us through niche marketing that will produce as many individual households as possible to which goods and debt may be sold. To reach and help our own culture in its specificity may mean being on the streets of our towns helping binge-drinkers escape violence and degradation, or offering safe places to which they can retreat; it does not mean validating binge drinking or niche marketing but looking underneath to discern what raging lack and nihilism drives that cultural practice. Why do people drink to excess not for rowdy fellowship so much as for oblivion? It may be that behind the casual sex and the drinking to reach unconsciousness lie the desire for transcendence, and certainly we need the wisdom to reach out and reveal the true desire hidden within the practice. But the 'seed' may be the 'unknown god' of spiritual hunger, rather than the practice that seeks to assuage it.

John's understanding of the role of the Holy Spirit is helpful in our searching of culture. For John, the Spirit is primarily an advocate, a defence counsel, who will teach the disciples everything (John 14.26) and 'sanctify them in the truth' (John 17.17). But in defending the truth, the advocate for the defence turns the tables on the world that would condemn the faithful and judges it. This idea lies behind the breathing of the Spirit on the apostles in the upper room, which is accompanied by Jesus' bestowal of authority to forgive or retain sins. The Spirit leads us to search for signs of his gifts: love, joy, peace, patience, kindness, generosity, faithfulness, gentleness and self-control, as Galatians 5.22–3 describes them. John was influenced greatly, as were many of the Church Fathers by the list in Isaiah 11.2: 'The spirit of the Lord shall rest upon him, the spirit of wisdom and understanding, the spirit of counsel and might, the spirit of knowledge and the fear of the Lord.' These gifts are truly gifted, in that they are charisms – graces from God – but they are also a *habitus*, and a practice that we inhabit: the house of wisdom. So we look at culture itself, not in the abstract but as a series of practices, and the Advocate guides us to evaluate them by means of the virtues in which he leads us. Like a defence lawyer he judges by means of a detailed reconstruction of events that form a connected narrative: he unveils the true story of what is going on.

The priesthood of all believers: unveiling the world

We have already established that the gathered people of God share through Christ and the Spirit in the divine liturgy of heaven. It is in Christ and the Church we worship even when we are in solitude like a hermit in his cell or, like Buzz Aldrin, who took communion alone after landing on the moon. Christians *together* are a royal priesthood, just as we are saved in the body of Christ. To become a Christian is to cease to be an atomized individual but to enter the life of communion. To know God, says St John, is to love one another. The unity and mutual indwelling in love of the faithful is itself the witness to the truth and the attractiveness of the gospel and the abiding of the Spirit. Our hierarchy is in the service of this participation, of 'a community that is essentially structured, where there are genuinely different roles, and the putting together of these different roles creates something new and different for all the parts that go up to make it'.[16]

Quite rightly, the role of the laity has been given new dignity in the contemporary Church, and enabled more participation in

16 Andrew Louth, 1989, *Denys the Areopagite*, London: Geoffrey Chapman, p. 132.

the Eucharistic liturgy itself. What tends to get forgotten in all this is the priesthood of the laity in the secular world: their specific mission is forgotten and unresourced. If our mission as the Church is to unveil and reveal the Divine ordering of the world and the true humanity, then that is the task of the laity to do this wherever they live and work. A recent visit to Paris revealed how much more seriously the working and family life of the laity is regarded in the ministry of the churches in that city. A typical urban parish church offered a range of classes in spiritual formation, as well as masses offered on behalf of various callings. There would be a study group for parents and educators, another for workers of a certain age and so on. There was a real attempt to allow these people to understand their role as the lay apostolate in daily life, where they too are called to mission. In work or home life they exercise wisdom and learn to discern virtuous practices and cultivate them. Moreover, home-workers, office and factory workers alike are all taking the elements of creation and making something with them. We are all involved in the Divine work of re-creation, as we seek to bring the world of people and things into relation with God and thus with each other. Auden again describes this activity:

You need not see what someone is doing
To know if it is his vocation,

You have only to watch his eyes:
A cook mixing a sauce, a surgeon

Making a primary incision,
A clerk completing a bill of lading,

Wear the same rapt expression,
Forgetting themselves in a function.

How beautiful it is,
That eye-on-the-object look.[17]

---

17 Auden, *Horae Canonicae* in *Collected Poems*, p. 630.

Recovering a Theology of Mission and Mediation

The Jewish faith has never lost this valuing of work, and provides blessing prayers for every possible activity. Our own tendency is only to direct the laity to 'testify' to their co-workers, forgetting that they are already testifying by the way they handle the money, fill in the forms, bathe the children or treat the customers. The wisdom books of the Old Testament and the Apocrypha are where one finds the furthest development in scripture of reflection upon practical work, and yet these books are also truly mystical. Similarly, the Gospel most influenced by the wisdom tradition, that of John, is also in many ways the most concerned with corporeal signs drawn from human work: water into wine, sheep-folds, vines, and most importantly, Christ's washing of the feet of his disciples at the last supper that urges us all to be both givers and receivers of service. This last sign shows us that service and work are truly sacramental: 'who sweep'st a room as for thy laws/ Makes that and the action fine' as George Herbert puts it.[18] That activity is a mode of priesthood because it is transformative in taking the matter of the world and making it into praise, and restoring it to order and connection with God and humanity. It is mission because it is following the words of Christ in Mark 16.15 to 'preach the gospel to the whole creation'.

The medieval period had a strong sense of this transformative work of the laity. It is evident in the organization of the extensive Corpus Christi processions, in which all trades were represented, and the Host paraded about the town to witness to the centrality of liturgical meaning in all human activity. The same is true of the mystery plays, in which vintners would enact the wedding at Cana, carpenters Noah's ark, and wool merchants the announcing of the nativity to the shepherds. The anti-Sabbath-breaking murals of the passion found on some church walls from the fourteenth century onwards, show how many trades were needed to furnish everything necessary for the crucifixion to take place.[19]

---

18 George Herbert, 1991, 'The Elixir' in *The Complete English Poems*, ed. John Tobin, Harmondsworth: Penguin, p. 174.

19 See Athene Reiss, 2000, *The Sunday Christ: Sabbatarianism in English Medieval Wall-Painting*, Oxford: Archaeopress.

They show a suffering Christ at the centre, with a variety of tools representing the various occupations of the parish. Not only do they suggest that those who work on Sunday crucify Christ again, but also they suggest that such practice attacks the socio-ecclesial body itself. This is again a concern in our own society, as Sunday opening disturbs family life and forces the values of the market onto every day with no respite.

The manner in which a medieval trade-guild would happily take on the staging of a play in which their own profession contributes nails or rope for the crucifixion shows the sophistication in which they understood the role of human work and making, and the need for transformative action. Blacksmiths both contributed to what was in fact a providential event that secured our salvation, but were also made aware of the violent use to which their productions could be put. Our contemporary mission to our own culture has the similar aim of revealing what is good, true and beautiful about management consultancy, horticulture or marquee-hiring, while judging their negative and destructive features. Most trades have the potential to be transformative: to be eucharistic in giving meaning and value to the matter with which they deal. Helping people to understand how they may already be participating in God's mission by the way they handle the guy-ropes or treat their clients is part of the mission of the Church. When Christ talked to the Samaritan woman at the well, he not only spoke to her about the living water he could offer, but he encouraged her to believe that she too could become 'a spring of water gushing up to eternal life' (John 3.14).

In the same way, the mission of the Church is to call all her children to mission, and specifically to mediation, so that we are all made aware of the way in which we touch, speak and handle the stuff of the world with veneration. John of Damascus expresses this mediatory attitude to matter forcibly:

I do not venerate matter, I venerate the Fashioner of matter, who became matter for my sake, and accepted to dwell in matter and through matter worked my salvation and I will not cease from reverencing matter through which my salvation was worked . . . Do not abuse matter, for it is not dishonourable.[20]

In the 28th canto of Dante's *Purgatorio*, his pilgrim self emerges from the fire of purged desire into the Earthly Paradise, which is the renewed Eden of restored human kind. He meets a mysterious female figure, Matelda, who represents this true, free and active humanity.[21] She sings, dances and gathers flowers, referring Dante to Psalm 92 for an explanation:

It is a good thing to give thanks to the LORD,
to sing praises to your name, O Most High;
to declare your steadfast love in the morning,
  and your faithfulness by night,
to the music of the lute and the harp,
to the melody of the lyre.
For you, O LORD, have made me glad by your work;
  at the works of your hands I sing for joy.
How great are your works, O LORD!
Your thoughts are very deep. (Psalm 92.1–5)

Matelda is responding to God's work in creation by praise in the form of action. She too 'makes' in the form of art, music and dance. Her flower-gathering is symbolic of positive human activity, all of which is now free worshipful response. The psalm goes on to describe the righteous as fruitful: 'in old age they still produce fruit; they are always green and full of sap' (Psalm 92.14). Matelda's fruitfulness is shown by the way in which she holds Dante as she pulls him through the stream of Lethe to bring him

---

20 John of Damascus, *Treatises on the Divine Images*, p. 29.
21 Dante Alighieri, 1973, *Purgatorio* 28: 67–9. 'She was smiling as she stood there on the opposite bank, arranging in her hands the many colours [of flowers] which that high land brings forth without seed' (Ella ridea da l'altra riva dritta/ trattando più color con le sue mani,/ che l'alta terra sanza seme gitta.) *The Divine Comedy: Purgatorio: Text*, ed. Charles Singleton, Princeton: Princeton University Press, pp. 306–7.

to Beatrice, the woman to whom he owes his vision of salvation. Matelda is a perfect image of mediation because in taking the stuff of the world she shows its created character: she unveils the Divine at work in our world. This is our mission also: to reveal to others the sanctity and intelligibility of reality, so that we may draw them to the renewal of life and vision available to them also through 'matter' in the form of the waters of Baptism.

Mission as abiding

One of the noticeable features of the Christ of John's Gospel is the way he spends time with the people he encounters. Not only does he engage in longer conversations with individuals than in the other three Gospels but the word used for this activity, *meno*, meaning to remain, dwell, abide or endure, and its cognate, *mone*, meaning home or dwelling are used also to describe Christ's relation with his Father: 'Those who love me will keep my word, and my Father will love them, and we will come to them and make our home with them [*monen*]' (John 14.23). The usage is both physical and literal, so that John the Baptist's two disciples in John 1.38 ask immediately where Jesus is staying (*meneis*), and then follow him there, to remain with him all that day (*emeinan*). John even gives the time when this 'abiding' began: four o'clock in the afternoon. And the long farewell discourse in the upper room that lasts five whole chapters is itself an example of abiding. It is also at the heart of the content of that farewell: 'Abide in me as I abide in you. Just as the branch cannot bear fruit by itself unless it abides in the vine, neither can you unless you abide in me' and 'As the Father has loved me, so I have loved you; abide in my love' (John 15.4–5, 9). Abiding in this sense has the strength of stability and the creative brooding of the Spirit as he hovers over the waters of chaos at creation. It has the sense of union without loss of selfhood that would later evolve into the Trinitarian doctrine of *perichoresis*, in which the three Divine persons 'dwell in one another . . . without coalescing or mingling, but cleaving to each other'.[22] Abiding is an act of love and attending, by which humanity is enabled to share the divine life: 'All mine are yours, and yours are mine; and I have been glorified in them' (John 17.10). It is through the mutual indwelling of abiding that Christ is with his disciples through the Spirit. Despite the prominence of individual characters in John, the emphasis is always on the *koinonia* of the friends. Knowledge of God is always a social reality that draws one into the circling of abiding. Even the intimate moments of reconnection with the Lord experienced by Mary Magdalene and by Thomas are redirected towards the group by Christ: 'Go to my brothers,' Christ tells Mary, and 'Blessed are those who have not seen and yet believe' to Thomas (John 20.17, 29).

We have stressed the element of abiding in mission because we are no longer in the period when the gospel had yet to be preached to the four corners of the earth. Even then, the missionary activity of the evangelist achieved authenticity by solidarity and co-existence with the people he or she sought to evangelize. And the best evangelism sought always the points of congruence between Christianity and the religious and ethical practices of the people to whom the gospel was being preached. Our call is to be sent in the sense of being with those with whom we live and work in a new way, calling them to a deeper and truer relation with God, each other, and the natural order. Our mission therefore is to be a *material* presence, mediating the treasures of the gospel and calling others to the mission of mediation and reconciliation in their turn. To abide has also the sense of service: to abide in Christ's love is to wash the feet, to love others in the sense that God loves us. For John uses the word for the serene outpouring of Divine loving-kindness, *agape*, to describe the love of the disciples for each other: 'This is my commandment, that you love (*agapate*) one another as I have loved (*egapesa*) you' (John 15.12).

---

22 John of Damascus, 1997, *Exposition of the Orthodox Faith*, in *A Select Library of the Nicene and Post-Nicene Fathers of the Christian Church*, second series, trans. Philip Schaff and Henry Wace, Edinburgh: T & T Clark/Grand Rapids MI: Eerdmans, vol. 9, 1, Ch. 14, p. 17.

Mission as being sent

We have earlier in this chapter argued, following Yves Congar, that being sent involves a new creation and a new relation with what has been before. We really have to avoid the imperialist model of mission 'from above' that 'implants' the message in an inert medium. But the language of sending is wholly biblical and in John's Gospel, as we have seen, is united with 'abiding'. In Galatians also, Paul speaks of the two together: 'God has sent the Spirit of his Son into our hearts, crying, "Abba! Father"' (Gal. 4.6). But the sonship that this indwelling effects means that we too are called, as Christ was, to be sent: this is very much the insight of the Swiss theologian Hans Urs von Balthasar. For him the Incarnation of Christ is of a piece with the procession of the Son from the Father: a begetting in which the Father freely gives life to the Son, and the Son is 'sent'. Similarly, the believer in Christ is 'sent':

When a human being becomes a person, theologically, by being given a unique vocation and mission, he is simultaneously deprivatized, made into a locus and a bearer of community. Theological persons are not monads clearly separated from each other in the same sense as natural conscious subjects: in fact the theological person radiates as far as his vocation and mission reaches. Insofar as he takes the initiative in carrying out this mission, this potential radiation becomes actual; and to that extent, *en Christoi* and in analogy with him, he opens up within his own person an area where others can receive freedom to act.[23]

For von Balthasar, the person in Christ is sent in being a space for others where they may be truly free and find themselves as 'sent'. This does not mean giving up what one is but hospitality and creative love, perhaps akin to the situation of a mother going about

---

23 Hans Urs von Balthasar, 1992, *Theo-Drama: Theological Dramatic Theory, Volume III, The Dramatic Personae: The Person in Christ*, trans. Graham Harrison, San Francisco: Ignatius Press, pp. 271–2.

her preparation of supper while her child does his homework at the kitchen table, confident and held in the warmth of the domestic space. It is being sent in the sense in which Christ speaks in John 15.13: 'no one has greater love than this, to lay down one's life for one's friends.' The atomized self dies but the one for others lives, and in living achieves fullest development as a person. Here mission is a kind of friendship, and the word 'friend' and its cognates is also central to the Gospel of John. This friendship offered in mission is one of generous self-giving: the self-giving of difference of the creation, and the self-giving of incarnation that leads to the cross. However, it is not a negative, life-denying self-sacrifice but a 'being sent' that allows us to be ourselves.

Mission and the Holy Spirit

It is common to complain that the role of the Holy Spirit is ignored in the Church, but there is a reason for this seeming neglect in that the Spirit is the bond of love between Father and Son as Augustine taught long ago:

> The communion of the Church's unity is as it were a work of the Holy Spirit Himself, with the participation of the Father and the Son, because in a way the Spirit Himself is the communion of the Father and the Son . . . The Father and the Son have the Spirit in common, because He is the Spirit of both of them.[24]

The Spirit is therefore felt rather than seen. He is indwelling and active – 'something far more deeply interfused', as Wordsworth struggled to express in 'Tintern Abbey' – and realized in action and in what Pierre Bourdieu, developing Marcel Mauss, calls *habitus*, meaning the embodied daily performance of beliefs and

---

24 Augustine of Hippo, Sermon XXI [LXXI Ben] in *Nicene and Post-Nicene Fathers*, first series, vol. 6, ed. Philip Schaff, 14 vols, Edinburgh and Grand Rapids MI: T & T Clark and Eerdmans , p. 330.

traditions that are acted rather than conceptualized.[25] According to Congar, 'He is the one who is *given* in order to produce everything that can be summarized as the community of the sons of God, the universal body of the only Son made man. He is, above all, the Gift.'[26] Our mission takes place in and through the work of the Holy Spirit. Like Christ we are driven by the Spirit, 'snatched away' by the spirit in the manner of Philip in Acts 8.39. In our baptism, the Holy Spirit overshadows us as he did our Lord in the Jordan: 'in the one Spirit we were all baptized into one body' (1 Cor. 12.13); the Holy Spirit is invoked in the *epiklesis* at the Eucharist to give us Christ and to give us ourselves in him. We are sealed by the Spirit at Confirmation.

In all these actions the Spirit unites: he unites us to Christ and to the Father as he unites us together: 'so that they may be one as we are one' (John 17.11). The mission of the Church is one mission, and it aims to make the whole of the human race one people. Although we may speak the truth in our own language, Pentecost means that this language is also common; we have diversity in unity. (It is telling that *Mission-shaped Church* misreads the speaking in many languages in Acts as 'translations' into multiplicity of cultures (p. 89), whereas the whole force of the story is to stress the undoing of Babel and the unity of the new disciples, who come to baptism that day.) There is no room in our conception of mission for an ecclesial apartheid, such as is expressed in the phrase 'mixed-economy church'. If Fresh Expressions is truly part of the Spirit's mission, then it belongs with the whole Church. Its leaders should say their daily office with the parochial clergy in whose parishes they work. Its outreach should be seen as part of the work of that parish and deanery rather than as some discrete entity. In practice, as we have already argued, much of this evangelistic work is already being undertaken by ordinary parishes. But you cannot have 'Church' without baptism and communion. Fresh Expressions activities will only live and flourish

---

25 See Marcel Mauss, 1973 [1935], 'Techniques of the Body', *Economy and Society*, 2, 1, pp. 70–88 and Pierre Bourdieu, 1977, *Outline of Theory and Practice*, Cambridge: Cambridge University Press.

26 Congar, *I Believe in the Holy Spirit*, p. 144.

in the long term if they are organically related to the vine, and if they are sustained by the *koinonia* of the body. Otherwise, they will be like the manna that fell from heaven but did not last, to which Christ contrasts himself as the truly and eternally sustaining 'bread of life' in John 6. The branches have to remain part of the vine, for alone they can do nothing.

This unity is not a vague 'lowest common denominator' of agreement but again participatory. As Gregory of Nyssa describes:

> Now the bond that creates this unity is glory. That the Holy Spirit is called glory no one can deny if he thinks carefully about the Lord's words: *The glory you gave to me, I have given to them.* In fact, he gave this glory to his disciples when he said to them: *Receive the Holy Spirit.* Although he had always possessed it, even before the world existed, he himself received this glory when he put on human nature. Then, when his human nature had been glorified by the Spirit, the glory of the Spirit was passed on to all his kin, beginning with his disciples. This is why he said: *The glory you gave to me, I have given to them, so that they may be one as we are one. With me in them and you in me, I want them to be perfectly one.*[27]

The scintillation of the divine light among us creates our unity, which is that of our source, and it is this same radiance that expresses our mission of cascading the love and light of God to the world. Paradoxically, the Son himself received this glory of the Spirit's indwelling when he was made man, so that it is humanity itself that is most human when seen as divinized. And it is the medium itself which is the focus of this participation, showing once again the holy and blessed nature of mediation in our common faith, as that which effects our sanctification.

---

27 Gregory of Nyssa, 1960–92, *Commentary on the Song of Songs* in *Gregorii Nysseni Opera/Gregory of Nyssa*, ed. Wernerus Jaeger and Hermannus Langerbeck, 10 vols, Leiden: Brill, 6, pp. 466–8.

7

The Parish

Whose heart does not lift when, amid the hubristic skyscrapers of the City of London, one spots a church spire or tower, dwarfed yet not erased by the temples to Mammon? Or coming upon a bright neo-Byzantine brick tower as abandoned take-away papers are blown around one's ankles in an out-of-town post-war estate? And yet this central emblem of Anglicanism, and the commitment to nation and community that it represents, is completely undervalued. One of the saddest elements of the original *Mission-shaped Church* report was its attitude to Christian tradition and to the parish church in particular. It seemed that the parish was being asked to die so that new forms of 'being church' might live. That this should be the Church's missionary response to the disastrous fragmentation of our society was itself tragic. It was also reminiscent of talks by opponents to women priests who would tell an audience of women that, as Christians, they should be humble, and therefore should not seek ordination. There was no suggestion that equal humility should be expected from the male members of the audience. In the same way *kenosis*, or self-emptying, is called for by *Mission-shaped Church* for the parish alone: 'the church is most true to itself when it gives itself up, in current cultural form, to be re-formed among those who do not know God's Son' (p. 89).

This attitude undergirds the paper/parable, 'Allotments' on the Fresh Expressions website by Steven Croft.[1] Some allotments that used to flourish have now lost their trade to a nearby supermarket. Their vegetables grow 'thin and straggly' and the smallholders

---

1 Steven Croft, 'Parable of the Allotments' at www.freshexpressions.org.uk.

blame the supermarket for their loss of trade as people no longer come to buy. The answer, they are told, is to diversify, create division of labour and produce more attractive produce. Most importantly, they need to tear down the walls both of their allotments and of their minds. The message is clear: parishes are allotments that are inward-looking and do not 'sell' the product. Instead of trying to reach people as a whole, they should find 'niche' markets and cultivate what Archbishop Rowan Williams has described as a 'mixed economy'.[2] The extended metaphor of this allegory is unclear and, unlike Christ's parable of the sower, which can be recognized by any gardener or farmer, this parable shows little understanding of the way in which allotments operate, let alone parishes. Barter and exchange are the norm among allotment holders. They offer an independent living free of the supermarket; they also offer friendship and society. In fact, they are one of the most popular and sought-after institutions in our whole culture, and one of the true signs of the Kingdom! In cities such as Nottingham and Birmingham, allotments are also naturally multi-racial, and bring people of diverse backgrounds together.

Of course, allotments are not Edens, as the 2007 film, *Grow Your Own*, about an old-established allotment community illustrated, making comedy out of the allotment-holders' resistance to a project to include refugee families, and parishes are equally capable of being inward-looking. But the picture of Croft's allegory of parishes as little fortresses which obscure the mission of God is a horrendous and unfair one. It also shows a complete misunderstanding of what parishes are about, assuming, indeed, that they could ever be equivalent to a supermarket or offer a commodity. It is the Fresh Expression that is the private, homogeneous

---

2 The first reference was in the Archbishop's address to General Synod at York in July 2003, available at www.archbishopofcanterbury.org/2195. The term is also used by proponents of Fresh Expressions to describe the Trinity: they seem blissfully unaware of the technical meaning of 'economy' in Trinitarian theology. They also define the Persons of the Trinity as separate 'identities'. See www.shareguide. org/section1/1/mixedeconomies. At this site there is also no attempt to explore the political and economic basis of this conception in contemporary political thought: PFIs being a highly controversial expression of 'mixed economy thinking in relation to the health service, for example.

unit principle 'plant', while the essence of the parish church is its inclusivity and its public character, as we argued in Chapter 4. Fresh Expressions is quite open about the marketing ideology behind the movement, which aims 'to increase *choice*' (p. 109). The ethos behind the parish church is that of service and rootedness, which is not invalidated by the fact that in urban areas, there will be some members of the congregation who may travel from another parish. The parish priest, even in the city, is responsible for all within the parochial bounds, who may call upon him or her for baptism, marriage or a funeral. It will be the aim of this chapter to defend the local church as a resource that is well placed to respond to the needs of our contemporary humanity, and as embodying a truer understanding of mission and anthropology than Fresh Expressions.

Our inheritance

From the very beginning, as we have already argued in Chapter 4, the Church stood against the segregation and stratification of society in the ancient world. The Church was wholly inclusive and soon also ubiquitous. Parishes in Britain developed naturally from the initial evangelization of these islands. Not only were churches founded in the towns and cities from the Roman period onwards, but also in the 'parochia', a term referring originally to those without citizenship in the Roman empire but, by the ninth century, applied to the Christian congregations in the countryside.[3] Monasteries and secular colleges of priests outside urban centres served these groups, and from the very beginning, as Bede's *Ecclesiastical History of the English People* makes clear, offered pastoral care and the sacraments to the people in their area. Bede writes to Bishop Egbert of York:

And because the places in the diocese under your authority are so far apart that it would take you more than the whole year on

---

3 Michel Lauwers, 2005, 'Paroisse, paroissiens et territoire. Remarques sur *parochia* dans les textes latins du Moyen Âge,' *Revues Mediévales, 49.*

your own to go through all of them and preach the word of God in every hamlet and field, it is clearly essential that you appoint others to help you in your holy work; thus priests should be appointed and teachers established who may preach the word of God and consecrate the holy mysteries in every small village, and above all perform the holy rites of baptism wherever the opportunity arises.[4]

'Parochia' in this pre-medieval period, thus refers to the family of communities closely tied to a particular *monasterium*.[5] The continuing existence of preaching-crosses marks places where people would gather to hear homilies and be blessed, even before they gained their own local church building. The Anglo-Saxon development of the Minster organization regularizes this structure, and along with it a whole series of chapels associated with the local minster centre of influence. The Minster Church at Southwell in Nottinghamshire, for example, drew its financial support from nearby farms and manors, which later became parishes, which were units both for tithe-raising purposes but also for pastoral care. By the early Middle Ages Britain was a complete complex of churches, chapels, monasteries and holy sites in which a parishioner would be baptized at the font in his parish church, where he might attend mass in his guild chapel but also have the opportunity to seek help in illness from the monks at a local religious house, and go on pilgrimage to a nearby saint's well or to his cathedral. The entire landscape, from the parish bounds beaten at Rogation to the road system itself, linked holy sites, with religious houses providing refuge on longer journeys from forest and bandit attack, with crosses marking the way. You can still get a feel of this religious topography on the East Coast Mainline, as

---

4 Bede, 1999, *Ecclesiastical History of the English People, The Greater Chronicle, Bede's Letter to Egbert*, ed. Judith McClure and Roger Collins, Oxford: Oxford University Press, *Letter to Egbert*, p. 347.

5 John Blair and Richard Sharpe (eds), 1992, *Pastoral Care before the Parish*, Leicester: Leicester University Press, p. 150, N. J. G. Pounds, 2000, *A History of the English Parish: The Culture of Religion from Augustine to Victoria*, Cambridge: Cambridge University Press, p. 21.

the train allows a glimpse of Peterborough Cathedral behind the more recent domes, passes the high Gothic spires of Grantham and Newark, and then takes you past York Minster; the ancient hulk of Durham; Newcastle, bringing Bede's Jarrow to mind; the Farne Islands, home to Cuthbert and Bartholomew; and the holy island of Lindisfarne, where the great illuminated gospel-book was created, in a reverse recapitulation of ecclesiastical history that reveals the ubiquity of what Will Coster and Andrew Spicer term 'veins of sacred force'.[6] In fact, the parish system, which was already territorially organized as early as AD 900 gave a symbolic unity to Britain that it lacked at the level of secular authority.[7] These boundaries were markers of economic and spiritual relations through the tithe system that supported the parish priest, and knit the people together in relations of mutual exchange.

From the beginning, churches were built on existing holy sites, so that there was continuity in the location of sacrality. This was a deliberate policy on the part of Gregory the Great, as his letter to Augustine, given in Bede, makes plain:

> I have decided after long deliberation about the English people, namely, that the idol temples of that race should by no means be destroyed, but only the idols in them. Take holy water and sprinkle it in those shrines, build altars and place relics in them . . . When these people see that their shrines are not destroyed they will be able to banish error from their hearts and be more ready to come to the places they are familiar with, but now recognizing and worshipping the true God.[8]

This meant that sites of Roman villas or even standing stones would be used for Christian churches. In northern Spain, there still survives a temple to the nymphs with a healing pool and murals of dancing girls, which was converted to Christian use as a

6 Will Coster and Andrew Spicer (eds), 2005, *Sacred Space in Early Modern Europe*, Cambridge: Cambridge University Press, p. 9.

7 See John Blair, 2005, 'Recent Work on Parish Formation in England: Some Comparisons and Contrasts with France,' *Revues Médiévales*, 49, pp. 33–44.

8 Bede, *Ecclesiastical History*, Book 1, Chapter 30, p. 57.

baptistery, with a church built above it. One of the holy well sites at Southwell Minster was formerly a Nymphaeum in the same way and no doubt there were many other examples of this mode of conversion.[9]

Britain by the twelfth century was 'a land of parishes', ranging from the churches in fields among the scattered farm settlements of Cornwall to the manor churches of Hampshire, which developed as the royal estates were parcelled out into manors.[10] Some parish churches evolved from cemetery chapels associated with the cult of relics.[11] In exchange for tithes and other oblations, the rector or vicar in his stead provided sacramental and pastoral care for all within the parish, and had especial authority through the possession of a font for baptism and a churchyard for burials. Churches were grouped into rural deaneries, whose clergy met in synod; the bishop's representative, the archdeacon, had authority over these deaneries, and chrism for baptism was, as now, collected from the cathedral church, where it had been given Episcopal blessing.

The rector was responsible for the upkeep of the chancel, and the laity the nave. The lay people were also responsible for providing mass-books and candles, and there are many examples of wills leaving bed-linen and kerchiefs to be made into altar-cloths.[12] Parishes were as important for secular local functions as for religious ones. Katherine French gives a list of witnesses to a baptism in Walton, Lancashire in 1379, who give a wide variety of reasons for being in church that day.[13] Only three out of the nine were present to hear mass; others went to buy and sell, to hear news of Ireland and 'to meet a man from Liverpool'. From the very

9 Malcolm Todd, 2005, 'Baths or Baptisteries? Holcombe, Lufton and their Analogues,' *Oxford Journal of Archaeology*, 24, 3, pp. 307–11.

10 Pounds, *History of the English Parish*, p. 5.

11 Louis Duchesne and M. L. McClure (eds), 1931, *Christian Worship: Its Origin and Development. A Study of the Latin Liturgy*, London: SPCK, p. 401.

12 See Eamon Duffy, 1992, *The Stripping of the Altars: Traditional Religion in England c. 1400–c. 1580*, New Haven and London: Yale University Press, p. 110f. Duffy emphasizes that altars were often under lay control.

13 Katherine French, 2001, *The People of the Parish: Community Life in a Late Medieval English Diocese*, Philadelphia PN: University of Philadelphia Press, 2001, p. 1.

beginning then, the parish church had wide functions, and a huge involvement from the laity, who also provided the pax bread for distribution after mass. It was local court, social service, and meeting-place for the whole people, who could all equally call on its spiritual services. As Martyn Percy points out, the parish church symbolized the sustainability of the community as such, saying, in effect, 'this is a viable, living community that can support itself and support its God.'[14]

One crucial aspect of the Reformation in Britain was that it did not lose this sense of total coverage. Under the Elizabethan settlement, the Church of England was not a Church among many but *the* Church for the English people, and the parish the main local administrative district, with the role of churchwardens even more important.[15] Indeed, at every stage of our Christian history, the idea of being there for everyone is always present. In earlier times this was natural in that the idea of an individual believer outside the social grouping was an unusual one. Our present understanding of the individual subject is a post-Enlightenment creation.

As a result of our history we thus have the most important collection of medieval parish churches in the world, without which our landscape, our cultural imagination and our faith is well nigh impossible to imagine. It is a stony sacrament of hospitality and a resource of incomparable value. It is important to state that even without its people, the church building is *already* a symbol of the out-flowing of the divine life, and the everlasting love of our heavenly Father. As a work of art it is very much a creation of lay piety, especially from the later Middle Ages, when the work of the guilds is most evident on church architecture. It is as true today. Priests may come and go but the lay people go on lovingly tending the churchyard – in the case of Lambley in Nottinghamshire, forcing shrubs into cross-shapes and planting bulbs in the shape

---

14 Martyn Percy, 2006, 'Many Rooms in My Father's House: The Changing Identity of the English Parish Church,' in *The Future of the Parish System: Shaping the Church of England for the 21st Century*, ed. Steven Croft, London: Church House Publishing, pp. 3–15 (p. 10).

15 See, for example, Lynn A. Botelho, 2004, *Old Age and the English Poor Law, 1500–1700*, Woodbridge: Boydell and Brewer, p. 20.

of holy signs. It was lay people of that parish who commissioned recently the lovely driftwood statue of Mary and Child by a local sculptor. The sunlight glances on the brass and makes it sparkle and the flowers shiver in the draught, while the silence is pregnant with the hopes and dreams of generations. And it does not take long for a building to acquire the sense of tradition and the history of prayer. It has only to be loved, treated decently, and prayed in. The more modern council-estate churches of Portsmouth and the Victorian Gothic churches of our northern industrial cities are just as eloquent, as loved and often as beautiful.

As long ago as the 1950s an agnostic Philip Larkin was bemused by visiting a church, but he admitted:

A serious house on serious earth it is,
In whose blent air all our compulsions meet,
Are recognized, and robed as destinies.
And that much never can be obsolete,
Since someone will forever be surprising
A hunger in himself to be more serious,
And gravitating with it to this ground,
Which, he once heard, was proper to grow wise in,
If only that so many dead lie round.[16]

In many parts of our country, the church building is the only architecture of character and merit in a place long abandoned by the supermarket chains – apart from their overpriced local incarnations – and long ago denuded by a Thatcherite government of its school playing-fields. The very presence of the building speaks of other values, other hopes. It expresses the truth we argued in the previous chapter, that in creation, the Word is active, and the Spirit breathes through every just and generous action. The presence of the Christian shrine is itself an expression of this truth that the place itself – suburb, ex-mining town or city – is holy. As John Donne writes in one of his sermons:

---

16 Philip Larkin, 1955, 'Church Going' in *The Less Deceived*, Hull: Marvell Press, p. 28.

But yet these places are not only consecrated and sanctified by your coming; but to be sanctified also for your coming; that so, as the Congregation sanctifies the place, the place may sanctify the Congregation too. They must accompany one another; holy people and holy places.[17]

Our need for a local place

Recovering a positive approach to our parish churches as a resource and a witness to God, allows us to use them strategically as agents for mission. For the parish church is a potent symbol. Despite the fact that the Church of England is doing its best to downplay its witness, the visual media make constant reference to the parish church building. One recent ITV Agatha Christie mystery transposed most of the action from the houses of the suspects in *Murder is Easy* to the parish church. This was a convenience, no doubt, because it brought all the characters together quite naturally, but it worked as a device precisely because the parish church is a shorthand way of signalling local community life, as it also does in the comic serial, *Jam and Jerusalem*, on the BBC.

In both cases, the church building is an expression of locality. The church evokes the sacred as at the heart of a place, and as granting it a cohesive identity. Importantly, the presence of a church building allows the place in which it is set to gather meaning as a community. In that sense, the parish church 'unveils' the created origin of humanity and its social character. One example of this creation of community is given by Samuel Wells in an article on liturgy and ethics, where he speaks of a church photography project, in which a group went out and took photographs of every sort of person and activity in the parish.[18] Displayed around the walls of the church by a single parents' group who met at the church, the interconnections between people and locality were revealed, and the whole area lay

---

17 From a sermon, quoted in John Moses (ed.) 2003, *One Equal Light: An Anthology of the Writings of John Donne*, Norwich: Canterbury Press, p. 225.

18 Wells, 'How Common Worship Forms Local Character', pp. 66–74 (p. 68).

open for intercession. Invited in, the people of the area could begin to see themselves as one neighbourhood. For a locality is not a given fact so much as a communal imaginative creation; like the nation state, a locality is an 'imagined community'.[19]

Fresh Expressions ideology is built upon the assumption that people are less localized, which is not actually the case for the poor ⎿ at all. Mobility is classed-based and affects primarily the middle classes. There are parishes in Nottingham, for example, where car ownership is only 43 percent or fewer of households, and where people are very unlikely to move.[20] A youth in such an area may spend hours in online gaming with others in Thailand or Alaska but belong to a gang that is at risk as soon as it moves beyond the invisible territorial barrier of its postcode. The atomization of modern life means that people are desperately in need of a sense of belonging, and the rise of gang culture is a negative outworking of this desire, especially necessary for those without strong family bonds. The (mostly middle-class) development of networks is similarly a way of making relations in a fragmented world.

In practice, most of the networks people make are local in character, from the book group to the school Parent Teacher Association or the badminton club. Although this is not the case with online networks, even here, the tendency to 'tweet' about one's current physical activity, such as tea-making or reading the newspaper, shows a need to 'earth' such activities in the embodied real. It is as if the activity has no meaning in itself until it is given social expression online, and in that way exhibits the same need for 'imagined community'. A hundred or even fifty years ago, many of these activities would have been part of the life of the local church, but as part of its natural out-flowing of creative life, not a

---

19 This is the title and leading idea of Benedict Anderson, 1983, *Imagined Communities*, London and New York: Verso. The parish is less of an imagined community than a nation because its size means people can relate face-to-face, whereas the nation necessarily cannot be visualized, and therefore has to be imagined.

20 A recent report into health needs in North and South Clifton revealed that in the Bridge area of Nottingham households without car ownership numbered 56.3 percent, while in Nottingham as a whole 44 percent of households had no access to a car (*Report on Clifton North and Clifton South Area Health Needs*, accessed at www.nomadplug.org.uk).

'church' in itself. The elective element in the badminton, football or sewing would have rendered it a part of a greater whole, not a complete expression of the church community. Many of the most successful so-called 'Fresh Expressions of Church' today are part of the larger mission of local churches. Often, the activities are an extension of what the parish has already been engaged in as a response to the needs of their local area. One example on the Fresh Expressions website, 'Tomatoes,' is a free Saturday morning cafe and discussion group run by the Church of the Martyrs, Leicester, for families coming to bring children to ballet class nearby. This is seen by the church people who organize it as an 'act of loving service', and they are clear that the activity is not 'Church' but part of building community and seeing Church as part of that community. It is a first step on a path towards discipleship, and the very clarity with which Peter Gilbert describes the modesty and yet authenticity of their aims, makes their work all the more successful, attracting regularly seventy to eighty people and their children.[21]

If the Church is truly to be incarnational, then she must be local, for there is no universality before complete immersion in the particularities of our own corporeality. Oliver O'Donovan emphasizes the fact that our love – including, of course, love of neighbour – can only ever be particular, and he finds divine warrant for this:

> The Divine Word, the intelligibility of God, is unlike the intelligibility of the world, in that it communicates itself in the particular; God makes himself known in election, the principle of particularity, and yet without prejudice to his universal processes of love. The phrase, 'Universal love' expresses the ultimate paradox of the divine presence in the world; for in all our experience of it, love is not universal but particular, intimate, and selective. The attempt to depict a form of human love which is without particularity, reciprocity or preference has never yielded anything but a cold monstrosity.[22]

---

21 See the full story at www.freshexpressions.org.uk/stories/tomatoes.
22 Oliver O'Donovan, 1989, 'The Loss of a Sense of Place,' *Irish Theological Quarterly*, 55, pp. 39–58 (p. 53).

The Parish

To be incarnational means to 'abide', to be part of where one lives and works, not to insert oneself in it as some implantation from outside. This is, to use Christological terms, an ecclesiology and a mission 'from below', that is faithful to embodiment and to place as God-given. This is true of the place one lives for a few months as for the home of decades. The authors of the 2005 report, *Presence and Engagement*, about the role of different faith communities in our common life, emphasize this point:

> To be present and engaged is to be incarnated, to be present in particular time and space, with the possibility of speaking particular words and taking a range of actions. Presence as incarnation is a gift of God, full of the possibility of abundant life; that is the purpose of incarnation – 'I have come that you might have life and have it abundantly.'

> [. . .] The Church of England has continued to understand itself to be called to be present corporately in all the localities of the country. At the heart of this understanding is the parish church, a Christian community called to be present and to engage actively with those who live in the neighbourhood irrespective of their faith or none. [. . .] It would be ironic if at a time when there is a growing acceptance of the significance of the local geographic community as a counter to the all pervasive globalising and centralising pressures, the church should move away from its historic commitment to people in a place.[23]

At a time when our localities are being stripped of their post offices, pubs and local shops, it would be cruel and ungenerous to abandon our parish churches and the commitment and solidarity they embody. As John Inge argues in his *Theology of Place*, in a globalized world, people are desperate for 'place' in the sense of a space that has value, and connects people geographically to

---

23 *Presence and Engagement*, at www.cofe.anglican.org/info/interfaith/presence.pdf, paras 3, 18 and 23.

155

their locality, and temporally to their past.[24] This is not to underestimate the financial cost of such a commitment, and the need for ways to ensure the burden of upkeep of a historic building does not fall completely on the often small community whose parish church it forms. It is, however, to assert that we should move away from a position that views our historic inheritance as a pure burden and an obstacle to mission, towards a commitment to the evangelistic and social value of the local church. For this is also a commitment to the poor, the marginalized and those unrepresented on Facebook.

Our need for a sacred place

It is not only the picturesque village church which is represented on television: every other urban detective television programme contains a scene in which a victim or perpetrator finds refuge in a crepuscular urban church in which the priest is, opportunely, just finishing an evening service or emerging from a confessional. Dead bodies, in such dramas, have an inherent tendency to appear in the most sacred parts of the church building. Here, the church building represents a sanctuary in the labyrinthine and violent inner-city. Even when violated, the holiness of the building offers significance and a depth of meaning to the death of the person found there.

For there is something quite uncompromising about a church building. Even when converted into a nightclub or a bijou residence, it speaks of values that are other. There is no faith anywhere without a concept of sacred places. Minority faith groups in our own country quickly raise money to build temples, mosques and gurdwaras. We date the beginning of religious practice itself to the arranging of the bodies of the dead in burial: these are the first shrines. And archaeologists now believe that the glorious cave paintings of Lascaux and elsewhere are religious in character.[25]

---

24 John Inge, 2003, *A Christian Theology of Place*, Aldershot: Ashgate, pp. 123–39.

25 Georges Bataille, 2005, *The Cradle of Humanity: Prehistoric Art and Culture*, New York: Zone Books.

The Parish

Stonehenge itself was at the centre of a complex sacred landscape of holy sites. One of the most moving aspects of Italian life even today is the sight of little shrines set into walls above shops, or in Switzerland the wayside crosses high up among the sound of cowbells. It is therefore not accidental that in our contemporary world, people quickly create shrines to their dead once more beside the road or at the sites of violent deaths. And Britain itself has such a wealth of holy sites, stones and great carved cross-shafts from the early Christian centuries, which still speaks to people independently of the faith. The presence of pieces of torn cloth on trees above holy wells put there by people influenced by New Age spirituality shows that the same unchurched audience that Fresh Expressions desires to reach is concerned with the power of holy places.

Christ's own mission was rooted in regular synagogue worship, and in frequent visits to the temple in Jerusalem, from which he famously evicted the money-changers with some violence to their stalls. Such a reaction does not speak of the unimportance of the sacred site, even if temple and ark fade before the presence of God himself, the 'temple not made with hands'. As we have argued, Christ as our 'temple' means that humanity, the city, the country and all creation is to be seen as holy: 'this is my body'. Since the Christian Church participates in God's mission as a community of indwelling and 'being sent', the new faith, once thrown out of the synagogues, naturally found new places to meet and worship in the houses of prominent members, which were big enough to contain them and, as soon as possible, gave witness by raising public buildings. Dura Europos in Syria, precisely dated to AD 231 by the careful mark of a founding member, contains the ruins of a house adapted for church use, with a dais for the altar table and bishop, and a pool for baptism.[26] The exciting discovery of a church dating from the same period inside what is now a prison at Megiddo in northern Israel, shows evidence of Christian soldiers worshipping with others (including four prominent women) inside

---

26 Harold W. Turner, 1979, *From Temple to Meeting House: The Phenomenology and Theology of Places of Worship*, The Hague: Walter de Gruyter, p. 158.

a Roman camp.[27] But long before Constantine's conversion that allowed the Church to build openly, great holiness accrued to the burial places of the martyrs, over which baptismal fonts would eventually be built. The Church Father Minucius Felix, *c.* 200 speaks of Romans complaining that Christian 'sacraria' (shrines) have sprung up all over the world and certainly by Eusebius's day, they were ubiquitous.[28]

We should not think, therefore, that the building of places of worship is some Constantinian accretion, or 'fall' from some nomadic ideal. Even the early house-churches were rather, house-mansions, since they had to be large enough to hold a meeting, and include a pool for baptism. The marking of sacred place is surely part of the nature of our embodiment that means we always need particular people and places. For it is from the particular that we learn to love; as G. K. Chesterton has pointed out, there is no universal patriotism that is not idealizing and vague.[29] To learn to love the world, we must first experience the holiness of the place in which we find ourselves. To regard a place as holy does not mean that it be necessarily a religious site *per se*, nor even that it be particularly beautiful. For Chesterton, a natural Thomist, it meant an attentiveness to the water tower or streetlight as real and separate from the self: 'Mine', he writes of his childhood, 'is a memory of a sort of white light on everything, cutting things out very clearly, and rather emphasising their solidity.'[30] Through the particularity of the object, he gained the sense of existence as existent: 'there *is* an Is.'[31] Seeing the tree or lamp-post as a tree or lamp-post is, however, to be aware of the object as mediated by a concept of arboreality, or of lamp-postiness; it is to be aware of it as formed, either by human making or divine creation. As the

---

27 Yotam Tepper and Leah Di Segni, 2006, *A Christian Prayer Hall of the Third Century at Kefar Othnay (Legio): Excavations at the Megiddo Prison 2005*, Tel Aviv: IAA.

28 Minucius Felix, *The Octavius*, in *The Ante-Nicene Fathers*, vol. 4, p. 177.

29 Chesterton, *Orthodoxy*, pp. 110–12.

30 G. K. Chesterton, 2001 [1936], *Autobiography*, Thirsk: House of Stratus, p. 26.

31 G. K. Chesterton, 1986 [1933], *Thomas Aquinas/ St Francis of Assisi*, San Francisco: Ignatius Press, p. 153.

object is disclosed, it opens itself therefore to its origin. It reveals existence to us as something with ultimate meaning, a meaning that is beyond the object itself, yet allows us to understand and appreciate it. For Thomas Aquinas and the medieval philosophers this was radiance: *claritas*.[32] Chesterton believed that children were natural Thomists in their clear-eyed perception of reality, and their play, he believed, was a mode of artistic creation. Knowing that they are playing, they too perceive form, meaning and radiance in their make-believe.[33]

Children respond to the beauty and reality of existence by collecting objects: stones, shells, buttons and other often-overlooked objects that they hoard in boxes. Their collections are a religious response to the wonder they perceive in the world. In the same way we build holy places. To create a Christian shrine or build a church is never to assert the supremacy in holiness of the part over against the whole. It is quite different from Durkheim's bi-polar view of a dualistic division between sacred and profane. Rather, it is to mark the otherness of the earth itself, and its created origin. A church marks the fact that the earth does not belong to us but to God, whose trustees we are. It is a way of marking the holiness and realism of the world that God made.

Bishop Alistair Redfern writes eloquently about the importance of the rural church building, which is frequently more important to its parish than the community itself: 'the church building stands for the dependability of God, and for God's power and presence as located, permanent and enduring . . . literally transcending the human world with its transitoriness and fallibilities.'[34]

In our rush to confine our understanding of 'Church' to the gathered human community, we are in danger of actually worshipping 'community' as such. This can often be the danger in the congregational emphasis of parts of the Episcopal Church of the

---

32 On *claritas* in Thomas, see Umberto Eco, 1988, *The Aesthetics of Thomas Aquinas*, trans. Hugh Bredin, Cambridge MS: Harvard University Press, pp. 64–121.

33 Chesterton, *Autobiography*, p. 26.

34 Alastair L. J. Redfern, 2004, 'Listening to the Anglican Tradition' in *Changing Rural Life: A Christian Response to Key Rural Issues*, ed. Jeremy Martineau, Leslie J. Francis and Peter Francis, Norwich: Canterbury Press, pp. 233–50 (p. 243).

United States, where the 'high' church liturgical practice of even the 'lowest' and most evangelical of churches belies the fact that the heart of the worship resides in celebration of the congregation as itself. This has been a danger also in the post-Vatican II Catholic Church, as the present Pope has become aware. And it can also be a danger in the successful suburban church in the United Kingdom. 'Abiding' without the sense of 'being sent' becomes mutual self-congratulation. The awful threats of global warming should call us away from this human self-centredness towards the importance of the whole cosmos as God's creation, of which we are a tiny part.

There is a beautiful poem by Alice Meynell about Portugal after its revolution that led, for a time, to the destruction of churches and outlawing of the Roman Catholic Church:[35]

And will they cast the altars down,
Scatter the chalice, crush the bread?
In field, in village, and in town
He hides an unregarded head;

Waits in the corn-lands far and near,
Bright in His sun, dark in His frost,
Sweet in the vine, ripe in the ear –
Lonely, unconsecrated Host.

The land is no less holy for the absence of religious practice, but Christ goes unrecognized: he lurks. A similar conception is expressed by the Russian theologian, Sergei Bulgakov, for whom the Holy Grail is not the legendary chalice that held the blood of Christ at the crucifixion, but the whole world. The earth is a giant grail, which holds the bodily fluids that poured from Christ's body and fell, unregarded, into the ground, to be part of it for ever.[36] For

---

35 Alice Meynell, 1924, 'In Portugal, 1912' in *The Poems of Alice Meynell: Complete Edition*, New York: Charles Scribner, p. 81.

36 Sergei Bulgakov, 1997, *The Holy Grail and the Eucharist*, trans. Boris Jakim, Hudson NY: Lindisfarne Books.

Bulgakov, the hidden water and blood of Christ is what allows the eschatological preparation of the world, and binds it totally to Christ. The mode in which Christ is present in the eucharistic elements is different but it is the same Christ.

Similarly, the church building is a little world of worship in which the unregarded holiness of the natural world of stone, wood and iron is brought into our consciousness, and related back to its Creator. The oaks all went from much of Sherwood Forest to build the ships to defend Britain against the Armada. But the fragments of glass that survive in the Forest churches are etched with acorns and oak leaves that preserve the beauty of that lost landscape. The Chapter House at Southwell Minster nearby is so alive with carvings of leaves of hawthorn and oak and hops and ivy that it caused the objective and usually unmoved architectural historian, Nikolaus Pevsner, to declaim:

> The inexhaustible delight in live form that can be touched with worshipping fingers and felt with all senses is ennobled . . . by the conviction that so much beauty can exist only because God is in every man and beast, in every herb and stone . . . Seen in this light, the leaves of Southwell assume a new significance as one of the purest symbols surviving in Britain of Western thought, our thought, in its loftiest mood.[37]

As D. H. Lawrence wrote of Lincoln Cathedral, so is every church 'a great involved seed, whereof the flower would be radiant life inconceivable, but whose beginning and end were the circle of silence'.[38] The church building is an expression of our worship: our human making as our response to our Divine creator. For it is our vocation as human beings to make things, to create beauty and life and colour: 'we make still by the law in which we're made' as Tolkien wrote in his poem, 'Mythopoeia'.[39] A church is a 'seed,'

---

37 Nikolaus Pevsner, 1945, *The Leaves of Southwell,* London: Penguin, p. 61.

38 D. H. Lawrence, 1958 [1916], *The Rainbow*, Harmondsworth: Penguin, p. 201.

39 J. R. R. Tolkien, 2001, 'Mythopoeia' in *Tree and Leaf*, London: HarperCollins, p. 89.

a pregnant place of holiness that allows us the critical distance we need from the value-free and debased empty spaces of secular modernity, so that we may go out from it to uncover and recreate holiness everywhere. As Stanley Hauerwas writes:

> The beauty, the goodness and the truth of our liturgy is tested by our being sent forth. If we are not jarred by the world to which we return, then something has gone wrong.[40]

Hauerwas reminds us that the beauty of our liturgy is not a merely aesthetic creation but a unity of the transcendentals: beauty, truth and goodness go together. And the beauty and power of the Christian idea of holiness comes from the cross: 'the beauty we have beheld in the gift of God's Son leaves its mark.'[41] Similarly, the holiness of the church building comes from its acknowledgement of suffering and death as parts of life that are taken up into the self-offering of the Son. Local priests take sick-communion using a set of vessels given for that purpose in memory of someone who was herself in pain for a long while. The Church marks the rage, the tears and the hard labour of generations. The affecting verses on tombs in many a churchyard record the many infant deaths of the past, or the dangerous realities of a living from the sea. A clerical colleague wanted to remove all the skull carvings on tombs from his church, arguing that they speak of death not life. Surely a better response to the realism of Jacobean piety would be to leave them but perhaps garland the tombs at Easter? As Alan Billings has forcibly argued, our ability to include death as part of experience is why we still matter to people in a world that sets its face against the physical facts of mortality.[42]

The church building is holy precisely because of its 'otherness', which is not a sign of its irrelevance but a source of its true power. Holding the cross and altar at its heart, it challenges the values of

---

40 Hauerwas, *Performing the Faith*, p. 164.
41 Hauerwas, *Performing the Faith*, p. 164.
42 Alan Billings, 2004, *Secular Lives: Sacred Hearts: The Role of the Church in a Time of No Religion*, London: SPCK, especially the chapter, 'Why funerals are overwhelmingly Christian', pp. 82–100.

secular power and secular ideas of success. In that sense it is set apart.

Our need for a public place that is inclusive

One of the most alienating aspects of life in the United States is the dearth of public space. In Virginia, for example, the countryside, outside the national park in the mountains, is private: the concept of the public footpath is an alien one, although to its credit, the (highly radical) local council is attempting to create a trail around Charlottesville. Attempting to walk the country lanes can cause suspicion that one is up to no good. Town centres have generally lost all centrality, as is beginning to be the case in the United Kingdom. Similarly, the Episcopal Church behaves more like a nonconformist 'gathered' church, with a strong sense of membership that is expressed by one's inclusion in a book of church members' photographs, and which can seem quite exclusive. This example is given because it is a warning to us of the tendency of the Fresh Expression Congregationalist model of Church, which is in accord with this American flight from the public and the communal.

The parish church, in contrast, is pre-eminently an inclusive place, from which no one is excluded. Anyone can walk into a service or a church building who wishes to do so. It is a sanctuary in the traditional place of resort, and a public resource. Again, encouraged by initiatives such as that of Sir Roy Strong, who wants to see churches again recovering their medieval function as meeting-places for the whole community and their varied functions, churches are opening up to community events.[43] There is nothing irreverent about badminton in the nave, or the local history society, or a post-office branch in the vestry. And the urban church as much as the rural one can fulfil this community need. A post office has just opened up in inner-city Nottingham, in a church adapted to joint community use in such a way as to increase rather than lose the sense of otherness and transcendence. Tewkesbury Abbey

---

43 Roy Strong, 2007, *A Little History of the English Country Church*, London: Jonathan Cape.

came into its own in the floods of 2007, when, as the highest point in the town, it became home to scores of people, something quite common in the history of fenland churches, whose bells would also ring out the warning. Traditionally, the parish bell rang out the death of any parishioner, with a stroke for each year of the deceased person's life.

The Anglican vision of the Church has always been that of a Church of sinners, a mixed body and not one of an elect. It is a Church of male and female, slave and free, all being one in Christ, and this image from Galatians 3.28 finds best expression in the openness and inclusivity of the parish church, in which all ages and backgrounds may be represented, and in which there is likely to be someone strange or disturbed at the back. We remember with fondness one very correct parish in the Anglo-Catholic tradition that patiently allowed a mentally ill man of the streets to blacken its holy statues by his over-enthusiastic pious lighting of votive lights week after week, and a cathedral that carried on its liturgy serenely while a disturbed person recited another service loudly in competition from behind the choir. Churches are one place where the housebound and sick are valued for their prayers and the elderly depended upon for their contribution, after society sees little role for them. People with Down's syndrome, with their love of pattern and movement, find a liturgical role, and small children with their spiritual realism give depth and vitality. In one Nottinghamshire village at garden-party time, a variety of men of the village will suddenly emerge, tools at the ready, to erect the tents. They attend the Songs of Praise service held later the same day but rarely appear again before the next August. Yet this work has strong religious meaning for them, and gives them a sense of belonging to the Church. No doubt, one could call this activity a 'Fresh Expression of Church' but it is not, in itself, 'Church' but rather an out-working of the Church. Only by connection with the whole worshipping action of the parish church does it become an expression of the faith, and so the men concerned understand it.

The occasional offices of baptism, confirmation, marriage and funerals are the traditional places where the inclusivity of the Church of England has been expressed. Today they are wonderful opportunities for preaching the gospel and re-connecting people to their spiritual roots. *Mission-shaped Church* like so much evangelicalism today, has little to say about these offices. Indeed, it is common for some evangelical clergy to actually refuse to perform a funeral for a non-churchgoer or deny baptism. Yet there is nothing that brings people closer to the realities of existence and their need for God than a death of someone they love or the birth of a child. These events make us realize intuitively that we are more than bodies, and that life is more than it seems. The funeral sermon allows the minister to view the life of the dead person in terms of the work of the Spirit in their lives and to connect that life to the Christian story. In the case of some disadvantaged people, the very granting of a meaningful narrative to a life that seemed chaotic and without form is an act of justice and blessing. One of the most moving things one of us did as a curate was to perform the funeral of a semi-homeless alcoholic. There was no one else in the chapel, not even the undertaker. As had been requested, however, his favourite hymn was sung: by the priest alone. Half way through his two closest friends arrived, worse for wear and unaware of the time. They were tremendously glad that his wishes were being carried out. Baptism too can be a revolutionary act of radical inclusion. In one parish a single mother, with no connection to the church, brought her child for baptism. The ceremony was made the centre of the patronal festival, so that the baby became the representative of the Church in that place and was processed with lights and flowers around the building, and offered cards specially made by the junior church. Who knows exactly what motives drive someone today to seek a baptism or a marriage? The inclusivity of the Church takes everyone to herself, and leads those who seek her sacraments beyond themselves to a new place. She does so both by being totally open to all who come, but also by preaching the whole gospel. There is no value in 'watering down' the faith.

Surely 'networks' and outreach work in small groups have been part of the Church since the Middle Ages, with a particular importance in the work of urban churches in the nineteenth and twentieth centuries, right up to recent times? There is great value in reaching out to people wherever they may be found, in skate-park or reading group. So far, Fresh Expressions is the common wisdom of our experience. Where we part company is in the idea that the book-group is 'Church' by itself: that the exclusive group can be separate from the Body, or be the Body on its own. This chapter has occasionally distanced itself from the gathered nature of the Episcopal Church in the United States. Yet where they are wholly admirable is in maintaining Christian formation for all sorts of adults, young people and children, offering groups on poetry and drama, music and detective fiction and many opportunities for so-cial service. This is particularly the effect of having a largely upper-middle-class congregation, all of whom are highly educated, but an African-American inner-city parish also offers a range of social and educative groups, though not on the same scale.

The problem with the Fresh Expressions approach is that it treats people as primarily individualized agents, even consumers, who are left within the arena of 'choice', not liberated from it. This is made painfully clear in the way in which a Cafe Church in Nottingham arranges communion. The elements are placed on a shelf, to one side, and anyone who would like to take communion helps himself, when he wishes. Henri de Lubac expresses clearly the theological mistake in this approach:

> In everything he does on the supernatural level the Christian acts *ut membrum Ecclesiae, ut pars Ecclesiae* [as a member of the Church, as a part of the Church] – Christ loves us individu-ally but not separately, saying to each of us, as he did to Moses, 'I know thee by name; he loves us in his Church, for which he shed his blood.[44]

To be a Christian is to exist in the Church: this communion of 'abiding', in which we are 'sent' as we open out to hospitality for others. We can go on enjoying hang-gliding or car maintenance but even our personal choices of enjoyment are opened up to hos-pitality and to the eucharistic action of engagement and mediation

---

44 De Lubac, *Splendour of the Church*, p. 45.

of the stuff of the universe. This eucharistic mediation is crucial because otherwise the family activities and the family home are in danger of becoming sites of consumer display. At the very point when the family unit has become vulnerable to isolation, fragmentation or partner break-up, the physical environment has received more attention in terms of money than ever before. And hobbies and groups have themselves become opportunities for self-expression through spending, and signs of social aspiration rather than communal endeavours. Children of the middle classes are ferried from one expensive activity to another, many of them competitive in character. They, too, are now sites for their parents' social aspiration and economic display.

The Church exists in a relation to all the activities of its parishioners, but as a mediation by which the activities may be celebrated in what is good about them, and judged by the values of the gospel. The Eucharist allows all our work and play to be brought into the offering of the Church, to be made visible, re-connected to our Creator, and to be received back, renewed in vision. It allows all our different identities, which each one of us traverses, to be brought together. Worship is not another elective activity in the way in which our hobbies are. There is indeed a role for the small house-group, and Anglicanism has learnt much from John Wesley, who saw the perfecting of faith supported both through sacramental common worship and through the smaller class meeting. But Wesley saw the two modes as mutually connected, as out-workings of the Church: the class meeting did not stand on its own.[45] Wesley himself travelled many miles and spoke in the open air to vast crowds of the poor. In that sense the whole world was his parish. He would declare the gospel wherever he found it right to do so. But he wished his evangelistic activities to strengthen the institutional Church and not substitute for it. Moreover, holiness was linked not only to moral and spiritual development but also to growth in the truth. There was a toughness and an intellectual integrity to the Wesleyan vision that is quite lacking in the Fresh Expressions

---

45 See David Lowes Watson, 2002, *The Early Methodist Class Meeting*, Eugene OR: Wipf and Stock.

approach, in which doctrine appears to be muted and the language of conversion also.

Our need for mediating structures

We have already made the theological case for mediation; there is also a dearth of mediating structures in British life as a whole. Local political parties and trade unions suffer the same problems as the Church in attracting support. Indeed, they have done much worse in terms of losing membership numbers, and even Greenpeace has seen its membership fall enormously in recent years, despite the ecological crisis.[46] People tend to feel that there is little point in such associations because political power seems so distant, and local planning consultations, for example, so easily overturned by central government. Globalization and big business make access to economic control seem equally distant. All this was noticed long ago by Pope Leo XIII in his encyclical, *Rerum Novarum*, subtitled, 'Capital and Labour', in which he sought to chart a Christian social vision that would avoid the denial of individual freedom in Marxism and the injustices of rampant capitalism.[47] He and later popes – and among Anglicans, John Neville Figgis – called for mediating institutions by which people could come together to make policy at the lowest possible level: the principle of subsidiarity, by which power should always be devolved as widely and locally as possible.[48] As John Paul II put it in *Centesimus Annus*:

> A community of a higher order should not interfere in the internal life of a community of a lower order, depriving the latter

---

46 On the fall of political party membership, see the briefing prepared by the Parliamentary Library at www.parliament.uk/commons/lib/research/briefings/snsg_05125.pdf.

47 All these encyclicals and other aspects of Catholic Social Teaching are combined in the 2005 *Compendium of the Social Doctrine of the Church*, Pontifical Council for Justice and Peace, London: Burns & Oates/Continuum for Libreria Editrice Vaticana.

48 *Compendium of the Social Doctrine of the Church*, pp. 93–6, John Neville Figgis, 1913, *Churches in the Modern State*, London: Longmans, Green and Co.

of its functions, but rather should support it in case of need and help to coordinate its activity with the activities of the rest of society, always with a view to the common good.[49]

The parish, in both ecclesial and secular form – the two being divided in 1894 except in the television comedy, *The Vicar of Dibley* – is a perfect example of this devolved and mediating structure. It is not an independent, free-floating entity, because it rests and is supported by the diocese and larger Church, but it is a site for the interweaving of the individual and the social at the local level. As such, when it works well in this way, it can be a sign for society as a whole, and enable the existence of other mediating structures: community and protest groups, inter-faith groups and so on. A good example is the network of churches, mosques and trade unions called London Citizens, which has made common cause to work for a living wage – gaining success at the LSE, the Olympics, HSBC and Barclays – and against debt servitude, in their anti-usury campaign. Maurice Glasman, one of its leaders, has no hesitation in celebrating the importance of parishes in joining and modelling the grassroots action that has led to so much success. For parishes can themselves be hospitable places that encourage and engender other mediating institutions that we so desperately need to revivify our political and social life. Precisely because of their public and visible character, parishes can relate to other faith communities in practical ways, or in social activities such as mosque/church cricket matches.

Indeed, the parish, rather than a sentimental ideal of a lost Christendom, is a springboard for mission and for engagement with the deepest needs of our contemporary culture. The parish is not just important in nurturing a sense of belonging but for configuring a vision of a humanity that embraces the local and the universal together, the whole cosmos human and non-human, the transcendent as well as the immanent.

---

49 John Paul II, 1991, *On the Hundredth Anniversary of Rerum Novarum (Centesimus Annus)*, Washington, DC: USCCB, 1991, no. 48.

8

Rebuilding a Christian Imaginary
in the Parish

Faith cannot be lived in any other way, including what is most spiritual in it, than in *the mediation of the body*, the body of a society, of a desire, of a tradition, of a history, of an institution, and so on. What is most spiritual always takes place in the most corporeal.[1]

Responding to secularization

It is very difficult to gauge exactly how secular Britain has become. One day in clerical dress we can be given a free ride on the bus from a youthful driver and asked for prayers, the next, gawped at as if from another planet by a group of school-children. Our, albeit limited, empirical observation of rural life suggests a familiarity with religious practice and in many places, growing congregations. Although for understandable reasons, the Anglican Church has withdrawn resources from the country to concentrate on areas of denser population, rural areas offer a direct access to people's lives and a still accepted and welcomed role for the country vicar. It is also true, however, that people in one generation have lost cultural familiarity with Christianity in the country as well as the city. As long ago as 1896, Fr Dolling in *Ten Years in a Portsmouth Slum*, noted the chasms of ignorance of who Christ might be among

---

1 Louis-Marie Chauvet, 2001, *The Sacraments: The Word of God at the Mercy of the Body*, trans. Madeleine Beaumont, Collegeville, MS: The Liturgical Press, p. xii.

Rebuilding a Christian Imaginary in the Parish
the desperately poor of Portsea in Victorian Britain, so this may
never have been a universal cultural familiarity.[2] Moreover, even
sociologists of religion such as Steve Bruce, Grace Davie and Callum Brown paint very different pictures of what is happening
and why.[3] The decline of religion was predicted by Weber and
Durkheim long ago, and yet the rage of the London-based media
and the Dawkinses of our own age are partly due to the resur-
gence of religious faith, especially in fundamentalist guise. Is secularization rampant individualism, or differentiation of multiple
sacred paths or religious groups? Is it the decline in prestige and
numbers of the churches? A quick survey of the literature reveals
one certainty: there is no consensus, and the picture is incredibly
complex. How is it, for example, that there is a revival in (capitalist) Asia or Africa, or so many believers in the individualist United
States?

The mistake of much Anglican policy is to assume that secularization is complete, and to respond by planning for decline and
shedding ever more of its traditions. Islam's revival in Britain by
contrast, owes much to the way in which it has held to its traditions but also offers a thoroughgoing critique of contemporary
morality and consumerist culture. Muslim women students wear
their headscarves with pride as a visible sign of this critique, and
Muslim students sustain the rigours of Ramadan as one central
emblem of their faith. Islam marks their daily pattern of life with
calls to prayer, affects their financial practice, their sexual and
family life. It reaches into every aspect of existence, and this is the

---

2 Robert R. Dolling, 1896, *Ten Years in a Portsmouth Slum*, London: Swan
Sonnenschein, p. 60.
3 See, for example, Steve Bruce, 1996, *Religion in the Modern World: From Ca-
thedrals to Religious Cults*, Oxford: Oxford University Press, Callum Brown, 2001,
The Death of Christian Britain: Understanding Secularism 1800–2000, Abingdon:
Routledge, Grace Davie, 1994, *Religion in Britain since 1945: Believing without
Belonging*, Oxford: Blackwell, Pippa Norris and Ronald Inglehart (eds), 2004,
The Secularisation Debate, Oxford: Oxford University Press, David Martin, 2003,
'On Secularisation and its Predictions: A Self-examination' in *Predicting Religion:
Christian, Secular and Alternative Futures*, ed. Grace Davie, Paul Heelas and Linda
Woodhead, London: Ashgate, pp. 30–8, Danièle Hervieu-Léger, 2000, *Religion as a
Chain of Memory*, trans. Simon Lee, New Brunswick, NJ: Rutgers University Press.

source of its power: it is a true *habitus*. Similarly, in the United States, despite the ostensibly private character of faith, not only is the public realm non-denominationally religious in tone but also the church, whether Nazarene or Episcopalian, offers a complete cultural embodiment, with an extensive extra-liturgical life of education and social service. American Christians know their Bible, their traditions and their history, and they have a wide range of customs and practices which earth the faith in the physical and corporeal. British Anglicans, on the contrary, have whittled away the core beliefs and equally the popular traditions that earthed those beliefs as non-essential. The attempt to separate the essence from the 'forms' has left us, paradoxically, with a non-intellectual yet abstracted faith that does not embrace the whole person. The veneration for the managerial medium of PowerPoint and its inclusion in worship to show jejune and often sentimental images is an index of how far we have lost our corporeal and imaginative bearings.

Above all, what we have lost since the 1960s and '70s is the extra-liturgical: the life of the parish in youth club and drama group, football club and choir. These activities had grown enormously in the period following World War II, following the One Nation service ethic that emerged out of the experience of total war.[4] In part these dwindled at the rise of television and the individualism of popular culture, just as other non-religious social activities declined in the same period. Callum Brown attributes their loss to the rise of paid employment among married women, who often sustained such activities.[5]

While there may still be large numbers of people who profess belief in God in Britain, there is no doubt that Christian stories and religious practice have been lost to many, not just outside the church but within it. At some point in the mid-twentieth century the Anglican Church lost her poise and confidence, so that there is a great need for a new presentation of the beauty and power of Christian faith, among Christians themselves as well as the

---

4 Brown, *Death of Christian Britain*, p. 170.
5 Brown, *Death of Christian Britain*, p. 191–2.

unchurched. Mission in this way begins with our own congregations. We need to offer a strong, confident and poised response on the level of intellect and apologetics to the secularist challenge but also practices that mediate a Christian vision of the whole of culture: a reassertion of the Christian imaginary, including everything from angels to church-clipping, pancake-tossing to ashing. Our own congregations often exist on a thin gruel of familiar stories and rituals. If we are to be truly missionary, then we need to offer a complete re-orientation of experience that is capable of expressing the truth that it is in God that 'we live and move and have our being' (Acts 17.28). The highly successful lay movements of renewal in the Roman Catholic Church embrace wholeheartedly the idea of a Christian culture that reconnects young people, in particular, with their own local traditions, and which reaches to the whole of experience: intellectual, moral and corporeal. For Luigi Giussani, the founder of 'Communion and Liberation', it is the function of a re-awakening of the religious sense 'to bring us closer to life in all its shimmering intensity'.[6]

In the sections that follow, we suggest just a few ways in which we can go about re-connecting with that latent imaginary, and re-establishing a hospitable and celebratory Christian culture. We offer 'trajectories, tactics and rhetorics' of resistance to secularization, following the advice of Michel de Certeau in his book, *The Practice of Everyday Life*, which shows how the weak may invent a counter-reality to the prevailing culture.[7] Some of what follows may strike chords, and already be part of the reader's own practice and experience. Often what is required is an intensification and emphasis upon what we are already doing, and doing it more openly and confidently. We have treasures, old and new, and are constantly re-inventing and renewing our traditions. But we do so according to what the sociologist Danièle Hervieu-Léger calls a 'chain of memory', to which we need to reconnect what she calls

---

6 Luigi Giussani, The *Religious Sense*, 1997, trans. John Zucchi, Montreal: McGill-Queens University Press, Foreword by Jean Bethke Elshstain, p. x.

7 Michel de Certeau, 1984 [1980], *The Practice of Everyday Life*, trans. Steven Rendall, Berkeley, CA: University of California Press, p. xix.

the 'amnesiacs' of our unchurched, disconnected culture.[8] It goes without saying that the parish is the natural local place for this project: 'home is where one starts from,' as T. S. Eliot states in *The Four Quartets*, 'and the end of all our exploring/ Will be to arrive where we started/ And know the place for the first time.'[9] In this rebuilding we need great poetry like Eliot's but, equally, traditional finger games, such as: 'here's the church, here's the steeple, look inside, here's all the people', the last accomplished by turning the interlaced fingers upwards to form a congregation.[10] Faith needs to live corporeally.

1 Redeeming time

> From one ancestor he made all the nations to inhabit the whole earth, and he allotted the times of their existence and the boundaries of the places where they would live, so that they would search for God and perhaps grope for him and find him (Acts 17.26–7a).

Restoring the rhythms of sacred and seasonal time

We live in a society dominated by time as a lack, in which there is never enough time, and in which a car stalling at traffic lights or a slow computer screen can cause actual rage. Seeking to communicate or travel ever more quickly, we can literally 'lose' time in the sense of temporality as God-given, not only as an aspect of our embodiment, but also as something to which God gave himself: not only did the God of the Israelites reveal his saving action in history, but in becoming a human being, the Son embraced time itself.

---

8 Hervieu-Léger, *Religion as a Chain of Memory*, p. 3.

9 T. S. Eliot, *Four Quartets, The Complete Poems and Plays*, 1980, London: Faber, pp. 117–45 (129, 145).

10 See the whole rhyme at Iona Opie, Peter Opie and Joan Hassall, *The Oxford Book of Nursery Rhymes*, 1957, Oxford: Oxford University Press, p. 8.

Rebuilding a Christian Imaginary in the Parish

Juliet B. Schor sparked off a furious debate by her book, *The Overworked Americans*, in which she argued that medieval peasants worked less hard then we do today.[11] Indeed, they worked long hours in back-breaking labour, but there were long periods also of inaction, and, in particular, many saints' days that were holidays. They lived by the rhythms of sacred time. Our first task, therefore, is to find ways to recover these rhythms, and to restore the value of time as a mediation of God. The parish church or cathedral is, of course, a visual embodiment of time, and traditionally time was marked on the side of parish churches in the form of mass dials: only the hours at which mass was likely to occur were included; for work ending-time there was the sunset. Seasons and the weather were the natural signals for a time to plant, to sleep and to wait. Following the deep truths of pagan religion, to which Christianity gave hospitality, the shape of the Christian year evolved, uniting the Jewish paschal and seasonal feasts to those of the pagan seasonal cycle. So we came to celebrate Christmas at the depth of winter, Easter in the spring at Passover, and the All Saints and All Souls feasts as the year was dying. The realities of seed-time and harvest had their place within the liturgical cycle, and one of the most unpopular aspects of the Reformation was the loss of the many saints' days to which Schor's book alludes and which had formerly been holidays free from work. Even in modern Britain the Christian year still shapes public time. American students often reflect on how different the year seems here in England to the aggressively secular dominance over public time in the States, in which only Thanksgiving survives as a truly national religious feast, but one now confined to the home. Yet the loss of Sunday as a non-commercial day and the re-ordering of Bank Holidays such as Whitsun away from their liturgical roots make ever more of a division between sacred and secular time.

There are, however, counter-movements. Initiatives by conservationists and ecologists to persuade us to eat seasonal and local food go along with attention to the natural, seasonal cycle, which

---

11 Juliet B. Schor, 1991, *The Overworked Americans: The Unexpected Decline of Leisure,* New York: Basic Books.

is already a sacred time, attentive to rhythms that unite us in physical and spiritual ways to a world beyond the self. The revival of paganism in New Age spirituality should not blind us to the fact that, as G. K. Chesterton wrote:

> All that genuinely remains of the ancient hymns or the ancient dances of Europe, all that has honestly come to us from the festivals of Phoebus or Pan, is to be found in the festivals of the Christian Church. If any one wants to hold the end of a chain which really goes back to the heathen mysteries, he had better take hold of a festoon of flowers at Easter or a string of sausages at Christmas.[12]

We noted in the previous chapter how the early Christians in Britain deliberately used pagan sites for worship. In fact, all that is best of pagan faith found a home in Christianity but purged of the sacrificial elements resulting from a religion of pure nature. Indeed, the dancing girls with their floral arches of a Roman temple mural in Spain still exist in the complex dances performed by village young people to celebrate the feast of Our Lady of Seafarers each August in the little fishing village of Camelle.

The link with pagan religion is particularly evident in relation to ceremonies that mark the changing seasons. The volume, *Common Worship Times and Seasons,* is full of services from the old agricultural year, and Plough Sunday, which traditionally marks the return to agricultural work after Christmas, still draws the crowds to churches such as Morton in Nottinghamshire, Burnham on Crouch in Essex or Knaresborough in Yorkshire to see the combine outside and the old, smaller plough within, hear ploughboy songs, and watch the morris men dance out of the church.[13] The ploughboy songs are not mere decorative heritage, for they are

---

12 G. K. Chesterton, 1905, *Heretics,* London: John Lane, pp. 156–7.

13 *Common Worship: Times and Seasons,* 2006, London: Church House Publishing, pp. 593–634, includes material for Lammas tide as well as Plough Sunday, Harvest and Rogation.

eloquent about the hardships of agricultural labour.[14] Furthermore, they are still being written, describing the life of a com-
bine-driver on the Canadian prairies, for example. Easter gardens
– themselves a Christian version of the old gardens of Adonis –
unite the death and resurrection of Christ to the rebirth of nature
in spring for urban and rural alike. Harvest Festival certainly has
both pagan and Jewish roots but is wholly benign, and is beginning
to be linked overtly with our religious duty towards sustainability.
In Todmorden in Lancashire, a strong 'guerilla gardening' movement, which planted vegetables on waste land and verges, was
taken up by the local council and the community as a whole, who
aim to become self-sufficient in fresh produce. Every year, the
fruits of this civic enterprise, which includes a part of the churchyard given over to vegetables, are offered in a giant harvest festival and picnic. People have a need to say 'thank you' and harvest
can be an excellent way of introducing religious practice into any
creative endeavour that can be said to have some 'fruit'. Another
simple way of marking the natural year along with the liturgical
is in the arrangement of flowers. Arrangers can be encouraged to
use local foliage and flowers, or at least ones actually in season
where possible: Michaelmas daisies, elderflower, late roses, winter
jasmine or evergreens. The Ecclesiological Society have mounted
some Victorian photographs at their website, which show that
our forbears made spectacular use of foliage alone to adorn the
church building, training it round pillars, and into garlands and
arches (www.ecclsoc.org/xmasforaldecoration.html).

Long ago the Church 'baptized' May celebrations by the proximity of Whitsun. At Lambley in Nottinghamshire there was also
Cowslip Sunday, the first in May, on which day people from the city
would walk out to the village, which was then a carpet of cowslips,
to buy great bunches from local people, or pick their own. The
men would tend to turn in to the pub, while the women and children went to the church, itself decorated with cowslips, for a special service. In the twentieth century, the hymn 'daises are our

---

14 See, for example, *Folk Songs*, ed. John Williamson Palmer, 1861, New York:
Scribner, p. 11: 'All the sweat o' your brow, boys,/ Will never get beer or bread'.

silver' was rewritten by the teacher and vicar to include cowslips and local Lambley landmarks and woods. Recently, individual maypoles, a Yorkshire custom remembered by one parishioner from her youth, were added to the celebration, to make arches to guide the congregation down to the stream. There they bless the beck or dumble, which is a Nottinghamshire word for a steep-sided, narrow stream-cutting, and a particularly rich natural habitat. The dearth of cowslips due to modern farming methods is being redressed by mass plantings after the service. The poet John Clare's Midsummer Cushions, which were arrangements of flowers placed in the windows of houses in his Northamptonshire village, were also revived recently. For tradition is always being restored and reinvented: once a congregation has done something twice, it becomes a custom. In Lambley, as in other parishes, a seasonal festival has taken on strong elements of conservation. Indeed, Cowslip Sunday in Winchester, following a massive replanting of cowslips on St Catherine's Down, seems to have been begun in 2002 as a conservation project.

May Day, as well as a seasonal celebration of spring, is a day in which we can celebrate time itself, as bringing fullness and possibility. This was the thought behind the association of the festival with workers in early socialism, as can be seen in Walter Crane's 'May Garland' and 'Workers' Maypole' poster designs, in which manual workers, both male and female dance with ribbons proclaiming 'eight-hour day' and 'leisure for all'.[15] The Roman Catholic Church celebrates the feast of St Joseph the Worker on 1 May for a similar reason of celebrating ordinary workers. Sometimes churches hold fairs on the May Bank Holiday, and include maypole dances, as at Wellow, a small village in Nottinghamshire, which has a huge maypole and an equally famous series of dances and processions. In the 1950s, every playground in urban Portsmouth, for example, had its metal maypole, showing that this custom was not merely a rural survival.

---

15 See Philip Sheldon Foner, 1986, *May Day: A Short History of the International Workers' Holiday*, New York: International Publishers, p. 67.

Rebuilding a Christian Imaginary in the Parish

One way of re-energizing such events in town and country would be to add to them the celebration of work, which, as we suggested in the previous chapter, should be seen as transformative action and part of God's mission in the world. Children could be encouraged to dress up to represent different trades, or trades and professions invited to participate as teams in some communal game, such as a tug-of-war, canoe race or five-a-side football, in aid of a community project. People who actually make things, such as joiners and bricklayers, could be invited to show others what they do, and quizzes could be held in which participants had to guess the function of particular tools and objects, celebrating, as Gerard Manley Hopkins puts it – 'áll trádes, their gear and tackle and trim'.[16] The role of the Church here is to make visible the productive use of time, and to value the positive aspects of work. This is in accord with the stress in Thomas Aquinas on action itself as good, the possible evil coming in the use to which we put our energy. So the parish priest can offer thanks for the energy, skill and thoughtfulness of workers, and their contribution to the common good, thus unveiling the positive mediation of work. In 2007, three English Catholic Dioceses held a 'May Day for Migrants' day, in which the contribution of migrant labour and culture was celebrated, and a mass of St Joseph the Worker, with music from the many cultures represented, was held in Westminster Cathedral. Parishes or deaneries could host similar celebrations in their own areas, especially those that rely on seasonal or immigrant labour.

Liturgical time of the Christian story is undergirded and orchestrated by natural time and seasons, and shares the latter's pattern of feast and fast, darkness and light. Recent years have seen a wealth of materials published to engage families and young people, in particular, in creative markings of the liturgical year, with the Jesse tree for Advent, chalk to mark and bless the house at Epiphany, and the travelling crib in which Mary and Joseph are taken from home to home. Some dioceses have excellent resources to offer parishes, such as Wakefield, which has a superb website, where

---

16 Gerard Manley Hopkins, 'Pied Beauty', *Poems and Prose*, ed. W. H. Gardner, 1972, Harmondsworth: Penguin, p. 31.

whole figures, story-cubes and badge-making kits may be booked, and materials are carefully organized according to the lectionary. School websites are also excellent places for materials to be given for family seasonal activities, and for information about the liturgical year. Woodlands School in Kent has the most visited of any school website, and specializes in providing material about British customs and traditions, with an excellent religious calendar.

It would be helpful, however, if the Church of England gathered the best of these together and promoted them centrally, with a careful theological underpinning for each practice and activity, so that good practice could be shared and a communal liturgical imaginary be developed. This could be an important resource for the local school, which is the mainstay of community in modern Britain, and the only socially uniting institution. If we are concerned to be truly missionary, the church school is the obvious place to begin, and to embody the Christian imaginary in a systematic way. For what we truly lack is a common culture, within the Church as well as outside. In the television comedy, *The Vicar of Dibley,* one can discern a very evident attempt to use the parish as a common imaginary, which reached its apogee in the wedding of Alice Tinker, the verger, that combined Anglican liturgy with the teletubbies. Every Parish Council meeting is littered with jokes about popular culture, which are held together by the character of the woman priest. The programme is reminiscent of Goth culture in that the obscene and scatological humour functions as a kind of grotesque realism, whereby a carnivalesque inversion – the vicar making smutty jokes – unites the community in a common humanity. Without the sacred figure of the vicar this would not work, nor would it without the rhythm of the liturgical year.

Every parish, however, has the marking of liturgical time in their own hands, with at least one bell to call the faithful to worship, and for the incumbent to ring before saying Morning and Evening Prayer daily as required by canon law. It is important that we do not allow this public marking of sacred time to be erased, and that we do all we can to encourage the art of change-ringing. There is nothing as exciting for children than to be allowed to help ring the bell calling people to the service, or the sanctus bell during Communion, because it produces such a gratifyingly loud and powerful noise and a dizzying feeling of power. At Granada, in Spain, the Archbishop invites all the children of the diocese to bring their own bell to the Cathedral on Easter Day. Several thousand bells all ringing at once is overwhelmingly celebratory and a fitting continuation of the old carnivalesque customs of the past that involved games, dances, exchanges of role and the *risus paschalis* or attempt to make the congregation laugh. Change-ringing is an art unique to Britain and Anglican tradition in the Commonwealth, and deserves to be celebrated as a religious act in itself. The poet Elizabeth Jennings writes in 'The Bell-Ringer' of how 'The bells renew the town, discover it/ And give it back itself again.'[17] The sound of the bells pealing out into the high air not only 'imagines' the parish as an entity but also calls it to a reality beyond itself. Bells can also be radical emblems of witness, as in the call of the Danish Churches to Christians all over the world to ring their bells 350 times at 3 p.m. on 13 December 2009, to shame the world leaders at the Climate Change Summit in Copenhagen into effective action.

We also have a rich tradition of liturgical colours with which to mark the different seasons. There is potential for extending the use of these colours as, for example, by the congregation dressing to match the priest in the appropriate colour at important festivals: everyone at one church in Lancaster would make an effort to appear in red at Pentecost, while in the United States, people wear white at Easter, and young girls mark the importance of Sunday by appearing in their party dresses. In the Midlands and North of England, the custom of the Easter bonnet lives on, and women and girls appear with whole habitats on their heads. We have gradually abandoned in Britain the idea that dress for church should be special in any way, and indeed, the more middle class the church, the more the people 'dress down'. West Indian members of a church in Lambeth regarded the jeans and tee-shirts of the urban professional members of the congregation with initial horror, then quiet bemusement. We do not need to return to the formality, the hats and gloves of an earlier Sunday convention,

---

17 Elizabeth Jennings, 1986, 'The Bell-Ringer', *Collected Poems: 1953–1985*, Manchester: Carcenet, p. 18.

but we could look as if we were at a celebration and not about to clean the car, especially on feast-days.

There is a role for liturgical colour to be used more systematically in public places, by employing it throughout the local church school, for example, as backing paper for displays of work, or stickers given out to award good work or behaviour at assembly. Church notices, diocesan magazines, all sorts of materials could be colour-coded. Church magazines should always make great reference to holy days, and noticeboards be decorated. Even when the church itself must be locked, the porch can be a site for seasonal material and meditation for when anyone passes by. Considerable numbers of ramblers and dog-walkers use public footpaths across churchyards in town and country, for example, while passengers often gaze idly at church notice boards from waiting bus windows. How much better to have seasonal colour and information than embarrassing puns or minatory declamations: to read, 'Today is the feast-day of Maximilian Kolbe, who exchanged places with a prisoner bound for execution in Auschwitz. Today we pray for all political prisoners', on 14 August would be much more arresting than such tired puns as 'What is missing from church: UR!'

Differences in seasons can be much more dramatically expressed, so as to create a shared seasonal psychology. Easter will look so much more joyful after a truly bare and workmanlike Lent. The effect of whole-scale stripping of the altar on Maundy Thursday, which is an activity that can employ children as well as adults, is truly moving and even shocking. The scarlet of Pentecost after the white of Easter can fill the whole building as children twirl large red streamers whenever the name of the Holy Spirit is mentioned. A patronal festival is a good opportunity for a birthday cake and encircling the building in the ceremony that used to be called 'church-clipping', from the Anglo-Saxon word for embrace, and is still performed at Painswick in Gloucestershire and Edgmond in Shropshire. We are not suggesting that every Sunday be filled with different seasonal activities but that we choreograph a stronger sense of drama and contrast, and help people to live physically and imaginatively in liturgical time.

This will involve the use of food, and a return to fasting as well as feasting. Oddly, the Lenten fast is still observed, although for reasons of health and dieting, by people with no connection to Christian faith. The reason, perhaps, lies in the value of fasting in itself, in training the body and in focusing the mind. It is sad that the Church abandons customs of so much intrinsic value out of a sense that the intellectual and moral is of higher spiritual value than anything physical and corporeal. Fasting also has been seen as too demanding, and abandoned out of an attempted kindness. That this is misguided is shown by the example of a parish in Derbyshire, which developed a successful family service early on a Sunday morning. This seems to go against every contemporary trend, which tells us that first, families cannot get their children ready in time for a 9.00 service, and second, that they are too busy with other activities. What happened was that parents bundled their children straight into the push-chair, had an enjoyable service with alert children who, after all, are usually awake very early anyway, and then ate a church breakfast together. In effect, they had both fasted and feasted.

Restoring liturgical time

Liturgy is a space in which we spend time generously, in the sense that we enter a different mode of temporality, in which there is a sense of movement and direction, but we relax into the giftedness of time: we use time itself as a medium of encounter with God. Here, we have the time for repetition: to use the doxology, 'Glory be to the Father . . .' again and again, to address Jesus as Lamb of God three times, to delight in the meditative repetition of a Taizé chant. Ben Quash in an insightful article, 'Making the Most of Time', explains the value of repetition thus:

> [Repetition] stands against the idea that each moment stands utterly unconnected from the moments around it – that every moment is self-enclosed, that we can be something completely different in this new moment from what we were in a previous

one and from what we will be in a future one. That would be the denial of time – another evasion of our real nature as temporal beings with debts to our past actions and obligations to our future ones. Repetition works with the grain of who we are, it helps us to learn more about who we are, and to grow in this knowledge.[18]

Here we see how repetition takes away from us the sense of autonomy and self-transcendence, and earths us in time and tradition, as the givenness of history.

Children also love repetition, as anyone who has had to read a particular favourite story to them knows all too well. It is not just comforting, but a positive pleasure for them, which allows them to receive reality afresh and more intensely. Repetition of a poem or story allows them to literally be shaped by time, as is the witness also of the great world religions, for all of which ritual repetition is a spiritual discipline that makes truth one's own. For repetition works both ways: it can make us aware of time itself in all its fullness of flow as Quash suggests, and model our temporal connectedness, but repetition can sometimes launch us into timelessness as we forget ourselves in the rhythmic pattern. Taking time in this way is, however, a practice that has to be taught to a modern congregation, who need to be weaned away from a functionalist view of time. The office of Morning Prayer in *Common Worship* is helpful here: 'The night has passed, and the day lies open before us; let us pray with one heart and mind' is a most beautiful invitation into time as an opening to possibility and fullness.[19]

Restoring memory

As well as drenching us in time in all its fullness and openness to possibility, the Church has been central as mediator of communal

---

18 Ben Quash, 'Making the Most of Time: Liturgy, Ethics and Time,' 2002, *Studies in Christian Ethics* 15, pp. 97–114 (106).

19 *Common Worship: Services and Prayers for the Church of England*, 2001, London: Church House Publishing, p. 32.

and individual memory. We see time itself in the churchyard and church building full of tablets, tombs and brasses. When we pray 'with angels and archangels and with all the company of heaven' the former worshippers of the place seem very present, as do those of the future: we hold time itself together in the proleptic anticipation of the *eschaton* in that moment at communion. New churches should always be built with generous space for burials of bodies or cremated remains. For otherwise our dead will be sent to the margins: the awful outer suburbia of the godless crematorium. And the congregation should be eager to preserve and beautify the churchyard, and to remember in prayer those who lie there in the democracy of the dead. For, as Alan Billings has pointed out, our faith can offer more consolation for mourners than a materialist understanding of death because Christianity teaches there is life after death and thus a possibility of continued connection and relationship with the dead person.[20] When we mark the 'year's mind' of the dead, it is as recalling people who are alive in eternity, not a mere memory. And, when the parish church is used along with or instead of the crematorium for a funeral, we can actually offer time. It is often very difficult to keep to the tight schedule of the crematorium, whereas the church takes its own time. We can also hold up the traffic as we walk up the road from the church to the cemetery as a mark of respect to the dead person, and to death's centrality in life.

At times of national mourning or local tragedy people look to the parish church as a resource. For there is often something quite melancholic in the private shrines people set up by the roadside or the school gate, in that each offering is separate and cellophane-wrapped. Yet the offerings huddle together as if seeking the communal expression of which they are not capable. When clergy or laity have some role in such a public mourning, it would be appropriate, with the permission of the family concerned, to offer to re-arrange and beautify such individual gestures, so as to show that the whole is greater than the parts, and to assert our communality. At Wootton Bassett in Wiltshire, down whose streets the cortèges of so many

---

20 Billings, *Secular Lives, Sacred Hearts*, p. 95.

young soldiers killed in Afghanistan make their way, passers-by or friends now throw single flowers on to the hearse, which then form part of the whole ritual in a moving and appropriate manner.

Caring for the memorials of the dead is not just a pious duty but also an important way of re-connecting us with our history and with each other. For Pope Benedict XVI 'Christian faith, by its very nature, includes the act of remembering; in this way, it brings about the unity of history and the unity of man before God, or rather: it can bring about the unity of history because God has given it memory.'[21] This was beautifully illustrated in one church, in which Remembrance Sunday was marked by a hotch-potch of formal remembrance with military honours and family service, in which each child would plant a cross for a person who had died in the two world wars. One year the two services were separated because the clergy believed that the children's noise in the two minutes' silence disturbed the British Legion. The Legion were, however, quite unhappy that the link with the present and the future was lost, and the children missed being present at such an awe-inspiring and serious event. For that parish *was* the community of children and elderly ex-soldiers, and each group felt diminished without the other. The communal memory held in God's eternity united them.

English schools now offer very little of connected, narrative history, although there is some provision for local history in Key Stage 2. One really effective programme to offer schools a history of Christian Britain was started in Southwell Minster in 1995. 'Time Travelling' offers a day of activities based in the Cathedral in which children learn about the history of the Church, her stories and practices, using prayer and craft, drama and exploration, following a pilgrimage model in which they enter the great west door in procession behind costumed guides. It is wildly popular and attracts several thousand children each year, with parishes using the materials to offer their own local versions. The leaders are careful to show how the Church today lives and worships, as

---

21 Joseph Ratzinger, 1987, *Principles of Catholic Theology* San Francisco: Ignatius Press, p. 23.

well as how Christianity came to the area and was expressed in the building of the Minster. Parish churches already have all the objects and people to make an effective 'time travelling' pilgrimage of their own. Children are fascinated by pulpits and eagle lecterns, by the smells and sights of the building itself, and love to dress up and sing like choristers or hold a churchwarden's wand of office. Nearly every parish has a local history group within it, who could be invited to give talks to an adult audience in the church about the history of the local area, in which the religious aspects will quite naturally find their place, good or bad, in the whole story.

For the Christian story in its historical dimension of the history of the Church is complex and often shaming, but equally often, an inspiring story. Our contemporary approach to history is too often one of unmasking of ideology and cynical emancipation from illusion. This is partly because we lack as a culture any shared values by which acts can be evaluated, so a negative version of the nineteenth-century-Whig-view of history as progress is what obtains, in the form of progress and escape *from* an evil past rather than *towards* a better future. This is true both in the amusing yet pernicious *Horrible Histories* books that entertain the young with a sense of the weirdness and ridiculousness of the past and in the way history is often taught in school, as well as on television, in which the reputation of a famous historical figure is deconstructed. The popular conception that religion causes war, as a knockdown argument used by atheists, needs challenging by a thick and rich and nuanced teaching of Christian history, which is as necessary for ordinands as it is for young children. Dee Dyas has published some wonderful visual material on the history of Christianity on CD ROM, and on pilgrimage, as part of a larger project to provide the background to the Bible and Christian culture without which much university humanities study is impossible.[22]

---

22 Dee Dyas, *Images of Salvation: The Story of the Bible through Medieval Art*, CD ROM; Dee Dyas and Esther Hughes, 2005, *The Bible in Western Culture: The Study Guide*, London: Routledge.

Redeeming memory

In thinking about the theology of time, we have to embrace our own contingency as a God-given gift and opportunity: in that sense we have both to abide and to be aware of ourselves as being sent, to give ourselves to time as opportunity and *kairos*. We have also to bear witness to our eternal destiny and our transcendence of temporality through the very acceptance of dying to atomized subjectivity and living in Christ's body: we have to remember our baptism, which takes us into a new mode of life and of time. Christian faith allows us above all to almost palpably touch time as a medium, since our history and practices make it visible. For 'without the meaning there is no time' as T. S. Eliot points out in 'The Rock'; only if there is a God and a creation can we speak of 'the fullness of time', since without divine intentionality all we have is flux.[23]

Without the transcendent dimension, however, the past equally remains fixed and over. The great liberation that Christianity offers human sinfulness is the fact of forgiveness, by which the past may be remembered differently. We assert this in every Communion service, which is also called a Eucharist, meaning a thanksgiving. We look at Christ's death differently, as a saving action which saves us now, and in which our chaotic and selfish past is 're-membered' by the death of Christ. One of the truly effective moments in Mel Gibson's controversial film, *The Passion of the Christ*, was the piercing of Christ's side. A stream of golden liquid, representing the water and blood, bathed Mary and John as they knelt by the cross, the stream caught in the sunlight. It was a tranquil moment of benediction, in which the violent suffering ended and its effects were creatively expressed in the birth of the Church. Another example of the transformation of the past can be found in Dante's *Paradiso*. Dante encounters notorious souls who had scandalous past lives, who are now scintillating in the Divine light and smile at their past sins, because they have been forgiven, and can now see their weakness as an opportunity for God's saving action. Their redemption of time is possible

---

23 T. S. Eliot, 1980, 'Choruses from "The Rock"', *Complete Poems and Plays*, p. 107.

because in Dante's vision of the afterlife, souls who have been purged are brought through the waters of Lethe, which brings forgetfulness of sin, and then drink of the stream of 'Eunöe', which restores memory of the good, so that the past is read redemptively.[24]

The Eucharist models to us the way we should behave in the whole of our lives, seeking reconciliation and forgiveness, and living in the redeemed present to which our baptism has brought us. The rite does not just offer 'cheap' forgiveness, because we call to mind our sins, confess, listen to the scriptures, intercede and bring to mind all that needs healing and justice in our world. But by the time we recite the Lord's Prayer after the conclusion of the Eucharistic prayer it takes on a new quality: it becomes not just a request but a reality. The priest presiding often opens his or her hands as if to receive, and to be open to the action of God. When Christ said the prayer it was less an expression of lack than of trustful giving-over of the temporal self in all its vulnerability and subjection to contingency to God as Father. And so it can become when the Church prays it over the Eucharistic gifts.

The Eucharist thus is itself the practice of all others that builds the Christian imaginary, and will be treated at length in the next chapter. In its structure we learn by habit and by doing, and often a congregation will know things in their bodies that they could not necessarily articulate. This does not mean that they are not learning but it means that our gestures, words and use of movement and silence need to be carefully crafted to enrich the value of the time together. And if a congregation is learning to enjoy temporality and to 'abide' in church, they will be ready to share time as a gift with others: to attend to the shop assistant instead of carrying on a parallel conversation on a mobile telephone; to be patient with an elderly person searching for change on the bus; to listen and sit with the lonely.

---

24 On this aspect of Dante's theology, see Miroslav Volf, 2006, *The End of Memory: Remembering Rightly in a Violent World*, Grand Rapids MI: Eerdmans, p. 135f. The souls are immersed in Lethe as in a spiritual baptism.

2 Space

Space is the Whom our loves are needed by,
Time is our choice of How to love and Why.[25]

Such is the change of orientation of experience of Auden's shepherds and wise men after seeing the Christ Child. Both time and
space have become shaped by the fullness and the humanity of
divine revelation. If time has become the *kairos* of opportunity
to love, space has lost its empty abstraction and become embodied. In his important study, *A Christian Theology of Place*,
John Inge spends a whole chapter surveying the various usages
of the terms 'space' and 'place' in philosophical, geographical
and sociological thought. The distinctions are various but (with
a very few exceptions, such as Michel de Certeau) a consensus
emerges historically in which space is abstract, empty and potentially infinite, while place, particularly since the end of the Middle
Ages, has become associated with locality, and limited 'placement'.[26] The turn to Phenomenology in continental philosophy
has sought, particularly in the work of Heidegger, to recover the
importance of situatedness and place as giving us the co-ordinates
for existence, but in modernity, as Inge points out, the international rich conquer space by quick travel and the international
poor endure space as migrant workers, and we lose our sense of
'placement'.

A renewed Christian imaginary needs, as has already been argued in the previous chapter, to restore a sense of placement and
embodiment, Our situatedness means more than being rooted in
a community but also involves mappings of the ways in which
knowledge and power operate in trajectories, as any child who has
had to negotiate a safe way home from school will understand.
It does not mean merely being at home in the world, but having
a set of co-ordinates by which to understand its complexity and
injustice, its fears and terrors. A world that has no room for the

---

25 Auden, *For the Time Being, Collected Poems*, p. 385.
26 Inge, *A Christian Theology of Place*, pp. 1–32.

sacred does its best to commodify place by treating it as empty space, as in the use of advertising in sporting locales. You cannot watch a bowler running up to the wicket in the Oval test match, without seeing the huge NPower logo superimposed on the grass. A similar understanding is behind the attempt to erect hoardings in fields by the side of motorways. A place is no longer itself but an opportunity for commodification.

The Christian imagination, however, can restore sacrality to 'empty' space, and allow it presence as a benign form of mediation rather than a barrier to true freedom in the 'I need space' sense. The 'empty' space of a parish church is quite different from the vacancy of the empty shop or office building. The building conveys a transcendence articulated and suspended by the spaces shaped by its architecture, and paradoxically an otherness that is one of presence, not absence. An empty church exudes a life of its own that is quite palpable. When furnishing a church or chapel, we should always think of how we shape the spaces between objects in such a way as to allow the worshipper or visitor to feel the space as generous and inspiring or intimate and palpable. Space experienced in this way becomes full like Traherne's 'lively lovely air', which for Gerard Manley Hopkins was 'world-mothering':

Wild air, world-mothering air,
Nestling me everywhere,
That each eyelash or hair
Girdles; goes home betwixt
Snowflake; that's fairly mixed
With, riddles, and is rife
In every least thing's life.[27]

For Hopkins the air is truly mediatory because it is akin to the Blessed Virgin Mary, who 'Let all God's glory through' the web

---

27 Thomas Traherne, 1988, 'Wonder,' in *Selected Writings*, Manchester: Carcenet, p. 20; Hopkins, 'The Blessed Virgin Compared to the Air We Breathe', *Poems and Prose*, pp. 54–58 (54).

of her selfhood.[28] Hers is a mediation that does not make that which it mediates more distant but closer, as the rainbow reveals the light in the raindrop.

Much can be done practically to allow us to be aware of the mediatory potential of space in church with the play of light and shadow, as well as proportion and materials. There is much value in candles, which give a warm depth to darkness and an equally beneficent light that is the polar opposite of the neon strip-light. After a December Christingle service, one young man told us that we should hold all our services in the dark. What was for his children a festival of light, for him had been rather one of the beauty of shadow. For the 'chiaroscuro' of a candlelit church does all the theological work for us: it speaks of a reality that is deep and nourishing, of a God who goes all the way down. The darkness it creates is warm yet mysterious, and its pools of light are gentle and alluring.

In the Middle Ages, not only was the feast of Christ's Presentation in the Temple a celebration of light – Christ being 'a light to lighten the Gentiles' in Simeon's canticle – but it was a time at which candles for the home were brought to be blessed as well as those for the procession.[29] It would be simple to revive this custom in our contemporary society in which candle use is fashionable for mealtimes, decoration and even bathing, and making the link between home and church a living and attractive one. Medieval Christians took candles home also to put in the hands of the sick and dying: a comfort and a light for their final journey.

The orchestration of light and dark is central also to the feasts of All Saints and All Souls, and particularly to All Hallows' Eve. All we do know of pre-Christian Samhain in Celtic areas is that it was a late harvest festival and marked the beginning of winter with bonfires and decisions about which animals to be slaughtered. The elements of turnip lanterns, misrule ceremonies such as 'Mischief Night' ('trick and treat' without the treat in swathes

---

28 Hopkins, *Poems and Prose*, p. 55.
29 Duffy, *Stripping of the Altars*, pp. 16–17.

of northern Britain), and ghosts all date from the Christian era.[30] The recent tendency in church circles for dressing-up as monsters to be seen as heathenish and even Satanic is a great mistake, since it cuts Christian practice off from its own popular out-workings, and rejects a wonderful opportunity to emphasize the true religious aspects of the custom.

Moreover, to deny expression of the monstrous and uncanny creatures of the dark is to give them over to a dualistic universe. Medieval churches are covered in monsters, particularly in northern Europe, because the imagination of the north delighted in the grotesque, and in stories of dragons. But in the Christian churches, all these weird creatures are put to use, either as gargoyles, to channel water off the roof, or as emblems of aspects of God's creative power, the word, 'monster' as Caroline Walker Bynum points out, being etymologically related to the Latin verb, *monstrare*, meaning 'to show'.[31] Monsters are illustrative of God's power, as for example, the great sea-monster, Leviathan, of the book of Job. God asks Job sarcastically if he can lead Leviathan round on a leash with a hole in its nose, and stresses the creature's terrifying power (Job 41.1–11). It is healthy and helpful to children, who tend to suffer nightmares and often find the dark of their own house terrifying, to dress up and play at being monsters. In Charlottesville, Virginia, they went 'trick and treating' among students on the 'lawn' before forming a procession and going to the local Episcopalian church for games, milk and peanut and jelly sandwiches. Another church in Virginia had a church lock-in for young people over Hallowe'en, with apple-bobbing and other traditional games, masks and lantern-making, ending with an All Saints Eucharist in the darkened church ablaze with candles.

If God is to be experienced in times of depression and fear as well as in easy circumstances, then he is God of the dark as of the light: 'the darkness and light to thee are both alike' as the psalmist

---

30 See Steve Roud, 2006, *The English Year: A Month by Month Guide to the Nation's Customs and Festivals from May Day to Mischief Night*, Harmondsworth: Penguin, pp. 322–3.

31 Caroline Walker Bynum, 2007, *Metamorphosis and Identity*, New York: Zone, pp. 37–75.

discovers (Psalm 139.12), while for the poet Henry Vaughan, the night is the time when God calls: 'his knocking time; the soul's dumb watch'. He concludes:

There is in God (some say)
A deep but dazzling darkness; as men here
Say it is late and dusky, because they
See not all clear;
O for that night! Where I in him
Might live invisible and dim.[32]

To truly open the Christian imaginary, we need the sense of mystery in sacred space in which Vaughan, like so many mystical writers, delights. Perhaps of all the subcultures to which young people adhere today, Goth culture, despite its ostensible negativity, is the most alert to the holy and mysterious. Indeed, it represents an inchoate grasping for holiness in a commodified world, in which the sacred can only be invoked by a kind of inversion. It is no accident that Goths, despite the black make-up and chains, are often the gentlest of individuals. This is not to suggest that we insert the gospel into Goth practice, but that we unveil the good desire for the sacred within it, and dip into the treasuries of Christian experience to direct and delight the need expressed.

To 'reclaim the night' for the Christian imaginary also involves making more incursions into public space after dusk. Our towns and cities change character at night because the only places open are pubs and clubs, and their customers young and often inebriated people. Sadly, many parishioners, even in rural areas, are too timid even to go out to an evening service. We were present once at an inner-city Easter Eve ceremony, at which we all piled outside to watch the lighting of a pretty spectacular Easter fire, which drew the fascinated attention of a number of young people and passers-by, who stayed to watch our antics. Nobody interfered but rather, respect was shown for a group of people concentrating

---

32 Henry Vaughan, 1983, 'The Night', *The Complete Poems*, ed. Alan Rudrum, Harmondsworth: Penguin, p. 290.

on their own activity. Advent or Candlemas are both times suitable for outdoor candlelit processions in the dark. People can meet to make the lanterns in all sorts of wonderful shapes before setting out round the streets, with drummers to add to the drama. Candlemas was once also marked by the lighting of a candle in the window of each house, which is in itself an assertion of the sacred in the dark, and a friendly presence for those out on the streets at night. In Ireland, candles were put in windows on Christmas Eve to light the way for the Christ Child, while the Moravian Church leaves one lighted candle in the window throughout Advent and Christmas and also make their own candles from beeswax for this custom. One cleric and his wife melt down ends of church candles, and colour them to sell at Christmas. The elements of making, recycling and participation in these customs are as important as the practice itself in the rebuilding of a Christian imaginary, for they put more of the self into what is made.

Writers who assume that communal practices have disappeared, often judge only from London, or the South East. In the Midlands and North of England, local uniformed organizations such as Scouts and Guides still march in their hundreds to city centre church or cathedral on St George's Day. Once, the Whit Walks of the Sunday School movement led thousands of children to march through the streets of northern cities behind their banners for their sports and treats. Indeed, in Manchester and other Lancashire towns, this custom still carries on, as it does in Kingswood, Bristol.[33] In Warrington, since the terrorist bomb of 1995, individual church walks have been amalgamated, and the walk has taken on the quality of an act of witness, which still draws about four thousand participants.

If space is to be mediatory, we all need to do a great deal more public walking, so that the street becomes an hospitable arena of meaning and presence. In some college towns in the US, as in Oxford and Cambridge, students process on foot in their gowns

---

33 Timothy Jenkins, 1999, *Religion in English Everyday Life: An Ethnographic Approach*, New York and Oxford: Berghahn Books, has made an extensive study of the complex meanings for different groups of the Kingswood Whit Walk (pp. 75–220).

through the streets to the Senate House or other place where they will graduate. In Oxford and Cambridge this is very much a purely 'gown' event but in Williamstown, Massachusetts, the students are followed by the whole town on foot, with pushchairs and dogs among the walkers. Many clergy go into schools for graduation assemblies, but why not suggest a walk from school to church for a short blessing and refreshments? Mourners do often appreciate the walk behind the coffin to the graveyard through the town or village where the dead person lived. Once brides walked from home to the church, and where this is practicable, it is a beautiful sight and full of meaning about the public nature of Christian marriage. Bridesmaids can hold a floral arch over the couple as they leave together, in the traditional way.

Rogation Sunday has traditionally been the time when the Church has mapped its space, maintained boundaries, and brought the sacred into the whole parish by the beating of the bounds. Eamon Duffy describes one medieval practice as involving a banner showing a dragon, whose tail would be chopped off for the return trip after the fields had been blessed.[34] There is enormous value in showing a Christian presence in all parts of the parish, and in rural areas the custom has been generally maintained, since it was deliberately included by the Reformers in the Elizabethan and later prayer books. George Herbert, in his prose work, *A Priest to the Temple*, writes that a parson:

> particularly he loves procession and maintains it, because there are contained therein four manifest advantages: First, A blessing of God for the fruits of the field: Secondly, Justice in the preservation of bounds: Thirdly, Charity in loving walking, and neighbourly accompanying one another, with reconciling of differences at that time, if there be any: Fourthly, Mercy by relieving the poor by a liberal distribution and largess.[35]

---

34 Duffy, *Stripping of the Altars*, pp. 279–81.
35 Herbert, *Complete English Poems*, p. 238.

Rebuilding a Christian Imaginary in the Parish

In Southwell, after a shortened Matins, the choir and servers with candle and lights set off up the lanes to the agricultural college, everyone following behind, and representative agricultural activities and animals are blessed en route, with an anthem and refreshments at the college. In one city parish, beating the bounds takes the form of stops at the parish businesses, several of which happen to be pubs. Add a band of some sort and a picnic, and the potential popularity of Rogation Sunday is immense. In Linton they offer a prize for the youngest and oldest walkers; while Welshpool holds an ecumenical walk, which this year included a steam-train ride.

Other opportunities for taking Christianity to the streets include Palm Sunday and Good Friday. A Palm Sunday procession on the Lizard in Cornwall, which included a number of small boys as Roman soldiers, actually brought people out of the shops and houses to join in the hymn, 'All glory, laud and honour', as the procession wound its picturesque way around the town centre. A Good Friday walk behind the cross is particularly appropriate, asserts powerfully the love of Christ for the whole world, and prevents faith from being confined to the private sphere. In one Gloucestershire village, the vicar and a handful of parishioners carried a cross round the village on Good Friday for the first time, stopping for brief prayers at each landmark or business. It seemed as if few had marked their progress but the Easter Day congregation was nearly doubled in size.

In the past, it was common to see clergy walking about their parishes or cycling. Today, busy and hurried, they dash off in their cars from meeting to meeting and thus miss all opportunity for casual and meaningful encounters. One inner-city colleague ventured into his local fish-and-chip shop in cloak and cassock to be teased as 'Darth Vader' but also greeted with affection and respect. A nun walks the Nottingham streets daily, praying for everyone she sees, and each street. A free-church minister in South London spent many hours chatting to shopkeepers and anyone he met in the street. When he died, the whole street market closed down as a mark of respect. Although he would have been proud to have been called an evangelical, he spent most of his time listening to the experiences of those he encountered, and was none the worse an evangelist for so doing. Leicester town-centre churches combined to organize a very imaginative garden beside the shopping centre, into which to invite shoppers to be still and peaceful. Clergy were on hand to pray in a space that was pure hospitality, and a different order of space from the commodified, commercial world.

The preceding chapter has already argued strongly for the importance of place and locality. In this, Christians are at one with the more prophetic and insightful of contemporary social currents. The movement 'Common Ground' is a good example of a communitarian initiative, which sees its task as 'linking of nature with culture, focussing upon the positive investment people can make in their own localities, championing popular democratic involvement, and by inspiring celebration as a starting point for action to improve the quality of our everyday places.'[36] One of its initiatives is the parish map, in which local people come together to discuss and map what matters to them in their locality, and to see it in a new way. Sometimes these maps are cartographic and include all the roads, but sometimes impressionistic. The same landmark or creature may appear more than once, seen from different perspectives. Although such projects might tend to the purely celebratory, they often point up tensions and difficulties, and habitats under threat.

The Situationists, a group of radical theorists of urban life of the mid-twentieth century, evolved the practice of the *dérive*, which can be put to good religious use.[37] *Dérive* means drift, and the idea is to experience space in a new way by following an arbitrary and aimless path through a city. Just taking each second right turn, for example, can bring one to the back of a familiar building, or find strange alleys or people, smells and light effects. It can be like turning the city inside out, and can also reveal hidden connections between places. The *dérive* can make the familiar strange, and in so doing, reveal the otherness of the world, and

---

36 www.commonground.org.uk.
37 James L. Penner, 1999, *The Situationist City and Guy Debord,* Boston: MIT Press, Merlin Coverley, 2006, *Psychogeography,* Harpenden: Pocket Essentials.

the peculiarity of each person in the sense of their individual particularity. It is a way of experiencing both the mystery of reality, and its otherness, by which we are made aware of its having been created by God.

A more organized way of understanding space as sacred is to follow an historical path using the insights of the *dérive*. Nottinghamshire has lost nearly all its coalmines, and communities can sometimes feel as if their past has been completely erased, but you can still with care trace their history in the landscape, from the grassed-over slagheaps to the meadow where the pit ponies had their summer holiday. Historical walks that trace the ways people walked to work or where they foraged for wood, or danced or boxed, give value and meaning to their existence as an act of faithful attention. These can become pilgrimages and acts of witness. Places are complex and conflicted sites, and understanding their richness, depth and variety of meaning is impossible if we just follow familiar routes or stay in a car. The psychogeographers, as their name suggests, believe that routes of drift can reveal the emotional and psychological meanings of places, as well as new meanings and interconnections. In the *dérive*, place can become an intense mode of mediation.

Pilgrimage is enjoying something of a revival, especially since the European Union has given such financial support to the Camino to Santiago de Compostela from many points all over the continent. The youth pilgrimage to Walsingham in our own country attracts hundreds of young people every year. For young people, a challenging walking pilgrimage is a fitting rite of passage, and our country is full of ancient holy sites to visit from Lindisfarne to Iona, Glastonbury to St David's. Research will also reveal local saints and traditional holy places and wells, suitable for a day-trip.

When one walks the Compostela route or any other one encounters people of all ages and motivations, and the walking itself is part of the experience; it is not simply defined as a pilgrimage 'to' somewhere. The attitude to space itself changes, from something empty to an intense experience of presence. We learn about ourselves and our capabilities, and about very different perspectives on life from those we encounter. In Spain, the pilgrim passes women still washing against stones; up and down Britain one can still encounter a traditional wanderer on the road, who follows a route from one safe sleeping-place to another. Pilgrimage, moreover, is not complete until the return home, when absence and the experiences you have gone through give a new perspective on home. The present Bishop of Bath and Wells, Peter Price, has recently walked in pilgrimage over three hundred miles round his own diocese, as the early bishops like Cuthbert would have done, and the response to his being out among his people has been amazing. For the Bishop too, it has been the best thing he has done in his ministry, meeting such interesting people and encountering the problems of his diocese head on.[38]

Finally, as well as ourselves taking to the streets in a variety of ways, we are in a position so often to offer space to others. As was argued in the chapter on mission, to be sent is to be opened up for others. This may mean the holding of service projects inside the church building or hall, such as breakfasts for the homeless, lunches for the housebound, toddler groups and so on. It may mean, as at Todmorden, opening the churchyard to productive agriculture. It might include offering space for public meetings or protest groups. These are activities we engage in primarily as a response to the gospel commands, but they also have a value in terms of the formation of our imagination. How do we decorate our hall, or parish room? Often such places are rather dreary. Why not invite a community art group to paint a mural expressing your church's aims and mission to the community? One church had a problem with graffiti sprayed on the hall, and even on the graves in the churchyard. They invited the perpetrators to spray a complete picture instead. Another way of dealing with this problem creatively instead of constant cleaning up and whitewashing of offensive drawings is to invite some creative person to transform the images into something positive and good, on the principle of turning swords into ploughshares. It could be a challenge to the A-level art group at the local school.

---

38 Interview with BBC Somerset, accessed at www.news.bbc.co.uk/local/somerset.

3 Stories

> I had always felt life first as a story: and if there is a story there
> is a story-teller.
>
> 'The Ethics of Elfland', G. K. Chesterton[39]

Stories make us what we are, and the sense of being a character
in a narrative is the beginning of the awakening of the religious
sense, in which life has shape and meaning, and our actions consequences. Stories are, indeed, practices themselves, and form our
actions.[40] We need to subject ourselves to the biblical narratives,
so that they begin to narrate us. And we need as many of them
as possible, so that we learn to interpret them one against the
other and all seen in the light of the gospel narrative. In this way,
we will quite naturally avoid modern literalism and equally modern liberal dismissal of anything that dares to question our contemporary understanding of reality. After a recent Bible quiz and
tug-of-war between fathers and children, we concluded, however,
that the modern child-in-the-pew knows only a few of the great
scriptural stories: Noah's ark, Jesus' birth, death and resurrection,
and a few parables. There seems a general tendency, even in high-
quality children's study material, to avoid the Old Testament, despite the obvious appeal of some of the most vivid and exciting
narratives one could imagine. One does not have to agree with the
adultery of King David or Gideon's military tactics to gain a great
deal from the tales, and children are quite sophisticated enough to
enjoy acting out whole story of John the Baptist including the beheading and presentation of the head on a platter, without thinking
that it is a good thing to murder a prophet. The important thing
is that they should be offered a multitude of stories, and that they
should inhabit them, so that they may be discussed, argued about
and understood in a Christian context. Unfortunately, the Church
has so lost her nerve about the Bible that even the adult Sunday lectionary avoids controversial material, while the so-called

---

39 Chesterton, *Orthodoxy*, p. 94.
40 De Certeau, *Practice of Everyday Life*, p. 81.

Pillar lectionary used in cathedrals at Evensong, is aimed deliberately at not offending the occasional visitor, and therefore omits whole swathes of biblical material. It also avoids ending a reading half way through a story, lest the putative visitor miss the point, completely ignoring the value of serial publication, with its 'cliffhanger' endings. Perhaps the visitors might actually want to find out what happens next for themselves! They would also realize that they are participating in an ongoing mode of life, and not a discrete and 'packaged' commodity.

Part of the reason why Bible stories fail to be grasped and remembered even when they have been narrated is due to the moralizing or bastardized manner in which they are presented to children. Often, illustrations to children's Bible stories are jokey in tone, with comic cartoon-like figures. The level of artwork in children's Bibles is often poor and unimaginative, and fails to give the stories the dignity and power they deserve. This is true also of many of the figures for tracing and cutting-out in Junior Church materials. There is no sense in which these are stories for adults, into which children can gain increasing understanding as they mature.

One way round this problem is to use the resources of internet image banks to provide paintings by great artists or Orthodox icons to enrich children's understanding of Bible stories. One Junior Church had a wonderful session on Jacob and the Angel, looking at different artists' attempts to reach to the mysterious nature of the encounter. Before the session the children were inclined to elide fairies and angels. Afterwards, they had a sense of the struggle for meaning, and the power of the sacred. The Godly Play movement, which adapts Montessori educational practice for Christian nurture, uses a range of objects to tell stories, and its manual deliberately suggests that these should be made of good materials and be of high quality. Some churches are fortunate to possess beautiful sets made for them by local artists, but if good materials are used, such as wood, even the rough and amateur quality of the carving makes them powerful emblems in which children can take great pleasure. Godly Play indeed, models the creative use of sacred time and space. The tone is meditative and slow-paced; the group meets around the tray, which becomes a sacred space in which the story is told and explored. Children are encouraged to be exploratory, creative and thoughtful.

Another successful initiative in which many parishes are already involved is the 'Open the Book' project (www.openthebook.net). This organization provides thirty scripts of Bible stories to be presented dramatically – and often with the children's participation – by a small group of volunteers in school assemblies over a year. There are also packs for a further two years. It is approved by the national curriculum authority, and has received wide acclaim from teachers and children alike. Potentially, if all three packs are used, a wonderful richness of narratives is made known. Furthermore, the group presenting week by week get to explore all these stories for themselves, and enrich the parish itself.

One of the most important ways in which we can regain our stories is through dramatic participation. In the Middle Ages every town and even village had its own plays based on stories from the Bible, lives of the saints and the moral struggle in all of us. In the early-twentieth century, George Bell with Martin Browne, revived the religious play at Canterbury Cathedral, attracting a range of writers that included John Masefield, Charles Williams, Dorothy Sayers and T. S. Eliot. This professional activity led to a great revival in amateur drama in the parish from the 1930s to the '70s, which as far as we are aware, has yet to be documented. One of us remembers as a teenager taking part in a Christopher Fry's *Boy with a Cart* in an ordinary inner-city parish as well as a musical version of the life of Mary using the music of *West Side Story*, and following a dramatized version of Bunyan's *Pilgrim's Progress,* in six weeks of a children's Lent course, with the most dramatic fights between Christian and Apollyon, and a terrifying Giant Despair.

It is quite possible to put on plays again in churches, as some still do, and the group Religious Drama Society (RADIUS, www.radius. org.uk) provides resources and advice. One Cambridge church mounts a yearly drama, which has included a dramatized history of their own church, which allowed them to understand how they had evolved and discern their mission in today's world. They also performed the medieval *Conversion of St Paul*, which involved players from four years to over eighty, with the children playing a herd of realistic demons and the PCC embodying with equal ease the seven deadly sins. Medieval plays work quite successfully today because they are very human, and often employ humour and comic scenes, without detracting from the serious nature of the story portrayed. Drama unites all ages and is particularly helpful for enthusing young people, who can act, write their own sketches and direct.

Drama is a key resource in re-building a Christian imaginary because it allows imagination and participation: it is an out-working of the Palm Sunday passion reading in which we find ourselves as the baying crowd, timorous disciples and Roman guards. We read ourselves into the biblical narrative as both saints and sinners. One of the most moving Good Friday acts of worship one of us attended was a children's service in which they enacted the events from Holy Week from Maundy Thursday through to the burial of Christ. They washed each other's hands, and slept in Gethsemane; they cried out for Barabbas. Each child in turn carried the large cross with great devotion, and the quality of their stillness at the death of Christ was intense. Again they were learning and interpreting the story with their bodies, and their performance was not so dissimilar from the popular 'creeping to the cross' of lay piety in the late Middle Ages.

Medieval Christians also decorated Easter Sepulchres, in which the host was housed along with the crucifix, from Good Friday until Easter Day.[41] Our equivalent is the altar of repose, and the Easter Garden. Traditionally, Easter Gardens were also made for home use, and an Easter sepulchre in one's front garden or window, could become a meaningful way of conveying the story to the neighbourhood. Parishes could also make outdoor ones in the graveyard, for passers-by to see, and to form the focus of outdoor Stations of the Cross. Stations of the Cross is a devotion that could be developed further as a way of allowing people to let the Christian story read their own lives. You could invite different parishioners to offer their meditation on the images from the perspective of their own experience of life. For it is a practice that works equally effectively as gaining an insight into Christ's journey

---

41 Duffy, *Stripping of the Altars*, pp. 29–31.

to death, and of those who suffer, or as illuminating aspects of one's own life. Stations can also be taken as posters to different locations, to allow, for example, inmates of a young offenders' institution or a care home to interpret their own lives in the light of the Passion story. And there are now versions available that include the whole story, right up to the resurrection, and others that avoid scenes not mentioned in the Gospels.

There is great beauty in a children's nativity play, performed with direct vigour and unself-conscious pride. And since there is no evidence that people of other faiths find such plays offensive – indeed, all the evidence points the other way – we should encourage our local church school to maintain the custom. In Italy, traditional plays are performed by adults in the street near the elaborate public crib scenes, with folk songs and real animals, following St Francis's example. In Rome, the Pope blesses mangers belonging to local children in St Peter's Square, which is a custom we could do in our own parishes for anyone who will display a crib scene in their home. It is a ceremony that can happen outdoors, with a collection for the homeless and asylum seekers, taken up in a manger-shaped box, reminding people of the holy family as first, unable to find an inn, and second, refugees in Egypt.

The origin of Christian drama is usually credited to the dramatizing of the arrival of the three Marys at the tomb at Matins on Easter morning, the *Quem Quaeritis* (whom do you seek?).[42] At Winchester and Canterbury by the tenth century, this took a dramatic form with a priest in a white alb as the angel 'sitting quietly' by the Easter sepulchre, and three monks in copes swinging incense, representing the women coming with sweet oils to anoint the body. The angel opens the curtain to show the women the grave-clothes, which they then take to show the clergy and then the laity that Christ has risen.[43] The play here has evolved quite

---

42 This is the view of Karl Young, 1933, *The Drama of the Medieval Church*, London: Clarendon Press, questioned by O. B. Hadison, 1965, *Christian Rite and Drama in the Middle Ages*, Baltimore: Johns Hopkins University Press, who stresses also the contribution of popular festive practices.

43 See Dunbar Ogden, 2003, *The Staging of Drama in the Medieval Church*, Newark, DE: University of Delaware, pp. 24–6.

naturally from the liturgical enaction. The Middle Ages developed actual plays from this, performed on their own, but they also tended to dramatize key events in the liturgical calendar in ways that did not detract from the action of the Eucharist itself, in which Christ's life, death and resurrection are re-enacted. Pentecost, for instance, was the occasion for a model dove to be lowered through the 'holy ghost hole' in the ceiling of the church, followed by rose petals or burning straw to represent the flames of his appearance, while the choir made wind noises.[44] These dramatic features were both highly popular and wholly educatory, and could be adapted for modern use. A dove lowered from the organ loft could be a safer modern substitute but we could still enjoy clouds of petals.

A great Protestant tradition of participating in the Christian story is through singing, by which we do not only enjoy ourselves and our harmony together but also learn the Christian stories and theology. As long ago as the fourth century, Ambrose of Milan wrote hymns to encourage the orthodox faithful during persecution by the Arian Empress. Choral singing of oratorios like Handel's *Samson* or *Messiah*, Benjamin Britten's *Noye's Fludde* or Haydn's *Creation* are a wonderful part of our heritage and often quite easy to sing. Parish churches are often the location of concerts at which these works are sung by choirs who may have no overt religious identity. They give an opportunity to offer a prayer thanking God for the creative power of the voice, or to give a short introduction explaining how the work relates to the scriptures. Come-and-sing *Messiahs* are very popular and a way of bringing people into church and learning more about the faith. One church in Nottinghamshire holds an art exhibition during its summer garden party, during which the organist plays his way through the whole hymnal, and quite a number of people come and join in for their favourite hymn.

An increasing number of churches are encouraging young instrumentalists to accompany their worship. In this way, the old tradition of the church band in the gallery is being revived. Carol-singing is a custom that could be more frequently practised

---

44 See Duffy, *Stripping of the Altars,* pp. 459–60.

outdoors, advertised in advance, and offered to businesses, pubs and private homes. Children love to sing at primary school age and in Brownie and Cub packs, but older people lose the chance to sing communally, although the success of television reality shows such as *The Choir* reveals how worthwhile communal singing can be. Yet Senior Schools no longer teach singing, nor expect hymn-singing at assemblies. Singing is a religious act that makes us aware of our physical embodiment, and of our voice as more than a utile instrument; it models communality when we sing together. It is such an obvious point but the church offers us a place to sing, and by singing we effect a larger harmony. One possible initiative that would benefit all schools would be a series of DVDs on the model of the old BBC radio programme, *Singing Together*. Children were taught a wide range of traditional songs, including religious ones, and no instruments were needed in the classroom. Our professional choirs in cathedrals and large churches, some of whom are already involved in the 'Sing Up' programme to encourage singing in schools, could easily put these together.

We are beginning in England, at last, to begin to value again our own cultural expressions, instead of sneering at them. Southwell's liveliest weekend of the year is that of the folk festival, when hundreds of tents appear in the fields and the pubs are full of fiddle players, morris men and clog dancers. The morris groups of Nottinghamshire discovered that the churches of Nottingham used to hire dancers to accompany them on their walk out to the Minster to pay the tax, or 'Southwell pence'. Of their own volition, the morris men revived the custom and now dance their way to the Minster, which is cleared of chairs for them all to dance inside. St Alban's Abbey has revived the play of the death of Alban, which now attracts crowds to see the giant puppets and attend the festal evensong. One parish in Hampshire uses a jazz band to accompany their procession through the streets and play for the Eucharist, and several jazz masses have been commissioned in recent years by British cathedrals.

Indeed, there are a number of religious artists and composers among the greatest of our age: James MacMillan and John Taverner in music, Geoffrey Hill, Les Murray and Michael Symonds-Roberts among the poets, Peter Howson and Robert Natkin among painters. The church has become a place of hospitality for all that is best in our culture, offering space and commissioning art, welcoming poetry readings, dance groups and brass bands, and social and community projects that aim at justice, reconciliation and the common good. So much is already going on, and the local church is already a hospitable opening to creativity: we just need to be more confident in advertising what we do, and in connecting up the various activities, so as to reveal their missionary character.

The emphasis on cultural practices in this chapter has been placed upon mediation and participation. We have given examples of practices that involve taking and honouring the stuff of the world, whether objects or people. To be taken up into the Christian story is to engage in a *habitus* of transformative action. As we stated in the opening chapter, we are made in the image of God as creative beings, and ones who seek to move others to be creative. We are made in the image of God as loving beings, and those who call others to engage in *koinonia*. Every participatory action works against the passive and the virtual, bringing us closer to other people, closer to the material world, and closer to God. For in every human activity we re-present the world as more than it seems. Football is called 'the beautiful game' because it has a quality of 'footballiness' that the activity manifests. In recognizing the beauty of footballing skill, we are making a sign, and turning the activity into a sacrament of that reality.[45] In this chapter, we have sought to show how time, space and story are equally capable of beauty, signification and sacramentality. We have also suggested that re-orientation of the body and the senses is as missionary an endeavour as any overt outreach, and that we need to recover the extra-liturgical, in which those committed or on the fringe may be drawn in to Christian practice and experience.

---

45 See David Jones, 1959, 'Art and Sacrament' in *Epoch and Artist: Selected Writings*, ed. Harman Grisewood, London: Faber, p. 153, where Jones uses the analogies of cricket and of birthday cakes.

9

Mediating Faith in the Parish:
a Liturgical Ethics

To be a Christian is to live a life constituted by the cross and the resurrection, and thus to live in an improvised performance of these events. Every event we encounter is put in the larger context of the Christian story and judged by Christ's whole action. This is achieved by what Stanley Hauerwas calls 'truthful performance' of the virtues.[1] Not only does Fresh Expressions ignore the liturgical, but also it is quite unclear as to how its practices embody an ethical programme, and a mode of Christian living. The parish through its whole life is empowered by liturgical praxis, and by the synergy between the Holy Spirit and the Christian body, which catches it up into the Divine life. How this works practically, though often unconsciously, is the subject of this chapter. We have argued that the parish as a mixed community is the appropriate site of reconciliation, where different sorts of people may learn to live together peaceably and with forgiveness. This is effected primarily through our Eucharistic life together.

As we demonstrated in the last chapter, it is because our faith is narrative in character that our understanding of the self is as a protagonist in a story. We are called upon to live out the scriptures, and to imitate in a non-repetitive and unique way the example of Christ. This makes our ethics not an abstract theory or even a series of rules but a cultivation of virtues, because virtues are the characteristics that enable us to follow Christ and live his story. When asked what the greatest commandment might be,

---

1 Hauerwas, *Performing the Faith*, p. 75.

For the Parish

Jesus said: 'You shall love the Lord your God with all your heart and with all your soul and with all your strength, and with all your mind, and your neighbour as yourself' (Luke 10.27). This is not only what we should do but it is our true end: 'to glorify God, and enjoy him for ever' as the shorter catechism of the 1647 Westminster Confession puts it.[2] Ethics or virtues are the kinds of ways of being that enable us to reach this end, and that have within them this end as their form or intelligibility.

The Christian life is lived as a series of practices and disciplines that we inhabit to learn the ways of heaven and to love God and our neighbour. It is an exercise of practical wisdom, called by Aristotle, *phronesis*, by which we try to embody and model true excellence.[3] The Greeks gave us the cardinal or 'hinge' virtues of fortitude, temperance, justice and prudence; Christianity gave us the theological virtues of faith, hope and love that are directly infused by God to direct our mode of life in practice, through the cardinal virtues. The theological virtues also direct us to God, and are unlimited in scope. They are what will allow us to be with God and to share his life. These virtues are inherently social and can only be developed in a community sharing common values.

We have seen in Chapter 1 how *Mission-shaped Church* seeks to downgrade forms and practices by describing them as garments, which may be discarded. In contrast, the New Testament is full of references to putting on armour or spiritual clothing as the medium of salvation. The apostle Paul, to whom we owe the whole vocabulary of Christian virtues, uses the language of garments to express the virtues: in Romans 13.14, believers are to 'put on the Lord Jesus Christ' himself as a piece of armour. In Ephesians 4.24 you are 'to clothe yourselves with the new self, created according to the likeness of God in true righteousness and holiness'. He is referring obliquely to the white robe of baptism but also to the reality that the baptized person has literally 'put on' Christ: in Christ 'God became man so that man might become God' in the words

---

2 Philip Shaff, 1977, *Creeds of Christendom, with a History and Critical Notes*, Grand Rapids MI: Baker Books, 1977), vol. 3, p. 676.

3 *Aristotle: The Nichomachean Ethics*, ed. Roger Crisp, 2000, Cambridge Texts in the History of Philosophy, Cambridge: Cambridge University Press, p. 107.

of Athanasius in his treatise on the incarnation.[4] The language of garments and robing is employed to suggest that virtues are like a habit, in the sense of a monastic habit: a piece of clothing that reveals one's vocation and discipline. A habit in both senses of practice and clothing is etymologically linked to the verb *habere*, which means 'to have' in Latin. Virtue here is like learning a craft or a musical instrument: through practice and embodiment we gain a skill.

The parish is where we begin to learn the grammar of the Christian life, to play ourselves like an instrument. It is the nursery of heaven where we encounter all ages and sorts of people, and where, as Paul writes in Colossians 3.10:

> [you] have clothed yourselves with the new self, which is being renewed in knowledge according to the image of its creator. In that renewal there is no longer Greek or Jew, circumcised and uncircumcised, barbarian, Scythian, slave and free; but Christ is all in all.

It is the place of peaceable difference, for all is also Christ.

The parish is where we learn to live in eternity through liturgy. We have already described how we learn there to waste time, and encounter space as sacred. We also put on the virtues in all that we do in worship. As Stanley Hauerwas, who is the most radical proponent of Christian virtue ethics, writes: 'liturgy is social action. Through it we are shaped to live rightly the story of God, and to become part of that story, and are thus able to recognise and respond to the saints in our midst.'[5] Samuel Wells shows in an article, 'How Common Worship Forms Local Character' how the Eucharistic liturgy nurtures us in ethics through cultivating in worshippers a series of skills learnt by practice and performance. Together, Hauerwas and Wells have co-edited *The Blackwell Companion to*

---

4 Athanasius, 1998, *Treatise on the Incarnation, Nicene and Post-Nicene Fathers*, second series, 4, ed. Philip Schaff and Henry Wace, Edinburgh and Grand Rapids MI: 54, 3, p. 65.

5 Stanley Hauerwas, 2001, *Christian Existence Today: Essays on Church, World and Living In Between*, Grand Rapids: Brazos, p. 107.

Christian Ethics in which the whole series of essays is structured around the Eucharist, including medical ethics and politics In this chapter, we shall follow the same structure, in order to make the point of the mediation section of this book, that Christianity is a form of life, a mediation of the mediating God. It is by our 'fruits', our practices that we are known but it is through them that we also learn. And we learn through our bodies, our senses, as well as our hearts and minds.

Gathering

Common Worship has emphasized the gathering of the congregation as part of the liturgy and not just a preparation. This is only possible where the group are not already segregated as in the Fresh Expressions model. The initial gathering section of the liturgy provides exercise of the following skills, according to Wells: naming the presence of God, the faculty of wonder, alertness, patience, expectation, an awareness of those absent and love for the lost.[6] It is not the gathering of a 'gathered Church' model of ecclesiology but a focusing of the people as representative of the whole human race. It is an assertion of the Church's priestly calling. Gathering, therefore, is not a retreat into a holy huddle but an opening of the world to God: the opening of a flower's petals to the sun.

We do not always need to be aware of every implication of our worship like this because, unconsciously, we are being shaped and oriented by its performance, again like the sunflower turning to the source of its life. This shaping begins as we are focused in the direction of the altar and the cross. In many churches the processional cross is brought in and we all stand up and orient ourselves to it: it marks the direction in which we are to travel. With it comes the gospel book, held aloft and put on the altar. In other traditions the same orientation is marked in different ways, as in the Bible resting on a cushion, placed centrally, to mark our gathering around the Word by which we are called.

---

6 Wells, 'How Common Worship Forms Local Character,' p. 67.

To step back and reflect upon the initial exchange of greetings in 'The Lord be with you. And also with you,' can be quite startling, when one realizes the depth of transformation implicit in a few simple words and gestures.[7] The greeting establishes the virtue of obedience, because as the priest gathers us by his or her greeting, we respond to the call as the call of God. We gather because we have been gathered. And in this exchange of greetings we have left behind the self-determination of the modern subject and entered the mode of inter-connection and hospitality to others. To respond to the greeting is to affirm the gatheredness of the others present; their value and integrity in Christ is affirmed in the same phrase that unites us in the one body, sharing the one Spirit.

Confession

In the act of confession we learn humility and vulnerability, and our incorporation in larger structures of sinfulness. The confession section begins with the collect for purity, which opens up the congregation to be read by God. We learn to depend on God in the *Kyrie eleison/* Lord have mercy. In the repetition of that ancient cry, we learn our constant need for God's forgiveness.[8] In receiving absolution worshippers, according to Wells

> Inhabit the clothes of their baptism. They learn the notions of adoption by the Father, justification through the Son, new birth in the Spirit, liberation from slavery, the resurrection of the body and vocation to a life of prayer and service. They realise that salvation is a gift to be received, not a reward to be earned.[9]

---

7 The rite envisaged by this chapter is that of 'Holy Communion' in *Common Worship*, pp. 166–329. The use of the pronoun 'for' rather than 'of' in the full title of the book '*for* the Church of England' (my italics) already dissipates the *koinonia* of the Church.

8 On the importance of repetition as reaffirming our constant need for forgiveness and beginning again, see Catherine Pickstock, 1998, *After Writing: On the Liturgical Consummation of Philosophy*, Oxford: Blackwell, pp. 183–90.

9 Wells, 'How Common Worship Forms Local Character', p. 69.

Incorporation into Christ necessarily takes us all through suffering and death to new life, and this is re-enacted in every act of confession. It allows us the ability to see our sin for what it is. And that, after all, was why we needed the Incarnation. Humanity failed to recognize the blockage of sinfulness that cut us off from our true end in God. In Christ's life and actions we see sin and its effect in the same moment that we see our hope of redemption. And this tells us what we are like as human beings. As Robert Roberts states, 'the historical fact that Christ died for sinners becomes an essential feature of human nature.'[10] So we can liturgically shout for Christ's death, or deny him as Peter did in the courtyard in the Passion reading on Palm Sunday, because the facing up to our own sinfulness immediately opens us to the virtue of hope, which orients us to forgiveness: 'while we were yet sinners, Christ died for us' (Rom. 5.6). Year by year we repeat the same narrative because through habit we learn to love, believe and hope, and to be forgiven as we forgive. And we have to learn forgiveness over and over again. How many of us rush off to church after quarrelling with our spouse or children, arriving late and flustered, to be re-ordered by the structural form of life we engage there, and reconciled at the peace?

Gloria

It is only after we have been re-oriented and have received forgiveness that we are able to offer praise. In the 'Gloria' we learn from the angels how to praise, since the first words of this most ancient of hymns are those the angels sang to the shepherds at the nativity. And their song is a concordat: 'and on earth peace, goodwill towards men'. It establishes the friendship between the heavenly and the earthly orders, which obtains throughout the Eucharist. We mention it again at the 'Sanctus': 'with angels, and archangels and with all the company of heaven'. The Sanctus itself is a biblical hymn sung by the seraphs in Isaiah's vision in the temple,

---

10 Quoted in Stanley Hauerwas and Charles Pinches, 1997, *Christians among the Virtues: Theological Conversations with Ancient and Modern Ethics*, Notre Dame IN: University of Notre Dame Press, p. 120.

and repeated by the four living beasts in John's vision of the throne in Revelation (Isa. 6.3; Rev. 4.8). The angels, who live in eternity, have intuitive and direct experience of God's presence, and thus only truthful speech. To unite our praise to theirs is to trust to mediation as God's communication, and to our companionship with other orders of being, which re-orients us from our sense of humanity being the centre of everything. The same sense of being taught how to praise is conveyed in the Book of Common Prayer, Morning and Evening Prayer by the petition, 'O Lord, open thou our lips'. Only by God's action can 'our mouths . . . show forth thy praise'.[11]

The Ministry of the Word

The collect begins this section by focusing the immediate needs of the congregation and the specificity of the day. It is already an act of interpretation that gives us a lens by which to make sense of the readings that follow. Character is formed through our hearing and interpreting of the Word of God in the scriptures. For the *Mission-shaped Church* report, 'the scriptures, particularly the New Testament centred on Christ, may be regarded as a gift of God *from the past*' (p. 89, my italics). They are contrasted with the work of the Spirit, bringing a gift from the future. When read liturgically in the Christian Church, however, the Bible is a *living* book, which speaks to us and forms us as a body. It shapes us in the present as we seek to understand and interpret, through Christ, the various readings from Old Testament, epistle and gospel in the light of our own embodied reality. The living Word makes us in the very act by which we ourselves speak the Word. As Stanley Hauerwas sees it, scripture is actually unintelligible without the interpretative community of the Church. For when read in the church, the scriptures give us knowledge as they act to transform us.

Gerard Loughlin, in his book, *Telling God's Story*, reminds us of the scene in Revelation 10.9–10, in which the seer eats the scroll

---

11 The Book of Common Prayer, n.d., London: Cambridge University Press, p. 72.

as instructed by the angel, and finds it both sweet and bitter.[12] So we must ingest the word of God, 'read, mark and inwardly digest' its truths, and be changed by them. Loughlin writes that this digestion makes us into 'living commentaries' on scripture.[13] The sermon at the Eucharist helps us in this digestion by finding a way to hold all three readings together and also a way to use them to understand what is going on in our world today. This does not mean that all is smooth and harmonious:

> At the same time, critical dissonances and disharmonies are awakened, identified, and in some instances, even accentuated. Whether these countervailing forces are taken up directly and explicitly addressed in the homily . . . the dissonances nonetheless do their work. The effect of such a reading practice is to set the various biblical passages in motion, encouraging them to reverberate and play off one another to generate specific melodies and harmonies, and sometimes harsh discords.[14]

Quite a degree of intellectual agility and suppleness is required by Christian worshippers, who are not allowed, by this method of presentation, to read scripture just on one level. Often without realizing it, we are embodying figural-type interpretation, whereby we both note the distance, to use a simple example, between the triumph of Moses and Miriam in the Exodus reading over the drowning of the Egyptians and their chariots and Christ's own death in the gospel reading, while at the same time seeing in the Exodus deliverance some anticipation of the redemptive work of Christ.

In many Anglican as well as Lutheran churches the gospel is processed. As Christ came down from the mountain to speak to the crowds, so the gospel goes right down into the heart of the people,

---

12 Gerard Loughlin, 1999, *Telling God's Story: Bible, Church and Narrative Theology*, Cambridge: Cambridge University Press, p. 103.

13 Loughlin, *Telling God's Story*, p. 103.

14 Jim Fodor, 2004, 'Reading the Scriptures: Rehearsing Identity, Practicing Character', *The Blackwell Companion to Christian Ethics*, ed. Stanley Hauerwas and Samuel Wells, Oxford: Blackwell, pp. 141–55 (pp. 146–7).

who all turn to follow it. In one church, the children all join the procession and surround the gospel reader, before skipping out for their own activities after the reading. In this procession, we recognize Christ himself, and the presence of the children helps us to see the procession as like the triumphant entry of Christ into Jerusalem on Palm Sunday. In our response of 'Alleluia,' again we reach for the words of the angels and we admit the power of the *living* Word, for 'alleluia' has the force of an imperative, meaning literally 'All Hail to Him who is!'[15] The gospel is appropriately read by a deacon or other minister, because the reading has to be detached as far as can be from the individual voice, which is why it is often intoned. The body is orchestrated to allow the sound free range. Jim Fodor describes such reading as 'rhapsodic', as if the lungs, throat and mouth of the reader become a 'sounding page'.[16] Some listeners to the gospel make a small sign of the cross on forehead, lips and breast to show their own acceptance of that word in their mind, their lips and their heart. Churches often encourage worshippers to listen to the gospel rather than follow the words on a sheet, so that it may enter by the ear, in the same manner as the Word himself was traditionally believed to have entered the body of Mary: 'blessed are those who hear the word of God and keep it' (Luke 11.28). As we look, listen and attend with our whole body to the gospel, so we are to attend with equal alertness to the word of God as we encounter it in our daily lives.

The creed logically follows the sermon, and completes the ministry of the Word, because it sums up all that we discern in the scriptures, and is itself a kind of food. In a series of Lent talks on the creed, *The School of Charity*, the spiritual writer, Evelyn Underhill, writes of our statements of belief as our equipment for the Christian journey, our maps and tins:

The spiritual life of man cannot be maintained on a diet of suggestive phrases and ideas. Only when we have found within the familiar externals of our religion, those vivid realities which these

---

15 *Catholic Encyclopaedia* at www.newadvent.org.
16 Fodor, 'Reading the Scriptures', p. 145.

externals enclose and keep safe, are we using our equipment
properly and getting the food we need. We must open the tins,
if we are to discover inside them the mysterious nourishment
of the soul.[17]

Historically, the creeds evolved out of the scriptures and the early
Christians' living experience of the nature of God. They were claimed,
personally, by the candidate for baptism, who would name his or her
own faith in their recitation. They are the deep grammatical structures of faith, which help us to direct our prayer rightly. But they
are also, as the title of Archbishop Rowan Williams's book of talks
on the creeds, tells us, 'Tokens of Trust'.[18] In them, we assert God's
trustworthiness, and we respond in joy and loyalty. Every time we
say the creed after the ministry of the Word, it gives us something
new, and opens to us further the reality of God. The Nicene Creed
is dramatic because it starts by dazzling us with the greatness and
otherness of God as Creator, and of the Son as one with God, but
then literally descends to the solidarity of the Incarnation. In the
Anglo-Catholic tradition the worshippers genuflect at this point,
to get up either after the statement, 'and was made man' or 'he
rose again'. To kneel at this point is very powerful as a theological
message, because God comes down to us, so that we might rise
with him. We name the Spirit and move from the nature of God
to the nature of the Church: as one, catholic and apostolic. The
creed challenges us as it sustains us, for it ends with our own life
with God: 'the resurrection of the body, and the life of the world
to come'. In reciting the creed we learn to model faith, hope and
love and we affirm the true end of life with God. The creed ac-
celerates time, and nests it within the eternal life of God, whither
we are bound, and into which we launch ourselves by anticipation
at the conclusion.

17 Evelyn Underhill, 1934, *The School of Charity: Meditations on the Christian Creed*, London: Longmans, Green and Co., pp. 2–3.
18 Rowan Williams, 2007, *Tokens of Trust: An Introduction to Christian Belief*, Norwich: Canterbury Press.

Intercession

The intercessions literally bring us back down to earth, as we seek to relate what we believe about the nature of reality and the true end of humanity, to the world and the Church as they are. Intercession is naturally an ethical practice, in which we are radical in seeking for a different world from the one we see. We name virtues and vices and seek the common good. The whole of experience is re-oriented and reconnected to God. It is our priestly work of unveiling, and the heart of our mission. Through faithful prayer we learn to name, identify and love our neighbour. In intercession we become aware of immediate and local needs and problems, such as the fatigue and isolation of those who look after the sick and housebound, which concerned one member of St John's parish in Bilborough in Nottingham, so that she started a carers' support group. Intercession, too, is a way in making central those who are marginal, by putting the concerns of the homeless, the disabled or the mentally ill at the heart of our prayer.

Samuel Wells also points out how we learn prudence about the limits of what we can ask, and fortitude and persistence as we carry on praying for peace in the Middle East, for example, that has yet to be a reality. Although intercession is so much part of our natural desire to ask things of God, it is also truly difficult. It is hard to keep on asking for justice that does not come. The needs of the world are so many and various that to shape them into a few phrases seems well nigh impossible. And it is a temptation to tell God what to do. Yet all this difficulty is part of the discipline – what has rightly been called 'the school of prayer'. By the feebleness of our own practical response, which the action of intercession tends to foreground, we are shamed into action.

The Peace and the Offertory

The giving of the peace begins the slow work of reconciliation for which the intercessions point the need. As we greet one another and offer the sign of peace, we do not just express a vague friendliness but a hope of peaceableness in our lives, as we say: 'peace be with you'. In turning right, left and behind, each of us models the virtue of peace that we seek. We can misuse the peace, either by rushing off to hug our friends, or by refusing the implications of the act by substituting a social, 'Good morning' for 'peace be with you'. But the gestures and the actions carry the meaning of re-connection. Indeed, the awkwardness of the greeting being given to people for whom one does not necessarily have easy comradeship or understanding is part of the ethical value of the act. For Paul Wadell:

> The amazing thing about the Eucharist is that it gathers together for a meal people who might never invite each other into their homes for dinner . . . One's table-companions may be strangers, misfits, malcontents, or even an assortment of enemies. There is no guarantee that in celebrating the Lord's Supper Christians will be surrounded by like-minded people.[19]

The peace we exchange is therefore an exercise in hope and faith that because we are not our own but Christ's, peace is a possibility on a new basis of existence. This new form of life gains its security not from possessions or power but from resting in God's love.

The offertory is a natural development from our intercession and peace. The peace comes down to us from the president who cascades the peace of Christ. In the procession of the bread, wine and money to the altar the people respond, as they bring matter of the world to be restored to its divine origin. The gifts are brought up by the laity, as if to model the offering of the world and the self, people and things, which are being restored to their true home by their priesthood. Ken Leech points out that in the offertory, the process of consecration has already begun:

> In a sense the bread and wine of the offertory are not ordinary . . . already, through the action of taking and offering, they are contained within the offering of the humanity of Christ, for they

---

19 Paul Wadell, 2004, 'Sharing Peace: Discipline and Trust', *The Blackwell Companion to Christian Ethics*, ed. Stanley Hauerwas and Samuel Wells, Oxford: Blackwell, pp. 289–301 (p. 294).

are the gift of the Church, the Body of the risen Christ . . . The Church in this act is being presented by Christ to himself. St Paul expresses it well. Christ, he says, loved the Church so much and gave his life for it, that we might sanctify and cleanse it with the washing of water (that is, Baptism) that he might *present it to himself*, a glorious Church, not having spot or wrinkle.[20]

The Church, enrobed in Christ, offers the world to God. Again, here the lay people assert their priesthood as those who work and live and transform the world by regarding it as God's creation. Here God's mission is enacted, as God becomes all in all.

The Eucharistic Prayer

In the Eucharistic Prayer, we enter into the mystery of the divine liturgy of love. As the president takes, blesses, breaks and shares the bread and wine, we do not merely stand like children with good table manners, waiting to be served. In some sense we participate in this mystery of our redemption. As we learn the skills of gratitude, and echo the great Jewish *berakoth* prayers of contemplative praise, we invoke the Holy Spirit to make the bread and wine Christ's body and blood for us. The Jewish *berakoth* were already, according to Louis Bouyer, an invitation for God to accomplish his design in the worshipper.[21] And in the post-communion prayer of the Eucharist, we offer ourselves, 'as a living sacrifice [. . .] to live and work to thy praise and glory'. In this way we offer ourselves also to be taken, blessed, broken and shared. We offer ourselves to the life of *koinonia*, of a breaking open of the self to relationality.

There is also a second ethical lesson embodied in the action, to which the Anglo-Catholic socialist tradition has long borne

---

20 Ken Leech, 1986, *True Prayer: An Invitation to Christian Spirituality*, London: Sheldon, pp. 103–4.

21 Louis Bouyer, 1968, *Eucharist: Theology and Spirituality of the Eucharistic Prayer*, trans. Charles Underhill Quinn, Notre Dame IN: University of Notre Dame Press, p. 48.

witness. Bishop Frank Weston shocked the 1923 Anglo-Catholic Congress by challenging them:

> Come out from before your tabernacles [containing the reserved Sacrament]. You cannot claim to worship Jesus in the table if you do not pity Jesus in the slum . . . If you say that an Anglo-Catholic has a right to hold his peace while his fellow citizens are living in hovels beneath the level of the streets, then I say to you, that you do not know the Lord Jesus in his Sacrament.[22]

For this tradition, the Incarnation gives ultimate value to every human being, in whom Christ is to be found. His 'real presence' is on the face of the child-worker and the prostitute; and the Eucharist is the revolutionary act by which this sacred truth is proclaimed. It is an act of equality, fraternity and liberty. We embody these values by the way in which we all receive and all kneel, raising our hands for the bread of life that sustains them, and united in fraternity by sharing from the one cup. We can, of course, tell the story badly by our liturgical practice, so that its ethical edge is lost or muted. But the words and gestures – the taking, blessing, breaking, sharing – are a faithful performance, although they take on an added prophetic power in the shanty-town, in the war zone, in a church containing people of opposed political views.

Sending out

To be drawn into the mystery of the action of Divine love is also to be commissioned and sent. The deacon's 'Go in peace to love and serve the Lord,' is a strong command. One of us once heard it proclaimed in loud chorus by the massed children of a Portsea parish, standing with their arms wide open on the altar steps, shooing us out. The peace in which we go, however, is a communal reality. We do not go out as individuals but as part of a new way of living: a new 'city' or *polis*. This is made clear to us in the blessing, in

---

22 Quoted in Ken Leech, 1981, *The Social God*, London: Sheldon, p. 21.

which the blessing is given not to us as individuals but 'among you'. There is a helpful study guide by John Thomson, *Doxa*, which uses meditation on what we do in the Eucharistic liturgy to explore our life as Christians as disciples in the world.[23] Each week the group of parishioners concentrates on one section of the liturgy and relates it to how we should live. In one parish they used the insights of the group to plan the sermon, in which the priest or reader would share the group's conclusions with the rest of the congregation, most of whom were not comfortable with discussion groups but would be prompted by what they heard to talk informally over coffee. In the sermon, the practices of service and loving-kindness already put into practice among this community could be shown as the effect of being grasped by the liturgy. Gradually they were learning how we should bear witness and how we are already being shaped to do so. They were learning the practices of discipleship, which Michael Cartwright describes as a life-long apprenticeship.[24]

It is wholly right that the sending out, forgiven, fed and blessed, should be part of our liturgy, in which we embody the gospel. But this brings us back again to mediation and mission. How can we be sent if not from someone and somewhere? 'How will they hear without a preacher?' (Rom. 10.14). In our sending out, the habits of virtue that we learn day by day become themselves the agents of mission: our testimony. And these are habits and virtues that are inherently communal and part of a tradition. Fr Luigi Giussani puts it eloquently:

> Unless we feel that our vocational group (the Christian com-
> munity to which we belong) is like a new, small segment of hu-
> manity that begins to disclose the mystery whereby Christ is the
> substance of all things and becomes a sign of it; unless we feel
> this in our daily lives and contacts, how can we live suspended
> from the mystery, how can we give praise and testify to it? How

---

23 John Thomson, 2007, *Doxa: A Discipleship Course*, London: Darton, Long-man and Todd.

24 Michael C. Cartwright, 2004, 'Being Sent: Witness', *The Blackwell Companion to Christian Ethics*, ed. Stanley Hauerwas and Samuel Wells, Oxford: Blackwell, pp. 481–94 (p. 488).

can we become supreme artists, able to touch the face of Christ and make it come alive, and with our mere touch, make everything that we touch a sign of his mysterious presence?[25]

No ethics is possible without a tradition and a community. 'The adolescent uses tradition as a sort of *explanatory* hypothesis,' says Fr Giussani in *The Risk of Education*. 'There cannot be a discovery, step or contact with reality that we initiate without some idea of possible meaning . . . that presents itself to the individual in formation with solidity, intensity and sureness.'[26] The Church and her practices, especially the Eucharist, are that tradition for us, who are all still 'in formation'. It is where virtue, as the word tradition from the Latin, *traditus*, indicates, is 'handed over'. Without a living tradition with which to engage, we are overcome by cynicism or by fanaticism: a one-sided view of reality. In communion, living eucharistically, we have true freedom in the sense of the satisfaction of our true desires. Like children born and raised in a loving home, we can grow to be exploratory, generous and outgoing: 'we are holy when we can embrace our neighbours and all of reality, turning this embrace into an adventure and a cry which proclaims that the substance of everything is Christ and that our embrace is not ours, but Christ's.'[27]

25 Luigi Giussani, 2001, *The Risk of Education: Discovering Our Ultimate Destiny*, trans. Rosanna M. Giammanco Frongia, New York: Crossroads, p. 44.
26 Giussani, *Risk of Education*, p. 53.
27 Giussani, *Risk of Education*, p. 44.

Conclusion

Mission-shaped Church and Fresh Expressions reveal a crisis of confidence in the Church of England. First of all, we lack confidence in the parish. Statistics concerning patterns of relation to the Church did not entail the Fresh Expressions movement and not, for instance, an attempt to revive the life of parishes where it is flagging. The response outlined in *Mission-shaped Church* is as much based on a lack of confidence in the parish (and in religion, but that is another story) as it is on 'empirical facts'. In contrast, the second half of this book has presented a vision of the vigour of the parish. Nowhere, of course, is the potential of the parish fully realized. It could not be. The strength of the parish is that its possibilities are endless. In many parishes the problem is more that the clergy and most committed laity are working too hard, not that they are working too little.

The report also demonstrates the lack of confidence in theology current in the Church of England. *Mission-shaped Church* is the least impressive theological publication from the Church of England that either of us can remember. We could go further and say that the report illustrates that the contemporary Church of England lacks a more general confidence in 'hard thinking' of every sort. The philosophical holes in the report bear witness to this, as does the light-weight nature of most of the sociology upon which the report relies so heavily. Or just consider that this, the definitive church report of the decade, was written by a committee where academic theologians were so singularly ill represented. In lay theological education and ordination training alike, people are tired of 'reflecting on experience' without any theological tools with which to do it.

Beyond this, we also lack confidence in our heritage as Anglicans. To write this at the present time is all the more incongruous. However else we interpret the current overtures from the Vatican towards members of the Anglican churches, they underline how valuable our 'Anglican patrimony' is to observers from other communions. While buying a second-hand Anglican history book recently, one of us was startled by the unprompted response of the assistant: 'thank God for the Church of England!' This book has attempted to direct us to what is good in our tradition, and the necessity of inspiring and equipping our members with an understanding of their faith that can enable them to say the same.

One reason that the Church of England has so little confidence in her own ancient and local expressions of the life of the Church is that she has so little confidence in *the Church* at all. We have demonstrated how Fresh Expressions literature reveals a singular lack confidence in the Church as the communal fact offered to us in the Christian gospel, and a central character in the history of God's work with human beings. Against this we need a renewed sense of the importance of the Church in the plan of God. This will require a rediscovery of the place of the Church in theology. In earlier chapters we have encountered some of the authors who will help us here coming from an Anglo-Catholic, Roman Catholic and Orthodox perspective. Just as important is the work of Church-minded evangelicals, who are also likely to be more immediately accessible to the average thinker about Fresh Expressions. There are writers such as Stanley Hauerwas, whom we have used throughout this book, and who appropriates the deeply ecclesial thought of figures from radical Protestantism such as John Howard Yoder.[1] There are Anglicans such as Oliver O'Donovan and the Bishop of Coventry, Christopher Cocksworth, whose book *Holding Together* might serve as a model of what we have

---

1 See, for instance, John Howard Yoder, 1992, *Body Politics: Five Practices of the Christian Community before the Watching World*, Nashville, TN: Discipleship Resources.

Conclusion

in mind.[2] There are also Reformed voices, such as Kevin DeYoung and Ted Kluck in the United States.[3]

Alongside renewed confidence, we need a concern for Christian nurture and maturity. Here Fresh Expressions and parishes should work closely together for their mutual benefit. Much that is most valuable in the Church of England's outlook would be speedily preserved if Fresh Expressions were recast as parish mission initiatives. This is, in fact, the way that many are functioning, despite the hope in *Mission-shaped Church* that these missionary gatherings would be given full autonomy. This sort of association would help both sides. The creativity of the Fresh Expressions pioneers would provoke the parishes to rediscover their innate possibilities for mission. In turn, the parish would provide a grounded community for education and practical discipleship.

These are vitally important questions. When it comes to Fresh Expressions leaders, the question must be whether it is healthy for them – upon whom so many burdens are laid – to be cut off from the nurture provided by a parish. There are also obvious difficulties when it comes to education and the provision of necessary theological resources if Fresh Expressions choose to pursue the model of autonomous local leadership. When it comes to the new disciples they hope to make, the question is whether Christian maturity does not involve the submission of the forms of our lives to the disciplines of the Church – and if so, whether it is helpful for the new convert, or the person brought back into the Church, to be steered away from the parishes. There is a clear tension in that the *Church of England* is simultaneously pointing to the liturgy as the principal place where Christians are taught and grow in discipleship, and yet also giving previously unknown permission for forms of Church of England life almost entirely dispensed from liturgical expectations. At the same time we have the former in the Liturgical Commission's

---

2 Christopher Cocksworth, 2008, *Holding Together: Gospel, Church and Spirit – The Essentials of Christian Identity*, Norwich: Canterbury Press.

3 Kevin DeYoung and Ted Kluck, 2009, *Why We Love the Church: In Praise of Institutions and Organized Religion,* Chicago, IL: Moody Press, and their 2009, *Why We're Not Emergent: (By Two Guys Who Should Be)*, Chicago, IL: Moody Press.

current mandate to pursue 'liturgical formation' and the latter in the theory – and even more in the practice – of Fresh Expressions.

In sketching the shape of a balanced Christian life we could do far worse than adopt the model of non-conformist chapels in the twentieth century: we need 'mission' services, and to attend to this with new diligence, but we also need 'fellowship' services – alongside something like the Fresh Expression there should be something like the parish community.

This book, and especially its first half, has cast itself first of all as a response to the report *Mission-shaped Church* and only secondarily to the ensuing literature. We have taken this approach, quite deliberately, because the report is the defining document. It legitimates whatever has followed on in practice. We are occasionally told by Fresh Expressions theorists that their world has moved on since the report was published. If so, and if it has moved in the direction of parish–Fresh Expression co-operation, it is to be welcomed. All the same, if that is true, we then need the Church to produce a new positioning document to supplant and correct the old one. This is exactly what has not happened. Instead, the fifth anniversary of the publication of *Mission-shaped Church* saw its reissuing with a new and celebratory preface.

A book such as this one could not say everything that needs to be said about *Mission-shaped Church* or Fresh Expressions. For one thing, there remains the task of exploring a shape of a closer relation between parishes and Fresh Expressions. This is something that could only adequately be begun from within conversations between both parties. Nor is even an initial critique of the ideas at work in Fresh Expressions thinking complete.

As the first of three examples to illustrate this, more work should be done on the importance of time, and especially on the abiding significance of Sunday worship for Christians as people of the resurrection. Then there is the claim that the parish church is marked and compromised by a 'come to us' mentality. This will seem almost incomprehensible for a great many parish priests. Unless it rests upon the elementary mistake of identifying the parish with the church building – which *is* something too heavy to be carried around – it reflects nothing of the Anglican model of the priest as active and visible in his or her community, or of the laity – who are equally the church – at work in the world. The people of the parish church are the ultimate example of its 'go to them' (rather than 'come to us') dynamic at work. In both of these ways, it is foundational to the parish that it is there for everyone, whereas the community at large might not even know that a particular Fresh Expression exists or where it is meeting.

As a third and final example, the empirical sociology behind this writing ought to be subjected to greater scrutiny. We have registered our worries that these writers elevate sociology over theology: the social sciences make good servants but bad masters. All the same, we welcome any attempt of Christian theology to work with an accurate picture of what the world happens to be like. It is just that we are not sure that the average Fresh Expressions writer works with sociology of great depth or with more than a certain rather small set of studies that support their own claims. As an example, we read in several places that it is no longer feasible to call Sunday our day for community worship because home ownership argues against it. The claim is that as more people own their own houses, they will choose to engage in DIY on the weekend rather than to be involved with their communities. On the contrary, there is good evidence to suggest the opposite trend: that home ownership tends to encourage enfranchisement and involvement in a community.[4]

There is also theological work left to be done. For one thing, we need a far more proficient theology of culture than the one on offer in this literature. We need something both far more theological and something that sees how constitutive culture is for all of us, rather than being a set of more or less peripheral 'life-style choices' concerning music and similar matters. We would also like to see careful exegesis of the key passages deployed in this writing – exegeses

---

4 'The main arguments for home ownership . . . are not primarily economic, but social. Home ownership . . . makes people more likely to vote in local elections and join clubs . . . In America homeowners are less likely to move than renters, so areas with a lot of homeowners are more stable . . . Homeowners are more likely to know who their representatives are; more likely to support local causes or parent-teacher associations and (this being America) more likely to go to church.' *The Economist*, 16 April 2009.

that drew on the best resources offered by biblical scholarship and the traditions of Christian doctrine. Nowhere is this more important than in the recurrent invocation of the 'dying to live' trope, which brings together hasty biblical interpretation, deficient Christology and not a little moral blackmail over members of the inherited church, urged to give up what they love and value when no similar sacrifices are being offered from the enthusiasts for *emergent church*.

Our final suggestions fall in the area of practical ecclesiology. We hope that more attention will be paid to the value of the pastoral offices for mission: offices such as marriage and burial. The daily offices of morning and evening prayer also offer opportunities, in their wise and humane consecration of the day and marking of time, not least in an educational setting. More generally, we need to think about the local church as guardian of place and history, as a place of both celebration and of resistance.

The parish church celebrates place and history precisely in the same gesture by which she sees beyond them to the One who transcends both space and time, and yet came to dwell within them. Parish churches may need to learn to let that celebration overflow onto the streets and greens of our towns and villages. All the same, this already happens to a considerable degree, and that is something which those who denigrate the parish tradition may need to learn in turn.

This sort of presence of the Church in public spaces lines up with a more conceptual presence – the involvement of the clergy and people in local advocacy, community organizing and debate. Here the parish church already occupies a pre-eminent place in many localities, and here her guardianship takes on a harder edge. Parish churches, their clergy and people, stand in the front line of the fight against exploitation, poverty and racism, for instance. Here we see the Church embodying her role as God's resistance movement – an idea so singularly absent in *Mission-shaped Church* and much that has followed.

Such work of resistance requires patterns of resistance to undergird it and renew the strength of those involved. This is what the practices and disciplines of the parish church provide. In this sense, the parish church is tougher than the average Fresh Expression. It lays greater emphasis on a life of conversion and resistance to sin, the world and the devil. It recognizes that the Christian life is an active one and that it is frequently difficult: the soil of our lives can be rocky, thorns grow readily and there are the birds of the air to contend with. For this we need the support offered by history, tradition, liturgy and by one another. Making the business of Christian faith 'easier' and ever more accommodated to contemporary life does not make it easier to hold on to. In this sense the inherited church is grittier than the average Fresh Expression, as we say, and yet the parish is also more open. It is there for everyone, and not just for the few marked out for conversion, for which end alone the Fresh Expression exists.

Bibliography

Afanasiev, Nicholas, 2007, *The Church of the Holy Spirit*, Notre Dame, IL: Notre Dame University Press.

Amiot, François, 1962, *The Key Concepts of St Paul*, Edinburgh: Nelson.

Anderson, Benedict, 1983, *Imagined Communities*, London and New York: Verso.

Anglican–Roman Catholic International Commission, 1999, *The Gift of Authority*, London: Catholic Truth Society.

Aquinas, Thomas, 1956, *Summa Contra Gentiles*, trans. Vernon J. Bourke, Notre Dame, IN: University of Notre Dame Press.

Aquinas, Thomas, 1920, *Summa Theologica,* trans. the Fathers of the English Dominican Province, 22 vols, London: Burns, Oates and Washbourne.

Aristotle, 2000, *The Nichomachean Ethics*, ed. Roger Crisp, Cambridge Texts in the History of Philosophy, Cambridge: Cambridge University Press.

Armstrong, Karen, 2009, *The Case for God: What Religion Really Means*, London: Bodley Head.

Athanasius, 1998, *Treatise on the Incarnation*, Nicene and Post-Nicene *Fathers*, second series, 4, 15 vols, ed. Philip Schaff and Henry Wace, Edinburgh and Grand Rapids MI: T & T Clark and Eerdmans.

Atkins, Martyn, 2008, 'What is the Essence of the Church?' in *Mission-shaped Questions: Defining Questions for Today's Church*, ed. Steven Croft, London: Church House Publishing, pp. 16–28.

Auden, W. H., 1991, *Collected Poems*, ed. Edward Mendelson, New York: Vintage.

Augustine of Hippo, 1945, *An Augustine Synthesis*, ed. Erich Przywara, London: Sheed & Ward.

Augustine of Hippo, 1991, Sermon XXI [LXXI Ben] in *Nicene and Post-Nicene Fathers*, first series, vol. 6, ed. Philip Schaff, 14 vols, Edinburgh and Grand Rapids MI: T & T Clark and Eerdmans.

Baillie, John, 1942, *Invitation to Pilgrimage*, London: Oxford University Press.

Balthasar, Hans Urs von, 2005, *Epilogue*, trans. Edward T. Oakes, San Francisco: Ignatius Press.

Bibliography

Balthasar, Hans Urs von, 1992, *Theo-Drama: Theological Dramatic Theory, Volume III, The Dramatic Personae: The Person in Christ*, trans. Graham Harrison, San Francisco: Ignatius Press.

Balthasar, Hans Urs von, 1982, *The Glory of the Lord: A Theological Aesthetics*, trans. Brian McNeil CRV, Andrew Louth, John Saward, Rowan Williams and Oliver Davies, 7 vols, Edinburgh: T&T Clark.

Bassler, Jouette M., 2007, *Navigating Paul: An Introduction to Key Theological Concepts*, Louisville, KY: Westminster John Knox Press.

Bataille, Georges, 2005, *The Cradle of Humanity: Prehistoric Art and Culture*, New York: Zone Books.

Bede, 2001, *Ecclesiastical History of the English People, The Greater Chronicle, Bede's Letter to Egbert*, ed. Judith McClure and Roger Collins, Oxford: Oxford University Press.

Billings, Alan, 2004, *Secular Lives: Sacred Hearts: The Role of the Church in a Time of No Religion*, London, SPCK.

Blair, John, 2005, 'Recent Work on Parish Formation in England: Some Comparisons and Contrasts with France', *Revues Médiévales*, 49, at http://medievales.revues.org/document1267.htm.

Blair, John and Richard Sharpe (eds), 1992, *Pastoral Care before the Parish*, Leicester: Leicester University Press.

The Book of Common Prayer, n.d., London: Cambridge University Press.

Bosch, David, 1995, *Believing in the Future: Towards a Missiology of Western Culture*, London: Continuum, 1995.

Botelho, Lynn A., 2004, *Old Age and the English Poor Law, 1500–1700*, Woodbridge: Boydell and Brewer.

Bourdieu, Pierre, 1977, *Outline of Theory and Practice*, Cambridge: Cambridge University Press.

Bouyer, Louis, 1968, *Eucharist: Theology and Spirituality of the Eucharistic Prayer*, trans. Charles Underhill Quinn, Notre Dame IN: University of Notre Dame Press.

Boyle, Nicholas, 1998, *Who Are We Now: Christian Humanism and the Global Market from Hegel to Heaney*, Notre Dame, IN: University of Notre Dame Press.

Brown, Callum, 2001, *The Death of Christian Britain: Understanding Secularism 1800–2000*, Abingdon: Routledge.

Bruce, Steve, 1996, *Religion in the Modern World: From Cathedrals to Religious Cults*, Oxford: Oxford University Press.

Bulgakov, Sergei, 1997, *The Holy Grail and the Eucharist*, trans. Boris Jakim, Hudson NY: Lindisfarne Books.

Bulgakov, Sergei, 1988, *The Orthodox Church*, Crestwood, NY: St Vladmir's Seminary Press.

Bynum, Carolyn Walker, 2007, *Metamorphosis and Identity*, New York: Zone.

For the Parish

Cartwright, Michael C., 2004, 'Being Sent: Witness', *The Blackwell Companion to Christian Ethics*, ed. Stanley Hauerwas and Samuel Wells, Oxford: Blackwell, pp. 481–94.

Certeau, Michel de, 1984 [1980], *The Practice of Everyday Life*, trans. Steven Rendall, Berkeley, CA: University of California Press.

Chauvet, Louis-Marie, 2001, *The Sacraments: The Word of God at the Mercy of the Body*, trans. Madeleine Beaumont, Collegeville MN: The Liturgical Press.

Chesterton, G. K., 2001 [1936], *Autobiography*, Thirsk: House of Stratus.

Chesterton, G. K., 1986 [1933], *Thomas Aquinas/St Francis of Assisi*, San Francisco: Ignatius Press.

Chesterton, G.K., *Orthodoxy*, 1957 [1908], London: Bodley Head.

Chesterton, G. K., 1905, *Heretics*, London: John Lane.

Cocksworth, Christopher, 2008, *Holding Together: Gospel, Church and Spirit – The Essentials of Christian Identity*, London: Canterbury Press.

Common Worship: Services and Prayers for the Church of England, 2000, London: Church House Publishing.

Common Worship: Times and Seasons, 2006, London: Church House Publishing.

Congar, Yves, 1999, *I Believe in the Holy Spirit*, trans. David Smith, New York: Crossroad.

Coster, Will and Andrew Spicer (eds), 2005, *Sacred Space in Early Modern Europe*, Cambridge: Cambridge University Press.

Croft, Steven, n.d.,'Parable of the Allotments' at www.freshexpressions.org.uk.

Croft, Steven (ed.), 2008, *Mission-Shaped Questions*, London: Church House Publishing.

Croft, Steven, 2006, 'Conclusion', *The Future of the Parish System*, London: Church House Publishing.

Croft, Steven, 2005, *Evangelism in a Spiritual Age: Communicating Faith in a Changing Culture*, London: Church House Publishing.

Croft, Steven 2005, *Moving on in a Mission-shaped Church*, London: Church House Publishing.

Croft, Steven, 2005, 'Transforming Evangelism' in *Evangelism in a Spiritual Age*, ed. Steven Croft, Rob Frost, Yvonne Richmond and Nick Spencer, London: Church House Publishing, pp. 126–147.

Croft, Steven, and Mobsy, Ian (eds), 2009, *Ancient Faith Future Mission: Fresh Expressions in the Sacramental Tradition*, Norwich: Canterbury Press.

Culler, Jonathan, 1976, *Saussure*, Glasgow: Fontana Press.

Damascus, John of, 2003, *Three Treatises on the Divine Images*, trans. Andrew Louth, Crestwood NY: St Vladimir's Seminary Press.

Bibliography

Damascus, John of, 1997, *Exposition of the Orthodox Faith in A Select Library of the Nicene and Post-Nicene Fathers of the Christian Church*, second series, trans. Philip Schaff and Henry Wace, Edinburgh: T&T Clark/Grand Rapids MI: Eerdmans, vol.9.

Dante Alighieri, 1973, *The Divine Comedy: Purgatorio: Text*, ed. Charles Singleton, Princeton: Princeton University Press.

Davie, Grace, 1994, *Religion in Britain since 1945: Believing without Belonging*, Oxford: Blackwell.

Davison, Andrew, 2010, 'Theology and the Future of the Church' in *Hope of Things to Come: Anglicanism and the Future*, ed. Mark Chapman, London: T&T Clark/Continuum, pp. 69–87.

Davison, Andrew, 2009, 'The mediating possibilities of absence in the thought of Simone Weil', *Theology*, 111, pp. 3–13.

Dearmer, Percy and Ralph Vaughan Williams (eds), 1906, *The English Hymnal*, London: Oxford University Press.

Dennett, Daniel, 2006, *Breaking the Spell: Religion as a Natural Phenomenon*, London: Viking.

Descartes, Rene, 1983, *Œuvres de Descartes*, ed. Charles Adam and Paul Tannery, 11 vols, Paris: Librairie Philosophique J. Vrin.

DeYoung, Kevin and Ted Kluck, 2009, *Why We Love the Church: In Praise of Institutions and Organized Religion*, Chicago, IL: Moody Press.

DeYoung, Kevin and Ted Kluck, 2009, *Why We're Not Emergent: (By Two Guys Who Should Be)*, Chicago, IL: Moody Press.

The Doctrine Commission of the Church of England, 1938, *Doctrine in the Church of England*, London: SPCK.

Dolling, Robert R., 1896, *Ten Years in a Portsmouth Slum*, London: Swan Sonnenschein.

Duchesne, Louis and M. L. McClure (eds), 1931, *Christian Worship: Its Origin and Development. A Study of the Latin Liturgy*, London: SPCK.

Duffy, Eamon, 1992, *The Stripping of the Altars: Traditional Religion in England c. 1400–c. 1580*, New Haven and London: Yale University Press.

Dunn, James, 2006, *The Theology of Paul the Apostle*, Grand Rapids, MI: Eerdmans.

Dyas, Dee, 2004, *Images of Salvation: The Story of the Bible through Medieval Art*, CD ROM.

Dyas, Dee and Esther Hughes, 2005, *The Bible in Western Culture: The Study Guide*, London: Routledge.

Eagleton, Terry, 2009, *Reason, Faith, and Revolution: Reflections on the God Debate*, New Haven, NY: Yale University Press.

Eagleton, Terry, 2008, *Trouble with Strangers*, Oxford: Wiley-Blackwell.

Eco, Umberto, 1988, *The Aesthetics of Thomas Aquinas*, trans. Hugh Bredin, Cambridge MA: Harvard University Press.

For the Parish

Eliot, T. S., 1980, *The Complete Poems and Plays*, London: Faber.

Eucharistic Presidency: A Theological Statement by the House of Bishops of the General Synod, 1997, London: Church House Publishing.

Figgis, John Neville, 1913, *Churches in the Modern State*, London: Longmans, Green and Co.

Fitzgerald, Allan (ed.), 1999, *Augustine through the Ages: An Encyclopedia*, Grand Rapids, MI: Eerdmans.

Fodor, Jim, 2004, 'Reading the Scriptures: Rehearsing Identity, Practicing Character', *The Blackwell Companion to Christian Ethics*, ed. Stanley Hauerwas and Samuel Wells, Oxford: Blackwell, pp. 141–55.

Foner, Philip Sheldon, 1986, *May Day: A Short History of the International Workers' Holiday*, New York: International Publishers.

French, Katherine, 2001, *The People of the Parish: Community Life in a Late Medieval English Diocese*, Philadelphia PN: University of Philadelphia Press.

www.freshexpressions.org.uk/stories/tomatoes.

Gaze, Sally, 2006, *Mission-shaped and Rural*, London: Church House Publishing.

Giussani, Luigi, 2001, *The Risk of Education: Discovering Our Ultimate Destiny*, trans. Rosanna M. Giammanco Frongia, New York: Crossroads.

Giussani, Luigi, 1997, *The Religious Sense*, trans. John Zucchi, Montreal: McGill-Queens University Press.

Gore, Charles, 1899, *St Paul's Epistle to the Romans*, London: John Murray.

Gorman, Michael J., 2004, *Apostle of the Crucified Lord: A Theological Introduction to Paul and His Letters*, Grand Rapids, MI: Eerdmans.

Gutiérrez, Gustavo, 1988, *A Theology of Liberation: History, Politics and Salvation*, trans. Caridad Inda and John Eagleson, Maryknoll, NY: Orbis.

Hadison, O. B., 1965, *Christian Rite and Drama in the Middle Ages*, Baltimore: Johns Hopkins University Press.

Hart, David Bentley, 2009, *Atheist Delusions: The Christian Revolution and its Fashionable Enemies*, New Haven: Yale University Press.

Hauerwas, Stanley, 2005, 'The Christian Difference, or Surviving Postmodernism' in *The Blackwell Companion to Postmodern Theology*, ed. Graham Ward, Oxford: Blackwell, pp. 144–61.

Hauerwas, Stanley, 2004, *Performing the Faith: Bonhoeffer and the Practice of Nonviolence*, London, SPCK.

Hauerwas, Stanley, 2001, *Christian Existence Today: Essays on Church, World and Living In Between*, Grand Rapids: Brazos.

Bibliography

Hauerwas, Stanley, 1996, 'The Liturgical Shape of the Christian Life' in *Essentials of Christian Community* ed. D. F. Ford and D. L. Stamps, Edinburgh: T&T Clark, pp. 35–46.

Hauerwas, Stanley and Charles Pinches, 1997, *Christians among the Virtues: Theological Conversations with Ancient and Modern Ethics*, Notre Dame IN: University of Notre Dame Press.

Hauerwas, Stanley and Samuel Wells (eds), 2004, *The Blackwell Companion to Christian Ethics*, Oxford, Blackwell.

Herbert, George, 1991, *The Complete English Poems,* ed. John Tobin, Harmondsworth: Penguin.

Hervieu-Legér, Danièle, 2000, *Religion as a Chain of Memory*, trans. Simon Lee, New Brunswick, NJ: Rutgers University Press.

Holland, Henry Scott, 1897, *God's City and the Coming of the Kingdom*, London: Longmans, Green and Co.

Hooker, Morna, 2003, *Paul*, Oxford: Oneworld.

Hope, Susan, 2006, *Mission-shaped Spirituality*. London: Church House Publishing.

Hopkins, Gerard Manley, 1972, *Poems and Prose*, ed. W. H. Gardner, Harmondsworth: Penguin.

House of Bishops of the Church of England, 1997, *Eucharistic Presidency: A Theological Statement by the House of Bishops of the General Synod.* London: Church House Publishing.

Hull, John, 2008, 'Mission-shaped and Kingdom Focused?' in *Mission-shaped Questions: Defining Questions for Today's Church*, ed. Steven Croft, London: Church House Publishing, pp. 114–32.

Hunsinger, George, 2003, 'Postliberal Theology' in *The Cambridge Companion to Postmodern Theology*, ed. Kevin Vanhoozer, Cambridge: Cambridge University Press, pp. 42–57.

Inge, John, 2003, *A Christian Theology of Place*, Aldershot: Ashgate.

Irenaeus of Lyons, 1995, *Against Heresies*, trans. Alexander Roberts and James Donaldson in *The Ante-Nicene Fathers*, vol. 1. Reprinted by Hendrickson Publishers.

Jenkins, Timothy, 1999, *Religion in English Everyday Life: An Ethnographic Approach*, New York and Oxford: Berghahn Books.

Jennings, Elizabeth, 1986, *Collected Poems: 1953–1985*, Manchester: Carcanet.

John Paul II, 1991, *On the Hundredth Anniversary of Rerum Novarum (Centesimus Annus)*, Washington, DC: USCCB.

Johnson, George and Mark Lakoff, 2003, *Metaphors We Live By*, Chicago: University of Chicago Press.

Jones, David, 1959, 'Art and Sacrament' in *Epoch and Artist: Selected Writings*, ed. Harman Grisewood, London: Faber.

Kant, Immanuel, 1998, *Religion within the Boundaries of Mere Reason*, trans. and ed. Allen Wood and George Di Giovanni, Cambridge: Cambridge University Press.

Kenny, Anthony, 1970, *Descartes: Philosophical Letters*, Oxford: Oxford University Press.

Kerr, Fergus, 1997 (2nd edn), *Theology after Wittgenstein*, Oxford: Blackwell.

Larkin, Philip, 1955, 'Church Going' in *The Less Deceived*, Hull: Marvell Press.

Lathem, Edward, 1966, *Interviews with Robert Frost*, New York: Holt, Rinehart and Winston.

Lauwers, Michel, 2005, 'Paroisse, paroissiens et territoire. Remarques sur *parochia* dans les textes latins du Moyen Âge', *Revues Mediévales*, 49 at www.medievales.revues.org/document1260.htm.

Lawrence, D. H., 1958 [1915], *The Rainbow*, Harmondsworth: Penguin.

Lee, Philip, 1992, *Against the Protestant Gnostics*, New York: Oxford University Press.

Leech, Ken, 1986, *True Prayer: An Invitation to Christian Spirituality*, London: Sheldon.

Leech, Ken, 1981, *The Social God*, London: Sheldon.

Lewis, C. S., 2000, '*On the Reading of Old Books*' in *C. S. Lewis: Essay Collection and Other Short Pieces*, ed. Walter Hooper, London: Fount, pp. 438–43.

Lindbeck, George, 1984, *The Nature of Doctrine: Religion and Theology in a Postliberal Age*, Philadelphia: Westminster Press.

Lohfink, Gerhard, 1985, *Jesus and Community: Social Dimension of Christian Faith*, trans. John P. Galvin, Minneapolis, MN: Augsburg Fortress.

Loughlin, Gerard, 1999, *Telling God's Story: Bible, Church and Narrative Theology*, Cambridge: Cambridge University Press.

Louth, Andrew, 1989, *Denys the Areopagite*, London: Geoffrey Chapman.

Lubac, Henri de, 2000, *Paradoxes of Faith*, San Francisco: Ignatius Press.

Lubac, Henri de, 1988, *Catholicism*, trans. Lancelot C. Sheppard and Elizabeth Englund, San Francisco: Ignatius Press.

Lubac, Henri de, 1956, *The Splendour of the Church*, trans. Michael Mason, London: Sheed and Ward.

Malcolm, Norman, 1984, *Ludwig Wittgenstein: A Memoir*, Oxford: Oxford University Press.

Bibliography

Martin, David, 2003, 'On Secularisation and its Predictions: A Self-examination' in *Predicting Religion: Christian, Secular and Alternative Futures*, ed. Grace Davie, Paul Heelas and Linda Woodhead, London: Ashgate, pp. 30–8.

Martyn, J. Louis, 2005, *Theological Issues in the Letters of Paul*, Edinburgh: T&T Clark.

Mascall, Eric, 1946, *Christ, the Christian and the Church*, London: Longmans, Green and Co.

Matthews, Melvyn, 2000, *Both Alike to Thee*, London: SPCK.

Mauss, Marcel, 1973 [1935], 'Techniques of the Body', *Economy and Society*, 2, 1, pp. 70–88.

McGavran, Donald, 1955, *Bridges to God*, London: World Dominion Press.

Meyenfeldt, F. H. von, 1950, *Het Hart (Leb, Lebab) in Het Oude Testament*, Leiden: Brill.

Meynell, Alice, 1924, *The Poems of Alice Meynell: Complete Edition*, New York: Charles Scribner.

Milbank, John, 2005, *The Suspended Middle: Henri de Lubac and the Debate Concerning the Supernatural*, London: SCM Press.

Minucius Felix, Marcus, 1994, *The Octavius*, in *The Ante-Nicene Fathers: Translations of the Fathers down to AD 325*, ed. Alexander Roberts and James Donaldson, rev. A. Cleveland Coxe, Edinburgh and Grand Rapids MI: T&T Clark and Eerdmans.

Mission and Public Affairs Council of the Church of England, 2004, *Mission-shaped Church: Church Planting and Fresh Expressions of Church in a Changing Context*, London: Church House Publishing.

Moses, John (ed.), 2003, *One Equal Light: An Anthology of the Writings of John Donne*, Norwich: Canterbury Press.

Muldoon, Paul, 2006, *The End of the Poem*, London: Faber.

Newbolt, W. C. E., 1899, *Religion*, London: Longmans, Green and Co.

Norris, Pippa and Ronald Inglehart (eds), 2004, *The Secularisation Debate*, Oxford: Oxford University Press.

Nyssa, Gregory of, 1960–92, *Commentary on the Song of Songs* in *Gregorii Nysseni Opera/Gregory of Nyssa*, ed. Wernerus Jaeger and Hermannus Langerbeck, 10 vols, Leiden: Brill, 6, pp. 466–8.

O'Donnell, Timothy Terrance, 1992, *The Heart of the Redeemer*, San Francisco: Ignatius Press.

O'Donovan, Oliver, 1989, 'The Loss of a Sense of Place', *Irish Theological Quarterly*, 55, pp. 39–58.

Ogden, Dunbar, 2003, *The Staging of Drama in the Medieval Church*, Newark, DE: University of Delaware.

For the Parish

Opie, Iona, Peter Opie, and Joan Hassall, 1957, *The Oxford Book of Nursery Rhymes*, Oxford: Oxford University Press.

Palmer, John Williamson (ed.), 1861, *Folk Songs*, New York: Scribner. Folk Songs.

Pecknold, C. C., 2005, *Transforming Postliberal Theology: George Lindbeck, Pragmatism and Scripture*, Edinburgh: T&T Clark.

Penner, James L., 1999, *The Situationist City and Guy Debord*, Boston: MIT Press.

Percy, Martyn, 2008, 'Old Tricks for New Dogs?' in *Evaluating Fresh Expressions*, ed. Louise Nelstrop and Martyn Percy, London: Canterbury Press, pp. 27–39.

Percy, Martyn, 2006, 'Many Rooms in my Father's House: The Changing Identity of the English Parish Church' in *The Future of the Parish System: Shaping the Church of England for the 21st Century*, ed. Steven Croft, London: Church House Publishing, pp. 3–15.

Pevsner, Nicholaus, 1945, *The Leaves of Southwell*, London: Penguin.

Pickstock, Catherine, 1998, *After Writing: On the Liturgical Consummation of Philosophy*, Oxford: Blackwell.

Pieper, Josef, 2001, *Scholasticism: Personalities and Problems of Medieval Philosophy*, South Bend, IN: St Augustine's Press.

Pontifical Council for Justice and Peace, 2005, *Compendium of the Social Doctrine of the Church*, London: Burns & Oates/Continuum for Libreria Editrice Vaticana.

Potapov, V, n.d., 'The Parable of the Sower' at www.stjohndc.org/Russian/parables/e_Par_1_01.htm.

Pounds, N. J. G., 2000, *A History of the English Parish: The Culture of Religion from Augustine to Victoria*, Cambridge: Cambridge University Press.

Pseudo-Dionysius, 1987, *The Complete Works*, trans. Colm Luibheid and Paul Rorem, London: SPCK.

Quash, Ben, 2002, 'Making the Most of Time: Liturgy, Ethics and Time', *Studies in Christian Ethics* 15, pp. 97–114.

Ramsey, Michael, 1956, *The Gospel and the Catholic Church*, London: Longmans, Green and Co.

Ratzinger, Joseph, 1987, *Principles of Catholic Theology*, San Francisco: Ignatius Press.

Redfern, Alastair, 2004, 'Listening to the Anglican Tradition' in *Changing Rural Life: A Christian Response to Key Rural Issues*, ed. Jeremy Martineau, Leslie J. Francis and Peter Francis, Norwich: Canterbury Press, pp. 233–50.

Bibliography

Reiss, Athene, 2000, *The Sunday Christ: Sabbatarianism in English Medieval Wall-Painting*, Oxford: Archaeopress.

Report on Clifton North and Clifton South Area Health Needs, accessed at www.nomadplug.org.uk.

Ridderbos, Herman N., 1977, *Paul*, trans. John Richard de Witt, London: SPCK.

Robinson, John, 1952, *The Body: A Study in Pauline Theology*, London: SCM Press.

Roud, Steve, 2006, *The English Year: A Month by Month Guide to the Nation's Customs and Festivals from May Day to Mischief Night*, Harmondsworth: Penguin.

Sallis, John, 2002, *On Translation*, Bloomington, IN: Indiana University Press.

Sanders, Carol, (ed.), 2004, *The Cambridge Companion to Saussure*, Cambridge: Cambridge University Press.

Sanders, E. P., 1991, *Paul*, Oxford: Oxford University Press.

Sanders, E. P., 1977, *Paul and Palestinian Judaism*, London: SCM Press.

Saussure, Ferdinand de, 1974, *Course in General Linguistics*, trans. Wade Baskin, Glasgow: Fontana.

Schor, Juliet B., 1991, *The Overworked Americans: The Unexpected Decline of Leisure*, New York: Basic Books.

Scruton, Roger, 2009, *Beauty*, Oxford: Oxford University Press.

Shaff, Philip, 1977, *Creeds of Christendom, with a History and Critical Notes*, vol. 3, Grand Rapids MI: Baker Books.

Sibbes, Richard, 1863, 'The Excellency of the Gospel above the Law' in *Complete Works*, 7 vols, Edinburgh: James Nichol.

Staniforth, Maxwell (trans.), 1968, *Epistle to Diognetus*, in *Early Christian Writings: The Apostolic Fathers*, Harmondsworth: Penguin.

Steiner, George, 1998, *After Babel: Aspects of Language and Translation*, New York: Oxford University Press.

Strong, Roy, 2007, *A Little History of the English Country Church*, London: Jonathan Cape.

Tanner, Norman P. (ed.), 1990, *Decrees of the Ecumenical Councils*, 2 vols, London: Sheed & Ward.

Temple, Frederick, 1888, *Twelve Sermons preached at the Consecration of Truro Cathedral*, Truro: no publisher given.

Tepper, Yotam, and Leah de Segni, 2006, *A Christian Prayer Hall of the Third Century at Kefar Othnay (Legio): Excavations at the Megiddo Prison 2005*, Tel-Aviv: IAA.

Thomson, John, 2007, *Doxa: A Discipleship Course*, London: Darton, Longman and Todd.

Tilby, Angela, 2008, 'What Questions Does Catholic Ecclesiology Pose for Contemporary Mission and Fresh Expressions?' in *Mission-shaped Questions*, ed. Steven Croft, London, Church House Publishing, pp. 78–89.

Todd, Malcolm, 2005, 'Baths or Baptisteries? Holcombe, Lufton and their Analogues', *Oxford Journal of Archaeology*, 24, 3, pp. 307–11.

Tolkien, J. R. R., 2001, *Tree and Leaf*, London: HarperCollins.

Torrance, James B., 1996, *Worship, Community, and the Triune God of Grace*, Carlisle: Paternoster Press.

Tracy, David, 1996 (2nd edn), *Blessed Rage for Order: The New Pluralism*, Chicago: University of Chicago Press.

Traherne, Thomas, 1988, *Selected Writings*, Manchester: Carcenet.

Turner, Denys, 1998, *The Darkness of God*, Cambridge: Cambridge University Press.

Turner, Harold W., 1979, *From Temple to Meeting House: The Phenomenology and Theology of Places of Worship*, The Hague: Walter de Gruyter.

Underhill, Evelyn, 1934, *The School of Charity: Meditations on the Christian Creed*, London: Longmans, Green and Co.

Vaughan, Henry, 1983, *The Complete Poems*, ed. Alan Rudrum, Harmondsworth: Penguin.

Volf, Miroslav, 2006, *The End of Memory: Remembering Rightly in a Violent World*, Grand Rapids MI: Eerdmans.

Wadell, Paul, 2004, 'Sharing Peace: Discipline and Trust', *The Blackwell Companion to Christian Ethics*, ed. Stanley Hauerwas and Samuel Wells, Oxford, Blackwell, pp. 289–301.

Ward, Graham, 2005, 'Introduction: "Where We Stand"' in *The Blackwell Companion to Postmodern Theology*, ed. Graham Ward, Oxford: Blackwell, pp. xii–xxvii.

Ward, Pete, 2008, *Participation and Mediation: A Practical Theology for the Liquid Church*, London: SCM Press.

Ward, Pete, 2002, *Liquid Church*, Carlisle: Paternoster Press.

Watkins, Silvestre Cornelius (ed.), 1944, *Anthology of American Negro Literature*, New York: The Modern Library.

Watson, David Lowes, 2002, *The Early Methodist Class Meeting*, Eugene OR: Wipf and Stock.

Webster, John, 2000, *Theology after Liberalism: A Reader*, Oxford: Blackwell.

Wells, Samuel, 2002, 'How Common Worship Helps Form Local Character', *Studies in Christian Ethics*. 15, pp. 66–74.

Williams, Raymond, 1988, *Keywords*, London: Fontana Press.

Bibliography

Williams, Rowan, 2009, 'Address to the Fresh Expressions National Pilgrimage, Coventry Cathedral, December 2008' in Steven Croft and Ian Mobsy (eds), *Ancient Faith Future Mission: Fresh Expressions in the Sacramental Tradition*, Norwich: Canterbury Press.

Williams, Rowan, 2007, *Tokens of Trust: An Introduction to Christian Belief*, Norwich: Canterbury Press.

Williams, Rowan, 2006, 'To What End Are We Made?' in *Who Is This Man?: Christ in the Renewal of the Church*, ed. Jonathan Baker and William Davage, London: Continuum.

Wittgenstein, Ludwig, 1980, *Culture and Value*, ed. G. H von Wright with Heikki Nyma, trans. Peter Winch, Oxford: Blackwell.

Wittgenstein, Ludwig, 1980, *Remarks on the Philosophy of Psychology*, ed. G. E. M. Anscombe, G. H. von Wright and Heikki Nyman, trans. G. E. M. Anscombe, C. G. Luckhardt and M. A. E. Aue, 2 vols, Oxford: Blackwell.

Wittgenstein, Ludwig, 1978 (3rd rev. edn), *Remarks on the Foundations of Mathematics*, ed. G. H. von Wright, R. Rhees and G. E. M. Anscombe, trans. G. E. M. Anscombe, Oxford: Blackwell.

Wittgenstein, Ludwig, 1953, *Philosophical Investigations*, trans. G. E. M. Anscombe, Oxford: Blackwell.

Wittgenstein, Ludwig, 1967, *Zettel*, ed. G. E. M. Anscombe and G. H. von Wright, trans. G. E. M. Anscombe, Oxford: Blackwell.

Woodward, James, Stephen Pattison and John Batton (eds), 2000, *The Blackwell Reader in Pastoral and Practical Theology*, Oxford: Blackwell.

Wright, N. T., 2005, *Paul: Fresh Perspectives*, London: SPCK.

Wright, N. T., 2005, *Scripture and the Authority of God*, London: SPCK.

Wright, N. T., 1991, 'ΧΡΙΣΤΟΣ as "Messiah" in Paul: Philemon 6' in *The Climax of the Covenant: Christ and the Law in Pauline Theology*, Edinburgh: T&T Clark, pp. 41–55.

Yoder, John Howard, 1992, *Body Politics: Five Practices of the Christian Community before the Watching World*, Nashville, TN: Discipleship Resources.

Ziesler, J. A., 1990, *Pauline Christianity*, Oxford: Oxford University Press.

Index

Index

Index

Lightning Source UK Ltd.
Milton Keynes UK
UKOW07f0142030315

247193UK00006B/118/P

THE LOST MOON
BOOK 1
EMMA T. SHANNON

Dedicated to the pink bird man who started it all.
If you know, you know. If you don't, well...maybe that's for the best.

Also by Emma T. Shannon

Song of the Hollow Duology
Song of the Hollow
Storm of the Gods

CONTENTS

CONTENT WARNING

THE EMERALD SEA SAGA is an adult fantasy series with magic, gods, and piracy. It is not for all audiences. This book includes the following: alcohol consumption, blood, childbirth, child sacrifice, cults, death (a lot), divorce, drug use, gun violence, infidelity (off-page, briefly mentioned occurrence in a character's past) plague, stillbirth, and violence. Reader discretion is strongly advised.

Author's Note

THERE IS A CAT in this book. While I cannot guarantee the safety of any human characters, I can promise you the cat (who is named after one of my childhood cats) survives until the end of the series. She might not get her dinner at the exact minute she expects it and will be kicked out of her sleeping spots, but she will remain alive and unscathed (even if she thinks she's starving to death because she hasn't eaten in thirty seconds). All future animal companions are also guaranteed to survive. The humans, though? No promises there.

EDYN

EDYLY

TWIN SERPENT
ISLES

♦SAFFRON

♦SELFOSA

EMERALD
SEA

CROW

KETH
MOUNTAIN

KETH
BAY

KETH RIVER

•LOCUS

SANDSUNNI• SANDSUNNI
DESERT

NORTH
RANGE

LYNCH•

LINWELL•

ARCHEPYLAGO

•WYVRON

STORMS
KEEP

♦KELSYN

ARALYTH

BROOK
GREEN

ICARUS
RIVER

ARAMORE

•MAYNE

GENDINE

•MERRIN

SAPPHIRE
SEA

ICARUS
MOUNTAINS

PORT
ICARUS•

ICARUS STRAIT

CARLON•

UNDYNE PORT
ISLAND

PORT 2•

PORT 1

PORT 5

PORT
K

CORSA

SERVEDIN
ISLAND

T

BELT
MOUNTAINS

VERIDIN

KOSE•

VERIDONIA

WANDERING
ISLE

FAIRAMORE•

SPIT BAY

VICIOUS
DESERT

SYRENIS

NAVAL
FORTRESS•

•CIRCEZ

KALWYL
ISLES

AME

BORELIN ISLE

SVALGBÄRD

ELLOEYNE

GELLO

ELLUF

ARBYN

AMAZONIA

BANLETTA

MORGOUSE
ISLAND

CORAVOU

NGLE OF FYLTH

SALTS
ATOLL

NORTH
AVOS

RUBY
SEA

RUBY
RIDGE

LEV

MERDYNE

JORIS
ISLAND

LYSS RAINFOREST

MELROSINE

HEL
ARCHIPELAGO

GLOSSARY

<u>The Kingdom of Gello</u>

King: Algernon Keats

Queen: Roisin Keats

Heir: Leianora Keats

<u>The Gods</u>

Poet: God of the sand, sea, and sky.

Dreamer: Goddess of the earth, trees, and life.

Lady Lightbringer: Goddess of war, justice, and strength. Patron goddess of the navy.

The Wanderer: Deity of debauchery, indulgence, sin, and adventure. Patron deity of the Wandering Isle.

Pronunciation Guide

<u>People:</u>

Anwir Helios: An-weer Heel-ee-os

Bartholomew Williams: Bar-thall-oh-mew Will-ee-ams

Thol: Thall

Czardas Rossi: Char-dash Ross-ee

Fynch Largos: Finch Lar-gos

Illie Valentine: Ill-ee Val-en-tine

Jonyth Commodore: Jone-ith Comm-oh-dore

Nathalia Divyne: Nah-tall-ee-ah Divine

Natha: Nah-tah

Nox Solveig: Nox Sol-vay

Pleo: Plee-oh

Vesperine Genevieve: Ves-per-een Gen-uh-veev

Places:

Amazonia: Am-ah-zone-ee-ah

Aralyth: Air-ah-lith

Archepylago: Arch-uh-pell-ay-go

Borelin Isle: Bore-uh-lin (Isle)

Edyn: Eden

Elluf: El-loof

Frys: Friss

Gello: Gel-oh

Hel Archipelago: Heel (Archipelago)

Ivenis Justyce Penitentiary: Ee-ven-iss Justice (Penitentiary)

Joris Island: Jor-is (Island)

Kalwyl Isles: Call-will (Isles)

Kelsyn: Kell-sin

Merdyne: Mare-dine

Morgouse Island: Mor-gose (Island)

Salts Atoll: Salts Atoll

Servedin Island: Serve-uh-din (Island)

Syrenis: Seer-en-iss

Triangle of Fylth: (Triangle of) Filth

Twin Serpent Isles: Twin Serpent Isles

Undyne Island: Un-dine (Island)

Veridin: Vair-uh-din

Cities:

Aramore: Air-ah-more

Arbyn: Are-bin

Brook Green: Brook Green

Carilon: Care-ih-lohn

Circez: Sir-keez

Corsa: Core-sah

Edylyn: Ed-uh-lin

Fjarg: F-yarg

Gelloiyne: Gel-oh-een

Lenwell: Lehn-well

Lev: Leev

Melrosine: Mel-rose-een

Saffron: Saff-rohn

Selfosa: Sell-foh-sah

Svalgbärd: S-valg-baerd

Veridonia: Vehr-ih-doh-nee-ah

Wyvron: Why-vron

BEFORE

THE GIRL'S HANDS BURNED as she plunged them into the salty sea, scrubbing stray scales from her calloused palms and rope-bitten fingers. Bits of brown wispy hair flew around her sweaty forehead, tugged free from its messy braid that hung down her back. Fish blood diluted, dissipating into pinkish clouds as it left her hands to be washed away at sea. As she stood, her arm hit the bucket of fish next to her, sending it tipping towards the water.

"No, no, no!" she cried out, scrambling to catch the bucket before her daily catch was lost. One decapitated fish slid back into the water before she caught the lip of the bucket, pulling it back to safety. Defeated, she sat down, dipping her clean hands into the bucket to count how many fish she had left. One...two...three... She had six. She should have had seven – enough for the week – but...fine. Six would do. She could make it work.

She watched the water, the cloudy plume of blood, and eyed a slim tentacle peeking precariously out of the rocks. An octopus – a young one, based on its size and difficulty choosing just one color. It wrapped its little tentacle around the dead fish, its flesh dancing between blue and red and grey, and pulled it back to its rocky home.

At least someone gets to eat, she thought with a huff. Hands once again sticky with scales, she wiped them on her apron and brushed her hair from her forehead. Grass crunched behind her, followed by the *thunk* of someone sitting next to her. He slid his boots off, then his socks, and bent to roll his trousers up.

"There's an octopus in there," the woman warned before he could stick his feet in the water and risk getting lines of tentacle hickeys.

The man stopped, hesitating for a second before resigning to simply let his feet warm in the sun. He was handsome, in a very particular way, his nose hooked and one of his teeth missing, but the woman thought he was the most beautiful person in the world.

"You should be resting," her husband said.

The woman let her hand fall to her swollen stomach. Eight months along, the little devil ready to pop at any moment. She was convinced his – for no girl would inflict eight months of torture on her mother – feet were currently in her ribs, rearranging her lungs and heart. At eight months, she *should* be at home resting, preparing for the babe, but her husband could catch a fish about as well as he could mend a shirt, which was to say he *couldn't*. His talents lay elsewhere, far away from the poles and nets needed for fishing.

"Half of fishing is just waiting for a bite," she pointed out.

Her husband reached over and tucked a strand of hair behind her ear. He looked at her like *she* was the most beautiful thing in the world, and in his world, she was. She still had acne and freckles from being in the sun so much. Her shoulders were wide, as were her hips, and she walked with a waddle now that her babe's head was constantly pressing into her pelvis. As gross as she felt, covered in scales and fish guts, her stomach swollen and painful, her husband never failed to make her feel beautiful. If only he could catch a fish; then she truly would be the luckiest woman alive.

"I caught seven," she said, gesturing to the bucket. "But I lost one. That little octopus got it."

"Well, now it owes you a favor. Maybe it was a god in disguise. Just watch; you'll find enough gold to make you the richest woman alive. You'll find out you're a lost princess. Our babe will be born divine." Her husband grinned and continued listing more and more ridiculous miracles.

The woman smiled and watched the water. The little octopus had politely set the fish bones aside and now crept slowly from its rock home as if hopeful more fish would fall from the sky. The woman was half tempted to give it another, but a kick from her babe reminded her that she was eating for two and couldn't spare anything. Not with the change in seasons coming soon, limiting what crops they could get at the market. She *should* be setting up more crab traps and nets so they could have more salted and dried meat in storage for winter. Though, the winters weren't ever harsh. They were god-blessed to have mild seasons. But the wind chill from the Seventh Spire, the tall mountain in the south, promised at least *some* snow. And with a babe on the way, they'd need as much food stored away as possible. Her husband would be returning to the sea for work in just a few short months, leaving the woman alone.

A ray of sunlight penetrated the water, startling the poor octopus, who now couldn't decide which shade of greenish blue to turn to blend in.

"Poor little god doesn't quite know how to use his body," the woman teased.

Her laugh was cut short when a sharp pain stabbed through her lower abdomen. Her monthly cycles before getting pregnant were always painful, but this sudden pain put them to shame. Her face twisted, the discomfort growing as the pulsing stab dragged on and on and on for what felt like an eternity but couldn't have been more than a few seconds.

Her husband said her name, but his voice was so distant, so warbled like he was underwater. She stood, clutching her belly. Slick fluid ran down her thighs, soaking her dress.

No, she thought. *No, little one, it's too early!*

Another contraction split through her abdomen, blurring her vision. She stumbled, losing her balance. The sky became her whole world for a moment, blue and vast and...

And something was falling, tearing through the blue like a burst of sunlight. The ray of light that had hit the water earlier wasn't from the sun; it was from the falling thing, and it had grown, turning brighter and brighter as the *thing* got closer.

She hit the water, too, salt filling her sinuses as she breathed in a mouthful of sea. Strong hands were around her in a second, heaving her out of the ocean and onto the grassy shore once more.

She sputtered, choking, and coughing up water. Then, with a shaky hand, she pointed to the sky.

"What –" she croaked, breathing hard through another contraction. Her husband ignored her, his focus on his wife instead of whatever was falling.

He picked her up, grunting under the weight, and carried her back to their small house. They'd talked about the plan for when the baby came. There would have been enough time for him to run to town to fetch a midwife, to draw a warm bath for her to give birth in, but that was over now. He placed her on their thin bed. The mattress did little to comfort her aching back, so he put a pillow under her spine, lifting her hips and hopefully cushioning her.

"I'm going to run a bath," he said. She just shook her head. Between heating the water and bringing enough buckets from the spigot outside, there would be no time. They weren't fortunate enough to have a house with running water inside.

"It's falling," she choked. Each breath smelled of salt. It made her sick. She turned and vomited all over the floor. The retching clenched her belly, sending more pain through her, bright and hot in her pelvis.

"What's falling?" her husband asked. He didn't wait for an answer. He shoved open the curtain separating their bedroom from the rest of the house and went to the stove. There was a pot of water already on the stove; he turned it on and rummaged around for the bangaloo bark tea they'd gotten from the market the week before. Bangaloo bark was used in medicine, commonly for cycle cramps and for helping with labor pains. His hands shook as he scooped some of the flaky, papery bark into the teapot. The kettle whistled, almost the same high-pitched note as the woman's scream; he quickly poured it into the pot and brought it, along with a cup, back to the bedroom.

"The moon!" she sobbed, clutching her belly. A red stain had seeped into the sheets. Part of the reason why she'd wanted to give birth in the bath, besides it helping with the pain, was because she had *not* wanted the work of cleaning blood from the sheets. She hadn't had to do it in a year now.

Her husband poured a cup of bangaloo bark tea, his hands shaking. "The moon...?" He went to hand her the cup, but she was gripping the sheets too tightly. He put it to her lips instead, holding it carefully as she drank.

When she pulled away, she said, through tears, "the moon is falling."

Outside, the tiny octopus shrank back into its little cavern, hiding against the darkness that had suddenly befallen the sky. The waves roiled; the sky was clotted with dark, tumultuous clouds. Lightning flashed, followed by thunder drowned out by the woman's screams.

Her husband quickly realized he was going to be the midwife. So, breathing slowly, he hiked up her skirts and nudged her legs aside.

"Breathe, love," he insisted. Mothers dying in childbirth was too common for his liking. "The moon isn't falling. That's impossible."

Wind rattled the windows. The bucket of fish outside had toppled over, long abandoned and forgotten. The woman's fishing nets tangled, her laundry flapping as it strained to hold on to the line.

She screamed again, the pain cresting all at once. It happened too fast. The babe was far too small to be causing her *this* much pain.

Soon, tiny cries filled the air and something warm and wet was pressed to her breast. Her child. A son – *of course.*

Crash!

Outside, whatever had been falling – it was not the moon, despite what the new mother thought – finally hit the ocean. In the sky, it looked tiny, nothing more than a little speck. But... it was giant. Huge. Big enough that it sucked the water down with it, and that water surged, a wave so big it towered over the Seventh Spire.

There was nowhere for it to go but *down.*

In the jungle to the north, all the animals had fled to the trees, as if the leafy canopy could protect them, from the smallest bangaloo tree frogs to the massive night panthers. The trees shook, leaves falling to the ground that was no longer a ground.

The river in the south had flooded completely, which wasn't unusual when there were great storms. The river's normal serpentine course was gone completely, years of erosion wiped away in a single moment.

The capital city far in the south had some of the best meteorologists in the world, but none of them could have predicted what was happening. Neither could the astronomers, nor the other scientists. A little girl had been outside when she saw the falling thing.

"The moon!" she said cheerfully, pointing to the streak of light that split through the grey.

The quakes could be felt throughout the entire country, and every single person knew at once what was happening. Tidal waves weren't uncommon.

Right...?

The day the moon fell a child was born, though his soul had already been picked out, and he would not be the reincarnated vessel of a god.

Because it wasn't the *moon* that fell, but a *god*. Something had injured him fatally, causing him to fall from the skies where he lived.

When his body hit the water, it was too late.

The god was dead.

PROLOGUE

THE BOY ON THE altar was going to die, but he was not afraid. He had not been afraid for a long time. Death was a mercy, the final one he would be granted, and he welcomed it with open arms. The pain would cease soon. The agonizing burn of metal biting into his wrists, deep enough to rub against his thin bones, the sting of salt in his eyes, the ache of being hurt over and over again until his body became numb... All of it would be washed away with the tide that would inevitably take him away. He had been wishing for death for the year he'd been strapped to the altar, and finally...*finally* it would be granted.

It had been twelve months, thirteen days, and nine hours since he had last seen his family. Twelve months, thirteen days, and nine hours since he'd been strapped to the altar, kicking, and screaming and begging to be let free. The fight in him had died after a few weeks. He'd given up completely.

You will be loved, they said. *You will be a hero. A savior. A martyr. Your family will be safe,* they promised.

It won't hurt, they lied.

The tide became a pendulum, swinging back and forth, ticking down to the moment of his promised demise. The sky was dark that day, heavy clouds threatening rain above him. His salt-dried hair fanned out around his head, tangled and pale. Scabs clung to his lips. He wore no clothes, save for the straps forcing his legs and arms down. There would be no chance of swimming away when the tidal wave came for him. There would be no option of escape. He would drown. He would be devoured. He would, without a crumb of doubt, die.

Thank the gods for that.

A year ago (twelve months, thirteen days, ten hours now), they came to his house – the small, rundown house that was more a glorified shack than anything – and went to the front door. They knocked twice and his mother answered. He could see that from where he was in the garden with his brothers. They all ducked behind overgrown bramble bushes, trying to see what was going on, pretending the robed figures were emissaries of some foreign royal here to tell them they were all princes and they'd be going to live in a palace (even though none of the boys *wanted* to live in a palace). The robed figures handed a pouch of coins to the boy's mother, and he knew, even if his younger brothers didn't, that they were likely *clients*. But his mother didn't invite them in the way she would her clients. She pointed to the garden, to the bramble bushes, and the boy *knew*.

He shoved his brothers away, telling them to run, to hide, to not look back no matter what. Slavery wasn't uncommon, and his mother was a selfish wench who wouldn't turn down a handful of coins even if it meant selling her own children. His brothers protested at first, but he screamed at them to go. He begged the eldest to watch over the younger ones, to protect them because he couldn't anymore.

The robed figures came just as the boys scattered, leaving only one behind. They took him, their grips like iron, and yanked a sack over his head, blocking out the world.

They dragged him down the dirt path leading to the harbor. They put him on a boat and bound his wrists behind his back, his ankles together.

You are destined for greatness, they told him.

Let me go! He screamed.

They gagged him after that. The rag had tasted of salt and iron. The winds were calm that day, so the robed figures rowed and rowed. The boy didn't know where they were taking him. He'd never been that far out at sea, especially not blindfolded.

Then, the boat ran into sand. The boy was dragged out and thrown over a shoulder. He kicked and writhed, squirming like a worm as he tried to escape. The figure did not relent. The figure did not set him down, not until they'd climbed up a hill and reached the altar. It was cold under the boy as he was laid on his back.

They removed his bindings first, leaving the sack over his head. Then, they removed his clothing. They clamped his wrists and feet down. They poured oil over his body, scented of lemon and sage and lavender. They massaged it into his skin and over his neck. They took the sack off his head and, before he could adjust to the change in light and scenery, rubbed more oil onto his face and through his hair. They brushed his brows and his lashes, they applied a salve to his lips, which they kissed, one by one – all six of them savoring the taste of his mouth and tongue.

They promised him he was a gift to the gods. That it wouldn't hurt. That his family would be safe and cared for. That he would be a *savior*.

For those first few months, he did not believe them. Not until the fight died and he became a shell of his former self, accepting the pampering and preparation without a word. As he grew, the bindings dug into his skin, creating raw wounds down to his bones that would've turned infectious had the figures not applied salves to them. They could not remove the bindings. Not until he was dead, and they could easily pick away the bits of flesh and bone that were left.

He screamed, too. He screamed until his throat bled and they threatened to sever his vocal cords because he did not need them. He told them to do it, please, just do it, *please,* and because he begged they didn't.

It had been two days since he'd last seen them. Had it not rained the day before, allowing him a few precious drops of water, he might have died of dehydration.

The tidal wave is coming now, they said before they left. They could not be on the island when it came. It was just the boy, all alone.

He wondered how his brothers were doing. If they missed him. If the youngest one, who had only been eight when he'd been taken, would remember him properly. If his wench of a mother had given birth to any more sons in the time he'd been gone.

The clouds gave out. The rain came in a few fat, sparse drops before it turned to a downpour. Something rumbled in the distance – not thunder. No, it was the tide this time. The tide that had pulled back like a slingshot raced towards him. He braced at first, some animalistic instinct, before relaxing completely.

It hit him with a colossal force that smacked his head against the stone altar. Salt filled his throat and his lungs, an icy cold that turned warm as the water in his lungs became iron, became blood, became the liquid death of drowning. He stopped holding his breath, opening his mouth to welcome in more, to drown before he could be devoured.

But it wasn't soon enough, for a pair of bioluminescent eyes, glowing the way plankton sometimes did in the rare summers, appeared in the darkness of the sea. The beast with angler fish eyes swam closer to the altar.

Let me die, the boy begged, though silently because he couldn't open his mouth.

You don't wish to live?

He had been begging for death for a year, but now...

Dark spots clouded his vision.

I don't want to die, he confessed.

You will not be allowed to touch the sun, the voice, both masculine and feminine and neither said. *You will become a creature of darkness. You will no longer be able to use your voice. You will no longer remember who you are.*

That was fine because the boy he'd been before was already dead.

The creature's mouth was on his. It drew out the air, the water, the blood. When he inhaled again, he did not inhale through his nose or mouth, but through his throat. Agonizing pain shot through his legs, but his ankles – not ankles anymore – were free from the bindings. As were his wrists. He blinked, eyes adjusting to the darkness he could now see through.

What is your name? the creature asked.

The boy said, "Victor."

The creature smiled with too many teeth. "Come, then, Victor. Do you wish for revenge? To inflict the same pain on those humans that they forced you to endure?"

He did. He so desperately did.

The creature took his hand and pulled him deep, deep, deep into the unforgiving sea.

Part One

1

Today was a perfect day to die. Dark skies made angrier with brewing tempests and wicked slashes of lightning, seawater darkened to a tumultuous black, waves cresting as they slammed into the hull of the *Silver Moon*. Rain came down in sideways sheets, soaking anyone who dared to be outside for more than a handful of seconds right to the bone. Even in his heavy green coat – the one that identified him faster than the black flag waving violently in the wind, the one that he wore in every wanted poster so that every child added the words *cloaked in green* to the skipping rope games they'd made up with his name sullied devilishly – Captain Nox Solveig (cloaked in green) looked like he'd just dived into the churning Emerald Sea below.

Of course, today would not be the day *he* died, because pirate captains as grand as he did not die. No, today would be the day he *finally* ended the existence of one of his many nemeses – Fleet Admiral Jonyth Commodore of the Imperial Navy.

Somewhere just north of the Wandering Isle in the Emerald Sea, only half an hour before, Gael, the navigator, shouted that he'd spotted a ship. A navy ship. And with his perfect vision, even through the deluge of rain, he made out the name of the ship, painted on the hull in blocky letters: the *Mary Jolene.* Named after the empress of the Aralyth Empire, Mary Jolene Helios, it was a ship every pirate in the Emerald Sea knew, because it was the ship captained by Jonyth Commodore.

"What are your orders, Cap?"

The master-at-arms of the *Silver Moon,* a curvy but muscular and talented woman named Kesh, appeared at Solveig's side. Despite the weather, she wore only a tight-fitting shirt that left her tattooed arms bare. Strapped to her back were two swords and she had at least three pistols at her hip, no less than a dozen knives strapped to the rest of her body. She looked up – nearly two feet shorter than Solveig, she had to crane her neck considerably.

"Load the cannons. Have Trudeau get as close to the *Jolene* as possible," Solveig ordered. "I'm going to board."

"They'll kill you," Kesh pointed out.

"They've been trying for years now." He winked. "I'll be fine. Help Zayn load the cannons."

Kesh gave a lazy salute, running first to the helmsman Trudeau to relay the orders before finding the gunner, Zayn, to help with the cannons.

"We should turn around." This came from the quartermaster. Scorpion was one of Solveig's closest friends – his second best friend if he really wanted to put a label on it. A tall man with dozens of tattoos and a shaved head, Scorpion was visually scarier than Solveig, even if he did like to spend his free time reading (and occasionally writing) poetry.

"And turn down the chance to sink the *Jolene* and put Jonyth in the green?" Solveig shook his head, drops of rain flying from his hair. "We charge on."

"The *Moon* is still recovering from that run-in with the Rabbit Pirates at Kelsyn. And Vern is out of commission right now. Prokofiev probably can't do much, either. Or Jamel."

"So, we're down three men," Solveig said. True, it was...unfortunate to have his bo'sun, doctor, and one of his sailors injured enough that they couldn't help. Well, Prokofiev wasn't injured, but as the doctor, he was tasked with keeping Vern stable, after he'd taken a bullet to the chest during a fight with the infamous Rabbit Pirates on the northern island Kelsyn, narrowly missing any vital organs.

"Three men," Scorpion argued. "And a busted ship. We should seek sanctuary on the Wandering Isle. Recoup and recover. Fix the *Moon*. We shouldn't be picking fights with the navy – with *Jonyth* – right now."

A muscle in Solveig's jaw feathered. "I didn't gain my reputation by fleeing."

"Your reputation won't mean a thing when you're dead."

The *Silver Moon* crested a wave nearly half its size. Solveig's organs rose and fell in time with the ship, creating a fluttery unease within. He'd fought the fleet admiral before. Once. Usually, it was the admirals and vice admirals and other wannabe-important officers that came after him. But they were skirting close to Aralyth territories. Of course, Jonyth would corner them.

If Jonyth was half as smart a man as he pretended to be he would have waited until *right* after the scrimmage with the Rabbit Pirates to attack.

"We're fighting," said Solveig.

Scorpion's shoulders sank a fraction. "Aye, captain."

The Aralyth Empire was the largest and most powerful of the four main ruling powers in the world. With territories that engulfed the Emerald Sea and most of the Sapphire Sea it, of course, came with a *very* powerful navy. And at the top of the food chain was Jonyth Commodore. Reporting directly to Emperor and Empress Helios, Jonyth had just as much influence as a king, rivaled only by the power the crown prince had. He was a formidable enemy, to say the least, and he would not go down without a fight.

Neither would Nox Solveig.

"Brace!" yelled Gael from his post at the crow's nest. His voice was all but drowned out by the wind and rain, but his message was enough of a warning.

The *Silver Moon* collided with the *Mary Jolene* in a clashing scrape of wood against wood. The *Moon* tipped precariously to the side – an inch more and it would capsize, but it steadied itself out with a crush against the waves.

"Fire!" Zayn screamed, and seconds later the roar of cannon fire sounded over the storm.

The *Jolene* returned fire of her own, each cannon sending the *Moon* rocking and shuddering, her hull splitting and allowing seawater to pour in.

Navy men from the *Jolene* leaped across the gap between the ships, swords drawn. In an instant, they were fighting, the pirates of the *Silver Moon* holding their ground. Distracting the navy. Creating an opening. Popping the collar of his coat, Solveig hopped from one ship to the other.

Despite being the fleet admiral and having more training than all the other officers on the ship, Jonyth was protected by a posse of sailors, all with a bloodthirsty gaze in their eyes. Solveig shifted into an offensive stance, hips square and knees bent as he sunk low –

And charged, cutting through the men like they were nothing. His boots had enough traction to keep him from slipping on the rain-slick deck, but as blood, thick and sticky, spilled, his footing became less sure. He sank lower, trying to lower his center of gravity to keep from falling. He sliced through the knees of another soldier before whirling around and impaling yet another with his cutlass.

Over the rain and brine and blood, he smelled smoke.

A navy sailor yelled, drawing Solveig's attention. The sailor hastily stabbed his sword, cutting nothing but air. With his sword in one hand, Solveig grabbed the man's arm and twisted it until it snapped with a crunch. The man screamed as his bone ripped through jagged skin.

It was carnage, raw and destructive and bloody. And standing amidst it all, calm as the eye of a storm, was Jonyth Commodore.

Solveig charged, barreling through the fight, sword slashing blindly as he cut his enemies down. With his cutlass in one hand, he balled his other into a fist and –

And slammed it right into the bridge of Jonyth Commodore's straight nose.

It shattered with a squelchy, wet crunch. Blood sprayed, a fine mist of it peppering Solveig's cheek before he had the chance to duck away, narrowly escaping the downward swing of Jonyth's sword. Bits of red hair were caught in the strike, falling to the soaked deck.

"Surrender!" Jonyth demanded, swinging his sword again. By a stroke of luck, Solveig slipped, sliding beneath the sword before he could get cut.

"I'd rather die," said Solveig with a grin. He swung his sword, the blade slicing through the air in a quicksilver flash.

Clash!

His sword met Jonyth's. Solveig pushed, leaning his weight into the blow as he tried to catch Jonyth off guard, even though the admiral had the same idea.

Solveig pushed and pushed, all his weight going into the strike, until...

Until he stepped to the side, forcing Jonyth to topple. He swiped his blade yet again. Blood spurted as the membrane-thin flesh of

Jonyth's cheek – stretching from his hairline across the broken bridge of his nose, narrowly missing his eye – split.

"I will kill you!" Jonyth screamed over the tumult, over the cacophony of metal against metal ringing like funeral bells.

"Go ahead and try!" laughed Solveig.

The admiral did try, wiping that smug grin off Solveig's face with a parry the pirate hadn't seen coming. Solveig barely managed to throw his own cutlass up to block the swing, but Jonyth's sword got far too close to Solveig's face for comfort.

Solveig spun around, gaining a better footing on a spot of deck not covered in blood. With his back no longer to the *Silver Moon* he was able to see... Flames. Tall, vicious flames licking at the storm clouds, plumes of smoke choking the rain and air. He couldn't see...*anyone*.

Not his feisty master-at-arms, Kesh. Not Trudeau, who was built like a bull and just as mean. Not wraithlike Zayn or Gael, who hated fighting more than anything. Definitely not Vern, who was injured, and Prokofiev, who was treating him. Not...not Scorpion, either, who wouldn't dream of going down without a fight.

The *Moon* groaned as her mainmast collapsed, the fire eating away too much of the wood.

In that vital split second of distraction, Jonyth struck. He knocked the sword from Solveig's grip and kicked his legs out from beneath him. *Thunk!* He hit the deck hard, teeth clacking as he bit through the tip of his tongue. Cold, sharp metal pressed against the lump in his throat.

"Surrender," Jonyth said coldly.

"Never."

Jonyth swiped, creating the thinnest of cuts. It blossomed red instantly, weeping lifeblood onto the front of Solveig's shirt, staining his green coat even more.

"By the will of the Empire of Aralyth, I place you under arrest." Jonyth grinned a wicked grin, his teeth stained red. "And by the request of his imperial majesty, Emperor Castros Helios of the Aralyth Empire, you are sentenced to die."

Jonyth pulled shackles from his pocket – because of *course,* he kept shackles in his pocket - and snapped them over Solveig's wrists.

"My crew!" He shouted desperately, craning his neck to see the *Moon.* What remained of it, at least. Half of it was already submerged, the other half burning. A captain was supposed to go down with his ship. He was supposed to be on that *damn* ship!

"They're dead," said Jonyth. "Good riddance. Though, a few of them *did* have nice bounties on their heads. I believe Kesh clocked in at...seventy-three million lune. Scorpion was just over a hundred million lune, was he not?"

Solveig gritted his teeth together so hard his jaw popped. His crew loved those bounties – the status they came with, the thrill of knowing they were very, very, *very* wanted. But now...now that was all they were reduced to. Seventy-three million lune. A hundred million lune.

His own bounty was five hundred million lune, enough to purchase a house the size of the Aralyth palace and have enough left over to live comfortably. Lune was the most common currency in the Aralyth Empire, printed on paper instead of the coins stone, kase and rine were. Anywhere in the world that was under Aralythian influence used their currency.

Without their heads, nobody would be collecting bounties on Kesh or Scorpion.

But Solveig...

Blood covered most of Jonyth's face, giving him a crimson mask that looked black in the night, illuminated only by the fire from the *Moon*.

"So, you're going to kill my crew, sink my ship, and threaten to kill me just to drag me back to Aralyth?" Solveig spat on Jonyth's blood-splattered boots. "Do you know how easy it would be to break out of your brig and kill you before we even dock?"

"Oh, you won't be getting out," the admiral promised.

A crack of burnt wood and a thundering splash drew Solveig's attention to the wreckage of his ship – his beloved ship he'd been sailing for six years, since he was freshly nineteen and determined to live out the dream he'd had since he was a child. *Gods,* how had the navy managed to incapacitate his crew? Scorpion alone should've been an unstoppable force, but...but there was no sign of *any* of them – not on the *Mary Jolene,* not on the *Silver Moon.* The cold waters of the Emerald Sea would've given them hypothermia if drowning didn't take them first...

The *Silver Moon* gave one last valiant stand before toppling, swallowed by the unforgiving sea.

Solveig's shackles were grabbed, and he was forced to his feet. Jonyth gave a violent tug, nearly sending Solveig to the deck. He slipped, only barely managing to widen his stance enough to keep from toppling over.

"I'll kill you," Solveig swore. "I'll kill you and send you to the green. Not even Poet will have mercy on your soul." He invoked the name of the god of the sea, even though it was risky to use the god's name in vain when in his realm.

"Cute," said Jonyth. "But, as I said, you won't be getting out. And I'll make sure *I* get the honor of relieving your filthy head from your shoulders."

As he was dragged towards the brig, Solveig frantically searched the waters, desperately looking for a sign – *any sign* – that *someone* from his crew had survived. Even in the tumult of the storm raging above, the waters surrounding the *Mary Jolene* seemed...eerily calm. He caught a flash of silver – a shark, no doubt, come to scavenge the not-yet-cold bodies of his crew – that crested before diving deep into the Emerald.

It was his last sight of the sea before he was taken below deck.

The brig on the *Silver Moon* was little more than a glorified storage closet, with a single cell that usually held buckets and fishing supplies.

The *Mary Jolene* couldn't have been more different. It made sense, since unlike pirates, the navy usually took their prisoners alive. And a ship as big as the *Jolene* held a *lot* of prisoners.

Yet Solveig was the only one. As they passed a row of tiny cells, Solveig realized his only companions were rusted buckets and a wiry cat who hissed when they got too close. Solveig was taken to the cell at the very end, furthest from the exit unless he could somehow force his way through a solid wall.

Jonyth threw him in, giving Solveig no chance to even think about catching himself before his face slammed into the wall opposite the bars.

Crunch.

Blood spurted from his nose, coating his upper lip instantly. Payback, no doubt, for breaking Jonyth's nose.

"Welcome to your first day of hell, pirate." Jonyth grabbed the front of Solveig's shackles, yanking them up and fixing them to a hook that hung from the ceiling.

Fine. He could climb up there. It would take a considerable amount of upper arm strength, but he –

Jonyth clamped another iron cuff around each of Solveig's ankles. He yanked so hard that Solveig fell on his ass with a *thunk* that caused his teeth to clack together. Jonyth clamped another chain to each cuff, locking them to the walls.

With his arms above his head and his legs spread apart with nowhere to go, Solveig was *stuck.*

Fine! He'd just have to escape when they moved him from the ship to the prison he'd stay in while he waited for his death sentence.

Boots clicked against the ground; another sailor joined Jonyth in the brig. The new navy sailor didn't have his jacket with the badges and stripes displaying his rank, but Solveig didn't recognize him as any of the admirals – or vice admirals, for that matter.

The sailor handed a syringe filled with liquid the color of polished rubies. It was too thin to be blood, too translucent, but Solveig panicked, nonetheless. He yanked on his restraints.

"What is that? *Commodore, I swear to Poet –* "

Solveig was cut off when the fleet admiral shoved the syringe into his jugular, forcing the liquid into his veins.

In an instant, a dizzying sensation engulfed Solveig. Colors and sounds blurred; his body felt ten times its weight, heavy and lethargic.

"Sinthoxine" said Jonyth as he handed the syringe back to the sailor. "Sinth. It's a sedative. It'll keep you complacent enough until we reach Ivenis Justyce."

Solveig's lucidity was already a swirling, eddying kaleidoscope of delusion and illusion.

Ivenis Justyce. The impenetrable prison on the coast of Aralyth where anyone who entered never came out alive. Only the worst of the worst were sentenced to Ivenis Justyce. Of *course,* Jonyth's worst nemesis – the pirate who had, only minutes ago, sliced open his face and shattered his nose – would go to Ivenis Justyce.

"M'crew..." Solveig slurred, his tongue too leaden to create anything more than two syllables of nonsense.

"Dead," said Jonyth. "Sinth comes in a gas form, too. And it's *very* flammable. You were supposed to be on the ship with them when they got gassed."

Solveig hadn't seen them because they'd all collapsed on the deck.

"M'g'nna'kill'you..." he garbled, lips slippery from the blood gushing from his broken nose.

Jonyth smirked. "Good luck with that, *pirate.*"

The world tilted sideways, blurring at the edges before going dark completely.

2

SOLVEIG BLINKED IN AND out of consciousness. His world became flashes of light, brief sights of the bars caging him in, sharp pricks of needles as more sinth was forced into his veins, and darkness. Lots and lots and *lots* of whirling, dizzying darkness. Time was a concept that did not pertain to him. Minutes might have passed. Weeks. Years. No, not that long. His bladder wasn't uncomfortably full yet. His hunger and thirst had been smothered – sated – by the sinth. Someone had set his nose, though both nostrils were clogged with dried blood.

His crew was dead. For the third time in his life, Solveig had lost his crew. For the *first* time in his life, Solveig was truly alone.

The door to his cell swung open. He'd gotten used to that by now. Jonyth would come give him another dose of sinth. He'd slip out of consciousness again. Rise, and repeat.

Only...this time, the familiar prick didn't come. Only...

Click... Clang.

The heavy chains holding his ankles to the anchors on the walls fell, no longer taut as they held him in place. The chain from the ceiling was unhooked next. Jonyth grabbed the chain holding Solveig's wrists together.

"We've made it to Ivenis Justyce Penitentiary," he said smugly.

Solveig wasn't lucid enough to even think of a witty response. All he could focus on was *not* falling on his face and re-breaking his nose as he stumbled after the fleet admiral, up a set of stairs that seemed ten miles long, across a deck scrubbed clean of blood and salt, down a gangplank that felt steeper than Keth Mountain in the north.

"That's him?" people began whispering as Jonyth paraded Solveig along the dock leading to the iron fortress that was Ivenis Justyce.

"He looks...greasier than his poster," another person whispered.

"He *is* wearing the coat. *Captain Nox Solveig, cloaked in green.*"

"Why can't he walk straight?"

"He doesn't even look scary."

"I bet I could push him into the water, and he'd sink."

"I thought he'd be taller..."

Solveig couldn't even lift his head to glare at the people whispering. It took all his focus to keep his eyes fixed on his feet, to make sure he didn't stumble and trip into the sea below.

"I was wondering when you'd show." A new voice – male, deep, accented. "When I heard you'd captured *Nox Solveig* I couldn't believe it."

Jonyth chuckled. "Why would I lie about that, Lakatos?"

Solveig didn't recognize the name.

A gloved hand grabbed his chin, forcing Solveig to look up. The man – Lakatos – was *massive,* much larger than Scorpion, one of the biggest men Solveig knew. His beard was greyed, and a burn covered half his face, creeping down his thick neck and disappearing beneath the collar of his heavy coat. It didn't take a genius to figure out that the medals and badges on Lakatos's breast marked him as the warden of Ivenis Justyce.

"*This* is Nox Solveig?" Lakatos sneered. "Unimpressive. He's scrawnier than I thought. How does Seven-B sound for a cell?"

"Sounds like hell," chuckled Jonyth. "Though, luckily for him, he won't be down there long. Not if things go to plan."

In a simple exchange of words, Solveig's fate was sealed. Warden Lakatos took the chains from Jonyth and yanked, forcing Solveig to stumble after as he was led into the belly of Ivenis Justyce.

The only mercy Solveig was granted in his delirious, sinth-high state was that they took the shaft to the bottom-most level of the prison. Whether it was because Lakatos simply didn't want to walk down all those stairs, Solveig was grateful, even as the shaft descended deeper and deeper.

When it reached the bottom, Lakatos tugged at his chains. The latest dose of sinth had begun to wear off, bringing with it a smidge of lucidity and a killer headache that started at the base of Solveig's skull and encapsulated his entire head. Even his *teeth* ached.

Lakatos unlocked a cell and led Solveig in. A quick glance at his new life showed he wouldn't be there long. The cell was barely big enough for him to lie down in, with a rusted bucket for him to do his business in and nothing else. Lakatos chained his wrists above his head, and his ankles to the walls, just like on the *Mary Jolene*.

"Try not to get too comfortable, pirate," Lakatos said with a hearty chuckle. He stepped out of the cell, locking it, then locking the heavy chain that wrapped around the bars. "You'll be out of here soon enough."

The warden made sure the locks were secure before going back to the shaft, leaving Solveig alone in the darkness.

He closed his eyes. It was too dark and too tiring to keep them open. In the silence, he said the names of each of his crew in his head.

Kesh. Trudeau. Zayn. Scorpion. Vern. Prokofiev. Gael. Jamel, and Von and Cliff and Charlie and Melody and Dime and Gabe and Amon and Rob and Petr.

All gone – all *dead* – because Solveig couldn't say no to a fight he had no chance of winning. He tipped his head back until his skull met the raw, harsh stone of the cell wall.

Ivenis Justyce was built on an island so tiny it never showed up on any maps just off the coast of Aralyth. It was close enough to the mainland that most of the people who worked there lived in Aramore, the capital city of Aralyth, but secluded enough that prisoners lucky enough to break out of their cells would be met with the harsh seas that would surely spare them no mercy. Seven-B, as cold and unfinished as it was, was likely built underground. The prisoners there wouldn't be able to dig their way free;

the only escape was *up*, and the place was crawling with jailers and pirates who would kill – quite literally – for a chance at freedom.

Metal bit into Solveig's wrists, scraping the already raw and sore skin, bursting the blistery scabs until blood trickled down his arms.

Kesh, Trudeau, Zayn, Vern, Prokofiev, Gael, Scorpion.

He repeated their names again and again, burning their faces – their voices, their laughs, their battle cries – into his memory. He would not forget them.

Water filled Solveig's mouth, forcing its way down his throat. His eyes flew open, and he choked. Water flew from his nose and out his mouth. *Drowning?!* How was he drowning?! Unless...

"You need to drink," came an unfamiliar voice. "Warden says we aren't allowed to let you die before the execution. So, drink."

The lip of a tin cup met Solveig's mouth again. He swallowed this time, the cold splash of water hitting his empty belly, making it twist uncomfortably. Without the sinth to keep him high, Solveig was *starving*.

"More," he croaked when the jailer took the cup away.

"I was told to keep you *alive*, not *comfortable*," the jailer scoffed. In the darkness of Seven-B, he couldn't make out the jailer's face, but he heard the locks clicking, and he was alone once more.

"Damn!" a woman's voice exclaimed once the click-clacking of the jailer's boots faded. "Who the hell are you to deserve such special treatment? You get to stay *alive?*"

Solveig blindly searched for the voice, but Seven-B had no light; he couldn't even see his own nose.

"I'm in the cell across from yours," the woman said. "I think. It's impossible to tell. I haven't had a cellmate in forever! The last one died of scurvy or the plague or something."

Solveig bristled. Great. Was *he* going to catch the plague just by sharing the cell the last prisoner died in?

The woman continued, "Don't worry. I think they cleaned the cell. The smell was *awful.* Ever been around a dead body that's been rotting for a week? I think rats got to it at one point. He was a cannibal, though. Hence why he was down here with me. Anyways. Why are *you* down here?"

If the last guy was a cannibal, what did that make this woman? She had an accent unfamiliar to Solveig, thick and full, almost with a staccato quality.

"I'm waiting for my execution," Solveig said, his throat hoarse and voice scratchy. Even in the soft tone he spoke in, the words were too loud, causing a splintering pounding in his skull.

"Death row!" the woman exclaimed. "*Unfortunate!* What did you do? Who did you piss off?"

"Jonyth Commodore," he grumbled.

The woman gasped as if she was some aristocratic lady receiving the latest court gossip. "He's still in the navy? Tell me more. I've been down here for almost four years now."

Four years. Nausea roiled in his gut. Four years... He couldn't be stuck down here for that long! He'd rather they just kill him now.

Still... He had nothing better to do. *And* he was going to die...

"Jonyth Commodore is the fleet admiral of the navy," he said, voice gaining confidence with each new word spoken. "He and I have been enemies since I started my own crew. Pirates of the Silver Moon. He killed my entire crew, I gave him a new scar, and now I'm here."

The woman groaned in delight. "Tell me more. Pirates of the Silver Moon? Never heard of them. You were the captain? Who did you sail with before? Anyone? Have you ever been to the Ruby?" The Ruby Sea – one of the four oceans in the world – was a southern ocean, bordering the Merdyne Empire in the south, along with the Amethyst Sea.

"I... Yes. I am – *was* – the captain. Sailed with the Serpent Pirates before, on the *Sea Wyrm* –" the woman squealed in delight. "I went to the Ruby with the *Sea Wyrm* a few times. Never with the *Moon.*"

Chains rattled, mixing with the groans and sighs from the woman. How lonely had she been to get *this* excited over a few bits of uninteresting information?

"Have you ever heard of the Ruby Pirates?" before Solveig could answer – he *had* heard of the bloodthirsty all-woman crew from the Merdyne Empire – the woman continued, "I sailed with them before they disbanded. I joined when I was a girl, but I became the bo'sun eventually."

Solveig's eyes went wide. He'd never encountered the Ruby Pirates, but he'd heard stories of them. His captain on the *Sea Wyrm*, Knight Hardy, fought alongside them on a few occasions. He always talked about how brutal they were, how they rivaled the Amazonian warriors in the north. *If you ever meet the Ruby Pirates, there are three people to watch out for,* he'd always said once he'd downed a few mugs of cinnamon rum too many. *Captain Mali, and her first and second mates, the Viper of the Sea, and the Witch of the Sea: Beryl Tchai and –*

"Vesperine Genevieve," whispered Solveig.

"So you *have* heard of me!" the Witch of the Sea beamed.

"You've been *here* this whole time?" Solveig's interest had been piqued. It was shortly after Captain Hardy died that news of the Ruby Pirates' fate spread across the world – Captain Mali *retired* (supposedly), the Viper of the Sea bargained with the emperor and empress of Merdyne Empire for freedom to live in peace, and while the rest of the pirates scattered, the Witch of the Sea *vanished*.

Sent to Ivenis Justyce Penitentiary, apparently.

"Be grateful you're a man," Vesperine Genevieve said. "The Justyce boys could care less if you're bleeding between your legs every month. Good luck to whoever has to scrape my blood from the floor of this cell after I die. There's four years' worth of it."

Solveig wasn't a woman. He never had to deal with the monthly bleeding. But Kesh – and a few others on his crew – did deal with the bleeding. Awkward as it was at first, he quickly got used to making sure they were stocked up on supplies (including stolen chocolates, ginger tea, and *lots* of cinnamon rum).

"Anyways," Vesperine Genevieve drawled. "What's your name, Cap?"

"Solveig," he answered. "Nox Solveig."

"Ah. You're a northerner. You use your last name instead of your first."

It had nothing to do with him being a northerner and more to do with the fact that all the greatest pirates used their surnames instead of their first names.

He didn't like his last name much, though, since it tied him to his mother, but she was dead, and he could not care less.

"Call me Ves," she added. *"Vesperine* is too long. Makes me sound like a princess." She made a gagging sound. "How long are they keeping you down here – you know?"

He did not know. Truthfully, he had no idea how much time had lapsed since the sinking of the *Silver Moon* and being thrown into Ivenis Justyce. The sinth had messed with his mind more than any amount of cinnamon rum could ever think to.

But...he would be getting out of Ivenis Justyce Penitentiary. Just not for long. He'd heard of prisoners being executed at the prison, but a prisoner as wanted as Solveig... They'd surely take him to the mainland. To the capital city, Aramore, where the royal family could watch as his head was lopped from his shoulders.

"What's your bounty?" Ves asked, startling Solveig from his thoughts of impending death.

"Five hundred million lune," he said. Once, he'd been proud of the massive number, the one that marked him as one of the top five most wanted pirates in the *world,* but now it just felt...empty.

Ves choked. "Five hundred *mill?!*" she made a baffled scoffing noise that echoed. "I was three hundred seventy mill. They didn't execute me, but my bounty said dead *or* alive. Bet the rat bastard who caught me is living *very* comfortably right now. Unlike *me*. With a bounty that high, I bet they're going to kill you. Publicly, probably. *Damn!* I wish I could see it. Not that I *want* you to die, Cap, but it's been a while since I've seen anything exciting."

Despite everything, Solveig chuckled. "It's a real damn shame I'm going to get executed. You would've made a mighty fine bo'sun."

Chains rattled as she must have waved her hand dismissively. "Perhaps in the next life, Cap. Pirates will always be pirates. If you make it to captain again, come find me and I'll be your second."

He thought of the silly pledge he and his brothers once swore, long ago when they were children, when they were all alive. *I will pledge my final breath to your name and my first to find you again.* His second oldest brother had come up with it and it was the promise they all shared.

"I will pledge my final breath to your name and my first to find you again," he whispered aloud, the words feeling much more real now.

"You swearing an oath to me, Cap?" Ves snorted.

"What? No. It's something... My brothers and I..." he shook his head. "It's nothing."

"No. Say the words again. Louder."

He did.

Ves let out a sigh. "Well, Nox Solveig. I will pledge my final breath to your name and my first to find you again. There. Now I'm bound to find you in our next lives to be your bo'sun."

He smiled. His lips were so chapped and dry that the skin split, spilling blood into his mouth. He didn't mind the taste.

"It's an honor to have you, Witch of the Sea," he said, and he meant it.

The days began to blur. He was fed only the most meager scraps every now and then but was given water regularly. Ves whined to the guards every time they came down, trying to weasel information out of them about the world outside Ivenis Justyce. Solveig listened closely, hoping for any news about his crew. Maybe someone survived. Maybe Jonyth had been bluffing about the sinth gas. Maybe this was all a horrific nightmare.

So far, Ves was only able to learn that bustles were back in fashion in Aralyth, the crown prince was starting to fall out of his father's favor, and an underwater volcano off the chain of islands that was Archepylago had erupted, adding *another* island to the country.

Useless information, really.

He started to learn that the guards came twice a day to give him water, and with fourteen visits to his cell, he must have been there a week. No matter how many times he begged Ves to ask the guards what *day it was,* she never did.

Footsteps sounded following the sound of the heavy iron door sliding open. Through the dark, Solveig shot Ves a look she couldn't see that said *ask-what-damned-day-it-is.*

But there was more than one set of footsteps. That was new. At least, for Solveig. The entourage brought lanterns with them, also something new. He squinted against the sudden new light, a headache already blooming behind his eyes.

The parade stopped outside his cell. Keys jingled, the door slid open, chains fell to the ground.

"Today," said the familiar voice of Lakatos, "is your lucky day, pirate. You're getting out of here."

Understanding washed over Solveig. *Ah,* he realized. Today he was to be escorted to the scaffold where he would die.

3

SEVEN JAILERS, THREE NAVY soldiers armed with loaded guns, the warden of Ivenis Justyce, Lakatos, and Jonyth Commodore, sporting an angry scab across his cheek, splitting the bridge of his very broken nose stood in a semicircle surrounding Solveig's cell. It was...well, underwhelming. He'd thought for sure there would be double that. Maybe a few admirals and vice admirals. The executioner. Emperor Castros Helios himself. Apparently, he only needed twelve people. *Gods* – were they going to pump him full of sinth, so he was high for his execution?

"All of you are here just to escort *me?*" Solveig, feigning *some* nonchalance. He could force himself to bare a lazy grin, but his heart thundered in his chest, his stomach clenched, and the primitive fear of death even *he* couldn't conquer threatened to take over.

"Silence," one of the marines snapped.

"Oh, I'll be silent enough soon," Solveig drawled. The navy men fixed their guns on Solveig, ready to shoot in case he made any sudden movements. He was tempted to flinch if only to see how they'd react.

Lakatos grabbed the front of Solveig's chains, yanking on them to lead him out like a dog on a leash.

"Today is a glorious day," Jonyth said, falling into pace next to Solveig. "Next, we'll have to execute *you.*"

In the dim light, Solveig could make out the shadowy outline of Ves. She lifted her head and grinned, white teeth flashing. "You wish, pretty boy. Cap and I will just come back to torment you in our next lives."

"Make sure she gets no dinner tonight," Lakatos calmly told one of the jailers.

"Oh, come *on!*" Ves groaned. "First you take away my only friend and now no dinner?!"

She was ignored, her protests soon drowning out as the posse ascended the steep stairs.

It was death enough to have to climb the thousand stairs from the bottom of Ivenis Justyce to the top, especially since Solveig hadn't eaten in weeks. He dragged his feet, too exhausted to walk properly. Maybe it wouldn't be too terrible to die high off sinth. At least he wouldn't be starving and weak and begging for death. A captain was supposed to go down with his ship. With his *crew.* He closed his eyes, sucking in a harsh breath, the stale air stinging his lungs. His crew had gone to the green, no doubt, but maybe he could find them in his next life.

The flames that had destroyed his ship flashed through his mind.

He had no fight left in him.

Jonyth Commodore seemed to realize that, too, as when they finally stepped out of the prison and into the sunlight, Solveig wasn't injected with any sinth to keep him submissive. He wasn't thrown into another cell either, the sloop he was led onto far too small to have a brig. It held a crew of three – two admirals and a captain. Solveig was forced to the ground, surrounded by Jonyth and his underlings.

"Ever been to Aramore?" Jonyth asked with a sneer. Solveig glared, wishing he could reach up and claw the scab off the man's face, to force the wound to go septic.

"Once," he answered. "Can't say I'm eager to go back."

"I was always curious," drawled Jonyth. Solveig groaned internally. "Where did you come from? I bet your mother was a whore. Probably didn't know who your father was."

Solveig ground his teeth together. His mother *had* been a whore, but she knew who his father was, even if Solveig didn't. He shared a father with one of his brothers.

"Doesn't matter," Solveig spat. "I'm not telling you anything."

"Shame. Well, I suppose some secrets ought to die with you. Any regrets, pirate? Anything you wish you could have seen or done?"

Plenty. He said, "Not killing you and not having it off with your mother."

Pain erupted in his face as Jonyth slammed the pommel of his sword into Solveig's jaw. He tasted blood. It took all his willpower to swallow the blood-thick saliva and not spit it onto Jonyth's face. It was still a long trip to Aralyth, and he didn't want to die just *yet*.

"I hear you have a few treasure caches hidden around the empire," one of the admirals mused, successfully capturing Solveig's attention. He *did* have some caches stashed around the empire – a few on the mainland and a handful on the scattered islands. He'd even managed to tuck one away on the Floating Isle just in case he ever ran into the mysterious moving island again.

"So what if I do?" Solveig snorted. He had maps leading to each of his caches, but those maps were gone with the *Silver Moon.* "It's not like I'm going to give up the locations of my treasures to the *navy.*"

"We'll find them," the admiral said. "Whatever gold you've hoarded over the years rightfully belongs to the empire, anyways."

Solveig clenched his jaw. According to Emperor Castros Helios, anyone born on Aralyth soil belonged to the empire. Anyone who died on Aralyth soil belonged to the empire. Any money made, anything sold, any goods brought in... All of it belonged to the Aralyth Empire. The rain that fell from the clouds that seemed to always suffocate the skies in the north? Aralyth's property. The sandy dunes in the desert of Sandsunni in the east? Every last grain belonged to Castros Helios. All the treasure in Solveig's caches – except for the one on the Floating Isle, as the island was sovereign – technically belonged to the empire, and when Solveig died, they'd just be taking it back.

"Fine," he said. "I'll tell you where one of them is."

Even Jonyth looked intrigued as all the soldiers eagerly awaited Solveig's answer.

He grinned lazily, teeth red with blood. "Jonyth, where does your mother live, again? I hid one of them in her pan—"

The pommel of Jonyth's sword collided with his jaw again. *That,* he thought with a grimace, *was deserved.*

The sun peeked through the dark clouds, as if it, too, wanted to witness the execution of Nox Solveig. Journalists and nosy onlookers bombarded Solveig and the navy men as they walked down the gangplank and onto the dock.

"Captain Solveig, a word?" one journalist asked.

"Where did you hide your treasure?" asked another.

"Is it true your crew is dead?"

"Did you really slay a kraken?"

("No, that was the Nameless God, remember?")

"Why didn't you just retire?"

"Move it!" Jonyth shouted over the crowd. He yanked on Solveig's chains, forcing him to stumble. The sun burned his eyes. He kept his head low, gaze focused on the dock, his hair a curtain over his face.

The crowd parted, clearing a path for the men to walk down. In the center of the square with a view of the ocean was the scaffold – a raised platform with a crossbeam and a wooden block. Solveig's heart thundered in his chest. That was it. The place where he was going to die. The gallows didn't have a rope, so he looked at the block instead. Beheading. At least it would be fast...

With each step he took, Solveig repeated one of his crew member's names.

Step. Kesh. *Step.* Trudeau. *Step.* Zayn. *Step.* Vern. *Step.* Prokofiev. *Step.* Gael. *Step.* Scorpion. *Step.* Ves, since she would join his crew in one lifetime or another.

Jonyth shoved Solveig to his knees before the wooden block. The admirals and vice admirals created a semicircle behind Solveig. Jonyth Commodore stood next to him, sword drawn. Of *course* it would be *Jonyth* who ended his life. Solveig fought the urge to roll his eyes. Above, a gull flew by. Solveig prayed to Poet – hell, to the Wanderer and Dreamer, two of the other gods, as well – that the bird would drop a steaming pile of –

"Today!" Jonyth's voice boomed over the crowd, those two syllables silencing the commotion at once. "Today, people of Aralyth, is a glorious day, because today is the day Nox Solveig is going to die."

Solveig sucked a harsh breath through his teeth. There *should* have been a *captain* in there. He'd earned that title. But title or no, all it took was one look at his green coat – which was more of a brown with all the dried blood on it – to know who he was. *Captain Nox Solveig, cloaked in green, set out to conquer the Emerald Sea. One day he'll go down to the drink. How many navy ships will he sink?*

He scoffed. Not nearly enough.

Jonyth held up a hand to silence the cheering. He reached into his coat pocket and pulled out a yellowed piece of paper. "Captain Solveig –" *there it was* "– you are found guilty of the following crimes: smuggling weapons; hijacking over three dozen naval vessels; sinking over two dozen naval vessels; interfering with maritime law; escaping a navy hold after being branded as a pirate –" he still remembered the searing pain of the burning brand being pressed into the flesh of his arm, a white *P* that couldn't be covered by any tattoos unless he did them himself, even though it had happened close to a decade ago. "– theft amounting to over a million lune; murder of multiple navy sailors; injuring a navy admiral."

He shot Solveig a glare. Solveig desperately wished to reach up and rip the scab off the wound he'd caused.

"Captain Solveig's bounty, as of his capture, totaled five hundred million lune, making him the second most wanted pirate in all four seas – Emerald, Amethyst, Sapphire, and Ruby." Jonyth rolled the paper back up and shoved it into his pocket. "For these crimes, I sentence you, Captain Nox Solveig, on this day, the seventeenth of Senmoon in the year 1153, with Lady Lightbringer as my witness, to death by beheading."

Seventeenth of Senmoon. The fight with the Rabbit Pirates had been on the thirtieth of Nakmoon, the sixth month of the year followed by Senmoon. That meant he'd spent three days high off sinth on the *Mary Jolene.* Nothing could placate the anger surging through his veins. Seventeen days. His crew had been dead for seventeen days and he was just now realizing it.

The crowd jeered, shouting a slew of slurs and curses that bounced right off Solveig. Seventeen days. His crew was likely all bones now, picked clean by the ocean beasts who had a taste for flesh.

At least he'd be joining their sorry souls soon. He'd gladly take whatever punishments they felt fit to deal out if it meant seeing them again.

I will pledge my final breath to your name, he'd promised Ves, whom he'd known for two weeks but already loved like a sister, *and my first to find you again.*

Jonyth sneered. "Any last words, pirate?" He unsheathed his sword, the blade glinting in the light as he raised it over his head.

"Seventy-three navy ships!" Solveig shouted to the crowd. He mustered up every last drop of waning strength and grinned. *"That's* how many I sank."

Jonyth shoved Solveig's head down, his chin cracking against the wooden block.

The blade descended like a swinging pendulum right for his neck.

Vesperine Genevieve had terrible luck when it came to making friends because she always ended up losing them. She'd decided, long into her sentence, that the sentence itself wasn't execution or to rot away in a prison cell in I. J. Pen (as she called it), but that she would die of boredom. For two measly weeks she'd had a friend, someone to talk to, to keep her company since she thrived off that. During those weeks, she'd refused to tell Captain Nox how much time had passed. She knew the hurt of losing a crew. Telling him how long they'd been gone would only hurt more. So, she kept it a secret and relished the friendship the pirate had to offer.

But now... Now, she was bored. *Again.*

She hadn't been chained to the walls or anything, and after half a year of telling the poor jailers they had to rip off her trousers and put a new pair on her every time she bled through them, she'd had her ankle shackles removed. All that was left were two cuffs on either wrist that could easily be chained together should she cause any problems. Her cell had only the barest of necessities – a bucket that acted as a chamber pot, a pile of dirt that acted as a bed (straw got moldy too fast and invited rats in), and, her personal favorite, the ball she'd snatched off a guard a year earlier. It was her only real source of entertainment these days.

I wonder how Cap's faring... she thought as she tossed the ball into the air and caught it with one hand. Who was she kidding? He was probably dead by now, hanging from his neck or with his head chopped off and on proud display...

She tossed the ball up again and began her second favorite hobby: singing shanties at the top of her lungs.

"Twin moons in the sky, for the third has died, aweigh anchor aweigh." She tossed the ball up and caught it again. *"The seas are dark, but the spirits are bright, we'll set the Ruby alight. Chart the course for the unknown way, aweigh anchor aweigh. Find the moon and the treasure tonight, we'll set the Ruby alight."*

Her ball bounced off the ceiling and landed smack on her face. Ves groaned and lay on her back, sprawled out to take up as much space as possible.

"Find the moon..." she murmured, that line from the shanty the Ruby Pirates sang day and night sticking out for some reason. "Ha. I found the blasted moon, but he's about to get his head chopped off."

She groaned again, just for the dramatics, and rolled onto her stomach. She'd made a vow to Solveig, one he'd returned. Unless she dropped dead now for her soul to somehow be reborn, there was no chance she and Sol would meet up again in their next lives. Not with her rotting in this cell.

She had once been one of the greatest pirates in the world. She sank an entire navy fleet. She slew a *kraken*.

(She conveniently left out the part about it being a juvenile that was barely the size of their ship. Anyone with a sword could've slain it, but she basked in the praise nonetheless.)

Footsteps sounded; she sat up quickly, just as a jailer stopped in front of her cell. The lad fumbled with his keys before sliding the door open just enough to push in a cup of water.

"Warden Justyce –" Lakatos Justyce was the descendant of Warden Ivenis, the founder of I. J. Pen "– said not to give you anything to eat, Witch."

Witch was an insult to most people, unless they were an actual witch, or if that was their title. Ves took no offense to it. She prided it if anything. She wasn't just *a* witch. She was *the* Witch of the Sea.

"I'm withering away to nothing but bones," she said dramatically. Even after four years of being locked away, her body had maintained most of its curves. With little to do, she would spend a lot of time exercising, toning her muscles that lay beneath a layer of softness.

"Rules are rules, Witch," the jailer said, the tiniest bit of sympathy in his tone.

"How am I supposed to bloody sard anyone when I'm nothing but a *skeleton?*" she moaned. She didn't need any light to know the poor jailer's face had flushed crimson at her profanity. He said nothing as he fumbled with the lock and hurried off, leaving Ves alone once more.

Ves stared at the ceiling, her grin fading to nothing. "Are you proud of me, Mali?" she whispered, invoking the name of her previous captain. "I took the fall once again. Poet, just smite me already."

The god of the sand, sea, and sky did not ascend from his watery home to smite Ves. Of course not. She had never been that lucky.

Solveig's mind was quiet in that perpetual state of waiting as the blade descended. He thought of the gods, their names flashing by all at once – The Wanderer, Poet, Dreamer, even Lady Lightbringer – as he briefly imagined what the afterlife would be like. He kept his eyes open, basking in the warmth of the sun for the last time. It was a shame he'd never see the two moons again.

And then, before the blade could sever his spine, his neck, his head from his shoulders, a voice rang out in the crowd.

"Wait!"

4

THE MAP SPLAYED OUT on the old counter beneath Illie Valentine's hands was, without a mote of doubt, a forgery. A shoddy one at that. Sarding fools always thought she couldn't tell the difference, but she was Illie Valentine, the best bloody mapmaker in the Veridin Kingdom.

"How much did you say you wanted this for?" she peered through her pale lashes, the same pink color as her hair, at the two rough sailors trying to swindle her. In the back room behind her, the door opened and closed. Elgar, the grandson of the old man who owned the shop, must be back from his smoke break. Illie silently willed him to stay put and to keep his nose out of her business.

"Five thousand lune," the shorter and rounder of the two said. He jabbed his grubby finger onto the paper. "This is a rare map.

It shows the Wandering Isle in the north. Maps ain't usually show that."

That's because, Illie thought as she forced a smile, the Wandering Isle never *went* to the north. It stuck close to the Midline, the strip of latitude right in the center, or below it. *That* was her first cue that the map was a cheap fake. The other was the quality of the paper – thin and brittle, brown but not from age, wrinkled. Quality maps were printed on thicker paper – the best ones were printed on waterproof paper or engraved onto metal. The cheap paper caused the ink to bleed at the edges, distorting the precise lines of the dozens of islands that made up the world.

Well, it wasn't even a map of Syrenis. Just the northern bit that included the Aralyth Empire, Edyn, the Twin Serpents, Kelsyn, the Borelin Isle, Archepylago, and the incorrectly placed Wandering Isle, right smack in the north Sapphire Sea on Aralyth's western coast.

The map was worth, at *most,* five kase coins, and that was being generous.

Crash!

Bloody Elgar must have knocked over a globe or something. Illie bit the inside of her cheek to keep the irritation off her face. Irritation wouldn't work. Not yet. Not while she was still trying to get these scammers to believe she was naïve.

Illie pushed her braid off her shoulder, the pink plait a stark contrast to the dull brown linen shirt she wore beneath her cream dress. She tapped one of her manicured nails against the map, right beneath the Wandering Isle. "Where did you say you found this?"

The swindlers exchanged a look. It was the taller, lankier one with a hooked nose and more gaps in his mouth than teeth, who spoke. "Port Icarus."

Now *that* was a lie if Illie ever heard one. Port Icarus, the coastal town at Aralyth's southernmost point, had exactly *one* mapmaking shop, and Illie knew the owner. Richard Ohms had trained with Illie's mentor and the owner of the shop Ink and Rose (maps, logs, and navigation supplies), Henry Quill back when they had been apprentices themselves. Richard Ohms, whom she'd met a handful of times, would rather die than even *think* of selling such a terrible map.

"Port Icarus?" Illie faked a gasp. "Oh, Aralythian maps are *such* better quality than Veridinian maps. Four thousand lune, you said?"

A vein bulged in the shorter man's forehead. "Five thousand."

"Mm... Right." Illie brushed herself off. "The owner is out, so let me have his grandson finish this."

The men exchanged a look, thinking they were *finally* getting somewhere.

"Elgar!" Illie called. "Elgar Quill, would you come here?"

Elgar Quill was two years Illie's junior, a lanky man who had grown into his feet but never lost his clumsiness. He reeked of sugar smoke and his glasses were crooked on his equally crooked nose. He was a mess, but he was a genius, so it could be excused as long as he didn't stand too close to Illie and let his smoke permeate her clothes.

He stumbled out of the back and quickly assessed the situation. Without needing to be told, he picked up the map, only to drop it quickly. "When did we start stocking such cheap paper?"

Illie liked Elgar to stay out of her business until precisely she was ready for his bluntness. She'd been dealing with the sailors for ten minutes now.

"We don't," Illie said sweetly. "These men are trying to sell us this map. They said Ohms made it."

Elgar fixed his glasses and examined the map closely. "This map is fake. The Wandering Isle doesn't go that far north. And Sapphire is spelled *S-A-P-H-I-R-E*. Only one P. How much do they want?"

"Five thousand," Illie said simply.

"Stone?"

"Lune."

Elgar burst out laughing. He crumpled up the map and threw it at the men. "Get out of my shop."

The men opened their mouths, no doubt ready to shout at the two, but the bell over the front door jingled and an old man walked in. He bent over a cane, his beard nearly touching the floor. Thick spectacles sat on his nose, and he smelled of salt.

"Watch it, old man," the tall man sneered when they tried to leave, only to have their path blocked. Illie grinned.

"Henry!" she exclaimed in greeting.

The color drained from the men's faces. Without lingering to witness the wrath of the infamous Henry Quill, they scurried outside, the bell jingling as they went.

"Have a nice day!" Illie said with one last bit of saccharine before letting her shoulders droop and her smile fall. She groaned, rubbing her face with both hands to massage the tension from her forehead.

"Are you scaring away my customers again?" Henry Quill asked. He rounded the counter and tapped Illie's ankle with his cane.

"Just the regular scammers," grumbled Illie, no longer faking sweetness. "Those two idiots thought they could sell me a forgery for five thousand lune. Said Ohms made it."

"They spelled Sapphire with only one P," added Elgar from the back.

Illie hoisted herself onto the counter. Inside the shop, she didn't wear any shoes, just her mismatched socks that had a layer of dust on the bottoms since she refused to sweep, and Elgar always *forgot*.

For the last fourteen years of her life, the Ink and Rose had been Illie's home. It was a quaint little shop with an apartment above where Illie lived, close enough to the Icarus Strait that she could taste the brine in the air. Most of the maps they sold were made by Henry Quill himself, though a fair share of them were made by Illie. Elgar preferred the art of preparing the papers and finalizing what Henry and Illie gave him, with titles and colors and landmark labels. The mural on the ceiling of the Ink and Rose, a massive map of the entire world with swirling sea serpents and golden krakens and frozen battles between the navy and pirates, had been painted by Elgar during the year Illie had been at sea with Henry when she was fifteen.

"I'm going to take a fifteen," Illie declared as she slid off the counter. "Oh. Argyle brought in a shipment about an hour ago. I've sorted through most of it and taken inventory, but I haven't had time to shelf it yet."

"Curse you, Illie!" shouted Elgar, who, no doubt, would be in charge of putting the shipment of parchment and ink away. Illie stuck her tongue out in his direction and skipped to the staircase leading up to her apartment.

The apartment once belonged to Henry, but after he'd taken her in when she was twelve, he gave it to her, instead going to live with his son's family. Sometimes, even after all those years, she would find herself staring at the ceiling – which had a mural to rival the one downstairs, with an indigo night sky speckled with diamond stars and the twin moons, both crescents, one waning and one waxing, on either side of the space – watching the shadows dance and distort and remember those first few days where she'd been terrified. It wasn't at all uncommon for apprentices to live with their masters, but Illie had run away from home, and for the first time in her life, she'd been completely alone.

Over the years, she'd decorated the apartment to be more *hers*. She draped vines of climbing asmyth, an almost sentient plant with spherical leaves and purple flowers that smelled *so* sweet, around the windows overlooking the Icarus Strait and had a few potted dwarf palms by the green chaise near the fireplace. Not a single mug in her kitchenette matched and every pot and pan had soot burns on their bottoms. It was a maximalist haven, with maps tacked to the walls like wallpaper, and it was all *hers*.

Well. Mostly hers.

"Mrrow?"

The tiny demon who shared the apartment with Illie rubbed her grey-and-black body against Illie's leg, sprinkling cat hair over her skirt. She had raised the little devil as a kitten ever since Henry gave it to her as a present eight years ago when Illie's loneliness spiked.

"Little devil, you." Illie scooped the tabby up and nuzzled her face against her belly. "If my curtains are shredded again, I'm going to feed you to the dogs."

The cat purred loudly.

Illie kissed her belly a few times before setting her down and spitting cat hair out. "Come on, Pleo. I don't have enough time to make tea, but I have just enough to work on that map."

Pleo continued to purr, tail swishing as she trailed after Illie into the bedroom.

Atop the desk that took up about as much space as the bed was an unfinished map of the world, held down by several old books. Illie pulled out the chair and flopped down, pulling one of the books close and opening it to the page she'd bookmarked with a spoon (since the spoon had been closer than any scraps of paper). She grabbed the wire spectacles balanced precariously on the edge of another book and slipped them over her nose to begin reading.

Rather, skimming, as she was only looking for very specific references.

There were legends that once, a thousand years ago, there had been five gods and three moons in the sky. For whatever reason, any mention of the extra god and moon had been wiped from the world. Some obscure maps and old books had references – drawings of a night sky with three moons, depictions of five gods instead of four, traces of plants and animals that simply did not exist anywhere in the world – and for the past year, it had become Illie's passion project to draw a map of the world and mark every reference to the moons, to the gods, to the long-forgotten flora and fauna on it.

She flipped the pages carefully, not wanting to rip the century-old paper. The book only cost her two stone since the owner of the used bookshop had just wanted it off his shelves, but it was old, so she had *some* care for it.

Aha! She sat up straighter, her heart fluttering through a skipped beat. In faded grey and white, there was an illustration of the Icarus Strait – she recognized that jagged shoreline and the big haystack rock peeking through the waves like a curious whale instantly – with two moons in the sky and...yes! That smudge behind a cloud *was* a third moon! A tiny sliver of a crescent, but a third moon no doubt.

The caption beneath the illustration read

Bowhead Rock, Icarus Strait, beneath the moonlight, seen from Carilon

J. Carmine

1023

Illie grabbed her pencil and made a note on her map of the year and the illustrator. Beneath it, she drew a picture of three crescent moons.

"Mrrow." Pleo rubbed herself against Illie's leg. She glanced at the clock atop one of the many cluttered shelves in her room. *Sard!* It had been almost twenty minutes!

"You were supposed to let me know when *fifteen* minutes were up!" she scolded her cat as she ripped off her spectacles and hurried for the door. "Not twenty!"

Pleo stuck her hind leg in the air and began licking the base of her tail.

Illie thundered down the stairs, bursting into the shop. A few pink hairs clung to her face, having been freed from her braid.

"I'm here!" she announced. Henry looked up from the map he'd been poring over. Elgar was nowhere to be seen – no doubt in the back organizing the shipment Illie had neglected to put away.

"I need you to make a delivery," Henry said. He reached under the counter and pulled out a tube – one of the ones used for transporting large maps. "I'd have Elgar do it, but you know how terrible he is with directions. You'd think a mapmaker would know how to get around town..."

Illie took the tube, glancing at the address label. *Mumford Scorn.* He lived on the other side of town, according to the label. The name was vaguely familiar, but Illie couldn't place it. She groaned and went to the stairs, shoving her feet into her raggedy boots. A quick peek at the window proved it was still sunny out, the summer heat devastating.

"I'll be back in an hour or so," she promised, grabbing her satchel from the bottom step, and slinging it over her shoulder. Tucking the tube under her arm, she slipped out of the Ink and Rose and into the summer sun.

"Wait!"

The cry rang out throughout the crowd, a deafening note that silenced the anticipation in one fell swoop. The blade stopped, mere hairs from Solveig's neck. If he so much as flinched the blade would bite into his flesh, right between his vertebrae. Still, he dared to glance up.

The crowd parted, creating a path for a man wearing a deep purple coat. His dark blue hair hung loose over his forehead in gentle, disgustingly perfect curls. Solveig knew that face. He'd seen it a million times, despite never in person.

Jonyth moved the sword a fraction away from Solveig's neck. "Your Highness," he said before dropping to one knee. The rest of the crowd followed suit, bowing to their prince.

"By the order of the crown I command you put a stop to this execution," demanded crown prince Anwir Helios, heir to the throne of the Aralyth Empire.

Anwir Helios was the lesser of two evils when it came to the eldest children of the emperor and empress. He was roughly Solveig's age, excellent with a sword, ex-navy, a notorious flirt, and quite possibly the most annoying person in the world, his voice grating Solveig's nerves more than Jonyth's ever could.

The prince climbed up the scaffold. Up close, the scent of vanilla and lilac smothered Solveig's senses. What kind of ex-navy sailor wore vanilla and lilac? This *was* Anwir Helios, and not his younger and more sadistic sister Iori Helios, right?

"Nox Solveig –" he said his name as *Sol-vig,* not *Sol-vay.* It didn't bother Solveig, though. It was his mother's name that was being tarnished, and he hated that wench. "Do you want to die today?"

Solveig didn't answer.

Anwir clenched his jaw. "Because if you don't, I'm going to offer you a deal. I'll ask you again; I presume you don't want to die?"

"I am quite fond of having my head attached to my shoulders, yes," Solveig sputtered.

The prince sighed heavily. "Of course. Right. Then, in exchange for your life, are you interested in working for me?"

"For the empire? I *would* rather die."

"For *me,* you moronic cad," the prince hissed. "Though, if you can find what I want, I will *ensure* you get the royal pardon."

The royal pardon. The shiny stamp that turned pirates into privateers, that made it legal for ruffians to do whatever they wanted with protection from the most influential – the most *powerful* – empire in the world. With the royal pardon... Solveig could get a ship. A crew. He could sail the world without worrying about the navy cutting him down.

It was far too good to be true.

Especially with how hushed Anwir was speaking, so only Solveig and Jonyth could hear.

Well, if he wasn't going to die here, what was the worst that could happen if he heard Anwir out?

"I've rented an inn just down the road from here. Admiral Commodore, I trust you can transport this...pirate...and rendezvous with me there in half an hour?"

Jonyth's face pinched like he'd just bitten into a lekim – a fruit more sour than unripe limes. As fleet admiral of the Aralythian navy, he was the *fourth* most powerful person in the empire, with just a bit more power than Princess Iori. To defy Anwir now would be to defy the prince, the empress, the entire realm.

How would his patron goddess, Lady Lightbringer, react?

Part of Solveig wanted to find out.

"Fine," Jonyth ground out. "Scaffold Inn? We'll be there." Then, to Solveig, he said, "If you so much as *blink* in a way I deem threatening, I will kill you with or without his highness's blessing. Understand?"

Solveig blinked as hard as he could. Jonyth scowled so viciously his blister popped, fresh blood oozing from the wound and slipping down his cheek.

"A shame," Solveig drawled, "that you weren't just a *second* faster to chop off my head. Care to remove my shackles, Commodore?"

"Don't even think about it, pirate," Jonyth snapped, and he grabbed Solveig's chains, yanking him to his feet and leading him down the platform.

Scaffold Inn was a rather grim place – two stories with rotting siding and gutters stuffed full of old seagull nests. The woman at the counter – at least, Solveig *assumed* it was a woman, but he couldn't be sure – grunted in their direction when Solveig and Jonyth entered. Wanted posters took up an entire wall; some of them crossed out. Solveig looked for his own – there! Right near the top, not crossed out yet. The picture was a few years old. His red hair was shorter, and he didn't have the thin scar through his brow, disappearing into his hairline. His green eyes were bright, his grin crooked, and his signature coat draped over his shoulders.

He quickly looked for another poster, one of a very old friend. His heart skipped a beat when he saw it still standing, not crossed out, even older than Solveig's. *Good.* He was still alive.

Anwir Helios stood by the roaring fire, a cup of tea in his hands. He sipped it politely. "Admiral Commodore. *Pirate.* Please. Have a seat. Miss Hazy will be leaving us shortly."

Miss Hazy, the woman behind the counter, grunted again before waddling to the back, leaving the three alone.

"Wait, when you said you rented the inn, you meant the *entire sarding inn?!*" Solveig choked in disbelief. He knew the royal family was loaded, but this...

He collapsed onto one of the *very* stiff chairs, grateful it wasn't the unfinished floor in Ivenis Justyce. He jangled his shackles dramatically, as if that would get either of his enemies to take them off.

Jonyth Commodore might have been an idiot for picking count-less fights with Solveig, but he wasn't stupid enough to set him loose. The admiral stayed standing, spine pin straight and chest puffed out ever so slightly.

"I have heard rumors that you are the second-best pirate in all four seas," Prince Anwir began. He sipped his tea. Solveig scowled. *Second-best.* He *should* have been *the* best, but the bloody Un-named God held that title. Anwir ignored him and continued, "You're good at sinking ships and causing problems. Tell me, pi-rate, are you any good at *finding* things?"

Solveig spread his legs, leaning back in the chair. "What, like, treasure? Like the Selfosa treasure I found a few years ago? Or the cache hidden by the infamous Roberts? The Ruby of Astoria?" Solveig and his crew had found all those treasures – gold and riches amounting to *billions* of lune. He'd given most of it to his crew, hiding the rest in various caches around the world or using it for repairs and supplies. The only one he hadn't sold was the Ruby of Astoria, a massive chunk of rock the size of his fist. He'd brought that one home, burying it in the empty grave belonging to his older brother, whose eyes had been the same color.

He'd found gems matching the eyes of each of his brothers, burying them all in their graves. If he'd cared about his mother, he would've put the hunk of emerald he'd dug up once in her grave, but he'd had it made into a ring – a ring that a certain admiral had *confiscated* when he'd been arrested.

When Solveig didn't say anything, Anwir set his teacup down and rubbed his face. One of his perfect indigo curls fell over his forehead. "Admiral Commodore, could you please step outside for a moment? I'd like to speak with the pirate in peace."

Jonyth bristled. "Your Highness, I'm not sure that's a good idea. Do you –"

"I'm going to pretend you didn't just tell me no, Jonyth, and tell you again to step outside."

As much as Solveig loathed Anwir Helios, he had to give the prince credit where it was due for talking down to Jonyth.

Jonyth's jaw feathered, but he nodded, marching out of the inn like a good little soldier.

Anwir sat down on the chair opposite Solveig. He steepled his fingers. "There is something I want you to find for me, pirate. If you can find it and bring it back to me, I will ensure you get the royal pardon. You'll be above the law. You can do whatever you want, as long as you don't harm the royal family of Aralyth, and you can live your life doing whatever it is you pirates do. Your name will be cleared. Your bounty will go away. You'll be paid a hefty sum."

There had to be a catch. Best as he could with his wrists still bound, Solveig crossed his arms over his chest. "And if I *don't* find this little treasure of yours?"

"Then you'll be right back up on the scaffold and your head will no longer be attached to your shoulders," Anwir said plainly.

"I don't have a ship," he said. "Jonyth sank mine. I don't have a crew, either."

Jonyth had killed them. Drugged them with sinth and let them sink with the *Silver Moon.* His chest tightened at the thought.

"Then collect a crew and get a ship. How much is your bounty? Five hundred million lune? I'll pay it now; use it to get a ship and supplies and whatever else you need."

Five hundred – Poet's bones, was the prince serious?! Solveig sat up straight. Who even *carried* that much money on them?! Solveig gnawed on his cheek. His throat had gone dry, tight with anticipation.

Anwir dropped his hands to his lap. "Of course, the royal pardon will extend to you and you, alone. Whatever crew you manage to scrape together won't be privy to that."

He sank into his chair again. Still... *He* would get pardoned. He would get five hundred million lune to buy a ship. He could sail the world again. *I will pledge my final breath to your name and my first to find you again.*

"What's the catch?" Solveig asked, teetering on the fine line between shaking Anwir's hand and accepting the gig right there and calling Jonyth back to finish up the execution. "What is it you want me to find? You're a prince. You have the entire navy at your beck and call. What is it you want that they can't find – that you have to *grovel* and ask *me* for help?"

Pink colored Anwir's cheeks. He squirmed uncomfortably before standing up and closing the distance in a few sure strides. He grabbed Solveig's jaw, gripping it hard as he yanked the pirate's head up.

"Are you a religious man, pirate?" Anwir asked.

"As religious as a man living in Poet's realm can be."

Anwir studied Solveig's face for a moment. The royal family of Aralyth had black eyes. It was a hereditary trait that trumped any other gene. Anwir and his sister Iori both had their father's black eyes, but Solveig had heard the youngest Helios child – Princess Faye, who wasn't even a year old yet – had inherited her mother's pale blue eyes.

"Lady Lightbringer, the Wanderer, Poet and Dreamer." Anwir let go of Solveig's jaw. "There are rumors that there was a *fifth* god at one time. The god of the moon – the third moon that legends say once existed."

Anwir leaned close, his perfect lips brushing against the dirty shell of Solveig's ear. "I want you to find the body of the dead god for me."

5

SUMMER WAS *SUPPOSED* TO be when Thol's garden flourished, but as he looked at the sad melon and tomato plants, his watering can hanging sadly from one hand, he had no choice but to accept defeat. Perhaps there was simply too much blood on his hands, his sins making the soil too basic to grow anything worthwhile. He nudged one of the melons – it was hardly bigger than his fist, looking more like a pathetic lime than anything else – with his foot. If not for the lush melons and tomatoes being sold at the market in town a mile or so from his house, Thol would have resigned to thinking it was just too early in the season.

No. He just had terrible luck with gardening.

He sat down with a grunt, abandoning the watering can in favor of scraping his long, coiled hair back, tying it at the nape of his neck to keep it off his face.

A spider scurried across its orb-like web when Thol got too close to where it stretched between tomato vines. Across his shoulder, wrapping from front to back, he had a tattoo of a web like the one on his tomatoes. There had been a time in his life where spiders made him *uneasy* (not scared, since he *refused* to be afraid of a little beast the size of his finger), but she had fixed that.

She also kept her garden alive, and Thol was tarnishing her name once again by all but killing the plants she'd loved. It was his first summer without her and he was struggling. As stubborn as he was, he would not let her garden die, not after only a year.

Thol stood and brushed dirt off his loose trousers. The spider peeked out from where it had hidden beneath a leaf, as if glad the massive man was leaving. The summer air was too warm for a jacket, but Thol grabbed one as he passed through his house regardless, if only to hide the murals of ink on his arms and neck. Of course, there was little he could do about the skull tattoos on his palms, or the letters stretching across his knuckles spelling out *PUNISHMENT.* At least the thorny vine inked around his left ring finger, since he wore his wedding band on a chain around his neck, looked somewhat normal.

Shoving his hands into his pockets, Thol began the walk to town. Midmorning was when the market was at its busiest, the streets crowded with townsfolk haggling for better prices while children ran amok, chasing stray cats with candy-sticky fingers. Thol watched a little girl with blonde braids stomp by and his heart squeezed painfully.

After living the retired life for nearly two years, Thol would have hoped the whispers would've stopped. But even with his tattoos covered, he still stuck out in any crowd – and not just because he was well over six feet tall, creeping closer to the seven-foot mark, or because he was built like a bear, or because he dressed like a farmer when he very clearly *wasn't* one.

Thol had once been a pirate, and it would take more than marriage to a civilian and two years of retirement to scrub his infamy from the minds of the townsfolk.

He kept his head low, ignoring the judgmental whispers as he headed to the botanist's.

The air inside the botany shop was a few degrees cooler, thanks to the dark curtains over the front windows. A bell chimed as he pushed the door open, drawing the attention of the clerk behind the counter. The girl wasn't the botanist – an apprentice, maybe – but with her wild mossy curls and thick spectacles, she sure looked the part.

"Good morning. How may I help –" she cut herself off suddenly when she took Thol in. Her face paled a few shades, and she took a nervous step back. "H-How may I help you, sir?" her voice became a stammer, nerves taking over.

Thol knew it was better to simply *not* smile, as the wicked grin he usually wore tended to scare people rather than placate them. Instead, he removed his hands from his pockets, showing he meant no harm, even if his tattoos screamed otherwise.

"I'm trying to keep a garden alive," he said, speaking slowly to not scare the poor, frazzled girl. "But it's...sad. My tomatoes are wilting, my melons are the size of pebbles, my cucumbers...well, they say size doesn't matter, but these won't get *any* job done."

Ignoring his phallic joke, the girl seemed to relax a bit. She grabbed a notebook and a pencil and scribbled something down, presumably Thol's predicament. "What else are you growing? Can you tell me about the soil? Your watering routine? How much sunlight it gets?"

For a brief second, Thol saw his wife in the girl. She used to light up when talking about her plants, shining brighter than the sun.

"Melons, tomatoes, cucumbers, beans and peppers, eggplant, korva, and some herbs...lavender, mint, thyme, I think. It's behind my house, but it gets decent sunlight. I water once a day, except that korva plant. I water that twice. The soil is..." he faltered. "Soil? I don't know. It looks like dirt to me."

The girl scribbled down a slew of notes. She pushed her spectacles up with her knuckle. "Is the korva in the same bed as everything else?"

Korva – a tuber that was like a potato mixed with a carrot, dark brown on the outside but a bright red on the inside – was a staple food for most sailors, since it didn't expire and could self-duplicate. His wife had always kept the plant tame, but since she was... Well, Thol could hardly corral it into one spot.

His expression must have said that, because the girl said, "That's probably your problem. The korva is leeching all the nutrients from the other plants, making it impossible for them to grow. If I were you, I'd try to relocate it. If that doesn't change anything, I'd add some calcium and bonemeal to the soil."

Thol's shoulders sagged with relief. "Thank you," he said, and he reached for his pocket. The girl flinched, so he moved quickly, pulling out a pouch. He opened it and produced a few lune bills and stone coins.

"Oh, no, I can't accept that," the girl said quickly.

"Because it's dirty money?" It wasn't, but convincing people to believe the truth was often harder than not.

"Because I didn't sell you anything. I just gave you some advice."

Thol set the money on the counter regardless. "I'll come back to let you know if it worked."

The girl stared at the tattoos across his knuckles, silent as he left the shop.

Illie took her time strolling through town. When she first began her apprenticeship with Henry, he'd taken her out, having her chart every street, every landmark, every address she found. Her first real map – not one of the ones drawn on the backs of napkins or on the walls of her childhood home – looked more like a handful of scribbles and poorly-spelled words than anything identifiable, but now, years later, she knew the city better than the back of her hand. She'd drawn no less than a dozen maps of Carilon since that first, terrible attempt. Ever since Veridin was all but successfully claimed by the Aralyth Empire, with Veridin's heir, Prince Elios Smythe, engaged to the wretched Princess Iori Helios, more and more people from Aralyth's reaches started visiting. And tourists, no matter how savvy they claimed to be with directions, *always* got lost, and *always* ended up in the Ink and Rose, desperate for a map and directions.

If Henry and Elgar were out, Illie would upcharge the tourists for a map that cost a handful of lune. Because tourists were gullible and Illie liked to buy only the nicest mapmaking tools.

The salty breeze knocked her pink braid off her shoulder, sending it to lay against her spine. She breathed in deeply, savoring the familiar scent of brine. Born and raised in Carilon, Illie had always felt the call to the sea. It didn't agree with her the first time she stepped foot on a boat – it took ages for Henry to stop teasing her about how she'd turned as green as the Emerald – but now she could sail on any boat and her stomach would stay settled.

She looked at the address on the tube again. Thirteen Ivy Alley. Despite Carilon's generous size, Illie knew all the shortcuts. Plus, Ivy Alley wasn't too far from where the Ink and Rose sat on Grommet Way. She'd be there in no time, even if she took a little detour...

Grinning to herself, Illie hastened her pace, squeezing past passersby to maze through narrow streets, the smell of the ocean getting stronger and stronger until she stepped off the cobblestone road and into the soft, sun-warmed sand. She closed her eyes, breathing in deeply, feeling the sun on her face, tasting the salt on her tongue. Birds squawked, flying over the massive Bowhead Rock, named after the whale it resembled when breaching. Tiny specks of ships dotted the horizon.

When she opened her eyes again, blinking a few times to adjust to the sun, she began walking, treading the length of sand just out of reach of the waves, following the beach towards Ivy Alley.

Thirteen Ivy Alley was a sliver of a house stuffed into a literal alley smothered in its namesake vine. Illie pushed a few stray vines away, ducking under the ones creeping down the awning to get to the door. She knocked twice, then took a step back to wait. Mumford Scorn didn't come to the door right away. She rocked on her heels, already bored of waiting. There was a newspaper on the doorstep. Henry got the paper, but Illie never read it. It made her stomach sour reading about Emperor Castros Helios's conquers.

But the headline of the folded paper on the doorstep of thirteen Ivy Alley caught Illie's attention. She bent down and picked it up, skimming over the words.

THE END OF AN ERA: NOX SOLVEIG TO BE EXECUTED TODAY.

Nox Solveig... As in the children's rhyme? Illie could name five pirates if she really tried. Still... From what she knew, Nox Solveig was the Aralythian navy's second most wanted. If he was to be executed, that could cause a chain of events worse than anything Solveig did during his reign.

The door swung open and an old man with an eye patch and a pipe hanging from his mouth glared at Illie. At once, she knew why the name seemed so familiar. Not because of Mumford Scorn himself, but Mumford Scorn *Junior,* his son and the lighthouse keeper who lived on Bowhead Rock. She'd met the man a few times and he always talked about how his father had the weathered look of a pirate despite not ever stepping foot on a ship.

"I have a delivery from Ink and Rose," she said, holding out the tube containing the map. As an afterthought, she held out the newspaper, too. "And your paper, I suppose."

His hardened gaze softened a fraction as he snatched both up. "Ah... My boy will appreciate this," he said around his pipe. "They feedin' you well at the shop?"

Illie blinked. "Pardon? It's a...it's a cartographer's shop. They don't *feed* me there." She hugged her waist, self-conscious of her willowy frame all of a sudden.

"Eh?" Mr. Scorn flipped through the paper, seemingly moved on from the topic. "Ah, they finally caught that scoundrel. I knew a Solveig once. Pretty woman. She was probably your age."

Illie just nodded, since she didn't know how to respond to an old man's rambling. "Well." She took a step back. "I ought to get back to the shop. Pleasure doing business with you, Mr. Scorn."

Mumford Scorn just went back inside, too engrossed in the paper to respond. Illie counted her blessings and hurried out of the alley.

With some time to spare and a few lune in her pockets, Illie decided to make a detour before returning to the Ink and Rose. Henry and Elgar could survive on their own for a bit longer, and Illie rarely got the free time to shop in the city. And she knew *just* where to go.

Carilon was big enough to have multiple bookshops, but the one Illie favored was the secondhand bookstore that was so hard to find only those who knew where exactly to look could stumble upon it. The cozy place was where she got all her old books she used for references on the third moon. With any luck, a new shipment would have come in since she'd last visited.

Scribe Books was located beneath a pub in a tiny space that was probably used as cellar storage at one point in time. She hurried down the uneven stairs and shouldered open the red door, the bell above jingling to announce her presence. Behind the counter was James, the man set to take over the shop when its current owner retired (or perished, since he was older than dirt). He looked up and grinned when he saw Illie.

"Fancy seeing you here!" he said. "You're just in time. I got a few books you might like."

Illie had never told anyone *what* she used the old books for – only that she liked books with old maps and with some religious subtext. James bent down, coming back up with a stack of books.

"For me?" she asked, grabbing the top one off the stack. She flipped through it absently. While she didn't outright see any references to the third moon, it seemed promising enough. "How much for them all?"

"Mm..." James drummed his fingers against the table. "Does ten lune for them all sound fair?"

Ten lune sounded like a steal. If James had been anyone else, she would've haggled, but she produced the crumpled bills and grabbed the books eagerly.

"Save me some good ones next time you get them," she called over her shoulder, pleased she didn't have to spend ages digging through the shelves of dusty books to find anything.

"You know I will." James winked.

Illie hugged her books to her chest, smiling to herself as she left the shop.

"I'm sorry, *what?*" Solveig asked.

"Unless you suddenly became deaf in the past thirty seconds, pirate, I'm almost positive you heard me," Anwir shot back. He scoffed, returning to his seat.

Solveig shook his head. He'd heard the prince all right, but... "The body of a dead god?" he snorted. "Maybe *you* took the sinth dosage I was supposed to get because you're making no sense. Gods don't die. That's what makes them *gods*. And even *if* one supposedly did die, how am I supposed to find its body? I don't suppose you have a convenient map laying around somewhere."

Anwir reached into the inner pocket of his purple velvet jacket and pulled out a rolled up scroll so ancient it looked one sudden movement away from crumbling to dust.

"Poet's bones, you *do* have a map," Solveig breathed.

Anwir didn't hand the map over. "Don't get your hopes up, pirate. If the map was any good, I would find it myself."

Solveig didn't let the words get to him. "So? Have the navy find it."

"Do you *want* to go back to the scaffold?" Anwir cocked a bale brow. "I can't have the navy go because the navy can't get involved. I... *liberated* the map from my father's private library. If you get caught with it, I will deny any responsibility. The navy will not cease to hunt you down, even though I will have paid your bounty. *You* alone will get the royal pardon *if* you can find this for me. Not your crew. Just you. Anything said in here *must* remain between you and me."

Had Solveig's old crew still been alive he would have refused the deal outright. If they didn't get their names cleared, it wouldn't be fair if *just* Solveig got to walk away. But... He *had* no crew. And he didn't plan on getting emotionally attached to whatever new one he scraped together. It was an unfortunate situation he could make amends with.

"Let me see the map," Solveig said.

Anwir held it closer. "You can *borrow* the map *if* you agree to my terms. I need this found by Zylfmoon."

Solveig silently counted the months in his head. "Half a year? There's no way. Let me see the sarding map so I can know how hard this will be."

Reluctantly, Anwir's shoulders drooped. "Fine," he said tightly. "Until Nakmoon." Eleven months. It was better than six, but... If he was going to gather a crew, get a ship, *and* sail around the world searching for a *body,* he wanted more legroom than what the prince offered.

Beggars, he knew better than most, couldn't afford to be choosers.

"Undo my shackles –" Solveig held out his manacled wrists, the chains clanking together "– and I'll do it. I want the map now, though. And the five hundred mil."

Anwir clenched his jaw. "People don't usually carry five hundred million lune on their person." He reached into his other pocket and procured a simple iron key. Solveig didn't bite back the smug smirk as Anwir, begrudgingly, slipped the key into the manacles and let them fall free.

In a heartbeat, Solveig was on his feet, towering over Anwir in a way that could make even royalty cower.

"There's a bank in town." Solveig plucked the map from the blanched prince. "I'll *patiently* wait here while you go fetch my lune."

Anwir's throat bobbed as he swallowed, forced to simply nod in agreement.

"One more thing." Solveig pocketed the map. He'd look at it later, once he had his money and he knew he'd be in the clear. "There's someone I want for my crew, but they're locked away in Ivenis Justyce."

Anwir narrowed his black eyes. "Whom?"

"Vesperine Genevieve."

"Ves – *her?!*" the prince sputtered. "You can't be serious. The Witch of the Sea?!"

"You're asking me to find something rather impossible." Solveig shrugged. "It seems only fair that I get the *Witch of the Sea* to help me. I'm *sure* Lakatos would be *ecstatic* to have her gone."

"And Admiral Commodore will skin me alive if he figures out *I* authorized her release..." Anwir grumbled to himself. He stood and scrubbed a hand through his hair. "Fine. If you're offering to babysit Genevieve, I'll authorize her *temporary* release. Stay here, pirate. I'll be back with your money."

Solveig sat down and crossed his ankle over his knee. "I look forward to it, princeling."

"Un*hand me!*" Ves screamed.

She was used to jailers coming to her cell, but not once, in all four years over her imprisonment at I. J. Pen did the jailers *grab* her. She writhed, kicking, and struggling. Had it been two or three men – and had she been less malnourished – she would have been able to fight them off with ease. But it took five men to hold her, to drag her out of the cell.

Sard! Did they decide *now* was the perfect time to finally stop putting her inevitable execution off?!

Lakatos Justyce, that filthy old man, stood at the top of the stairs when the jailers finally managed to drag Ves up, after half an hour of struggle. He somehow managed to look more irritated than Ves, and he hadn't just spent thirty minutes wrestling a bunch of juveniles.

"If one more thing goes wrong today," Lakatos lamented, "I'm going to step down from my position. It's your lucky day, Witch."

Ves narrowed her eyes, not trusting a single thing that came from Lakatos.

The warden sighed through his nose. "Your sentence is up."

She scoffed. "What, that's it? You're sending me to the gallows now? I curse you, Justyce! My ghost will return and haunt you for the rest of your miserable life!"

"You're free," Lakatos said.

What.

Ves recoiled, blinking in surprise.

"Prince Anwir signed the papers." Lakatos ground his teeth together, clearly upset that he was losing one of his most valuable prisoners. "You're free to go. Under one condition. Someone bought you."

What what what.

Slavery wasn't unheard of, but it was *supposedly* outlawed in Aralyth. But that only included the mainland. Someone from one of the annexed islands could have easily paid to have Ves as their slave. Her stomach soured. Death was preferable to *slavery.*

The second she got out of this place, she promised herself, she would take a sword to the gut to keep from being a slave.

"You *do* know how much I'm worth, right? Three hundred –" Ves started, but Lakatos cut her off with an exasperated shake of his head.

"Only your head is worth that much, and I don't think that's what you were bought for," the warden grumbled.

Ves's stomach sank deeper than the furthest depths of the Sapphire Sea.

"Give her some sinth," Lakatos instructed. A man wearing a navy uniform stepped up to Ves, pulling out a syringe

Ves screamed, kicking and lashing as she tried to fight off the navy sailor, but the prick of a needle sliding into her neck cut her off. She had just enough time to hurl a few more insults at Lakatos before her world went dark.

When Ves opened her heavy, bloodshot eyes, the world a blur of sensations and stimuli, she saw the green jacket first. Then, she took in the man that wore it – tall, muscular beneath ill-fitting prisoner clothes, stubble on a sword-sharp jaw, reddish hair that hung over green eyes.

Ves grinned a lopsided, still-riding-on-the-last-dregs-of-a-high grin. "You know, I thought you'd be taller," she said to the captain she'd only seen the blobby outline of.

Nox Solveig held out a hand. "I *could* be a whole head shorter, though. I have recently found myself in possession of a bit of freedom and a lot of money. I think I could use a bo'sun."

Ves took his hand and stood. "Well, Cap. Looks like you've got the *finest* bo'sun in the four seas."

6

"I SWEAR, IF *ONE* person even *insinuates* coarse salt can be substituted for fine salt, I will *lose my sarding mind.*"

Nathalia Divyne slammed her hands against the slim counter space between two hot stovetops, sending a bowl of mixed herbs toppling over. She barely managed to grab it before she lost the entire mix but didn't try to stop the eggs that rolled off now that the bowl, they were leaning against was moved. They splattered against the ground, one after the other, eggshells and yolk dangerously close to her polished shoes.

"Um... Miss Divyne...?" a quiet voice came from Natha's side.

"*What?*" she whirled on the poor cook, nearly slipping on the broken eggs.

The young cook recoiled. "I...um...I can take those from you. The spices. Jarod wanted me to tell you he found some salt – *good* salt – in the back."

Natha nearly sobbed in relief. She thrust the bowl into the cook's hands and stomped off, trailing egg yolk behind her as she went to track down that insufferable Jarod.

She found him in the breakroom, a pipe hanging from his mouth. She crossed her arms over her chest and tapped her foot impatiently.

"I swear to every god that there is, if this salt is *coarse* – " Natha started, but Jarod, a chef of some prestige but nowhere near Natha's level, held up a jar full of white grains. It could have been sugar, which would be *rather* unfortunate for the stuffed squid it was needed for, but Natha knew better.

She snatched up the jar. "Put that disgusting thing out," she snapped. "No smoking anywhere near my kitchen."

"Yes, ma'am," Jarod grumbled. Natha didn't linger to see if he'd followed her orders, instead going back to the kitchen.

While Natha didn't own the restaurant, she was the head chef, and she had worked herself to the bone to get there. As much as she loved cooking and creating her own recipes, she was stuck with a staff so incompetent it was a bloody miracle she hadn't suffered an aneurism. Yet. The slate board in the breakroom cheekily reading *DAYS SINCE THE LAST INCIDENT* had to be divided into three columns: burns, cuts, and near-death experiences, all but the latter having big, fat zeroes under them.

(It had been three days since the last near-death experience. Someone had learned *very* quickly why running with a knife between two chefs cooking with hot oil was a quick way to see the gods.)

She considered adding a fourth column – *DAYS SINCE NATHA LAST CONSIDERED FRYING ALL HER COOKS.*

There would also be a zero because she wanted to dunk the head of the nearest unfortunate soul into the bubbling vat of broth *someone* neglected to stir.

Natha bit the inside of her cheek and grabbed a spoon, shoving through the crowd to get to the pot before it boiled over. She turned the heat down, stirring with precise flicks of her wrist to dredge up the garlic and onions from the bottom. The rhythmic motion calmed her, bringing her to a lull of peace. Absently, she grabbed a jar of paprika and sprinkled three shakes into the broth.

The main course for that evening's dinner would be fried squid tentacles stuffed with herbs, served with roast vegetables and a savory vinegar-based sauce. Soup always came before dinner, no matter what, so the light broth paired with warm bread would be first. Even though it was *hours* before dinner, Natha couldn't help but think about the chocolate and cream pastries, drizzled with honey and sugar, that she would make for dessert.

When the broth reached a steady simmer, she covered the pot and put the spoon in the sink. The dishwasher, a young lad, hurried over and got to work cleaning.

Wiping her hands on her apron, Natha slipped out of the kitchen, going through the back door to the outside of the restaurant. Overcast clouds hung low in the sky, pregnant with rain that would fall at any given moment. Even in summer the weather was unpredictable, especially this close to the coast. If she blocked out the scent of oil and spices clinging to her apron, Natha could smell the sea in the distance.

She sighed and pulled off her apron, rolling it up in her arms. She popped her head back in and tossed her apron to the nearest person. "I'm going shopping!" she announced. "Do *not* add anything to the soup. Absolutely nothing. Keep it covered. I'll be back in a few hours."

There was a chorus of *Yes ma'am*. Natha couldn't help but smile to herself. At least those heathens of hers could act like they knew who was boss. She shook out her messy bun, the blonde waves falling over her shoulders for a moment before she scraped them back up, pulling them off her face as she began walking to the harbor.

Natha knew she should have gone to the market earlier because now she had to squeeze through a crowd so thick it gave her a migraine. Located on the pier stretching over the harbor, the market was a mix of smushed stalls and permanent buildings where anyone could sell their wares. Anything from clothing to wines costing thousands of lune could be found there. There were a handful of shops Natha frequented – she was grateful she never had to go to the fishmonger's stall, since he always brought her the best catch every morning – but the one she needed now was the spice and tea shop. Normally, she could have made it there in less than a minute, but after squeezing through the crowd and mazing her way there, by the time she pushed open the door and breathed in the aroma of spice, it had been nearly ten.

"Natha!" the shopkeeper, an older woman with grey coils and a figure like a ball, beamed. "Haven't seen you in a while, hon. What can I get ya?"

Natha pinched the bridge of her nose, trying to alleviate the tension building behind her eyes. "I have a list," she murmured, fishing out the scrap of paper from her pocket. She placed it on the counter.

"You want a cuppa?" the woman, Shar, asked as she picked up the paper.

"No," grumbled Natha. "Unless it's a cuppa of your strongest booze. I don't smoke, but I'm tempted to start."

Shar pulled down a jar of salt from the shelf behind the counter and measured out enough to fill a sack. She tied it off and got to work with the next spice – cayenne, which Natha could never get enough of. "Smokin' will kill you, hon. What you need is a massage, a thing of chocolates, and a good night's sleep."

Natha leaned against the counter, propping her elbows up and holding her chin in her hands. "What I *need* is a competent staff, better wages, someone to sard, and...well, I can't deny those other things, too."

She didn't need a mirror to know the dark circles under her eyes were blacker than night. It had been months since she'd actually slept through the night. Usually, she had to add a splash of cinnamon rum to a cup of hot lavender milk just so she could sleep long enough to dream, and even that was rare. Her blood sang to be elsewhere, far away from this place. She loved her job, but... She hated the people she worked with. She hated their incompetence, their inability to follow her recipes. To use the *right* salt because *she* knew the difference.

"Not gonna sugarcoat it, hon. You look like hot garbage." Shar filled another sack with lemongrass.

"Yeah, well, divorce does that to a woman," Natha sighed.

It was no secret Natha had gotten divorced only a few months ago. Her ex-husband had been in a higher social circle – Natha's first mistake – and gossip traveled faster than the Alkenio Plague amongst the elite.

Shar offered her a look of sympathy that did nothing to calm Natha.

"You hear the news?" Shar asked, changing the subject from Natha's messy divorce. "They were going to execute that one pirate this morning, but it got interrupted. Now he and that Witch of the Sea are both free."

Natha frowned. "The Witch of the Sea?" she'd been a girl when the infamous Ruby Pirates terrorized the seas. She'd never met them, but she saw their ship once, in the distance. The Witch of the Sea had vanished four years ago.

"Mmhmm," Shar drawled. "Her bail got paid. Apparently, they were keepin' her in the Ivenis Justyce Penitentiary. She'd better not come here and stir up unnecessary trouble."

Pirates were the absolute last thing Natha needed to deal with right now. If her staff found out about it, there would be no calming them down. Her head ached at the thought of having to wrangle a dozen chefs while maintaining *some* order in her kitchen.

"You know that poppyseed tea?" Natha asked. "Add some of that to my personal tab. Please."

"Nu uh, hon. That's on the house. You need it more than I need your stone." Shar grabbed the jar of poppyseed tea – a sweet blend that helped with minor pain and sleep problems – and filled a pouch. "That all?"

"Yes. Thank you, Shar. I'll think about the massage and chocolates, but I don't have a day off for a while." Natha grabbed the bag with all her goods.

"You could always quit."

"I love cooking too much to do that."

Natha hoisted the bag onto her hip and left the shop. Her head throbbed the entire way back to the restaurant.

"Well, Cap, what's the plan?" Ves crossed her arms, sizing Solveig up. She was nearly half a foot taller than him, so she didn't need to try very hard. There was an island to the east – Amazonia -- inhabited by warrior women who were bigger and stronger than most men. Solveig had a hunch Ves had some of that blood in her veins.

"Jonyth is required to give us an hour head start before he unleashes the navy on us," Solveig said. Technically, they only had fifty minutes left since it had taken Ves ten to devour everything in the inn's kitchen and regain the strength the sinth leeched from her.

The deal Solveig had with Anwir extended *only* to Anwir. Jonyth could still pursue the pirates. He could still capture and execute them. He almost had *more* of an incentive to catch them now. Solveig couldn't reveal anything about his agreement, not even with Ves or anyone else he might have join his crew. But...he did have a fat sack of money (the bank had *not* been happy when Anwir asked for five hundred million lune in cash) and a bo'sun. All he needed now was a ship. And a map.

"I have someone else I want on my crew," Solveig continued. "We need to find a ship. I'd rather not spend any lune right now. You know how to steal a boat?"

"Do I know how to steal a boat." Ves burst out laughing. Lucky her – the sinth didn't have lasting effects as it did with Solveig. "Of course. Who's this mysterious person you want to join?"

Solveig didn't answer right away, too busy thinking about where his old friend might be. He'd ripped the wanted poster off the inn's wall, shoving it into his pocket with the ancient map.

"An old friend," he finally said. "I have a treasure cache that I want to get, too. It should have some supplies to last us until we find a sanctuary city."

Sanctuary cities were aplenty, even under the strict rule of the Aralyth Empire. The Wanderer, god of debauchery and sin, was worshipped in the cities run by pirates. Booze was cheap and abundant, brothels were just as frequent as taverns, and there was a strict *no navy* law enforced in every sanctuary city in the world. It would be a good place to form a better plan, to find a crew, to hash out the details of the mysterious dead god.

Ves turned her head towards the sky, a smile gracing her full lips. "I never thought I'd feel the sun on my skin again," she breathed.

"Wait until next month. Ulamoon heat is the worst." At least, the areas bisected by the midline suffered the worst Ulamoon heat. Being from north of the Midline, Solveig never developed a fondness for the heat.

"You say that now, but you've never gone swimming in the Ruby in Ulamoon," Ves practically purred. She rubbed her arms, her flimsy Ivenis Justyce clothing doing little to protect her from the sun's rays. "So. Where are we going to find this friend of yours?"

Solveig had been dreading the question because he simply did not know. He'd lost track of his friend three years ago when their old captain died. His friend had taken over and Solveig left to start his own crew.

Thinking about his crew made his stomach sink like a rock.

"I think he returned up north, on the other side of the Icarus River." It was a hunch backed by nothing but a feeling that his friend would have returned to the area they'd grown up in. Then again, Solveig hadn't returned to that area since he'd buried the last gemstone at his brothers' graves. He wouldn't ever return there, not even when *he* died. Two of those graves were empty, and someone would erect a third empty one when Solveig finally went to the green.

Ves groaned loudly, drawing a few wary looks from passersby. Jonyth Commodore, reluctantly, announced to the town that they were not to touch the two pirates for a full hour. The townsfolk, scared as they were, seemed to have a morbid fascination with the two, watching from behind closed curtains and as they swept the same area on their porch over and over again.

The marina soon came into view. The *Mary Jolene* was moored there, beside a few other naval ships. Solveig hoped Ves wouldn't be foolish enough to steal one of those. They needed something small and fast – a sloop, maybe, or a schooner. A brigantine if they were lucky, but those would be harder to man with just two people.

Ves stopped at the dock, hands on her full hips as she scanned the marina. While she was busy ogling the ships, Solveig took the chance to study her. For two weeks, she'd just been a voice in the darkness. Now she was here, physical, corporeal – tall and curvy with biceps as big as Solveig's and thighs *bigger* than his torso. Her unruly curls were held back by a single scrap of fabric torn from her shirt. She was *powerful*. Solveig silently thanked Poet she was on his side because she would be a formidable enemy.

He did *not* want to know what it felt like to have his skull crushed by those thighs.

"That one."

Ves's voice pulled Solveig from his thoughts. He followed where she pointed – a sloop rocking gently in the waves.

"You sure?" Solveig narrowed his eyes to get a better look. The deck seemed empty, with a few barrels and cannons. "I know we have an hour of immunity, but I doubt Jonyth would be pleased if we tossed the crew overboard."

"It's empty," Ves said confidently.

"How do you know?" Solveig hurried after her as she began walking down the dock to where the sloop was moored.

"I just do."

The sloop – named the *Dargason* – was a slim beauty, recently made based on the still-fresh polish on the railings. For a ship named after a mythical sea beast, Solveig assumed it *had* to be lethal and wickedly fast.

"Well!" Ves grinned at the *Dargason*, like a proud mother. "Orders, Cap? A bo'sun and a captain hardly make for a good crew, but you're *Nox Solveig*, and I'm the Witch of the Sea. I think we can make do."

Solveig crouched to undo the mooring line. "Get this ship ready to sail. See if you can find a map. Take inventory."

"Aye, Cap."

Ves gave a lazy salute and hopped up the gangplank with surprising energy for someone who just spent four years in prison. She made quick work of ensuring everything was secure before lowering the mainmast sails. Solveig kicked the mooring lines off the dock and climbed onto the ship. Ves shoved her weight against the windlass, cursing at its initial stick before the anchor started to raise.

Solveig grabbed the pegs of the wheel, testing their firmness absently. As captain, he knew how to do every job – from scrubbing the decks to making some repairs, to keeping the cannons ready and reading the currents (the only job he'd ever been banned from was cooking, because he somehow managed to burn noodles) –

but he hadn't been the primary helmsman in ages. He closed his eyes, honing his other senses.

Gulls squawked overhead. Waves lapped against the side of the ship. Brine and fish clotted the air. The wood beneath his fingers was smooth and polished. Ves had made her way beneath the deck – he could hear her rummaging around.

"HEY!"

Solveig opened his eyes. The *Dargason* had drifted from the dock, no longer trapped by an anchor or mooring lines, but that didn't stop a man from running towards them.

Ah. The owner of the ship.

Solveig grinned. He held up a hand and waved. "Sorry, lad!" he called to the man who was older than he. "I'm untouchable by the navy for the next half hour! You can fight for your ship *after* that!"

Solveig grabbed the wheel and yanked, forcing the ship right. He bent his knees, legs going lax to rise and fall with the waves. He gave the man another wave just as a summer gust filled the sails and propelled the *Dargason* forward, away from the city where he was supposed to die.

Half an hour later, the continent of Aralyth far behind them, vanished into the horizon, a chill swept down Solveig's spine. Eleven months to avoid capture and to find the body of an ancient god.

He'd worked with worse odds before.

Only when night fell in a sheet of darkness, the twin moons crescents in the starry sky, did Solveig feel confident he'd put enough distance between the *Dargason* and Aralyth.

Ves came up the stairs to the quarterdeck, a map in one hand and a mug in the other. She'd been *ecstatic* to find a bathtub in the captain's quarters and spent a good hour soaking in it. There were no clothes aboard the ship to fit her, so she'd chopped up a sheet and turned it into a loose dress. Solveig had traded his prisoner garb for a linen shirt and loose trousers, grateful to toss the striped clothes into the sea.

"Map or booze?" Ves asked, leaning against the railing, her curls whipping around her face. Even in the dim moonlight, the ring through her bottom lip glinted.

"Map," Solveig said. "I can drink *after* I know where we're going."

"Then you can get your own rum." Ves held out the map.

Solveig grabbed it, splaying it haphazardly against the wheel. He fished his compass from his pocket – stolen from the captain's quarters – watching the needle spin and settle on north. A glimpse at the sky, at the red-tinted star above the two moons, was enough to confirm the compass was accurate. The north star, Aster – a name that had Solveig wanting to throw up – seemed to stay fixed between the two moons, Mene and Sin, though it, for whatever reason, always pointed north. Every sailor was taught the importance of several names before they first stepped foot on a boat – Poet, god of the sea and sky; Mene and Sin, the moons; the Sapphire, Emerald, Ruby, and Amethyst, the four seas; and Aster.

"This map is two years old," he murmured absently, glancing at the cartographer's signature in the corner. The letters were either initials or the number *four*. He tapped his finger against the map. "The Wandering Isle was between the Salts Atoll and Joris Island two years ago."

"The Wandering Isle was in the Triangle of Fylth when I was arrested." Ves took a long gulp of her drink. *"Gods!* I *missed* cinnamon rum."

She guzzled the rest of the spiced drink while Solveig studied the map. He had a cache on the westernmost island of Archepylago, but the ship was on a set course north. The next closest one, without going further north to the Twin Serpent Isles, was in Brook Green, an Aralythian town small enough the navy had no real presence but big enough to hide a bit of treasure.

Solveig traced his finger along the jagged coastline.

"Don't you need a sextant?" Ves hiccuped. She leaned back, staring at the night sky. "If we get lost and die at sea, I will come back to haunt you."

Solveig shook his head. "The ocean and I have a mutual understanding of each other. We'll be fine." Besides, he had the stars and moon to guide him, and Brook Green wasn't too far from where they were.

"You should use the bath, Cap. Get something to eat. *Sleep.*" Ves straightened and thrust her hip against Solveig, knocking him away from the wheel. "I'll man the ship for a while. I suppose I can wake you if something happens, but I *am* the Witch of the Sea. I fought a kraken and sank a navy fleet."

Sighing, Solveig handed her the map and compass. "Wake me before dawn. We should reach Brook Green by sunrise."

"Aye, Cap."

Solveig managed a tiny smile. His crew was dead, but... He had a new one now. His friends would forgive him for living, wouldn't they?

He pushed open the door to the captain's quarters and, after a second, locked the door. Strangely, he trusted Ves with his life, but... Anwir had been clear. He couldn't share this with anyone.

Solveig sat at the desk and carefully took the ancient map from his pocket, gently unfolding it, weighing the corners down with whatever he could find – a letter opener, a wax seal, a polished bit of pyrite, an empty mug. Ves must have lit the oil lamp when she'd been down here earlier. Solveig pulled it close, the flickering flame casting an orange glow over the map.

A poorly drawn version of the world was penned in dark brown ink – ink that *might* have been red at one point. It was missing several islands – two of the three that made up the Triangle of Fylth: Servedin and Morgouse; the Wandering Isle; Undyne; and Kelsyn, along with a few smaller islands whose names Solveig didn't know.

He moved his hand from where it rested on the map, realizing the scribbles around the border weren't scribbles at all, but...*words.*

Beneath a shadow on the Endless Sea
Where the moon once sat upon the waves
The child who watches with a dead eye
A memory forgotten, a field of graves.

North of refuse and east of swindler
Through caverns of salt and blue glow
The child, and slave to eternal night
Will bring the horizon the moons sink below.

In chains of the child who once was small
Then coveted, now lost to the sun and time
By thirteen chimes of the clock of the dead
A city of gold gifted to the maritime.

A kiss from the writer to see through midnight
A song which death can never touch
To find the core go first up then down
The name of the third moon is such.

The map itself was so outdated it could hardly be reliable, the shapes and sizes of the islands that *were* there too distorted to be accurate. But it wasn't the map itself that pointed to the dead god; it was the *poem* written along the border.

How did Anwir figure out from this *that there's a dead god out there?* Solveig rubbed his forehead. Right. This...this was a treasure map. Whoever created it wouldn't just draw a massive *X* to mark where a divine cadaver was hidden.

Solveig pushed his makeshift paperweights aside and folded the map, tucking it into his pocket for safekeeping. Once they stopped at Brook Green, Solveig would find some books to help decipher the code. But, for now, Ves was right – he needed to rest. *Desperately.*

He bathed quickly with cold water, scrubbing salt and grime from his body, and put on his stolen clothes once dry. He climbed into the sizeable cot, atop the blankets, and fell asleep quickly.

7

Natha got home late. Far later than normal, thanks to a dinner crowd she hadn't anticipated and a restaurant owner who overbooked the reservations and left Natha scrambling to make enough to satisfy everyone.

A year ago, she would have come home to a clean house with dinner sitting on the table for her and a bath already drawn. A lot changed in one year, and now she came home to a practically empty apartment. She had no desire to make dinner for herself, even though she loved to cook, so she filled a kettle with water and let it heat up while she went to shower. At least her small apartment had plumbing because if she couldn't peel off her clothes and stand under a stream of hot water after a long day, she would have gone insane.

She tipped her head back, letting water sluice over her face. *You could just not show up tomorrow,* that traitorous voice whispered in the back of her head.

"I need money," she grumbled out loud, silencing that voice. Divorce was messy and expensive and Natha had gotten the short end of an already short stick.

She washed quickly and got out, dressing in only a robe so she could massage her special lotion into her arms. While the cream did nothing to hide the mottled scars stretching from her fingers to past her elbows, it did help with the pain that persisted even years after healing.

Returning to the kitchen, she poured herself a cup of poppyseed tea and grabbed the newspaper that had been delivered while she was at work. She brought both to her bedroom, where she settled into her bed, her back and feet screaming in relief as she sank into the mattress. She took a sip of tea and opened the newspaper, hoping to find something interesting – or at least something so boring it would put her right to sleep.

Besides the front page filling Natha in on the story of the pirate captain who evaded execution and ran off with the Witch of the Sea, there was a lot of *nothing* in the paper. Sipping her tea, she flipped to the end. Right before the gossip columns and romance advice (which she avoided like the plague because the last thing she needed in her life was romance) was the Navy's Most Wanted. She skimmed them, taking in the names and sketched faces. Working at a restaurant right on the coast in a capital city, she was bound to get pirates as customers. If she could catch one of the Top Five, she could retire, open her own private business, spend the rest of her life drinking wine, eating chocolates, and cooking for people who *actually* appreciated her work.

Fifth: Ryuu Nova of the *Dragon King*. He wasn't terrible to look at, if his drawing did him any justice, and the bounty of four hundred fifty million lune was even more enticing, but the Dragon Pirates were notoriously violent and picked fights with anything that moved.

Fourth was Bonny Reed of the *Moon Rabbit,* captain of the Rabbit Pirates. She was also decent eye candy, with curls that looked like living flames, but it was no secret that she'd been married before and refused to entertain anyone else after her wife died.

Third was Ellery Anor, captain of the *Eldwode's Revenge.* Just a million shy of the five hundred title Nox Solveig held at second place, there were rumors that Anor had mentored the navy's number one most wanted.

Natha traced her finger over the empty space where the first most wanted pirate's portrait should have been. Nobody knew what they looked like, only that they were the strongest pirate, even though they'd made their first appearance only three years ago. The Unnamed God, captain of the Unnamed Pirates, worth *nine hundred million lune.*

Nine hundred million. She could buy the palace. She'd be the richest woman in the kingdom. Her ex-husband would look *pitiful* next to her.

"*Ah,*" she whispered lazily to herself. The poppyseed tea coursed through her body, lulling her into a calm. "*Nathalia Zimmer, is that you?* It's Nathalia Divyne now. *Oh, please, take me back! Please be my wife again! I'll do anything!* Go sard yourself with a cutlass..." She chuckled at the lovely visual of her ex-husband shoving a cutlass where the sun didn't shine.

She fell asleep sitting up. She did not sleep for long before the nightmares began.

Ves kept her gaze on the dark sea, watchful even though she couldn't sense anything amiss. Sighing, she leaned against the wheel, watching as the gentle waves rocked the *Dargason.*

The gods never fraternized with humans, but they did, occasionally, gift a drop of their power to the mortals. It wasn't hereditary and happened at random, but those who were divine touched were *powerful.* Ves was god-blessed by the goddess of the earth, trees and life – Dreamer – to *see* living things where people normally couldn't. At the marina, she had scanned the ships, looking for one that was empty. The *Dargason* didn't have anyone in it, and besides the harbor seal swimming beneath it, it was void of life completely.

(There was a pod of dolphins to the left, swimming a quarter mile beneath the surface of the sea, too many fish to count, and an albatross above the clouds).

Of the blessings Dreamer could have given, it wasn't the worst. Ves knew other god-blessed pirates who had it way worse.

She glanced at the compass and turned the wheel a fraction, setting the *Dargason* back on course.

"Twin moons in the sky, for the third has died, aweigh anchor aweigh. The seas are dark, but the spirits are bright, we'll set the Ruby alight. Chart the course for the unknown way, aweigh anchor aweigh. Find the moon and the treasure tonight, we'll set the Ruby alight." As she softly sang to herself, she wondered, not for the first time in the past four years but the first time since she'd been granted freedom, what her old crew was up to. If they were even still *alive*.

They *had* to be. She refused to be the last one alive. It meant little now, though. She'd already gone ahead and pledged her loyalty to a new captain. A new captain who had *actually* gotten her out of prison. None of the ex-Ruby Pirates had managed to do that. *Very* few people made it out of I. J. Pen alive.

Ves was just happy to be out at sea again.

Ves knocked on the captain's door the next day. They'd taken turns sleeping and keeping watch throughout the night, but for most of the morning, Solveig had hidden himself away in his quarters.

"What?" came her captain's response. Dull footsteps shuffled across the ground and the door swung open.

"Well, Cap!" she grinned a wicked grin. "The cannons are loaded and – here – I have a sword for you."

Ves tossed the blade she'd found when doing inventory the day before. Solveig caught it with ease. "What's this for?"

"Cutting down your enemies," she answered simply. "There's an enemy ship approaching. Well, it could be a merchant. Or a fishing boat. Regardless, it's our enemy and while we aren't flying any colors, it might do us good to at least raid them."

Something flashed across Solveig's face – *excitement?*

"This'll be our debut fight as pirates," Solveig said, mostly to himself but loud enough Ves still heard it.

Her palms itched in anticipation. *Her* first fight in four years. "What're the orders?"

Solveig paused, strategizing silently in less than thirty seconds. She had a hunch he was clever – how else would his bounty skyrocket to five hundred million? – but it was something else seeing that cleverness in action.

"Block their bow and gun them down," he instructed, sliding his new cutlass into his belt. Without a sheath, it hung limply, and Ves bit her tongue to keep from making a dirty joke as Solveig continued. "Get us as close as possible so we can board."

"We?"

"The last time I left my crew on the ship so I could fight, they all died, and I got arrested."

"And you met me."

Solveig scowled. "Focus. You're a clever woman, Ves. This is the first show in the *Witch of the Sea Revival Tour*. And we need supplies. Water –"

"Rum."

"Rum, yes, we need that." Solveig turned to see the incoming ship. Ves followed his gaze and…her heart skipped a beat.

They were flying colors – a pirate ship. A small one, smaller than the *Dargason*. She could tell the crew – ten in total – were all drunk. It would be an easy fight. *Too* easy for her first in four years, but at least she got to do *something*.

"Get the cannons ready," Solveig instructed as he went to grab the helm.

"Aye, Cap." Ves grinned and ran to the cannons.

The *Dargason*, small as it was, only had six cannons, three per side. It would be crowded and messy, but six cannons firing at the enemy ship would be *so* much more efficient. Ves sliced through the ropes tying the portside cannons down and shoved them starboard. She felt around her jacket and trousers, knowing she'd put a box of matches *somewhere* – there! She pulled the box free just as the *Dargason* approached the enemy ship.

"Permission to fire?" she drawled, leaning against one of the guns.

"If you have to ask my permission before launching an attack, this alliance might not work." Solveig steadied the *Dargason* as best as he could.

Clear skies blessed them, the waves around the ship minimal. Ves noted a lone whale swimming deep below; if she inched closer to the surface, she would cause both ships to rock dangerously. Ves silently told the creature to stay down where it was safe for everyone.

As soon as the *Dargason* was close enough to the enemy ship that Ves could make out the wiry hairs on one of the pirate's upper lips, she struck a match and lit the fuses – one after the other until all six were burning and her fingers were warm from the flame.

Bang! Bang! Bang!

The cannons fired, each one hitting true, shattering wood with an acrid burning smell. Cannons tore through the ship's hull, letting seawater spill in dangerously. They were at such an angle the enemy ship *couldn't* launch a counterattack, not with cannons.

Ves reloaded quickly, firing again. As the cannons launched, Ves counted the people on the ship. Seven on the deck, one at the helm, two still below.

That was where the goods were. They were trying to secure what treasure they had before Ves and Solveig could siege the ship.

"This would be a million times easier if we had a bigger crew," grumbled Solveig as he hopped over the railing to land on the main deck.

"You saying ten people is too many for you to handle, Cap?" Ves tossed a spent match into the sea below.

"I said it would be *easier,*" he shot back.

One of the enemy pirates fired a pistol. Solveig jumped aside, narrowly missing the shot as the bullet landed in the deck.

"Poet's blood – I *just* stole this ship!" Solveig yelled at the enemy.

"Here." Ves took the pistol she'd swiped from the captain's quarters out of her belt and handed it grip-first to Solveig.

He took it without question and fired, hitting the fool who'd shot at him right between the brows. He tossed the gun back to Ves and jumped onto the railing, balancing precariously on the slim bit of polished wood. Below, the whale let out a mournful note before swimming deeper.

Solveig jumped, landing on the other ship's deck with a *thud.* He drew his cutlass and struck, slamming his blade into the fleshy bit between another pirate's shoulder and neck. He ripped the sword free, drawing a stream of blood and a slew of gurgled screams.

Ves launched one more round of cannons before crossing after her captain, sword drawn and eyes wild. She met Solveig's gaze and nodded once. He nodded in understanding, fighting off another pirate to clear a path.

She took it, running across the deck and cutting down a drunk who tried to get in her way. *Foolish man.* Had they forgotten who she was?

Ves followed the sight of the two pirates below deck, running down a flight of stairs to the dark, dank quarters. The two men looked up, frightened as mice before a cat, and stepped in front of the crate they'd been crouched before just a moment prior.

"Now, lads," she drawled. "I don't know what's in that box there, but I *really* want to find out. You can be a couple of good boys and give it to me, or I can fight you for it." She brandished her sword, making sure the fools saw the blood on the blade. "And I'm absolutely *positive* I can win."

The fools did not want to be good boys.

The taller of the two charged, holding nothing but a dagger that would satisfy some but could hardly be worth bragging over. He lunged, slashing through the air in a frantic arc.

Ves threw up her cutlass, knocking the dagger out of Tall Fool's hand. It skittered across the floor, helplessly out of reach.

"*Poet,*" Tall Fool cursed.

"The name's Vesperine Genevieve, actually." Ves grabbed the man's collar and shoved him against the wall so hard the wood splintered. He kicked helplessly, trying to get down. Ves grinned. "Though you might know me as the Witch of the Sea."

She buried her sword into his gut, skewering him to the wall. She left him there, twitching and dying, and turned her attention to Short Fool.

The blasted idiot had wet himself.

"Just give me that box and I won't kill you," she promised.

Short Fool, the spineless bastard he was, nodded and shoved the crate towards Ves. She caught a glimpse of gold through the slats. *Bingo.* She scooped the crate up, easily balancing it on one hip.

"Men are *such* idiots. Don't they know never to trust a witch?"

Short Fool's eyes went wide. He opened his mouth, probably to plead for his life, but Ves had already pulled the trigger on her pistol, the iron ball already buried in the man's brain. She blew the steam away from the barrel and hurried back upstairs just as the ship rocked dangerously and seawater started to crash in.

Solveig didn't recognize the flag the pirates flew, and that was just fine. As long as the scrawny small fries didn't send his ass flying to the green, who they were wouldn't bother him.

One of the pirates charged at Solveig, cutlass drawn and ready to slice, but he blocked it. Metal scratched against metal. The drunk pirate caved, the weight too much. He hit the ground, at the mercy of Solveig's sword. Solveig sliced clean through flesh and sinew, opening the pirate's throat in a splash of red.

Solveig cut down another pirate just as the ship lurched. The belly of it must be filling with water, he thought. It would go down soon. A sloop of its size would succumb to half a barrel of seawater.

He turned to face the last pirate, blood dripping from the blade of his sword.

"Wh-who are you?" the drunk pirate slurred. Apparently not even his imminent death was sobering enough.

Solveig grinned. *"Captain Nox Solveig, cloaked in green. Set out to conquer the Emerald Sea."*

The pirate's eyes went wide in realization, but it was too late. Solveig slid his sword into the man's belly. He ripped it free as Ves bounded up the stairs, a crate balanced on her hip.

"I'm taking this back to the *Dargason!*" she called cheerfully.

Solveig ought to have joined her, but the sloop hadn't sunk *yet* and there was still pillaging to do. He crouched down, swiping weapons and jewels from the dead pirates. All of his plunder went into his pockets, except...

He paused, staring at the moonstone ring he'd grabbed. It fitted onto his littlest finger perfectly. *A sign,* he realized with a tiny smile.

Creeeeeaaaaak.

The ship dipped. Water must have filled the hull, forcing the bow down. Solveig hardly had enough time – he'd have to make do.

The captain's quarters were obvious since it was the only other door besides the stairs Ves had gone down earlier, so Solveig went there. He would have liked to have the leisure to examine everything and take only what was important, but he didn't, so he grabbed what he could fit into his arms – a handful of maps, a few old books, a jewelry box whose weight was promising, a jewel encrusted dagger, a pouch of stone coins.

The ship lurched; Solveig slid across the floor, caught off guard. He grabbed one last book, shoving it into his pocket, before running out.

Ves stood on the *Dargason,* a rather unstable plank of wood between the ships. It would do. Clutching his plunder, Solveig jumped onto the plank and ran across. Once on the *Dargason* he dumped his pilfered goods onto the deck and watched as the enemy ship sank beneath the waves.

"Well!" Ves sat down next to the crate. "That felt *good.* When we get to Brook Green, I'm getting myself some *nice* weapons. A pistol, a sword, some knives..."

Solveig picked up the dagger and tossed it to her. "Here. You can have this."

Her brown eyes lit up as she caught the dagger. The gilded hilt was wrapped in supple leather, though the pommel held a fat topaz the color of the setting sun. More tiny gems – rubies and garnets and citrine – decorated the rest of the hilt, twinkling like the sunrise on the ocean.

"We need an accountant," she said, sifting through the jewels Solveig had dumped on the ground.

"Typically, the bo'sun *is* the accountant." Solveig sat and crossed his legs. He rubbed the smooth moonstone on his ring absently.

"I need a ledger and a pen, then." She picked up a pearl necklace and toyed with the stones. "River pearl. Worth less than ocean pearl. I'd wager... Ten grand."

Solveig chuckled. "See? You're perfect for the job. Here. What about this?" he handed her a solid gold bracelet.

Ves weighed it absently. "Fifteen grand. Though, I might keep this for myself. It's pretty." She slid the bracelet over her hand, admiring the way it gleamed in the sun.

"When we get to Brook Green, you can take whatever treasure you want to be exchanged for lune." Solveig grabbed one of the maps and unfolded it. It was of Aralyth. He did a double take when he saw the tiny print of his hometown. It never appeared on any maps. *Strange.*

"Yeah, yeah, and I'll get some supplies. Food, rum, water, gunpowder?" Ves pulled the strip of fabric from her hair only to scrape the mass of curls back so she could braid it.

"And anything else you might find important. Maybe get yourself a fancy new ledger."

"Aye, Cap."

Solveig couldn't help but smile. It didn't reach his eyes, though. Because as good as it felt to have a crew again, he knew he was damning Ves just by having her with him.

"Welcome in – oh!" The moss-haired girl looked up from the newspaper when Thol walked into the botanist's that morning. She folded the paper and pushed it aside. "You again."

Thol's lips quirked up into a tiny smile. "Me again."

"How's the garden?" She leaned forward, eager. She didn't look at his tattoos – not directly, at least.

"Better," he answered. He'd moved the stubborn korva plant and the rest of his garden practically flourished overnight. "Much better. You were right. I... Want to plant some flowers. Wild-flowers. I was planning on going to get some seeds after this, but...you're the expert. What's your advice for growing successful wildflowers?"

Her gaze flicked to his exposed chest, where a splash of colorful wildflowers had been inked into his dark skin, right over his heart. A reminder. A promise. A secret carried to the grave.

"Wildflowers got their name for a reason." She pushed her spectacles up her nose. "They grow anywhere and everywhere. They're resilient. You can get by with just sprinkling seeds in your garden and they'll thrive. Do you have a yard?"

Thol nodded, even though he didn't plan on planting the wild-flowers there.

The girl continued, "Just spread the seeds over your grass. You'll attract plenty of honeybees. If you're interested in beekeeping..." she trailed off, rambling to herself about how delicious wildflower honey is in tea. "Regardless! Let me know if you have any success. I have a friend who runs a stall in the market. She sells seeds of every type. Tell her I sent you and she'll give you a good deal."

Thol knew he'd get a good deal regardless as the shopkeeper would likely just want him gone before his foreboding presence scared away any potential clientele, but he kept that pessimism to himself. He was trying very hard not to be pessimistic these days, a feat easier said than done.

"Your tattoos," the girl blurted as Thol turned to leave. He paused and lifted a brow. He had *dozens* of tattoos. It was easier to list the spaces where he didn't have any. The girl, flustered and blushing crimson, said, "On your chest. The flowers."

Thol pulled his linen shirt aside to reveal the whole piece – a bouquet over his heart, covering a twisted mass of scar tissue. Baby's breath, red carnations, chrysanthemums and clovers, irises and daisies and forget-me-nots, poppies and roses and salvias and violets – all painting a rainbow of floral affection. Hidden amongst the petals were initials only he knew – *M. W.* and *E. W.*

"My wife designed it," he said.

"She has good taste."

"She did," he said, solemn. As he left the botanist's, he touched the flowers on his chest and smiled.

8

VES TIED THE MOORING lines, her knots precise despite the salt-stiff ropes. It had been two days since their run-in with the small fry pirates and they had just now arrived in Brook Green.

Solveig hopped off the *Dargason,* landing on the dock with a *thud.* The morning sun shone bright in the sky, but despite the summer humidity, he wore his green coat.

"You have the list?" Solveig asked Ves.

"Aye, Cap." She plucked a scrap of paper from her bosom – Solveig had no idea *why* she'd keep it there – and waved it flippantly. "Two hours, aye? I bet I could fit a decent sard in –"

"Ves."

"Right. Business first."

Solveig's lips quirked up. "Two hours. Do *not* get into any trouble."

"Where's the fun in that?"

"Without me."

Ves grinned a wicked grin. *"Aye,* Cap."

She saluted lazily before stuffing her hands into her pockets and walking down the dock. Solveig watched her go, knowing she might not come back. If she didn't, he wouldn't blame her. She finally tasted freedom after four years of being locked away, trapped in the dark. The oath she swore was hardly binding.

Still...

Solveig scraped his hair back, tying it loosely at the nape of his neck, and followed his bo'sun's lead.

Collect his cache and find information about his friend's whereabouts. Those were Solveig's goals. The wanted poster sat snuggly in his jacket's inner pocket, next to Anwir's map.

Brook Green greeted him with a lively throng of people – school children in a line following their teacher, a pair of women gossiping about the neighbor's mistress, a teenage couple dancing to an out-of-tune accordion. Despite its name, the town boasted a color scheme of mostly blues and whites. He passed a small temple for Lady Lightbringer, a group of women huddled at the shrine inside, bowed in prayer.

Lady Lightbringer, the patron deity of the navy and goddess of justice, tended to frown upon pirates. She and the deity of debauchery, the Wanderer constantly butted heads, or so the legends claimed.

Solveig passed the temple, going a few doors down to the Ink Drop, a tavern where the bartenders would turn a blind eye to piracy for a few extra stone. It was the kind of place his friend used to frequent. He pushed open the door, stalking up to the polished bar and taking a seat.

"Be right with you, love," the busty barmaid said without looking up from the glass she was polishing. *Definitely* the place his friend would like.

Solveig reached into his pocket and took out the folded poster. The barmaid turned around and leaned across the counter.

"Oh," she purred, giving Solveig a face full of pale bosom. "Ain't you a pretty thing? What'll it be, love?"

"Information, if you have it." Solveig took out two stone coins and slid them across the bar. "I'm looking for someone."

"Ain't we all? Who's the lucky someone?" She tucked the coins into the front of her dress. Solveig tried not to stare, to figure out *how* the coins wouldn't fall and get lost.

He unfolded the poster and showed the picture to the woman. "As far as I'm aware, he's still alive."

The barmaid twisted her painted lips up as she thought. Solveig held his breath, only to let it go when she shook her head. "Ain't seen him. Maybe try the Stone Well. Just up the street. Might have better luck there."

Solveig tucked the poster into his pocket and gave the barmaid a crumpled lune bill. "Thanks anyway." He stood and left, ignoring the barmaid as she tried to convince him to stay a while longer.

Solveig tried the Stone Well. When they had nothing, they directed him to a nicer tavern. They had nothing, either, instead telling him to check out Connor's, a bawdy tavern right on the beach. After he got nothing, he gave up, deciding to fetch his cache since the two-hour mark was fast approaching and he needed to meet with Ves.

Defeated, Solveig slinked through the streets to the Brook Green Bank, a tiny building next to the town hall. Normally, pirates had no business going inside banks, unless they planned on robbing it. Still, Solveig went inside and walked right up to the counter where a mousy man sat, scribbling in a notebook that he *quickly* shut when he noticed Solveig.

"G-good day, sir!" the man said in a nasally voice. "How may I help you?"

"I have a safe I want to access," Solveig said. "Number thirty-seven, under the name Nolan Holst."

"I presume you're Mister Holst?" the man dug through a drawer, pulling out a key.

"You presume correctly." It was one of Solveig's many fake identities – the one he typically used for banking and other important things.

The reedy banker stood and gestured for Solveig to follow. He followed the man into a back room full of lock boxes. The man handed Solveig the key to safe thirty-seven. "Let me know if you have anything else you need."

Solveig waited for the man to leave before he looked at the key – one somehow charmed to react to his blood. It had a tag – *HOLST* – attached to it. Solveig bit his thumb hard enough to draw blood, letting a few drops fall onto the iron key. It changed shape, morphing into something that would fit into the lock. Solveig slid it in and unlocked the safe.

His Brook Green cache was a smaller one, with only about five thousand lune in cash, a compass, a medical kit, and a bottle of cinnamon rum – *very* old, by the look of it. He pulled everything out, stuffing the various items into his pockets. When he closed the safe, it locked, and the key returned to its regular shape.

Solveig tossed the key at the banker and left without another word.

With half an hour until he had to meet Ves, Solveig decided to pass through the street market. There were a few things he needed that he didn't include on his list, and it wouldn't hurt to ask a few more people...

The first stall Solveig went to belonged to a glass smith.

"I need a lens," Solveig said without preamble. "A magnifying one. Something small and discrete, like...like a jeweler's lens."

The smith, a stocky man with a massive mustache, raised his equally massive eyebrows. "A jeweler's lens? I have a bit of glass that would work, but I'd need to set it in something."

"How long will it take?"

"About fifteen minutes, if you have the lune."

Solveig dug into his pocket and grabbed a fistful of paper bills. His fingers brushed against the poster. Slowly, he pulled both out. "This man. Have you seen him recently? I'm looking for him?"

The smith studied the poster, then shook his head. "Sorry, lad. I'll get the lens for you. Come back in fifteen and it'll be ready."

Jaw set, Solveig turned to walk away. Only...a soft tap on his shoulder caused him to pause.

"Um... Excuse me?" a woman's voice sounded. Solveig glanced over his shoulder. A girl with mossy hair and spectacles looked up at him, sheepish. "I know the man you're looking for. I-I mean, I know where he is. He hasn't done anything illegal in recent years, though. Are you looking to arrest him?"

Finally! Solveig grinned. "Arrest him? Why would I want to arrest my best friend?"

Ves flipped her shiny dagger into the air absently, catching it without even looking where it landed. She eyed the young boy – far too young to be working at the docks, but she couldn't say anything, since *she* joined the Ruby Pirates when she was ten – who rolled a barrel of clean water up the gangplank. *The next ship,* she promised herself, *will have running water.*

She tossed the dagger into the air again, catching the hilt and seamlessly shoving it into her belt. She took out her brand-new pocket watch, checking the time for the dozenth time. Solveig was late.

"That's good, lad," she said to the boy after he'd righted the barrel. She tossed him a few lune. As he scurried off, she looked up through her lashes to see a newcomer. "You're late." "You're early," Solveig said, even though that was a lie. "She ready to sail?"

"She is now." Ves put her watch back in her pocket and hopped over the railing, landing on the dock with a thud.

She untied the mooring lines and kicked them into the water. Solveig raised the anchor; Ves hurried back onto the ship as the gentle waves pushed it from the dock.

"Where to now?" She sat on one of the barrels and pulled out her dagger again, using the point to clean under her nails.

"Lenwell."

Lenwell. Ves had been to the major city once or twice on an errand. The booze was good, the brothels better, and while it wasn't a sanctuary city by any means, it did have an underground that catered to gangs – both pirate and not. Still... Going to such a major city didn't seem like the best idea. Brook Green had no navy presence. Lenwell did.

The booze was good, and the brothels were better *because* Lenwell housed a navy academy – one of the many institutes around the globe where young cadets could learn how to fire a pistol and slay a pirate and protect the *wonderful* empire. A place *full* of little twerps desperate to do something to catch Admiral Commodore's attention. Catching Ves and Solveig would be just the thing to get them promoted from cadet to captain.

"I know you're the captain and all, but can I veto that?" Ves asked.

Solveig gripped the helm. "The man I want to make my quartermaster is there. We're going. Lower the sails, would you? There's a good southern wind."

Ves groaned and dragged herself off the barrel. She loosened the ropes holding the sails up, grommets sliding as the sails filled with wind, propelling the *Dargason* forward.

"Did you take inventory?" Solveig asked before Ves could argue going to Lenwell again.

"Not counting whatever you brought in your cache, aye." Five barrels of fresh water, one barrel of cinnamon rum, a pantry of food to last them a week, a new headband for her unruly curls, a ledger with an orange leather cover *and* a matching, orange-tinted glass pen, a pocket watch, and a cheap set of stays to last her until she could get *properly* fitted.

They pinched under her arms and were just a bit too tight around her stomach, but they provided support for her chest, and that was all she cared about.

"I hear Lenwell has a good shopping district. Some of Aralyth's best ateliers are there," Solveig mused.

Damn that man. Damn him for having excellent points.

"I will be using *your* lune to buy myself a *very* nice corset," she shot back.

"Fine by me." Solveig grinned. "I'll just take it out of your allowance."

It had been nearly a week since Thol last saw the botanist's apprentice. Nearly a week since he'd scattered wildflower seeds around the two graves at the back of his house overlooking the sea below. Tiny blossoms of color sprinkled throughout the grass, blowing gently in the breeze.

Thol placed a bundle of baby's breath against the smaller grave. It was empty since the babe was buried with her mother in the other one, but she deserved her own mark. Another breeze blew, pushing the baby's breath to lay against the larger grave. His heart ached at the sight.

With a sigh, Thol kissed both graves and grabbed his trowel and watering can, bringing both back into his house. As he passed through the kitchen, he lit the stove to warm a pot of water for coffee.

Knock, knock, knock!

Thol froze in his tracks. Sometimes when the newsboy rode by, he threw the paper too hard, and it bounced off the door. But he'd already come that morning and it only ever made two thuds at most.

Knock, knock!

He'd given up piracy. He avoided the navy like the plague. The kettle whistled; Thol poured himself a cup of tea just to give his hands something to do so he wouldn't reach for the pistol he kept stashed in the wall.

"Go away," he said through the door. "I'm not interested in whatever you have to sell. I'm *retired.* Got it? Re. Ti. Red. *Retired.*"

There was a pause. Then...

"You won't even open up for an old friend?"

Thol dropped the teacup. It shattered on the floor, but he didn't care. In two strides he was at the door, ripping it open, and...

"Nox." Thol grabbed his friend by the collar and yanked him inside, crushing him in a suffocating hug.

"Can't – breathe –" Nox Solveig writhed in Thol's grip. Thol let go quickly.

"I heard you were going to be *executed,*" Thol said accusingly. "How are you here?"

Solveig rubbed his face, pushing his red hair out of his eyes. "It's a *long* story."

Thol just stared at Solveig, unspeaking. It was Solveig who eventually broke the silence by saying, "That's a new tattoo. And *retired?* Is *that* why I haven't heard of the *Sea Wyrm* in a while? I kept hoping I'd hear stories about your crew, but nobody ever talked about you anymore. Just the *Unnamed God,* whoever that is."

"The *Wyrm* sank," Thol explained. He stepped over the broken cup and sat on the chaise beneath a window. "Three years ago."

The *Sea Wyrm* had gone through one too many battles, her hull giving out after years of sailing. Thol sank her himself and retired as captain. He stayed behind in Wyvron, the capital of Archepylago, before moving to Lenwell with...her.

"A year after the Ruby Pirates disbanded, then," Solveig murmured. "The end of an era, I suppose. Except the other big names are still around... Eldwode, Rabbit, Dragon..."

Thol clenched his hands into fists, the word *PUNISHMENT* clear across his knuckles. "Nox. Why are you here?"

"Can't I visit my best friend after finding him again?" Solveig sat on the chair opposite the chaise and crossed his ankle over his knee.

Thol raised a dark brow. Solveig sighed. "I cheated death and now I'm gathering a crew to find a priceless treasure. I want you to be my first mate."

"No," Thol said without hesitation. He gave up piracy. He swore never to sail under the colors of the free again.

Solveig's grin fell in an instant. "Thol," he tried. "I... You... We made a promise."

"When we were kids, Nox. I'm retired. Find someone else." Thol stood, going to where he'd broken his teacup. He crouched down and began picking up the pieces.

Solveig stood. "What, did three years of *retirement* turn you into a coward? Because that's what it seems like to me. It seems like you became a coward. What happened to you, huh? What happened in those three years to kill *Captain Bartholomew Williams?* What would V—"

Thol dropped the ceramic shards and slammed his hands onto the floor. One of the shards bit into his palm, slicing just shy of the skull inked there. "I lost my wife, Nox."

Tears burned his eyes, hotter than fire. He looked up; Solveig stood there, still as a statue, face blanched.

"You got married?" Solveig whispered.

"I got married." Thol looked at the cut, at his palm slick with blood. "And she died. A year ago, she died giving birth to a still-born."

Solveig's eyes went wide. He murmured something under his breath before saying, "You...had a child..."

"The key word being *had.*"

Thol turned his back to Solveig to go to the kitchen. He grabbed a rag off the counter and pressed it against his palm, stanching the blood.

"Thol, I had no idea..." Solveig said gently.

"No, because you were too busy gallivanting on some *high seas* adventure. Look where that got you," Thol snapped.

Solveig flinched.

Sard. "Nox, I..."

"No." Solveig grabbed the doorknob. "No, you're right. You're right. I'm... I'm sorry for coming here. I'll leave you alone. I'm sorry about your wife and your babe. What...what was her name?"

Thol gripped the rag so tight his knuckles turned white. "Meadow." He closed his eyes, imagining her smile, her wheat-like hair, her eyes that shone like pink diamonds, the way her nose crinkled when she smiled, the freckles that covered her body because of the hours she spent under the sun, tending to the garden she loved more than almost anything.

It was the same kind of love Thol had for the sea.

He inhaled deeply through his nose. "What's this treasure you're looking for?"

"I...am bound not to say. But it's something massive. Something that will make us the most famous pirates to ever live," Solveig said.

"How big of a crew do you have? What's your ship like?" Thol knew the *Silver Moon* sank in the fight that ended with Solveig being arrested – it had been all over the news.

"It's just me and a bo'sun right now. Vesperine Genevieve. We... Have a sloop. A stolen sloop..."

Thol looked at his hand. The bleeding had stopped. "You're going to need a bigger ship than that."

Solveig scowled. Even though he was an adult, Thol couldn't help but treat him like his kid brother, since they *were* brothers – sworn brothers.

Thol said, "I have a brigantine. She hasn't been used in a while, but she's good. Reliable. Brought Meadow and me here from Wyvron." Though he hadn't sailed in years, his ship had a permanent spot at the harbor, and Thol regularly went to make sure she was in sailing condition.

"I'm not going to take your ship, Thol," Solveig said flatly.

"No, you're not," Thol said. "She's still *my* ship. But you can captain her. I'll join your crew."

9

Something swatted Illie's face, drawing her out of sleep. *Partially* out of sleep. She groaned and rolled over, hugging her pillow closer to her chest.

Swat!

She groaned again. "Fi'mo'm'nis," she slurred, barely able to string together a coherent sentence.

She was swatted again. This time, she sat up to see Pleo curled up next to her, tail moving back and forth as she watched sunrays dance across the walls. Illie spat out the bit of hair that had made its way into her mouth and rubbed the sleep from her gritty eyes.

"It's my day *off,*" she sleepily scolded.

Pleo chirped, whiskers twitching as she watched her sunny prey. Her tail whacked Illie again before she pounced, attacking the wall.

Illie lay back down and stared at the ceiling. It was her day off, the Ink and Rose closed, but she didn't like spending the whole day cooped up in bed. With a heavy sigh, she threw back the blankets.

Something clattered to the floor, scaring a hiss out of Pleo. Illie lazily looked down to see a few books on the ground. *Right.* She'd fallen asleep reading. She stood and quickly made her bed before grabbing the books to place on her desk. One of them had fallen open; she closed it, the page crinkling under the cover. She set the stack on her desk and shuffled out of her bedroom to the kitchen. As she heated up a pot of water for tea, she opened the curtains and windows, letting in the warm morning air. She plucked her watering can from its place on the windowsill and filled it up, watering all the plants, finishing just as the kettle whistled.

Illie yawned and shuffled back to the kitchen. She poured the water into a cup and opened her pantry, sifting through the collection of teas until she picked out a black tea.

Pleo came running into the living room, meowing loudly as she wove between Illie's legs.

"Yes, yes, I know," murmured Illie. She set her tea down, going back to the pantry to fetch Pleo's food. She filled the cat's bowl and set it down before she could get yelled at again. Pleo satisfied, Illie took her tea and an apple from the bowl on the counter and went back to her room.

Sitting at her desk, Illie pulled the book she'd been reading the day before towards her, opening to the marked page to resume her research. She flipped through the pages, sipping on her tea as she skimmed over the blocks of uninformative text, only stopping when she found a section dedicated to the gods. She set her cup down and began reading.

Illie wasn't the most religious person in the world. She prayed to the gods when convenient and celebrated religious holidays, but she didn't go to any temples, she didn't have any altars or idols in her apartment, and she used the gods' names in vain. Constantly. Still, she knew the basics of each god, and she knew *very* well that god-blessed people existed.

Lady Lightbringer was the goddess of war, justice, and strength. Not only was she idolized by the navy, but she was their patron, blessing the higher-ups and their ships. She constantly butted heads with the genderless deity of debauchery, indulgence, sin and adventure, the Wanderer. There was a reason no navy base had been set up on the Wandering Isle, and it wasn't just because the island moved constantly. Illie wasn't *lawless*, but she liked the idea of adventure. Of the two, she preferred to pray to the Wanderer.

Poet, the other god Illie found herself praying to, was the god of the sand, sea, and sky. She heard stories from sailors and fishermen claiming they'd seen Poet – as a massive kraken, as a fish-human-hybrid, as a legendary siren, as a leviathan – but nobody could agree on what he looked like. Illie had been at sea long enough to know to *always* pray to Poet when on a ship, no matter how religious she was. Sailors considered it bad luck to name their boats after the god since it was seen as an invitation to sink the ship.

Dreamer, Poet's star-crossed lover, was the goddess of the earth, trees, and life. As she was rumored to live in the mountains, she only embraced her lover during Titan Waves, the massive mountain-high waves that happened at random. Illie had never seen a Titan Wave before, but she'd studied weather patterns and the ocean's behavior enough to know that if the sea started to recede suddenly, not even high ground would be a mercy. She thought it was romantic, two gods of opposite realms desperate for one fleeting moment together that they didn't care who they damned.

She slumped over her book, groaning loudly. Maybe it wasn't romantic at all, and *she* was just starved for affection. How embarrassing.

She sat up and pushed the book aside, reaching for a different one. She flipped to the middle and began reading.

Though... She couldn't keep her mind from wandering. From thinking about Poet and Dreamer and their Titan Waves.

A sinking feeling – *longing* – filled her stomach, heavy as rocks. It wasn't *affection* she was starved for; it was *adventure*.

Ves had been given two very simple tasks when they arrived in Lenwell: don't get into trouble, and don't go near the navy base. Easy. Four years was long enough for most people to forget what she looked like, and she had no plans to stir up trouble. When Solveig went off to find the house he said his friend lived in, Ves went into the city, seeking out a tavern to get something to drink

And to eavesdrop.

She found a place at the bar and ordered a mug of cinnamon rum. The bartender slid the chilled mug of dark booze over. Ves paid in lune and brought the drink to her lips. She drank slowly, tamping down her divine powers to *listen* to the flurry of conversations around her.

"Mister Previn was caught sleeping with his neighbor –"

"Ugh. If I have to eat one more helping of cucumber soup, I will divorce the woman."

"That's what I heard! It can track the Wandering Isle in real time –"

"That Rossi lad is putting on a concert soon. We should go."

"Did you see the ring Prince Elios got for Princess Iori?"

Wait.

Ves scanned the room, trying to find that one conversation again. She spied the couple sitting at a table, close enough for Ves to eavesdrop without being caught. She shifted slightly, trying to hear better.

"Haven't seen you around here," a new voice said. Ves shuddered, glancing to see the man next to her.

"Probably because I haven't been here," she murmured into her booze.

"There's talk about them putting it on display, but I doubt something that valuable will ever be seen by the public –"

"You lookin' for a guide?" the man asked, clearly not getting the hint. His breath smelled like stale beer.

"You can't handle me," she said plainly. *Don't get into any fights, Ves. Don't cause trouble. You do* not *want to end up in I. J. Pen. again.* Her grip on her mug tightened, her golden rings clacking against the glass.

"*Of course, the navy has it. For now, at least. They're probably just holding it so they can transport it to Aramore –*"

"I think I'm *perfectly* capable of handling you." The man placed his grubby hand on her thigh. Ves saw red.

Don't cause trouble don't cause trouble don't cause trouble –

Sorry, Cap.

Her knife was in her hand in an instant, pressed into the man's side, concealed by the cover of the bar. One quick flick of her wrist and the blade would sink into his diaphragm.

The man knew it, too. He froze, going completely stiff, not even *breathing*. And he thought he could handle Ves. *Cute.*

"I told you," she said calmly, pressing the knife harder and watching the color drain from the man's face, "You can't handle me. Now, how about you let me finish my drink in peace and stop harassing women who are clearly out of your league?"

"You're insane, lady," the man hissed.

Ves just grinned. "I'm a witch, actually."

The man left without another word. Ves returned to her cinnamon rum, but when she went to eavesdrop again, she found the couple had already gone.

Ves returned to the *Dargason* to see Solveig rolling a barrel down the gangplank. Crates and barrels and old chests were stacked on the dock in a haphazard array.

"What are you doing?" she demanded.

Solveig looked up. "Oh, good. You're back. Here, you can help. We're abandoning ship."

Abandoning – "Poet's blood, what did you *do*, Cap?!"

Before Solveig could answer, a massive man walked over to them. His dark skin was colored with dozens of tattoos and iridescent discs hung from stretched ears. His long, dark twisted locks had been tied up off his face, showing off sharp cheekbones and a neat beard. When he reached to grab a barrel, she saw the word *PUNISHMENT* across his knuckles.

"This is our new quartermaster," Solveig said plainly. "Bartholomew Williams. Thol, meet Ves, our bo'sun."

Thol was several shades darker than Ves and only an inch or so taller – which was something because *she* was *tall*. Ves crossed her arms and looked him up and down.

"Thol has a ship he's letting us use," Solveig explained. "It's bigger. And it has running water and working plumbing. The *Serenity*."

Ves uncrossed her arms and thrust out a hand for her quartermaster to shake. "Well! I'll let you boys do the heavy labor while *I* go enjoy a nice, hot shower."

Solveig said something to her – an insult, an order, she didn't care – but Ves was already walking off, spying the polished red hull of the *Serenity*.

It was a beautiful ship, far nicer than the stolen *Dargason*. The figurehead was just as lovely as the rest of the brigantine. Ves paused to stare at it. Carved from rich, dark wood, a woman holding a star to her chest seemed almost lifelike, her hair billowing out around her slim face, her eyes covered by a blindfold that seemed *too* lifelike to be made from wood.

Approving the ship with a simple nod, Ves marched up the gangplank. She did a cursory inspection of the deck before slipping through one of the doors. There was a galley and a dining room, captain's quarters with a *massive* bed, a few empty rooms – some big enough to be barracks, others the size of medical rooms or storage space – and... *Gods,* she'd found it. A washroom located through one of the barracks. She wasted no time testing the toilet, the sink, the massive bath, and separate shower. They all had running water. Warm water!

"Well. Don't mind if I do." She turned the shower on and peeled off her clothes, dropping them into a pile on the tiled floor. She stepped under the warm stream of water, sighing happily as it soaked her hair and skin.

It probably would have been smart to find soap *before* getting in, but it was too late. She was already in paradise, determined to take the longest shower of her life after four years of sitting in her own filth. No amount of scrubbing could get the dirty film that clung to her skin after being locked away in I. J. Pen.

The water finally ran cold. Ves turned it off and stepped out, searching the room until she found a stash of towels. She dried off and braided her damp hair, putting her clothes back on before skipping out, humming her shanty as she went to find the men.

She found them on the main deck, putting supplies away.

"Oh!" she said, catching their attention. "By the way, I overheard something important while I was in town."

"I thought you went shopping," Solveig murmured.

Ves waved her hand flippantly. "I'll go shopping in the next town. Navy wives clog the ateliers here, anyway. But that's not the point. The *point* is that the navy has something I think we could use."

Thol leaned against the railing, one thick brow arched. "Are you going to elaborate, or is that the end of the story?"

Ves flipped him off. She said, "I *heard* that there is a map that tracks the Wandering Isle's location in real-time and that the navy has it."

Solveig and Thol exchanged a look.

It was Solveig who finally spoke. "I thought you wanted nothing to do with the navy. Was that whole *I don't want to go to Lenwell because the navy is there* spiel just an act?"

Maybe solitary confinement in I. J. Pen. wasn't such a terrible fate.

"I don't want to mess with the navy," she shot back. "But, you know, *maybe a map of a moving island will be helpful?*"

Thol pinched the bridge of his nose. He had a bit of scar tissue over the bridge. It had been broken at least once, and now would be forever slightly crooked.

"It's just a map," Solveig said. "How hard can a piece of paper be to steal? I say we get it. Ves is right; knowing where the Wandering Isle is would give us an advantage."

Natha had zero expectations when walking through the back door
of the restaurant that morning and yet somehow even those expectations weren't met.

She'd gotten up early that morning and read the paper while she
drank two cups of coffee. She dressed in her usual black attire, tied
back her hair, and left to meet the fishmonger at the restaurant
like she did every morning. She knew there would be a pile of
dishes in the sink and crumbs all over the floor. She knew the chefs
responsible for preparing breakfast would be sitting in the back,
sharing a sugar cigarette – the non-harmful yet just as addicting
alternative to tobacco, with smoke that acted like oxygen in the
lungs and smelled sickeningly sweet – and gossiping – probably
about Natha's divorce – instead of working.

She unlocked the door and stepped inside, pausing long enough
to grab her apron before the familiar knock from the fishmonger
came. She let him in.

"Mornin', Miss Divyne," the man said with a gap-toothed grin.
"I got a good catch for ya today. Swordfish, sawfish, green squid..."

Already Natha was planning out recipes. She could grill the
swordfish with lemon and parsley, serving it with onions and peppers. Green squid was a sweeter alternative to the regular squid, its
minty color giving it its name. It would be good in a soup or as a
pallet cleanser.

"Miss Divyne?" The fishmonger asked, pulling her attention
back to the present.

"Sorry," she murmured. "What did you say?"

"I asked if you wanted me to put them in the icebox for ya," he repeated.

"No, no, one of my –" she paused, realization suddenly settling on her shoulders, weighing her down.

Slowly, she turned, scanning the kitchen. Even if her useless chefs had been in the back, gossiping and smoking sugar, they would have come out when they heard her to avoid getting in trouble. They *always* did. And they were at leasr smart enough to turn on their stoves and pretend to look busy.

But the kitchen was silent. *Too* silent.

"I'll be right back," she said. She marched straight to the break-room door and shoved it open.

The lights were off; the air didn't smell of sugar smoke. She checked the bathroom next and gave the restaurant floor a cursory glance. She usually had three people for breakfast but there was *nobody.* Not a single person in the whole building except for her and the fishmonger.

"Miss Divyne?" the fishmonger called. Natha's eyes burned. She swallowed hard.

"Yeah," she said, defeated. "Put it in the icebox. Please. And thank you."

She took a deep breath, blinking back tears, and went to her stove. She turned the knob, lighting the flame, and got to work gathering ingredients – flour, eggs, a block of cheese, milk, and cream. If her cooks decided not to show up, she would have to do it herself.

The fishmonger got to work bringing the cuts of fish to the icebox while Natha cracked eggs into a bowl and whisked them up. Since she was the only person there, breakfast would have to be simple – crepes and omelets, fried toast with syrup and sugar, and pancakes with chocolate and blueberries. Easy. She could do it all with her eyes closed.

And she *had,* back at the Royal Academy of Culinary Arts. She'd cooked an entire platter with her eyes blindfolded for an exam and passed it with flying colors.

The door creaked shut, leaving Natha alone in the kitchen. For the first time in nearly a year, she started to hum, the gentle tune becoming a full blown song. She danced around the stove, flipping crepes and pancakes, mixing omelets and dipping toast in an eggy batter. Natha was not god-blessed or royalty, but she was a damn good cook.

By the time she finished serving the last stack of crepes – layered with cream and fresh strawberries sliced paper thin – the door swung open and mindless chatter killed her singing. Her gaze went stony, her grip on her spatula iron.

"Oh! Chef. Didn't know you were here early," one of her pathetic cooks said cheerfully.

"It's almost nine in the morning," Natha said coolly.

"Huh," the second arrival said as he tied his apron around his waist.

"On a Poetsday," she gritted. The first day of a two-day weekend, Poetsday was always the busiest of the week, which meant the breakfast crew had to get there *extra* early and the dinner crew always stayed late.

"*Oh!*" the third arrival cursed. "Sard, it is! I thought it was Dreamsday!" the *second* weekend day, and the *slowest* day of the week.

"Well, looks like you got everything done, Chef," the first cook said with a grin.

Had Natha been a fraction weaker than she pretended to be, she would have broken down in tears. She wasn't even thirty yet, but she swore she'd find a grey hair or two if her hair didn't fall out from stress completely.

She inhaled through her nose, then pointed at the door.

"Get out of my kitchen," she said as calmly as she possibly could. "And don't think about coming back."

"Wait, Chef," the second fool tried to plead. "Seriously. We thought it was Dreamsday. We went out drinking last night and lost track of time... It was an honest mistake! You can't just *fire* us."

"Get. Out. Of. My. Kitchen." She ground her teeth together so hard her jaw screamed in protest. "If I have to ask again, I will start throwing knives, and you know I don't miss. Get. Out."

They left. Not after sweeping bowls onto the ground and shouting obscenities at Natha. But they left, and the waiters came in to take the plates out to the customers, and Natha fell to her knees and began to sob.

Thol had not gotten up that morning expecting to be reunited with his best friend. He had not expected to join his best friend's pirate crew, holding only one station above *Vesperine Genevieve*. The fact that she was still alive was an enigma, and one Thol didn't have the brain capacity to delve into.

It had been a few years since he gave up piracy. He never thought he'd step onto another ship again, never thought the *Serenity* would become a pirate vessel.

He stared at the poorly drawn sketch he'd made in a hasty handful of seconds, wondering how his life had come to this. How he'd been roped in by a Solveig to do something so *utterly* stupid it might just border on genius.

Ves had asked him if he'd made his pledge, and Solveig had to sheepishly explain that the pledge they'd made up as kids was the oath he now had his crew swear. An oath Thol had already made years and years ago, the cosmic scales of divinity once again bringing Thol back to where he'd started.

Thol never actually visited the navy academy. Aside from seeing the outside of it, he didn't know what the inside held. For all he knew, those people Ves eavesdropped on *were* navy sailors planting a trap. Maybe in those four unaccounted years, Ves had become a navy sailor and *she* was the one leading them to their doom.

No. That didn't make sense. When Solveig and Thol were busy moving things from the *Dargason* to the *Serenity*, Solveig told Thol about his brief stay at Ivenis Justyce. About the Sinthoxine, how he was to be executed, how, in the very bowels of the most impregnable prison in the *entire world,* he had found the Witch of the Sea and befriended her.

That part was believable. Enemy or not, Thol had no doubt Solveig considered Ves his friend. He'd always been good at making friends with anyone.

In the tiny village they'd grown up in before either of them set out to sea, there was a goose that liked to destroy gardens and bite anyone who got close. Thol went to that yellow house at the top of the bluff one day and found Solveig sitting in the grass, the damn goose next to him, listening intently as Solveig spun a story about pirates and sirens.

Thol chuckled at the memory.

"Are you laughing at my plan, Flower Boy?" Ves put her hands on her hips.

Thol blinked. *Flower Boy?* Now *that* was a new one. "I wasn't listening. Apologies."

Ves rubbed her face. "Here's an idea, Cap: promote *me* to quartermaster and *demote* Flowers here to bo'sun."

Solveig quirked his lips into the whisper of a smile. "The plan's simple. Sneak in, take the map, leave before they even realize it's gone."

"The academy is huge," Thol deadpanned, even though he knew Solveig's plan was more detailed than that.

"We split up," Ves chimed in. "The academy's divided into three rough sections anyway – sections that the map would be in. I doubt they're keeping some priceless map in the *barracks.*" She tapped the rough drawing. "The record archives, the training hall, and the common area. The map could be in any of them."

"The archives mostly hold files on the enrolled cadets," Thol said, repeating what he'd overheard people say before. "But the training hall also includes lecture rooms, for classes on seafaring and navigation and whatnot. The common area is where they'd greet higher-ups. I hear there's a particularly gaudy portrait of Jonyth Commodore there."

Ves groaned dramatically. Thol barely had any sympathy. They were breaking into a *navy building*. It wouldn't be *easy*.

Then again, hadn't Vesperine Genevieve been responsible for sinking an entire fleet?

"Ves, you'll take the archives. Thol, you'll cover the training hall," Solveig said as he pointed to each section on the horrible drawing. "I'll take the common area."

"Shouldn't one of us take the common area instead?" Ves asked. Thol had to agree. Neither of them was as notoriously known as Solveig. He wasn't exactly *subtle,* either, with red hair, and that green coat he always wore.

"I'm shorter than both of you," Solveig quipped. "I'll blend in better. Oh, that's the second part of the plan. We need to steal uniforms. At least that way if we *are* inevitably caught, it won't be as quickly. They'll be looking for pirates, not...navy cadets."

"This is a terrible idea," grumbled Thol.

"We're all going to die, aren't we?" Ves sighed.

"Maybe," Solveig said with a wicked grin. "But that's half the fun of being a pirate, isn't it?"

There he is. Thol couldn't help the smile that tugged on his lips. There was that insane delinquent he'd befriended all those years ago. There was the kid who befriended a goose; the kid who snuck onto a pirate ship and demanded to join the crew; the kid who became a man worth five hundred million lune – the second most wanted in *all of Syrenis.*

There was his best friend again, after too many years apart. Pride swelled in his heart, for the first time in forever – since he'd felt that first kick of his unborn daughter in Meadow's belly. This wasn't just his best friend. Nox Solveig was his *captain.*

Ves pulled her knife from her belt and tossed it in the air, catching it without looking. "When do we plan on breaking in, Cap?"

"There's only one time when the building is closed to the public," Thol interjected. "Because all the sailors are fast asleep."

The three of them exchanged a glance.

"There's your answer," Solveig drawled lazily. "We'll break in tonight."

10

THOUGH NIGHT HAD FALLEN, the sky was still bright, illuminated by the two moons and a smattering of constellations that shone like diamonds against the inky swath of indigo. Had the streetlamps not been lit to illuminate the streets of Lenwell, Solveig had a feeling he wouldn't have any trouble seeing.

Ves and Thol spent the afternoon preparing the *Serenity* for departure since none of them wanted to stick around long after stealing from the navy. Ves had gone into town to snag some uniforms off a drying line and Thol went to finish some business, leaving Solveig to pace restlessly until they both returned.

And now, with the cover of night to protect them, Ves, Thol, and Solveig crept through the alleys, ill-fitting uniforms hiding their identities. For the most part. Solveig loathed parting with his coat, and his red hair stood out starkly against the pristine white uniform that was too tight in the shoulders. Nothing could conceal Thol's tattoos – not even gloves since his arms and neck were also covered. And Ves... Well, Ves looked *very* out of place, her uniform too baggy in the waist and too tight in the chest, her mess of curls untamed and her lip ring violating at least three different dress code rules.

The academy came into sight, moonlight reflecting off the roof, giving it an almost ethereal look. Lady Lightbringer supported the navy completely; Solveig didn't doubt it looked ethereal on purpose. He stopped in his tracks and held out a hand to stop the others.

"One hour," he whispered, reminding them of the plan. "Then we meet at the *Serenity,* no matter what. Thol, you're *sure* you're fine with this? It's not too late to back out."

Something unreadable crossed Thol's face, but he nodded, solemn.

"One. Hour," Solveig repeated.

He looked at the academy, visions of sinth and Jonyth and dark prison cells and burning ships sparking his mind. He shook those thoughts away and shifted to the balls of his feet, running towards the academy.

The common area consisted of three main spaces: the foyer, the mess hall, and the gathering hall. Solveig had quickly ruled out the possibility of the priceless map being stored where a bunch of hungry navy cadets dined. Logically, it would be in the gathering hall instead of the foyer – the space where cadets could collect for leisure, to play cards or read or smoke sugar cigarettes. The foyer seemed too...open. Too easy for anyone to snatch the map and get away with it.

Solveig made quick use of the pins Ves had lent him, unlocking the door in a matter of seconds. He slid the borrowed pins into his pocket and slipped inside. Darkness greeted him, a long stretch illuminated sparsely by sconces on the walls. He scanned his surroundings before clinging to one of the walls, walking slowly.

In the dim light, he could make out a few portraits and drawings framed on the walls – admirals, professors, ships... Despite himself, he stopped when he came face-to-face with an unfortunately familiar scowl. Even without the new scar splitting across his cheek and nose, Solveig recognized Jonyth Commodore instantly.

He had an entire hour to find the map and meet the others back at the *Serenity*. Plenty of time...

Reaching into his belt, Solveig pulled out a dagger. It was stupid. It would get them caught. But he didn't care. *This is payback for all those doses of sinth,* he thought as he jammed the knife into the portrait, splitting the oil-covered canvas with little resistance. He tore, mimicking the slash he'd made that fateful day weeks ago, giving an artificial scar to the painted Jonyth. When that wasn't enough, he tore another slash, the satisfying *riiiiiiiip* sending tingles down his spine.

Take that, Jonyth, he thought smugly. He admired his work for a moment, relishing how the jagged edges of canvas cast shadows over the rest of the portrait, before returning his dagger to his belt and continuing down the hall.

Just as he was about to turn down a corridor, footsteps sounded, the unmistakable clicking of boots on tile.

Solveig froze. Heart pounding against his ribs, he nervously looked around, trying to find *somewhere* to hide

"Yeah, right," a navy cadet snorted. "All that sugar's probably gone to his head. He had no idea what he saw."

"Hey, don't get mad at me," a second cadet said. "I'm just telling you what *I* heard through the grapevine."

With nowhere to hide in such a short amount of time, Solveig went with plan B. He puffed out his chest, putting on the same swagger he'd seen Jonyth ooze, and turned the corner to go down the corridor.

"Evening," he said to the cadets as he passed them.

"Evening," one of the cadets said without even looking up. "Lightbringer bless you."

Solveig bristled but repeated the phrase back. The cadets continued, still arguing about whether someone had actually seen a mermaid or not. Once their voices faded, his shoulders relaxed, and he let out the breath he'd been holding.

Wanting to get out of there before the cadets saw what he'd done to Jonyth's portrait, Solveig hurried down the corridor to the recreational room.

Sneaking in through a window was by far the hardest part of the entire heist, and even *after* he'd managed to squeeze his way

through the tiny opening not designed for broad shoulders to fit through horizontally, Thol grumbled to himself about how *he* should have been the one to waltz in through the front door, not Solveig.

He pulled his locks back, tying them into a messy bun to keep them off his neck, and scanned the room he'd found himself in. The training hall was set up on the second and third floors of the academy, with the classrooms on the third floor and the sparring rooms below. Having climbed through a second-floor window, Thol realized he was in a padded room with practice swords lined up against the wall. Made of whittled wood, the practice swords were no better than the sticks he'd used in pretend fights as a kid.

Spying the door across from the window, Thol abandoned the practice swords and strode over, letting go of a breath when the door – unlocked, thank Poet – swung open. He stepped into the dark hall, eyes struggling to adjust to the lack of moonlight, and picked a direction at random, hoping to come across a staircase since only an idiot (though who in the navy *wasn't* one?) would keep a priceless artifact where cadets who could hardly handle swords or guns trained.

Solveig had been wrong about one thing; just because he was shorter didn't mean he was any sneakier. Despite his massive size, Thol had the uncanny talent of being deathly silent. He was like a shark, predatory and still, able to sneak through the shadows without a sound. (He had a tattoo of a shark on his leg for that reason). The corridor of the training hall became his reef and Thol slipped into the tiger shark he'd once been.

Thol found a staircase at the end of the hall, one set of stairs going down to the part of the academy Solveig prowled, the other going up. Ducking to fit through the doorframe, Thol began his ascent, taking two steps at a time to reach the third floor.

A long hallway lined with doors greeted him once he arrived at the top. Some classroom doors were open, revealing lecture rooms with desks pushed about and windows letting in the moonlight, illuminating the floor in a river of silver. Thol peered into one of the classrooms. A slate board with the remaining scribbles from the day's lecture on currents took up most of the furthest wall. Next to it was a small shrine to Lady Lightbringer, another to Poet. All sailors, it seemed, worshipped the god of the sea and sky.

He went to the next door, pushing it open to see another classroom. The next three doors all led to more classes. *How dull,* he thought with a frown. *Why join the navy and sit through lectures when you can just get on a ship and experience the world for yourself?*

He closed the door and sighed through his nose. Unless there was a class to teach cadets how to track down an island that moved like it was alive, the map wouldn't be there. It would have to be in an office belonging to a professor.

There *was* a fourth floor, and the barracks were in a separate conjoined building. The fourth floor had to be the offices. If the map was going to be here, it would be in one of them.

He glanced over his shoulder. The stairs didn't go up anymore. There had to be another staircase somewhere. But...where? If he wanted to put his shoulders through hell again, he could climb out the window at the end of the hall and scale the building.

As if on cue, an ache surged across his shoulders from where he'd had to squeeze them to get through the window.

And four stories off the ground, hanging on by a very literal edge? Absolutely not.

He started opening doors at random, hoping a staircase would be hidden behind one.

Near the massive window, he found a narrow staircase. A plaque on the wall, barely lit up by the moonlight, read *ADMINISTRA-TION AND OFFICES.* Perfect. Pressing his hand against the wall so he knew where he was going, Thol stepped into the dark once again.

It wasn't until he reached the top of the stairs that it suddenly struck him.

This was a massive naval academy – the biggest in all of Aralyth.

Why weren't there any guards?

His stomach sank to his feet. There weren't any guards because this was either a trap, one they'd stupidly walked into, taking the bait, and surrendering to an unknown ambush.

Or... There were no guards because all the soldiers were watching over a priceless artifact. One that would be transported to Aramore – one that was probably being *prepared for transport.*

Solveig wasn't a silent fighter; if he'd been in a scuffle with the navy, Thol would've heard it, even three stories above. That meant...

Ves.

The map was in the archives, and Ves was down there, alone, a minnow in shark-infested waters.

Thol flew down the stairs, stealth be damned. He had to get Solveig, and he had to warn Ves before it was too late.

Ves pressed her back against the wall, peering through the gaps between books, tracking the paces the navy soldier on the other side of the shelf made. Besides her, there were nine people in the archives. When she'd first slipped in fifteen minutes ago, there were zero.

Which meant it was either a trap *or* the map was down here somewhere, amongst the dusty books and old ledgers.

She held her breath as the soldier walked off, vanishing behind another shelf. Guard lowered a fraction, she started scanning the shelf shielding her. The books were older than dirt, their titles irrelevant to the Wandering Isle. She brushed her fingers against the cracked spines.

Crack.

Every muscle in her body went taut as the wooden shelf bowed, cracking right in the center. Footsteps shuffled closer. Ves eyed the shelf nervously. Carefully, she picked up one of the books stacked on top of the others and stuffed it into the waistband of her trousers, just to get it out of the way. When the shelf didn't instantly crack, she scooted across the stone ground, putting three more shelves between her and the broken one.

Crash!

Books and wood fell to the floor as the shelf finally gave out. Footsteps ran towards it, lights from lanterns illuminating the spot she'd *just* been in.

"What is it?" a navy soldier asked, rounding the corner.

"Just a broken shelf," the man with the lantern grumbled. "I'm telling you; they need to upgrade the storage down here. I bet these shelves are older than both of us."

As if to prove a point, he kicked the base of the shelf, causing more books to topple over. In their distraction, Ves slinked to another hiding spot, trying to get as much distance between her and the navy.

"Come on," the first man said. "There's nothing down here. The others are playing cards; they'll deal us in the next round."

The second man eyed the broken shelf once more before deciding cleaning the books was not his job. He shrugged and followed his friend to archives' entrance, where the other seven huddled, playing a game of cards and blocking Ves's only escape route.

Unless she killed all nine men, she was trapped. If she didn't have Thol and Solveig to worry about, she would do it in a heartbeat. But killing them would alert the rest of the navy to their presence, and she did *not* have even the slightest desire to deal with any soldiers, not at all. She'd be sent right back to I. J. Pen. and that was the *last* thing she wanted. Death was a better outcome than being stuck in that dingy cell. At least in death she wouldn't have to worry about bathing.

Sighing, she let her ability take over. Nine humans, all men, huddled by the entrance. She could guess their ages and heights, but what use was there in that?

If I was a map to the Wandering Isle, where would I be...? Ha. Probably in Aramore, far from here. She snorted, then quickly covered her mouth with her hand, heart speeding up as she waited, still as death, to see if the navy soldiers found her.

She counted to thirty, then to a hundred, before relaxing.

Well, there was only one way to go, and that was deeper into the belly of the archives. Steeling herself, Ves sank low on her feet and shuffled further in.

It's a map, she chided. *How hard can it be to steal? You've stolen worse, after all.*

She delved deeper into the belly of the archives, skimming each shelf to see if there was an out-of-place map amongst the old books.

You stole a priceless gemstone before, remember? She smiled at the memory, at the phantom weight and warmth of the garnet she'd pilfered when she was little more than a girl.

You stole a rare hibiscus flower from Empress Nefeli's garden. Empress Nefeli of Merdyne prized her exotic garden above most other things. Ves had been a child when she snuck over the gate and picked the prettiest pink bloom. She was lucky Empress Nefeli was *Princess Nefeli* back then, just a few years older than Ves and uninterested in punishment.

You stole the heart of that Amazonian warrior...

Ves paused, something shiny catching her eye. A glint of metal amongst the old paper, something so *very* out of place. Glancing over her shoulder, she made sure the nine cadets were still by the door. Then, slowly, careful not to disturb the papers on either side of the thin sheet of tin, she pulled it free.

A lithograph. A *lithograph*. Of course! The damn map wouldn't be on paper. Paper was easily destroyed, but a lithograph? They were sturdier, they were more valuable. In the dim light, she coul make out the outline of Aralyth. Mountains and forests and rivers were imprinted deep into the sheet, perfect calligraphy spelling out *Keth Mountain* and *Icarus River* and *North Range*. She spotted Lenwell, north of Brook Green and Aramore, labeled with the universal symbol for *navy*. In the bottom corner was a signature – initials *H. Q.*

Ves set the lithograph down right where she'd found it.

The map to the Wandering Isle was supposedly being prepared for transport to Aramore. The safest way would be by train, avoiding the uncertainties the sea had to offer. But if nobody was supposed to *know*, it would make sense to put the map on a navy ship and sail it down to Aramore. After all, what pirates would raid a navy vessel without knowing what was on it? Lithographs couldn't be rolled up the way paper maps could, so it wouldn't be in a tube. It had to be in a box – a padded crate, a *chest*.

And then she saw it. The tiny spark of life, the yellow-gold aura of a person, a human, emerging from nowhere. Ves shoved herself against the wall, shrinking into the shadows as much as she could.

She didn't dare *breathe,* eyes tracking the aura as it became the shape of a human.

Her stomach sank. It wasn't a cadet, like the nine by the door. Even through the dim light she could make out the stripes on his sleeves, the badges and medals at his breast, and the air of confidence and authority he walked with.

Not a cadet. A sarding *commander.*

The highest ranks at the academy were usually lieutenants, as professors were retired officers. So...what was a *commander* doing here? And where had he come from? The only thing that interfered with Ves's ability to see the auras of life was distance. She could see up to a mile in any direction, not hindered by water or clouds or buildings.

Biting the inside of her cheek, Ves tiptoed deeper, trying to find where the commander had come from.

The entire room smelled of sugar smoke – sweet, slightly acrid, way too suffocating. Solveig frowned in distaste as the residual smoke filled his lungs, turning to oxygen and leaving a film of saccharine at the back of his throat.

Ignoring the smell as best as he could, Solveig looked around the room. A billiards table sat abandoned, a deck of cards tossed haphazardly atop it. Portraits of graduated cadets lined one wall. Curious, Solveig peered at it, trying to see if he recognized anyone.

He'd made it through the third row of framed portraits before someone behind him cleared their throat. Solveig jumped, reaching for his dagger as he turned around, already thinking up several excuses.

"If I was Jonyth Commodore, you'd be dead," Thol lazed, leaning against the doorframe.

"If you were Jonyth Commodore I would have smelled your bull a mile away," Solveig grumbled, though he let his shoulders relax. "Did you find anything?"

Thol shook his head. "I have a hunch, though."

Solveig turned back to the portraits long enough to tilt one askew. "And...?"

"And I think this is a trap."

Solveig froze. A trap?

His eyes widened. "The map's in the archives," he said. "Ves."

"She's in danger," Thol said. He stood up straight. "I think everyone on duty is down there right now."

Solveig stopped listening. He pushed past Thol and picked a direction, hoping the archives would be close. Navy or not, he had to save Ves. He couldn't let anything happen to his crew again.

"Nox, wait," Thol hissed. His footsteps thundered behind Solveig, but Solveig didn't stop. "Nox!"

Thol grabbed his shoulder, forcing him to a halt.

"First of all, the archives aren't even this way." Thol shook his head. "Second... We need a *plan*. If the archives are crawling with the navy, we can't just burst in, guns blazing. Be smart about things for once."

"When am I anything *but* smart?"

Thol just raised an eyebrow.

"We need a *plan,*" he repeated. "And with your permission, *captain,* I have one."

There was a *door* embedded in the wall, so faint and inconspicuous that if she hadn't been looking for it, Ves would have missed it completely. Eyeing the ten auras out of the corner of her eye, Ves approached the door, fingertips brushing against it. She couldn't see a lock or a *doorknob* for that matter. How was it supposed to open?

She stared at the door. She couldn't detect any life behind it – human, animal, insect, *nothing.*

It was like a massive wall was blocking her sight.

The hairs on the back of her neck stood on end, dread slithering down her throat to coil in her belly like a snake.

That's when she noticed the tiny hole next to the door. It was perfectly round, no bigger than a kase coin – just big enough for a finger to fit.

Ves swallowed her unease and slowly held her finger out, pushing it into the hole.

Something gave way with the tiniest, faintest *click.* In the silence of the archives, it was deafening.

Then, the door slid open, and she saw *it.*

11

It sat on a plush pillow atop a raised pedestal, no bigger than a book. Next to it was a wooden crate, the word *FRAGILE* stamped on the side as if *that* would deter anyone who came to steal it. Ves took a tentative step closer, just close enough to see the outline of the lithograph. It wasn't printed on tin or slate or any material she could recognize – it was as thin as paper but had the milky, shimmery iridescence of moonstone or opal, like the mapmaker had printed the thing on a precious rock instead of cheap metal. Another step and she could make out the jagged coastline of the Wandering Isle. She held her breath, waiting, and then...

It *moved*. So slightly, the movement so minuscule that anyone who didn't know what they were looking at wouldn't have caught it, but it moved. Ves stepped closer, closer still, and stared at the map. The Wandering Isle never went north of the midline for whatever reason. Even without the compass in the corner –

without the damn *coordinates* displayed at the top, degrees moving minutely – she could tell where it was. Just north of the frozen country of Frys, floating along lazily with seemingly no purpose.

The map is real...

Somehow, probably with a god-blessed gift, someone had been able to create a map tracking every movement the Wandering Isle made.

Mapmakers always put their signature on the map, some sort of symbol to identify them as the creator. *H. Q.,* like the initials on the first lithograph Ves found, was one of the most common across the Aralyth Empire. Part of Ves expected to see those familiar initials in the corner, but...

Three crescent moons, two back-to-back with the third stacked on top, were printed in the corner, just below the compass rose. She reached out, brushing her fingertips against it and –

At once, all the sconces in the room turned on, flooding the small space with bright, sterile light. Ten auras were quickly approaching – *sard!*

Ves grabbed the map and shoved it into her waistband. It was cool against her skin, though had a strange humming, vibrating sensation.

The door she'd just come through started to close – some stupid alarm system she overlooked that must have triggered when she grabbed the lithograph.

Oh, well, she thought, dashing for the door. *Too late for subtlety now.*

She slid through the door mere seconds before it shut, no doubt locking from the outside. Had she been even a *millisecond* slower, she would be trapped and at the mercy of the navy.

Ves would *not* be returning to I. J. Pen. anytime soon.

She picked a direction at random, running in the opposite path of the ten auras. If she'd learned anything in the twenty minutes she'd been down in the archives, it was that the place was a *maze.* A labyrinthine cage of dusty books and mildew-scented walls. She was a rabbit in an unfamiliar warren.

But she was clever if nothing else, and she was stubborn. And she *hated* the navy with a passion that burned brighter than the sun and both moons.

She would get her gods-damned captain the gods-damned map so he could find whatever gods-damned treasure it was he wanted. And when he became a very rich man, she would become a very rich woman, and she would buy a very expensive house – with a pool, a massive kitchen, and a *very* deep wine cellar – right on the coast of Merdyne, so she could sit on the beach and drink cinnamon rum and watch the sunset every sarding day –

Gold flashed in the corner of her eye. Ves dared a glance over her shoulder, her stomach flopping when she saw a cadet rounding the corner, stopping when *he* saw *her.*

Well, there goes being subtle.

In a flash, she pulled her dagger free, brandishing it with the intent to throw it. He was a kid – barely out of his teen years – brainwashed into thinking Lady Lightbringer and her shiny navy were the greatest things the world had to offer.

But Aralyth had no draft. The cadet was here because he wanted to be, not because anyone forced him to. If he wanted adventure, he could have become a pirate. If he needed money, there were brothels that would pay a pretty kase. If it was duty, well... There were more gods out there besides Lightbringer.

And Ves hadn't gotten her nickname for no reason.

She struck, fast as a viper, deadlier than a shark, the blade burying itself hilt-deep into the cadet's throat. Before his eyes could widen, before he could even *realize* he was going to die, Ves tore the knife free, dodging the spray of blood with the precision of a dancer, refusing to get any on her skin. She spent four years bleeding on herself; she could do without *more* blood.

The cadet collapsed, but Ves was already moving, retracing her steps to get back to the entrance. To get back to her *crew*.

"There!" A voice called, followed by a flurry of footsteps.

Six revolver barrels were trained on her in an instant.

Ves slowly, nonchalantly, raised her hands. "Look, boys," she drawled. "I don't want any trouble."

Her words didn't even have the chance to settle before she threw her knife, the blade slicing through the air.

Thunk!

It landed, wet and meaty, in the eye of one of the cadets. He collapsed to the ground, screaming, clawing at his face, trying to get the dagger – the pretty dagger she didn't want to lose – out.

"Fire at will!" one of the cadets shouted.

Ves was already running when the first round was fired. She ducked behind a bookshelf, pausing long enough to brush her fingers against the warmth of the lithograph. Good. It was still there.

She spotted the broken shelf out of the corner of her eye. At least she was going the right way...

Escape would come later. For now, she had seven cadets and a commander to deal with, to take out before they realized she wasn't working alone.

"Alright, then," she murmured to herself. "Let's see just how rusty you got."

"How is that any better than marching in, swords drawn?" Solveig asked as he kept pace with Thol – a considerable feat considering just how fast the insanely tall man was compared to Solveig.

There was a plant called Lightbringer's Kiss that, until five minutes ago, was completely unknown to Solveig. It was a red flowering plant in the shape of a heart that glowed blue at night. It grew everywhere, like a weed, but it was *especially* abundant around navy strongholds.

"It's just a flower," Solveig had said when Thol explained the plant. "We're going to give the navy *flowers?*"

"Their seeds are incredibly potent," Thol had said. "Think of opium from poppy seeds, only a hundred times stronger. If you get enough of them and crush them into a powder, it'll lace the air with a sleeping drug."

Solveig, despite wanting nothing more than forcing the navy into a deep sleep, couldn't help but think of Sinthoxine.

Thol came to a sudden stop. Solveig crashed into his back.

"What was that for?" Solveig hissed, rubbing his nose with his arm, his hands too full of heart-shaped blue flowers. He swallowed back a sneeze.

"Gunshots," Thol breathed.

Solveig went silent, listening over the night for the explosions.

Bang! Bang bang!

He nearly dropped his armful of Lightbringer's Kiss. *Ves!*

"Plan B?" Solveig croaked, fear already coursing through his veins. Visions of his old crew dying, sinking, drowning while high on sinth...

"You're the captain," said Thol, who, for the first time in his life held a position below Solveig.

Solveig paused, waiting to hear if there were more gunshots. When there weren't he said, "Plan A and a half. We drug the navy, and we fight like hell. We aren't leaving without Ves or that map."

Thol's lips tugged into a half smile. "As you command, Captain."

Solveig bit the inside of his cheek. With gunshots... It would only be a matter of time until the other cadets woke, until higher officers came to their aid.

Until Jonyth Commodore realized it was *Solveig* stirring up trouble in Lenwell.

He shoved those thoughts aside. Ves was in trouble, Witch of the Sea or not, and he was her captain. It was his job to rescue her, whether she truly needed rescuing. Clutching the Lightbringer's Kiss to his chest, careful not to inhale too much of the dusty blue pollen, Solveig passed Thol, pausing outside the archives door long enough to lift his leg and kick, forcing the door inwards.

Three cadets, eyes wide and guns clutched awkwardly to their chests greeted Solveig.

Solveig grinned a wicked grin, teeth flashing in the dim light. He threw the Lightbringer's Kiss into the air, holding on to only a single handful.

"Surprise!" he said, and he grabbed the shirt of one of the cadets, yanking him close and shoving the opium-like flowers into his face.

"Wait –" the second cadet cried, but Thol was quicker, forcing a fistful of flowers into the cadet's mouth before he could even think about squeezing the trigger on his revolver.

Both cadets crumpled, one after the other, unconscious before they even hit the ground.

"Guns blazing?" Solveig asked, making a mock gun with his forefinger and thumb.

"Guns blazing," Thol said.

Solveig scooped up one of the abandoned pistols and ran, following the distant shouting. There was no telling how many navy men crawled amongst the shelves, hungry for pirate blood. Anyone –

Shing!

Metal whizzed through the air, slicing a few strands of red hair before burying in one of the shelves mere inches from Solveig's head. He froze, going completely still to not catch another stray dagger.

A cadet – no, a private – stared at Solveig, eyes wide and face blanched. He was panting, chest heaving, like throwing that dagger had cost him everything.

Solveig raised his stolen gun and fired without hesitation. The private cried out in agony, knees buckling as bone split, the bullet tearing straight through his lower leg. Blood sprayed, splattering on the precious books and maps.

Maps!

There was no time to stop and see if any of the maps lined up with the ancient one Anwir gave him; Solveig grabbed the oldest-looking one from a shelf and shoved it into his waistband to look at later. The private screamed in pain, writhing as he cradled his leg. Keeping him alive was risky, especially when he'd yap to the higher ups about who broke in. The last thing Solveig needed was Jonyth on his trail.

Solveig slammed his boot into the private's head, knocking him out to give him *some* mercy. More than the navy had ever given him.

Bang!

Gunshots too close for comfort rang out, followed by a heavy *crash!* Solveig spun around just in time to catch a plume of dust rising in the distance.

"There's a commander!" Ves screeched.

A *commander?!*

Ves slid over a waist-high shelf, flicking her wrist behind her. A blade flew through the air, too fast to comprehend.

"Wait, don't!" Solveig tried to warn her. "Drugged flowers!"

Ves, despite her hurry, paused just long enough to stare at Solveig, to see if he was serious.

Bang!

A bullet whizzed through the air, followed by Ves's scream. Her hand flew to her left arm, clutching it tightly as, even in the dim light, red blossomed, soaking through the fabric of her stolen uniform instantly.

"Get to Thol!" he shouted, voice authoritative. He was her captain; he would *not* sit by and let her get hurt again.

"Oh, piss off, Cap!" She argued, of course. She held her other hand out, palm to the ceiling, concentrating on her fingers.

A fist collided with Solveig's jaw.

His teeth rattled, mouth filling with iron when he bit into his tongue. Without pausing to see who had hit him, Solveig acted.

He grabbed the arm of the attacker, gripping it *hard*, and *yanking*. As the attacker stumbled forward, Solveig swept his leg out, hitting the man behind the knees to knock him down.

As the attacker went down, he grabbed Solveig's middle, dragging him down, too. Only then did Solveig realize the rank of the man.

This wasn't a cadet. This was the commander.

Solveig buried his fist into the commander's gut, wishing it was a knife instead of knuckles. Blood dribbled down his lip, into the stubble along his jaw. He spat a mouthful at the commander.

The commander grinned a wicked grin.

And at once, the world went...still. Silent. It was Solveig and the commander, and they were no longer in the archives.

They were nowhere, everywhere, in a dark expanse of just them.

"CAP!" Ves screeched.

Thol curled his fingers into a pair of fists, holding them so *punis* and *hment* joined together to spell out the fate of the cadet in front of him. He cracked his fist against the cadet's cheek, knocking him unconscious in one swoop. Hardly waiting for the cadet's limp body to fall, Thol ran, following the direction of Ves's scream.

"Ves?" he asked when he found her. "What's wrong? Where's... Where did Nox go?"

Ves turned to him, her eyes wide and full of a harried, frazzled, unreadable expression that made Thol's stomach queasy.

"He's *gone,*" she blabbered. "He was just here, fighting the commander, and now I can't sense *either of them.* I don't know *where they went.* Oh, *sard,* this *sarding hurts!*"

He noticed the blood then, the way she held her arm tightly.

She sucked in a breath through her teeth. "It just grazed me. I'm fine. Where in the *sarding sard did our captain go?!*"

Thol popped his knuckles, making fists that spelled *PUNISH-MENT* once again. Footsteps sounded; a cadet came running, brandishing a sword. Thol swung, knocking him out with a single, unfocused punch.

"Did you get the map, at least?" Thol shook out his hand.

"Yes, I got the map, Flowers," she snapped.

"Just checking, Witch."

"In here!" A voice shouted, followed by a stampede of footsteps, boots against the hard ground, the click of guns being readied and the *shing* of swords being drawn.

Thol stepped closer to Ves. She pressed her back against Thol's, a dagger in her hand. Where had she even gotten it?

"I really didn't want to fight the navy," she groaned. "I was promised a shopping spree."

"I was promised retirement," grumbled Thol. He clenched his fists, raising them with the intent of fighting. "But we're pirates, Witch. Fighting the navy's what we do."

"You're in charge, first mate," she reminded him. The footsteps drew closer.

"Fight like hell," Thol said. "And don't die."

He couldn't see her, but he knew she was grinning.

The navy men – cadets and privates and lower-ranking sailors – rounded a corner and stopped, guns drawn and aimed at the two pirates. For a precious split second, nothing happened. There was a lull, a pause, a hesitation on both sides as they each waited for the other to make the first move.

"FIRE!"

Explosions rang out, but Thol was faster, deadlier, and he was already in the thrall, fists striking jaws and guts. He struck rapidly, not caring who or what he hit.

Bam, bam, bam! His mind relaxed, breathing falling into pace. Fighting was just another dance. He didn't care where Ves was, only what he was doing, only that his punches landed.

He grabbed the arm of a soldier and yanked, ripping him off his feet and using him to knock another three navy sailors down. He dropped the weaponized man and tackled another, throwing him to the floor. Bullets shot past his face, narrowly missing his jaw, his ears, his hair. His knuckles started to ache, flesh threatening to split as it stretched taut over bone, colliding again and again and again, a rapid hellfire raining down.

Outranked or not, Thol had the urge to protect Solveig, no matter what.

People didn't just disappear. Solveig had to be here somewhere.

He would make sure the archives were safe when his captain returned.

12

"Nox Solveig, I presume?" the commander drawled. He spat a bloody tooth on the ground. Solveig wished he'd punched harder, hard enough to loosen *two* teeth.

"There should be a captain at the beginning of that," Solveig said.

"Admiral Commodore told us about your little escape." At that, Solveig frowned. Escape? He hadn't *escaped*. If he'd escaped, he would have *some* dignity left. No. He'd been given a temporary pardon, an hour's head start to escape Jonyth to find whatever it was Anwir wanted.

"Jonyth Commodore couldn't even hold me down." Solveig felt for his pistol. It wasn't at his hip. *There.* It must have fallen in the scuffle. It lay a few feet away, unnoticed by the commander. Solveig didn't give it more than a glance, not wanting to draw the commander's attention to it. He said, "What makes you think *you* can catch me?"

Wrong thing to say.

The commander twisted his face into a contortion of rage. He drew his sword and swung, a deadly arc of silver splitting the air far too close to Solveig.

Solveig narrowly jumped back in time, the blade skimming where his torso had just been.

Without wasting any more time, Solveig ran, diving for the abandoned pistol and grabbing it. He aimed and squeezed the trigger.

Click.

No, no, no, no, no, no, no –

Click. Click. Click.

The blasted thing wasn't even *loaded!*

Solveig's heart thrummed against his ribs. He threw the pistol. The gun hit the commander in the shoulder, hard.

Armed with nothing but his hands, Solveig clenched his fingers into fists and charged, wasting no time.

He swung, hardly waiting to see if his punches landed before swinging again and again.

"You're more pathetic than I thought, *Captain* Solveig," the commander spat.

The commander thrust his blade up. Solveig had no weapon of his own to block it. He threw up his arm, wincing as metal sliced through flesh.

"So are you, Commander," Solveig shot back.

He reached for the blade, desperate to pry it free and have it as his own. The commander caught on; he swung the sword, the sharp edge cutting into Solveig's palm.

Solveig did his best to ignore the rivulets of blood sluicing down his palm and dripping onto the floor. He could worry about his injuries later – *after* he won the fight.

The commander swung again, but Solveig was quicker this time, diving to the floor, his knees crashing hard against the ground. He grabbed the gun and thrust it up just as the sword came down. Solveig pushed all his strength into holding the gun up, forcing the sword back and back and back and –

Solveig suddenly rolled to the side, so fast that the commander was up against gravity. The commander stumbled forward, his balance gone. Solveig sprang to his feet and tackled the commander, wresting the sword from his hands in the moment of distraction.

Solveig leveled the blade, the tip right against the commander's throat.

"Surrender," said Solveig.

"Never," hissed the commander.

Maybe he needed to stop offering his enemies mercy.

Faster than lightning, Solveig struck. He tore the blade across the commander's throat. Flesh tore, ripping like flimsy fabric. Blood sprayed.

The commander's eyes went wide. He choked, gurgling, and drowning in his own thick blood. It spilled down his chin.

He collapsed, and so, too, did the strange darkness that had surrounded them.

Back again in the archives, a slew of bodies – most unconscious, some not – around them. Ves spun around to face Solveig first, like she knew he'd returned.

"Cap!" she exclaimed.

"Back to the ship!" Solveig ordered.

He took off running, jumping over bodies in the race to the stairs. Cold night air greeted him with a kiss on his cheeks, a relief from the blazing summer sun that had beat down on them all day. Sparing only a glance over his shoulder to make sure Ves and Thol were following, Solveig gripped his stolen sword tightly and ran for the harbor.

An hour after fleeing Lenwell, Ves, Thol and Solveig gathered on the deck, a barrel acting as a table for the map Ves laid out.

A lithograph, printed on some shiny rock-like material, the familiar shape of the Wandering Isle moving ever so slowly across the expanse.

Solveig picked at the bandage wrapped around his palm, eyes tracking the coordinates as they changed. Ves had done it. She'd found the map and stolen it, and now... Now they knew where the Wandering Isle was at all times. They didn't have to rely on luck to find it or to avoid the doldrums it caused in its wake.

He reached out, brushing his fingers against the precise lines. The lithograph seemed to hum beneath the pads of his fingers, warm and radiant. *Alive.*

Ves sat on the deck with a dramatic huff. A bottle of cinnamon rum, unopened, clattered against the polished wood, knocked over in her theatrics. She grabbed it and pried out the cork, taking a generous swig. After gulping it down like it was water and wiping her mouth with the back of her hand, she sighed heavily.

"I don't know about you boys," she said, "but I think I'm going to take a *long* bath, then go right to sleep. Wake me if anything exciting happens. Or don't. I don't care."

She stood, took another drink, and started for the door leading to the designated *women's quarters.*

"You going to share the rum?" Thol asked.

Ves just laughed and flipped her middle finger to him over her shoulder.

Solveig waited until her door was shut before saying, "What business did you have to attend earlier?"

Thol looked up from the map. "There's a girl who works at the botanist's. I asked her to take care of my wife's garden while I'm away."

His wife. Reunited with his best friend for less than a day, Solveig had already forgotten about Thol's...marriage.

"Your –" he started, but Thol stopped him with a subtle shake of his head.

"I'll talk about her when I'm ready," he said.

Solveig looked back at the map, at the shifting coordinates. The Wanderer themselves must have played a role in its creation. Or someone god blessed. The longer he thought about it, the more Solveig realized the navy commander must have been divine touched to create...shields. Vacuums of some sort, little pockets where nothing else existed.

"Sorry I dragged you out of retirement," Solveig said.

"No, you're not," Thol said.

Solveig looked at his sworn brother with a grin. "You're right. I'm not. I'm beyond happy to have you back."

Thol lazily punched Solveig's shoulder. He said, "You're the only idiot who could drag me out of retirement. If anyone else tried, they'd get a face full of punishment."

Grinning wider, Solveig leaned all the way back, until he was laying on the deck, staring up at the starry sky. "You don't have to tell me about your missus, but how about this: you tell me about how you became the captain of the *Sea Wyrm,* and I tell you about the crew *I* captained?"

Thol silently moved around the barrel, laying down next to Solveig. Solveig didn't have to look over to tell where Thol's gaze landed – the reddish star shining brighter than all the others.

"It happened not long after you left..." Thol began.

Illie hunched over the table in the back room of the Ink and Rose, sucking on her bottom lip as she carefully traced a line she'd drawn a dozen times before. She could draw the continent of Veridin with her eyes closed, yet she still kept her hand slow and steady as she drew the northern coast with the care and precision she'd had since the first time she drew it, years and years ago.

With one final stroke of her pencil, the continent was whole. Illie let out the breath she'd been holding and sat back to examine her work. While she lacked Elgar's flair for intricate details and artistic extravagance, she'd managed to label all the major cities and landmarks: the Belt Mountains, bisected by the Cage Pass; the Vicious Desert curled around the Spit Bay; the Vern Mountains south of Veridonia; the Icarus Strait in the north, Bowhead Rock jutting out just off the coast; the Sapphire Sea to the west, the Emerald Sea to the east, and the Amethyst Sea in the south.

She picked up an ink quill and scribbled her initials – *I. V.* – in the corner, branding the map as hers.

"Elgar!" she shouted, leaning back in her chair. "Map's ready to be inked!"

Usually, Illie would ink the maps she drew, but with a backlog of work to be done, she had to shoulder some of the work to Elgar, who, despite grumbling about tracing over her work, was happy to get out of running the front desk. Elgar slipped into the back and wordlessly grabbed the map.

Illie reached into the drawer beneath her desk and pulled out a fresh sheet of paper. As she affixed it to the table, securing the corners with paperweights and making sure it was completely straight, she looked at the list tacked to the wall. Beneath *map of Veridin* was her next task: *Triangle of Fylth, isle triad (no cities listed, leave middle blank).*

With one hand, she dug through another drawer, pulling out the notebook she'd brought with her on her two global journies.

She flipped through the worn, dogeared pages until she found the sketch of the three islands with all her cartographic notes.

She picked up her pencil, twirling it over her fingers a few times before sketching out the lines of the imaginary triangle. Years of practice made her hand steady and sure; she could draw a straight line with little more than a flick of her wrist. Still, she pulled out the ruler she'd made specifically for charting degrees and the triangulation surveys she'd calculated during her trip around the world, and she lay it against each of the lines, making sure they lined up with the etches in the ruler. Frowning, she erased one of the lines and redrew it a fraction to the left.

Maps of the Triangle of Fylth were incredibly popular among treasure hunters. Leaving them mostly blank was for the special treasure hunters who wanted to chart where shipwrecks lay beneath the tumultuous waves of the infamous expanse of sea. Some people claimed the god Poet lived beneath the Triangle, and it was his fury at the people who dared to cross that caused so many ships to sink there.

Satisfied with her lines, Illie started sketching out the dramatic outline of Servedin, an island that would be less identifiable without the Jes Bay that split deep into it. Before she could finish the southern coast's curve, the bell above the door jingled.

"If you want me to ink your maps, *you* get it," Elgar shouted from his desk deeper in the back. Illie groaned but shoved her chair back and stood. She tucked a strand of pink hair behind her ear and rounded the corner to the counter.

She froze, still as a statue, when she saw the people standing in her shop.

Pirates were among the most common customers in any map-making shop, but they almost always knew to treat the cartographers with respect, lest they get a faulty map that would send them straight to their watery doom. Pirates usually gave the best tips, keener to be out a few extra lune than lost in the middle of nowhere because the coordinates on their maps were purposely off. They were better than the navy, who paid the minimum price with snark and disrespect, trusting Lady Lightbringer to guide them to the right place.

There were six of them, all bulky men smelling of salt and gunpowder, greasy hands touching the maps on the walls and the inventory on the shelves, smudging pristine parchment with oil and deck polish. Illie bristled, hackles raised. There were *countless* signs on the walls and shelves instructing patrons *DO NOT TOUCH* and *YOU BREAK IT, YOU BUY IT.*

Either the pirates didn't know how to read (unlikely, since most pirates *had* to know how to read at a basic level) or they simply did not care.

Illie put her palms flat on the counter, a trick of submission. Make the pirates think she was unarmed, unable to fight, because her hands were in plain sight, ignoring the fact that she didn't wear shoes inside and could use her foot to pry open the drawer beneath the counter where a loaded revolver and a dagger sat (Henry's necessary anti-theft measures he'd only implemented *after* hiring a young, impressionable girl as his apprentice).

"Well, well, well," the biggest of the pirates – the one wearing a red coat – drawled. He stepped closer to the counter, leaning down. His breath stank of fish and sugar smoke. Illie schooled her expression, doing everything in her power to not scrunch up her nose in disgust. The pirate continued, "Where's the mapmaker, pretty girl?"

Illie lifted her chin, defiant. "I'm the mapmaker," she said. It was true, after all. Henry was basically retired, and Elgar preferred art over actual cartography.

The pirate tossed his head back and laughed, a full belly laugh that had the rest of his crusty crew laughing, too. Heat rose to Illie's cheeks. She dug her nails into the wood countertop and pulled the hidden drawer open with her foot.

"She's a cheeky one!" the pirate – Illie guessed he was the captain – said. "Really, lass. Where's the mapmaker. You might be a cute doll, but I won't ask twice."

Illie sucked in a harsh breath through her nose. She said, as calmly as she could, "I am the mapmaker."

The pirates exchanged a look Illie knew meant bad news.

She snuck her big toe beneath the gun, trying to leverage it out without making it obvious.

"I am," she said as slowly and carefully as she could, "the mapmaker. What can I help you with?"

The captain slammed his hands on the counter. Illie flinched, quickly sweeping her skirt over the open drawer so the pirate couldn't see what was inside.

"See, I find that a bit hard to believe," he lazed, drawing out his syllables in a way meant to be demeaning. "Mapmaking is a man's job."

The words were out before Illie could stop them. "What I have between my legs has *nothing* to do with my ability as a cartographer. You're clearly *projecting.*"

As soon as the words were out, followed by a silence so thick and heavy it would've been more stifling than a lead quilt, Illie knew she messed up. She needed the gun *now* if she wanted to even *imagine* living to see the next five minutes.

Yet the silence was shattered, not by gunshots or Illie's bloody death rattle, but rather... by *laughter.*

For a single, naïve second, Illie's shoulders relaxed. The pirates wouldn't have her head for her emasculating quip.

Her naivety didn't last long. Not with the hand suddenly wrapped around her throat, thumb pressing harshly into her jugular. She stiffened, not daring to even blink lest she find her neck snapped like a flower stem.

"It was cute the first time," the captain said, jaw against her ear. "But it's annoying now. Had you not gone and said that, I would have spared you. But nothing pisses me off more than smug little brats who think they rule the world. If you're so insistent on being the mapmaker, doll, I'll treat you like one."

Illie swallowed hard, her throat constricted against the roughness of his palm.

"There is a map I want. A map *to* the Wandering Isle. Not of it; *to it.*" He let go of Illie's throat. She reached up, rubbing her sore neck as she coughed, desperate to get a decent breath of air into her aching lungs.

"Th-there's no such thing," she sputtered. "You ca-an't track an island that m-moves."

"You're the mapmaker, Dollie," the pirate said. "Make it for me. I'll be back in two days to collect."

"We require a deposit upfront. Fifty percent," she said, her tongue once again moving before she could tell it to stop.

The pirate raised a bushy brow. "Your deposit is your life, Dollie. If you can make it, you'll get payment. However much lune you want. But if you fail..."

One of the other pirates grinned and ran his thumb across his neck.

The captain just shrugged. "I'll be taking that *deposit* back."

The pirates, all of them, left, not before pulling down a stack of paper from a shelf and scattering it on the floor to step on.

The door closed. Illie slumped against the counter. Her body trembled, fear surging through her veins.

"Illie?" Elgar poked his head out from the back, *finally* deciding to show up after the threat was already gone.

"I'm fine," she said, kicking the drawer shut. "I'm fine. Can... Just... Please watch the counter for me."

Not waiting for a response, she rounded the corner and crouched down, picking up the ruined paper. She gathered it all into a stack, which she dropped in front of Elgar. She stomped to the stairs, shoving her feet into her boots, and left the Ink and Rose without an explanation, determined to find Henry.

13

Sunshine beat down on the city of Carilon, the sand hot, the sea water warm, the day *perfect*. Moored at the harbor, their dues paid to the harbormaster who was more than happy to turn a blind eye to the colorless pirate ship at the dock with a few extra lune tossed in, the *Serenity* bobbed gently in the lapping waves.

It had been four days since their scuffle with the navy in Lenwell. Four days of sailing through currents that pushed them down the coast far faster than Solveig would have expected. Four days to study the lithograph of the moving Wandering Isle.

To study the ancient map Anwir had given him, to make sense of the words scribbled around the border.

The map Solveig had grabbed from the navy archives turned out to be incredibly uninteresting and useless – a map of the tiny island Gello, one of the three making the triad that formed the Triangle of Fylth. Not wanting to throw it away, Solveig had tacked it to the wall in his quarters for a bit of decoration.

He stood on the deck of the *Serenity*, eyes closed as he breathed in the warm summer breeze, salt filling his sinuses in a way that was familiar and...soothing.

A palm smacked his back hard enough to draw him from his peace.

"You gonna just stand there all day, or are you gonna come into town with us?" Ves asked. With her hair tied back, held off her face with a strip of fabric, and her outfit of tight trousers tucked into tall boots and a blouse that cut *low,* leaving *very* little to imagination, she looked more like a pirate than a tourist.

"I'll come with you," Solveig said, raking his hand through his red hair. "But I am *not* sitting in an atelier while you try on every bit of clothing they have."

Ves stuck out her bottom lip in a dramatic pout.

"Don't think about asking me, either," Thol called as he hopped down the steps to the main deck. He wore his shirt unbuttoned, exposing the array of tattoos across his toned chest, the sleeves rolled up past his elbows, his *PUNISHMENT* on display.

Ves groaned loudly. "You both are no fun. Petition to have our next crew member be a girl. I need *someone* I can go shopping with."

"You can *shop* with us." Solveig hopped over the railing, landing on the dock hard enough to shake it, water spilling over the sides. "But I have no desire to sit for hours while you try to figure out *what* to buy."

"Half the fun of shopping is trying stuff on," she argued, her tone light and playful, even as she jumped over the railing, landing even harder beside Solveig. He threw out his arms, quickly catching his balance before he could topple into the warm, clear water below.

"Thol, back me up here," Solveig whined.

"You can complain *after* you've been married to a woman," Thol said as he walked down the gangplank, far more civilized than both Solveig and Ves.

He secured the mooring lines, triple-checking that they were tight. Solveig watched, silent. Married to a woman... He never envisioned himself marrying *anyone*. The thought of settling down with anyone – woman *or* man – seemed...too domestic. He'd have to give up piracy, and...*Poet,* what if he somehow had children? Solveig struggled with remembering to drink water instead of rum most of the time and he could hardly keep himself out of trouble. Adding an actual child to the mix...

He shoved those thoughts aside, instead focusing on the task at hand: get supplies, lie low for a bit while they shook the navy off their tail, and talk to a cartographer about the lithograph. Solveig planned on sailing for the Wandering Isle after leaving Carilon – and making a final stop in Veridin, further down the eastern coast. If anyone knew about the body of a dead, forgotten god, wouldn't it be the people whose very home was constantly being moved by another god?

Carilon, being one of the bigger cities in the Veridin Kingdom, was made up of colorful buildings squished close together, sand from the beach tracked onto the cobblestone streets. Ivy-woven pergolas stretched from rooftop to rooftop, creating a canopy of shade over some places, shielding outdoor café seating from the harsh summer sun and offering a bit of respite for children tired after chasing each other with sticks shaped to look like swords. As he passed an alley, Solveig saw a trio of kids skipping rope, chanting a familiar rhyme.

"Captain Nox Solveig, cloaked in green, set out to conquer the Emerald Sea..."

He shoved his hands into the pockets of his green coat, suddenly wishing he'd left it on the *Serenity.* The kids didn't look up from their game, too concentrated on counting the navy ships Solveig legendarily sank as the third hopped over the rope.

"Oh, my *gods,"* Ves suddenly exclaimed, the sound of children laughing fading beneath her voice. "Do you smell that?"

Thol lifted his chin, eyes closing for a brief second. "Smells...sweet."

Solveig's mouth was already watering. "Whatever it is, I want it."

"I think it's coming from the café over there." Ves pointed at a dusty pink building, a cream-and-rose awning framing the massive window taking up nearly the entire front wall. Wire tables stretched onto the street, the people sitting at them chatting idly as they nibbled sugary pastries – *definitely* the source of the sweet aroma.

As if on cue, Solveig's stomach let out a whale-like grumble.

"Change of plans," he said, determined. "We can gather supplies *after* we try whatever those things are."

Ever loyal was his crew as they followed him into the café. A woman stood behind the counter, flour dusting her apron and her hair stuffed into a crooked bonnet.

"I'll be just with you," she said without looking up from the stack of receipts she was wrist-deep digging through. When she finally looked up, something dark crossed her round face. She cleared her throat and said, "Wh-what can I get you?"

Ves all but smushed her face against the glass display case, ogling the confections and deserts ready to be eaten. Paper thin dough wrapped around cream and fresh berries, miniature cakes piled high with rich chocolate frosting, decadent tarts with perfect lemon filling, cone-shaped sweets with slivered almonds and raspberries, and oozing chocolate...

"That," Ves said, pointing at the latter. "Three of those." She jabbed her thumb against the glass a few more times, leaving unsightly smudges behind.

The woman's throat bobbed, and she nodded stiffly, nervously. With hands that trembled, she reached into the case, plucking out three of the raspberry treats. The café had gone silent. Solveig glanced over his shoulder. Everyone inside had gone still, busying themselves with the paper or looking at the walls.

Slowly, Solveig reached into his pocket.

The woman dropped the pastries on the counter and held her hands up in surrender instantly. "Please don't shoot," she whispered, not moving an inch.

Solveig's brow creased. He may be a pirate, but he wasn't going to rob some quaint bakery of three desserts... He pulled his hand from his pocket and set a few crumpled lune on the counter.

"You know who we are?" Solveig asked, watching as Ves scooped up the paper parcels.

The woman shook her head quickly. "N-no, sir. No, I don't. I... You're pirates, aren't you? You're with those..." she didn't finish her sentence.

"Those...?" Thol prompted, hiding his tattooed hands before she could see them and connect the dots.

"A week or so ago, these pirates came into town." She spoke in a hushed tone now, so faint it was barely audible. "They've taken over. They're capturing women and killing anyone who defies them. You're not with them, are you?"

Ves's excitement dwindled to nothing, her face steeling. "Who are they."

The woman swallowed hard again. She gathered up the lune, gripping the bills tightly. "I... I heard they're calling themselves the Redcoat Pirates."

A little too close to Solveig's signature green coat, but he wasn't calling his three-man crew the *Greencoat Pirates*.

Ves hugged the parcels close as Thol asked, "Where might we find these *Redcoat Pirates?*"

"Why?" the woman breathed.

"So we can run them out of town," Solveig said. He grinned, giving the woman a savvy wink. "And *we* can claim Carilon and put it under *our* protection."

The woman's eyes went glassy, fogging up with tears. She sucked her bottom lip between her teeth and said, "I hear they're up at the lighthouse on Bowhead Rock. You'll need to find someone to take you up there. The lighthouse keeper hasn't responded to any messages lately..."

"Aye," Ves said. "And when we come back, I expect more desserts from you." She took the woman's hand and kissed the back of it. "Seem like a decent payment for getting rid of these vermin?"

Tears rolled down her flushed cheeks, but the woman nodded. She whispered a thank you, so very soft, as the three left the café.

"Let's go to Lenwell to get supplies," mocked Ves between bites of her sugary pastry. *"We won't fight the navy. Let's go to Carilon to get more supplies, we won't fight pirates."*

She slid down the wall she'd been leaning against and sat, unceremoniously, on the cobblestone ground, nibbling on her treat like a child on the verge of a tantrum. She wasn't really upset about the idea of fighting pirates. In fact, she *wanted* to.

But her captain seemed to have a penchant for attracting danger where there shouldn't be any.

"Ves," Thol warned.

"I'm curious, Cap," she said, ignoring him. "Why did you agree to run those Redcoats out of town? It's not *our* problem. And claiming a city as big as Carilon as our territory... We'll basically be telling the navy *we're right here! Come get us!*"

Solveig licked powdered sugar from his fingers before saying, "Carilon is an important port city. If we control Carilon, we control the Icarus Strait. If we control the Icarus Strait, the navy will have to go around Aralyth or Veridin to cross from the Emerald to the Sapphire."

Ves popped the last bite of her pastry in her mouth, chewing slowly as she considered. Controlling the regulation of goods that passed through the Icarus Strait would make them some of the richest people in the Emerald Sea. And she *did* want more of those raspberry pastries...

Who was she kidding? She was *itching* for a good fight. A filthy fight with no rules, the kind she'd only get when fighting another pirate. Four years in prison did nothing to soothe her temper.

"I want to go shopping, first," she said, hauling herself to her feet. "We can fight these Redcoats *after* I get some new clothes." *And a collection of soaps, and some cosmetics, and a pretty dagger since the last one is back in Lenwell...*

"Fine," Solveig said. "But *you're* in charge of securing passage to Bowhead Rock."

Ves held up her middle finger, though it didn't hide the grin on her face.

"I'll meet you boys back at the *Serenity* in two hours, then. Don't get into any trouble while I'm away."

"Wouldn't dream of it." Solveig grinned.

Ves did not believe his words for a single second.

She brushed the dust and dirt from her trousers and picked a direction at random, heading deeper into the belly of Carilon.

Veridin was the only of the three continents to be ruled by a kingdom and not an empire. Crown Prince Elios Smythe, the eldest child of King Argos and Queen Lydia – and the eldest of the five royal children – was engaged to Princess Iori of Aralyth. While Ves didn't care too much about politics and royal drama outside of Merdyne – and even then, she didn't keep up with the empress there after leaving the continent – she felt *some* pity for Prince Elios. After all, Iori was nothing less than a psychopath. Ves didn't doubt that as soon as she had the Veridin crown on her head, she'd relieve Elios of *his* head. Veridin and its measly territories would be under Aralyth's iron grip

The sooner the entire Helios line died out, the better the entire world would be.

Ves shoved her hands into her pockets, breathing in the salty air. Her knuckles brushed against the leather purse stuffed full of lune – lune she was *supposed* to spend on supplies, but now that they had a quartermaster to deal with inventory and shopping, she could use it to buy some frivolous things.

A striped awning caught her eye. She stumbled, backtracking to read the sign over the door.

Lilly's Atelier.

Perfect.

She pushed open the door, the bell jingling to alert her presence. A soft floral scent overwhelmed her instantly, gentle violin music playing from a phonograph somewhere in the back. An older woman with greying hair and fine wrinkles slipped from behind the curtain.

"How can I – oh." The woman pushed her glasses up her nose and took an instinctual step back.

Great.

Ves put on her kindest, friendliest smile. "I need a wardrobe refresh," she said. "I have the lune to pay. Think you can help me?"

Four years in prison had slimmed Ves down a size or two, but she was still considerably curvy, with muscular arms and legs, an ample bosom with hips to match, and her height posed another issue most ateliers didn't want to invest time into handling.

The woman blinked a few times. "Y-yes, of course," she stammered. "My name is Lilly. Can I get you tea? Coffee? I'll need to take your measurements. Do you have color or style preferences?"

Perfect.

"Tea is fine," she said. "Sugar and cream if you will. Extra of both. I'm fine with any colors. I like my clothing loose and not restrictive. I don't care much for skirts, but I need a good corset for my chest."

Lilly stood up taller. She gave Ves a once over before nodding and disappearing into the back. She returned a minute or two later, holding a steaming cup of tea, a notebook, and a measuring tape.

"Are you a sailor?" Lilly asked. She snaked the tape around Ves's middle, pausing to jot down the number before measuring her hips.

"Of a sort," Ves answered truthfully. She held the teacup close to her face, breathing in the steam despite the heat outside. "I'm Ves."

Better safe than sorry, especially when someone was eager to fit Ves for clothes.

"Are you from Merdyne?" Lilly measured her bosom next, nearly using the entire length of tape to get the numbers.

"Born and raised," she said proudly. "I was born in North Avos, but I moved to Melrosine when I was a kid."

"You crossed the Ruby Ridge that young?" Lilly jotted down a few numbers.

The Ruby Ridge, a formidable spine of mountains that isolated North Avos from the rest of Merdyne, was impassable in the colder months, but in that stretch of time between spring and summer, they opened enough to let travelers through. Ves had only been two – she couldn't remember the trek at all – but her parents used to say they made the journey in less than a week.

"Can't remember it," she admitted.

"No bother." Lilly measured Ves's height, cursing under her breath when she realized Ves stood taller than most men. "Merdyne is lovely this time of year. Hot, but too hot for any bugs. And if you get that southern Amethyst wind..."

Ves knew *exactly* what Lilly spoke of. The Amethyst Sea bordering the southern coast of Merdyne where she grew up was colder than the northern Ruby Sea. Even when the summer heat was intolerable, scalding as though the sun was *right there*, the Amethyst remained cool, bringing down the hellish heat.

"I think that's all I need for now." Lilly stepped back and looked over her notes. "I'm going to get a few samples. Be honest with me and tell me what you don't like."

Ves nodded and sat on the chaise, sipping her tea as she looked around the shop. Lilly the seamstress was the only other person in the shop, her aura faint as she rummaged through the back.

She returned a few minutes later with an armful of fabric. Ves grinned widely.

"Let's see if any of these will suit you," Lilly said.

Illie had cried three times that day and it wasn't even noon. She'd spent the entire day before researching the Wandering Isle, trying to figure out how to make a map *move*. Between getting four hours of sporadic sleep, the headache she was nursing, and the realization that she was going to die, she felt justified in her crying.

Even if she'd cried once every hour she'd been awake.

She sat in the back, hunched over her desk.

"Gah!" She crumpled up the paper she'd been drawing on and threw it at the wall. It hit it with a sad thunk, falling into the mountain of other discarded sketches.

She couldn't even *draw* the Wandering Isle anymore. Every time she tried to draw the familiar star-shaped island, it ended up looking like a mishappen blob.

Jingle!

Every single muscle in her body went taut as the bell above the door rang. She sank into her chair, hoping Henry or Elgar would get it.

Sard, she realized with a jolt. Elgar was running deliveries and Henry hadn't come to the shop yet. Illie dug her nails deep into her palms. She snatched a letter opener from one of her desk drawers and stood slowly, concealing the makeshift blade in her sleeve. Quietly, she tiptoed around the corner.

"It hasn't been two days yet!" she called, hoping that if it *was* the pirates, she'd scare them off.

"What?" a feminine voice called back.

Well, sard.

Illie scrambled out of the back, hurrying to the counter. There, she saw her customer. The woman was *tall.* A gold ring bisected her full bottom lip and her mane of curls fanned out behind her head like a storm cloud. There was something familiar about her, but Illie couldn't place it.

"Sorry about that," Illie hurried to say. "I thought you were someone else. Welcome to the Ink and Rose, maps, logs and navigation supplies. Can I help you?"

The woman narrowed her sage green eyes. They contrasted with the warm brown of her skin, a color combination unusual in Veridin.

She held up three fingers. "Three things: a sextant, a star chart, and directions to someone who can bring me to Bowhead Rock."

Between bloodthirsty pirates and idiots trying to scam Illie, the requests were...oddly reasonable. *Normal,* even.

Illie stepped around the counter, gliding over to one of the many shelves in the shop. She skimmed over a few of the displayed sextants, settling on a lightweight one. Bronze in color, the only thing that stood out about it was the kraken engraved on the side. It was the prettiest of the bunch, and Illie would be happy to give it to a woman who clearly understood the importance of beauty.

"One sextant," she said, placing it back on the counter. She then dug through one of the barrels, grabbing a map of the night sky, drawn by Henry himself. She unrolled it, showing it to the woman before adding it to the counter. "And one star chart."

The woman crossed her arms, one dark brow cocked. "How much?"

"Five hundred for the sextant, one hundred for the map." A discounted price, since Illie didn't feel like haggling with anyone.

The woman pulled out six hundred-lune bills and set them down. "And directions?"

"Why do you want to get to Bowhead Rock?" she asked, counting the bills and shoving them into the register. She scribbled a handwritten receipt, keeping a carbon copy for the ledger.

"There are some pirates there," she drawled, "and I want to kick their asses."

Pirates. Could they be *the* pirates? The ones Illie would be killed by tomorrow? She swallowed hard, her throat bobbing. If this woman could fight them and win – and she *could,* given her massive size and the way she seemed to loom over everyone and everything – Illie wouldn't have to draw the impossible map. She wouldn't have to die.

"I can take you," she blurted.

The woman paused, then grinned a wicked grin. "Well, that was easy. When can you do it?"

"I have to be here until four in the afternoon." Her heart sped up, pounding hard against her ribs, though she couldn't tell if it was from anxiety or...*excitement.*

The woman gathered up her sextant and map. "My crew and I are on the *Serenity.* It's the red brigantine in the harbor. Come meet us there when you're free." She turned to leave, but...

"Wait!" Illie called out. "I... What's your name?" She didn't offer up her own.

"Ves," the woman said over her shoulder. "I'll see you tonight, Pinkie."

When she left, the bell jingling as the door opened and shut, Illie collapsed to her knees, the letter opener falling from her sleeve.

She couldn't tell if she'd just made a massive mistake or not.

But...she was *excited.*

As soon as Elgar and Henry left for the day, a little after four, Illie locked the shop door and rushed upstairs to her apartment. She yanked off her dress, tossing it on the living room floor as she hurried to her bedroom, where she changed into a pair of dark trousers and a loose linen shirt. She braided her hair back as tightly as she could and ran back downstairs, hopping into her boots and rushing out of the shop.

With the sun still high in the sky and the people of Carilon still meandering about, she couldn't exactly *run* to the marina. Still, she walked as quickly as she could, weaving through alleys and taking as many shortcuts as possible.

Finally at the marina, the scent of brine overwhelming, Illie went not to the *Serenity,* but to Henry's old ship. He kept a rowboat on a line behind it, one that could easily get a few people to the back of Bowhead Rock, where the precarious staircase leading up to the top where the lighthouse was.

Illie quickly inspected the rowboat, making sure there were no holes or leaks and that both oars were tucked safely beneath the benches. Everyone at the harbor knew Illie was Henry's ward, so no one would question it when she took the small boat out.

Satisfied, she peered around the marina, spotting the red hull of the *Serenity* easily. She puffed out her chest and rolled her shoulders back, trying to look as brave as possible, not at all like she'd cried three times that morning.

Three people were on the deck of the ship, talking about something Illie couldn't hear. She recognized the only woman as Ves, but the other two...

She narrowed her eyes, staring at the red-haired man. There was something about him...

"Pinkie!" Ves suddenly called, waving down at her. "Come on up! We're going over the plan."

Illie's face flushed a shade darker than her hair, but she scrambled up the gangplank. It wasn't until she saw the discarded green coat next to the red-headed man that she realized who he was.

"You're…" she breathed.

But the man held out his hand and grinned. "Nox Solveig, at your service. Captain of this ship and the one who is going to kick the Redcoat's asses so hard even Lightbringer won't be able to protect them."

Illie stared at his hand for a heartbeat before carefully taking it. "I-Illie Valentine," she stammered. "Mapmaker, navigator, and the one who will get you to Bowhead."

"You've already met me," Ves boasted. "Vesperine Genevieve, Witch of the Sea. The flower boy is Bartholomew Williams, former captain of the *Sea Wyrm,* but you can call him Thol because *Bartholomew* is an *ugly* name."

If Thol, who was even *bigger* than Ves, was bothered by her words, he didn't show it.

"I thought you were supposed to be dead," Illie blurted.

Nox Solveig blinked. Then, he burst out laughing. "If I had a lune for every person who thought I was dead, I'd be rich enough to retire now. You hear that, Ves? Word of my execution reached *Veridin.* I'm that famous!"

"Famously annoying," grumbled Ves. "Don't scare Pinkie off. We need her."

We need her.

Illie had never been needed before, not like this. Warmth swelled in her chest.

"I can fight, too," she said suddenly, drawing the attention of all three pirates to her. "I… I mean, the pirates you're planning on fighting… They… Threatened me. Told me to make them an impossible map or they'd kill me. So, I want to fight them, too. Just give me a weapon and I –"

"Woah, woah." Solveig put his hands up, stopping Illie mid-sentence. "We don't know you. For all we know, you could be working with the Redcoats. Why would we give you a weapon when you could very well turn around and, quite literally, stab us in the back?"

Illie looked away, sheepish. "You... You can't trust me. I'm a stranger. But I'm not stupid; I wouldn't go up against *Nox Solveig* and the *Witch of the Sea.*"

Thol grumbled something about not being included, to which Solveig murmured something about *retirement.*

Illie crossed her arms over her chest, trying to look as brave as possible. She said, "You're borrowing my boat. Without me, you'd have to find someone else willing to take you to Bowhead, and with those pirates occupying it, *good luck.* If you want my help, you have to let me fight, too." Then, after a beat, she added, "Please."

Solveig looked at Ves, who just shrugged and said, "You're the captain, Cap. And if you get defeated by Pinkie here, you probably deserved it."

She leaned close to her captain and whispered something Illie couldn't hear.

Then, to her surprise, Solveig said, "Fine." He pulled a dagger from his belt, flipping it around in his hand before holding it out hilt-first. Illie took it, careful not to drop it, and slipped it into her belt.

She said, "Follow me, then. I hope you're ready for a hike since there's only one way up the rock."

14

BOWHEAD ROCK LOOMED LIKE a goliath, reaching towards the sky, unforgiving as tumultuous waves crashed against its base. The tiny rowboat the four of them had been stuffed into rocked precariously, threatening to capsize with each wave that beat against it. Sea birds circled above, tiny stains against the bright blue of the late afternoon.

A tiny, tiny, *tiny* staircase, narrower than Solveig's foot with steps far too steep, snaked up the back of the rock, protected only by a flimsy rope that whipped in the sea breeze. Solveig didn't have a problem with heights. Growing up on the tallest point in his village quashed any potential phobias, but...

Well, the stairs leading up the rock could certainly change that.

"You expect us," he said tightly, "to *walk up there? What* happens if we slip and fall? Because that doesn't look very *sturdy.*"

The pink-haired cartographer, Illie, just shrugged. "Then you'd better hope you can swim. Oh, and watch out for the sharks. They're particularly hungry this time of day."

"*Sharks?*" hissed Ves.

Illie grinned, holding back laughter. "Kidding. About the sharks, not the swimming. One of you toss me the line."

Before Solveig could tell her to get the line herself, Illie jumped from the rowboat, landing on the eroded ledge at the base of the rock. She bent her knees, throwing out her arms to keep from slipping on the thin layer of algae. Once she was steady, she held out her hands, expectant.

Thol grabbed the rope and tossed it to her. She caught it and, with surprising strength given her willowy figure, reeled the boat in. She tied the mooring line to a hook affixed to the rock. Thol climbed out first, followed by Ves. Solveig stepped out last, craning his neck back to see the top of the rock.

"It's a long way up," said Thol. "We have just enough time to go over the plan once more."

Solveig grabbed the salt-stiff rope, gripping it tightly as he went up the first makeshift step, then the next.

"What kind of map did these fools want you to make?" Solveig heard Ves ask. He didn't dare look up from his feet, lest he trip.

"A moving map," Illie replied. "They wanted some map of the Wandering Isle that could *move.* I'm an excellent cartographer, but I'm not a *god.* "

Solveig *did* look up at her words, though he only saw the back of her head, her pink braid whipping in the wind.

"A moving map, huh?" Ves asked. Solveig couldn't see her face, but he knew she was grinning. They dissolved into conversation, ignoring Thol's request to go over the plan again.

Solveig skipped a step, catching up to Thol as best as he could. The stairs were too narrow to walk side-by-side, but he was used to being in Thol's shadow.

The royal pardon will extend to you and you, alone. Whatever crew you manage to scrape together won't be privy to that.

Anwir Helios's words suddenly came back, assaulting Solveig's mind. He sucked in a harsh breath through his teeth.

All the reason to get what Anwir wants and...

And what? Beg for his crew to be pardoned? Pay off their bounties? Refuse to hand over the corpse of a god until Anwir agreed the *whole* crew could be saved?

No, none of that would even work. The only way to ensure the safety of his crew would be to topple the Helios empire completely. To remove Castros Helios, his heir, *and* the next in the line of succession, Iori.

If someone else sat on the Empire's throne, someone who didn't wish for the eradication of pirates...

A gust of wind smacked Solveig right in the face, tearing his hair off his forehead and stealing his balance. He gripped the rope railing tighter, willing himself to not slip on the slick rock steps.

"I'm starting to think this was a terrible idea," Solveig ground out from between clenched teeth.

"I didn't think you were scared of heights," drawled Thol, without looking over his shoulder to face Solveig.

"I'm not," Solveig hissed, though he wasn't so sure himself anymore.

"You grew up on a house on a hill," Thol continued. "You have no reason to dislike heights."

"I also grew up on a *ship,* and you don't see me complaining about the high seas," Solveig shot back.

From up ahead, Ves called, "If you two are done bickering, we should go over the plan again."

Solveig held his middle finger up to Thol's back. As if he had eyes on the back of his head, Thol returned the gesture over his shoulder.

An iron tang coated the back of Illie's throat as she neared the final steps of Bowhead Rock. Her lungs strained, but she refrained from gulping in any greedy breaths, just so she wouldn't seem *too* out of shape to the pirates behind her. Not for the first time in their spontaneous hike did Illie thank Poet she had her back to the others, so they wouldn't see how flushed and sweaty she'd gotten.

Halfway up the rock, the winds switched from northern, pushing against their backs, to southern, a welcome change as it cooled her face and dried some of the sweat clinging to her underarms and chest. That same wind brushed against her reddened cheeks as she clambered up the final step, onto the somewhat flat summit of the rock.

She threw her arms in the air, silently celebrating the hardest part of the entire adventure.

Because that's what this was, wasn't it? An *adventure* – a real one, with dangerous environments and pirates and an impending fight. If everything went to plan, Carilon would be under Nox Solveig's control – his *protection*. Illie wouldn't have to worry about making an impossible map.

And maybe...

No.

She lowered her arms, her triumphant smile falling. All she'd done was lead some pirates to the top of Bowhead Rock. Even though she claimed to be determined to fight, Illie knew she didn't have it in her. She'd just get in the way.

A hand clapped her shoulder, causing her to jump.

"Well!" Ves exclaimed, grinning down at her. "The hard part's done. Now we just have to kick some ass and get back *down.*"

Illie's stomach twisted. The fluttery sensation snaked around her heart, squeezing like a boa.

Shaking away the feeling of dread, she lifted her hand and pointed to the lighthouse partially hidden by a rocky outcrop. "If the pirates are here," she said, mouth going dry as she thought of the lighthouse keeper, Mumford Scorn Junior, and his father, who had bought a map recently. Was he okay? "They would probably be in there. The...the lighthouse keeper lives there."

"Ugh, civilians," Ves groaned. "I assume you *don't* want us to let the lighthouse keeper be a casualty?"

"Finding a good one is a lot harder than you'd think," Illie grumbled. "Nobody likes living in isolation."

"Tell me about it," grumbled Ves.

"We don't have all day," Solveig said, pushing past Ves and Illie, heading in the direction of the lighthouse.

Pulling her knife from her belt and gripping it tightly, Illie forced her feet to move, forced herself to follow him.

Focused on her feet, Illie didn't realize Solveig had stopped until she ran right into his back, sparks flooding her vision from the sharp pain in her nose. She rubbed it, taking a step back.

"What –" she started but peeking over his shoulder caused her words to fall flat.

Seven pirates lounged in a patch of grass, discarded bottles and crates surrounding them. Illie recognized the captain instantly – he was the only one with a red coat after all. A bottle of cinnamon rum dangled from his fingers, a lazy smirk tugging on his lips.

"Lookie here," the captain crooned. "Little miss cartographer got *scared* and ran off with her tail between her legs."

Another drunken pirate piped up, "I wouldn't mind getting between her legs."

Illie's face flushed. She stepped behind Solveig, hoping he would shield her from the humiliation.

The captain dropped his bottle and stood. "And who do you think *you* are? This is our territory. You know the pirate code, don't you?"

"'If a pirate steps onto another's territory not seeking refuge or sanctuary, he is there for a fight,'" Solveig quoted. He popped his knuckles and drew his cutlass. "Good thing I'm here for a fight. Captain Nox Solveig, at your service. And *you* are?"

"A cheap knockoff, it looks like," snickered Ves.

Click.

One of the Redcoats aimed a revolver right between her eyes. Ves, to her credit, didn't even flinch. She didn't hold up her hands or even pretend to act scared. If anything, she looked *bored* at the prospect of being threatened with a gun.

"Phillippe Rouge," the captain said. "Captain of the Redcoat Pirates, and warlord of Carlion."

"It's *Carilon*," Illie hissed. As soon as the words were out, she clapped her hand over her mouth, silently praying Phillippe Rouge hadn't heard her. Gods knew they needed no more reason to kill her.

Whether he heard her or not, Rouge didn't say anything. Not to her, at least, for all his attention was, dangerously, on Solveig.

"Isn't Nox Solveig supposed to be dead?" Rouge cocked a brow. "Doesn't that make *you* the cheap knockoff? I heard the Pirates of the Silver Moon were killed."

Solveig tensed, back rigid.

Out of the corner of her eye, Illie caught a glimpse of movement. The tail of a coat, the glint of silver –

"LOOK OUT!" she cried.

The Redcoat swung his sword, the careening arc swinging toward Solveig's neck –

Slice!

Blood sprayed, but not Solveig's. The Redcoat's arms fell to the ground, twin meaty slaps against the grass. The Redcoat's eyes went wide, the pain not quite setting in as he slowly realized what had happened.

Thol had happened, moving so fast he'd been nothing but a blur. With Rouge's attention narrowed in on Solveig, he hadn't noticed Thol drawing a weapon and moving to the side, getting a better stance to attack. To defend his captain.

Thol swung his blade out, snapping the blood from it.

Rouge's face twisted up in crimson fury, a vein popping out on his forehead. *"ATTACK!"* he shouted, voice cracking.

Ves whispered something to Solveig, so soft Illie couldn't hear it, and pulled two daggers from her belt, not giving her words any time to settle before she charged, swinging and slicing with deadly grace.

As much as she'd begged to, Illie knew she couldn't fight, but she *could* do something else. With the Redcoats and Solveig's tiny crew busy, forgetting Illie's presence in the heat of the melee, she took off running toward the lighthouse.

Please be alive please be alive please be alive. She repeated the mantra over and over, praying to whatever gods cared to listen, that the lighthouse keeper was still alive in there.

She shoved her shoulder against the wooden arched door, expecting to be met with resistance, only –

"Oof!"

She stumbled, hurrying to catch her balance before she got a mouthful of wrought iron, the stair's railing far too close for comfort as she tumbled inside.

Brushing herself off, Illie looked around. She'd never been inside a lighthouse before but was still surprised at how...*narrow* it was. She doubted she could hold her arms out and walk up the winding stairs like that.

"Hello?" she called out, cringing at how her voice echoed. "Mister Scorn? Are you here?"

She grabbed the railing, ignoring the burn in her legs protesting her plan to climb more stairs. "Mister Scorn?" she called again, taking the stairs two at a time.

Fifteen stairs up, Illie realized it probably would've been easier to just yell at the top of her lungs until Mumford Scorn, if he was even there, showed himself.

"Misterrrrrrr Scooooooorn!" she yelled, her voice warping as it echoed, rising to the top of the monolithic lighthouse. "It's me, Illie Valentine, the cartographer! I'm here to... To rescue you!"

It sounded a lot less dumb in her head.

Sighing, she skipped up the next few steps, only –

Creeeeaaaaak.

She stopped, body tensing. Slowly, slowly, slowly she reached for her dagger while hesitantly asking, "Mister Scorn, is that you?"

"Well, well, well," drawled a voice that most definitely did *not* belong to Mister Scorn. "Wha' 'ave we 'ere?"

Illie looked over her shoulder. Another Redcoat pirate stood a few steps below her, trousers loose around his bare hips, no shirt to hide the array of scars and trashy tattoos across his less-than-toned torso. She swallowed hard, fear bubbling in her chest.

The pirate climbed up a step. "I don' recall you bein' one've the lassies we took."

One of the... Her eyes went wider than the moons. These pirates weren't just threatening *her,* they were kidnapping other women from Carilon, too.

Fight or flight instincts kicked in; Illie gripped her knife tightly and started running, adrenaline pumping her legs to get her up and up and up the stairs, closer to the top where...

Where *what?* Where she would be cornered?

No. She refused to die on this rock so close to where she'd been born. Illie wanted *adventure.* If she was going to die one day, she wanted to die at sea, in some distant country, in a jungle untouched by mankind. She would not die in a stupid lighthouse, and she *certainly* would not die at the hand of a greasy, filthy pirate.

Footsteps thundered behind her, the clang of boots on iron steps. The pirate was taller than Illie, probably more in shape, too, and would catch up easily. She ignored the burn in her thighs, the dizziness that washed over her as she spiraled higher and higher. She had to get to the top. She had to get outside. There was one last ace up her sleeve, and she'd throw it at this pirate before he could kill –

"*Ah!*" she screamed. Blood flooded the back of her throat, pooling in her mouth, hot and fast. She choked on it, barely able to spit it out before she could swallow it. Stars clouded her vision, followed by the numbing pain erupting across her brow.

It took a precious second to realize she had fallen, splitting her brow open on one of the steps and biting deep into her tongue.

Splaying her hands on the steps, she tried to push herself up, only... A hand grabbed her ankle, yanking her down. Her hands slipped, palms shredding under the iron. *That* would be a problem for later. Her knife slid between the cracks, falling helplessly to the bottom of the stairs with a clatter she couldn't hear over her own screaming.

"Let me go!" she shrieked. Illie kicked at the pirate. The heel of her boot met his nose with a satisfying *crunch*.

He let go, hands flying to cradle his broken nose. Illie scrambled to her feet, skipping up the stairs with less surety now. Her head swam, vision clotted with stars and the vestiges of black fog around the edges.

"You wench!" the pirate shouted. "When I get my hands on you!"

She drowned out his threat. She just had to get to the top. The top, the top, the top...

Daylight filtered in, bright and gold, and she knew she would be there soon.

Illie made it to the top of the stairs with a choked sob. She pushed past the beacon, smearing bloody handprints on the glass. Fresh air smacked her in the face the moment she stepped onto the observation deck. *Perfect.*

She breathed it in, let it fill her lungs to the brim. When the pirate staggered onto the deck, she reached out to grab that air.

It fitted in her hands like a rope, frozen and with little resistance. She tugged at it before whipping it out, the wind smacking into the pirate and sending him flying backward. He hit the beacon hard. The glass cracked.

Illie let go of the wind only to grab a new gale, a feisty one. When the pirate rose to his feet, spitting a bloody tooth out as he did, she threw the wind at him again. Her palms started to burn, not from the cuts, but from the *cold*.

Illie Valentine was Poet-blessed to control the winds, but it came at a cost – she would be dealt frost burns the longer she held onto the freezing air. It wasn't a power she used often, since she got burned after one or two winds, but it was the only thing she could think to use against the pirate.

He got up again, this time charging. Illie grabbed the wind again, screaming as the burns engulfed her hands, the cold too extreme it was *hot*.

"*Get! Away!*" she screamed.

She threw the wind around the pirate, hard and fast. It smacked into his torso, stealing his balance, and sending him into the railing. He flipped over it and plummeted head-first to the ground.

Illie fell to her knees before she could hear the splatter. Her hands trembled, the skin bright red and blistered. Tears streaked down her cheeks, the adrenaline from the chase finally wearing off, leaving the pain from her frost burns and bitten tongue and split brow as blinding as ever.

Below, the clash and clang of swords drew her out of her panic.

Solveig. Ves. Thol. She couldn't just *abandon* them. They were stronger pirates than her – not that she *was* a pirate, but she *had* just killed a man – and didn't seem like they'd need help, but...she dragged them up this rock. She'd promised to help. Mumford Scorn Junior didn't seem to be in the lighthouse, either...

It's just for a few more seconds, she told herself as she hauled herself to her feet. *Pain is temporary. Death is forever.*

With aching hands, Illie gripped the railing.

And then she jumped.

15

BLOOD DRIPPED FROM SOLVEIG'S face like sweat, the same color as his hair, a harsh contrast to the white of his teeth as he *grinned,* a vicious snarl that betrayed no emotions besides bloodlust and thrill. He sliced his cutlass in a perfect arc, met with little resistance even as he lopped an oncoming Redcoat's arm clean off.

A violent wind tore through the air, tossing Solveig off balance.

"Gun!" shouted Ves.

Solveig ducked just as a bullet whizzed by, dangerously close to where he'd been standing just a second ago.

He put the grip of his cutlass between his teeth and dove, tackling a Redcoat by the waist and pinning him to the ground. He spat his cutlass out, catching it with one hand.

"You pathetic worms will rue the day you decided to make Carilon yours," Solveig said between clenched teeth, the blood of the Redcoat's comrades dripping onto his face, "Because Carilon is *mine.*"

Solveig swiped the blade, slicing a grim smile into the Redcoat's throat. Then, he stood, arms out.

"Who's next?!" he shouted over the tumult.

"Captain Nox Solveig, cloaked in green," drawled Rouge as he stalked close. Solveig scrunched up his face in annoyance. He'd pronounced his name as *Sol-vig,* the way Solveig would as a child when he was annoyed with his mother.

"Yes, yes, I know the rhyme," Solveig said lazily.

"I heard you were going to the gallows."

"And I've never heard of you, yet here we are."

Rouge twisted his mouth into a feral snarl. He ran, feet splashing in the muddy grass, and swung his sword.

It met Solveig's with a clash. Solveig leaned into the parry, forcing Rouge to stumble.

Solveig hooked his cutlass beneath Rouge's, arcing it up to pry it from Rouge's grip. The sword flew through the air, landing in the grass a few feet away.

Rouge met Solveig's gaze. For a heartbeat, neither moved. Neither dared to breathe.

Then, Rouge ran, going for his abandoned sword.

"Oh, no you don't," growled Solveig, and he took off running after the pirate.

Just then, in a blur of pink, something – no, *someone* – fell from the sky, landing between Rouge and his sword. *Illie.* Where had she come from?! Solveig glanced up – the lighthouse? How had she survived a fall from *there?*

Illie stood somewhat ungracefully, looked around, and pulled the sword from the ground. She flinched as though holding the blade hurt, but to her credit, she didn't drop it.

"Looking for this?" she asked, one brow cocked.

"You filthy wench!" Rouge hissed. "If you know what's good for you, give that to me. I'll even forgive your little lie about being a cartographer."

Both of Illie's brows arched at that. Her gaze drifted over Rouge's shoulder to meet Solveig's. "If you own a Veridinian map," she drawled, "I *guarantee* I made it. My name is Illie sarding Valentine, and I am the *best damn mapmaker in Veridin.*"

She reeled her arm back, then threw the cutlass. It sailed over Rouge's head. Solveig acted fast, shoving his own cutlass between his teeth to grab the other sword's grip. With it safely in his hand, he pulled the blade from his mouth.

"You've gone and made her mad," said Solveig. He held both swords out, ready to attack. "And you lost your weapon. If you were smart, you'd surrender now."

"And lose the opportunity to fight Nox Solveig?" Rouge grinned. Solveig's stomach sank.

In one swift motion, Rouge had Illie pinned against him, his arm locked over her throat so she couldn't escape, no matter how hard she thrashed. A pistol appeared in his hand, safety flipped off and finger hovering over the trigger.

Slowly, slowly, slowly, Solveig lowered his swords, setting them on the ground and holding his hands up. Ves and Thol were still fighting; he could rely on them to watch his back for a minute. Illie was an *innocent*. He couldn't let this low-class pirate kill her because Solveig decided to fight dirty. This was *his* fight after all, not hers.

"Smart," said Rouge. "But you forget one thing, Solveig. We're pirates. We don't follow the rules."

He squeezed the trigger, the bang met with a feminine scream – one of pain unlike anything felt before.

"Help!"

The voice was so soft, so weak, that Thol would have easily missed it over the melee had he not been standing right next to the rock where it had sounded. He punched an oncoming pirate square in the nose and turned toward the rock. At first, he didn't see anything other than moss and bird droppings, but – *there*. A pair of gold eyes staring intently at him, wider than saucers and full of fear.

Thol crouched down, the split in the rock obvious now, revealing the mouth of a rather tight cave and the round face of a young girl, barely in her teenage years at the most.

They're capturing women and killing anyone who defies them.

When the woman at the bakery said that Thol assumed the Red-coat Pirates were capturing *women*. Not girls barely old enough to have their first monthly bleed.

"Hello," Thol said as kindly as he could. It probably didn't help that he had blood sprayed across his face and raw knuckles from all the punching he'd been doing.

The girl blinked. "Tia is sick," she said. "Can you help? Please?"

Maybe the blood and split knuckles didn't scare the girl because she saw right through it. Being married had made Thol *soft*. Fatherhood – for however brief he experienced it – made him...trustworthy.

He smiled the way he would have smiled had his daughter lived. "I don't think I can fit inside the cave. Can you bring Tia to me? How many of you are in there? What's your name?"

The golden-eyed girl just blinked again. "There was twenty, but now there's nineteen. I'm Mary. I... I think I can bring her. We can't leave the cave, though."

It was then that Thol saw the shimmery veil, membrane-thin and taut as it stretched across the mouth of the little cave. A barrier of sorts. One of the pirates must have been divine touched... No matter. Divine touched or not, Thol could break it down. He gave another smile and said, "You are very brave, Mary. I'm Thol. I will help you."

Mary's eyes lit up like fireworks. She nodded once and disappeared into the darkness of the cave. He could hear soft talking but drowned it out as he got to work on the fickle barrier. He balled his hands into fists and punched.

Pain blossomed behind his eyes. His knuckles split, leaving raw, bloody wounds stretching over his hands. Blood trickled between the cracks of his fingers.

He reached for his sword. Behind him, footsteps pounded closer. He spun around, abandoning the veil for a moment to subdue his attacker –

Splat!

A knife soared through the air and buried itself deep into the oncoming attacker's eye socket. *Where are all these pirates even coming from?!* They must have a ship docked somewhere or a base Thol hadn't seen yet.

"Don't you know to never turn your back to the enemy?" Ves sauntered over, flipping a knife absently. "What are you doing over here? The fight's over there." She nodded in the direction of the melee.

Thol glanced at the veil. "You're too big to fit, too..." he murmured.

"Excuse me?"

"Too tall," he quickly rectified. "To fit into the cave. There're apparently nineteen girls stuck in here, and one of them is sick. They're *girls,* Witch. Children. But one of the pirates is divine touched, so they can't get out."

Ves stared at the cave. "Eighteen girls," she said. "One is very weak. And one...I think there's a man in there, too. One's coming now."

Just then, Mary reappeared at the mouth of the cave. "Ford is trying to move Tia," she said before Thol could question what Ves had said.

"Which pirate put you in here?" Thol asked.

Mary shrank into the darkness. "Th-the big one..." she whispered. "W-with no hair and a b-big mustache."

Thol wracked his brain, trying to recall if he'd seen such a pirate. Ves sighed heavily. "We haven't seen him," she said. "But we will find him and kick his ass so hard even Lady Lightbringer will pity him. Hang in there, kid. You're safe now."

Mary nodded and rubbed her eyes with the back of her wrist. Thol stood, blade drawn.

"Let's figure out where all these pirates are coming from, Flowers," Ves said.

Thol rolled his eyes at the nickname but followed Ves.

Illie tore through the air, falling too fast. The anticipation of pain hurt more than the actuality of it, she knew, but she still hesitated. Before she could splatter on the earth, she grabbed a gale – eyes burning at the raw pain – and used it to slow her descent.

Too many things happened at once. She grabbed a sword and threw it. She was yanked against the captain of the Redcoats. Solveig set down his weapons.

The captain of the Redcoat Pirates squeezed the trigger of his pistol.

Illie's own pain was irrelevant compared to the life of Nox Solveig. She twisted, grabbing a wind, and whipping it out, snapping the bullet off its trajectory. She screamed as her palms split, blisters bursting in an oozy mess of blood and clear fluid.

The bullet whizzed past Solveig's head, narrowly missing by a few split hairs.

Rouge cursed and aimed his gun again. Illie took the moment of distraction to bite down on his forearm hard enough that blood exploded in her mouth. She gagged – *disgusting!* – but didn't let go.

"You stupid wench!" Rouge screamed. He tried to shake her off, but Illie held firm, even when he slammed the butt of his gun against her temple. Stars burst in her vision, dizzying and bright.

He hit her again. Only then did she let go, spitting a mouthful of blood on his boots. His grip had loosened enough so she could slide beneath his arm, stumbling just out of his range.

"Are you alright?" she asked Solveig.

"I should be asking *you* that," he hissed. Illie just shrugged. She could let the panic and pain take over later once she was safe.

She rolled her sleeves up and shifted her stance. Rouge spat, "The little kitty cat has claws. It's a shame they're too small to do anything."

"This kitty cat also has teeth, and she isn't afraid to bite." She shot a glance over her shoulder. "Give me a sword," she said to Solveig.

"Can you even use it?" he asked.

"It can't be that hard."

He shrugged and tossed one of his two cutlasses to her. She caught it with both hands, staggering under the sudden weight and the pain of her raw blisters rubbing against the leather-wrapped hilt. Sarding *hell!* Maybe it *would* be that hard...

Two against one. Two swords against a gun.

Illie wasn't a pirate. She was a cartographer. A mapmaker. A navigator who knew the stars better than she knew her own face, who could chart the world without batting an eye.

She let out a roar and swung, begging the winds to work in her favor. She brought the blade down as an explosion sounded – the pistol firing. The blade met resistance, thick and heavy.

Crunch!

She couldn't pull the blade free, no matter how hard she tried, but it didn't matter anymore.

She fell to her knees as the mostly decapitated body of Captain Rouge crumpled to the ground.

Ves's stomach wouldn't stop twisting. Pirates capturing young women to use for their own gain wasn't unusual. But when she'd sailed with the Ruby Pirates, the only captives they ever took were men. Women and children were always, without a doubt, spared. A rule that got messy when the navy started enlisting female troops, but one whose morals stuck with her, even four years later. Thol seemed to have the same beliefs, but did Solveig? She owed him her life, but if he allowed such young girls to be taken hostage...

"There isn't a lot of hiding space," she murmured, mostly to herself. Eyes peeled, she kept looking for another spark of life, something unfamiliar. From the corner of her eye, those little sparks kept dying out. All she could do was pray one of those souls didn't belong to Solveig.

"If this bald man can create barriers, we have to assume he could be anywhere," Thol said. "If we kill him, the barrier will break."

"That's usually how godly powers work, yes." Ves couldn't manipulate anything physical with her ability, so she could only guess, but it *seemed* logical enough.

She sighed out through her nose, forcing her shoulders to relax as she focused harder. She pushed the cluster of souls in the cave out of her mind, along with the flickering ones on the battlefield, until the only souls she could see were Thol's and a few tiny sparks too high up to belong to anything other than seabirds.

"You have a soft spot for young girls, Flowers," Ves murmured as she concentrated, filtering the flitting seabirds out of her range of sight.

"I had a daughter," he said. "Fatherhood will do that to you."

"Sappy."

Then... *There.* A tiny spark in the corner of her vision, faint and hidden, but *there.* Behind the lighthouse stood a tall outcrop of basalt, but behind that... That must be where the other pirates were hiding. They could see the fight themselves, but they were completely hidden.

Unless someone with the ability to see souls knew where to look.

Ves grabbed Thol's wrist. "Got him," she said with a feline grin. "Let's go kick some ass."

She didn't bother coming up with a plan, because the only thing she cared about was sending Baldie to the drink. Behind her, the chaos of gunshots and screams and clashing swords drowned out, all her senses tunneling in on the bright soul just behind the chunk of basalt. Licking her lips, she pulled two (stolen) daggers from her belt and charged.

Pirates who hid from battle, pirates who captured young girls, pirates who threw up barriers seconds too late, trapping their enemies with them, were nothing but a bunch of sniveling cowards. And cowards like them deserved to *die*.

She was the Witch of the Sea, the ex-bo'sun of the Ruby Pirates, the current bo'sun sailing under Nox Solveig, and she feared no man.

Her blades sang, splitting through the air, through flesh and sinew, painting the basalt red, red, *red*. Coward pirates barely had a chance to scream as she sliced through them, one by one, felling her enemies with crimson smiles to their throats. Souls flickered out, falling to the carnage that was Vesperine Genevieve.

A man charged her. Ves spun and shoved her blade under his chin. She slammed her palm against the pommel, forcing it through his mouth and into his brain with a wet *crunch*. He collapsed when she yanked it free with an arced spray of warm blood.

In her periphery, she saw the silent blur that was Thol chasing down a tall man. He looked like an egg. Ves snorted. Sarding fool.

If – *when* – Thol got his hands on him, he would crack like an egg. Jealous as she was, the kill belonged to him.

If only because it was the fatherly thing to do – killing a man to free a bunch of kids.

"Got you, wench. You're *mine.*" A pair of grubby mitts grabbed Ves by the bicep. She turned to see a greasy pirate with a missing tooth and a whole lot of gumption gripping her arm. He was built like a stick, if sticks could grow stringy hair and have beer bellies, so she yanked her arm free with ease.

"Ew," she scoffed. "I prefer women, thank you."

She shoved her knife into his eye socket. The pirate screamed in agony, the wails drowning out the squelchy pop of his eyeball bursting. She pulled the blade free. His eye had been skewered on it like an olive.

"Ew!" She frantically shook the eye off her knife. It hit the still-writhing form of the pirate before rolling pathetically across the dirt.

Suddenly, the ground shuddered. Had they been on solid ground – or a sarding ship – Ves wouldn't have batted an eye. Earthquakes happened all the time, a result of Dreamer shifting and moving, and seaquakes could be felt on the surface if Poet was particularly angry. But Ves was not on the ground, and she was not on a ship. She was on a rock that, to her understanding, should not suddenly *tremble.*

Ves had never seen any of the gods, and she wasn't sure if they would show up in her vision, but she still desperately glanced around, trying to see if Poet or Dreamer was moving about or if Bowhead Rock just decided that now, after standing tall for millennia, would be the perfect time to crumble and collapse.

There were no gods.

The rock shuddered again. The gauzy veil that had been hastily thrown over the area shattered into a million tiny star-shards.

Thol –

Ves spun around just in time to see Thol flinging the blood off of a sword he must have picked up off a corpse, the fresh body of a rather egg-shaped man at his feet.

He dropped the sword and took off running. He glanced over his shoulder and stumbled.

"*VES!*" he shouted.

The pain came before she could register his warning. No, not the pain. The sticky wetness, the tear of her shirt and flesh, the realization that she'd been cut came first.

Then, Thol's warning.

Then, the pain struck.

Oh, *gods,* the *pain.* It obliterated her at once, a harrowing rip like a million magma blades rained down on her. The world tilted. No, *she* did, falling victim to heavy gravity that tugged her down and down. Bile bubbled in her throat. Her lungs were *paralyzed.*

With the last vestiges of her strength, Ves spun and grabbed the jaw of her attacker. In one quick flick of her wrists, she snapped his neck. Then, with trembling hands, she reached back, her stomach sinking when her fingers came away slick with blood.

To Thol, she yelled, "*GO!*"

Those girls needed him. They needed medical attention more than she did. She was the Witch of the sarding Seas. She had survived worse.

She could survive this.

A gunshot rang out, followed by a bright soul blinking from existence. Shivering, Ves took a stumbling step.

She could survive, she could survive, she could survive –

The basalt seemed to rise to greet her as she fell to her knees.

Dreamer, do not *let me die here,* she prayed inwardly as the assaulting black splotches obliterated her vision. *I was promised an adventure, and I will sarding get it.*

If the goddess answered at all, Ves didn't hear it. Her consciousness slipped away in a blink, gone just like the souls she had watched vanish from the fight.

She was the Witch of the Sea. She'd survived Ivenis Justyce Penitentiary for four years. She would be *fine.* At least, that's what Thol kept telling himself as he abandoned her, bleeding from a laceration to her back – given to her by a coward who couldn't face her from the front – to run for the cave.

She will be fine. He repeated the mantra over and over. *Those girls need you. They aren't as strong as her.*

Sarding damnit, Ves, if you die –

Thol shook his head to clear that thought from his mind. She *wouldn't* die. She was part of his crew, and as first mate, it was *his* responsibility to make sure his crew was okay.

Swallowing the acrid conflict that had materialized in his throat, Thol jumped over a chunk of basalt, skidding to a stop before the mouth of the tiny cavern.

Mary stood just inside, hesitant as she stuck her hand out. Next to her was a man far too tall to be stuck in the tiny space, his back shaped like a *C* as he hunched over a girl with skin so pale and waxy, Thol thought for a moment that she was already dead. Mary's eyes lit up, though, when she saw him.

"Thol!" she cried in a voice that made his heart palpitate. She was just a kid, yet that spark in her eyes hadn't been extinguished.

"The barrier's gone." To prove it, he reached in and took her hand, gently pulling her into the afternoon light. Her eyes turned glassy, and she hugged him with all her minimal strength. Startled, all he could do was hug back, careful not to crush her tiny form.

Slowly, one by one, the rest of the captured emerged from the cage, huddling around Thol. Not a single one, save for the man – Ford, Mary had called him – was over the age of twenty by the looks of it. The oldest of the girls had to be in their late teens at the oldest, with acne smattered over their malnourished faces and girlish features not yet shaped by maturity.

The youngest couldn't have been older than ten.

She shuffled over to Thol and smushed her little face into his bicep.

Ford broke the silence. "She needs a doctor," he said, nodding down at Tia. Now that she was in the light, Thol could see the fluttery, barely-there rise and fall of her chest. Fever leeched her skin of its luster, leaving her cheeks flushed an unnatural red.

Carefully pulling away from Mary and the younger girl, Thol took Tia from Ford's arm. Ford breathed a sigh of relief, his twiggy arms clearly not used to holding up much weight.

"Is there a doctor in Carilon?" Thol demanded.

Ford nodded. "I have a boat moored on the eastern side of the rock. It will be big enough to bring everyone back."

"I have three more with me," Thol said. "One is injured –"

"*Thol!*"

He turned to see Illie running towards him. Her hands were blistered and red, her fingertips blackened. Her pink hair had been freed from its braid and now hung in loose strings over her face. There was no sign of Solveig.

"Where's Nox?" he asked, tamping down the panic that surged through his veins.

Illie stopped and doubled over, panting hard. "He – he's... He..." she gulped in a few breaths. "Shot! He was shot, but he's alive, but he's bleeding." When she stood upright, her eyes went wide and she gasped, "Mumford Scorn?!"

Ford – Mumford Scorn, apparently – stared at Illie with a confused recognition masked over his face. He shook his head. "You said someone was shot? Take me to him. I can wrap the wound. My ship is fast. It'll get him to Carilon quickly."

Illie nodded. "Where's Ves?"

"Behind me. She was slashed. She needs a doctor, too. I can carry her on my back. But I can't carry Nox. Where was he shot?"

"The shoulder. Mister Scorn, can you help me get Ves? Then you can help Solveig and we can get off this sarding rock." When Mumford Scorn nodded quickly, Illie took off in the direction Thol had left Ves.

Thol looked at the pale girl in his arms, then at the semicircle the others formed around him. He wasn't a doctor by any means, but he, like everyone else in the world, knew the signs of the Alkenio Plague, a devastatingly deadly disease that wiped out a good chunk of the population twenty-four years ago. There was no cure – at least, not one that anyone knew of – and cases were still far from rare. The signs of the plague were taught to everyone: irises that turned silver, a high fever, skin that, despite being feverish, turned black like frostbite had taken hold, blood that oozed from the various orifices, and the stench of rot as the infected victim's internal organs turned to mush.

He would never forget the wet thunk a plague body made when tumbling into a grave.

To Thol's relief, Tia didn't have any of the symptoms other than the fever. With her eyes closed, he couldn't tell if her irises had turned silver, but if she really did have the plague, everyone else in the cave with her would be sick, too, and nobody showed any signs of having caught it.

Illie and Mumford Scorn returned moments later, holding Ves between them. Sweat dripped from her pallid face, clinging to her curls. Her shirt was shredded and wrapped around her torso like a makeshift blanket.

"Help her up," Thol said, crouching down. Illie and Mumford Scorn awkwardly helped Ves onto Thol's back. She loosely wrapped her arms around his shoulders. *Good.* She was still conscious.

"I can walk," Ves grumbled weakly.

"That's a lie and we both know it," Thol shot back. "Hold on tight. If you fall, I can't catch you."

Ves's head fell forward, her face pressed against his shoulder. It would be awkward carrying someone nearly his height down a steep rock, but she was crew, and Thol didn't leave crew behind.

"You smell like fish guts, Flowers," Ves whispered. Her words slurred together like she was hanging onto the barest threads of consciousness.

"I doubt you smell any better," Thol shot back. If engaging in conversation kept her awake, so be it. "Can you move your toes?" He hadn't seen how deep the pirate slashed into her back. If he'd severed her spinal cord...

"Yes, I can move my sarding toes." She flexed her foot, weakly nudging it against Thol's thighs.

Illie and Mumford returned again, this time dragging Solveig with them. He held a bunched-up strip of fabric torn from his own shirt against his shoulder. Illie clutched her hands to her chest. The bleeding on her face had stopped, leaving dry, crusty flakes of blood behind. Solveig's coat sat on her shoulders, swallowing her.

"Let's get off this sarding rock already," Thol said. In his arms, Tia stirred, her breathing shallow. Without waiting, he started walking, his pace quick as he followed Mumford Scorn to the western side of Bowhead Rock.

16

Ves slowly blinked awake, her eyes fuzzy in the sudden bright light of the strange room she was in. Sunlight spilled through a window blocked by only a gauzy, gossamer-thin curtain, bathing the otherwise sad, beige room in a swath of gold. The scent of sugary fried dough made her mouth water. She sat up quickly – too fast. Lightning pain struck her from behind, radiating from shoulder to hip in a diagonal slash.

"Careful!" Solveig said. "If I have to bribe the doctor to stitch you up again, I have a feeling he'll be sewing my mouth shut."

Again?

Groaning, Ves reluctantly lay back down. She did not have the chest for stomach sleeping, but someone had stacked a few pillows beneath her waist and hips so her breasts wouldn't be squished. She turned her head, cheek flat against another pillow, to face Solveig. He wore a loose linen shirt, the outline of bandages peeking through as they wrapped around his shoulder. His signature coat had been draped over the chair opposite the one he sat on, a plate of pastries stacked on the table between the two.

Ves pointed. "I want one."

"You don't want to know how the others are? How long you've been out? Why I had to bribe the doctor?" Solveig cocked a brow.

"Those aren't as important as food, Cap. I. J. Pen. Four years. Give me."

Chuckling, Solveig picked one out – a delicious crescent moon of buttery, flaky dough – and handed it to her. Crumbs rained down over the bed, but Ves ignored it and gobbled the thing up. Then, licking crumbs from her fingers, she stared at Solveig, expectant.

He picked out a fruit scone for himself and turned it over in his hand. "You've been out just under a day. Seventy stitches, by the way. I only needed six." He gestured with the scone to his bandaged shoulder. "You move in your sleep. Pulled a few free. Thol is fine. A few split knuckles, but he's used to that. Illie needed two stitches in her eyebrow, and she somehow had *frostbite,* but she's fine now. She and Thol are back at the *Serenity.*"

"And the girls?" she pointed to the plate again. Solveig tossed her a cookie stuffed full of gooey chocolate chunks.

He bit into his scone and chewed thoughtfully, swallowing before answering, "All fine. The sick one is here, in a different room. Caught some virus and had a fever, but she'll make a full recovery. Carilon's ours now."

"Jonyth won't be happy about that," she said between bites.

"Jonyth can shove it where the sun doesn't shine," he said bitterly.

Ves finished her cookie, almost sad that it was gone. At least the woman at the bakery had come through with her promise to supply them with desserts.

"What happened to your shoulder?" she asked.

Solveig finished his scone in two bites. "Rouge shot me just before Illie nearly beheaded him."

"Illie?! That tiny pink thing?!" Ves started to sit up, only to be assaulted by a sharp pain again. Right. She'd been slashed across the back and apparently needed seventy stitches. She flattened herself as best as she could.

"It must have been adrenaline. The sword got stuck halfway, but she made the killing blow." He scraped his fingers through his hair, the ring on his pinky glinting in the sunlight. "I didn't know she had that kind of fight in her. I'm tempted to ask her to join us."

"A navigator would be good," Ves mused. *As would having another lady on the crew.* "Maybe a navigator would keep you from going on tangents and side quests."

There were two things Ves knew about Solveig's situation: he needed to find a treasure, and Anwir Helios was behind the scheme. She could only guess what Prince Anwir wanted, and Solveig stubbornly refused to tell her what it was – much less where they were supposed to be going.

"My *tangents* and *side quests* got us a ship, an impossible map, a quartermaster, and reign over Carilon," Solveig said defensively. "All things relevant to finding Anwir's blasted treasure."

Ves closed her eyes, drowning out his grumbling. "Bring me more of those moon-shaped things. And some cinnamon rum."

"You're not the captain."

"No." she smiled to herself. "But you're going to do it anyway."

She heard the chair scrape against the ground, then the swoosh of fabric as Solveig undoubtedly grabbed his coat and slung it over his shoulders. His footsteps were soft as he left.

Sometime between getting on Mumford Scorn's ship and now, Illie must have collapsed from exhaustion since she had no idea how she ended up in the hospital, hands wrapped in thick layers of bandages and a steaming cup of spiced milk warming her fingers. She hardly paid attention as a nurse flitted about checking her vitals, and recounting to her how she'd needed two stitches to her eyebrow and that she was the unluckiest girl in Carilon to have somehow contracted frostbite in the middle of summer.

She stared at the creamy milk, steam curling around her nose. Solveig came in once to tell her everyone was fine, but he was quickly scolded by the same nurse as before and chased out with a broom and threats to chop his arm clean off if he didn't *rest*. Even though he grinned the whole time, Illie couldn't help but feel...*weak*. If she had grabbed the air around that final bullet, Solveig wouldn't have gotten shot. It was her fault, really. Her fault for taking his second weapon, her fault for not being strong enough, her fault for not actually beheading Rouge – for not killing him sooner.

Mumford Scorn visited her next. He awkwardly thanked her and told her about how, when the Redcoat Pirates came, he tried to fight back, only to be outmatched and shoved into the cave.

By the time he left and Thol arrived, the spiced milk had gone cold.

If her hands didn't heal properly, she might never draw again. Her mapmaking career would be over before it ever truly got to begin, all because of some pirates. No. Not because of pirates; because of her own *weakness.*

The mug was suddenly plucked from her hands. Illie looked up to see Thol holding it between his thumb and middle finger. "You should talk to Nox about frostbite," he said without preamble. "He had it once, ages and ages ago. I heard you beheaded Rouge."

She stared at her bandaged hands. "The sword didn't go all the way through."

"I didn't expect it to. There're lots of muscles and bones in the neck that make beheading someone hard." He sat on one of the wooden chairs, putting the mug on the other. "I cried when I made my first kill. Had nightmares for a week."

Despite it all, Illie snorted. "You? I don't believe it."

"I was also a kid." He smirked. "Nox cried for *two* weeks, *and* he wet the bed. He'll deny it, but I was in the hammock beneath him when it happened."

A smile tugged on Illie's lips. "No way."

"He was nicknamed *Piss Boy* for a solid month before our captain banned the name."

If Illie had more of her strength back, she would get up and find Solveig *just* to whisper that name in his ear.

"You're a cartographer," Thol said. "Does –"

She cut him off quickly. "I can't make a map that tracks the Wandering Isle. It's impossible."

He blinked. "We already have one of those. We don't need another. I was going to ask if being a cartographer means you're artistic."

Already have one? These pirates had a map that tracked the Wandering Isle?! Such a thing couldn't exist, but... Her mouth watered, her stomach warming as her heart palpitated. More than anything in the world, Illie wanted – no, *needed* – to see that map.

"I'm... Not. But my master's grandson, Elgar Quill, is. Why?"

"I need something designed for me. How fast would he be able to work?"

She lifted her shoulders in a shrug. "Depends. Once they let me out of here, I'll take you to him. *But...* I want to see that map. Just to look at it, nothing else."

Thol grinned. "Deal."

Two and a half hours later, after being freed from the hospital and making a stop at the Ink and Rose to let Thol relay the details of his project to Elgar and to feed Pleo, Illie found herself on the deck of the *Serenity*.

"In here," said Thol, waving her to an ajar door.

Illie hurried over, slipping through the door into what she could only guess were the captain's quarters. A cot with blankets strewn across it hung in one corner. Beneath a row of windows was a cluttered desk. Illie had to step over discarded scabbards and clothes to get to it. Amidst the mess, she spotted three wanted posters – one for Solveig himself, one for Ves, and one for Thol.

Illie snorted. "Your name really is *Bartholomew?* I thought Ves made that up."

He shot her a glare that only made her laugh.

Turning back to the desk, Illie glimpsed at a scrap of paper, a handwritten note scribbled on it. She only caught the last two lines before Thol slammed a shimmery lithograph atop the papers.

Illie's eyes widened until they resembled the twin moons Mene and Sin. If not for the rapid numbers flitting to indicate a change in degrees, she would have assumed it was just another standard lithograph, a map carved into a piece of thin metal – or...shimmery...rock in this case. But...it was *moving*. This map somehow managed to capture the floating island's actual movement, a feat she thought impossible.

Her mouth practically salivated as she reached out to touch the map, only to recoil last second. It wasn't hers to touch.

Never in her life had Illie loved a map more. She wanted – no, she *needed* – to know how it worked.

She needed to recreate it. Her hands itched for her tools, for a piece of parchment and a nub of charcoal to start sketching.

"How is he in his mid-twenties and he still doesn't know how to clean up after himself?" Thol grumbled, dragging Illie's focus from the lithograph for a second. She glanced over to see him picking up the discarded clothes and tossing them into a pile in the corner.

Having lived with two of them for most of her life, Illie knew better than most how childish grown men could be. Especially when it came to cleaning up. She ran her finger absently against the edge of the lithograph. "Still? Have you and Solveig known each other for a long time?"

Thol kicked a pair of trousers into the pile. "We grew up together," he said. "His mother was slightly better than my father, so I all but lived at his house. And we sailed together for a while until he set out to form his own crew. He's my brother."

"Is that why you call him *Nox* instead of *Solveig?*" It wasn't uncommon for people to go by their surnames instead of their given names, especially for men. Women who identified themselves by their surnames were either praised as being progressive or shunned for being too confident. Illie's surname was also a common male name, and she didn't like her blood family enough to want to be identified by their name.

He nodded once. "He started going by Solveig after breaking away from the *Sea Wyrm*. Said all the best pirates went by their last names. Solveig was his mother's name, and he hated her, so gods know why he uses it."

As much as Illie wanted to pry – she knew a thing or two about hating mothers – she knew it wasn't Thol's place to free the skeletons in Solveig's closet, nor was it her place to snoop into his past. She was just a mapmaker who happened to have goals that aligned with his for a brief stint. Nothing more. Nothing less.

Thol turned to pick up a few scabbards off the ground. With his back turned, Illie lifted the edge of the lithograph – it was warm, and it *hummed* against her fingertips – to glimpse at the paper beneath it.

To find the core go first up then down
The name of the third moon is such.

The third moon...

She knew then, wholly and without a sliver of doubt, that fate had dragged Ves into the Ink and Rose for a reason. She had *longed* for an adventure, and now...

Now, she just needed to figure out how to insert herself into this one.

Ves was released from the hospital after two days, though Solveig thought she should've stayed an extra day. Despite needing seventy stitches, she got out of bed and marched out of the hospital herself without even hinting at being in pain.

Solveig waited for her outside, arms crossed, a grin plastered on his face.

"I want a bath, rum, and a feast so big even ole Castros would find it gluttonous," she said without preface.

"You're not supposed to get your stitches wet, we have rum on the ship, and Thol's been receiving *generous* edible donations from the townsfolk." His grin widened.

When he had first seen his bo'sun bleeding – when he'd first seen how deep she'd been cut, layers of flesh and muscle lacerated by a rough blade – panic had set in. He couldn't lose his crew, not again. He didn't sleep, even though he was injured, too, and the pain medicine that had been fed into his veins made him drowsy. Instead, he stayed up until the moons vanished beyond the horizon and the sun painted the sky in shades of lavender and pink haze, praying to Poet and Dreamer, the Wanderer, even Lady Lightbringer that Ves would survive.

Seeing her now, Solveig had no idea why he'd doubted her resilience.

She wore her trousers, but her shirt had been damaged during the fight, too stiff with blood to be salvaged, so she tied her hospital gown around her chest. Her hair was a mess, dried blood clinging to the ends, the curls double their usual size, frizzed from the humid summer air. But despite the dark smudges beneath her eyes, she smiled so wide her dimples could be seen from clear across the country.

"Any monetary donations?" she asked as she followed Solveig.

"Some." A pang of guilt tugged at his stomach. He should tell her about the money Anwir Helios had given him, but... His tongue went leaden when he tried to form the words.

Swallowing his guilt, he shoved his hands into his pockets and continued to the harbor, ignoring the shouts of praise that followed.

It was a strange thing to be seen as a hero. As a boy, between games of pirates and pretending to be in the navy, when he was alone, he would play hero. He'd venture down the hill into town to scale trees and rescue kittens or save dolls from older bullies.

But Solveig was a pirate now. He wasn't a hero; he was *Captain Nox Solveig,* the infamous killer who razed and pillaged and took down seventy-three navy ships.

Yet, despite it all, the people of Carilon considered him their savior.

Heroism tasted like two bottles of cinnamon rum too many. It tasted like *shame.*

The *Serenity* bobbed gently in the waves, sails furled, and anchor lowered. Lounging against a stack of crates, tinted spectacles covering his eyes, and a bottle of cinnamon rum in hand was Thol. Next to him, with an open book balanced on her knees and wire spectacles on her nose, was, to Solveig's surprise, Illie. She was the first to notice Solveig and Ves.

Shoving her book aside and standing, she called, "You're back!"

"What's in those crates?" Ves pointed to the ones Thol sat against as she marched up the gangplank. "Food, rum, money?"

Illie peered through the slats. "Looks like fish. Do you have an icebox?" She pushed her spectacles onto the top of her head.

"Flower boy's the only one who isn't injured." Ves sat down and stretched, reaching for her toes. "He can put it away."

Without looking up from his rum, Thol held up a bandaged hand.

Ves ripped off her shoe and chucked it at his head.

"If you spill my rum," he said, the boot landing on the deck after just missing his head, "I won't tell you where I put the rest of it."

Ves let out a long string of curses. She threw her other boot at Thol.

Illie picked up her book and cradled it against her chest, un-speaking as she watched Thol and Ves launch into a rather childish fight. She shifted awkwardly.

"We'll depart in the morning," Solveig said to her. "It's best we don't stay here too long. Word of what we did will be reaching Jonyth – the navy – soon, and it's better for everyone if we're long gone before they show up."

Illie's shoulders sagged. "Right," she murmured. "But you'll be here overnight, right?"

Solveig cocked a brow. He knew better than to blindly trust anyone, but nothing about this girl screamed *navy spy*. It would be smarter to leave now, to put as much distance between the *Serenity* and Carilon as possible, but he knew his crew was too exhausted to sail now. He couldn't be certain Thol had even *slept* since the fight on Bowhead Rock

"I-I just mean... I..." Illie stammered, her ears turning as pink as her hair. "A banquet! You should have a banquet! Celebrate your victory. Wh-who knows? Maybe you'll get more people bringing you gifts tonight!"

Not a navy spy. But she *was* planning something.

Solveig turned his gaze to the sea, just past Ves and Thol, who were still squabbling (rum *had* been spilled. A lot of it, all over the deck and Ves's trousers), to where the sky met the sea in a blur of white, a horizon he longed to reach.

The dead god had to be out there, somewhere.

"I know about the third moon," Illie blurted at the same time Solveig said, "Join my crew."

Again, at the same time: "What?"

And again: "No, you."

Solveig didn't say anything, instead gesturing for her to speak first. She sucked in a breath and said, "Thol showed me the map of the Wandering Isle and I saw a note on your desk that said something about the third moon, and I *know* about the third moon. I've been charting every mention of it on a world map because I believe it did exist once, and I can help you. I can copy my notes for you and –"

Solveig held his hands up, cutting her off. At least she had just seen his notes and not the actual map, which was tucked safely in the inner pocket of his green coat.

The third moon. That elusive final line to the clue on the map Anwir Helios had given him. Was that truly the connecting piece, the bridge Solveig needed to find the dead god – to get the royal pardon and sail the four seas without worry? Anwir seemed to think it was.

Illie was the key. The last piece Solveig needed.

"I need a navigator," Solveig said.

Illie sucked her bottom lip between her teeth.

Solveig said, "Join my crew."

But before Illie could answer, there was a shout from the dock below.

Illie and Solveig both rushed to the railing to see the fuss. Solveig reached for the cutlass at his hip but lowered his hand when he saw, from the corner of his eye, Illie waving at the man below. He was short and bespeckled, and he held a large, wrapped package against his chest. The man eyed Solveig nervously. Rather, he eyed Solveig's *coat*.

"That's Elgar Quill," Illie said, like that would explain everything.

"Let him up!" Thol scrambled away from Ves and her antics, hurrying to the railing. "He has something important."

Solveig waved the boy up. Elgar Quill stumbled up the gangplank, a rabbit amongst hungry wolves once he reached the deck. With shaky hands, he handed the package to Thol.

"Grandfather is wondering when you'll be back," Elgar stage whispered to Illie.

"Tell him I'll be back soon. And make sure Pleo has food, please," she whispered back. Elgar Quill nodded and hurried off the *Serenity*.

Thol smoothed out the package and held it out to Solveig. "This," he said, "is for you. *Captain*. I think it's time you got this."

Frowning, Solveig picked at the tape. "What is it?" he asked, not one for surprises.

Thol, knowing that, just grinned. "You'll see."

Solveig tore the tape, ripping the brown paper and letting it fall to the deck. His heart thudded against his ribs when the gift was revealed. He didn't need to unfold the bolt of fabric, dark as ink, to know what it was.

All proper pirates needed a black flag. The colors of the *free*.

Even though Solveig himself was anything *but* free.

Letting the last bits of paper fall, Solveig, with shaky hands, slowly unfolded the flag.

He wasn't much of a crier. Crying only damaged his reputation. Captain Nox Solveig, cloaked in green, didn't cry. But as he stared at the flag, tears pricked his eyes, welling up and threatening to spill.

It wasn't just any flag; it was the flag they had used when Solveig was a boy, pretending to be a fearsome pirate.

A crescent moon had been painted on the center, stabbed by a sword. Dripping from the tip of the sword, as if the moon itself was bleeding, were five gemstones: an emerald, an amethyst, a sapphire, a ruby, and a glittering moonstone. The only change was that the gem inlaid in the sword's pommel was an emerald now, not a polished piece of brown tourmaline like it was when they were children.

Solveig looked up from the flag to meet the gaze of his best friend.

"I asked Illie for a favor," Thol explained. "All pirates need a flag. I figured –"

Solveig cut him off by crushing him in a hug.

"Thank you," he whispered to his oldest, closest friend. "They would have loved this."

"They would be proud of you," Thol whispered back.

Pulling away, Solveig turned to Illie. He said again, "Join my crew."

Illie glanced at Thol. She nervously wet her lips, inhaled softly, and said, "I have a few things I need to bring. And I need to tell my master I'm leaving. And... And I want to bring my cat. She's a good mouser and she'll stay out of the way."

"Oh! A cat!" Ves clapped her hands together. "We do need a cat."

Solveig inclined his head in a nod. He had more than enough lune at his disposal to feed a *cat*.

"Then... Then..." She took a deep breath. "I will pledge my final breath to your name. And my first to find you again."

Solveig grinned. "Welcome," he said. "Thol, get the cinnamon rum. We have a navigator now; I think that's cause for celebration."

PART TWO

17

NATHA WIPED THE TEARS from under her eyes with the backs of her forefingers. She blinked a few times to get the last tears out of her vision and forced a smile. Tucked in the back closet with the door locked from the inside, she was about as alone as she could get in the busy kitchen, but not for long. Her crying break only lasted five minutes, and that was far too long.

That morning, the owner of the restaurant came in when Natha was busy preparing for breakfast and told her she would be responsible for the catering at a gala.

It wasn't an unusual request. Natha did catering for galas all the time, though not as frequently now as she'd done in school. She didn't have a problem with it. Coming up with a menu, preparing the dishes, all of it was *fun*.

But usually, she had a few *weeks* at *minimum* to prepare.

The gala was that evening, and the owner decided less than ten hours' notice was all Natha was deserving of.

She relayed the news to her chefs, telling them to prepare with a basic set of entrées while she hastily made a menu. When she'd finished with that and given recipes out, she learned two chefs quit, three had decided to make four dozen of the *same* entrée *each,* and one discovered he was sick halfway through cooking and everything he'd made had to be scrapped.

It was noon now, and Natha had already made most of everything herself, as usual, when she simply broke down.

She took a few deep breaths to calm herself and stood, smoothing the wrinkles from her uniform and opening the door. She stepped out into the kitchen and went right back to work. If she could keep busy, she wouldn't have the time to let her mind wander. She wouldn't think about how horrible her life had become, how miserable she was, how maybe throwing herself into the Emerald Sea would be better than slaving away at a job she once loved but now loathed.

With so little time to prepare, the menu was simple. The gala was to be held at the Royal Veridin Museum of History, so Natha decided local Veridinian recipes would be favored. She picked three main courses: black cod served over creamy potatoes and marinated asparagus, drizzled with a basil and sun tomato vinaigrette; blue lobster smothered in melted butter mixed with parsley and thyme, with roasted korva coated in salt and pepper; and one of Natha's favorite dishes – black fish eggs tossed with cheese-filled noodles and a lemon-butter sauce.

She picked three desserts, too, though with the time crunch, she couldn't make the rather involved dishes she would have usually paired with the three main courses. Instead, she settled on an almond cake, a fluffy mousse made of honey, fresh lemon, and mint, and a rich dark chocolate tart with sweet orange and a coffee ganache.

Simple things, really, made less simple by the incompetence of her employees and the lack of time to get everything ready.

At least she was required to attend the gala. While she didn't care much for dressing up, she did like the fact that she was getting paid to listen to live music and look at old art and artifacts.

She grabbed a knife, twirling it over her fingers before chopping a bunch of basil leaves into tiny pieces. She scraped the basil into a mortar already filled with chopped sun tomatoes – a golden tomato that only grew in the summer months and, when cut open, resembled little halved sunbursts. They were delicious when cooked – especially atop bread with olives and salt and a dribble of olive oil – but could be eaten raw, too.

Natha ground the basil and tomatoes until they became a pulpy mash. She drizzled in a splash of olive oil and mixed it up with the pestle. The tangy aroma of basil filled the air, reminding Natha that cooking wasn't supposed to be a chore.

She grabbed the bottle of vinegar and poured it into a larger bowl, measuring with her heart more than anything else. When she was satisfied with how much of the tangy dark liquid was in the bowl, she scraped the basil-tomato mix in and whisked it together.

When that was finished, she tugged her pocket watch free from her trousers.

Four hours left.

She'd, unfortunately, worked with worse odds before.

"Look me in the eyes and tell me, *specifically* – word for word – what you were told *not to do.*"

Something told Fynch Largos his closest friend, Czardas Rossi, was not pleased with him, but he was too busy tossing pebbles in the air and blindly catching them to put his finger on *why*.

"Are you even listening?" scolded Czardas.

Fynch tossed the pebbles, one after the other, in rapid succession, hitting the targets he'd set up on the other side of the room – a bottle that promptly shattered, a book that slid to the ground with a *thunk,* and Czardas's block of rosin that cracked but was too sticky to fall.

"You were not supposed –" Czardas started, but Fynch finished for him. "Not supposed to follow you. Yeah. I know. *But...* consider this. I didn't *follow* you. We just happened to be going to the same place at the same time."

Czardas put his bow in the same hand he was holding the neck of his violin and pinched the bridge of his nose. Hard.

"Fynch, in *what* version of this universe would you go to a museum for a gala where you have to *pay to enter?*"

It was a harsh question, and by the look of shock on Czardas's face, after he said the words, he knew it. Czardas Rossi had grown up with *very* wealthy parents. He'd never wanted for anything. Never spent a day worrying about where he'd get his next drink of water, when he'd get his next meal, if he would be mugged in his sleep and never wake up again.

Unlike Fynch, who was born at the very bottom of the social food chain and had looted garbage cans for a scrap of dinner more than once.

"Maybe I just want to hear you perform...?" Fynch tried. He took another pebble from his pocket and flicked it at the wall. It hit a fly, killing it.

"You've been listening to me practice for a week straight," Czardas deadpanned.

The truth was, Fynch just wanted to go to the Exhibition Gala at the Royal Veridin Museum of History because he was Czardas's unofficial bodyguard, and who knew what kind of scoundrels would be sneaking in with the intent of slaying the famous Czardas Rossi?

And there was a new exhibit at the museum Fynch was itching to get his hands on.

But mainly, he wanted to make sure Czardas was safe, especially since Czardas had dedicated so much of his life to keeping *Fynch* safe. Just safe. Not out of trouble, since Fynch always sniffed that out, but safe.

"If you cause *any* problems tonight, I will disown you," Czardas threatened. He tucked his violin between his cheek and shoulder and placed the bow over the strings.

Fynch didn't know the first thing about music, other than that it sounded nice. Czardas didn't just *play* music. He breathed it to life with each pull of his bow, his fingers dancing up and down the strings faster than a bullet. It was mesmerizing to hear him play, even more so to *watch*. Fynch held his breath, tense with anticipation.

Czardas closed his eyes and began to play, running through the trills and slurs of the dance he'd been playing nonstop for weeks now. Czardas claimed it wasn't a difficult piece, but his fingers moved so fast they became a blur.

Excitement bubbled in Fynch's belly, his heart swooping and dipping and soaring in time with the arpeggiated runs. He bit his tongue, heart galloping faster and faster as the melody swelled, hitting a climax that ruptured Fynch's flesh in goosebumps before tumbling into a release so divine only the gods themselves seemed capable of creating.

Czardas groaned loudly. "It's still not *right.*"

Fynch tossed a pebble in his direction, purposely missing his mane of unruly curls by a hair. With hair that couldn't be tamed and warm brown skin interrupted by patches of paler flesh, Czardas easily stood out amongst the elite Veridinian class. He was the antithesis to Fynch, who had messy blonde hair, green eyes, and a crooked nose, yet they were thick as thieves, even if Fynch was the only thief between them.

"What's not right?" Fynch asked because there wasn't a single musical bone in his body. To him, the song sounded perfect.

After living with Czardas for most of his life, Fynch *should* have understood music better, but he didn't. Just as Czardas didn't know the art of pickpocketing or sharpshooting.

"I'm still too flat on the high notes," Czardas grumbled.

Fynch procured another pebble from his pocket and lazily tossed it into the air. Maybe he did know more about music than he let on because he said, "Have you tried *overshooting* it? Go higher than you think you should?"

It was a sharpshooting technique, but maybe it could be applied to music, too.

Czardas stared at him blankly. Then, he brought his violin up and began playing the section right before the wispy high notes. This time, he kept his eyes open, fixated on the neck of his instrument, on his fingers dancing over the strings.

He shot his fingers further up the neck suddenly, the pressure of his bow lightening to the faintest of whispers.

"Aha!" Czardas exclaimed, triumphant. "You're a genius, F! Now I just need remember to overshoot... Ah! I have to go. Just... Just *stay here,* got it? Don't move. Don't touch anything. Just sit here and I'll bring you something to eat."

Fynch had a criminal sweet tooth. As if on cue, his stomach grumbled uncomfortably. "Dessert," he demanded. "And don't *worry,* Czar. I won't move a *muscle.*"

Czardas glared but nodded once. Straightening out his waist-coat, he hurried out of the backroom and into the museum where he would perform.

Fynch Largos was a thief, but he was also, unfortunately, a liar. Security would be too focused on the gala to notice Fynch sneaking around. The opportunity was simply too good to miss.

Sorry, Czar, Fynch thought to himself as he tiptoed over to the vent grate just high enough for him to jump to. *I promise I won't get caught, and I promise I'll be right back here when you're done.*

Fynch wiggled into the vent. He'd find the new exhibit, pocket it, and return to make sure Czardas was safe.

He passed over a grate, pausing long enough to glance down at the crowd of wealthy people. He just *knew* their pockets would be overflowing with lune, practically *begging* to be stolen. Next to a piano was Czardas, already mid-song. A group stood around him, watching in awe, as if they had never seen a violinist worth his salt in their lives.

Huffing, Fynch continued on.

The vent started to get narrower and narrower, making it harder for Fynch to shimmy his way through. He came to another grate and peered through, scanning the room it showcased to make sure there was no one. Positive he was alone, Fynch wrested the grate out of place and wriggled down, landing as silent as a cat on the balls of his feet.

The Royal Veridin Museum of History was the largest histo-ry museum in the entire kingdom – though, in a few years, it would change its name to the Royal *Aralyth* Museum of History, Veridonia Branch, when Prince What's-His-Name married Princess-Who-Cares – and so it boasted the most exhibits, stuffed full of countless – *priceless* – relics.

The room Fynch landed in was a square with three paintings on each of the red-painted walls. Beneath a landscape painting of a creature with a clock for an eye was a door. Fynch didn't care for art, mostly because it was too difficult to steal, impossible to resell, and he thought it was all ugly anyway. The relic Fynch wanted wouldn't be in this wing of the museum.

As he walked through the door, clinging to the shadows like a wraith, he debated if the relic he wanted would be in the *religion* wing or the *history* wing.

Once upon a time – according to legends Fynch wasn't sure he truly believed – instead of *four* major kingdoms, *four* oceans, and *four* gods, there had been five. Veridin, Aralyth, Merdyne, Gello, and *another*. The Emerald, the Sapphire, the Ruby, the Amethyst, and *another*. Poet, Dreamer, the Wanderer, Lady Lightbringer, *and one more*. One that was forgotten, scrubbed from the world, from the records, from everything except a strange relic recently discovered and brought here, to Veridin, to be put on display.

From what he'd gathered, experts weren't exactly sure *what* it was; they only knew that it was important and very, *very* old.

And *very old* and *very important* typically meant *very expensive*. The lune he'd get from pawning it would change his life. Fynch thought he deserved a better life.

He sneaked down a lengthy corridor, the painted eyes of the long dead watching him as he went.

It looks like a compass of sorts, he recalled eavesdropping.

Some sort of religious icon?

There are three crescent moons engraved on it.

There's an inscription, but not in any language anyone knows.

Footsteps drew near. Fynch held his breath and dove through a doorway, narrowly pressing his back against the wall as a drunken gala guest stumbled down the hall right where he had just been. The lingering smell of sugar smoke followed. He sighed out the breath he'd been holding and examined his surroundings.

Still in the art wing, but there, next to the door across the room from where he stood, he spotted a small plaque not affixed to any paintings. He hurried over.

Archaeology and Ancient Religion

The arrow beneath the label pointed to the doorway. In his debate about whether the relic would be in a theology wing or a history one, he completely overlooked the obvious: archaeology.

Grinning like an addict who'd just cleared his gambling debt in one fell swoop, Fynch slipped through the doorway.

And there it was.

Seated on a pedestal, protected by the thinnest shields of glass – *glass,* of all things – was...

Well, Fynch wasn't really sure *what* it was. It looked like a compass but also like a pocket watch or a compact mirror. Big enough to fit in his palm and circular in shape, it had two separate faces: one with a needle that spun aimlessly, like a broken magnet desperately searching for north, but no cardinal labels. Just...a few splotches of ink. The other face was shimmery, pearlescent with rainbow slashes of blues and reds and greens. It looked like someone had sliced off a sliver of the moon and painted nonsensical numbers around its circumference.

One.

Ten.

Five.

Thirty.

Zero.

Five again.

Six.

Well, it didn't matter what it meant. All Fynch cared about was snagging it and returning to the backroom to wait for Czardas.

The rock in his pocket was the *perfect* size and weight. He wouldn't trip any alarms, and even if he did, the guards were too drunk and too far away to reach him before he could get away.

He placed his fingers – he lacked fingerprints, thanks to a stupidly genius idea involving fire – on the glass and lifted.

Maybe the gala wouldn't be so bad. As the head chef, Natha had zero obligations to serve the guests, so she *was* a guest. Of sorts. She had to linger near the table and be ready to rush to the makeshift kitchen (a storage closet where all the extra food was kept warm or cool at steady temperatures) at a moment's notice.

She wore the second fanciest dress she owned as the first was nothing more than ashes. She'd burned her wedding dress after the divorce. This one was a deep red, a color that matched her eyes almost perfectly, as well as her lips. It hugged her hips and torso, the collar reaching her chin. With no sleeves, her shoulders were on full display, though the skirts fanned out in a rather impractical train. She wore gloves (white silk, of course) to cover her arms because, even after so many years, she wasn't confident enough to show the world her ugly past.

Since she was working, Natha couldn't drink, but that didn't stop her from grabbing a narrow flute full of sparkling white grape juice. Coffee, her preferred drink, would be served *after* dessert, so the non-alcoholic wine would have to do for now. She sipped on it, letting the bubbles pop over her tongue.

All things considered, the gala turned out nicely. *And* Natha had dragged herself out of her tiny flat, put on some makeup and a nice dress, and was actually at the first social gathering she'd dared attend since the divorce. Her ex-husband, last she'd heard, was off on some mission at Emperor Castros Helios's discretion. He was a navy captain, but with Veridin just a few years away from being part of the Aralyth Empire, he followed Castros's orders as well as King Argos Smythe's.

Argos Smythe was a coward in every way. Probably why he agreed to sell his eldest son to Castros Helios's witch of a daughter. Royal gossip intrigued Natha, especially since she had not only studied at the Royal Culinary Academy of Veridin but had also served the royal family her dishes on more than one occasion. She'd been invited to be the palace's royal chef once but declined when her ex-husband said it was a terrible idea.

Marrying him was a terrible idea.

Sipping on her juice, Natha surveyed the crowd. Most of the guests were seated at the array of cloth-covered tables, happily eating her creations. She heard rumors that the queen, Lydia Smythe, would be attending with her two youngest daughters, the twins Haru and Vivian. Natha remembered clearly when the girls were toddlers. She was one of the few outside the royal court who remembered Vivian's transition, too. But as she looked from table to table, she couldn't spot them.

"I can take your glass, ma'am," a server said, startling her. Before she could swipe her leg out and pin the poor server to the ground, she held out her empty, lipstick-smudged glass. The server, unsuspecting of Natha's fight or...well, just fight instincts, walked off to gather more empty flutes.

Soon, more servers came out to take the empty plates off the tables, only to replace them with dessert. A smile – rarer than most things these days – graced Natha's lips as the guests delved into her ccooking.

"Ah...excuse me, ma'am?"

Natha looked up to see a young man standing before her. He had dark skin broken up by paler patches, and under his arm was a violin. She knew him instantly. Czardas Rossi, the musician. He was younger than she was, but *everyone* in Veridonia, the capital city of Veridin, knew who the man was. He could play over thirty instruments, though his preferred was the violin. He was so talented that the gossip columns in the newspaper insisted there was a god of music who had blessed Czardas.

Natha knew it was garbage, though. Talent and hard work outweighed being divine touched.

Czardas said, "Did you make everything? To eat, that is." When she arched a brow and nodded once, he continued, "It's very, *very* good. Um... Do you think there's extra? I have a friend who wasn't able to make it, but I promised I'd bring him something."

Her chest swelled with pride. Not only did *Czardas Rossi* like her cooking, he also wanted to *take some home.* To *share.*

This was why Natha cooked. She loved the precise balance of ingredients, and the way she could make anything taste good, but more than that, she loved it when people *enjoyed* what she made.

"I –" she started, but she didn't get to finish that sentence. A kid, no older than Rossi himself, ran past in a streak of blond hair and black clothes. He clutched something to his chest as he ran.

Behind him were four guards, chasing with pistols drawn.

All the color drained from Czardas's face.

"Fynch Largos," he hissed under his breath. Turning to Natha, he said, "Never mind. Sorry for bothering you. I have to go."

And with that, he took off running, too.

Maybe Fynch should have come up with a more solid plan, because *grab the relic and run* wasn't working out.

As far as he knew, he hadn't tripped any alarms. The glass cover slid off nicely, and he was able to quickly swap the relic for the stone in his pocket, returning the glass before any sirens could sound. He *knew* walking calmly to a vent and crawling back to the room he was supposed to wait in was the smart thing to do, but Fynch wasn't exactly the smartest.

So, instead of remaining calm and inconspicuous, once he had the relic clutched to his chest, he decided to walk the halls back to the back room.

And instead of keeping the relic in his pocket – instead of pretending to be a drunken gala guest when he passed a pair of guards – he kept it out, and when they saw the glint of moonstone and asked Fynch what he was holding, well...

He booked it.

Fynch wasn't the tallest person alive – far from it, really – and years of running from authorities had given him a bit of an athletic advantage over the lumbering guards. As he ducked through different rooms, slipping through open doorways, and mazing his way through the museum to shake the guards long enough to find a vent to squeeze through, he let one *crucial* detail slide.

There were far more than two guards at the Royal Veridin Museum of History.

Sarding sard! He cursed to himself.

Running through a door into the art wing, Fynch came face-to-face – rather, face-to-chest – with a massive guard. He tipped his head back to take in the full mountain of muscle. The color drained from his cheeks. Fynch swallowed hard.

"I...uh...got lost?" he tried, his voice little more than a soft, mousy squeak.

"Get him!" one of the two guards from before shouted, finally caught up.

Muscles lunged, sweeping his arms out to catch Fynch, but Fynch was quicker. He ducked beneath Muscles' arms and took off running. Violin music rang out in the near distance. The gala was close, and where the gala was Czardas was.

Except Fynch had *explicitly* promised not to get into trouble, so he couldn't face Czardas, not with three guards chasing him in a game of wolves and rabbits.

No. He had to get out of the museum. He could use his knowledge of the streets to his advantage to shake the guards before returning home.

Fynch *really* didn't want to go to jail *again*.

Thundering footsteps shook the ground beneath Fynch's feet. Fast as he was, the guards were gaining on him.

Absent chatter and faint piano music drew closer and closer. It would be risky to run through the gala, but... What choice did he have?

Sard, sard, sard! Sorry, Czar.

At the very last second, Fynch turned and bolted through an open doorway, causing the guards to stumble and backtrack, buying him a few precious seconds. Clutching the relic to his chest, he shoved past guests, praying to any of the gods who cared to listen that Czardas wasn't among them. Slipping and weaving through the throng, Fynch finally reached the other side. He dared a glance over his shoulder, his shoulders relaxing a fraction at the sight of the guards struggling to get through with the same ease.

Not wanting to waste any more time, Fynch ran right for the front doors. He shoved them open with his shoulder and jumped down the steps, vanishing into a dark alley.

He waited until he was three blocks from the museum before slowing to a walk. His chest ached with each heaving breath he took, his sinuses screaming in burning agony.

"You had better be worth more than a handful of lune," he grumbled to the relic as he shoved it into his pocket.

Instead of going home, Fynch wandered the city, twisting and turning until he was absolutely positive he wasn't being followed.

It was close to sunrise when Fynch finally scaled the trellis that snaked up the back of Czardas's parents' house. Czardas kept his window unlocked, making it easy for Fynch to open it from the outside and climb in. He expected Czardas to be in bed, asleep, so he tiptoed to the bookcase against the far wall – the bookcase that, when a certain book was pulled out of place, opened a hallway to the hidden library where Fynch lived.

Click.

Light flooded the room, freezing Fynch in his tracks. He peered over to see Czardas standing between him and the bookcase, arms crossed.

"You," said Czardas, "have a *lot* of explaining to do."

18

Sunshine beat down on Illie's cheeks, the smell of salt thick in the air. Wisps of pink hair whipped free from her braid, her skirts twisting around her ankles as the gentle sea breeze met them head on. A southeast wind, no more than five knots – though she didn't have an anemometer, she knew the winds better than most.

Illie had been a pirate for six days.

In those six days, her hands had healed nicely, leaving only minimal scabbing and the faintest feeling of pins and needles in her fingertips. Her eyebrow wouldn't scar – a shame, as Ves said since all pirates needed scars.

In those six days, she had also learned a lot about her crew.

Without a proper cook, they took turns in the kitchen. Ves was banned from stepping foot in the galley because, well, it would be better to drink seawater than attempt to digest anything she made.

Thol was the best cook of them all, and even then, he wasn't the best.

The ship's cabins were divided into women's quarters and men's quarters, though only Thol occupied those since Solveig tended to sleep in the captain's quarters. Illie shared with Ves, who, despite saying she wanted nothing to do with Illie's cat Pleo, tended to coax the tabby into sleeping with her. She also had nightmares, ones that shook Illie from her sleep. Ves refused to speak about them, and Illie didn't push her.

Ves liked to drink, and when she'd had a few cups of cinnamon rum, she liked to sing. She was good at it, and she often sang a shanty with a line that bugged Illie – one about the third moon. But drunk Ves couldn't bother stringing together a coherent sentence, and sober Ves refused to sing – refused to even acknowledge the things Drunk Ves did.

Thol was the only one who preferred evenings, so when the sun set and the others went to sleep, he stayed up to man the helm. The four of them took turns at the helm, Illie more so than the others. She was the first to wake, the first to take over sailing, the first to make sure the *Serenity* had survived the night.

She leaned over the railing to catch a glimpse of the figurehead. The *Serenity* was a beautiful ship. Anyone with eyes could see that. She was a brigantine, perfect for sailing the four seas, painted a deep red like she was created to be a pirate ship and nothing else.

"We should be arriving at Veridonia in the next day or so," she said when she heard footsteps approaching. She glanced over her shoulder to see Solveig, his green coat draped over his shoulders, red hair tousled by the (five knots speed) wind.

"After we get that thing you mentioned," he said, "I'll need your help charting a course. I want to see that map you made and use that as a reference."

Her map of all the locations where the third moon had been mentioned. Because Solveig wanted to find the third moon, though he didn't explain *why* or *how* or what those two lines in his quarters hinted at. Regardless, she knew more about the mysterious lost moon than anyone else.

Of the many books Illie brought with her, one of them had a drawing of a compass. Illie would have ignored it if not for the caption beneath it:

Believed to be an ancient navigational tool from the lost civilization that worshipped the third moon

It took a lot of digging and combing through different newspapers to figure out that the compass was a real thing and that it was currently on display in the Royal Veridin Museum of History in Veridonia. She'd shown the picture to Solveig and, to her surprise, the captain – *her* captain – agreed to go.

She turned to face Solveig, leaning against the railing lazily as she met his gaze. He was easy on the eyes, all things considered, but even if he wasn't her captain, Illie had no desire to pursue anything.

"When are you going to tell me why you want to find the third moon?" she asked, a brow cocked.

"When are *you* going to tell *me* why you want to find it?" he shot back.

Touché.

She held up two fingers. "One: I want an adventure. I missed sailing. I missed being at sea with no end in sight. Finding the lost moon seemed to be the best way to go about that. Two: I read something once that mentioned it, and it bothered me. So, I kept reading, and every country in the *world* has *some* reference to the third moon. *Every. Single. Country.* All of them, Sol. That breaks the gap between myth and reality. If Edyn *and* Fjarg –" the northernmost country and the southernmost one "– both have books or artworks with three moons instead of two, it has to be real. I want to prove that it's real. I want to find out what happened to it because a moon can't just *vanish.*"

A salty spray kicked up the side of the ship. Illie narrowed her eyes.

"Ves!" she called to the bo'sun, who lazed against the helm, clearly bored. "Starboard two degrees."

Ves grabbed the pegs and shifted the *Serenity* ever so slightly.

"You're good at that," Solveig said, jumping on the opportunity to change the subject. "How long have you been sailing?"

"I sailed around the world twice," she said plainly. "But I'm blessed by Poet, so it makes it easier."

"By Poet, huh?" He scratched at the stubble along his jaw. "My mother once said my father was blessed by Poet, too."

Divine blessings weren't hereditary. The gods chose people at random to share a sliver of their powers with. Neither of Illie's parents nor her younger sister were blessed.

Illie couldn't help but notice, though, how Solveig phrased it like his father was gone. Her own father died nineteen years ago when she was seven.

"Is your father...dead?" she asked, unsure of how else to say it.

Solveig shrugged. "No idea. Never met him. He knocked my mother up and left. She said he looked like my brother, though. Same hair and eyes. And he was supposedly blessed by Poet."

Illie looked at the ocean, not knowing how to handle that confession. Sure, her own family life was messy. Her father and sister were dead, she'd run away from home when she was a child, and Henry and Elgar were more family than her mother and her stuffy noble family were.

"Come to think of it," Solveig murmured, "Thol might know more about my father..." he grumbled something to himself; Illie didn't strain to listen.

"*Caaaaaap!*" Ves called. "Your turn! I want to take a bath before we arrive!"

Illie snorted. "Better listen to her, Sol," she said. "She will whine to me for hours if she doesn't get her bath."

"Trust me," he groaned. "I know. Everyone in the Emerald Sea will hear her whining."

Illie smiled, watching as her captain went to take over the helm.

"Fynch Largos, I am going to *kill you*," seethed Czardas through clenched teeth. After hearing Fynch's story, Czardas had to physically restrain himself from attacking his best friend.

"In my defense," pleaded Fynch, "I figured I could sell it. I need the money."

"I feed you!" Czardas cried, only to remember too late he wasn't supposed to be awake, and his parents wouldn't hesitate to barge in if they thought something was amiss. Lowering his voice to a hiss, he continued: "I give you a place to live, no charge. I give you clothes and access to books and...and you *still* need money?!"

Fynch narrowed his eyes. But despite the fire in them, his shoulders slumped, and he looked away. "I can't stay here forever, Czar. I can't keep mooching off you. I... I need to pay you back and I need to get out of your hair before your ma and da get wind of me being here."

So *that's* what this was about. Fynch didn't want to live with Czardas anymore.

Czardas sat on his bed, trying – and failing, quite miserably – not to look too dejected. Fynch, that bloody, selfish fool.

"You *can* stay here," he whispered. "As long as I'm here, you can stay here. I want to move out eventually, anyway. There's a flat I've been eyeing, a condo that overlooks the port... There would be enough space for both of us. And I make enough money, so you don't have to steal anymore –"

"Czar," said Fynch, voice flat. "I would rather die than survive on your charity."

"So, you stole so you could get away from me."

Fynch cringed. "Can we talk about this in the morning? I'm tired –"

The slap echoed through the room. Czardas didn't feel the sting on his palm until after he saw the red mark on Fynch's freckled cheek. His stomach sank with the realization of what he'd done.

That should have stopped him from yelling at Fynch.

But it didn't.

"You are such a sarding *idiot!*" he snapped. He grabbed the front of Fynch's shirt and shook him. "I can't keep bailing you out of jail, F. I don't *want you to leave!* You need to stop stealing. Seriously!"

"I'm not like you," said Fynch, his voice barely even loud enough to be considered a whisper. "I don't got money. I'm not talented. The only things I'm good at are stealing and shooting. Navy won't take me, so it's not like I can do anything with those things."

Czardas glanced away, Fynch's words a harsh blow. When they were not more than boys, Fynch wanted to join the navy more than anything else in the world. He had the talent for it; he wasn't just an excellent shot – he could hit a moving target the size of a fly from a quarter mile away. With his eyes closed.

But Fynch, unlike his older brother, couldn't join the navy. His criminal history was too much. He'd been arrested a few years ago for an armed robbery, and there were *still* whispers about it throughout Veridonia.

As much as Czardas wanted to sweep the whole thing under the rug, he couldn't.

But Fynch was right; they could discuss this in the morning.

He rubbed the bridge of his nose. "Shower before you sleep, F. You smell like sweat."

Fynch's shoulders slumped – with relief or disappointment, Czardas was too tired to know – and he hurried to the bookcase, tugging on the false book to open the hidden hallway. Once the door slid shut, Czardas sat on his bed and held his head in his hands.

Fynch sarding Largos was going to be the absolute death of him.

Ves lunged, striking as fast and as deadly as a viper, her cutlass splitting the air in two as it arced down. Metal clashed against metal, deafeningly blocked at the very last second.

"You have to be *faster.*" Ves pushed her weight into the blow. She slid her blade against Illie's and struck again, going low, forcing Illie to react just as quickly.

"I still think we should be practicing with – sard! – with fake swords!" Illie's parry was sloppy, a fraction too slow. She lost her grip on her cutlass; it clattered to the ground and skidded just out of reach. *"Sard!"*

"Your enemies won't be using fake swords." Ves dashed for the discarded blade at the same time Illie dove for it.

Illie grabbed the hilt just as Ves brought her blade down, burying it in the deck mere inches from Illie's face.

"Hey!" shouted Thol from the helm. "Do *not* mess up my ship!"

Ves, foolishly, looked to the helm, an apology forming on her tongue (though by *apology,* Ves planned on cursing Thol out). Illie grasped the moment of distraction. She grabbed her cutlass and struck, slamming the pommel of it into Ves's shin.

Ves's eyes widened as blunt pain shot up her leg. She yelped, sounding like a seagull being strangled. Swallowing her discomfort, she narrowed her lethal gaze on Illie. The smug grin fell from Illie's face instantly.

"No killing on my ship either!" Thol yelled lazily.

"You play dirty," Ves hissed through her teeth. Illie hadn't struck hard enough to break her bone, but there would be a *nasty* bruise on her shin for a while. "Good. Pirates always play dirty."

She yanked her cutlass free and sheathed it at her hip. While she *preferred* knives, she could wield a sword just fine. After all, what was a sword, if not an oversized dagger? Plundering the Redcoat Pirates back in Carilon left Solveig's crew with more swords at their disposal than knives, so until she used her allowance to buy some pretty blades when they docked in Veridonia, a cutlass would have to do.

"Don't go for my knees this time." Ves backed up a few feet and drew her sword again. "Don't worry, Pinkie. I'm not gonna *actually* hurt you. And don't worry about hurting me. I promise I can take it."

It had barely been a week since Ves had woken up with a row of stitches down her back. While most of the wound had scabbed over and there was no real risk of her popping her sutures, she couldn't sleep on her back, and if she twisted too much, sharp pain accosted her spine. It would take a lot longer than six days to fully heal, but Ves didn't have that kind of time.

Ves shifted her hips, knees bent and center of gravity low. While she preferred to attack hard and fast, leaving no room for mercy, Illie was the opposite. She was cautious, overthinking every move she made.

Not the kind of fighting style a pirate should have.

Ves decided not to give Illie any time to overthink.

She darted out, sword singing through the air – a silver bolt of lightning that struck deadly and true. Instead of aiming for Illie's weak spots – her exposed flank, her thighs, her throat, her shoulder – she went for Illie's sword, thundering attacks on the metal like it was the sea that took her parents' lives incarnate.

Illie stumbled back, weakly parrying each blow, though her arms trembled under the weight.

Ves brought down her cutlass; Illie threw hers up to block. She was faster for once, striking before Ves could finish her sword's parabolic dive. The suddenness of it threw Ves off guard, off balance. She took a fraction of a step back, giving Illie enough of an opening to strike again.

Illie's sword crashed against the upper third of Ves's, the unbalanced point where, with enough force, Ves would lose all control over her blade, especially if she wasn't paying attention – if she wasn't anticipating it.

She, of course, wasn't.

The sword fell from Ves's grip before she could stop it. Metal met wood, and metal won. The sword buried itself in the deck.

"Ves!" snapped Thol. "Who's going to patch these holes?! We don't have a shipwright!"

She ignored him, instead going for her sword. She yanked it free and thrust it up, creating a barrier mere seconds before Illie brought hers down again.

"You favor your left side," Solveig said, startling them both. Illie retracted her attack.

Solveig pushed himself off the railing he'd been lounging against. Illie's cat, Pleo, rubbed herself against his legs.

"You favor your left," he repeated. "You're left-handed, aren't you?" when Illie nodded he continued: "You keep leaning into that, and you leave your right completely open. You've never used a sword before, have you?"

Illie lowered her sword, the tip dragging against the deck (Thol didn't protest. He just groaned very, very loudly and very, very pointedly). "No," she admitted. "Not before Bowhead Rock. I've used a knife and a spear a few times, but never a sword. I... I need to learn, though. I don't want to be reliant on the wind..."

Learning that Illie was blessed by Poet was the biggest betrayal Ves had dealt with in years. Of course, the only other girl on the ship would be blessed by *Poet,* not *Dreamer,* like Ves was. A true travesty, almost as tragic as when Solveig asked her to help Illie control her powers when Ves couldn't do anything more than spot souls.

(A pod of dolphins swam beneath the *Serenity* with at least two seals).

"We could break her arm," Ves suggested. Jokingly. Mostly. Her previous captain, Captain Mali, broke Ves's arm once when she was hardly even a teenager. She'd injured her right wrist, and instead of treating it, Mali broke it further, forcing Ves to learn to use her left hand when fighting. It wasn't until later that she learned Mali made the break worse so it could heal properly because if she let it be, Ves likely would have never been able to use her right hand again, but at least she'd gotten ambidexterity out of it.

"We don't have a doctor, either," Thol called from the helm.

Ves tugged down her lower eyelid and stuck her tongue out at him.

"When you grab the winds," Solveig said, ignoring Ves and Thol, "what does it feel like?"

Illie glanced at her palm. "Like...grabbing a rope. A really, really, *really* cold rope."

"What, we freeze a rope and give *that* to her?" Ves snorted at the absurdity of the idea.

Solveig rolled his eyes. "No. But maybe giving her a *not-frozen* rope to practice with could help."

It wasn't a bad idea. Far better than Ves's plan to break Illie's arm. Plenty of spare rope was lying around, and it would help build some muscle so Illie's twiggy arms didn't tremble whenever she parried against Ves.

"Port of Veridonia spotted, Nox!" Thol said.

Illie dropped her sword and scurried up to the helm. "There's a cove just east of the port. If we want to avoid detection, we should go there. The tides are low enough to careen. They'll be low for the next three hours before you won't be able to beach anymore."

Ves sheathed her sword and scooped up Pleo, nuzzling her face against the tabby's furry belly. "She's good," she murmured to her captain. "Pinkie. She has a lot of fight in her. With a bit of training, she'll be wicked. Good thing she has the Witch of the Sea to train her."

Solveig snorted. "Yeah, right. If anything, you're scaring her."

Ves nuzzled her cheek against Pleo's side, savoring the fluffy warmth before the cat squirmed and jumped free, padding off to find a sunny spot to sleep in.

"You wound me, Cap." She put her hand over her heart, gasping dramatically.

He raked a hand through his hair. "Are you sure you're up for a heist?"

As *if* her back injury would keep Ves from breaking into a museum to steal some relic. Piracy was all about two things: plundering and pillaging. Besides, it was just a *museum.* How hard could breaking in be? She'd have Illie with her, anyway, in case things went wrong.

Well. Illie could hardly drag Ves back to the *Serenity* if things *did* go wrong.

If not for Ves's ability to see souls, she would have volunteered Solveig or Thol to go with Illie. But, of *course,* she was the only one capable of pulling it off.

"I'll be *fine,* Cap. I stole the map to the Wandering Isle, remember?" she cocked a brow. "I can handle a measly little museum."

"I'm going to town to get some supplies." Thol ducked his head into Solveig's quarters. "The girls tore up my deck. Do you need anything?"

Solveig draped his arms over the map on his desk, hiding it from Thol's view. Half an hour ago, the *Serenity* careened on the sand of a small cove. Illie and Ves took off for their heist, and Thol had busied himself by patching holes and scraping barnacles off the keel.

"Answers," grumbled Solveig. "No. Find a place to eat, though. I'm going to go crazy if I have to eat korva one more time."

"Sure you don't want Ves to cook?"

Solveig looked up from his map, color leeched from his face. He would much rather eat mushy korva for the dozenth time in a row than eat whatever inedible concoction Ves managed to throw together. She was somehow a worse cook than *he* was. Nausea squeezed his stomach, taking any shred of an appetite he might've had.

Thol grinned. "Joking. I'll be back in an hour or so. I'm invoking my powers as quartermaster and assigning Ves to deck polishing duty when she gets back."

He slipped out, closing the door behind him. Solveig's shoulders slumped. He looked at the ancient map spread out before him.

"I don't know what you want me to find, Anwir," he grumbled, eyes darting over the words written along the map's borders.

He grabbed a mostly blank piece of paper and a nub of graphite. He'd tried analyzing each individual line, but maybe that wasn't what he needed to do.

Maybe he needed to look at it section by section instead.

Beneath a shadow on the Endless Sea, where the moon once sat upon the waves. The child who watches with a dead eye, a memory forgotten, a field of graves.

Solveig dragged his hand over his face. Nowhere on the map was there an ocean called the *Endless Sea*. None of it made any sense! He shifted the map to read the next section.

North of refuse and east of swindler, through caverns of salt and blue glow. The child, and slave to eternal night, will bring the horizon the moons sink below.

North and east. Those were two directions he knew. He drew two smudges on the paper – one for refuse and one for swindler. Then, north of one and east of the other, he drew an *X*. If he just knew what in Poet's name *refuse* and *swindler* meant, he could actually chart a course.

"Salt..." he murmured, tapping his graphite against the paper. He shot a glance at the map pinned to the wall.

The Salts Atoll was a ring of islands in the Ruby Sea. He'd never been, but he knew it was under the rule of the Merdyne Empire, and Emperor Castros Helios wanted to get his filthy hands on it. The atoll got its name from the ring of Salt Coral around the exterior circumference, a strange organism that, when filtering seawater, created salt deposits on its exterior, like crystalline growths. Those deposits could be harvested without hurting the coral, creating a safer alternative to the salt mines at the base of the North Range in Aralyth.

If the Salts Atoll was what the map referenced, then *refuse* had to be either Merdyne itself or the Hel Archipelago in the south, and *swindler* had to be Aralyth's Joris Island.

Solveig quickly labeled the marks on his makeshift map.

In chains of the child who once was small, then coveted, now lost to the sun and time. By thirteen chimes of the clock of the dead, a city of gold gifted to the maritime.

Well... Salt... salt was as precious as gold, right?

The final section – *a kiss from the writer to see through the midnight, a song which death can never touch. To find the core go first up then down, the name of the third moon is such* – made no sense, even compared to the rest of the strange riddle. Ignoring it completely, Solveig shifted his attention to the map on the wall. He'd have to talk with Illie, but...

The Salts Atoll. That seemed to be where the map was leading them.

19

THOL WAS NOT A shipwright by any means. He could patch a hole and polish a deck just fine, but anything else was out of his element. The *Serenity* hadn't succumbed to any real damage (yet, thank the gods), but her keel was crusted with barnacles and kelp, and there were those damn holes in the deck courtesy of Ves and Illie.

He slipped into town unnoticed and picked a direction at random, hoping to find a shipbuilding district to get the supplies needed to pretty the *Serenity* up.

Summer sun, harsh and unforgiving, accosted his face and shoulders. Tugging the elastic band off his wrist with his teeth, he scraped his long locks into a bun at the back of his head, tying it off despite how messy it surely looked.

Veridonia, the biggest city – and the capital city – in Veridin, was the bustling center for trade and education within the Veridin Kingdom. Boasting the Royal Veridin Academy and all its branches – music, culinary arts, fine arts, history, science and mathematics, and literature – it was no wonder the city was as crowded as it was. Nobody spared Thol a second glance despite his stature. Even a man as big as him didn't stick out as he navigated through the streets.

Gulls squawked overhead, muddling the chatter of people hurrying to work or school or to get their shopping done. A train of children with bright backpacks clung to a rope led by a young schoolteacher. Thol watched as she confidently brought them through the busy square to the schoolhouse on the other side. He had grown up in a tiny town – he couldn't imagine being brought up *here*.

"Oof!"

Something – no, someone – crashed into Thol. He glanced down to see someone brushing themself off. The kid was at least a foot smaller and built like a reed; it was a wonder they didn't completely fall over after running into Thol.

Thol raised a dark brow. "You alright?"

The kid looked up, green eyes wide and full of fear.

Thol realized then that the purse of money tucked in his inner pocket was gone.

"Sorry about that," the thief stammered. "I guess I was spaced out."

Thol held out his hand. "Sure. Mind returning my money to me?"

The thief's eyes went even wider. Their hand drifted to the front of their trousers where Thol's purse was no doubt stashed. They shifted, ready to run, but Thol was faster. He grabbed the thief's wrist.

"I wasn't asking," he said coolly. "Return it to me. If you can point me in the direction of the shipbuilding district, I'll let you keep some."

Gritting his teeth, the thief snatched the purse from their trousers and shoved it at Thol's chest. "Go to the pier. You'll find someone who can help you there. L-look, just don't tell the navy. Please."

Still holding their wrist, Thol used his teeth to open the purse. He grabbed a few lune bills and dropped them in the thief's outstretched hand.

"Trust me," he said as he let go. "I want to be involved with the navy even less than you." To prove his point, he waved, the first five letters of his *PUNISHMENT* tattoo on full display.

The thief stood there, completely frozen, as Thol began walking to the strip of dock in the distance, stretched far out over the glimmering Emerald Sea.

When he glanced over his shoulder a moment later, the thief was gone, vanished into the throng to try their little scheme with someone more gullible. Thol shook his head and headed straight for the pier.

Illie had never pulled off a heist during the day. Granted, she'd never pulled off any sort of heist before, but she always imagined they'd be done at night. The whole way to the museum Illie's mind raced as it tried to come up with every possible way to sneak inside without being caught.

It didn't occur to her that they could simply walk in through the front door.

Ves strode into the Royal Veridin Museum of History, chin held high like she was Queen Lydia Smythe herself. Illie scrambled after, trying to muster up a scrap of that same confidence.

The museum was strangely empty, though it made sense since most people were at work or school this time of day. Still, the hairs on the back of Illie's neck stood on end, and her stomach flip-flopped a half-beat behind the arrhythmic thrumming of her heart.

You're a pirate, she reminded herself, falling into step with Ves. Aloud, she said, "My guess is it would be in the history wing."

"Aye. If you think so, Pinkie." Ves started humming absently, walking past a few open archways with ease. It bothered Illie that she was so damn *calm* about the whole ordeal.

Then again, Ves had been a pirate for a lot longer than Illie's measly six days. If anyone could be nonchalant about stealing a priceless relic from a museum, it would be Vesperine Genevieve.

Nobody knew what they were doing. The museum was oddly empty anyway, and if it was open to the public, Ves and Illie had every right to be there.

At least, that's what Illie kept telling herself.

Soon, Illie spotted a plaque marking the history wing. Without thinking, she took Ves's wrist and led her through the arch.

"Bit forward of you, Pinkie," Ves murmured. Illie ignored her, dropping her wrist and scanning the room.

"It looks like a compass," Illie whispered, imagining the picture from her book. Just a compass. It wouldn't be that hard to find, right?

Ves had the decoy stuffed somewhere on her person – a regular compass they'd just so happened to have swiped from the Redcoat Pirates. Illie had asked no less than a dozen times on the walk from the *Serenity* to the RVMH if Ves still had it.

She resisted the urge to ask again now.

Illie walked over to a display case and peered inside. A few coins and bits of shrapnel sat on velvet cushions – relics, according to the placard inside, from the Aralythian Conquest two-hundred-something years ago. Illie hardly knew her world history, especially history from an empire she wasn't part of, but she knew, vaguely, that the emperor at the time, starving for power, invaded Servedin Island and Joris Island, killing thousands, and razing the settlements to the ground, and absorbing both into the Aralyth Empire.

She went to the next case, spotting more ephemera from the Aralythian Conquest.

"I'm going to the next room," said Ves.

"Me too." Illie tore away from the case. "I'm willing to bet it'll be in a room dedicated to nautical history or seafaring history."

Surely, the museum curators didn't know the true purpose of the compass. If they did, why wasn't the missing third moon common knowledge? Why did Illie learn about it from random passages and pictures in old books?

Ves vanished into the next room. Illie paused, looking over her shoulder at the case of reliquaries from the Aralythian Conquest.

"You said it's a compass, right?" Ves called from the other room, even though she surely *knew* it was.

Poet's breath.

Illie all but ran into the next room – one marked *archaeology* – hardly managing to skid to a stop before the case Ves stared at. And there it was, sat on a velvet pillow. It...

It looked rather ordinary, all things considered. The spare compass Ves had seemed fancier.

"Okay," Illie whispered. "You make sure no one is around. I'll lift the case and you –"

But Ves, of course, ignored her. She grabbed the sides of the glass case and lifted it. Illie braced, ready to be accosted by wailing alarms and armed guards.

"What are you doing?" she hissed, watching in horror as Ves reached in and grabbed the compass. She slid it between her breasts and put the fake compass – where she'd stashed it, Illie didn't know – on the pillow.

"Got our compass, Pinkie." Ves beamed. "What? You really thought I couldn't do it? I am Vesperine sarding Genevieve. There's nothing I can't do."

Except break out of prison, thought Illie in a desperate attempt to keep the anxious nerves at bay.

It didn't work, of course. Her stomach squeezed, intestines skipping rope around her other organs, nauseating and violent. Her heart beat a rapid tattoo, her mind racing with one thought alone – *get out of here get out of here get out of here.*

"Let's go," said Ves casually, as if the prospect of being caught and tossed back into prison didn't faze her.

Illie had to remind herself *again* that she'd only been a pirate for six days.

She eyed the duped compass and hurried after Ves, who was murmuring something about being hungry and how she would definitely exploit Solveig's generosity to buy dinner.

A thought struck her, sudden and sharp as a bullet, as she passed the threshold of the RVMH, hot on Ves's heels.

Nox Solveig had been sentenced to the gallows.

How had he survived? And how did he have enough money to sustain a crew without dipping into the stash of pillaged treasure they'd acquired?

Who in Poet's name was Nox Solveig?

Nox Solveig was hungry and bored and covered in graphite smudges.

Thol hadn't returned yet. Neither had the girls. It was just him and Pleo on the ship, and Pleo was little help in solving his map dilemma. She sat on his feet, purring loudly as she (supposedly) slept, though he couldn't be too sure – her flicking tail was enough of a sign that if he even thought about moving, he'd wind up with tiny fangs in his leg.

He scraped his fingers through his hair, forcing it off his face for a half second before it fell right back into place.

Outside his door, the deck creaked, followed by a loud clatter that woke Pleo up. Solveig snatched up his map and shoved it into his pocket before hurrying out to see the commotion.

Thol shoved a few buckets across the deck with his foot.

"Ves and Illie make it back yet?" he asked without looking up from the armful of wood planks he'd scooped up.

"Not yet." Solveig crossed his arms and leaned against the closed door. "Need help?"

"You're technically still injured."

"And *you're* technically retired."

Still, Solveig walked over and picked up a wooden scraper, tossing it absently from hand to hand.

"It'll be like the old days," he said with a grin. "Back when we were just boys."

When Solveig and Thol were nothing more than apprentices on the *Sea Wyrm*, Captain Hardy assigned all the worst chores to them. Scrubbing toilets and swabbing the deck, scraping mold from the bathtubs and barnacles from the hull had been their responsibility.

"It'll teach you how to be a good sailor," Captain Hardy scolded whenever Thol and Solveig complained. *"A good sailor knows how to read a map, how to chart the stars, how to sail a ship, and how to keep her pristine."*

Thol rolled his eyes but picked up another scraper and hopped over the side of the boat, landing in the sand with a dull *thud*. Solveig followed, forcing a smile when he landed to hide the grimace the shock of pain from his shoulder caused.

He sat down, legs stretched out before him, and slid his scraper against the keel, forcing barnacles to split off the wood. His shoulder screamed in protest, causing him to favor one arm over the other.

"I can't believe *you* retired," he said. He picked a few stringy bits of seaweed that had been tangled in the barnacles free with his fingers.

"I can't believe you got caught by the navy," Thol shot back.

Guilt knotted in his belly in the form of nausea. His old crew, his friends, had been killed, and it was his fault. He didn't deserve a second chance, not when they were nothing but bones at the bottom of the Emerald now.

Thol tossed the chunks of barnacles he'd scraped off into the shallow waters. "Her name," he said, his tone softer now, the gentleness he reserved for those he cared about creeping through, "was Meadow. I'll tell you how we met."

Thol wiped the sweat from his brow with the back of his hand, forgetting momentarily that he was covered in polish. It wouldn't be until later that he realized he'd smeared polish over his forehead. He'd been working at the docks in Wyvron, Archepylago for just over

a year, after the Sea Wyrm *had been discharged and now sat at the bottom of the Emerald Sea. With his hands constantly covered in grease, the tattoos that marked him as Bartholomew Williams remained hidden, and it was easy to pop his collar to hide the other tattoos on his neck.*

"Williams!" Another dockhand tossed a rag to Thol. He caught it and wiped the sweat off his neck. "Take a fifteen, man. Get something to drink. It's hotter than Lady Lightbringer's tits out here."

"I guarantee she will smite you if you say that again." Thol wadded the rag up and threw it back. "Railing's polished. Haven't started the deck yet."

The other dockhand groaned dramatically. "I take it back. No break for you. Get back here and help me polish the deck."

Thol held up his middle finger and hopped off the ship. "Too late!" He called in a singsong voice. Ignoring his friend's playful protests, Thol left the marina, going to a tavern right on the beach.

It was crowded during the lunch rush, but Thol managed to find a table by the window, where he could look out at the glistening waves of the Emerald.

"Um. Sir?" A soft voice caught his attention. He looked over and... There she was.

With long hair the color of wheat and a round face, thick lashes fanned over pink eyes... She was the most beautiful person Thol had ever seen. She was so slim he figured he could grab her waist with just one hand (never mind the fact that his hands were massive*). She wore a dark purple dress and Thol decided it was his new most favorite color.*

"*Sir?*" the woman prompted again.

Thol's cheeks flushed with embarrassment when he realized he'd been caught staring.

"*You...um....*" she tapped her forehead. "*Have a big grease stain.*"

Thol quickly reached up to scrub it away. The woman laughed and handed him a napkin. He scrubbed his forehead, trying blindly to get rid of the smear of polish.

"*Here.*" The woman took the napkin. "*Do...um...do you mind if I...?*"

Thol did not mind whatever she planned on doing, and when she licked the pad of her thumb to wipe away the smudge his stomach flopped so hard that he nearly puked.

"*There!*" she pulled back and beamed, clearly proud of her work. "*Now, what can I get for you?*"

"*You,*" Thol blurted, his tongue working on its own. The woman's cheeks and ears flushed pink. Thol clumsily threw out his hands and desperately tried to fix the situation. "*I-I mean, I'll... I'll... Something to drink would be nice?*"

Still blushing, the woman laughed. "*I'll be right back, then.*" She turned and walked off, disappearing into the crowd.

Thol didn't expect her to come back. She probably went to the kitchen to beg a different waitress to bring Thol his drink. Groaning, he put his head in his hands. What had gotten into him? He'd been with plenty of women before. Granted, women at brothels or ladies he met at taverns whom he invited up to his rented room at some rundown inn (because most land-dwelling ladies couldn't handle *rolling around with a pirate on a ship). So, what was different about this pink-eyed girl? Why did* she *make him so flustered?*

"Meadow."

Thol looked up to see the same girl holding a pair of mugs filled with a cinnamon-colored liquid. She set one down, then slid into the seat opposite Thol, keeping the other for herself.

"My name's Meadow," she said. "Do you mind if I, um, if I sit with you?"

"Yes!" Thol exclaimed. "I... I mean, yes, please sit. No, I don't mind. I'm Bartholomew. But you can call me Thol."

She chuckled and took a sip of her cinnamon rum. For such a small, dainty woman, she sure seemed to be able to handle her booze. Thol sipped his. It promptly went down the wrong tube, and he began coughing and sputtering as he tried to clear his throat. When he finally managed to, he realized he'd practically spat a mouthful of rum all over Meadow, soaking her bosom and dress. She blinked twice, and Thol knew he'd just ruined any chances he might have had with her.

Then, she burst out laughing. A full belly laugh, her grin so wide her eyes crinkled into half-moon crescents. She leaned back in her seat, causing it to topple over. When she hit the ground, she laughed harder, *drawing the attention of everyone in the tavern.*

Thol scrambled to his feet, rushing to her side to help her up. She leaned against him heavily, face right against his chest, nose where his heart was. She clutched his arms and continued to laugh.

When she finally pulled away, tears ran down her face, smearing the kohl that had been lining her eyes. She beamed brighter than the sun. She said, "I like you, Thol. Come back again tomorrow at the same time. I'll give you free rum if you let me drink with you."

Thol wouldn't realize until much later that he'd fallen head over heels for the woman named Meadow right then and there.

20

DURING THE ENTIRE WALK back to the *Serenity,* Ves's heart thundered against her ribs, stealing the air from her lungs and sending her stomach into an acrobatic performance. The compass was warm against her heart, nestled snugly in her bosom. It was surprising how few people thought to look *there* for treasures when pickpocketing someone. Ves kept all her important things squished between her breasts.

Illie was a nervous wreck, even more so than Ves, fidgeting the entire time and murmuring protests when Ves led them in circles, mazing through the streets of Veridonia in case they'd been followed out of the museum.

Despite the nerves, Ves paused at a newspaper vendor. She took a few stone coins from her pocket and set them on the counter, grabbing a paper in exchange.

"We need to get back to the ship," Illie hissed.

"We're going," said Ves through her teeth. She skimmed the front page, a strange mix of relief and disappointment flooding her when the article was about Prince Anwir Helios and his supposed push for engagement and *not* about her crew. Their little stunt at Bowhead Rock should have gotten the front page...

As she walked, relying on Illie as her guide, she flipped through the pages until she found the navy's most wanted list.

Captain Ryuu Nova of the *Dragon King.* Captain Bonny Reed of the *Moon Rabbit.* Captain Ellery Anor of the *Eldwode's Revenge.*

And... sard it, Nox Solveig sat right there in second place. Somehow, the navy had gotten wind of the *Serenity*'s existence since her name was right next to Solveig's. She'd hoped their escapades at Lenwell and Carilon would have shot Solveig up to be the *first* most wanted. But...no. Even though he had control over Carilon and the Icarus Strait, even though he'd escaped death at the gallows, even though Jonyth Commodore *loathed* him, there was still a pirate the navy wanted dead or alive more.

The Unnamed God.

Ves knew nothing about the pirate captain, but she wasn't the minority. Nobody knew a thing about him, only that he was worth *nine hundred million lune.* He sailed with the Unnamed Pirates, but that was it. He didn't even have a picture attached to his name like the other four pirates did.

Odd.

She rolled up the newspaper and stuck it in her pocket, figuring Solveig might want to take a look.

"Relax, Pinkie," said Ves.

Illie, who seemed incapable of relaxing, toyed with the end of her braid. "I'm fine," she grumbled. "I'll be fine once we're on the ship and the compass is locked away."

"Rel*aaaaax.*" Ves grinned. "You're a pirate, Pinkie. Pirates ain't scared of commoners. You're *fiiiiine.*"

Illie grumbled something that sounded a lot like she *wasn't* fine, but Ves tactfully ignored her, instead focusing on slipping through the alleys to get back to the cove where the *Serenity* was.

Thol and Solveig sat in the sand, talking back and forth and laughing as they scraped barnacles off the *Serenity*'s keel. Ves couldn't help the smile that crept across her face. It had been so long – too long – since she'd had a crew like this. A *family* like this.

Pulling the rolled-up paper from her pocket, she sauntered over to her captain and quartermaster, knocking both of them on the head with the newspaper.

"Compass acquired," she said, tugging it from her bosom. She dropped it in Solveig's lap. "I'm going to go change. I hope you found somewhere good to eat because I'm *starving.*"

Without waiting for a response, she skipped up the gangplank and to the washroom on the women's side of the ship. It was no small miracle that the *Serenity* was big enough to have gendered quarters *and* gendered bathrooms. Even though she trusted Solveig and Thol, there was still freedom in being able to shower alone. Something she missed *terribly* after four years of being locked away and left to rot in her own filth.

She turned the faucet on and peeled off her clothes as she waited for the water to heat up. She dug a towel out from the cabinet mounted to the wall and set it aside, along with the soaps she'd been collecting – jasmine blossom and peach tea and an absolutely *divine* mango pineapple bar that smelled good enough to eat.

"*Twin moons in the sky, for the third has died, aweigh anchor aweigh,*" she sang softly, stepping into the shower and letting the warm, fresh water cascade over her body. She avoided getting her hair wet since it would take an eon and a half to dry properly, even with the blazing summer sun.

She lathered the mango pineapple soap between her hands and started scrubbing her body.

"*The seas are dark, but the spirits are bright, we'll set the Ruby alight. Chart the course for the unknown way, aweigh anchor aweigh. Find the moon and the treasure tonight, we'll set the Ruby alight.*"

The soap sluiced over her body and down the drain. She lingered under the water for a moment longer before turning the faucet off and grabbing her towel. She dried off quickly and scurried to her wardrobe, picking out a causal outfit of loose trousers and a billowy poet's blouse. Making sure her hair was tied back and she had no less than six knives strapped to her body, she waltzed onto the deck and down the gangplank to join the others.

If *one more thing* went wrong Natha would lose her mind *again*.

All she wanted was a competent line of cooks in her kitchen. Chefs who *respected* her and her authority. Chefs who could read a sarding recipe and *follow it.*

Apparently, that was too much to ask for.

She had not studied at the Royal Veridian Academy of Culinary Arts just to deal with a bunch of adult children who couldn't fathom the difference between *pheasant* and *pheasant fish* – a type of flying fish with an extra-long tail fin like that on the bird it was named after.

"What is this?" she asked, gesturing to the plate of roasted pheasant, drenched in a jus that was, admittedly, perfectly crafted.

"Uh, pheasant, Chef," the idiot cook said.

Natha gritted her teeth so hard her jaw nearly cracked. "And what did the recipe ask for?"

"Pheasant, Chef...?" the cook stammered.

It took every last minuscule drop of her waning self-control not to throttle the cook right then and there. She dug her nails deep into her palms, leaving pale crescent-shaped pockmarks behind.

"Pheasant *fish,*" she said as calmly as she could. "The poultry was supposed to be for *tomorrow's lunch.*"

The cook just shrugged. "Oops? We can change the menu?"

She imagined bashing her head against a wall over and over since the headache *that* would cause would be favorable to the headache these *idiots* were causing her. She sucked in a deep breath and said, "Fine. Fine! Pheasant for dinner tonight. I'm going to change the menu before it gets handed out. Hear that, everyone?! If I come back and things are messed up again, I will fire all of you!"

Truthfully, she didn't have the authority to fire anyone, nor could she *hire* anyone – the owner was in charge of both things, which was why Natha was left with a grossly incompetent staff. But the threat still stood, and hopefully, it would scare the cooks into doing something right for once.

Grumbling to herself, she marched out of the kitchen and to the office where the owner's assistant sat, clacking away at a typewriter.

"Change in the menu," she said, exhausted. The assistant, a young girl who thought she was better than everyone, looked over the rim of her tortoiseshell spectacles. Natha continued, "Switch tonight's dinner with tomorrow's lunch."

The assistant shifted the sugar-smoke cigarette in her mouth, dragging it across her bottom lip and tucking it into the other corner. "Why?"

Oh, there was that metaphorical wall again.

"Because there was a mishap in the kitchen. Please, just change it."

The assistant sucked in a mouthful of sugar smoke, letting it fill her lungs with sweet oxygen before exhaling a cloud of white. "Aren't you responsible for the kitchen? If you were capable of doing your job, there wouldn't be any *mishaps.*"

Natha imagined grabbing the assistant's gauzy scarf. She imagined dragging the assistant over the desk and throwing her over her shoulder and onto the floor. She imagined locking the girl's legs and pinning her hips to the ground as she held that stupid scarf and used it as reins to smash the girl's head against the Merdyne-imported rug over and over and over until it was no longer an ugly burnt orange but a sticky red –

"Just. Change. It," she hissed. *"Please."*

"Take better care of your staff. I already had the menus printed, so this little correction will be taken right out of your paycheck." She plucked the cigarette from her lips, holding it between two manicured fingers. "Now, go. I have a lot of unnecessary work to do now, no thanks to *you."*

As Natha turned to leave, relieved that she didn't have to fight the assistant to get what she wanted, she heard the girl mutter under her breath, "You should have just stayed married to that husband of yours. Women like you belong at home, disciplined by a man."

One more thing, she told herself, slamming the door harder than she needed to, hoping it would scare the assistant. *One more bloody sarding thing...*

She marched back to the kitchen, head held high.

Everything has gone wrong already, she thought as she washed her hands and went back to her stove. *What else could possibly go wrong?*

Half an hour into the dinner crowd a few hours later, Natha realized she'd made the mistake of speaking too early.

Everything, apparently, could go wrong.

Czardas was at the music hall, practicing with the Royal Veridian Chamber Orchestra for an upcoming concert, which meant Fynch was alone.

Which meant... he was responsible for finding his own dinner if he didn't want to go to bed with an empty stomach again.

On the nights Czardas was home, he'd sneak up some leftovers from whatever elaborate meal his family's private cooks concocted. But with no one to feed him, Fynch was left to fend for himself. With no money – all of it went into a hidden cache, a private trove of riches he'd use one day to buy himself freedom – Fynch had to steal.

He skulked through the streets, clinging to the shadows as he scoped out which place to sneak into. As he was debating between two smaller joints, the smell of roast bird filled his senses. Mouth watering, Fynch crept across the street to the busy waterfront restaurant. As he slid into the alley next to it, he caught sight of a group walking through the front door. He wouldn't have paid them any mind, except one of them stuck out. The tall man he'd tried to rob earlier – the one who'd caught him red-handed. He thought of the lune he'd been given, crumpled money he put right in his cache, next to the compass from the museum.

The tall man disappeared inside the restaurant. Shaking his head, Fynch slipped into the alley, searching for a bin to loot or a back door to slide through.

He found the back door easily enough. Now, all he had to do was wait. Crouched low, he watched the door closely. It didn't take long before it opened, and someone stepped outside, a bag of trash in their hands. They dropped the bag and stuck a sugar cigarette between their lips, distracted.

Fynch lunged, darting through the door before it could close and pressing his back against a shelf. He exhaled sharply, hoping the idiot would take a lengthy smoke break and return only when Fynch was ready to rush out the door again.

For now... He looked around the storage room, trying to find something he could eat. While he *could* eat flour and raw potatoes – he'd definitely eaten worse – the empty pit in his stomach demanded more.

It would be risky, but...

Back close to the wall, Fynch tiptoed closer to the door leading to the kitchen. He could hear the yelling and clatter of pots and pans, the sizzle of bubbly oil, the shouts of *"Table three, please!"* and *"Where is the salt?"* They seemed distracted enough. It would be in and out, then back to the alley where he could quickly eat and run back to the Rossi Estate.

Easy.

He peered through the circular window on the door, eyeing the chefs and, most importantly, the counter with countless plates full of delicious food. All he had to do was swipe one of those plates and go. He robbed a museum; he could rob a kitchen.

When no one was facing the door, Fynch shouldered it open and slid into the kitchen. He held his breath and walked as slowly and inconspicuously as he could to the counter –

"Hey! What are you doing in here?" a voice said from behind Fynch. He stiffened at once, completely paralyzed.

"Uh –" he started.

Then, he dove for one of the plates, grabbing it – *sard*, it was hot! – and bolting for the door. Not the door he'd come through... The swinging doors leading into the restaurant itself.

"Thief!" the person yelled.

"Oh, no, you don't," an accented voice swore. He risked a glance over his shoulder to see a blonde woman shoving through the crowd of cooks to get to him.

Heart in his throat, Fynch *ran*. Too late for subtlety now; he had to get *out*. Clutching the plate to his chest like it was the most priceless treasure in the world, he streaked through the restaurant, narrowly dodging tables and staff. He spied the tall man sitting with his friends through the chaos, but he didn't waste a second more.

He ran outside and down the street, not pausing until he couldn't see the restaurant anymore. Breathing hard and fast, Fynch stepped into an alley and sat down on the dank cobblestone. With his bare hands, he picked up the roasted meat and sank his teeth into it.

Victory tasted a lot like cooked pheasant.

The place Thol picked out was the fanciest restaurant Solveig had ever stepped foot in with the intent of sitting down to eat. The menu, of course, lacked cinnamon rum – only taverns and pubs served the drink – but Solveig wanted to keep his wits about him, anyway.

After they ordered and the waitstaff left, Solveig leaned close to the others. "I have a destination figured out," he said, his voice somewhat hushed, even though the chatter from the other patrons would have drowned him out regardless. "Illie, I'll need you to chart a course once we get back."

"Where're we going, Cap?" Ves stuck a toothpick in her mouth and chewed on it absently. She knew that Anwir Helios had tasked Solveig with finding something, and Thol knew Solveig was searching for a treasure – and Illie knew about the third moon – but that was it, and he intended on keeping their knowledge limited.

After all, he'd made a deal with Anwir.

"The Salts Atoll," he said.

Ves plucked the toothpick from between her teeth, her grin bright enough to light up the entire city of Veridonia. "The Merdyne Empire? Ah! I can't *wait* to return to the Ruby Sea!"

Illie drummed her fingers against the table. "We'll have to skirt around Joris Island. It'll be easier to go north of it, assuming the Wandering Isle isn't in our way. It's a good thing we have that lithograph. Otherwise we wouldn't know its location until it's too late..."

"I vote we stop at Undyne to pick up a shipwright first," said Thol, clearly still bitter about the lacerations in the *Serenity*'s deck.

Solveig opened his mouth, but before he could remind the crew about the time crunch and the impossibility of this whole scavenger hunt, someone tore from the kitchen, running through the restaurant and out the front door.

Then came a shout from inside the kitchen. "That is *it!*" a woman yelled. "I quit! I! Sarding! Quit!"

The doors swung open, and a blonde woman stormed out, looking both furious and on the verge of tears.

"Oh, divine Dreamer..." Ves whispered.

The woman, dressed like a chef with a white coat, rubbed her eyes with the back of her hand.

"Hey." Ves waved to the woman. "Hey! Come sit with us."

"What are you *doing?*" hissed Solveig.

Ves ignored him. "There's room. Join us."

The woman looked them over. Solveig frowned, hoping she would just walk away, but she pulled out the empty chair between Ves and Thol and sat down.

Solveig shot Thol a look. What was Ves *thinking?*

Clearly, she *wasn't* thinking, especially not when she waved a waiter over and asked for a glass of wine and another plate to be brought out. *Never mind that it's* my *money,* thought Solveig.

Well. *Anwir's* money.

"We need a cook, don't we, Cap?" Ves asked. "Unless you want *me* to cook again?"

Solveig almost lost his appetite right then and there, but he swallowed back the memory of Ves's attempted cooking.

"Wait," the nameless woman said, holding her hands up. "What are you talking about? I don't even know who you are. I need to go." She started to stand, but Ves grabbed her wrist first.

Two things happened in the span of a single heartbeat, almost too fast for Solveig to realize what.

Ves was on the floor, on her back, gasping for air as the wind was snatched from her lungs – and probably, he realized, because her back was still injured.

The woman was standing over her, and that's when the second thing happened. Solveig got a good look at her face. At her features. At her pale blonde hair braided tightly down her back and at her eyes, the color of rubies sparkling in the sunlight.

He *knew* those features.

Ves choked on a breath as she sat up, then pulled herself back onto her chair. She tucked a stray curl behind her ear and grinned a dimpled grin. "I want to keep her, Cap."

Illie toyed with the edge of her napkin. "She's a human, Ves. You can't just adopt her like she's a cat or something."

The woman looked at Solveig, a strange array of confusion and realization painting those features he hadn't seen in fourteen years. She said slowly, "I know you. You're Nox Solveig, aren't you? I could turn you in right now and get your bounty. Five hundred million lune. Do you know what I could do with five hundred million lune? I could turn my entire life around. Why *shouldn't* I turn you in?"

He was flattered that he was recognized. But the flattery ended there. He couldn't go back to Ivenis Justyce now. He couldn't face Jonyth and the gallows, not when he was *so close*, not when he knew where Anwir's bloody map led.

"Because," said Thol, nodding his thanks to the waiter who set five plates on the table, "we need a cook. And because you're the only person who can, quite literally, sweep Vesperine Genevieve off her feet."

He picked up his glass and took a long, pointed sip.

"I'm Illie Valentine," Illie said, quickly shifting the conversation to make it seem more inviting. "Navigator and best sarding cartographer in the world. You know of Sol, and that's Ves, the Witch of the Sea. And that's Thol. He's gentler than he looks. I know that look on your face. It used to be *my* look. It's the face of longing, of wanting more. You want a grand adventure, don't you?"

The woman's shoulders slumped. Solveig held his breath, waiting for her to make a run for it to report them to the navy, but... To his surprise, she sat down. "Nathalia Divyne," she said. "But you can call me Natha. You're *lucky* I want nothing to do with the navy. Otherwise you'd be in chains, and I'd be a *very* rich woman."

Solveig stabbed his fork into his pheasant, a bite-sized silken chunk sliding free with ease. He nearly moaned when it hit his tongue, the taste unlike anything he'd ever had before. Even though he knew nothing about spices, he just knew the blend of rosemary, thyme, and bay was *perfect*. The sauce, a rich red wine, only enhanced the savory flavor.

Natha took a bite of hers and instantly grimaced. "Too much salt," she murmured, though she took another bite.

"Did you make this?" Ves gestured to her plate with her fork. "See? This is why we need a cook. I can't make this."

Natha stared at her food for a blink too long. "I... I am – was – the head chef. This is my recipe. But nobody else knows how to follow a recipe. I should have tested it before allowing it to be served. It's terrible."

Solveig knew what terrible tasted like, no thanks to Ves, and this was far from it.

Finished with his meal a while later, Solveig stuck a toothpick between his teeth and leaned back in his chair. Natha, surprisingly, had stayed with them the entire time and still hadn't gotten up to leave.

"Do you –" she started, but the slamming of doors being thrown open cut her off. Solveig turned, his stomach sinking to his feet.

Navy sailors, a whole squadron of them, scanned the restaurant, swords at their hips and guns in their hands.

"Oh, no," whispered Natha, her face as white as the tablecloth.

The sailors exchanged a look before marching over to Solveig's table. A man with ginger curls and a sneer plastered on his (unfortunately, conventionally attractive) face smirked. A commander, based on the badge on his breast.

"Well, well, well," he drawled. "Look what the cat dragged in. Was the divorce really so bad that you had to cozy up with thieves and pirates just to feel something? What would Adrian think?"

Natha clenched her gloved hands into fists. She stood, almost eye-to-eye with the commander. "Adrian," she said slowly, "is the one who divorced *me.*"

"A pity. You know, you were always a wench," the commander said, still grinning like a feral beast. "You should have been with me, not my brother."

As Solveig's mind raced, trying to piece together the familial links and how Natha was the ex-sister-in-law of the commander, she struck. In a blur, Natha was on the commander, legs wrapped around his neck in a gravity-defying move that had him flipped over her and onto the ground.

She dropped to the ground with all the grace of a cat and brushed her coat off. "Well," she said, looking from the sputtering commander to the other navy men to Solveig. "I suppose even I can't be forgiven for attacking the navy. You said you needed a cook, right?"

Solveig pulled his revolver free, ignoring the pain in his ribs from his week-old injury and grinned. "That I did."

"Hey!" Illie shouted.

A pair of navy men held her restrained, a third busy patting her down as if looking for something. Four more sailors did the same with Ves, who put up more of a fight.

The compass, he realized. Somehow, the navy must have found out that Illie and Ves stole the compass from the museum and tracked them here.

Sard it all!

To Natha, he said, "I'm assuming you know how to fight?"

She nodded. "And I've been *itching* to put these fools in their place for a *while* now."

"Good," he said. "Well then, welcome to the crew."

With that, all hell broke loose.

21

THE COMPASS HAD BEEN a fake – some sort of tracker that led the navy right to them. Illie *knew* it had been too easy.

She had not given up her easy life to be a pirate just to be caught less than a week into her adventure. She would not be taken, not until she learned the truth about the moons.

She lifted her foot and brought it down hard, slamming her heel into the toes of one of the navy sailors. He yelped in pain, his grip on her loosening just enough for her to wriggle free and knee the other sailor between his legs.

Illie Valentine was a pirate, and she would make a sarding name for herself no matter what.

Swiping a steak knife off the table, she brandished it like a dagger. The first sailor – Toes, she decided to call him – cursed and pulled his pistol from the holster at his hip.

She smirked. "Bullets can't hurt me," she chided. There was just enough of a breeze coming through the open doors for her to grab.

Toes fired just as Illie grasped the wind and whipped the bullet off its trajectory. It hit a picture on the wall just behind her, the glass shattering. In the precious seconds it took Toes to realize she hadn't been lying, she lunged, swinging her knife wildly.

It's an extension of yourself, she heard Ves's voice scold. *Treat it like one, not like some foreign limb.*

Maybe Ves was actually scolding her. Illie didn't have the time to sort through what was real and what wasn't.

Pretend it's your wind, she told herself.

She raised her arm and brought the knife down. A jolt of surprise shocked her when the blade severed cloth and flesh. She stumbled back as a spray of hot, metallic blood spattered across her face. Toes looked as shocked as she felt. He dropped his gun and pressed his hand against his collarbone where she'd slashed, his uniform stained crimson.

"Switch with me, Pinkie!" Ves suddenly thrust the hilt of a gun into Illie's hands, snatching the bloodied dinner knife instead.

She stared at the flintlock. She *could* shoot. Henry had drilled that skill into her since all sailors needed to know how. Her hands were already starting to blister from the wind she'd grabbed.

The other soldier who'd been holding her – Jewels – grabbed her braid and yanked, forcing her head back. She cried out, flailing blindly, smashing the butt of her gun into his hand to try and get him to *let go.*

Damn it!

She pointed her flintlock at the ceiling and squeezed the trigger. *BANG!*

Jewels let go of her braid, covering his head as he ducked to avoid the falling glass from a light that exploded.

An idea struck her then. Grabbing the edge of the tablecloth, she pulled, ripping it off the table and sending plates and glasses clattering to the ground. She swung the cloth out; when it was in the air, she turned to the others.

"Flip the table!" she cried.

Thol slammed his fist into a man's face and grabbed the lip of the table, flipping it over smoothly. Illie dove behind it, grateful for the superficial bit of cover it provided.

Around her, patrons of the restaurant raced for the door, bottlenecking as they desperately tried to get away before they could be caught up in the crossfire. A woman with a hat that took up half her face pointed at Illie and screamed. Like *that* would do anything. She debated, if only for a sliver of a second, shooting at the woman to scare her off, but decided her scant bullets couldn't be wasted on someone so meaningless.

Peering out from around the table, she watched as the tablecloth fluttered to the ground, a successful diversion.

She aimed at Jewels' hulking figure, wanting to take him out for hurting her, but from the corner of her eye, a navy sailor charged, cutlass brandished and poised, ready to stab through Solveig's back.

Without thinking, she swiveled her gun and fired. It grazed the man's arm, causing him to drop his sword before he could skewer Solveig.

Not enough!

Gritting her teeth together, she reached out and grabbed the wind. *Obey me,* she commanded it. *You are mine to control.*

She let the wind fill her hand until she couldn't stand the burning cold. Then, she let it out, a violent surge, a tempest from the bowels of hell that raked across the restaurant, knocking into the navy men and snaking around her crew, sparing them, *obeying her.*

"Got you," a voice said. Illie's eyes went wide as the barrel of a gun pressed against her temple, and Jewels grinned down at her.

If Natha's day hadn't already been ruined, seeing her ex-brother-in-law's sneering face would have done the trick tenfold. Commander Adam Zimmer, her ex-husband's younger brother, was even more disgusting and more of an ass than Captain Adrian Zimmer was. Before she married Adrian, Adam had tried more than once to steal her instead, as if she'd go for someone with *less* of a title and *less* of a personality. That behavior didn't stop when she married Adrian; Adam tried getting Natha drunk enough to say yes to sleeping with him on her *wedding night.*

She was glad she was done with that wretched family.

Even if they weren't done with her.

Adam sucked in a breath, trying to refill his lungs. Slowly, he stood. "You," he hissed, "are going to regret that."

Natha narrowed her eyes. She wasn't scared of him, not anymore. Adam Zimmer was less than dirt. "What part?" she asked coyly. "Decking you? Joining a pirate crew?"

Fury contorted his features; his face boiled, turning the same shade as his red hair.

Natha's heart thundered against her ribs. She balled her hands into fists, channeling her fear into anger, into drivel and passion.

Adrian Zimmer never beat her, but Natha always feared he would. He was away from home more often than not, and when he was, she would sneak out to the navy training base. All it took was a bat of her eyelashes and a freshly cooked meal to convince the navy to teach her how to fight. Adrian never found out, and Natha continued to practice when she was alone.

She did not give Adam a chance to attack her.

She aimed for his abdomen, wrapping her arms around it and ramming into him with all her strength. He stumbled back but didn't fall.

"Sard you, Nathalia," he growled. He swung, his fist colliding with her cheek *hard*.

Blood filled her mouth. She ducked under his arms and scrambled to get distance between them. She spat a glob of blood out and grinned, teeth red. "Sard you, Adam."

She didn't hesitate, didn't give him an opening to attack, before charging. She went low, diving for his leg. He'd been navy trained,

too, and knew to keep his knees loose and bent. Perfect for grabbing.

Natha forced her shoulder into Adam's pelvis, shoving him off
his feet and over her shoulder. He hit a table with a *crash*, plates
shattering, and people screaming.

It's not enough. The fight wouldn't be over until one of them
stopped moving.

Arms wrapped around her throat suddenly. She threw her hand
up, creating a valuable pocket of space between her trachea and the
beefy forearm of another navy goon. Gravity would not be on her
side this time. She'd have to fight *extra* dirty.

Opening her mouth, she bit down. *Hard.* Blood splashed
against her tongue, acrid and vile. Still, she didn't let go, not even as
the goon cried out and tried shaking her off like she was a naughty
kitten.

Crunch!

The goon let go; Natha fell to the ground. She rolled out of
the way, not before watching the pirate Thol shake his fist out,
knuckles split and red with the goon's blood.

"Thanks," she huffed.

"Duck," he replied.

She did so quickly, just as Thol punched another goon, one who
had been skulking up behind her, square in the nose with a wet
crunch.

"Thanks," she said. *"Again."*

Thol grinned. "Welcome to the crew."

Belly full, Fynch pressed his back against the alley, eyeing the back door of the restaurant, the empty plate clutched to his chest. Returning it was stupid, especially when he'd almost been caught in the first place, but...

Well, he'd almost been caught, and now guilt ate at his insides, so he had to at *least* return the plate to make up for something. All he had to do was slip inside, dump it into the sink, and escape. Then he could run back home and act like he hadn't been out stealing when Czardas returned.

Poet's breath, he simply could not handle another chastising from Czardas.

And he *really* did not want to see Czardas disappointed again, even though all Fynch seemed to be good at was crawling beneath Czardas's bar of standards.

The door didn't open. Fynch sighed through his nose. He'd already been waiting for at least fifteen minutes. Oh well. He'd just have to be *extra* fast, then...

Holding his breath, he peeled himself from the wall and pushed the door open. Nothing. No chatter from the kitchen, no dishes being washed, no oil bubbling on the stoves... Curious, he stepped inside, slipping from the storage area full of shelves and into the heart of the kitchen itself.

Empty.

The sound of gunshots and clashing swords and shouting, however, bled through the double doors.

He set the plate on a counter and crept over to the door, peering through the window to see the commotion.

Tables had been flipped. Navy men brandishing swords and guns surrounded a group – the same group as before. Fynch recognized the tall man instantly.

"Trust me. I want to be involved with the navy even less than you," the man had said.

Something fluttered in his stomach – butterflies, only...more aggressive. Moths, sirens, vicious things that tore at the lining of his belly, making his heart skip one breathless beat after another.

Pirates.

They were *pirates!* Actual pirates, here in Veridonia, right in front of him. No wonder Fynch couldn't snatch the tall man's money; *he was a pirate!* Nervous, giddy laughter bubbled up his throat.

There had been a time in Fynch's life, long ago, when he was still young and naïve and innocent, when he'd wanted – more than anything – to join the navy. But with his criminal record, the only way Fynch could step foot on a ship was if he was a stowaway or a pirate.

The idea crossed his mind in a brief flash. Fynch, a pirate, with pistols in his hands, salt in his hair, and the wind in his face. Fynch, who didn't have to worry about disappointing Czardas or his family or whether the Rossi family would kick him out, forcing him back onto the streets to fend for himself. Instead of people being *disappointed* when he stole, they would *encourage* it.

A pirate...

The door swung open, smacking Fynch in the nose hard enough that stars danced across his vision. He reached up, cupping his nose, blinking back the sudden rush of tears, when a hand grabbed his wrist.

"I found another one!" the navy man barked.

Another one...? Oh, sard, they thought Fynch was *with* the pirates. He squirmed, trying to get free. At least he hadn't been recognized yet. If the navy realized who he was – if they connected the dots and linked Fynch with the stolen compass from the museum – he'd be right back in jail, and no one would bail him out this time. His family cut him off completely, and Czardas wouldn't know where he was being kept. He'd die behind bars if he wasn't hanged first.

"Feisty little lass," grumbled the navy man, his grip on Fynch tightening.

Fynch narrowed his eyes. At once, he dove for the revolver at the man's hip. Ripping it free, he aimed the barrel between the man's eyes.

"I'm a *man,*" he hissed, curling his finger over the trigger and squeezing it.

Bang!

Blood and brains sprayed over the wall. He was out of the kitchen before the man's body could hit the ground.

His options were limited beyond belief, but at least he had a gun. Thank the Wanderer for that.

It dawned on him at once, the moment he stepped into the fray, the severity of what he'd just done. Fynch's crimes in the past were limited to stealing. Even though his siblings blamed him for his mother's death, he'd never actually killed anyone.

At least, not until now.

Piracy sounded more and more tempting.

Fynch had killed a man. A navy private. He couldn't stay in Veridonia anymore. He probably couldn't even stay in the entire Veridin Kingdom.

What would Czardas think?

I told you so, he thought.

Five pirates. At least triple that in navy men. He should run now while everyone was distracted.

And risk leading them back to Czardas? Yeah, right.

He raised the revolver, the gun a comforting weight in his hand, and shot, hardly even aiming since he knew the bullet would strike true.

And it did, right through the skull of a burly man before he could bring his sword through the neck of a *very* tall woman.

Spinning the pistol around his finger, he turned and fired again and again, hitting the hands of two more enemies and knocking their weapons away.

He fired again, hitting a man sneaking up behind the pink-haired girl. Before the man's body could hit the ground, Fynch dove behind a flipped table, seeking cover before anyone could fire back at him. Pistols usually held six bullets; Fynch had wasted five. Until he found another weapon, he only had one shot left. Anyone else wouldn't favor those odds.

Fynch did, though, because he wasn't anyone else. Because he was the best damn sharpshooter this side of the Emerald.

Sucking in a breath, he peered around the table. The five pirates still stood, fighting the navy off one by one. The tall man had his back against the blonde woman's – the chef who had chased him earlier, he realized. Both fought with their fists. The tall woman used...used *steak knives* to fend off her enemies, while the man in the green coat used a cutlass. The pink haired girl held a gun, though her hands trembled; Fynch could see that from across the room. She was scared, just as he was, but holding a gun seemed to worsen her fear while it solidified Fynch's. He could do *anything* with a gun in his hand.

Anything except, it seemed, realize someone had snuck up behind him.

He turned, eyes widening in shock as the navy man grabbed a fistful of his hair and wrenched his head back, only to slam his face into the table. Pain exploded in his sinuses, flooding his vision with stars. It wasn't the first time he'd had his face hit, nor would it be the last if he kept his lifestyle up, but the sudden, hot gush of blood from his nose wasn't something he'd ever get used to. Nor was the hardness that fell on his tongue. He spat, a sliver of his *tooth* clinking on the floor. In the second before his face was slammed against the table again, he brushed the tip of his tongue against his upper teeth, his stomach sinking when he felt the sharp slope cutting through his front incisor.

His face hit the table again. His head throbbed, pressure building up behind his eyes. He'd been in enough scrapes to know that just a few more hits would leave permanent damage if he was lucky.

He'd be dead if he wasn't.

One shot. That was all Fynch had left. One shot, one chance to save his life. He needed to survive long enough to give Czardas the money he'd gathered over the years.

He needed to live long enough to say goodbye.

The man's grip tightened; he pulled Fynch's head back, ready to crush him into the table again. With less than a second to react, he struck.

Fynch aimed the gun over his shoulder, an impossibly blind setup, and squeezed the trigger.

Bang!

Heart in his throat and breath fled from his lungs, Fynch braced. He'd never missed a shot in his life; what were the odds he'd miss now?

Thunk.

The man's hand slid from Fynch's hair. He collapsed to the ground, his head nothing more than a pulpy mash of brains and shattered bone.

Lightheaded, Fynch turned and vomited his stolen meal all over the floor.

"Where'd you learn how to fight?" Thol asked as he punched a navy sailor in the jaw, then grabbed him and threw him aside like trash.

"The navy," said Natha, whose back was pressed against his as she ducked under the commander's fists.

"But you're not navy? Watch out." Thol swept his leg out, tripping another sailor. He grabbed the shoulders of yet another and smashed his head into theirs.

"My ex-husband was," she said.

Gunshots rang out. That was never a good sign. Gunshots alerted people that there was a fight. Gunshots would draw more of the navy to them.

Thol grimaced, the shock of pain shooting from his split knuckles souring his stomach. Still, he swung his fists again. Natha was crew now, and he didn't give up on crew. From the way she fought, she didn't need a *lick* of protecting, but defending? He could offer her all the support he had.

Crew.

Technically, Thol's fourth crew. There was that first one, the one that pretended to sail under the crescent moon flag. The Serpent Pirates he crewed with, then the ones he captained. And now... Here he was, a Solveig pirate yet again.

A sailor charged at him, knife waving wildly. Thol smacked the blade away with ease. He cracked the man's head over his knee, letting his unconscious form slide to the ground.

Shouting came from the kitchen. *"I found another one!"*

Another one...?

Oh, no.

Thol saw the blond kid dart behind a table, recognizing him instantly. The cheeky thief who had tried to rob him earlier. Why were *they* here?

The moment of distraction cost Thol. A fist slammed into his stomach, forcing the air out of his lungs. Over the melee, he could *hear* Meadow scolding him, telling him it would leave a terrible bruise if he didn't take care of it.

"Can you hold your own?" he asked over his shoulder.

"You calling me weak?" Natha shot back.

He nodded, the confirmation all he needed. He shoved the man who'd punched him to the ground and raced across the floor to where Solveig was. Natha might be crew, but Nox was his captain, and Thol would be damned if he lost another Solveig.

"They want Ves and Illie," panted Solveig. He swung his cutlass one-handed. A sheen of sweat glistened on his forehead, his skin waxy and void of all color.

Pain. He's in pain. That idiot, fighting so soon after being injured... But being reckless was something every Solveig had in common. Thol had been around them long enough to know that, unfortunate as it was. Nothing he could say would get Solveig to put the sword down and run back to the *Serenity.*

Until he could convince Solveig to abandon the fight, Thol had to protect his captain.

He pummeled his fists, throwing punches one after another in violent succession, crunching noses and shattering jaws and wrenching away the weapons of anyone who dared to get close.

People said to never bring fists to a sword fight because those without a weapon were doomed to lose.

Clearly, those people had never met Thol.

As she jabbed her dinner knife into the eye of a navy sailor, Ves realized she should probably admit that the compass she'd taken – the compass she gave to Solveig, leading the navy right to them – was a fake. Ves was never wrong.

But... But this was all her fault, really.

At least you led the navy to us, she thought, slashing her blade across a throat before abandoning it in the sternum of someone else, *and not to the* Serenity. *At least we still have a way to escape.*

Pitiful crumbs, honestly.

She swiped another abandoned knife off a nearby table and threw it in a perfect twisting spiral. *Thunk!* She paused to admire her work, grinning at the sight of the blade buried to the hilt in the skull of her enemy. Around her, souls blinked out of existence, but the four that mattered stayed bright. Solveig, Thol, Illie, and Natha. As long as those souls stayed burning bright, she couldn't care less what other ones were extinguished.

Ves slashed her knife, hot blood spraying on her face, dribbling into her mouth. *Disgusting.* As she wiped it away with her thumb, she heard the whisper from one navy sailor to another – three words that made her freeze, that stopped the battle completely until she was suspended in time, neither breathing nor thinking.

"Ivenis Justyce Penitentiary."

No. *No!* Ves would *never* return to that hellhole, not in this life nor the next, nor any of her other lives after that. She'd made a *pledge.* She...She...

She would rather *die* than go back there.

Spinning around, she grabbed the fool who dared to utter those words in her presence by the front of his shirt.

"If you wish for mercy," she growled, her voice steel, "then you will tell me what you just said."

Had she not been blessed by Dreamer, Ves would have assumed his soul had left his body behind with how pale and limp he became. The sour stink of urine filled her senses; she didn't have to look down to notice the dark stain spreading across the man's trousers.

"A-Admiral Commodore," he stammered. "H-he sent word that he will be arriving soon, with Captain Zimmer. H-he'll bring y-you to Ivenis –"

Ves slammed her knife into his skull, leaving it there as he crumpled to the ground.

Sard sard sard sard sard!

Solveig. She needed to tell Solveig. They needed to get out of there before *Jonyth* arrived. She took a step towards him, only to stumble. Her knees gave out as a wave of pain erupted from her back. Blood seeped through her shirt, and she knew at once she'd messed up. Her stitches tore, fresh scabs breaking with them.

"Cap!" she shouted. "It's Jonyth! He's coming!"

She hit the ground. Suddenly, a blur of blond hair was before her. *Navy?* No, he – she? – wasn't in the uniform.

"I'm only doing this 'cause I owe your friend," the boy said. He fired off three rounds, hitting soldiers from clear across the room. "Don't tell anyone you saw me here, and we'll be even."

Natha had to end this. It was her fight, after all.

Get them to your level, her teacher's voice rang in her head. *If you can get them on the ground, you will have the advantage.*

Most men have a common weakness. Sometimes, it doesn't hurt to exploit it.

Adam put some distance between himself and Natha. Smart, on his end, especially with how fatigued Natha was becoming. Her stomach cramped, and her lungs ached; her arms were limp noodles, cooked and soggy, and hardly able to stay still.

She sucked in a breath.

Get him on the ground.

Win the fight.

When she exhaled, she put most of her remaining strength into one move and bolted. Instead of tackling Adam to the ground, instead of flipping him over her shoulder like she was used to, she brought her foot up in a straight-legged kick.

One that landed *right* between his legs.

The color leeched from his face, vanishing along with his breath and any attack he might have been planning. For a heartbeat, nothing happened, and Natha froze, too, her mind racing as she tried to figure out *why* her ultimate move wouldn't work.

And then he collapsed, hands clutching his precious manhood. He folded to his knees, then to his side, curled in a moaning fetal position.

Natha pounced, straddling his waist. She swung her fist, pummeling his face one punch after another after another after another after –

Someone grabbed her wrist. Thol.

"That's enough," he said.

Blood covered her clothes, though it wasn't hers. It was the same blood on her hand, the same blood soaking into the floor, the same blood that caked Adam's face. She stumbled to her feet, all but collapsing into Thol. Adam's face had begun to swell like a balloon, bruised and bloody, and all her fault.

He was a bad man, she reminded herself.

"Jonyth is coming!" shouted Solveig, drawing her attention away from Adam. "We have to get out of here before he does!"

"You have anything at home you need to bring?" Thol asked her. She nodded numbly. Her cookbooks, her rare knives, her clothes... The divorce had left her with nothing, but she needed that nothing. Thol called to Solveig: "We'll meet you in fifteen. Circle around. Storm's Keep!"

Natha had no idea what that meant. Storm's Keep was the capital city of Kelsyn. Was that where they were going? She'd never been, considering how far north Kelsyn was from Veridin...

Thol tugged on her wrist, drawing her away from Adam. She spared the chaos one final glance before running out of the restaurant.

Her heart beat a violent tattoo, throbbing with each footfall as she ran through the familiar streets. The sun had set, the bleeding watercolors of dusk swathing the sky in pinks and oranges and dusty purples – a backdrop reflected on the ocean waves as the first sprinkling of stars peppered the expanse between the two moons. Gas lamps flickered on, one after the other, illuminating the street congested by carriages and wagons and people hurrying home after work on foot. Crowded as it was, at least the evening rush would provide enough cover for Natha and Thol to escape.

"This way," she hissed, turning down an alley that, at first glance, looked to be a dead end. But halfway through, there was another narrow corridor that cut between two buildings.

A woman standing on her back deck, sweeping, paused long enough to look up as Thol and Natha ran by.

Darting through a few more alleys and mazing between buggies on main streets, Natha soon stopped at the doorstep of her flat. She sucked in a couple of greedy breaths before unlocking the door and slipping inside.

"Keep watch," she instructed Thol.

It was a small miracle, she thought as she pulled her favorite clothes from her dresser and knocked her prized cosmetics off her vanity, that she hadn't fully unpacked after moving in.

And that Adrian had kept most of her things in the divorce just to spite her.

She found her luggage set – two leather suitcases that her parents had given her when she left for university – and began piling her things in haphazardly. Clothes, cosmetics, and ointment for her arms. Then to the kitchen for her cookbooks, knives, and her poppyseed tea. With both bags full, she grabbed them and hurried to the front door.

"How far is the pier from here?" Thol grabbed her bags from her. She shakily locked the door – she didn't know why. It just felt right.

"Not far at all. It's just – oh, *sard!*"

Men in white uniforms stood across the street, shoving their way through the crowd. The navy.

Thol noticed them, too. He cursed under his breath.

The pier was a five-minute walk, but the rush hour crowd would turn that into fifteen minutes if they were lucky. They didn't have the luxury of time, especially now that the navy had tracked them down. Running on nothing but adrenaline, Natha couldn't afford to fight again. Her stamina was only good for short bursts, not all-out battles.

"I know a shortcut," she said suddenly, thinking of the corridor they'd run through earlier. "Follow me. Where on the pier do we need to go?"

She hopped off the porch and slipped into the side yard, moving slowly so as not to draw the navy's attention. If they planned on breaking in to see if she was home, at least they'd be slowed down by the locked door.

"The very end," said Thol. "We have to time it just right, or it won't work."

She nodded once. "Try to look inconspicuous. The navy is looking for suspicious people."

Stepping out of the corridor and onto another busy street, she dared a glance over her shoulder. They weren't being followed. Yet.

"I'm nearly seven feet tall," grumbled Thol, who was, Natha stupidly realized, incapable of being inconspicuous.

Through a throng of people, the sign over the pier was noticeable. A horse-drawn wagon cut in front of them, blocking the view of the pier for a split second. When it passed, a clear shot opened up.

"Stop right there!" a voice shouted from behind.

"RUN!" Natha screeched.

She took off running, abandoning the inconspicuous façade she'd just donned, shoving her way through oblivious people to get onto the dock. Thol raced beside her, matching her pace even though he could run faster if she wasn't there to slow him down.

At the very end of the pier, barely visible over the shops and through the evening haze, a ship cut over the waters. At the top of the mainmast flew a black flag – a moon, though the details were too far for her to make out. A *pirate ship.*

A bullet whizzed by her ear, splitting a few loose blonde hairs. She stumbled, cursing loudly.

"Sard this," grumbled Thol. "I had a wife, so do not think anything of this. It is a necessity."

Before Natha could ask what he was talking about, an arm wrapped around her waist, and she was picked up and thrown over Thol's shoulder. She gasped, not used to being...being *manhandled* like this, but humiliating as it was, they were moving faster now. The navy was behind them, reloading guns and taking aim.

"They're going to shoot!" she screamed.

"Then we dodge," he shot back. "Almost..."

The end of the pier had to be getting close. Shops Natha recognized passed in a blur. She saw Shar closing up her store, doing a double-take when she realized that the tall man running by had *Natha* over his shoulder. She called out, but Natha couldn't say anything.

"Thol, they're going to shoot!" she warned again.

"Brace!" was all he had to say.

She turned her brain off, since that was all she could do with such a short warning, and *braced*.

For a heartbeat, they were in the air. For a heartbeat, she wondered if they were going to fall into the ocean below and that would be it.

Crash! Natha slipped off Thol's shoulder, hitting the solid wood of a deck. Her teeth clacked together harshly.

"Sloppier than Storm's Keep," drawled Nox Solveig.

Natha looked through her disheveled hair. Thol stood next to her, her abandoned luggage discarded on the deck. Illie stood at the helm of the ship, Ves sitting next to her. And there was Solveig, arms crossed over his chest, a grin on his face.

Thol rubbed the bridge of his nose. "The navy caught up to us."

"Then start firing the cannons," the captain ordered.

"Aye," said Thol, and he went to do just that.

Solveig turned to her, holding out a hand to help her up. She grabbed it, letting him pull her to her feet. "There's an oath I have my crew swear when they join. I won't force you to say it, but if you want to join us, it's the only way I'll know I can trust you."

He paused, waiting for her to nod. When she did, he continued, "'I will pledge my final breath to your name, and my first to find you again.'"

That was it? Natha was expecting some sort of blood oath, something that would tie her to Solveig's ruthless mercy for the rest of her days. He was the second most wanted pirate in the world – *Captain Nox Solveig cloaked in green.* The pirate who had escaped the gallows, the pirate the world wanted gone.

She licked her dry lips and said, in the strongest voice she could muster, "I will pledge my final breath to your name, and my first to find you again."

"Hear that?!" Solveig shouted to the rest of his – *their* – crew. He grinned widely. "Well, Natha, welcome aboard the *Serenity.*"

Czardas returned home late that evening, long after the sun had set. His violin case weighed against his shoulder, dragging him into a lopsided stand as he kicked off his shoes and shuffled upstairs. He poked his head into the parlor to greet his parents before going straight to his room. Dropping his violin on his bed, he pulled back the secret book and slipped into the hidden library.

Nine years ago, when he was thirteen, and Fynch was ten, Czardas had discovered the library. There were no windows and no other doors. The walls were coated in dust, and the furniture looked one breath away from collapsing. But there were books. *So* many books. Most were at least a century old, some even older. He loved those books, the ones lost to time. The once-loved tomes forgotten by everyone but Fynch and Czardas.

He trailed his hand along the spines, glimpsing at the titles as he walked deeper into the library. *The Old Fisherman. The Islander. The Histories of Mu. Beauty of the Beast. The Lost Princess.*

There was one book that he liked better than most: a book of music from a composer he'd never heard of. He wasn't even sure it was written for the violin – in fact, while he could read the notes perfectly, he had no idea *what* instrument it was meant for. But he loved that music, and he played the *Eldoria Symphony* whenever he could.

"There you are," he said, rounding a corner to find Fynch curled up on his makeshift bed – a nest-like pile of blankets and pillows.

Fynch lifted his head, and Czardas's stomach sank. His cheeks were swollen and puffy, bruises forming over his cheekbones and on his jaw. His nose was crooked – freshly broken judging by the crust of blood on his upper lip – and his tooth... It was chipped badly.

"What happened?" Czardas demanded. He knelt next to his friend, touching his cheek and recoiling quickly when Fynch flinched.

"Doesn't matter," grumbled Fynch.

"It *does* matter!" exclaimed Czardas. He licked his thumb and wiped away the flakes of blood. "Who did this to you? Tell me, and I'll make sure they face punishment."

"It's my fault," he murmured. He spoke with a lisp now, no thanks to his tooth. "Don't worry about me, Czar. I'm going to be leaving soon. I won't bother you anymore."

Czardas's stomach sank. Leaving? Fynch was *leaving?* He couldn't! What was he supposed to do with Fynch gone?

"I messed up," Fynch whispered. "So, I have to leave. I'm sorry. I... Thank you. For being my friend."

Czardas grabbed a lock of Fynch's hair and tugged on it. "You must've hit your head hard," he said, "because only an idiot would think like that. I'm not letting you leave, F. Not by yourself, at least. We've been over this. Wherever you go, *I* go."

Veridonia wasn't big enough for Czardas, anyway. If he wanted a life of performing concert after concert, playing the same songs written by his father until he died, he wouldn't have memorized the entirety of the *Eldoria Symphony.* He wouldn't play it in the quiet of his room where no one could hear. He wanted to know who wrote the symphony.

He wanted to write a symphony just like it.

Czardas smiled one of his rare smiles. "So," he said. "When do we leave?"

INTERLUDE

JONYTH COMMODORE SHOVED EVERYTHING off his desk aboard the *Mary Jolene,* the crashing clatter of books and papers and half-empty bottles of cinnamon rum not nearly as satisfying as he'd hoped.

"What do you *mean* they got away?" he seethed.

Captain Adrian Zimmer stood ramrod straight, hands clasped behind his back, fingers no doubt fidgeting. The corner of his mouth twisted as he chewed the inside of his cheek.

Jonyth slammed his hands on the table, causing it to shake. "Are the people in Veridonia too incompetent to chase down *four* pirates?!"

"F-five, sir," said Zimmer. "They have a fifth now."

"Is that supposed to be better?!"

"Sir," he said slowly. "I request permission to pursue. They assaulted my brother, Commander Adam Zimmer. I visited him in the hospital. He told me who the fifth pirate is, sir."

Jonyth narrowed his eyes into dangerous slits, the muscle movement tugging on his newest scar, courtesy of Nox Solveig.

Zimmer shifted his weight from one leg to the other. "Nathalia Zimmer, sir. My ex-wife. Sir."

Jonyth collapsed in his chair, raking his hands through his hair. "Permission granted. Do *not* disappoint me, Captain, lest you wish to bear the brunt of my anger."

Zimmer dipped his head in a nod. "You won't be disappointed, sir."

Jonyth knew better than to get his hopes up. "For your sake, you'd better pray to Lady Lightbringer that that's true."

Zimmer saluted and left, leaving Jonyth alone in his office. He opened his desk drawer and pulled out four wanted posters – three old and one new.

Bartholomew Williams, four hundred fifteen million lune. Vesperine Genevieve, the Witch of the Sea, three hundred seventy million lune. Illie Valentine, ten million lune for her part in the Bowhead Rock Incident.

And Nox *sarding* Solveig, his grinning face taunting Jonyth over the bounty of five hundred million lune. Money Prince Anwir had given him, along with a head start to find...find *something*.

Whatever that something was, Jonyth would find it first, and he would not spare Nox Solveig again, no matter what anyone said.

He pulled a dagger from his belt and slammed it into Nox Solveig's forehead, the paper crinkling and tearing.

"I should have killed you when I had the chance," he hissed. He opened the drawer again, looking at the vials of green, red, and blue liquid. Sinthoxine. Sinthide. Sinthephane. He'd fill Solveig's veins with the drug and slice his sword through his head.

Pirates deserved to die, and Nox Solveig was far from an exception.

22

Somewhere on the Emerald Sea, west of Veridin and south of Undyne, according to Illie, who sat cross-legged on the deck, soaking in the sun with her maps and books spread out before her, Pleo purring as she bared her belly to the late morning sky, the doldrums struck.

There were no coordinates that marked a specific stretch of sea where the wind refused to blow, but there were two things that, without fail, always seemed to cause them: areas above the sea where Poet slept and the path the Wandering Isle recently crossed.

Solveig had given the lithograph of the Wandering Isle to Illie, but even without it, he was willing to bet the island had been here as recently as a few weeks ago. That, or there was a sleeping god lurking beneath the waves. Religious as he was, Solveig didn't like the idea of a deity strong enough to obliterate them all without batting an eye beneath their ship. The *Serenity* wasn't close enough to the Salts Atoll yet for Solveig to consider the doldrums being caused by Anwir's strange dead god.

The door to the kitchen swung open, and Natha sauntered out, holding a tray full of drinks. She walked around the deck, handing one to everyone.

"Iced raspberry tea with mint-and-lemon ice cubes and a honey syrup," she explained when Solveig took his.

He took a sip, his eyes going wide at the perfect combination of sweet and sour. The cold ice slithered down his throat, a welcome relief to the hot summer air. Natha had been with them for just over a week, and it was the best decision Solveig had ever made. Somehow, even with their simple ingredients, she managed to make something new every day. And she *enjoyed* it. Over the days, her face had brightened, her eyes taking on a glow that hadn't been there before. She even made things for Pleo to eat, creating decadent displays of fish and eggs and chicken for the cat, who was growing quite fat and lazy despite her job as a mouser.

"It's delicious," Solveig said, licking the sticky syrup from his lips.

"Of course, it is," she said. "Everything I make is delicious." She tucked her tray under her arm before continuing: "We're going to be stuck here a while, aren't we?"

Solveig gulped the rest of his drink and held the cool glass between his hands, condensation beading on the edge and sliding onto his fingers. The *Serenity* found herself trapped in the doldrums since yesterday evening, and the skies showed no signs of wind. Even Illie struggled to grasp a gust big enough to shoot the *Serenity* out of the stagnancy. Her hands were bandaged, and, despite the heat, she wore two pairs of socks over each hand to protect against the wind chill as she tried again and again to grab one.

As if she could read Solveig's mind from across the deck, she looked up from her book and said, "The bad news is that we might be stuck here a while. Until I can find a gale strong enough to move us, we can't go anywhere. The good news, though, is that anyone chasing us will *also* be stuck, and they won't have someone Poet-blessed to get them out."

"We need a *shipwright,*" grumbled Thol as he hopped down the ladder leading up to the crow's nest. "And we need oars."

The *Serenity,* it turned out, had more issues than Thol and Solveig previously thought. She should have had eight oars on each side, but she had four.

In total.

Solveig set his glass on the deck and scraped his hand through his hair, forcing the sweat-slick red locks back. "I don't think we're going to be finding a shipwright out here," he shot back. "Unless the mer are real and one of them has the ability to conjure twelve more oars out of thin air, we're stuck for now."

Ves, who had been sunbathing at the bow, sprawled supine with only a breastband and loose trousers on, sat up, her hair a dark cloud of messy curls. She spotted her drink and snatched it up, eyelids fluttering closed as she drank deeply.

"Arguing isn't going to move us," she hollered. "Jony Boy hasn't found us. What does it matter if we're stuck for a little bit? At least the weather's nice."

Solveig clenched his jaw, thinking of the time constraint Anwir had given him. Eleven months. It was nearing the end of Senmoon. If they made it out of the doldrums soon, they could reach the Salts Atoll by the beginning of Ulamoon – when the southern heat would be the most brutal.

He closed his eyes. It had been nearly a month since his old crew had died at Jonyth's hand. As his new crew argued about oars and wind and getting out of the doldrums, he repeated the names of his old friends silently.

Gael. Prokofiev. Vern. Zayn. Trudeau. Kesh. Scorpion. Jamel, Von, Cliff, Charlie, Melody, Dyme, Gabe, Amon, Rob, Petr.

Jonyth would pay for what he did to them. A scar across his face wasn't enough of a punishment for drugging and drowning his crew, for setting fire to his ship and letting it sink to the bottom of the ocean, never to be seen again.

It had been nothing short of luck that landed Solveig on the *Silver Moon* all those years ago, freshly an adult and fresh off the *Sea Wyrm*. He built his crew from nothing, and built his reputation from less. A few sunken navy fleets and a few run-ins with Jonyth Commodore ending in frustrating stalemates later, and Captain Nox Solveig (cloaked in green) became the second most wanted pirate in the world.

Solveig needed to kill Jonyth Commodore and Emperor Castros Helios before he could lose his crew again.

He would not lose his fourth crew. His fourth family.

"Sol. Soooooool. Hey, Captain Solveig!"

Illie's voice snapped him from his thoughts. She was still sitting at the desk, books before her and spectacles balanced on her flat nose, a map weighed down with her empty glass, a compass, one of her boots, and Pleo splayed out.

"I've charted a course," she said. "Come take a look at it, will you?"

"Thanks for the drink," he said to Natha before hopping down the stairs to where Illie sat.

The map was a standard one, depicting Syrenis as a whole. She had the lithograph of the Wandering Isle in front of her as well, its coordinates changing ever so slightly. With a red pencil, Illie had drawn lines over the paper map, with notes scribbled next to them. One route circled north of Joris Island, skirting south of the Triangle of Fylth to get to the northern island in the atoll. The second course went south of Joris, narrowly avoiding crossing into the Amethyst Sea to get to the southern islands of the Salts Atoll. While the southern course would be faster, the Wandering Isle had plopped itself right in the middle, between Joris and the Hel Archipelago.

Without the lithograph, it would be impossible to maneuver around the Wandering Isle. Its unpredictability made it dangerous. But... they had the lithograph, and the navy didn't. It would be a prime opportunity to throw them off their trail, to get rid of them, and buy some precious time.

But the navy – *Jonyth* – would expect them to go south since both Servedin Island and Joris Island were under Aralyth's rule. The stretch of sea the *Serenity* would have to cross through was Emperor Helios's domain. Jonyth would plan on Solveig avoiding Aralyth territory in favor of Merdyne territory, Wandering Isle or not. By going north, Solveig would confuse Jonyth enough to buy some precious time.

And then there was the Salts Atoll. Solveig was nearly positive the map was pointing him there, but... The atoll was big, both the islands themselves and the coral barrier around it, as well as the lagoon in the center.

If Solveig was an ancient god, where would he have gone to die?

A deep lagoon surrounded by a protective chain of islands and shallow waters laden with keel-ripping coral?

"What's the easiest way into the atoll?" he asked, tapping the middle of the eight islands.

"Probably through the west. There's a deep channel here..." She took her red pencil and traced a line between two islands. "But getting in and out is tricky. It would be easier to drop anchor before we reach the reef and take a smaller boat through. We can borrow a sloop from the locals if you want to go to the lagoon. But...why?"

Solveig stared at the map, Illie's voice becoming background gibberish.

The lagoon was almost a perfect circle as if something spherical had fallen in the middle of the atoll. As if a *moon* had fallen there.

"What do you know about the lost moon?" he blurted suddenly. Illie seemed to know the most about the strange legend.

She looked up, startled. Slowly, she set her pencil down. "Every culture in the world mentions the third moon in one way or another. Ves told me the Ruby Pirates had a shanty they used to sing that mentioned the third moon."

She grabbed one of her books and flipped through the pages, pausing when she found a crinkled one, the paper folded like an accordion, as though she'd shoved it back toward the spine and forgotten about it. Frowning, she smoothed it out.

"You mean *Burn the Ruby?*" Ves suddenly appeared by their side. She flopped down, startling Pleo enough to cause her to scramble off in search of a quieter sunny spot. The unweighted corner of the map curled up. *"Twin moons in the sky, for the third has died, aweigh anchor aweigh. The seas are dark, but the spirits are bright, we'll set the Ruby alight. Chart the course for the unknown way, aweigh anchor aweigh. Find the moon and the treasure tonight, we'll set the Ruby alight."*

Find the moon and the treasure tonight. The words almost matched those on Anwir's map. The weight of the ancient paper turned leaden against Solveig's chest, where it rested safely.

Solveig's brow creased. "What does that mean?" he asked, interrupting Ves as she began singing the song. "'Find the moon and the treasure tonight.' What does that mean?"

She lifted her shoulders in a lazy shrug. "There's a story in Merdyne about how there were once three moons. One got too close to the sea and couldn't rise with its siblings. Something about it missing caused flooding and the seas to change, but I don't really know. It's just a story Captain Mali used to tell."

"The third moon?" Natha folded herself on the deck, peering at the map. "The Salts Atoll? If I might make a request, Captain, I'd like to get some of the coral salt there. I've only cooked with it once."

"If we're stuck here," grumbled Thol, as he, too, sat down, "we should discuss a plan."

The third moon. The Salts Atoll. Anwir's map and Ves's song. Solveig frowned, wracking his brain as he tried to figure out how it all connected, what it all meant. He'd never heard of a third moon. However, growing up in a town so small where he knew everyone did not leave much room for old legends to circulate.

Ves murmured something to Thol about no one around them for miles, not even anything bigger than guppies beneath them.

"This might be a coincidence," said Illie, her voice strained as she fought a nervous shake. "But I just found something that is *really* weird. Listen to this."

She took a breath and began reading from her book: "'One hundred days of darkness will arise, a millennium after the third moon dies. A tower black and cold as night, a ward against the unknown plight. A prisoner trapped in eternal dark, a centennial sennight, a lull in the lark. A chain with a broken link, a chased dream that will not sink. Through moonstone and haze, at the end of all days. To the north and bound, the dream can be found.'"

A hush settled over the deck. Even the gentle waves lapping at the sides of the *Serenity* seemed to cease, the doldrums seizing the breath from Solveig's lungs.

"What...?" he asked slowly, shattering the doldrum silence to look at Illie's book. The page was darker in color than the others – thicker, almost – like it had been transplanted there. There was nothing to provide any context, no filigree around the border, no page number, *nothing*. Just the words, written in six stanzas – *written*, with ink that had bled over the years, not typed like the words on the other pages.

He read the poem again.

No. It wasn't a poem. It was too heavy, too...too *important* to be a poem. It had the same severity to it as the riddle on Anwir's map.

To the north and bound, the dream can be found.

"Well," he said. "I suppose that settles it. Illie, set a course to enter the Salts Atoll from the north. It's going to be rough, and we'll be crossing through Aralyth territory, but this has to be a divine message."

If he were an ancient god, Solveig decided, going to the Salts Atoll would be the *perfect* place to die.

"You don't have to do this." Fynch shoved his treasury of gold and lune and other stolen goods into a canvas rucksack. He'd pulled it all from its hiding place in his library, along with the compass from the museum, which he wore on a cord around his neck, tucked into his shirt.

"Yes, I do." Czardas pulled a few books off the shelves, flipping through them quickly and putting some in his own rucksack, placing the others back on their shelf. "We're in this together, F. Don't forget that."

"There's a difference, though. I have nowhere else to go. You have a family. A life. A reputation. All of that."

His new lisp irritated him, forcing him to speak slower as he tried to avoid invoking it.

He grabbed his spare clothes and stuffed them in the bag, too, along with the pistol he swiped from the restaurant fight. Czardas, surprisingly, had already packed his things, moving quickly as if he'd anticipated running away for some time. He had three bags in total, compared to Fynch's single rucksack, though one of the bags held canteens of water and food from the Rossi kitchen, and the other was his beloved violin case, sheets of music tucked inside, nestled against the instrument.

"And?" Czardas slipped another book into his rucksack. Fynch had tried telling him bringing *books* would just slow them down, but Czardas, who was, unfortunately, just as stubborn, kept packing them.

"And you shouldn't be throwing all of that away for *me.*" He tugged the leather strings tight and fastened the buckle to his bag. Heavy, but it would have to do. Everything he owned fit inside the single bag.

He'd run away enough times to know better than to overpack, to own more than the barest of necessities.

"I'm not throwing anything away," Czardas said. "I *want* to go with you, F. I'm *bored* here. And I'm sick of being treated like a child by everyone. I'm twenty-two years old. I'm not a musical prodigy anymore, and I shouldn't have to ask for my parents' approval before doing *anything*. Speaking of which, I want to stop by the bank before we go. I just need to transfer my funds to an account they don't have access to so we can spend money without them tracking us down."

Fynch's hands twitched at the thought of going to a bank, but he dug his nails into his palms to quash those ideas. He was in enough trouble as is; he didn't need to rob a bank on top of that.

"Why?" he whispered, looking at the rucksack in his hands. Even though they'd been friends for most of Fynch's life, he couldn't understand why, out of everyone in the world, Czardas chose *him*. He could have a dozen upper-class, aristocratic snobs for best friends, but he chose Fynch. Fynch, the street rat. Fynch, the criminal who'd been in a jail cell more than once. Fynch, who was incapable of going anywhere without causing problems.

Czardas cinched up his back and heaved it over his shoulder. He nudged the less heavy food bag towards Fynch with his foot and picked up his violin case, slinging the strap over his chest.

"Because," he said simply like that single word held all the answers in the world. "You're my best friend, F. Our friendship might've cost me a rine in the first place, but I wouldn't trade it for anything."

Fynch slung both his bags over his shoulders. "You're an idiot for following me."

To that, Czardas just smiled. "I'm *your* idiot, then. And that makes you *my* idiot."

If there was one thing Fynch could not understand, even at six years old, it was why his parents decided having so many kids was a good idea when they simply could not afford to feed them all. He was right in the middle of them all, with three older siblings and a younger twin brother and sister duo. His father died three years ago, when the twins were one, leaving Fynch's mother behind to take care of all the snot-nosed brats. His oldest brother, eleven years old, wasn't old enough to work a legitimate job, but he brought home scrapes of rine every day from scrubbing barnacles off the keels of ships at the Veridonia marina instead of going to school. His two older sisters did go to school but picked wildflowers at the end of the day and sold them to passersby. His younger brother and sister, who were four, weren't old enough to leave their mother's side.

Fynch learned how to pick pockets quickly, practicing on his siblings, then his neighbors, then going into public to slip his little hands into the purses of strangers. He was small for his age and fast, making it easy to pilfer coins and scurry into alleys to hide and count his wares.

Soon, he learned that rich people liked to flaunt their wealth, bringing purses full of crisp lune bills wherever they went, and so he started frequenting the wealthier part of the city, where the palace was. It was difficult at first, avoiding the royal guards to snatch watches and rings from anyone who stopped to admire the Veridin Palace, where King Argos and Queen Lydia and their five children lived. But he learned their schedules fast, and he learned that aris-

tocrats liked to bring expensive gifts for the three-year-old prince and princess.

If his mother suspected he stole the stuffed bear plushies for his brother and sister from the prince and princess, she didn't say anything.

Lately, Fynch discovered that going to galas and concerts was the jackpot. Tons of rich people meandering aimlessly, not paying attention to their belongings at all.

It was evening – time for Fynch to be at home, though he knew his mother wouldn't worry too much since she was used to her four older children being out past sundown – and Fynch clung to the walls of the Royal Veridian Concert Hall's lobby. The concert had just finished, and the attendees cluttered the lobby as they sipped champagne, laughed, and discussed the musical genius of Duke Rossi. Fynch didn't know who Duke Rossi was, nor did he care. All he wanted was some money so his mother could buy bread that wasn't stale or riddled with mold.

A few feet away, sipping from a glass of orange juice, was a boy a few years older than Fynch. He had hair so curly and wild it looked like a mane, and his brown skin was splattered with vitiligo spots a shade or two darker than Fynch's pale complexion.

Jealousy tore through Fynch at once. The boy wore brand new shoes, shiny and polished, and trousers that ended just above his knees, leaving a sliver of skin between the hem and his gartered socks. His shirt was pressed, not a wrinkle nor hole nor stain in sight, unlike the tattered canvas shirt Fynch wore (it had been his brother's first, passed down to Fynch after being patched with scraps of mismatched *fabric when Fynch declared he did not want to be like his sisters, but like his brother).*

The boy sipped his juice, oblivious. Bingo. Clinging to the wall, Fynch skulked through the crowd to the boy's side. When the boy looked away, scanning the throng of people for something – no, someone – Fynch slid his hand into the boy's pocket, fingers closing around the cool metal of a rine coin. He pulled it free, slipping it into his own pocket. Just as he took a tiptoe step back, ready to find a wealthier mark to rob, the boy spoke.

"Hey," he said, his voice accented, though it didn't match Fynch's sloppy accent. "Did you take my coin?"

Fynch, not used to being caught, stared at the boy. The boy was missing one of his front teeth, and Fynch felt a strange surge of relief to know that even rich brats lost their teeth. He'd lost one of his teeth, too – his first one – just a few days ago. The gap where his canine once was felt strangely gummy and empty, the taste of iron still faint on his tongue. He gave the tooth to his sisters to sell, as they sold theirs, and it kept him up at night, knowing that someone else had his tooth.

"Uh," Fynch said lamely, unsure of how to get away without making a scene. The boy would no doubt yell, drawing all the attention to Fynch. He couldn't get caught. He wouldn't, not until he had something substantial to bring home. "No...?"

The boy gripped his glass tighter. "Yes, you did. You're a terrible liar."

The audacity! The gall of this strange boy to call Fynch a liar – and a terrible one at that! He scoffed. "No, I'm not."

"Yes, you are," the boy argued. "I was going to use that coin to buy an ice cream later. Now I can't."

Fynch didn't know what ice cream was, but it sounded delicious. His stomach, that traitor, grumbled loudly. The whale song imitation didn't go unnoticed. The boy's shoulders relaxed.

"I can ask Mother to buy me one," he mused. "What's your name?"

"Fynch," he said since he was too stunned to even think of a lie. Then, he added, "I'm a boy."

The boy eyed Fynch's atrocious haircut. He'd taken scissors to the blonde locks, hacking away at them until his hair didn't brush against his shoulders but curled around his ears. When his mother found out what he'd done, she calmly evened it out, cutting it very, very short. Spikes of blonde stuck up haphazardly, making him look like a particularly angry kitten.

"I'm Czardas," the boy said. Char-dash, the r rolled in a way that left Fynch repeating the pronunciation softly to himself. He was so engrossed in mimicking that rolled r that he nearly missed what the boy said next. "Czardas Rossi. I'm going to be a duke one day and a musician, just like my father. You can keep the coin."

Rossi. Rossi.

"Your da is Duke Rossi?" Fynch blurted. Did that make Czardas royalty?

"Mhm." Czardas finished his juice. "But he doesn't have any real power. My mother is the Rossi Duchess, and she made my father duke when she married him. I'm a Rossi by blood, so I get to inherit the duchy when I'm old enough."

Fynch didn't understand what half those words meant, but he didn't say anything. The only thing worse than rich people being disgusted by the poor was when they pitied them, treating them like infants because they weren't born with blue blood.

But Czardas, instead of explaining the situation out of pity to Fynch, said, "Do you want some juice?"

And so, five minutes later, the boys were seated in oversized plush armchairs before a roaring fire, crystal flutes of orange juice in their hands.

Fynch dug into his pocket and pulled out the rine. He held it out to Czardas.

To his surprise, Czardas pushed Fynch's hand back. "You keep it," he said. "On one condition."

Fynch tensed. Here it was. The pity. The anger. The –

"Be my friend."

What?

Fynch blinked twice, trying to figure out if he'd heard that right. Him? Friends with a future duke?

"I mean it," Czardas pressed. "Be my friend. I don't have any friends, and I like you."

Fynch chugged his juice to avoid answering, only to promptly choke on it. Juice spewed from his nose, burning his sinuses. He choked, coughing and sputtering as he tried to clear his throat. Cheeks red, he glanced at Czardas, expecting to see a look of horror plastered on his perfect features.

Instead, Czardas was laughing. He laughed so hard that he tumbled from his chair onto the ground, juice spilling. He continued to laugh, which made Fynch laugh until his stomach felt like bursting.

"Okay," he said with a grin so wide it hurt. "I'll be your friend."

That night, as she sat on the deck with her map and compass, a breeze sifted through Illie's hair. Shoving her map into the pocket of her dress, she grabbed her thick makeshift gloves and yanked them over her hands.

"Wind!" she shouted to the others.

"Thol, to the helm!" Solveig instructed. "Ves, help me get the sails down!"

"Aye, Cap!" Ves climbed the mast, skillfully untying the sails and letting them fall free.

Natha joined Thol at the helm. Thol grabbed the pegs of the wheel, ready for Illie.

She sucked in a breath. It would hurt, but she could get used to the pain. Pain, after all, was temporary, and death – the fate that would meet them should they linger in the doldrums any longer – was very, very permanent.

Illie reached out and grabbed the wind like a rope. She yanked, forcing it into submission and throwing it at the sails. The sails filled, puffing out taut.

The *Serenity* jolted forward. Illie clenched her jaw, teeth gritting as the burn seeped through her gloves and bandages to assault her palms. She yanked harder, driving more wind into the sails.

"Starboard!" she yelled. "Hard starboard! Do not stop turning until I tell you to!"

Thol spun the wheel, the rudder shifting beneath the ship and spinning the *Serenity* to the right. She dug her heels into the deck, fighting against the burn and the feisty wind, throwing all of it into the sails.

A bit more... She could *feel* the currents shifting beneath the ship, driving out of the doldrums and into familiar waters.

The wind grew stronger, filling the sails without her assistance. She let go at once, the raw pain suddenly sharp. Tears pricked her eyes, and she tore the gloves and bandages off, revealing wet blisters on her palms and fingers.

"You did it!" shouted Ves. "We did it! We're out!"

She ran across the deck and tackled Illie in a hug so hard she couldn't breathe, especially not when her face was thoroughly smushed against Ves's bosom.

Still, she smiled. She wasn't the greatest fighter, and her powers were still weak, but she'd done it. She'd saved her crew from the doldrums.

Ves rained kisses down on her hair. It hadn't taken long for Illie to learn that Ves expressed her affection through physical intimacy. Illie didn't mind, especially not now when she was so giddy with excitement that the praise only fueled her swelling ego.

Pulling away, she raised her arms in the air and let out a whoop.

More arms were around her then. Thol's grip strangled her, his beefy arms bigger than her torso. Solveig was a bit more hesitant, but when he hugged her, he smelled of salt and cinnamon. Natha gave one of her rare smiles, red lips stretched wide across her face.

"When you're done smothering me," Illie gasped, though she wasn't *too* upset by the group hug, "the *Serenity* needs to go fifteen degrees port. There's a current between Joris and Servedin I want to catch.

"You heard her," said Solveig. "Fifteen degrees port. Next stop, the Salts Atoll."

23

THOL STOOD AT THE sink, dragging a razor slowly along his jaw, shaping his beard until it was just how he liked it – well, how Meadow used to like it. Most of the mirror was fogged from the shower he took, though he'd cleared a small area to trim his beard and tie back his twisted hair. Pirate or not, he cared about his hygiene. Having a wife did that to a man.

The door opened with a squeak. Thol didn't look up from the bottle of aftershave – a tingly combination of rum and aloe juice that he picked up in Veridonia – as he opened it and splashed some on his cheeks. "Good morning, Nox."

Typically, Thol preferred evenings and fought to get out of bed each morning, while Solveig was up with the sun. The crew drew straws to pick the order of shifts to make sure the *Serenity* didn't stray off course and that no storms or enemies attacked them when they were vulnerable. Last night, Thol got the very first shift, while Solveig had the last one.

He washed his hands and turned to face his captain. Solveig looked half-dead, his hair a bird's nest and his skin sallow. His shirt was on crooked, his trousers backward, and he wore one boot and one sock. He held his coat in one hand, dragging it behind him like a blanket.

Thol snorted. "Why are you even up?"

"Natha said if I don't get out of bed, I don't get breakfast, and I can wait until lunch," he murmured in his gravelly, sleep-thick voice. "Where are your clothes?"

"I'm more properly dressed than you," Thol said calmly. It was far from the truth, though, since he only wore a towel wrapped around his hips.

Solveig grumbled something incoherent. He leaned against the partition wall and closed his eyes. For a moment, he didn't move. Thol frowned.

"Nox."

Solveig startled. "I'm up," he slurred. "I'm awake. For the love of Poet, put some sarding clothes on."

"Why?" Thol grinned. "Jealous?"

"Of what? You being ugly? In your dreams." Solveig yawned and rubbed his face. The bandages wrapped around his shoulder pulled taut. "Get out of here. I'm gonna shower. If Natha doesn't save me anything, she's fired."

"You can't fire your crew, Nox."

Solveig held up his middle finger defiantly. Chuckling, Thol left the washroom. He dressed quickly and went to the deck to join the others.

Illie and Ves were in the middle of a skirmish, swords clashing loudly. They danced across the deck, avoiding a stack of papers weighed down by a jug of cinnamon rum.

The scent of something savory and sweet wafted from the galley. The smell of fried bread and cinnamon slammed into Thol violently, whisking him back to a simpler time two years ago.

Thol visited the tavern every day for two weeks straight. When Meadow brought him a plate of that day's special, she slid into the seat across from him. Crispy, golden bread, soaked in eggs and fried to perfection drowned in syrup and sugar and blueberries, still hot from the stove. "If you're not going to ask me out," said Meadow, picking a blueberry from his plate and rolling it between her fingers, "then I suppose I'll have to do it."

Thol paused, his fork halfway to his mouth.

"I'm off at four." She popped the berry into her mouth and chewed slowly. "I have to go home and change, but I'll be ready by five." She grabbed a napkin and the pen from her pocket and scribbled an address. Thirty-seven Cliffside (the blue house) was written in her...surprisingly sloppy handwriting.

Thol set his fork down and picked up the napkin, careful not to let any syrup drip onto it.

"Wear something nice, but not anything too fancy." She licked syrup from her fingers as she stood. *"I'll see you tonight, Thol."*

When she winked, he damn near had a heart attack.

That evening, a quarter to six, Thol stood outside thirty-seven Cliffside, dressed in a dark linen shirt and trousers that, surprisingly, didn't have any stains or holes. He gathered his hair at the nape of his neck, exposing the ink there. There wasn't anything he could do to hide the skulls on his palms or the PUNISHMENT on his knuckles, but Meadow never seemed to mind.

He raised his hand to knock, worried that he might be too early, when the door swung open and Thol fell head over heels for the woman named Meadow again.

She wore a sundress, the pale purple fabric dotted with embroidered forget-me-nots, her pale legs on full display. She'd tied her hair back, but a few wispy strands fell across her face. Her rose eyes sparkled like diamonds, matching the flush of her cheeks as she grinned.

"You look beautiful," he blurted. The nerves kicked in then because he stammered: *"You always look beautiful. I'm not saying otherwise. You just look* extra *beautiful right now. Beautiful...ler. That's not a word."*

She grabbed the front of his shirt and pulled him close, dusting a lipsticked kiss on his cheek. *"You look beautifuler too. Come on. I hope you're hungry."*

She laced her fingers with his – her hand was so small, so delicate, and he worried he might crush it, until she started dragging him along, heading for the strip of sandy beach just beyond her home. For some reason, he'd worried – panicked – that she would bring him to an expensive restaurant based on the dress code she'd given him, but... she led him to a shack with a thatched roof and an open bar. Meadow slid into one of the seats and patted the one next to her.

"It might not look like much, but this place has the best noodles in the entire world. It's my favorite food, and I want to share it with you. Because you're my favorite person."

She said it with so much nonchalance, without even blushing or stammering.

The man behind the bar slid over two bowls of steaming noodle soup adorned with flakes of seaweed and thin slices of meat. Meadow picked up the pair of wooden sticks next to the bowl and expertly fished out a bite of slippery noodles.

Thol stared at his sticks. He watched Meadow out of the corner of his eye and tried to mimic her. As hard as he tried, he couldn't pick up anything.

Meadow snorted. "Here," she said, reaching over with her own sticks and picking up a bite of noodles and meat. "Say ahhhh."

He did. She fed him the bite. He closed his eyes, savoring the taste. When he finished, he said: "I think I love you."

"Oh," said Meadow, "that much is obvious. The feeling is mutual, Thol. I don't call just anyone my favorite. Just you."

Already he was figuring out how many hours he'd have to work to afford a ring.

She fed him another bite, then showed him how to hold the sticks, explaining how they had to balance between his fingers just right, or *else he wouldn't have proper control over them. It took more tries than he cared to admit before he finally figured it out.*

Later that evening, their bellies full, Thol held Meadow's hand and walked her down the stretch of beach. She stepped through the foam, waves lapping at her ankles and the hem of her dress.

"Tell me a story about the sea," she said. When she turned to face him, the sun's rays hit her eyes just right, flecking the pink with gold.

He faltered. Most of his stories would be too gruesome for a civilian to handle, even if that civilian was Meadow.

"There's a boy I used to sail with," he started, deciding the stories of him would be the safest to tell. "We grew up together and had sworn brotherhood to each other when we were too young to understand the severity of such oaths. Our captain didn't like taking in kids, but he let my friend – my brother – Nox and me join, so long as we could keep up with the work.

"We didn't, at first. Two kids on a ship of hardened men were bound to cause nothing but trouble. One night, when Nox and I were sleeping – he only got to sleep on the bottom bunk after an incident that earned him the nickname Piss Boy, but that's a story for a different time – our captain woke us up. At first, we thought we were under attack, but he just led us to the deck and pointed out at the sea. You know why the oceans got their names, right? Because of the color of the bioluminescence that happens sometimes. It's a rare phenomenon. We were on the Emerald Sea at the time, and even though it was dark – both moons were new – the entire ocean lit up green. Only the three of us were awake, and only the three of us got to witness it. It was...it was incredible. Nox cried, actually. I almost

did." He paused, bending down to pick up a shell. He polished the sand off it with his thumb and handed it to Meadow. The curve of the shell was the same pale pink as her eyes.

"It was moments like that that kept me at sea," he finished. "She's unforgiving and ruthless, but she's beautiful, and that beauty was worth her fury."

"Was?" questioned Meadow as she turned the shell over in her hand.

"I'm retired now," he said.

"Good," she said. "If we get married, I would have asked you to give up piracy regardless."

"How –"

"I have your wanted poster hanging in my bedroom." She grinned. "Duh."

Solveig leaned against the shower wall, eyes closed. Warm water sluiced over his shoulders, seeping into his bandage, and slicking his hair to his face. If he lingered any longer, he might just fall asleep again.

During his shift at the helm, he'd read over the riddle on the map and the prophecy from Illie's book, trying to figure them both out. The riddle had to be pointing them to the Salts Atoll, and it made sense for the third moon to be in the lagoon. But what did that mean? Was the third moon the god? Surely, they had been dead for a long time. Did godly bodies decay the same way mortal flesh did? Would there even be anything left for Solveig to take back to Anwir?

His heart stuttered when he thought of Anwir, and he didn't know why. Chalking those thoughts up to sleep deprivation, Solveig turned off the water and shook out his hair. Toweling off, he put on his clothes – only then awake enough to realize how much of a mess he'd been – and went out to join the others on the deck.

The *Serenity* had a large galley fit with a dining hall, but when the sun was out, and the air wasn't sticky and humid, the crew – his crew – liked to sit on the deck to eat.

He sat, joining the circle just as Natha brought out a tray full of fried bread and sliced fruit. The others already sipped on cups of coffee and tea. Thol slid a cup of black tea, brewed weak, to Solveig as he took a plate from Natha.

Thol pushed his food around his plate. Solveig frowned. "Eat your oranges," he said between mouthfuls. "You don't want to get scurvy, do you?"

"We need a ship's doctor," Thol said. "And a shipwright and a proper helmsman because *you* need sleep."

Solveig couldn't argue with that. But they couldn't afford to stop and search for more crew members. Especially not now when Jonyth Commodore was hot on their tail. Solveig had to get the *Serenity* to the Salts Atoll to find the corpse of a dead god – and somehow a missing moon – and bring the dead god back to Aramore to give to Anwir Helios (again, his heart stuttered) in exchange for a single royal pardon.

And *then* he had to kill Jonyth and Castros Helios so none of his friends would be punished for their piracy.

And then... Then what?

He stuffed a bite of syrupy bread in his mouth and chewed slowly, so deep in thought that he forgot to blink.

What would happen after? After he got the pardon and advanced to privateer, after he abolished the Helios reign, after...after he was free?

Well, he was being too optimistic. Anything could happen between now and then. Solveig's survival – his success – wasn't exactly a guarantee.

Anything could happen, and the odds hadn't been in Solveig's favor lately.

"It should only be another two weeks before we reach the Atoll," said Illie, breaking the silence. "If we don't get stuck in the doldrums again, that is."

"And if we don't make any more stops to go shopping, only to get into a fight," added Ves.

Two weeks. Maybe asking Anwir for a year *had* been too greedy.

Illie licked the syrup off her fork. "The Wandering Isle is, according to the lithograph, south of us. We shouldn't run into it. The closest bit of land to us right now is Veridin's southeast peninsula, and it would take us several days to get there. No stops for a while unless you want to stop at Servedin or Joris."

Natha murmured something about fishing and korva stew under her breath.

"Eat," Solveig hissed at Thol.

"You're not my ma," said Thol, but he took a bite regardless, and Solveig watched as the tension melted from his shoulders. "You're not Mistress Solveig, either."

Sol-vig.

Solveig, despite grinning, held up his middle finger. What had once been an insult was now nothing more than an inside joke between the sworn brothers.

"Of all the ships in the harbor," hissed Czardas, despite Fynch's hand clasped over his mouth, *"Why,* on Dreamer's green earth, did you choose *this one?"*

Stuffed tighter than sardines in a storage cell, smushed between crates and their bags, so close together they were practically one entity, Czardas realized he should not have let Fynch choose which ship to stow away on.

Because Fynch, clever as he could be – *Fynch,* with his *criminal record* – chose a navy ship.

"Nobody would think to stowaway on a navy ship," Fynch whispered back. He shifted, one of his legs flopping overtop Czardas's. "They won't even *check.* I promise. Now, shut up, or they *will* start checking."

Judging by the rocking of the ship, Czardas knew it would be too late for the navy to toss them back in Veridonia, but they wouldn't be safe from the cells or from being thrown into Poet's domain.

Maybe Czardas was a bit too impulsive...

Fynch shifted again, his elbow burying itself in Czardas's oblique. *Hard.* Czardas stifled a groan.

"Stop moving," he whispered, grabbing Fynch's ear and giving it a tug. Gods, this was a terrible idea. No way would it work; no way would they find freedom. Each time the ship crested a wave, the crates slid, knocking into the boys and, more importantly, into Czardas's violin case. If he opened it to find even *one* thing wrong – a snapped string, a shifted bridge, *anything* – he would personally smite both Fynch and the navy.

And Poet, too, since it was his ocean and his waves causing all the movement.

"You stop moving," Fynch shot back. "And stop talking!"

The ship, the *Meredith,* crested another wave, sending Czardas's stomach to his throat. He swallowed his unease but didn't say anything further if only to get Fynch to stop squirming and pressing his palm against his mouth. As much as he cherished Fynch, he did *not* trust that hand to be even *remotely* clean.

Sighing through his nose, he leaned his head back against a crate, peering at the light slipping through the cracks in the floorboards above. His parents would have noticed his absence by now. Not that he cared. He was twenty-two years old, old enough to make his own decisions, old enough to sneak onto a navy ship to start a new life. They'd be disappointed, though, and no amount of freedom could revoke the sour feeling in his belly at the thought of his parents being *disappointed.*

He wasn't cut out to be a duke, though. Yet that was the fate that awaited him back in Veridin. If his mother died or got too old, she would give up her power to Czardas. Unlike his father, he was a full-blooded Rossi, so he wouldn't have the option to pass his duke duties off to someone else so he could focus on music.

Music was all Czardas cared about. Not fame. Not power or wealth or influence. Just music. He could play forty-seven instruments, though he technically knew how to play fifty, even though his skills in those remaining three were abysmal at best. He could sing. He could compose music while he slept. Nothing else in the world mattered to him as long as he had his music.

And as long as he had Fynch.

Fynch leaned his head against Czardas's shoulder. "I wonder," he whispered, "where we will end up. Any guesses?"

So much for not talking.

Czardas hummed softly, melodizing with the waves outside. "We'll likely go to Kalwyl, to the naval fortress there. Or maybe Joris."

Fynch huffed softly. "Boring. Where do you *hope* we'll end up, then? I hope it's somewhere interesting."

"F, you don't know your geography," Czardas muttered. "And you've never left Veridonia, so *everywhere* would be interesting." He paused, listening to the waves for a moment longer before adding, "I hope we go to Merdyne. Or Elluf."

Both countries were known for their music, but Elluf was home to a three-stringed lute-like instrument Czardas longed to learn. He'd only heard it played once and since Elluf was an independent country, it was impossible to find anyone able to teach him.

"Well, *I* hope we go to the Wandering Isle," drawled Fynch. "I think –"

Czardas held his hand up, cutting Fynch off mid-sentence. Over the waves, he could hear the navy men above talking. He listened intently, hoping for a clue as to where they were headed.

"The admiral seems to think they'd head south," someone said. "Since they've been going south this whole time."

"They must be heading to Merdyne," someone else replied. "The Witch of the Sea is from there; she must be trying to return. In that case, it would make sense for them to cross into the Amethyst and then into the Ruby..."

"But...?" the first man prompted. Footsteps creaked overhead.

"But they have a master navigator with them," the second man said. "And Nox Solveig is clever. They won't go south; they'll go north, between Joris and Servedin. Set a course to follow them. And officer?"

"Yes, Commander Zimmer?"

Fynch went as pale as a sheet.

"Take Nox Solveig alive," Commander Zimmer instructed. "And leave my ex-wife to me. *I* will deal with her."

"Yes, Commander."

Their footsteps sounded across the deck.

"So," whispered Fynch in a shaky breath. "As soon as we stop, we're getting off this ship."

24

THE MIDMORNING SUN SHONE brightly in the sky, creating a dazzling display over the deep blue waves when Ves spotted the influx of souls.

She lowered her knives, halting the practice fight against Illie, and counted. Fifty-four. *Sard.*

"Ves?" Illie asked. She sheathed her sword – she was, admittedly, getting better at it, even building some muscle on those twig arms of hers – and followed Ves's line of sight, trying, and failing, to see what she saw.

Fifty-four people. That could be a merchant ship. It could be a group of fishermen.

But deep down, even without seeing the ship itself, Ves knew that was too optimistic. It wasn't a merchant ship or a fishing vessel.

No. It was the navy, finally caught up to them.

Even though she'd been locked away, hidden from the world, and left to rot underground for four years, Ves was born of the salt. She knew these waters better than the back of her hand. The *Serenity* was closer to Servedin than Joris, far away enough to avoid the naval fortress on the northern tip of Joris Island. There was no reason for the navy to be there.

Unless it was to follow the *Serenity*.

Sard it all! Dreamer's teeth, the crew was *not* ready to fight the navy. Ves's back still ached, even though the wound was mostly healed. The scar tissue pulled taut whenever she bent or twisted, still tender from when she was sliced at Bowhead Rock weeks ago. Solveig was in worse shape, his arm still practically useless. Illie... She could wield a sword with some decency, but could she hold her own against the navy? Absolutely *not*. And the *Serenity*... She was fast, but not nearly as fast as a navy ship.

You are Vesperine Genevieve, she told herself, repeating the mantra that had kept her alive for those four years spent in I. J. Pen. *You are the Witch of the Sea. You have sunk entire fleets. You slew a kraken, baby or not. You are blessed by Dreamer herself. You sailed for Merdyne, and now you sail with Solveig.*

She didn't have as much power as Thol or Solveig, being only the bo'sun, but she was loud, and she could see things the others couldn't, so she shouted, *"NAVY!"*

There was a lull, a pregnant pause, as her words settled like dust.

And then, at once, everyone jumped into action.

Thol claimed the helm – the *Serenity,* after all, was his – while Solveig climbed the mast, hoisting their colors high.

"Are we fighting or fleeing?" asked Natha, who slipped from the galley. She scraped her hair up into a high tail and cracked her knuckles.

"If the navy is this close, they've no doubt spotted us." Solveig hopped onto the deck, his green coat billowing behind him. "They're faster than us, and the winds aren't fast enough to let us outrun them. We fight. And we *win.*"

And we win. No room for error. No room for death. They would take on the navy and they would follow their captain's orders to win.

We fight and we win.

Ves grinned. Her crew was in no shape to fight, but when had that stopped them before? In Lenwell, against the cadets? On Bowhead Rock? In Veridonia, where they were so unprepared, they had to rely on steak knives to fight?

Before, when Ves and Solveig were alone, fleeing the navy on a stolen ship and fighting amateur pirates?

She owed Solveig her life because he had given it back to her.

Without him, she would still be rotting in that dark underground cell in I. J. Pen. She would still be at the mercy of Lakatos Justyce, the warden who loathed her enough he sometimes forgot she existed.

It wasn't just Solveig, though. She had Thol, who would laugh at her jokes and pretend to hate her drunken singing, even though he was hiding a smile behind a mug of cinnamon rum. She had Illie, who was her friend, the expert navigator who fought with them when she didn't have to, who woke up every morning to train with Ves because she wanted to be stronger, who let Ves braid her hair and, in turn, tried braiding Ves's curls, who was her first female friend in four years. And she had Natha, who smiled like the sun, who could fight harder than the others, who could flip Ves over her shoulder without breaking a sweat, who cooked for them all without question, who fought with them and joined them without a second thought.

It wasn't the Ruby Pirates, but it was...it was better. The pirates of the *Serenity* were her family.

She drew her knives and shouted, *"Aye, Cap!"*

There was simply no way the navy had caught up with the *Serenity*. She was *fast*. But... The navy likely avoided the doldrums, unlike the *Serenity*. Thol couldn't see the ship yet, but he didn't doubt Ves's ability for a second. She liked to be *incredibly* annoying with it. More than once, she would walk onto the deck and announce how many fish were beneath the ship.

"Where is it?" he called to Ves, who was scanning the horizon intently, a cat searching for a mouse.

"To the north!" she called back.

Glancing at his compass, Thol spun the wheel, shifting the helm to direct the *Serenity* hard port until the compass's needle balanced right above the *N*. A gale blew over his shoulders. *Perfect.* If everything else went to sard, at least Illie would have a backup weapon. They had two divine touched pirates on the crew, and while one's ability was *far* more useful in combat than the other's, it was an advantage, nonetheless.

He brushed his fingers against the ink on his chest, the tiny *M. W.* and *E. W.* tattooed there, silently asking his wife and daughter to keep him and his crew safe.

I'm sorry I returned to piracy, he thought, hoping somehow, somewhere, Meadow would hear him. *But I couldn't let Nox do this alone. He's my brother, and I will not lose another one of those.*

You know *family is the most important thing to me,* he imagined Meadow chiding. The ghost of a smile graced his lips.

Within a few minutes, the blobby silhouette of a ship appeared on the horizon.

"Fifty-four enemies," said Ves as she paced the deck, clearly restless. As childish as she could be at times, with her drunken singing and fish statistics, she seemed to be the most bloodthirsty of them all.

Not that Thol blamed her. She'd spent four years locked away and wanted her vengeance. She was the *Witch of the Sea,* after all. Few were as fearsome as her.

It was a sarding good thing she was on *his* side because she had proved herself to be a formidable enemy.

Fifty-four enemies. It seemed like a rather small number, especially compared to some of the fights Thol had been in when he sailed on the *Sea Wyrm.*

Solveig grabbed one of Ves's curls and tugged. "Will you *stop* pacing? You're stressing me out. It's just one ship. We can handle it."

"What if it's the *Mary Jolene?*" she asked. Admiral Jonyth Commodore's ship.

Solveig scrunched his face into a grimace. "Then I'll kill Jonyth, and we won't have to deal with him ever again." "I am *not* going back to I. J. Pen.," she shot back.

Thol turned the wheel. It would be best to block the navy's ship by going perpendicular to them, effectively cutting off their escape route and giving the *Serenity* the upper hand. If they were lucky, they could pump the enemy's ship full of cannonballs and sink it before things got too bloody, but pirates were rarely lucky.

"What's the plan?" he called to Solveig, even though he'd already cemented one out on his own.

"You're my first mate, Thol," Solveig said. "I trust your judgment. If Jonyth is on that ship, leave him to me. He is going to pay for what he did to my friends."

Natha added, "If there is a Captain Adrian Zimmer, let me handle him."

Her ex-husband. After the fight at the restaurant in Veridonia, Natha had explained to them that she'd been married to the divine touched Captain Adrian Zimmer but split in a messy divorce. It made sense that she wanted revenge. Thol would grant her that much, as would, he knew, Solveig.

"Crossing the T," explained Thol. "Do not cross over until Nox gives the signal. Ves, you and Illie man the cannons. Nox and Natha, I want you on offense."

"Bossy," said Solveig, though he gave a lazy salute.

"Aye, Flowers," chimed Ves.

The navy ship grew closer, the inkblot becoming a frigate, the telltale bust of Lady Lightbringer carved on the figurehead. Only the navy dared to invoke the gods by plastering one on every one of their ships.

Thol clenched his teeth, grinding them together. Fifty-four enemies.

He spun the wheel, willing the *Serenity* to go faster. Poet must have been on his side today, as the ship obeyed, drawing closer and closer, until Thol could read the name painted on the navy ship's hull.

The *Meredith*.

"Sard me," cursed Natha. "That's Adrian's ship. How the *hell* did he find us?!"

The *Meredith* was a captain's ship. This wouldn't be an easy fight. Thol hated to admit it, but they were outnumbered.

Severely so.

"Illie!" he barked. "If you can, I need some wind. I'm going to cut them off before they can get too close."

Guilt wrapped around his stomach. Illie still had little control over her powers; the thick gloves she wore whenever she used them were not enough to keep out the inevitable frostbite.

Natha darted back into the galley while Illie reached out, gripping seemingly nothing. She threw her arms out, cracking an invisible whip that filled the sails to the brim, shooting the *Serenity* forward, closer to the imminent *Meredith*. Natha returned with a bowl of warm water; Illie shucked off her gloves and plunged her hands into the bowl to warm her fingers and palms before the frostbite could get to her.

Thol fought against the waves, turning the *Serenity* parallel, her port side against the bow of the *Meredith*.

"Ves, Illie, get to the cannons," Solveig instructed, marching across the deck with his cutlass drawn. His ring glinted in the morning light.

Illie pulled her gloves back on and dashed to the cannons. She watched as Ves aimed, then did the same thing.

"FIRE!" ordered Solveig.

Bang! Bang! Bang! The cannons shot, one after the other, zipping through the air to embed in the wooden hull of the *Meredith*. Wood splintered, charred as it flew into the air in bits of shrapnel. Already, Ves and Illie were reloading the cannons along the side of the *Serenity*, firing them when Solveig commanded.

Bang! Bang! Bang!

Solveig darted for the sails, tying them up so they wouldn't be a target anymore.

"Uh... Cap?" Ves's hands hovered over the cannons, her gaze fixed on the *Meredith*. "I can't sense the souls anymore. They just blinked out, all at once. That only happens when someone dies or when they get too far away. It's only ever happened once before when we were in Lenwell."

When she, Thol, and Solveig stole the lithograph.

"I can't grab the wind, either," said Illie as she flexed her gloved hands.

"Incoming!" yelled Natha, grabbing everyone's attention as a rope sailed through the air. It wrapped around the railing.

Thol's eyes widened. He knew this trick – this *dirty,* pirate trick. Letting go of the helm, he dashed for the rope while shouting, "Everyone sarding *brace!"*

He was fast, but the *Meredith* was faster. She moved with grace and speed and divine control, and at once, the roles were reversed. The *Serenity* was yanked into submission.

Thol gripped the railing tight, trying to keep from falling as he worked on the knot.

"Adrian is divine touched!" Natha was the first to regain her catlike balance as the *Serenity* bobbed precariously up and down in the waves. "He can control the outcome of probability! He's blessed by Lady Lightbringer!"

"You didn't think that was important to tell us *sooner?!"* hissed Ves. She rose to her feet, knees bent to reacquaint herself with the rocking ship.

"I try not to think about my ex-husband," Natha shot back. "He's a gambler! He will control the probabilities of *everything* he can. He must have seen an outcome where our roles were reversed and took it. He's *dangerous!"*

Thol finally got the knot undone. He let it fall into the sea below, but his efforts were for naught. A plank of wood thunked on the railing. A crossing binding the ships together.

Sard.

His eyes darted across the ship, searching for – *there.* Solveig stood still as a statue; all color drained from his face, and his grip on his cutlass slackened until he was hardly even holding onto the blade.

Sarding hell. Thol had seen him like this only three other times in his life.

"Captain!" he yelled, desperate to pull Solveig out of whatever panicked state he'd found himself in. "Nox!"

Bang!

The *Serenity* lurched violently, shaken by the cannonball that breached her hull.

"Not my sarding ship, you sons of wenches!" Thol cursed. Then, he shouted to his captain again: *"Nox Solveig, snap out of it!"*

"Permission to cross!" Ves eyed the enemy ship hungrily, ready to attack.

For whatever reason, *that* snapped Solveig out of his stupor because he shouted, "Permission *denied!*"

The ship rocked, the explosions from cannon fire far too close for Fynch to be comfortable.

Right now, it was a gamble. He and Czardas could stay on the navy ship, or they could chance running over to the other ship. Fynch wanted to be as far from the navy – as far from the man who shared the same family name as the commander from the restaurant in Veridonia – as possible. But Czardas...

He turned to his friend, prepared to explain that the other ship would probably be safer, even though it was most likely a pirate vessel.

"We need to get on that other ship," Czardas, to his surprise, hissed. "This one is going to sink if it gets hit anymore."

Well, at least he didn't have to explain why staying was a terrible idea.

Fynch grabbed his bags and slung them over his shoulders, only to pause. No, he needed to be smarter about this. He shrugged one bag off and dug through it, returning it to its place once his pistol was in his hand.

"Let's go," he said, cringing, as he had been for the past few days, at the severity of his new lisp.

Czardas clutched his violin close and nodded.

Fynch listened to the thundering footsteps on the deck above, waiting for a lull. Once there was a pause, a bit of quiet, he shoved open the door and darted out.

The ship was in shambles. Wood, acrid and smoldering, littered the corridor, damp with seawater that filtered in through the holes. Cannons fired in violent rounds, shaking the ship with each blow. Fynch bent his knees, ducking down in an attempt to keep from falling over each time the ship rocked. It would be suicide to go to the deck, but he prayed the navy would be too involved in the fight to realize two stowaways were sneaking off.

He spotted the stairs leading up and waved for Czardas to follow. Dashing up them, he paused. The deck was in even more of a disarray. The pirate ship – it *was* a pirate ship, Fynch knew, because the black flag whipped in the wind. It wasn't one he recognized – a moon impaled by a sword that dripped five gems – but it was, without a doubt, a pirate flag.

And then he saw a flash of green, and he *knew* who the pirates were.

"Are you *sure* stowing away on a pirate ship is the best idea?" whispered Czardas. Fynch pulled him behind one of the masts, hiding both of them from sight.

"I fought with them," he said. "In Veridonia. Briefly. Just… Trust me, Czar. They're our best bet right now. And *you* said we needed to get off this ship. Unless you'd rather stay here?"

"I'd rather not get involved in any fights, F, but I trust you."

A dangerous game, a risky gamble, a terrible decision all things considered, but Fynch just grinned and spun his pistol around his forefinger. Today, he would make sure the navy realized they had made a fatal mistake in not letting him join. Because if Fynch Largos wasn't with them, he was against them.

Fynch grabbed Czardas's hand. "Ready?"

Czardas groaned, "No."

"Good. Let's go."

Fynch took off running, dashing across the deck towards the other ship – the *Serenity,* based on the name painted on the hull. A plank had been laid out between the two ships – *bingo.* Gripping Czardas's wrist tighter, Fynch made a beeline for the plank. If he faltered and looked into the water, he would lose his balance.

He wasn't scared of the ocean, but it made him uneasy. He was an excellent swimmer, but the ocean was merciless. It would not hesitate to devour him.

Explosions sounded behind him, their heat licking at his ankles. Sucking in a breath, he went for it, running across the plank as fast as he could, his grip on Czardas iron.

His foot caught, and Fynch tumbled forward, careening too close to the edge of the plank. *Sarding sard –*

"You!" a voice cried.

Someone grabbed his free arm and pulled both Fynch and Czardas onto the solid deck. He blinked and looked up (and up and up and up –) to see a familiar face.

"I don't have time for you," said the tall woman he'd defended in Veridonia. "Get out of the way. I have people to kill."

Fynch glanced at Czardas, giving an uneasy grin. "See? We're safe."

"Well, well, well," a booming voice said, startling Fynch. He turned around, finally putting a face to the voice he'd been stuck listening to for days now.

Captain Adrian Zimmer had crossed over, a wicked grin plastered on his face.

Natha's body went colder than an ice box, her stomach souring as it flipped in violent acrobatics. Every hair on her body stood on end, flesh pocked with goosebumps.

"Nathalia Zimmer," drawled her ex-husband. The battle went silent around her, a muffled nothingness as her ears homed in on the steady thunk of Adrian's boots across the deck. She'd envisioned this moment countless times before, but now that he was here, all the snarky responses she'd dreamed up vanished.

Adrian had never hurt her physically, but for the duration of their two-year marriage, Natha found herself wishing more often than not that she was dead because if she was a corpse in the ground, she wouldn't have to deal with him.

She cursed herself for falling for his pretty face and his charming wit. She cursed herself for cutting ties with her family after both her sisters died, for ignoring her mother when she pleaded with Natha to take things slowly, to court Adrian longer before accepting his proposal. She cursed herself for being too weak to leave him sooner.

Her mouth went dry, cotton-stuffed.

You're a pirate, she reminded herself. Pirates didn't fear the navy. They didn't fear anything. *You're a pirate on Nox Solveig's crew. You are sailing the world to find the lost moon.*

She channeled as much faux strength as possible, pretending she was carefree Illie, pretending she was brave Ves. Slowly, she turned around and faced her ex-husband for the first time since he left her sobbing in the courtroom after taking everything she ever had.

"It's Natha Divyne now," she said calmly, saying those words she'd practiced in the darkness of her dinky flat over and over again.

"R*iiiiiiii*ght." He grinned a shark's grin, one that stretched from ear to ear but didn't quite reach his eyes.

She knew that grin. He was going to try to coerce her into submission.

He could try all he sarding wanted; she would not give in. She would *never* give in to him again.

She balled her hands into tight fists, letting them hang by her hips. Adrian fought dirty, so she would just have to fight dirtier. She would have to be faster than his god touched ability.

"You know I never wanted to hurt you, Nathalia," he continued. "But if you're siding with *pirates* now, I have no choice."

"If you didn't want to hurt me, you wouldn't have brought home divorce papers out of the blue and taken everything with you." She clenched her jaw and ran, bolting for him only to duck low, escaping his fists as he went for the punch.

Behind him now, she kicked out, her foot meeting the backs of his knees. He stumbled, though he regained his balance quickly. *Too* quickly. Natha didn't have the chance to get out of his range.

Adrian grabbed a fistful of her hair and yanked. Pain erupted along her crown, the *ripping* of hairs being torn from her scalp deafening.

"You've always been like this," he scolded, as if she were nothing more than a toddler. "You've always made everything about you. *I* didn't do anything wrong. *You're* the one who agreed to marry me, and *you* also signed the divorce papers. I'm not the bad guy, Nathalia."

She kicked and writhed, clawing at his hand, desperate to pry it from her hair. All she wanted to do was curl up and cry. He was right. Everything was Natha's fault. She was pathetic and weak and –

She was a sarding *pirate*.

"No," she said coldly, mustering every bit of Illie and Ves and Thol and Solveig into her voice. *"You* gave me no choice. You gave me the papers. You divorced *me* because you're *weak*. You're a spineless coward who divorced me because you were upset I walked in on you *cheating."*

In their bed, no less. She had burned those linens after.

He tugged on her hair. "Oh, Nathalia. I told you I did that because of you. It was your fault. If you'd just been a bit more attentive..."

She shrieked. *"I was working! I had to work!"*

He chuckled dryly. "Women don't work."

That was the final straw. She had not spent her entire life studying at the most prestigious university – she hadn't cooked for the royal family – just for her ex-husband to tell her *women don't work.*

She bit the inside of her cheek, knowing the pain would be brutal, but brief. She twisted, pulling out of Adrian's grip, landing her knee right between his legs.

"Tell that to the sarding *queen!"* she screamed.

Adrian doubled over, pain stealing the color from his face. Locks of her pale hair tangled around his fingers, torn from her scalp. Natha balled her hands into fists, panting hard as she tried to catch her breath. Her throat burned, sandpapery from all the screaming.

The clashing of swords and cannon explosions became a fishbowl, muddled and distorted.

She *could* defeat Adrian. She just had to be faster than him. She had to be *unpredictable.*

She sucked in a breath through her teeth. As she exhaled, she said, "Marrying you was the worst mistake I've ever made."

Fury steeled his eyes, turning them into twin stormy seas.

"I am going to kill you," he seethed.

The Natha he knew would have bowed in submission at those words, too afraid of death to invoke his wrath further. But that Natha was gone. That Natha drowned herself in spirits and the bath in her shoddy flat after she returned her ring and two years of her life to him.

This Natha was a sarding pirate, and she didn't fear death, not anymore.

So, she grinned and said, "I'd like to see you try."

As Illie shoved cannonballs into the cannons, one after the other, lighting the fuses in succession, she tried to reach for the wind. For as long as she could remember, the wind had always been *right* there. Whether she wanted to or not, she could reach out and grab it, except for those hours in the doldrums. But even then, she could feel the whispering gales slipping through her fingers like wispy strands of angel hair.

Except for now.

Now, it was like a wall had been erected between her and her ability. She couldn't grab the tempests no matter how hard she tried. It was as if someone had *taken* that power from her, rendering her as normal as anyone not divine touched.

Without her powers...

No, she scolded herself. Her powers didn't define her. She hadn't beheaded Captain Rouge with the wind; she'd done that with pure adrenaline and a too-heavy sword.

She fired another cannon. It missed its target completely, hitting the water with a heavy *splash!*

"Come *on!*" she hissed, panic thickening her throat, making her voice heavy. "Come on, Poet. Give it *back!*"

She tore her makeshift glove off with her teeth and grasped at the air. Nothing.

There wasn't enough time for this! She yanked her glove back on and drew her cutlass, grateful to still have it sheathed at her hip. Now would be the final test, her debut shot at displaying the skills Ves had taught her.

Poet, she hoped she could do it.

Gripping the sword with both hands, elbows loose like her knees, she spun around, locking eyes with an enemy.

There was a difference between these navy men and the Redcoat Pirates at Bowhead Rock. There was a difference between the navy now and the navy in Veridonia.

The difference was that these ones weren't attacking her yet. *She* had the opening to make the first move, and that was what gave her a flutter of hesitation. If she attacked first, she wouldn't be killing in self-defense. She'd be murdering in cold blood, just like a real pirate.

To hell with it. There was already a bounty on her head.

Illie charged, praying to Poet that her power would return, that she wouldn't trip and make a fool of herself, that she would be able to remember Ves's lessons and take down the enemy, preferably without any bloodshed, without getting killed herself.

No pressure.

A war cry escaped from her lips, muted by the sounds of battle surrounding her. With a *clash,* her sword met the navy man's. She leaned into the blow; he leaned back. Metal gritted against metal, the screams of two blades battling for dominance nearly as deafening as the thundering of Illie's heart in her throat. Nausea churned, bile rising up her gullet.

She had given up a quiet life of drawing maps for *this.*

Oh, gods, she was going to die.

The navy man pulled his sword back and swung it in a downward arc, too fast for Illie to parry. She closed her eyes, praying that the death that loomed above her would be quick, that her next life would be more forgiving.

I will pledge my final breath to your name, she had vowed, *and my first to find you again.*

Her unbreakable *oath.*

I'm sorry, Sol, she thought. *I will find you again. I –*
BANG!

Blood sprayed across her face, hot and thick, followed by the clatter of a sword and the baritone scream of a man unused to pain.

She peeked one eye open and saw the navy man gripping his hand tightly, trying desperately to staunch the blood spurting out in a scarlet geyser. His hand... Gods, it was a mangled mess of meat and shredded bone, more blood than anything else.

Her nausea swam to her vision. She stumbled back, weakly holding her sword.

"Stop wasting bullets!" someone hissed.

"He was going to kill her!" another unfamiliar voice – accented and lisped so thickly she had to repeat the words in her head a few times before she understood what had been said – shot back.

Her vision swam, drunken, as she turned to see a blonde...girl – no, a boy? It was impossible to tell, and frankly, at the moment, she couldn't care less – reloading a gun. Neither he nor the curly-haired boy next to him wore navy fatigues, but Illie didn't recognize them.

She steadied herself, darting away from the bleeding man before he could enact his vengeance on her. His blood slipped between her lips, settling on her tongue like a stack of kase coins.

Shrugging her shoulder to wipe her face, Illie tried reaching for the wind again.

"You must be divine blessed," chided a voice she didn't recognize. "That means with our little *trick,* you are completely and utterly *useless.*"

Solveig stood on the deck of the *Serenity,* but he also stood on the deck of the *Silver Moon.* The ghosts of his friends danced around him, asking for permission to cross, telling Solveig to stay with them, demanding retreat because they couldn't take on Jonyth and the *Mary Jolene.*

He regretted a lot of things about that day, but mostly he regretted not fleeing when he had the chance. He regretted giving Jonyth the opening to drug his crew with sinth and letting them drown. He regretted letting his ego get the best of him.

And yet...

And yet, here he stood, at the bow of the *Serenity,* smoke and ash raining down, his green coat billowing behind him, once again against the navy.

Once again making the same decision that cost him the lives of his crew.

How many more lives would the navy take? How many more of Solveig's loved ones would they put in the ground?

He hadn't even been a teenager when the navy marched into that tiny town he'd grown up in, leaving with soot on their coats and blood on their hands. When they spotted the childish black flag, clearly meant for a kid's game, and took it as a threat, one worth a round of Lady Lightbringer-endorsed bullets.

When they rearranged the world, making the youngest the oldest.

Shock glued him to the ground, his muscles and bones stiff, like he'd been encased in a tomb of ice.

It was happening again. The navy had come to take everything from him again. His old crew, Tuo –

"Nox Solveig!"

Thol barreled into him, knocking him off balance. He stumbled, hardly managing to catch himself before he could topple to the ground.

"They're going to take everything away," Solveig whispered, his voice once proud and now nothing more than broken glass shards.

"Not if you fight back," said Thol. He hadn't been there the day the navy came; he didn't know the pain firsthand the way Solveig did.

But he had lost brothers that day, too, and the pain of finding out afterward must have hurt just as much as watching too many bullets enter too-small bodies.

"You need to snap out of it, Nox," Thol growled. "Or the navy will continue to take from you. You have to *fight back.* How does that rhyme go? *Captain Nox Solveig, cloaked in green, set out to conquer the Emerald Sea. One day he'll go down to the drink –"*

"How many navy ships will he sink?" finished Solveig.

He'd sunk seventy-three. He would sink seventy-three more before he considered the score even. One hundred forty-six ships for the lives of two boys whose only crime was flying a pretend flag.

The *Meredith* would be seventy-four. He promised himself that, gripping his cutlass with grim determination, a taut smile slashed across his face.

"I'm crossing over," said Solveig. "You stay here and protect the ship, the crew. They have a drug – sinth – that can be turned into a gas. If that happens, do *not* breathe it in. I'm not letting –"

Solveig didn't get to finish his sentence.

A cannonball tore through the *Serenity*'s hull, rocking her like a branch in the wind. She groaned, dipping closer to the waves below.

Sarding hell. She was going to *sink*.

That was enough to get Solveig's attention. They had to end the fight now before the ship could go down.

He spun around, figuring out where his crew was. Thol was with him, and Ves was busy fighting off navy men while reloading the cannons in a desperate yet futile attempt to fire back. He caught a glimpse of Illie's pink braid and spotted Natha with who could only be the navy fleet's captain.

And there was a blond kid with a dark-skinned boy next to him, the former firing a gun and the latter struggling to use a broadsword as a rapier.

"Nox," said Thol, "we won't lose this fight. I promise."

"If you break that promise," Solveig said through clenched teeth, "I will never forgive you."

Thol cracked his knuckles, eyes darting over the melee as he figured out who to attack. "I still have to tell you the rest of the story about Meadow, remember? I'll see you when we win this."

His heart somersaulted in his ribs, squished against his lungs. Solveig nodded once and watched as Thol ran off to tackle a navy sailor, leaving him alone in the eye of the storm.

He eyed the *Meredith.*

It would not be hard at all to sink it.

The sword weighed a ton and a half, even when Czardas held it with both hands. Maybe it wasn't truly that heavy, and his shaky hands and bone-deep anxiety made it seem like it weighed a ton and a half, but regardless of the reason, it dragged him down.

He'd tried holding it like a rapier at first, one arm straight and the other bent back, but his arms were built for holding up weightless violins and violas, not steel swords forged for pirates. It had been lying discarded on the deck of the pirate ship, and nobody seemed to be looking for it, so he picked it up under the guise of being helpful, only to regret it instantly.

But Fynch had seen him holding it, so it was too late to admit to his weakness. Czardas gripped the leather-wrapped hilt tighter, the rigidity of it biting into his palms, rubbing against soft flesh where an expert swordsman would have calluses.

Fynch cursed suddenly, snapping Czardas's attention to him. Fynch scanned the deck anxiously, fiddling with his pistol. "I ran out of ammo," he said. "Look, Czar, can you find me some? I'm sure they have a stash somewhere. If we help them out, they can't get too mad. Maybe they'll give us a ride – oh, that doesn't matter right now. Just find me some bullets!"

Czardas shoved the sword back into its scabbard and tucked that into his belt, the weight harsh against his thigh but manageable.

He nodded once, sharply, and took off running across the deck, pretending he knew where he was going.

One of the doors was locked and wouldn't budge no matter how hard he shoved his weight against it, but the second door beneath the quarterdeck swung open suddenly. He stumbled, nearly tripping into the room.

A cabin, he realized, the sunlight streaming in from behind him illuminating the rows of cots. Chests were bolted neatly against the wall, and on a desk was a vase of dried flowers. Czardas stepped into the room, dashing for the chests. Most, he found, were locked, but one pried open with a creak.

Empty.

Sard it!

He slammed it shut and stood. There wouldn't be ammo in a cabin. He needed to get below deck somehow, where the storage would surely be.

He left the cabin and tried two of the other doors. One led to a dining area with a door that surely led to the galley, and the other opened to another cabin. A puffed-up grey tabby hissed at Czardas before darting into an open chest.

The final door led to a staircase leading down, and Czardas nearly sobbed with relief.

That is until he descended the steps only to be met with ankle-deep seawater.

He cursed. Weren't ships supposed to have carpenters to fix holes *before* the hull filled with water?

Before he could decide to turn back, though, he saw it – a crate stacked on a bolted shelf labeled *AMMO.*

Maybe the gods decided to take pity on him. Or maybe the pirates who owned the ship were sarding idiots who thought keeping their ammo in plain sight was smart.

The ship careened forward, unsteady. The lights above swayed, flickering and sputtering in a threat to go out. *Hurry up,* they seemed to taunt.

He descended another step. Seawater seeped through his trousers and – his stomach soured – his socks. There were few things in this world Czardas loathed more than wet socks – snapped violin strings, piccolos, and soggy bread came close, though.

Swallowing his discomfort, he lunged for the box, staggering under its unexpected weight. He clutched it to his chest, treasuring it as he bolted up the stairs.

"Took you long enough!" exclaimed Fynch when he returned. He kicked open the crate and dug out some bullets, expertly loading them into his pistol and firing without skipping a beat.

Fynch turned and beamed a chipped-tooth grin.

Czardas swallowed. "I... I think I need to fix the ship," he said. He'd crafted a guitar once. It couldn't be *too* different...right?

But Fynch didn't answer. He dug out more bullets and continued to shoot, each shot perfect.

Keep him safe, he prayed to whichever gods might be listening. Sucking in a breath, lungs filling with soot and ash and smoke, Czardas ran for the stairs again.

25

Ves chanted her mantra as she abandoned the cannons, re-alizing they were useless in the position they were in.

I will not return to I. J. Pen.

I will not return to I. J. Pen.

I will not return to I. J. Pen.

She brandished her knives and threw them, one after the other, at a navy man aiming his gun at her. They sailed just shy of his head, embedding hilt-deep in the mainmast.

Ves never missed. She was the Witch of the Sea, and the Witch of the Sea could cut down a man fifteen feet away with her sarding eyes closed.

She tried grasping for her second sight, tried filtering out the corporeal bodies around her in favor of the golden souls, but there was nothing. She had become blind, her sight stolen from her.

Her breath shallowed. *I will not return to I. J. Pen.*

She grabbed another knife from her belt and threw it at the same man. It missed just as he fired. Ves didn't think; she just dove to the ground, hitting the deck before her brains could paint the wood red. Her heart thundered against her ribs.

Natha's ex-husband was blessed by sarding Lady Lightbringer. This was all *his* fault. She clenched her jaw so hard her teeth ached.

She was going to kill that fool that shot at her –

Boots slammed down next to her head. She rolled to her back and jumped to her feet, eye-to-eye with...with a *woman*. She wore navy colors, but the emblem at her breast indicated her status. Vice-captain. Natha's ex-husband's second in command.

Ves got a good look at the woman. It was a damn shame she was with the navy. She was all muscle, tall enough to have some Amazonian blood in her veins like Ves did. Her hair was a dark blue, threaded with silver, and her face, while harsh, had a sort of cold, callous beauty to it.

"If it isn't the Witch of the Sea," the vice-captain said smugly. "I remember when you were arrested all those years ago."

Ves scoffed. "Were you still *vice*-captain back then?" her fingers inched toward her belt, seeking the last knife she had sheathed there. Unless she managed to get to the mast to pull her other blades free, she was down to one eight-inch weapon against a sword.

Terrible odds, even without Natha's ex-husband's power intervening.

"You're one to talk," said the vice-captain. "You were the boatswain back then, and you're the boatswain now."

She said it like the rank was miles below that of vice-captain. As if the navy didn't have three dozen of those already.

Ves shrugged, nonchalant. "I'm the second mate, too."

And then, she struck.

Her knife met the blade of the vice-captain's sword, metal clashing against metal. In a battle of strength, a dagger was virtually useless against a sword.

But daggers could move faster, and Ves was a viper.

She swept her leg out, kicking the vice-captain in the shin. She forced her knife along the sword's blade, arcing it around to swipe close to the woman's face. Bits of grey-blue hair fluttered to the deck, lost amongst the ash.

Blood pumped hard and hot in her ears, deafening. Adrenaline surged through her veins, more addictive and intoxicating than a barrel of cinnamon rum. Her knife danced over her knuckles, her grip on it changing from a defensive hold to an offensive one. Instead of slicing down, she jabbed, stabbing through air and fabric, nicking the unprotected flesh beneath.

She met some resistance, the muscle hard and striated. Instead of pushing harder, Ves ripped her knife free and spun around the vice-captain. It was a dance, really. A dance that lacked music and choreography, but Ves knew how to dance, and she *liked* to do it.

"You *wench!*" cried the vice-captain. She pressed the heel of her palm against the injury to her oblique, her jacket already morphing from a pristine white to a sticky crimson.

"You're one to talk." She tossed her knife from hand to hand, carefree.

The vice-captain's face twisted into a snarl. She lunged, stabbing the space Ves had occupied mere seconds before. Ves darted under the blade, sliding between the vice-captain's legs.

"You're going to rot in Ivenis Justyce for this," snarled the V. C.

Adrenaline was replaced, in that moment, with pure, undiluted *rage.*

"I will not return to sarding I. J. Pen!" Ves screamed.

She shoved her knife between her teeth and grabbed the woman's middle. She couldn't see what beasties lurked beneath the waves, but if they were smart, they would know to avoid a fight between ships. It didn't matter. Ves had sworn an oath, anyway. If she couldn't help Solveig in this life, she'd just have to help him in the next one.

The V. C. screamed, but her cries were lost to the wind. Ves held her tightly, refusing to let her go.

They crashed into the water.

It was strange, Ves thought as she began to sink. Even though it was summer, and the air above was sweltering, the Emerald Sea was so very cold.

Around her, as her eyes began to close, she could see the faintest tendrils of gold.

Thol swung his fist, cracking his knuckles into the jaw of a sergeant. He'd picked the biggest man amongst the navy's crew, a man not nearly as tall as he was but wider, arms and legs cord-

EMMA T. SHANNON

ed with thicker muscles. There was a part of him – perhaps the husbandly part, or maybe the paternal part that never got a chance to properly shine – that wanted to help Natha fight since she was so outnumbered, especially with her ex-husband's divine ability to alter probability into his favor.

He shook out his hand and punched again, leaving an angry red splotch mirrored to the one he'd delivered moments before.

"I know who you are," the sergeant spat, bloody spittle spraying across Thol's face. How the man could still talk was beyond him, but that just meant he needed more punches to the face. He continued: "Bartholomew Williams. Ex-captain of the *Sea Wyrm*. You might've dropped off the radar for a few years, but you're still worth a pretty rine."

Sixth most wanted, last he checked. A number that would have Meadow dragging him in by the ear to shout at him until everyone in Lenwell was *well* aware of his dirty laundry.

Thol kicked high, aiming to leave a nice boot print on the man's face. The sergeant was faster, grabbing Thol's ankle and yanking him off balance. Thol stumbled.

He couldn't fall. He couldn't break his promise to Solveig.

It would hurt, but it would simply have to do.

He swung his leg, arcing it through the air and dragging the sergeant with it. His hip screamed in pain, his thigh muscles turning to jelly under the excessive weight, but it was enough to throw the sergeant across the deck.

The sergeant hit the railing hard enough to splinter the wood. Thol held his breath, knowing it wouldn't be that easy. A sergeant reporting directly to a captain couldn't be taken out by a single hit. If he could, he was no different from the privates and cadets Thol had faced up until now.

The man groaned, slowly rising to his feet as he dusted splinters and soot off his ruined uniform.

Right. Too easy. The odds weren't supposed to be in his favor right now.

He tilted his head to either side, popping the tension along his spine. His hip ached. Pain was irrelevant. It would go away eventually, but death... Death would be permanent, and as much as he missed Meadow and Evangeline and his brothers, he wasn't ready to see them again so soon.

The sergeant balled his hands into fists. Thol did the same.

Thol charged, his gait irregular but deathly fast all the same. The sergeant met him halfway.

Bodies collided; Thol's fist met the sergeant's jaw. The sergeant's fist met Thol's stomach.

Jumping back quickly, Thol spat out a globby string of bloody saliva. It coated the back of his teeth. He sucked in a breath and charged again. Without losing momentum, he hooked his elbow around the sergeant's throat and dragged him to the deck.

Thol straddled the other man, pinning him to the deck. The sergeant thrashed, legs writhing and hands scratching at Thol's arms, but Thol did not relent.

"You know who I am," he said coldly. "You know what the letters on my knuckles mean. So, before I give it to you, I need you to tell me something. Jonyth Commodore. Does he know of our location?"

"As if I'd tell you," the sergeant spat.

Thol lifted one shoulder in a nonchalant shrug as if to say *suit yourself.*

Then he slammed his fists into the man's nose, one after the other, the twin blows of punishment cracking into cartilage and shattering it with a wet *crunch.*

The sergeant cried out, tears spilling from his blackened eyes.

"Does Jonyth Commodore know where we are?" he asked again.

"I don't know!" the sergeant cried. "We met him in Veridonia, but he didn't follow us. We wouldn't have spotted your ship if we didn't have Captain Zimmer with us!"

Interesting...

Zimmer was Natha's ex-husband. Peeved as he was that she decided to keep that bit of information to herself, Thol really couldn't fault her. But he changed things. If he hadn't been blessed by Lady Lightbringer, the *Serenity* could have sunk the *Meredith* ages ago.

There had to be a loophole. Every divine power had a weakness. Ves could see souls, but only at a certain distance. Illie got frostbite whenever she grabbed the wind. The Redcoat Pirate at Bowhead Rock seemed to only be able to create one barrier at a time.

Divine abilities were just that – *abilities.* They were doled out randomly, and whoever got the power only had a single enhancement. Abilities were one of a kind but *could* be repeated after the original user died. There might have been another mortal decades ago who could wrangle the winds, but after their death the power returned to Poet, who gifted it to Illie. Adrian Zimmer could control probabilities.

Blessed by Lady Lightbringer to be a gambler.

Gunshots sounded too close for comfort. Thol looked up from the sergeant to see that same blond thief from Veridonia standing by the mainmast, firing round after round, hitting hands and legs – not fatal shots, but...*accurate ones.*

Either Zimmer's probability blessing didn't extend to that little thief or...

There was a limit to how much Zimmer could control at once.

And that little rapscallion had managed to avoid being ensnared in it.

Thol punched the sergeant one more time, feeling the fight finally seep out of him. He slumped to the deck, limp. Unconscious, based on the fluttering pulse in his throat.

For good measure, Thol dealt him one last round of *PUNISHMENT* to the face before standing up, the bite of pain radiating from his freshly split knuckles throbbing in time with his heart.

The thief fired another round before diving for the box of ammo. There still wasn't time to linger on the pain in his leg and hip; Thol ran for the thief.

The flickering overhead lights were going to give Czardas a migraine. He could already feel the dull throb budding behind his eye as he tore apart a crate (previously housing silks that were, unfortunately, ruined by the water, so he felt slightly less bad about discarding them).

Patching a hole was, in fact, nothing at all like sculpting a guitar.

Czardas found pretty quickly that he wouldn't be finding any hammers or nails, so he made sure to keep the nails already in the boards from the crates accounted for. He slammed his weight against the wood over and over, bruises blossoming on his shoulder, but so far, one of the holes had been patched.

One.

One.

The water gushing in from the other half-dozen holes showed no signs of stopping. The water was nearly to Czardas's knees, and while he wasn't the tallest man around, it was still a considerable depth for a *ship*.

The lights flickered again, several of the kerosene lamps sputtering out completely. He waded through the cold, dark water, two pieces of wood riddled with crooked nails in his grip. He listened for the sound of rushing water, spotting the next hole just above the waterline.

Lovely.

He crouched down and shoved one of the wood planks against the hole. Then, with all his might, he slammed his hip against it. The wood creaked, nails embedding in the hull. He slammed into it once more for good measure before applying the other plank, staunching the leak as effectively as he could. Water still dribbled in, though slower now. The pirates would be able to properly patch it later, after they won the fight.

Let them focus on winning for now.

Czardas felt around for the broken crate, hissing when his finger met a jutting nail. It tore through his flesh, inviting stinging salt-water in. Black spots clouded his vision, the throbbing in his head encompassing his cheekbone and teeth as it sank deeper. The ship beneath him swayed, tilting and twisting in a dizzying way no ship should move.

He swallowed back the nausea that had started churning in his belly, knowing he had nothing in his stomach he could spare regurgitating. Breaking off another plank, he searched for the next hole.

Bang!

The ship rocked violently. Czardas stumbled, unable to catch his balance before he fell to his knees. He threw out his hands to break his fall.

Pain shot up his arm, all the way to his cheek and ear, and down to his soaked toes. Eyes wide, he gulped down the scream that threatened to slip past his lips and reveal to everyone above deck what he was doing.

Slowly, he pulled his hand out of the water. Gravity took care of the worst part; he didn't have to see the nail or the board it was stuck to attached to his palm, but he did, even in the dim light, see the dark splotch of blood slicking his palm, gathered around the hole where the nail had just been.

It's fine, he told himself, because it had to be. He couldn't afford for it to be anything *but* fine!

He just wouldn't be able to play fast runs on the violin for a while, but he could still sing, so music wasn't completely stolen from him.

He picked up the board, mindful of the bloody nail, and got to his feet. The next hole was further up; he stood on his toes and reached. The skin around his wound pulled taut, drawing tears out of his eyes.

Ignoring it, he shoved the board in and reached for another. Three holes had been patched. The water wasn't flowing in as quickly now, but it was past his knees. Any more hits and the ship would capsize. Anymore –

Bang!

The cannonball tore through the hull mere *inches* from Czardas's head. Water rushed in.

He took a breath and, channeling his singer's lungs, screamed, *"Help!"*

It wasn't until his words settled that he realized nobody on the ship, save for Fynch, knew what his voice sounded like. And Fynch... He was needed up there, loath as Czardas was to admit it.

Footsteps thundered down the stairs, followed by the sloshing of water. Czardas narrowed his eyes, trying to see through the dark and the migraine-induced haze. A man stood in the water. While it was knee-deep for Czardas, the water barely reached the man's mid-calf. He was *massive,* and Czardas's stomach sank with the realization that this giant would be the death of him.

"Where's the hole?" the man asked. He grabbed a crate and ripped it apart with his bare hands, making it seem as easy as tearing through parchment.

Czardas stared.

"The sarding navy," the man grumbled. He sloshed through the water, finding another hole without Czardas's help. "This is *my* ship. What do they think they're doing, blowing holes in her? Are you Czardas?"

"I –"

"The blond thief told me to help you."

Fynch.

"I'm Thol," the pirate said. He slammed his fist into the board, nailing it to the wall. "Sarding Nox... I *told* him we needed a shipwright. Come on, kid. Since you're down here, you're going to help. Find a bucket and help me get this water out of here before we all drown."

Illie slowly turned to face a navy sailor – a navigator, by the compass he wore around his neck and the ink smudges on his hands. Of *course,* Poet would pair her with another navigator.

The navigator grinned. "I'll tell you since it would be a pity for you to die without knowing. There is a type of rock that suppresses all divine abilities. Dwalenite. If you crush it up and mix it with paint, you can coat an entire ship in it and anyone close enough will feel its effect."

Her stomach twisted. She wasn't able to grab the wind be-cause...because of *paint?*

The navigator continued, "But if you take a shot of the stim-ulant Sinthephane, the companion to the depressant Sinthoxine, you will be able to use your abilities when no one else can."

Sinthephane. She'd never heard of it, and she wasn't sure she wanted to. If it could reverse the suppressant, it couldn't be good.

And the *navy* had it.

Illie had, she concluded with a sick sense of dread, two options: find a shot of Sinthephane to get her powers back or defeat the navigator with her meager sword skills.

One, unfortunately, seemed a lot more feasible than the other.

She tightened her grip on her cutlass, Ves's lessons rushing through her mind.

Strike true and fast. Don't falter, don't hesitate, don't die.

She swung the sword.

Clang!

It met the navigator's sword. He was quicker, withdrawing from the blow and attacking again, cutting the tip of his blade danger-ously close to her stomach, tearing through fabric but not skin. She jumped back, wishing she was in better shape.

Survive, she told herself, preparing for another parry. *And you can get in shape.*

Wind whipped around her, mocking. What was the point of being blessed by the gods when a rock could take it away? Why would they allow their divinity to be overshadowed by something mortals made?

Give it back, Poet! Give me back my ability! Let me harness the winds again!

The breeze tore through her hair, seeping into her pores.

The navigator struck again; Illie barely threw her cutlass up in time to deflect. Heart thundering in her ears, her hands went numb with adrenaline – with the fear that she would be cut down any moment now. That she would die. That she would never find the sarding third moon.

You beheaded a pirate! She kicked the navigator in the shin, gaining a sliver of leverage. She swung her blade in a downward arc. *You sailed the world twice. You are a sarding pirate, and you are blessed by the* gods!

She swung; the navigator met her blow. She stumbled back, his force stronger than her noodle arms could handle. He pressed harder, forcing her back against the railing. She dared a glance at the sea below, tumultuous from the cannon fire and fight above.

"You're nothing without your power," chuckled the navigator.

"And you're a son of a wench who probably doesn't even know what a barometric gradient is!" she screamed.

His face twisted with rage. He struck fast – too fast for Illie to block. Her sword flew from her hands, sailing through the air and skidding out of reach. Heart in her throat, she stared at the navigator.

In one last futile attempt to save herself, she tossed up her hands.

And felt the wind nestle into her palm.

Had the situation been any different, Illie would have marveled at the sudden return of her powers. She would have realized it wasn't nearly as cold as she was used to. She would have tried to figure out how, without taking Sinthephane, she was able to override the Dwalenite.

But Illie was about to die, so her fight-or-flight instincts took over, kicking any curiosities out of her head to make room for more adrenaline.

Welcome back, she whispered to the wind.

She gripped it tightly and swung, the rope-like gale lassoing around the navigator. She yanked, pulling him off his feet and throwing him through the air.

He hit the mainmast with a crack that could have been his spine or the wood splintering. Or, she realized with a sick sense of relish, *both.*

The wind curled around her wrist, snakelike, as if it were sentient. She let it; the cold wasn't as bothersome yet. The pinpricks of ice seeped through her gloves, but it wasn't the harsh ache of frostbite. She whispered, *"Thank you."*

The gale cinched tighter around her arm before vanishing to the skies again. Curious, she reached out, grabbing a different breeze.

Illie grinned. Her ability was back.

And then, in a blur so fast she nearly missed it, Ves and someone else tore through the air, diving overboard and landing in the sea with a *splash.*

26

FYNCH KNEW, INEVITABLY, HIS luck would one day run out, but that day simply could not be today. Not with the streak he was having, hitting his mark perfectly every single time.

He'd learned how to shoot when he was far too young to be around guns. Maybe it was luck, maybe it was pure talent that had him knocking the bottles and cans he set up at the end of the alley without fail. Maybe he was blessed by one of the gods – the Wanderer, most likely – to be a perfect shot. If not for his criminal record, Fynch could have joined the navy. He could have ranked *high* as a sniper, given his skill.

But Fynch was a criminal, and now he was siding with pirates, so his chances of following his brother's footsteps were nonexistent. That didn't mean he wasn't skilled enough, though. He was sarding *good* at shooting.

He turned his focus to the navy ship. The way things were, the navy, undeniably, had the advantage. They'd cornered the pirates, trapping them in a cage only escapable through death.

Fynch Largos would not die here.

He aimed, closing one eye to perfect the target. It was an impossible shot, one that would fail if he didn't do it *just* right.

The navy ship's mainmast held on by a single rope, and if that rope snapped, the mast would crumble. They wouldn't be able to chase after the pirates.

He held his breath, ready to shoot, when two people darted in front of him, going right over the railing. If not for the fact that he *recognized* one of them, he wouldn't have cared.

The curly-haired pirate. The one he'd defended in Veridonia. Time stilled. Nobody went after her; maybe because they trusted her to get out alive. But even Fynch knew the waters beneath a fight were dangerous, unpredictable, and by falling in, the pirate had all but sealed her death sentence.

All things considered, Fynch excelled at swimming. He'd been taught at a young age, along with his brother and sisters, and while he'd never *needed* the skill before, he certainly possessed it.

Sard it to hell!

Fynch never pictured himself as a hero, but as he blindly pulled the trigger, hoping – somehow knowing – it would meet its mark, threw his pistol into the crate of ammo, and ran for the railing, he decided if he was going to die, he might as well die heroically.

There wasn't time to hesitate, not as he threw himself over the railing, falling through the air and breaking the surface of the sea.

He sank lower and lower, eyes stinging as he desperately searched for the pirate woman. *There!* Swimming deeper, he grabbed her wrist. The other person she'd dived in with was already swimming toward the surface.

The pirate's eyes were closed, bubbles escaping from her full lips.

Come on! He desperately thought. He wrapped his arms around her torso, but she was too heavy, sinking deeper and pulling Fynch with her.

Bubbles slipped from his mouth, his oxygen depleting the longer he stayed beneath the waves. The bloody clouds in the water would attract sharks soon – bigger creatures, too, if his luck really had finally run out.

A flash of silver darted through the murky ocean, a glint of scales catching the faintest rays of sunlight. *A shark...?* No, sharks didn't *gleam* in the light.

Adrenaline pumped through his body, forcing Fynch to kick his legs. Soaked clothes and a heavy pirate tried to drag him down, but the fear of being devoured by some sea beast kept him going. The murky shapes of the ships sharpened, their outlines definable.

As if aided by Poet himself, Fynch broke the surface. He gasped for air, sputtering sea water out of his mouth.

"Help!" he yelled, struggling to keep afloat with the pirate woman who was still dead weight. "I need a line!"

The pirate with pink hair looked over the railing before disappearing. When she returned, she had a rope. Fynch grabbed it with one hand, awkwardly looping it around the pirate's middle. The pink haired pirate struggled with the makeshift pulley, tugging her companion up the side of the red ship.

A few minutes later, when she returned with the rope for Fynch, a silver spinal fin crested the waves. He grabbed the rope, scurrying up the side of the ship. Collapsing on the deck, he caught his breath before peering back into the water.

The fin was gone.

The last time Solveig stood on the deck of a navy ship, his crew died. He was drugged with sinth and taken away to Ivenis Justyce Penitentiary to await execution.

The similarities were too much for him to have even a shred of confidence.

Now, standing on the deck of the navy's *Meredith*, Solveig looked over his shoulder every thirty seconds, ensuring the *Serenity* still bobbed on the waves, his crew alive.

He swallowed the rock-like lump in his throat and darted across the deck. Sinking a ship while *on* it was a lot harder than sinking it from outside, but he would have to make do. At least most of the navy was on the *Serenity*.

The easiest way to sink a ship was to fill it with water, so Solveig found the doorway leading beneath the main deck.

Before he could descend the steps into the water-filled space, a bang cracked through the air, followed by the splitting of wood.

Crash!

He spun just in time to watch the mainmast topple, breaking through the railing and flipping over to land in the ocean with a splash so big the spray hit his face.

The *Meredith* tipped precariously to the side, weighed down by the broken mast.

Oh, sard it to hell and back...

The *Meredith* leaned further to the side; Solveig slid across the deck, gravity stronger than he claimed to be. Ironic how fate could be. The last time he'd been on a navy ship, his crew died. And now *he* would die.

Solveig sat in the crow's nest of the Sea Wyrm, *arms crossed, and his too-big hat tipped over his brow. A month had passed since Captain Hardy banned the nickname* Piss Boy, *but the whole incident had bruised Solveig's ego like an overripe peach.*

"There you are."

He tipped his hat back just enough to see Thol peering into the crow's nest. At seventeen, he already looked like a full-grown man, with a neat beard across his jaw and his twisted hair piled at the back of his head in a messy bun. The tattoos on his palms – two skulls – still had the irritated bruising around the edges from when he'd gotten them three days ago.

"Go away," mumbled Solveig.

"Nox," Thol sighed.

"Don't call me that. Call me Solveig. All the best pirates go by their surnames." Not to mention, he loathed his first name. It was, in his opinion, the ugliest of all the names his wench of a mother thought up.

Thol heaved himself into the crow's nest, shoving Solveig aside with his hip so his massive self could fit.

"I don't go by my surname," he pointed out. *"But I don't go by Bartholomew, either. Fine, Solveig. I'll call you that."*

He said it the wrong way – Sol-vig. The same way they'd pronounce Mistress Solveig's name whenever they were irritated at her.

Solveig dug his blunt nails into his palms, hardly resisting the urge to throttle Thol right then and there. He dragged his knees to his chest.

Truthfully, he wasn't really upset about the Piss Boy incident anymore. Sure, his face would turn the same red color as his hair when people make snickering jabs about the thing, but that wasn't why he was upset.

He was upset because he was weak.

He'd sparred with the other younger pirates aboard the Sea Wyrm but never once won. He sparred with Thol exactly twice before realizing he would never be able to go up against his sworn brother in a fair fight. He was weak. Absolutely, pathetically weak and he would never survive as a pirate.

And that truth, above all else, hurt.

It hurt like a blunt sword had buried itself in his chest and twisted each time he thought about it – each time he realized he should have died that day the navy came to destroy the children who flew a pre-

tend pirate flag. He should be buried in the ground with the others, not masquerading as a pirate who cried when he killed someone and couldn't hold a sword against someone in a scrimmage.

"Scoot over," Thol instructed, nudging Solveig aside with his hip. Then, he wrapped Solveig in a chokehold and ruffled his hair with his knuckles. "You're sulking. Ah, before you deny it, the entire crew can see it. It's like you have this cloud of doom around you. I won't say who you remind me of, but I think you know. All you need is a notebook and a ridiculous quill and a silk hat."

Solveig did know because there was only one person in the world who made being a gloomy poet his entire personality.

Still, even though that someone was dead and buried, Solveig cracked a smile, albeit a faint one that faded as soon as he remembered why he had climbed up the crow's nest.

"Thol," he said. "Tonight, when everyone is asleep, will you spar with me?"

"Why not –"

"I don't want anyone to watch."

There was a pause, a moment where only the waves splashing against the sides of the Sea Wyrm *and the chatter of the crew below could be heard.*

Then, "Is that *why you're sulking? Because I keep kicking your ass?"*

Solveig's stomach twisted; his eyes and ears burned. "Will you, or won't you?"

"Fine," said Thol. "But you have to stop sulking. There's only room for one gloomy poet with your name, Solveig, and it can't be you."

Cold enveloped Solveig, but not the icy wet of seawater. No, this...this was different. This was something he had never felt before, like liquid ice had wrapped around his torso, crushing him in a hypothermic hug.

There wasn't anything there, but the corporeal rope seeped frost into his bones.

"Hold on!" shouted Illie, and his first thought was *hold onto* what?

Illie. *Illie!*

She grabbed her wind-rope and tugged, pulling Solveig up the side of the sinking ship. Her arms shook and sweat beaded at her brow, but she kept pulling.

If the wind was this cold wrapped around Solveig, he could only imagine how could it was in her hands.

He grabbed at the invisible cord between them, though his hands went through it. He wasn't divine touched.

Illie screeched. At once, Solveig began slipping, the cold rope around his waist dimming until he could only feel the faintest whisper. He clawed at the deck, nails splitting as splinters slid beneath the beds.

The rope wound itself around his torso again, and Illie resumed tugging. As soon as he could, he grabbed the railing and pulled himself to his feet.

"Catch me if I miss," he called to his navigator. Her nose and cheeks were flushed pink, her lips tinged blue.

Sucking in a breath, Solveig steadied himself, then jumped, crossing the distance between the two ships with ease.

Landed, he dashed over to Illie and grabbed her hands, holding them tightly, trying to force his body heat through her gloves.

"Sol..." she whispered, teeth chattering.

"You did good, Illie," he said, and he meant it.

He shrugged off his coat and draped it over her shoulders.

"Keep this safe for me," he said. "They'll be retreating soon."

Tears welled in her golden eyes. She sucked her bottom lip between her teeth and nodded. If she opened her mouth to speak, she would cry instead; he saw the sob forming as a lump in her throat that she tried and tried to swallow.

"We're going to have to take a detour," he said as gently as he could. "Chart a route to Undyne, master navigator."

"A-aye, Ca-ca-captain," she stammered. Fat tears rolled down her cheeks, dripping onto her knees. She tucked her hands into Solveig's coat. "V-Ves is h-hiding. She almost d-drowned."

Sard.

The *Serenity* would be lucky to make it out of this fight.

Still, he nodded. "Go be with her. Keep her safe. I trust you."

He looked for the rest of his crew and spotted only Natha, still fighting the navy captain. He trusted Thol, too, and knew a petty fight wouldn't be enough to bring him down.

So, he took the sword that lay at Illie's feet and went off to defend his cook.

Try Adrian Zimmer did, each blow he threw aimed to be a lethal one. Natha had stopped thinking, stopped doing anything but letting the adrenaline take over. It pulsed through her veins, tidal waves of hormonal fury surging with each rapid beat of her heart.

He punched; she blocked it with her shin, her kick higher than she realized she was capable of.

Gritting his teeth, Adrian grabbed her ankle and yanked, trying to throw her off balance, but Natha was quicker. She brought her leg down fast, breaking out of his grip and landing a sideways kick in his oblique. The solid wall of muscle reverberated pain up her leg, settling in her hip.

It was a pain she could heal later with a hot bath and plenty of rest. A pain that she could deal with after she won because if she lost, she would be dead.

"You *wench!*" he shouted.

"I wasn't one until I met you!"

He was holding back, she realized. Even with his claim to want her dead, he was holding back.

That sarding *bastard!*

Maybe he never would have hurt her during their fights leading up to the divorce. Maybe he would just scream at her and demean her and make sure she knew every derogatory name in the book.

Because to him, she was a woman – one raised in a life of luxury and comfort – and to him, women would always be *weak*.

Natha was not weak, and she would use his own foolishness against him. If he wanted a submissive wench for an opponent, he would sarding get one.

He took a step forward with his right foot – his tell. Adrian always stepped with his right foot before striking. A weird thing for Natha to know, considering he'd never hit *her*, but a fact she knew like the backs of her scarred hands.

(Hands that were hidden behind gloves now because he always commented how gross the scars were, engraining the self-consciousness deep in her psyche).

She did not brace. She did not throw up her own hands to block the fisted blow. Instead, she let his knuckles collide with her cheekbone, *hard*.

Pain struck, knuckles meeting bone in a flash that she felt in her teeth. Her head whipped to the side, blood rushing to the spot that was most definitely already bruising.

Adrian's eyes went saucer-wide. He hated Natha. He wanted her dead, or so he'd claimed. But when she stumbled back, clutching her tender cheek, she saw the fear in his eyes. The *regret*.

What sort of Lady Lightbringer-blessed navy captain punched an unarmed *woman?*

Where are your probabilities now? She thought, smug.

And then she attacked, snatching that sliver of a moment, that tiny crumb of leverage where Adrian Zimmer was too stunned by his own actions to even think about twisting the probabilities into his favor.

She swung her leg, slamming her calf into his head.

Adrian stumbled. The probabilities shifted in Natha's favor the moment he began to fall.

She was not finished.

Natha jumped, straddling his waist and pinning him to the ground. She punched his face over and over. Blood gushed from his nose – broken, after a good crunch to it with the heel of her palm – slicking her fists, but she didn't stop.

"You ungrateful sarding ass!" she screamed. "I gave up my entire life for you! I spent *years* in misery because of you. I did *everything* for you, and you still cheated on me! You still divorced me and dragged my sarding name through the mud! I hate you! I hate you, I hate you, *I HATE YOU!*"

She reeled her fist back, ready to land another blow, but someone grabbed her wrist.

Déjà vu washed over her, taking with it her adrenaline.

"That's enough," said her captain. "We need to leave before they send reinforcements."

She punched Adrian Zimmer one more time, anyway, and when she stood, she kicked him in the side.

Two privates ran over, grabbing Adrian under his arms and dragging him off the *Serenity* to a waiting rowboat.

The *Meredith*, Natha saw with wide eyes, was *gone*.

The navy had lost; the fools were *retreating*.

She'd done it. She'd finally stood up to Adrian Zimmer, even though it was too late. All those comments – about her body, about her scars, about what she'd done with her life, about how she wasn't a real woman because she prioritized work over popping out Zimmer heirs – came rushing in, smothering her.

Natha's knees gave out; Solveig caught her before she could collapse to the bloody deck.

"I've got you," he said, his voice full of more kindness than Adrian Zimmer had ever shown in his entire pathetic life. "I have you, Natha. You're safe. You can rest."

She leaned into him, tears streaming down her cheeks. She buried her face in his chest, the smell of smoke and salt overwhelming but...comforting.

Solveig held her up when her legs gave out again. He didn't so much as scoff when she got tears and snot all over his shirt.

"I'm an embarrassment of a woman." Solveig's chest muffled her words. She gripped the back of his shirt tightly, fingers trembling.

"No," he said. "The only embarrassment of a woman to ever exist was my mother. You are strong, Natha. You are the greatest cook to exist – the greatest cook in all of Syrenis. You are not an embarrassment of a woman; that captain was an embarrassment of a man."

He pried her off just enough to see her splotchy, snot-streaked face. She tipped her head back to meet his gaze, her bottom lip slick with saliva and trembling.

He said, "You are part of my crew, Natha. And I am *honored* to sail with you."

The two kids stood ramrod straight, their wrists bound with salt-stiff rope in front of them.

"The little one dragged me out," Ves was saying. She had a blanket draped over her shoulders, despite the summer heat. Illie sat next to her, her hands curled up for warmth. She'd given Solveig his coat back, though Natha wore it now.

Natha stared aimlessly at the horizon. She'd tried going to the galley to cook something, but Solveig just grabbed her by the shoulders and forced her to sit. He forced all his crew to sit, exhausted as they were. Even Thol, whose only injuries were his split knuckles.

"She did?" Solveig had a hard time believing the blonde wraith was capable of pulling *Ves* – a massive woman more muscle than not – out of the sea.

"I'm a *boy,*" the blond snapped. "And yes, I pulled her out. I also saved her skin in Veridonia."

"You!" Natha exclaimed, her first words since the fight. Even though it had been hours ago, her face still had the tell-tale puffiness of someone who had bawled their eyes out.

Thol, Solveig, and the dark-skinned boy managed to get all the water out of the *Serenity,* though her patches would hardly hold until the Salts Atoll. The boy hadn't protested when Solveig tied him up. The blond, however, put up a fight.

"You're the little thief who stole from me!" Natha continued.

The boy paled. "Sorry, miss. Hungry. At least I returned the plate…"

Natha muttered something about that good-for-nothing restaurant and how she should have done more damage before she left.

Solveig pinched the bridge of his nose. "Who even are you two? Where did you come from?"

"I'm Czardas Rossi," the dark-skinned boy said. "That's Fynch Largos. Just...ignore him. He talks too much. We were stowaways on the navy's ship."

"The blond is an excellent shot," Thol piped up. "Didn't miss a single target."

"I'm the best shooter in the world," Fynch Largos boasted. "You need a sharpshooter on your crew, don't you? Well, here I am."

After the fight, Thol recounted Fynch's performance. He had been the one to shoot the rope holding the *Meredith*'s mainmast up, causing the ship to sink. Loath as he was to admit it, Solveig knew the boy had been pivotal in their victory.

The other one, though...

Solveig's gaze slid to Czardas Rossi. "What can you do?"

"I'm a musician," said Czardas. He glanced at Natha, though it was fleeting.

"We don't need a musician."

Fynch butted in: "If you want me, you get him, too. We're a two-for-one deal. Where I go, he goes. If you want a sharpshooter, you get a musician, too."

Great. Solveig had been the (second) greatest pirate in the world once. Now, he was reduced to a nanny.

"You have to pledge your life – and all your next lives – to the captain," Ves said calmly. She braided Illie's hair into a pink crown, as Illie's hands were too injured to make the precise movements.

"We don't –" Solveig started. Two kids?! It would be a disaster! The crew was supposed to be small. Only *he* would get that royal pardon.

"'I will pledge my final breath to your name, and my first to find you again,'" supplied Thol, that traitor.

"I will pledge my final breath to your name, and my first to find you again." Fynch grinned smugly, not at all bothered by the idea of signing his soul off to a pirate.

Czardas hesitated before repeating the phrase. "I...will pledge my final breath to your name, and my first to find you again."

Thol smiled. As did Ves and Illie, and probably Natha, too, though her back was to them.

Solveig smacked his hand against his face, shaking his head. "Fine. Fine! We have a gunner and a musician. Happy? Welcome aboard the *Serenity.*"

Jonyth Commodore watched the blackened edges of the missive curl into themselves before crumbling to ash, devoured by the fire roaring in the hearth.

He pretended he was on the *Mary Jolene* and not in one of the many guest rooms inside the Veridin Palace.

He pretended the missive was the *Serenity* and not just a piece of paper detailing Captain Zimmer's failure.

The seabird carrying the missive had arrived from Zimmer half an hour ago, but it was dated the day before. He'd wanted to throttle the bird for being so sarding slow, but the royal advisor had been in the courtyard with Jonyth when the creature arrived. He waited until he was in his room to let his anger get the best of him.

Flames consumed the last of the paper, but it didn't matter. Jonyth had the contents memorized.

Admiral,

It is with my deepest regret and guilt that I must inform you that Captain Nox Solveig and the crew of the Serenity *escaped. Even with the use of my ability, the sinth E. and the Dwalenite, the pirates were victorious. The* Meredith *did not survive the fight. I will put in a formal request to have a replacement ship when I return to Veridonia.*

The pirates are stronger than we anticipated. There are seven of them now. I was at least able to get their names, which I listed below.

Nox Solveig, Vesperine Genevieve, Bartholomew Williams, Nathalia Divyne, Illie Valentine, Czardas Rossi, and Fynch Largos.

Captain Adrian Zimmer.

Jonyth stopped pacing long enough to sit at the desk, pulling out a piece of paper and a quill. He wrote a missive of his own, sealing it with a drop of wax and getting up to visit the aviary.

"I need your fastest bird," he told the boy tending to the birds. He held out the scroll.

The boy took it and attached it to a sleek black raven. The bird hopped on one foot before taking off, flying to the sea.

Bonny,
There is a ship in the southern Emerald Sea called the Serenity.
Take it out. Leave no survivors.
I will ensure you get the title of privateer if you do.

J.

PART THREE

27

"Get your grubby hands away." Natha whacked Fynch across the knuckles with her wooden spoon. "You've been here long enough to know the rule: kitchen is off limits to everyone but *me*. Go on. Get." She waved her spoon at him, shooing him away like he was a pest.

He *was* a pest, lingering by the galley whenever he smelled what she was cooking, ready to snatch a plate as if she never made enough.

"But –" he started to protest.

She brandished her spoon. "I will call you when dinner is ready. Does it look ready?"

He peered at the pan on the stove. She'd made a pasta dish – small noodles cooked in a bone broth with roasted vegetables and *plenty* of garlic. Ves had been asking for spicier foods, so she made a chili oil to drizzle over it once the noodles were cooked, along with the shredded garlic-slathered chicken warming in the oven. It was a simple dish, but one that made the entire *Serenity* smell divine.

"It *smells* ready," Fynch said.

She whacked him with the spoon again.

"Get out of my kitchen," she scolded. "If I catch you in here again, I'll feed your portion to the fish."

In the handful of days since Fynch joined the crew, he'd put on a bit of lean weight. At first, he would sneak into the galley at night and eat as much as he could, only to pass out on the floor and get caught in the morning. He still had some bad habits to break, but he wasn't stealing from the galley anymore.

Well, he *tried* to steal, but Natha had little patience.

She set the wooden spoon down and picked up a *clean* one, using it to stir the creamy pasta around, making sure none of it stuck to the bottom of the pan.

"You're still here," she said without looking up, sensing Fynch's looming presence like it was a stain. She gripped the neck of her spoon tightly, knuckles white beneath her gloves.

She did not have to wear the gloves anymore, especially not now that Adrian Zimmer was out of the picture and she'd started her life over, but she'd been self-conscious of the scars for nearly her entire life; keeping them hidden was the only thing she knew.

"Captain told me to entertain myself," he said like he was nothing more than a bored toddler. "And I'm hungry, and dinner smells done."

"Dinner isn't done," she said sharply. "Go scrub the deck if you need something to do. I am not your babysitter."

"That's exactly what Captain told me."

She imagined bashing her head into the wall.

At least he isn't one of your employees, she told herself. If he was, she wouldn't be able to avoid his idiocy. He was...he was crew. He was on her side, annoying as he was.

"Do you *want* to be smacked with the spoon again?" she picked up a pinch of the finely chopped parsley she'd set aside and sprinkled it over the pasta. "Fine. Taste this. Then get out of my kitchen."

She grabbed a clean spoon and scooped up a small bite. She handed it to Fynch, who grabbed it and stuffed it in his mouth. He closed his eyes, chewing slowly.

The little brat had good taste.

"The door is right there," she said, refusing to let her pleasure show. Of course, he liked her cooking. It was *her* cooking.

"Could be cooked a bit longer," he said. "Noodles are too chewy."

She threw her wooden spoon at him.

He scampered out of the galley, shouting, "It's really good, Miss Nathalia!" as he ran.

Natha looked at the pasta again, unable to hide the tiny smile that tugged on her lips.

Huh. She really had found herself a family, hadn't she? All it took was beating her ex-husband to a pulp for her to realize she didn't need a fancy manor for a home or rooms full of expensive trinkets or fake friends who hid vile smiles behind exotic fans and gaudy jewels.

She just needed a ship, a galley, and six people (and one cat) who ate everything she cooked.

She set her spoon down and peeled off her gloves, setting them on a clean stretch of counter. The burns looked wet in the evening light, but they had healed years ago. After all, she had only been a child when she got them.

Fynch did not want to swab the deck. For whatever reason, he'd assumed that was Thol's job. Fynch kept the cannons in pristine condition and the ammo organized, but he refused to touch a mop.

Natha had been one of the last people Fynch visited. He went to bug Czardas first, but his friend was too busy singing with Ves while she wrote up a list of things needed in Undyne. Illie sat in the crow's nest, maps and books spread out around her and her cat, Pleo, sleeping on her lap. Thol was at the helm, of course, sailing the ship toward the island Undyne, Solveig next to him, a mug of cinnamon rum in his hands, the golden liquid spilling over the sides whenever he laughed.

He *could* go annoy Solveig, but the captain would just tell him to polish the cannons or make himself useful and that he was running a pirate crew, not a governess's house.

(Fynch knew what a governess was only because Czardas had one as a boy, and he would always gush about how pretty she was. Fynch thought her nose was too big for her face).

Groaning loudly as to alert the rest of the crew to his boredom, Fynch sulked to the men's quarters, the living space he shared with Czardas and Thol.

It was a major upgrade to the library floor he'd grown used to, with his own hammock and wardrobe (even though it was the size of him. Still, he hardly needed anything bigger) and access to a washroom with a toilet, a bathtub, *and* a shower.

He climbed into his hammock, nestling into the blankets and fixing his gaze on the ceiling. As he shifted, something dug into his hip. Cursing, he looted around until he grabbed something solid – a book.

His brow drew together. It was one of Czardas's books. He must have dropped it in the wrong hammock when he finished reading earlier.

Well, he thought, flipping open the front cover. *Not like I have anything better to do…*

He nestled into his blankets, skimming over the title – *Legends From the Emerald Sea* – before beginning to read.

Of the five oceans, the largest, vastest, and deepest is the Emerald Sea. Home to sirens and krakens and a bestiary of other creatures, the Emerald Sea covers over a third of Syrenis. It is also the ocean in which Poet dwells, though his exact location is unknown. Some speculate he lives in the Triangle of Fylth, the hostile stretch of sea between the islands Servedin, Morgouse, and Gello.

Fynch flipped through the pages, already bored. His hopes for this being a fantastical account of the different myths from the islands scattered across the Emerald were quashed as he continued to skim over dense paragraphs about the history of the ocean and what islands were in it.

A *lot* of sarding isles were in it. It was the biggest ocean and the most densely populated.

A picture stopped his flipping. Fynch's hand hovered over the page, brow furrowed as he took in the image.

Before he could figure out what the coiled...*creature* was, Natha's voice rang out: *"Time to eat!"*

He slammed the book shut and scrambled to his feet, racing to the dining room like it had been months since he last ate.

Illie couldn't sleep that night. She stared at the ceiling, wide awake, her hammock swaying gently as the *Serenity* coasted over soft waves. No moonlight shone through the portholes; dark clouds had covered the night sky before the sun could set. It unnerved her, but she hadn't picked up on any weather changes, and she'd been tracking it all day, meticulously measuring the wind and humidity and currents.

Pleo lay on her chest, purring so loudly that Illie's entire body vibrated. Illie absently stroked the dark stripe running down her back.

Something was not right, and it was *killing* her.

She flexed the hand not currently petting the cat, unable to see the mostly healed blisters on her palm in the dark.

Sighing, she climbed out of her hammock, cradling Pleo to her chest. Careful not to wake Ves, she tiptoed out of the room and up the stairs to the main deck. Natha stood at the helm, head tipped back as she watched the sky.

Pleo wriggled out of her grip, running back to the warm hammock she'd been so rudely taken from.

"What are you doing up?" Natha asked.

Something is wrong something is wrong something is wrong.

She shook the annoying voice out of her head, walking to the helm and sitting on the floor at Natha's feet.

"Can't sleep."

Natha sighed. "I've been there. If you watch the helm for five minutes, I can make you something to drink. To help you relax."

The nagging sensation of something being *wrong* would keep Illie up, warm drink or not.

Dread twisted in her belly, harsh enough to make her nauseated.

"I need to wake Sol," she whispered, clambering to her feet. "Something is –"

Lightning streaked across the sky, so bright it lit the entire horizon up.

No more than five seconds later came the thunder, a deafening boom that rocked the ship. Natha gripped the wheel tightly, refusing to fall even though her knees threatened to collapse.

Illie wasn't paying attention to Natha, though. Her gaze had been drawn to the horizon. The lightning faded, leaving nothing but inky darkness in its wake, but she was *sure* she'd seen something.

"Natha," she whispered, slowly rising to her feet. "Go wake Sol. And everyone else."

She held her breath. Lightning flashed again, and her dread shifted to tangible fear. Her stomach flipped to her throat; her legs went numb.

"Oh, sard it," breathed Natha when she saw what Illie had seen.

There, on the horizon, beneath a swirling mass of thunder clouds alive with slithering lightning, was the beginning of a funnel.

A *massive* tornadic funnel of seawater and wind – wind she could not touch. Wind that was too powerful for her pathetic grasp, for the weak powers Poet had given her.

"Sol!" she cried, forcing herself out of her stupor. Natha nodded once, jumping down the stairs and throwing all her weight against Solveig's door.

Illie had faced waterspouts a few times in her double voyages around the world, but they were meager ones, ones that just rose a dozen feet in the air and dissipated with a splash. She'd never seen one this big, this violent before. Poet himself had materialized his anger and wrath into both his realms – the sky *and* the sea.

And the *Serenity* was about to face the brunt of it.

Her fingertips tingled, aching to grab the winds that had picked up speed, whipping her braid off her face.

Focus, she told herself. Natha would get the others up. They'd be able to help. But for now...

It was too late to outfit the *Serenity* with her storm jib, especially since Illie didn't even know where the sarding thing was.

"Reduce the speed," she murmured, running for the lines to pull the sails up. Her arms turned to rubber under the weight; her feet scraped against the deck, searching frantically for traction that simply would not appear.

Suddenly, the line was taken from her grip. Solveig yanked on it, pulling the sail up before it could get destroyed.

"Waterspout," she gasped to her captain.

Rain came all at once, without warning. Where there had been none before, buckets of it poured down, gallons upon gallons soaking the *Serenity*. Illie's hair clung to her face, the fabric of her shirt sucking against her skin. She peeled at it, but the fabric was too heavy to deal with.

She scraped her hair off her face, blinking water off her lashes and spitting it off her lips.

"Everyone to the middle of the ship!" Solveig shouted. He finished tying the line – Thol, thank Poet, had gotten the other sails secured – and grabbed Illie's wrist. "Come on. Are you a good sailor?"

Not a good enough sailor to avoid this storm! She wanted to cry, but the words turned leaden in her throat. She glanced at the helm – the wheel spun helplessly. There was no way she could wrangle that beast.

"Never mind. Thol can handle it. You know weather, right?" when she nodded meekly, he said, "Good. You're going to get us out of this storm."

Poet, god of the sky and sea, you had better *get us out of this storm.* Praying, Solveig realized, would be useless now, but the fate of the *Serenity* was in Poet's hands.

Terrible, *terrible* odds.

His crew huddled in the center of the deck, soaked and shivering. Raindrops streaked down Illie's cheeks – or maybe they were tears. Czardas clutched Fynch's hand so tight his knuckles turned white.

A wave began to crest, rising high, peaking white at the top. His heart fluttered in his throat.

Thol nudged the *Serenity* to face the wave head-on. She crashed through it; water sprayed onto the deck. Fynch slid, slipping with the ship. Ves grabbed his wrist and pulled him close, nearly crushing him.

"We need a line!" Illie shouted over the wind. "We need to secure ourselves to the railing. Anyone could fall overboard at this rate!"

"And what happens if the ship goes down?" Czardas shouted back.

"She won't!" yelled Thol from the helm. He spun the wheel, forcing the *Serenity* to summit another wave. "Tie yourselves to the railing. A little help with directions, Illie?"

She patted her pockets, pulling out a compass. Even Solveig could see that the needle spun wildly, uselessly. She sucked her bottom lip between her teeth, struggling to figure out *where* to go.

Sard it all. Solveig could not afford to be turned around now. Not with the *Serenity* so damaged. Not with Jonyth so close to catching up.

Not with his freedom so sarding close.

Static charged the air, tugging all the hairs on Solveig's neck and arms erect. Lightning lit up the sky, illuminating the twister barreling closer and closer.

Ves threw a rope, which Solveig barely caught. He looped it around his waist three times, making sure the knot was secure. The others all sported the same line, a tether keeping them secured to the *Serenity* and away from the tumultuous waves below.

I'm sorry, lass, he thought to the ship. First the damage from the *Meredith,* now this...

It would take nothing short of a miracle to get the *Serenity* to Undyne, and miracles were allergic to Solveig.

He gripped the rope tightly. *My name is Nox Solveig,* he told himself. *They will fear my name.*

My name is Nox Solveig. I am born of the salt. The salt will not take me back until I decide I'm ready.

"BRACE!" yelled Thol, his raw bass voice hardly audible over the tempestuous fury that was Poet.

Winds slammed into the *Serenity,* hard and fast, unforgiving, shoving waves into the hardly patched hull with the force of a *god.* Solveig's boots lost traction; his stomach careened, flipping to his throat. He grappled at the line, not ready to trust how sturdy the knots were.

Lightning bolted across the sky. The waterspout was too close now. Any closer and the *Serenity* would be gulped up and torn to shreds.

"THOL!" screamed Ves. She pulled Czardas and Fynch close, her bosom a shield to protect the young boys from inevitable death.

It would not be a quick death, either. It would be gruesome, the winds shredding the ship and her crew. If that didn't kill them, they would fall into the icy Emerald and drown.

The *Silver Moon*'s crew flashed across Solveig's mind. Maybe he would be reunited with them sooner than he'd thought. Maybe he would never find Anwir's treasure, whatever it really was.

The *Serenity* tilted sideways.

Lightning illuminated the sky, ghastly.

Illuminated the wave that crested taller than Keth Mountain in northern Aralyth.

He stupidly tipped his head back to watch as the wave loomed over the ship...

...and came crashing down.

28

"*Where are –*"

"*Rope – stuck –*"

"*Burns!*"

"*What –*"

"*Help!*"

The sounds were too muffled. Too distorted. The air had turned too cold. Solveig couldn't keep up with any of it.

He closed his eyes.

His mother was sick. Everyone pretended to care, everyone doled out false pity (but nothing more), everyone told him how strong he was, how brave he was, how unfortunate it was that he was going through this.

Truthfully, Nox just wanted his mother to die faster. Mistress Solveig was a monstrous wench, and the world would be a much better place with her six feet in the dirt.

Except that was a bad idea because her corpse would rot the earth.

Nox just wanted her gone.

Nobody really pitied her. If they did, they'd bring medicine, food for Nox, anything other than mournful looks cast at a distance.

The Alkenio Plague ran rampant amongst the lower class, and as often as she called herself a madame, Mistress Solveig was the lowest of the low. Nox hadn't been surprised when her gums blackened, when she started to cough, when her irises turned silver, when she was stuck in her bed, quarantined in her room (the only bedroom in the tiny house), but he still checked himself in the mirror every day, worried he might have caught it, too. He hadn't. It was just Mistress Solveig, as though Lady Lightbringer had decided to show Nox a sliver of justice.

Nox sat in the dirt beneath the overgrown trees in the abandoned apple orchard that was technically Solveig property but, like everything else in her life, was forgotten years ago. He poked at a particularly fat grub with the flat end of a stick.

Leaves crunched. He didn't even look up to know that Thol was sitting next to him.

Thol, seventeen, eyed the grub. "Five stone if you eat it."

Nox, twelve, was not in the mood. He wasn't in the mood for anything. The navy's arrival was still too raw. The graves in the yard were still too fresh. The realization that his mother was going to die of the plague and Nox would be the only Solveig left in the entire world was too much.

"Are you upset about your ma?" Thol was starting to look like an adult, with twisted hair and the shadow of stubble along his jaw. He wore discs of moonstone in his stretched lobes, as he always had, but Nox stared at them for a while, watching the opalescence glimmer in the late afternoon light.

The grub inched away quickly, glad to be away from Nox's stick.

"I won't miss her," he grumbled. "I hate her. She ruined my life. She ruined everyone's lives. I'll be glad when she's gone. I just..."

Tears prickled his eyes.

"There's a pirate ship at the marina," Thol said, expertly shifting the conversation before Nox could start sobbing over his wench of a mother. "We should visit. Maybe they'll let us join if we beg. Or we can sneak on... I heard they'll be here for another week or so."

In another week or so, Nox would be orphaned. He would be completely alone in the world, save for his sworn brother Thol – Thol who, years and years and years ago, exchanged a cup of stolen rum (mixed with a lot of fruit juice) and shook his bloody palm with Nox.

He would be the only Solveig left, and that burden was simply too much for a twelve-year-old to bear alone.

He poked his stick into the mulchy dirt, disturbing half-rotten leaves and a few ants searching for fallen apples.

"Nox," said Thol flatly. "You and I are gonna visit the pirates. You've always wanted to be a pirate."

Not true. Not true. *It hadn't been his dream at first because he wasn't the first to dream it. He'd been the youngest once, and he was, as of a few months ago, the youngest again.*

He was the eldest, too, but it was hard being both when he was the only one left.

"Fine," he grumbled.

Mistress Solveig died in her sleep, alone and forgotten, which was too good for her. When Nox peered in through the window the next morning to check on her and saw her bloated, rigor mortis body, flies buzzing around her head, he just stepped down and began walking away.

Good. She deserved to die.

Nox found Thol in the apple orchard. Together, they buried Mistress Solveig. Together, they spat on her grave. Together, they went to town and slipped into a tavern, and confronted the pirate, whom they later learned was named Captain Hardy. Together, they snuck onto his ship.

Together, they left their tiny town for good and set sail, fulfilling the dream of the four who had left them behind.

Solveig blinked against the bright light, head throbbing in tandem with his heart. He tried to swallow, his throat tight and cotton-stuffed.

Shapes began to materialize, dark and blobby at first, then more defined. He pressed the heel of his palm against his eye socket, trying to minimize the dull ache building behind his sinuses.

Why was I dreaming about when Ma died? He wondered, blinking a few more times to clear the salty fuzz from his brain.

Then, without warning, his stomach lurched, and he spewed out gallons of seawater and bile and whatever other contents had previously been in his gut.

The storm. The waterspout. The wave.

His crew!

Wiping his mouth with the back of his hand, he scrambled to his feet, only to be pulled down by...by a line. The rope was still securely tied around his hips, the end frayed and soaked. With shaky hands, he clawed at it, finally getting it loose enough to slip off.

He shoved it aside and looked around. The mainmast was cracked, the railing mostly gone.

And his crew... His *crew.* They were all sprawled out on the deck, soaked but breathing. *Alive.*

A compass! If they were to survive, Solveig needed to figure out where the ship had ended up. He patted his pockets, searching for a compass –

The pocket where he kept Anwir's map was...strangely empty.

Dread encased him all at once. If he lost that sarding map, it was all over. No dead god. No lost moon. No pardon. No freedom.

Solveig would be right back at the gallows, only this time there would be no royal intervention to keep his head attached to his shoulders.

"'Beneath a shadow on the Endless Sea, where the moon once sat upon the waves... The child who watches with a dead eye, a memory forgotten, a field of graves –' Hey! I was looking at that!" Fynch exclaimed, reaching for the map as Solveig snatched it away.

Though a bit damp, the map hadn't been damaged at all. The ink hadn't smudged or run; the thin, ancient paper hadn't torn.

The only problem – and it was a rather *big* problem – was that now Fynch Largos knew about the map Solveig had sworn to keep a secret.

Well, there goes the royal pardon. Anwir would kill Solveig himself once he learned of the broken promise.

"What's with all the yelling?" grumbled Ves. She peeled herself off the deck slowly, wraithlike, and shoved her curls off her forehead. She took one look at the rope around her waist before slicing through it with a knife pulled from gods know where.

"Captain Solveig had a map in his pocket, but he took it from me," explained Fynch, like he was somehow in the right. His hair stuck to his face, making him look like a sad, wet dog.

A pity, then, that Solveig preferred cats.

"A map?" chimed Illie. She untangled herself from the rope and stumbled over, walking with a drunken gait. "Let me see."

He didn't give it to her. Instead, Thol, with his eerie ability to creep without making a sound, plucked the map from Solveig's hand.

He cleared his throat, gravelly from the salt, and read aloud:

> *"Beneath a shadow on the Endless Sea*
> *Where the moon once sat upon the waves*
> *The child who watches with a dead eye*
> *A memory forgotten, a field of graves.*
>
> *North of refuse and east of swindler*
> *Through caverns of salt and blue glow*
> *The child, and slave to eternal night*
> *Will bring the horizon the moons sink below.*
>
> *In chains of the child who once was small*
> *Then coveted, now lost to the sun and time*
> *By thirteen chimes of the clock of the dead*
> *A city of gold gifted to the maritime.*
>
> *A kiss from the writer to see through midnight*
> *A song which death can never touch*
> *To find the core go first up then down*
> *The name of the third moon is such."*

"Nox," he said slowly. "What is this?"

Illie peered over Thol's shoulder. "This type of map is very, very, *very* old. I'm talking hundreds – if not *thousands* – of years old. Where did you even find this?"

Dread turned to ice deep in his belly.

"He was keeping it in his pocket," said Fynch unhelpfully.

Czardas, who had awoken and joined the group, smacked Fynch upside the head. "You sarding idiot, you can't just *steal from our captain.*"

Fynch rubbed the base of his skull, but he didn't look the least bit shameful.

There was no hiding it now. Solveig snatched the map back and shoved it into his pocket, pretending it would be safe there.

"When I was at the gallows," he began. Everyone in the crew – Fynch and Czardas included – knew that he and Ves had spent time in Ivenis Justyce Penitentiary and he had been sent to the chopping block. "Jonyth Commodore was stopped before he could kill me. Stopped by Anwir Helios, the crown prince of the sarding Aralyth Empire."

There was a collective gasp, an exchange of uneasy looks, a slate of betrayal from his sworn brother.

Still, Solveig continued. "Anwir gave me a choice: either I go back to the gallows and accept my fate, or I take this map and find a treasure for him. The body of a dead god. He paid my bounty so I could hire a crew and buy a ship, since Jonyth killed and sank my last one, and promised a royal pardon if I returned with the body of his god in a year."

It wasn't *technically* a lie.

But it wasn't the full truth, and by omitting the most important detail – the detail that only *Nox Solveig* would get the pardon, and if his crew waltzed into Aramore they would hang from the gallows at best, be sent to Ivenis Justyce at worst – it was almost *worse* than outright lying.

And maybe he should have told the truth because there was a *joy* that danced from member to member of his crew – a joy at the possibility of being *forgiven,* of being allowed to sail the seas as they pleased without having to worry about the navy because the most powerful empire in all Syrenis *protected them.*

He should have told the truth.

Gods, he should have.

Because if he had, he would not be getting punched by the first half of *PUNISHMENT,* right in his tender jaw with enough force to make him see stars.

"What is *wrong with you?!*" Thol snapped. "Why would you hide something like this from me? From *us?* We are your *crew,* Nox. We swore an oath, and this is what you do? You hide things from us?"

Illie added, her voice whisper soft, "Were we even going to the Salts Atoll? What about the lost moon? If I'm supposed to be your navigator, why couldn't you trust me with a map?"

Her words, spoken in such a broken tone – glass shattered that could never be repaired – almost hurt more than Thol's fist.

Czardas and Fynch hadn't known Solveig long enough to be truly, deeply hurt by his secrecy, but Czardas still shook his head, disappointed. "We could have helped. Probably."

"And if you didn't want us to find the map, you should've hidden it somewhere else," said Fynch.

"*Shut up,*" Czardas hissed, shoving Fynch hard enough to cause the boy to stumble.

"You're working for Anwir Helios?" asked Natha. "For the Helios family?"

She was from Veridonia, the kingdom whose first son was
promised to the wretched Iori Helios, Anwir's tyrannous little
sister. The future queen of Veridonia, the future ruler of Natha's
home. Working for that very family was as deep of a betrayal as it
got.

"Is no one going to say it?" Ves snapped, and Solveig's stomach
sank. It was one thing to incur the wrath of *PUNISHMENT,*
but the Witch of the Sea? The woman who sank an entire naval
fleet and killed a kraken? The woman who was sentenced to four
years and counting in the lowest level of Ivenis Justyce Penitentiary,
Seven-B?

There was a reason Solveig wanted Ves on his crew. He did not
want to make an enemy of her.

And yet.

And yet, he had. He'd kept something so petty from her – from
all of them – because, for some *idiotic* reason, he had decided it
would be better to follow the orders of a prince than to trust his
crew.

They would never trust him again. Not that he blamed them;
he wouldn't trust himself if he was in their shoes. If old Captain
Hardy had kept something from his men, Solveig would never
have forgiven him, nor would he have believed another word that
came out of his mouth.

But Anwir –

No. Anwir wasn't to blame; Solveig alone was.

His shoulders slumped, defeat weighing him down. "I'm sorry," he said because it was the only thing he possibly *could* say. "I didn't want to put any of you in danger by telling you. Jonyth slaughtered my old crew; I can't have that happening to you."

"Maybe, *Solveig,*" hissed Ves, "you should have thought of that before keeping things from us. What kind of captain keeps things from his crew? Not a very good one."

"We can argue later," interjected Illie. She looked as uncomfortable as Solveig felt, shoulders tense and lips twitching as she tried to figure out what to say next. "The ship is badly damaged. We should make sure she's still operable and get back on course for Undyne –"

"Oh, sard the ship!" shouted Ves. "You are in *no* position to order us around, *navigator.* I outrank you, so shut up."

Thol stepped between the two women; Natha grabbed Ves's wrist, but Ves smacked her away.

"I outrank the both of you," Thol said. "So you *both* need to shut up. Illie, check our course. Ves, go take inventory. I don't care that it's *my* job; I'm assigning it to you. Czardas and Fynch, clean the deck. Natha... Frankly, I don't care what you do. Nox, you're coming with me."

"Yes," muttered Solveig, because even though he was the captain, he was still Thol's younger sworn brother, and no matter what, he would always be inclined to answer to him.

Thol gestured for him to follow; Solveig hung his head and obeyed, trailing Thol below deck to gather supplies to make any repairs.

"I hate you right now," Thol said, shoving wooden planks into Solveig's arms. "The only reason I'm not leaving is because I swore an oath – not to you, to *him.*"

Him.

Solveig swallowed the lump in his throat. "Be mad at me later, after you've listened to my reasoning. After we've fixed the ship up and are back on track to Undyne."

Thol just huffed and went back to the deck.

"I don't know much about pirate flags." Fynch ambushed them, speaking without any preamble. "But black flags mean pirates, right?"

Both Thol and Solveig just blinked. Fynch was, as it seemed, allergic to context.

Thankfully, he continued to ramble: "Cause Illie spotted a ship and it's coming to us, and it *might* be help, it *might* be another ship that was caught in the storm, or it *might* be pirates."

"Why...why do you say that?" Solveig asked slowly. The tension between him and Thol was thick enough to eat. Enemies would only worsen that.

Fynch gestured to the horizon, like that might help. "She said she couldn't see the name of the ship, but she saw that they were flying a black –"

"Oh, for the love of Poet, *get to the point!*" Czardas shouldered Fynch out of the way. "They were flying colors. A black flag with what looked to be a rabbit on a moon."

If Solveig thought things could not get much worse, he was proven very, *very* wrong with those words.

All the color drained from his face; Czardas and Fynch saw it – they both scrambled to ask their captain what was wrong.

It was funny how things worked, how things seemed to make a perfect circle where no circles should exist. The very pirates he'd fought, landing him with a dead crew and a burning ship and veins full of Sinthoxine, had found him again.

"Bonny Reed," whispered Thol.

"Sard it to hell!" Solveig laughed because there was a strange bit of irony in the whole situation. "The Rabbit Pirates have found us."

29

NATHA KNEW OF THE Rabbit Pirates, partially because of the *wanted* section in the newspaper she combed through every day and partially because, well, when she was younger and not tied down to Adrian Zimmer, she'd developed a schoolgirl crush on the captain, Bonny Reed. In her mind, it was perfectly reasonable: Bonny Reed would never know of her existence, and anyone with eyes would agree that she was beautiful. She wasn't the most beautiful woman in the world – that title had been given to Empress Nefeli of Merdyne – but she was damn near close to it.

Bonny Reed, she silently recited, remembering the newspapers from Veridonia. *Fourth most wanted. Captain of the Rabbit Pirates, sailing with the* Moon Rabbit. *Bounty of four hundred eighty million lune.*

"What's the likelihood that they're not here to attack us?" she asked. The *Serenity* was in shambles, the crew was pissed at each other, they still hadn't fully recovered from their fight against Zimmer and his men. Going up against Reed would be a death sentence for them all. The Rabbit Pirates outnumbered them ten to one, the *Moon Rabbit* twice the size of the *Serenity,* at *least.*

"Slim," said Solveig grimly. "The only scenario where they wouldn't attack us is if their ship is abandoned and the whole crew is dead. Reed and I... We don't get along."

Natha cursed silently.

Well! Piped up that unhelpful little voice in the back of her head. *At least you get to see Bonny Reed before you die!*

"We need to prepare for a fight," said Thol. "The *Serenity* is in no shape to outrun a galleon of that size."

He muttered something about the *Serenity* being in no shape to fight, either, but it seemed Natha was the only one to hear his grievance.

She clenched her hands into fists, scars pulling taut beneath her damp sleeves. "Well," she said. "At least it's a good day to die."

Fynch grabbed as many guns as his arms could carry – it was surprising how many were stashed on the *Serenity* – and made sure each was loaded with full rounds. He shoved them into his belt, into holsters strapped across his chest, into his boots, anywhere they could fit and be easy to grab. The last thing he wanted was to be caught in a fight with no weapon, and reloading took too much precious time.

"What am I supposed to do?" asked Czardas, who only knew how to wield a rapier – the only weapon the *Serenity* did not have, apparently.

"Do I look like the captain?" Fynch shoved another pistol into his boot, grateful that the *Moon Rabbit* was far enough away that he'd been able to change into dry clothes – they all had, thankfully.

"Right now, you're the only one I trust, and I'm starting to think that's a terrible mistake."

Maybe stealing from Solveig had been a bad idea in hindsight, but *Czardas* didn't have any reason to be mad at Fynch. That was supposed to be *Solveig*.

"Go ask the *captain,*" he snapped. "I don't suppose you can just *serenade* them into leaving us alone."

Fynch didn't have any reason to be mad at Czardas, either, but he'd always been good at holding grudges for stupid reasons.

He checked the last two pistols, making sure they were loaded, before twirling them around his forefingers.

Fourteen guns would hardly be enough to stop a massive pirate crew, but Fynch would try.

Illie put on her thickest pair of gloves, tight over her wrapped hands, and prayed to Poet that there would be no Dwalenite, no Sinthephane to stop her from using her abilities. Without her abilities, she was useless. She couldn't take down opponents three times her size like Natha; she couldn't throw knives with expert precision like Ves; she couldn't shoot a target a hundred yards away with her eyes closed like Fynch; her punches weren't strong like Thol's; she couldn't use a sword like Solveig; she couldn't even reload cannons or make repairs as quickly as Czardas.

But she could control the winds and turn them into whips that obeyed her every command. She could wrap them around her body, serpent-like, and invoke the wrath of Poet through her hands.

So long as there wasn't any Dwalenite to stop her.

The *Moon Rabbit* was close enough that she could see the colors on the flag without a spyglass. Her fingers itched to grab the wind, to make sure her ability was still there. Checking would be too great of a risk. Reliant on her ability as she was, she simply couldn't risk burning her hands with frostbite before the battle had begun.

She glanced at Ves, who was perched at the helm, polishing her sharpened knives. She *could* ask her if she could see the Rabbit Pirates' souls, but their fight was still a fresh wound, one Illie didn't want to pour salt in yet.

She went to Thol instead. He looked up from his knuckle wrapping – the strips of fabric protected his still-raw split knuckles that had yet to scab over properly but revealed the *PUNISHMENT* tattoo he was so infamous for – when he heard her soft approach.

"If you do me a favor," she said slowly, carefully, in case he, too, was mad at her for overstepping bounds, "I will owe you."

He tied off the bandage and flexed his fingers. "You don't have to owe me anything. We're crew; crew is supposed to work together."

He was mad, just not at her.

She almost – *almost* – pitied Solveig for incurring Thol's wrath.

But he was a liar, and he had kept something so vitally important from everyone else, so she was mad at him, too.

"I... I need to ask Ves if she can see any souls," she said, then felt a wave of guilt because she hadn't explained the Dwalenite in detail. She had told the others that Adrian Zimmer's ship had been coated in something that kept god blessed abilities at bay and there was a drug to counteract it, but that was it.

"Because of that paint?" he cocked a brow.

"Dwalenite," she said. "I don't want to grab the winds yet and risk frostbite, but..." she trailed off.

"Tie your hair back so they can't grab it," was all he said before marching to the quarterdeck.

Shucking off her gloves, Illie wrapped her braid in a tight bun at the back of her head.

A moment later Thol yelled: "She can see them!"

Relief crashed down on her, washing away a weight that had settled on her shoulders. But...it was short-lived because Thol added: "She counted eighty."

Czardas piled a stack of wooden planks close to the doorway beneath the deck. After the rush to fix the *Serenity*'s hull during the fight against Adrian Zimmer, Czardas and Thol found as many supplies as possible to repair the ship should another fight catch them unprepared. Boxes of nails, hammers, and rubber mallets were lined up next to the planks. With little fighting experience and the slimmest bit of shipwright experience, he decided he would do best making small repairs and staying out of the way so the others could fight their battle.

For someone born on a stage and raised beneath a spotlight, it was...odd to be behind the scenes now.

Not that he could truly complain. Behind the scenes was safe. Behind the scenes would keep him from getting killed.

His hand throbbed beneath the bandage he wore. The puncture from when he'd slammed a nail through his palm was mostly healed, thanks to a grueling cleaning with half a bottle of cinnamon rum, but it still ached every now and then, especially when he flexed his tendons. Playing the violin had become difficult, so he – reluctantly – kept the case stuffed in his wardrobe (closed, because the last time he left it open, Illie's cat Pleo decided it was the perfect place to sleep).

He shoved his other hand through his curls, forcing them off his face long enough for him to stack a few more boards.

Footsteps creaked on the stairs; Czardas spun around to see Thol lingering in the doorway.

"The supplies are all ready," Czardas said. "Cannonballs are by the cannons. Bullets are wherever Fynch stashed them. Pleo is sleeping in Illie's wardrobe."

"After this is over, I'll teach you how to throw a proper punch," Thol said.

The last thing Czardas wanted was to use his hands – his perfect hands, crafted for creating music – for violence, but he just nodded.

Thol started for the stairs, only to pause and glance over his shoulder. "It's going to be dangerous down here. You could get hit with a stray cannonball. You could get swept out to sea."

He'd already considered both those possibilities. The chances of him dying were higher than the chances of him surviving.

But at least he would die doing something to protect his crew.

His crew. His…his *family*. The people who saw him as Czardas, not *Czardas Rossi* the famous musician, not *Czardas Rossi* the future Rossi duke. Just Czardas.

He didn't mind the idea of dying as *just Czardas* if it meant he did something important with his life – something more important than playing the same symphony to the same crowd every other night.

"I know," he said. "But someone has to make sure the *Serenity* doesn't sink, and that person must be me."

Thol's lips quirked into a half smile. "You're braver than the rest of us, then. Don't die, Rossi. Our adventure has only just begun."

If not for the oath she swore deep in the bowels of I. J. Pen. and the bloodlust surging through her veins like her own personal strain of Sinthoxine, Ves would have left her captain to fight alone. She wanted to. Dreamer's teeth, she wanted to. Nobody kept secrets that big from their crew and expected forgiveness.

But she swore an oath, and she had spent four years locked away, unable to give into the cravings for violence, so Ves shoved her knives into the sheaths bedecked across her body and watched with her other sight as the *Moon Rabbit* charged toward the *Serenity*, black flag whipping in the wind, cannons brandished, eighty souls glowing like beacons.

Eighty enemies.

Rookie numbers compared to what she'd done before.

Witch of the Sea. She had sunk an entire fleet once. She could sink this ship by herself, too, but where was the fun in that?

She wanted Solveig to suffer a little bit, too.

Her gaze narrowed, homed in not on the souls but on the ship itself, on the way it tore through the waves faster than the *Serenity* could ever dream of going. The figurehead came into full view – a woman with rabbit ears and a sphere in her hands that, once the ship got closer, resembled a single moon.

An ironic symbol, considering it was the third moon they were trying to find.

The *Moon Rabbit* showed no signs of slowing, no signs of pivoting to block off the *Serenity* in the typical "crossing the T" formation pirates at sea favored.

She squinted.

A glint of silver caught the light, and her stomach sank to the very bottom of the Emerald Sea.

Bonny Reed wasn't going to stop or switch to usual tactics. Her ship's figurehead wasn't just another busty woman like Serenity was.

She was a weapon. Out of her shoulders, out of the moon, out of the space around her jutted massive spikes.

Reed was going to slam her ship into the *Serenity,* skewer it to cross over, to slaughter Ves and her crew, and leave their ship as nothing but flotsam.

Even with the distance she was at, Ves could make out the cloud of curls that was Bonny Reed, her hair like living flames, like a puddle of freshly spilled blood, the kind that would attract only the deadliest of sea predators to feast.

Without a master helmsman to maneuver the *Serenity* out of the *Moon Rabbit*'s trajectory, she was screwed.

Ves's daggers suddenly felt more like butter knives than actual weapons.

I need to tell them, the unhelpful voice that sounded a lot like Captain Mali piped up in the back of her head.

Ordering the crew around after she'd just snapped at Illie for insubordination would be hypocrisy, and Ves was no hypocrite.

She swallowed around the dread materialized as a lump in her throat

The *Moon Rabbit* was close enough now that Ves could see the twisted grin on Reed's face.

Sard it to hell. Hypocrisy be *damned.*

"Starboard!" she screamed. *"Everyone starboard, NOW!"*

Ves's scream rang out, barely settling before Thol saw the spikes jutting out of the *Moon Rabbit*'s bow. He'd just come up the stairs when he heard the shout. Praying Czardas heard the warning, he grabbed Fynch's upper arm and dragged him to the other side of the ship.

The *Moon Rabbit* hit the *Serenity* mere *seconds* later.

The *Serenity* tipped, impaled like a fish. Waves crashed over the railing, sluicing water across the deck.

"Stay on our turf!" shouted Solveig. "No crossing over. No taking hostages. No taking treasure. We fight to survive, and then we flee. Nobody is allowed to die!"

"Aye, Captain!" said Thol. He could be angry later; now...now he had to *fight*.

"Aye, Captain!" the rest of the crew – Illie, Ves, Natha, Fynch, even Czardas below deck – returned.

Solveig's green coat whipped in the wind. His cutlass hung by his side, shining silver and sharp.

Pride, despite his anger, swelled in Thol's chest. That was his best friend, his sworn brother. The man he'd sailed with before and stepped out of retirement to sail with again. The man he had, one rainy night sixteen years ago, sworn to protect.

The man he had promised his final breath to, the man he would, in the next life and the one after, find and serve again.

The man before him was all of those, and he was also the second most wanted pirate in the world. The pirate with a bounty of five hundred million lune on his head, the one who escaped death at the gallows because the heir to the Aralyth Empire needed his skills.

The man who had gotten them out of so many scrapes before – the navy cadets in Lenwell, the Rouge Pirates at Bowhead Rock, the navy in Veridonia, Adrian Zimmer and his crew...

Thol let go of Fynch when the boy started to squirm.

"If you can somehow sink their ship with a single shot," muttered Thol, "I will forever be in your debt."

"A debt that can be paid with bands of lune, gold, and enough food to keep my stomach full 'til I die?" Fynch grinned. "You've got yourself a deal, old man."

"Fynch," said Solveig without looking over his shoulder. A shiver ran down Thol's spine. That was Captain Hardy's voice. That was the ice-cold tone of a captain who had looked Death in the eye and laughed. "I want you to shoot their flag. Destroy it. They might have made the first move, but we will hurt them more."

Thol watched as Fynch's face split into a grin so wide his own cheeks hurt. *"Aye,* captain."

He spun his pistol around his forefinger before taking aim and firing – one round after the other after the other. Three consecutive shots tore through flammable fabric.

Flames ate away at the flag, leaving a gaping hole in the middle.

There was no going back now. Either they would win, or they would die trying.

30

THE FLAG BURNED, ASH raining down on the deck of the *Moon Rabbit* like snow. Bonny Reed grinned down at Solveig; Solveig grinned back. There wasn't a single bit of humor in either smile, just teeth and bloodlust and wrath.

"Well, well, well," she drawled, her accent thick – like Solveig's own subtle lilt, only ten times harsher and less understandable. "Noxy Solveig. What happened to your last ship, hm? Your last crew? They really that replaceable?"

Ice spidered down his spine.

"Don't act dumb, Reed. We both know you know what happened," he spat.

Reed's grin stretched wider, red lips pulled taut across a freckled face. She truly was beautiful, if not for the predatory hunger gleaming in her olivine eyes. Red curls almost rivaled Ves's, fanned around a slim, pale face marred with more freckles than there were stars in the night sky. She still wore her wedding band on her left hand. In fact, it was the only ring she wore, like Solveig with his moonstone ring.

"I cannot *wait* to gut you," she purred.

Then, viper quick, she struck.

Not Solveig, not any of his crew, but...*herself.*

She shoved a syringe into her jugular, pumping her veins full of an unnaturally green liquid. *Sith,* logic told him, but sinth was red.

Reed cackled. Her veins, beneath freckled skin, glowed the same lime green as a python's scales. Deadly. Venomous.

The color flooded her irises, her gums, her tongue. And when she struck, for real this time, Solveig was so distracted by the not-rightness of it all that he was distracted.

That he caught her blow – the swing of a boot – with the side of his face.

He stumbled, head whipped to the side from the force of the steel toe cracking into his cheekbone, hard enough that the bone should have broken but by some miracle or another, it didn't. At least, he didn't think it broke, but with that single kick, adrenaline surged, blocking any logic and numbing his pain.

"*Attack!*" yelled Reed.

"Take them down!" ordered Solveig. He spat out a glob of bloody saliva.

Reed's grin didn't falter. She brought her leg up, then swung it down like an axe. Solveig threw up his sword, blocking her blow with the flat edge of his blade. Reed forced her weight into the kick, trying to snap Solveig's cutlass clean in two.

Moving quickly, he ducked out of the way, pulling his cutlass with him. Reed stumbled, gravity catching up to her.

Solveig was fast, but Reed... She was faster. Whatever drug she'd injected in herself made her *superhuman.*

He fought her once, winning by mere scraps. She fought dirty, ignoring all the rules, but she was not divine touched. As far as he was aware, she was a normal human. A very strong human.

But the way she moved, darting through the air in a blur, grabbing Solveig's wrist and twisting it back...

There was nothing human about that.

She squeezed his wrist, trying to activate his reflexes and get him to drop the sword. He kicked her in the stomach, forcing her to stumble back in surprise, if nothing else.

"Ohhhh," she cooed. "I see why Jony Boy is so obsessed with you."

Jony Boy?

For the second time during their brief fight, Solveig was distracted, and this time, he deserved it when Reed kicked him in the ribs hard enough that he *felt* them snap.

He coughed up blood, nerves screaming in agony.

Bonny sarding Reed hadn't stumbled upon the *Serenity* by chance.

She had been sent by *Jonyth Commodore.*

There was no coming back from destroying the Rabbit Pirates' flag. Fynch hadn't quite made a name for himself; he could have hidden below deck with Czardas and waited the fight out with Bonny Reed and her crew none the wiser, but *he* destroyed their flag. He shot three rounds through it, setting it ablaze and turning it to ash.

You're a sniper, he reminded himself. With the cannons as useless as they were, he couldn't fire them. He had to rely on his pistols.

And what better place for a sniper than as high up as he could go?

He fit one of his pistols between his teeth and darted for the ladder leading to the crow's nest. It was the best vantage point for a sniper but also the most dangerous. If the mast tipped, Fynch was as good as dead.

Ignoring the fight beneath him, he climbed higher and higher until he tumbled into the crow's nest.

From so high up, he could survey the battle. At least a third of the Rabbit Pirates had boarded the *Serenity,* if not more. Solveig was in the middle of a fight with the redheaded captain, and he quickly spotted the others – tall Ves, taller Thol, pink-haired Illie, Natha with her white coat.

Gods, he prayed as he aimed both his pistols at the pirates on the *Moon Rabbit, please keep Czardas safe. Protect him. If someone needs to die, spare him and let it be me.*

He fired round after round, hitting his mark cleanly each time. Bullets tore through skulls, through hands raised with weapons, through throats and chests. First blood had been Bonny Reed's claim, but the first kill?

That was all Fynch.

Click. Click.

He dropped the pistols, replacing them with two from his belt.

Then, he saw it. The target he needed to take out to shift the tides, to put the favor in his court.

A grey-haired woman with gloves and a long coat checking the pulses of the pirates Fynch shot and wrapping bandages around bloodied wounds.

The ship's doctor.

As long as she was alive, she would keep the pirates in fighting condition. As long as she was alive, Fynch's crew, with their lack of a doctor, would be on the losing end.

He had to kill *her.*

He aimed both pistols at the back of her unsuspecting head, fingers curling around the triggers.

Natha pressed her back against Ves's, relying on her for cover for a few precious moments while she caught her breath.

"You good?" Ves glanced over her shoulder.

Natha wiped her upper lip with the back of her hand, grimacing at the sheen of blood left behind. Some bastard decided her face would look better with his fist in it, and she hadn't been able to move out of the way fast enough to evade the punch. She wriggled her nose, making sure it wasn't broken, just bloody.

"Does *pissed off to all hell* count as 'good'?" Natha asked.

Ves slashed her knife horizontally across a pirate's throat, sending a hot spray of blood soaking her face.

"It means you're not dead, Love, so I'd count that as a good thing."

A pirate charged at Natha, drawing a groan out of her. She reached back, putting her hands on Ves's shoulders, using her as an anchor as she jumped up, planting both feet into the pirate's chest and knocking him back.

"Someone is about to die." Natha landed on the deck silently. "The next idiot who tries to put their hands on me is getting a snapped spine and a one-way ticket to reincarnation."

"Well, damn, Blondie." Ves threw one of her knives and turned around, cutting down a pirate who was charging at Natha. "You want to talk about it, girl-to-girl?"

She absolutely did. For so long, after the divorce, nobody bothered to ask Natha how *she* felt. How *she* was handling being uprooted and abandoned.

She swung her leg out, clocking a pirate in the side and throwing him back.

"I divorced Adrian Zimmer because he was cheating on me," she said, letting all her hurt out. "Well, it didn't go well. He kept the house and almost everything in it because money bought the judge's favor and he had a sway with the royal family that even *I* lacked, despite me being close with them for years!"

A pirate ran; she grabbed his arm, twisting it back so far it snapped. He let out a scream; Natha kicked him in the face, his nose crunching under the heel of her boot.

She continued, "He always said I worked too much. That I, as a woman, belong at home. I think he married me because of my pedigree – I'm from a noble family, too, just a *lesser* one – so I could give him *pure* babies. I am not having children. Not now, not ever, no *thank you.*"

A scream tore through the air behind her. She glanced back just in time to get a face full of pirate blood. As if she needed anything else to make her day worse.

Another pirate snuck up on her, reaching for her throat. Groaning, Natha kneed him between the legs. She grabbed his shirt and yanked, tearing off a piece of fabric. She scrubbed at her face with it, getting as much blood off as she could.

"I'm a professional chef!" she exclaimed. "I studied at the greatest school in the *world*. I am, quite possibly, the best chef on Syrenis. He was a mediocre navy captain at *best*. If either of us should have quit our job to manage the household, it should have been *him*. Him! So, we get divorced, my life becomes hell, my cooks are the most incapable idiots in the world, and now here I am, bleeding because some *sarding wench kicked me in the face!*"

She dove between Ves's legs, narrowly escaping a grubby hand that had been aiming to grab her hair.

"Well, Blondie, seems like you've earned the right to punch a few fools in the face." Ves helped Natha up with one hand, the other busy carving an enemy's eye out. The screams didn't even rattle

Natha. Ves chuckled, "We should get drunk after this. Go tear up Cap's clothes or something."

Natha's heart fluttered at the idea. She grinned one of her rare grins. "All the more reason to stay alive, then."

Don't fail me now, Poet, prayed Illie. She sucked in a breath and reached out, nearly laughing from the sheer delight of feeling a wind slither into her waiting grip. It slithered around her arm, colder than ice, waiting for an order.

"Go," she breathed.

She reared her arm back and whipped the wind out, knocking three enemy pirates down like dominoes. Calling the wind back, it coiled around her arm again, patient. Waiting.

Freezing.

She bit her inner cheek. It was cold, but she could handle the cold a bit longer. She had no choice but to, lest she let her crew die.

BANG! Without even thinking, she threw the wind, knocking the enemy's bullet off course. It whizzed past her ear, singeing the stray wisps of hair that fell free from her braid.

The frost burn tingled her fingertips beneath her gloves. She grabbed another gale, stretching it like taffy. If she could somehow knock the *Moon Rabbit* off the *Serenity*...

Come on, she thought, projecting her words to the frisky gale in her hand. It squirmed, writhing like a sentient worm, a snake ready to strike. *Give me your best.*

She threw it as hard as she could. Her shoulder snapped, the pain reverberating all the way to her toes. The wind raced, whipping faster than it had been made to go, crashing into the side of the *Moon Rabbit* with enough force to rock the ship.

But not enough force to pry it off.

And then *she* was flying across the deck.

She hit the railing hard enough to knock the breath out of her lungs. Gasping like a beached fish, she struggled to her feet, reaching for the wind that had been taken from her.

Glowing green eyes and a matching absinthe grin filled her vision, the smell of alcohol and fish assaulting her senses. A greasy pirate stared down at her, everything about the way he moved *unnatural.* Jagged, rigid, like he was a puppet.

"You must be Illie Valentine," he drawled. "Divine touched navigator. Only worth ten mill, but I can make do. What'll it be, princess? Dead?" he pulled a knife from his belt and ran his glowing tongue over the blade. "Or alive?"

Below the deck, Czardas hammered boards into place, trying desperately to patch the holes torn open by the *Moon Rabbit.*

He had narrowly escaped being skewered, Ves's earlier warning just loud enough to get him to move out of the way. The same could not be said for the *Serenity.*

Water poured into the hull, sloshing around his ankles. There was no time to toss it out; he had to focus.

Three holes had been patched so far.

At least a dozen remained.

The *Serenity* creaked beneath his feet, an agonized moan.

"I'm sorry," he murmured, hammering the last nail in before grabbing another board and a handful of nails, moving to the next hole. "I'm sorry, girl."

The *Serenity* groaned again.

Czardas knew how to read sounds, and the sounds the ship was making were painful.

She was dying, and only Czardas knew it.

31

SLIDING HER KNIFE ACROSS the throat of one pirate, Ves shoved the blade through the eye of another. She ripped it free, squealing in disgust when his eyeball stayed on the blade like an olive. A very juicy, bloody olive.

She flicked it away as fast as she could.

"Squeamish?" asked Natha. She punched an oncoming enemy twice before kicking him both in the chest and the jaw. She flipped through the air and landed silently on the balls of her feet.

"Women can't be squeamish." Ves swung her blade in an upward arc, cutting an assailant's hand off at the wrist. Blood rained down. She didn't even flinch. "But it's *gross* when their eyes come out."

Swords clattered around them, mixed with gunshots and the sounds of screaming and bodies falling into the ocean. Ves's heart thundered against her ribs. There was no time to pause and make sure her crew was alive. The second she looked away from the fight was the second she forfeited her life.

And she had *just* gotten that life back.

She spun, stabbing her knife through the cheek of one pirate, tearing it free and jamming it through the soft spot under another's chin.

Blood slicked her skin, sluicing over her cheeks and chest, turning her yellow shirt crimson. She grinned, feral, bestial.

The Witch of the Sea was back.

The more she moved, the faster she spun, the more the scab on her back pulled taut. Any more outrageous movements and the scab would tear.

Her wound would reopen.

That, she decided, would be a problem for *Future Vesperine*.

She jammed her knife into the sliver of fleshy space between another pirate's ribs. She started to pull the blade free.

A hand grabbed her wrist, grip hard enough even *she* couldn't pull free.

"You've Amazonian blood in your veins," said a woman. A woman whose gaze Ves had to tip her head back to meet. She grinned, gums the same burning green as her eyes. "So do I."

She slammed the heel of her palm into Ves's nose.

The doctor did not fall. Blood did not bloom. Even at a distance, Fynch could see that.

Someone had intervened. Someone had stepped between the doctor and the bullet. They stared in Fynch's direction, holding something pinched between two fingers.

He didn't have to see it to know what they held.

A single spent bullet. One meant for a doctor's skull.

Somehow, someone had *grabbed* it midair.

His stomach flipped, an unfamiliar sense of dread turning his adrenaline into something much worse. He pressed his back against the crow's nest, like that would somehow protect him as the someone with the bullet stepped closer to the *Serenity*.

They pulled their arm back and threw.

The bullet soared through the air with the same velocity it would have had it been shot from a gun.

Oh, gods – he started to helplessly pray.

The bullet tore through wood and fabric, flesh and muscle and bone, and wood again as it went through the crow's nest and Fynch's chest and right out of the crow's nest again.

His eyes went wide, body not quite registering the pain yet.

Stop the bleeding, a voice ordered in his head. His brother's voice – one he'd tried so hard to forget, back to haunt him now that he was going to die.

He laughed, a wet, gurgled sound as blood spilled over his bottom lip and chin.

I'm going to die, he thought. *I'm going to die, and nobody is going to realize it until it's too late.*

Blood spurted from the wound. His heart shuddered, pumping out more blood, blood that filled his mouth when he tried to exhale, wet and sticky. He pressed his hand to the wound, somehow still surprised when it came back slick and red.

With a shaky hand, he lifted his pistol and fired until it clicked, the chamber empty.

He took a gasping, rattling breath and dropped his pistol over the side of the crow's nest.

Through the adrenaline, the dull throb began to pulse, spreading white-hot from his chest to each of his limbs. His brain fought a foggy haze, screaming at his body to get up, get up, get up and stop *dying!*

But his body simply could not move, not as it slumped down. Blood seeped into his trousers, and, through the shock-filled hysteria, he laughed again. It was several weeks too early for him to be bleeding through his pants, yet here he was.

He was unconscious before his head hit the railing.

Thol would always be the first target in a fight. It was something he'd gotten used to at a very young age because even at a young age, he had been anything *but* a small boy. He had never met his mother, and his father had decided he did not want a son when Thol was four, so he couldn't ask him about her, but he always suspected his mother was from the island Amazonia – an all-women warrior tribe under Merdyne's rule. Amazonians were tall and muscular by design, and Thol's father had been a shrimp of a man.

Amazonian blood or not, Thol was tall, and being tall meant he stood out.

And standing out in a fight meant he was a target.

He had no reason, then, to be surprised when a sword slashed across his chest, threatening to reopen the thick, old scar he already had and narrowly missing his memorial tattoo.

He still was surprised, though.

Because only *once* in his life had someone dared to cut him.

He skidded across the deck, fingers brushing against the wound and coming back red. It stung, but that was a good thing. If he couldn't feel it, it was too deep, and he wouldn't survive the fight. Shallow wounds hurt more, but he had a better chance of surviving.

He balled his hands into fists, ignoring the sting of split knuckles beneath his shoddy wrappings. The joint in his pinky finger throbbed dully. Fractured, most likely, if he was lucky. Shattered if he wasn't.

The pirate flung his sword out, flicking Thol's blood off the blade to mar the deck of the *Serenity*.

"I have heard of you," the pirate said. "Bartholomew Williams. The pirate who fights with his fists. Somehow, I was expecting you to be more...well...*exceptional.*"

He charged, sword held high.

Thol curled his hands into fists, knowing it was foolish to fight against steel with his bare hands.

He swung anyway.

Natha had half a second to watch Ves's nose break before her hair was yanked, and she was on her back, the wind knocked from her lungs and eyes staring unfocused on the descending boot of her enemy. She rolled to the side, narrowly avoiding being crushed. Inhuman green eyes stared at her.

The pirate moved too fast, faster than any living thing Natha had ever seen, and she had seen rats scurrying out of her storeroom, fish darting through the waves, her ex-husband jumping out of her bed after she walked in on him with another woman.

The pirate grabbed Natha's throat and pinned her to the deck, squeezing her windpipe. Kicking and thrashing, she clawed at the pirate's wrist, desperate to get a breath into her panicked lungs.

She brought up her foot, slamming it between his legs. His grip loosened just enough for Natha to squirm out.

The pirate darted again, and before she could blink, she was on the deck again.

No. Not on it.

Wood splintered around her as she was slammed *through* the deck.

She cried out in pain as wood splinters stabbed into her unprotected sides, as the pirate squeezed her throat and shoved her down *harder.*

Wetness seeped across her back, soaking her shirt. *Sarding hell,* she managed to think. Blood –

No. It was cold. *Very* cold. Not blood, then. Not blood, but *seawater*.

The knife slid through Illie's shoulder slowly, drawing an agonized scream from her. The green-eyed pirate laughed and twisted the blade. Tears flooded her eyes as she screamed and screamed.

Wind! She begged, but her hands were trembling too much to grab hold of a gale.

"Oh, you're a screamer," cooed the pirate. He leaned close and ran his tongue along her face, licking the tears she'd shed. "I think I'll take you alive just to hear your pretty screams again."

He ripped the knife out and pressed the blade to her throat. Panic made her legs numb. Blades weren't supposed to be taken out of wounds. It would only cause the person to bleed out.

She was bleeding out.

Illie knew what blood looked like. Every moon since she turned twelve, she dealt with blood. Her sister had perished after coughing blood into their mother's fancy silk handkerchiefs. When she held the wind for too long, her frostbitten blisters would burst bloody.

But she stared at the wound as it squired her lifeblood out, and she, stupidly, thought, *it's very red.*

The dawning that she was going to die settled over her in the form of another stupid thought. *Mary, Baba, I guess I'll be seeing you again sooner than I thought. Mama, Henry, Elgar, Pleo... I'm sorry.*

The perverted pirate pressed the blade harder.

She squeezed her eyes shut and braced, praying to Poet her death would be quick. "You'd kill me," she hissed, "if you weren't a sarding coward."

32

REED KICKED SOLVEIG IN the aching, broken ribs hard enough to send stars to his cloudy vision. He stumbled back, coughing up another glob of blood that splattered on the *Serenity*'s deck.

She cracked her neck and stalked closer, her eyes burning that inhuman green.

"I heard Jony Boy killed your crew with Sinthoxine," she said casually, calmly, as if it wasn't one of the most devastating things to have happened to Solveig. "And I'm sure Zimmer would have used Sinthephane. That's navy only."

She drew her sword and twirled it through the air. Solveig clutched his broken ribs.

"But this... This makes you *stronger*. Faster. A hundred times so." Her grin stretched impossibly wider. "It's *Sinthide*. And it's what's going to kill *you.*"

In the fraction of a heartbeat, Solveig was thrown across the deck. Reed dug the heel of her boot into his ribs, crushing the already broken bones. He arched his back off the deck, screaming as pain unlike anything he'd ever felt before tore through every fiber of his being.

She had him in the air again just as fast, gripping him by the collar and holding him a few feet off the deck with just one hand, the other still holding her sword.

She angled the sword, prepared to skewer him with it. Heart beating faster and faster, he clawed uselessly at her hand, knowing that if he did not get out of her grip in the next second, he would die.

Captain Nox Solveig, cloaked in green, set out to conquer the Emerald Sea. One day he'll go down to the drink. How many navy ships will he sink?

Solveig was not divine touched. He had not trained with the navy only to decide piracy was more appealing. His father was not a pirate – not that he knew. He'd never met the deadbeat. He didn't come from a long line of sailors. His mother had been a wench up until the day she died alone in her bed, and there was nothing special about wenches. He was just a human.

Just a man.

What could a man do against someone inhuman?

What could a man do against Death?

It was inevitable that he would die at sea, that he would die today, but his crew. His *crew*. He would not let another crew die.

Spots danced in the corners of his eyes. His hands spasmed. If he didn't do something soon, it would all be over.

There was a second part to the oath, one that Solveig whispered to each of his crew members so softly only the gods were his witnesses.

I will pledge my final breath to your name and my first to find you again, they said.

And he, in response, whispered, *I will carry you to the ends of the earth and never let them forget your name.*

He could not be defeated now. He hadn't fulfilled his oath.

Reed thrust her sword.

Solveig kicked her in the stomach.

The blade sliced across his thigh, ripping through muscled flesh and drawing blood, stopping just short of his chest.

Even with Sinthide coursing through her veins, Bonny Reed was still human, too.

She doubled over, instinctively protecting her squishy organs, and that was enough for Solveig to tear himself out of her grip.

Without skipping a beat, he swung his cutlass.

She flung hers up, blocking his blow.

Solveig jumped back and swung again, feinting left before swinging at full strength to the right.

Reed moved faster than she should have, sliding under the blow and jamming the pommel of her own blade into Solveig's side.

Shattering *more* ribs.

He stumbled, feet losing traction as he slid over blood and sea-water. Moving his arms was becoming more and more tedious.

He could hardly hold his sword with all the strain on his chest. The cutlass dipped; his shoulders tensed. It became a conscious motion to relax them. Clenched shoulders would slow him down. Clenched shoulders would lead to sloppy blows.

Go for the unguarded areas, a tiny voice whispered in his head. *Confidence trumps weight. Force trumps weight. If you believe you can cut through bone, you sure as hell can.*

He shifted his feet, sinking low on bent knees. Blood streaked from his nose, from his mouth. His green coat billowed in the wind.

Around him was carnage, raw and destructive and bloody. And standing amidst it all, furious as the heart of a storm, was Nox Solveig.

He moved first, darting toward Reed. She raised her sword to defend. Solveig swung in a clear attack...

Only it was a feint.

He went low, slashing upward. His cutlass met little resistance as it severed bones and muscle.

Reed's hand fell to the deck with a meaty thunk. The blood that squirted from the stump was more serpentine green than oxidated red.

She screamed, and Solveig struck again, grasping that precious second of pause to cut her *other* hand off. It, too, fell to the deck, along with her blade.

Ragged and panting hard, struggling to get a decent breath around his ribs, he pointed the tip of his sword at her throat. "Surrender," he demanded. "Retreat."

"No!" she spat. Her true eye color bled around the edges of the green, her tongue and gums dulling to a muddled shade of greenish-pinkish-brown.

"You will regret that."

He kicked her hands away – not like she could reach them regardless. She had been defeated, whether she would admit to it.

It was time to protect the rest of his crew.

Solveig spotted Ves first, engaged with another woman nearly her size. Ves ducked under the other woman's punch, but she wasn't fast enough. A fist collided with her jaw. She stumbled, nearly falling.

Thol threw up his arms, blocking a sword before it could strike him in the face. Metal tore through flesh like it was paper, slicing to the bone.

Illie was thrown to the deck and pinned there, blade above her throat, ready to pierce. She didn't fight, didn't reach for the winds.

Natha and Fynch were nowhere to be seen, and that...

That was somehow worse.

I will carry you to the ends of the earth and never let them forget your name.

He hadn't found the lost moon. He hadn't brought his crew on the grand adventure they all longed for. Instead, he'd damned them all. He got one crew killed, and now...now he was about to lose another.

I want you to find the body of the dead god for me, Anwir had said.

Why in Poet's name am I thinking about Anwir *when my crew is about to sarding die?!*

No. Not Anwir. The god. The dead god of the third moon – the moon Ves sang about, the moon Illie dreamed about, the moon he promised he would bring his crew to, and the moon that was absent from the sky as the other two, Mene and Sin, rose in the lavender haze of dusk.

Aster, the brightest star, was there, too, and that...

That, not the moons, not the screams of his crew, was what caused him to move.

Solveig grabbed the front of Reed's shirt and dragged her to the *Serenity*'s broken railing.

"My name!" he shouted, drawing everyone's attention toward him. "My name is Nox Solveig. *Captain* Nox Solveig. Your captain can no longer swim."

It was true. Blood gushed from her matching stumps, getting all over Solveig's boots.

"If you wish to save her life, you will surrender now."

He leaned down, lips brushing against Reed's ear. "You will tell Jonyth that if he wants to kill me, he has to do it himself."

And then, holding Bonny Reed to his chest, Nox Solveig fell backward into the Emerald Sea.

33

"YOU CANNOT DIE," WHISPERED a voice – a voice so familiar yet unrecognizable. It filled Solveig's head like cotton. *"You can't!"*

His eyes were closed. Or perhaps they weren't. It was too dark, really. Open or not, everything surrounding him was pitch black.

"Nox! Wake up!"

Ves sat on the deck, her body so sore she was unable to move, watching as the Amazonian woman dove off the side of the *Serenity* to fetch her captain.

Then, she saw the amputated hands and promptly threw up.

And *then,* stomach sufficiently emptied, she got to her feet and raced to the side of the ship, desperately searching the waves, filtering out the flitting souls of fishes and distant whales as she searched for the only soul that mattered.

He had lied to her. But he was her sarding *captain*.

Nox Solveig, where are you?

She counted one soul – the Amazonian, sinking deeper and deeper. Her sight strained.

There! Another soul, and another, entwined tightly, and another, a fourth soul glimmering...silver. A color she had never seen before, but it didn't matter right now.

She started climbing over the railing when something cold wrapped around her arms, pulling her back.

Illie.

"Are you trying to get yourself killed?" Blood wept from her arm, far too much to be normal. Ves faltered, reaching out to press her hand against the wound.

Thunk, thunk, thunk –

Splash!

Ves didn't see him jump in, but she saw his soul diving down and, moments later, four souls resurfacing – the Amazonian with Reed and...

"Give me a rope!" Thol shouted. Solveig slumped over his shoulder, not moving. She couldn't tell if he was breathing.

Illie moved first, whipping out a rope of wind. It must have wrapped around Thol's hand because he was being pulled out and Illie was tugging on something only she could see. Blood spurted from her wound under the new strain.

Thol collapsed on the deck with Solveig. He wasted no time pressing his hands against his chest, forcing water out and air in.

Ves's eyes welled with tears as she watched.

"His soul," she whispered. "It's still there. It's faint, but it's there."

Thol simply nodded and continued with his compressions.

Ves spun around the deck, searching for the rest of her crewmates. Two souls beneath the deck, bright and alive, and one...

One soul flickering, dying.

Gathering up what little strength she had left, the Witch of the Sea bolted for the crow's nest, praying she wasn't too late.

Fynch sat in a puddle of his own blood, skin ashen and face slick with sweat. His breathing was shallow – a gasping wheeze barely even there. Blood blossomed in a grim flower on his chest, right over his lung.

In his hand, his grip so loose it hardly counted, was a pistol without a single bullet left in the chamber.

"Stay in there, Little Bird," she whispered, silently thanking Dreamer that his soul was still there, that he was still alive. "I'm going to fix you up. You are not allowed to die on me, Birdie."

She brushed a lock of damp hair off his sweaty face.

"Illie!" she called. "I need you to make a net out of your winds. I need to get Birdie down, but I can't risk moving him too much. He's... He's barely breathing. I'm going to jump."

She scooped Fynch up, careful not to move his legs too much. She tried to keep him in a sitting position, cursing when more blood wept from the wound.

"I got you, Birdie," she breathed.

His soul flickered weakly in response.

"Cooperate," Illie commanded the wind. She grasped at a flitting gale, wrangling it into a forced submission.

Never in her life had she been able to hold more than one wind at a time, but as she stepped on the first gale, she reached for a second. Her hands burned, the cold so intense it felt like hellfire wrapped around her hands.

She gritted her teeth together, swallowing back a scream. Between her bleeding shoulder and the frostbite spreading down her fingers, the pain was more than anything she'd ever known before.

One wind in each hand, she forced them together, creating a blanketed current.

"Sarding cooperate!" she hissed, snapping the wind like a whip to get it to settle down.

It did, after one last bout of rebellious coiling, flattening into a breeze so still it hardly seemed to be there at all.

She had no way of knowing whether it would hold.

She had no choice but to believe it would.

Sucking in a breath, she yelled, "It's ready!"

She prayed to Poet, to any of the gods who gave a damn to listen, that the wind would break Ves's fall. That she and Fynch would survive. She still closed her eyes, turning her head when Ves leaped over the side of the crow's nest.

The patches would have to make do. Czardas had done everything he could, but by the time the spikes receded, there were more holes letting seawater in and no more boards to keep it out.

Natha lay in the shallowest water, Czardas's torn waistcoat tied around her head to stanch the bleeding there. She'd fallen from the deck above, bruised and bloody and hardly conscious. She was teetering on the edge of unconsciousness now, so Czardas did the only thing he could think of to keep her awake.

He sang.

Well, he hummed since the song didn't have any words. The *Eldoria Symphony* was, as far as he was concerned, strictly instrumental, so he hummed as loudly as he could, ignoring the volume markers he'd memorized, hoping it would be enough to keep Natha from slipping into unconsciousness as he smashed up crates and shoved the splintered boards against the holes.

"One..." Natha croaked, voice bubbly from the water. "One...over here..."

He paused humming to look over. She pointed at a board floating in the shallow water – a deck board, broken but... Big enough to patch one of the smaller gaps. He'd run out of *actual* boards several holes ago.

"You're a genius, Miss Natha," he gushed and dove for the board, grabbing it and nailing it to the biggest remaining hole before another surge of water could rush in.

"The...song..." she whispered. "What...?"

"It's..." he hammered the last nail in, ignoring his throbbing palm. "It's a symphony I found in the hidden library at my estate. The *Eldoria Symphony*. I don't know where it came from, but it's my favorite thing to play."

Natha sighed out, softly. "It's nice... I think I'm going to sleep now, Czardas. Thank you for keeping –"

She didn't finish the sentence.

Czardas dropped his hammer and rushed over to her, shaking her shoulder. "Miss Natha? Miss Natha, wake up!"

She didn't wake up, but the water by her nose rippled ever so slightly. Unconscious, but by the mercy of all four gods, *alive.*

Thol slammed his broken fist into Solveig's ribs, the cracking of bone and cartilage deafening.

"Wake up," he demanded. "Nox, wake up. I can't lose you. I can't lose you, too. Not after I just got you back. You're my sarding *brother!*"

He only cried twice in his life: when Captain Hardy died and when his wife and daughter died. He didn't cry when his other brothers were taken from him.

He cried now, tears slipping down his cheeks.

"Wake *up*, Nox!"

He slammed his fist into Solveig's chest again, the second half of *PUNISHMENT.*

Solveig coughed out a mouthful of water and gasped in a lungful of air.

34

ONE WEEK LATER...

Solveig stood at the bow of the *Serenity*, nursing a mug of cinnamon rum. His ribs had been bandaged so tightly that he felt like a mannequin every time he tried to move, but the pain wasn't as sharp now as it had been the past few days.

Illie strode up behind him, a newspaper clutched in her bandaged hand. Her other arm was nestled against her chest in a makeshift sling. Luckily, she hadn't broken any bones, but the wound was still deep enough that Thol, the stand-in surgeon until they found one (he claimed there was one in Servedin who could help – someone named Isra), instructed her to wear the sling until he was sure the scab wouldn't reopen.

"There's good news and bad news," she said, her voice light enough to suggest otherwise. "Bad news: none of our bounties went up. Unfortunately. I was hoping I could break a hundred million."

Her bounty of ten million lune was still extraordinarily high for an upcoming pirate like herself.

"Good news, though: we *all* have bounties, and we are all wanted dead or alive." She held out the newspaper. Solveig stiffly took it and skimmed the posters.

Czardas Rossi, eight hundred thousand lune. Nathalia Divyne, eight hundred fifty thousand lune. Illie Valentine, ten million lune. Fynch Largos, sixty-nine million lune. Vesperine Genevieve, three hundred seventy million lune. Bartholomew Williams, four hundred fifteen million lune.

Nox Solveig, five hundred million sarding lune.

Next to the posters was the list of the navy's most wanted. He still sat comfortably in the second place, but Bonny Reed wasn't there anymore. Ryuu Nova had taken her spot at fourth, and in fifth...

Bartholomew Williams.

Pride swelled in his chest seeing his brother's name there.

Just then, the door to the ex-closet-current-surgeon's-room swung open, and Ves stumbled out. She hardly made an appearance nowadays, preferring to stay in the cramped room to make sure no souls flickered out.

Natha had sustained two broken ribs and a concussion that turned her into a raging wench two days after the battle against the Rabbit Pirates when she decided her headache had to be everyone's problem. After plenty of sugary coffee and lots of rest, she was back to normal, spending all her time in the galley.

Ves only suffered a broken nose that she set back into place herself with minimal fuss. She'd been the one to stitch Thol's chest and set his fractured hand. She'd also been the one to scold him for jumping into the Emerald with an open wound.

Besides a healthy dose of shock, Czardas had come out unscathed. He, along with Illie and Solveig, were the least injured, even though Solveig needed ten stitches in his leg and had eleven broken ribs.

"He's awake," Ves gasped, breathless. *"He's awake!"*

There was only one *he* she could be referring to.

Solveig dropped his cinnamon rum and the newspaper, racing Illie to the open door. Thol and Natha were right behind.

Czardas sat on the edge of the thin cot, tears streaming down his cheeks as he hugged Fynch as tightly as he could.

Fynch, who had been unconscious for the past seven days, barely surviving a bullet wound to the lung, just sat still, dazed.

In those precious moments after Ves jumped from the crow's nest with him, landing in Illie's net of wind, it was a race against time and death. Thol had the most medical knowledge, even though that was a rather generous title, so he was the one to make sure the bullet was out. He was the one to stitch the wound, to seal Fynch's lung back together.

For seven days, he was unconscious, and nobody thought he would ever wake up.

"What...?" Fynch whispered, his voice gravelly and raspy. Then, the pain must have caught up to him because he flinched, shoving Czardas away. Pleo, who had been sleeping contentedly on Fynch's freshly abandoned pillow, picked up her head, opening one lazy eye to observe what had disturbed her.

Czardas explained everything. The fight, Ves getting him down, Thol bringing him back to life, all of it. And Fynch just sat there, silently absorbing it all.

Then, softly, he said, "There was a man on the other ship who threw a bullet at me faster than my guns can shoot. I want to learn how to do that. I want to be the greatest sharpshooter Syrenis has ever seen."

Czardas rubbed his eyes with the back of his sleeve. "I want to learn the origin of the *Eldoria Symphony* and write one of my own."

It was a soft, intimate moment between friends. Friends who never thought they'd see each other again. Friends who transcended the boundaries set by the word, becoming *brothers* instead.

But they weren't alone. They had a crew.

Natha spoke up first: "I want to visit every island in the world. I want ingredients from every land so I can make something Syrenis has never seen before."

Then Ves, who was crying but trying very hard to keep her tears to herself (Solveig made a point of not looking at her tear-stained face): "I want the world to remember my name. Those who forgot the Witch of the Sea will remember who I am for the rest of time."

Illie said softly, "I want to make a map of the world like the lithograph of the Wandering Isle. One that moves with the tides and currents, one that tracks every subtle motion there is. And... And I want to find the missing moon."

Thol smiled one of his rare smiles. "I want to be the strongest pirate in the world." The true meaning behind his words was left unspoken: *I don't want to lose another brother ever again.*

Solveig thought of the map in his pocket – the map that somehow survived his ocean plunge. Thousands of miles away, Prince Anwir Helios sat on his throne, waiting for Solveig to return with an impossible treasure. The body of a dead god. The legendary third moon.

Taking a breath, he put his hand over his heart and said, "As your captain, I will carry you to the ends of the earth and never let them forget your name. I will lead you to the greatest treasure of all time."

He grinned, and his crew grinned back.

"I will bring you to the lost moon."

Epilogue

Jonyth Commodore was not usually a smoker, but he lit four sugar cigarettes and stuffed them all in his mouth, breathing in the sickly-sweet oxygen and exhaling a plume of smoke.

Bonny Reed, bandaged stumps locked together with Dwalenite cuffs and veins full of Sinthoxine, glared at him as she was pulled through the gaping doorway of Ivenis Justyce Penitentiary, dragged by Lakatos Justyce, the warden himself.

He lit a fifth cigarette and gnawed on the ends.

Bonny Reed was supposed to have killed Nox Solveig. How was that idiot still alive?

Three navy admirals stood off to the side, watching Jonyth as he stormed back to the *Mary Jolene*.

Prince Anwir Helios stood at the gangplank, arms crossed. "You should be celebrating, Commodore. Another pirate was just locked away."

If the man before him had been anything other than a prince, Jonyth would have used his face as an ashtray for his five cigarettes. He swallowed a cloud of smoke instead and spat the cigarettes out, smushing them out with his boot.

"Don't be so smug, your Highness," hissed Jonyth. The crown prince and the navy fleet admiral had the same power. Nobody else could talk down to the heir of the Aralyth Empire the way Jonyth did.

"If I knew you would struggle to catch a single pirate, I wouldn't have given him a head start." Anwir uncrossed his arms, following Jonyth up the gangplank and onto the polished deck of the *Mary Jolene.* "I thought you were stronger and cleverer than a meager pirate."

The scar on his face throbbed, as if the mere mention of Nox Solveig was enough to get it to hurt. He dug his nails into his palms, fury boiling in his chest.

"He's not just *a* pirate," growled Jonyth. "He's a demon."

"He isn't even your most wanted."

The Unnamed God was another of Jonyth's problems, but nowhere near as big of a thorn in his side as Solveig was. Oh, how he wanted to strangle that son of a wench...

"Solveig gave me a message," Bonny Reed had spat when the Dwalenite cuffs snapped closed over her wrists. *"If you want him dead, go after him yourself."*

If not for the will of Emperor Castros Helios, Jonyth would. He would hunt Solveig down and gut him like a fish.

But Emperor Helios had other plans. Let his influence smother the Veridin Kingdom. Secure a marriage for Anwir. In the newspaper that day, next to the smug poster of Nox sarding Solveig, was an article that had piqued the interest of Emperor Helios and the distaste of Anwir: the king of Gello was sick. Quarantined. If it was the plague, he'd be dead soon, and his daughter, Princess Leianora, would become the queen.

Jonyth reached for the pack of sugar cigarettes. Anwir grabbed his wrist, stopping him from stuffing another five between his teeth.

"Are you a coward, Commodore?"

Rage struck Jonyth right in the gut. He dropped the cigarette he'd been holding, letting it bounce and roll to the edge of the deck, teetering close to the railing.

Jonyth Commodore was *not* a coward. He didn't claw through the ranks, going from cadet to private, commander to captain, vice admiral to admiral to fleet admiral for nothing. He had *earned* his position, his title, his power, his prowess.

He regretted not swinging his sword faster that day at the gallows.

"You're the one who freed him," seethed Jonyth. "Why are you against him now?"

The prince lazily leaned against the railing, dark hair blowing in the summer breeze. "Why not?" he said with a regal air of nonchalance that only pissed Jonyth off more. "I want him to bring me something. Doesn't mean I'm rooting for him. Doesn't mean I don't want him to struggle. This is all a game to me, Commodore. The world will be mine one day. Why not remind its people of that fact?"

His Helios eyes slid over to Jonyth, oily and dark.

Before Jonyth could commit regicide, he stormed to his quarters, slamming the door behind him and locking it for good measure.

He swept everything off his desk, letting it clatter to the floor in a mess that would only irritate him more when he inevitably had to clean it later. Papers scattered, ink pots shattered, and a single flyer floated down, landing unscathed atop the mess.

Jonyth grabbed it and slammed it against the wall, pinning it there with the dagger he'd kept at his hip, the blade buried in Nox Solveig's forehead.

A coward, huh?

Jonyth Commodore was not a coward. He was ruthless, and he would not stop until Nox Solveig was dead.

The man who had no name (and ironically no divine blood in his veins, despite the nickname) leaned back in his chair, eye skimming over the newspaper in the dim light of his cabin. His ship rocked gently in the waves, stationary a mile or so off the coast of the Wandering Isle.

Not many things caught his attention these days, but this certainly did.

He knew the names, of course, because for a man without a name himself, he was quite good at remembering the names of others, and he knew their faces. Their bounties.

Seeing those names printed on the paper beneath the infamous words *dead or alive* did not draw his attention. He had those words printed beneath the made-up name given to him by the very people who wanted him dead. Even the pictures – faces that might have made his heart skip a beat once, but no more (mainly due to the fact that he simply refused to acknowledge the presence of the organ anymore) – didn't catch his eye.

It was the article printed on the next page, squished next to a piece about royal drama and the occupancy in Servedin that pulled his attention.

Captain Nox Solveig of the *Serenity* defeats Captain Bonny Reed of the Rabbit Pirates. Reed sent to Ivenis Justyce Penitentiary to await punishment. Rabbit Pirates disband.

"Nox Solveig..." he murmured, pronouncing the name the way it appeared written. Just because he was good at names did not mean he was good at saying them correctly.

Or perhaps he did know it was *Sol-vay* and not *Sol-vig*, but he simply did not care to correct it.

Beneath the mask that covered every inch of his face – including his eyes – he grinned.

"I'm coming, Nox Solveig," he said to himself. He set the paper down and reached up, unfastening his mask and setting it down. Alone in the darkness of his cabin aboard the *Nameless* he tipped his head back, bare face angled to stare at the mural painted on the ceiling.

A night sky with three moons stared back.

The Unnamed God touched his fingers to his chest, right above his heart, in a silent oath. *"Wait for me."*

To be continued...

ACKNOWLEDGEMENTS

FOR ME, THE ACKNOWLEDGEMENTS part of a book is good for two things: thanking the army of people who helped me get here and serving as a "behind the scenes" look into what the author (me!) is really like when they aren't writing epic battles and what-not.

Hi!

First, I want to thank my mum for reading this before anyone else (my mum only likes books with romance, short chapters, and no cliffhangers. Oops). And also just for being the greatest mum in the world. To my dad, who doesn't really like to read but would read to me when I was younger, fueling my love of weird books from the start. I guarantee you won't read this book but maybe you'll read the acknowledgements for funsies? Also, thank you for answering all my weird medical-related questions. Why use Google when your dad knows everything?

A special thank you to my sister Penny who, when I started obsessing over pirates, threw gasoline into the fire. I wrote 99% of this book under all your goober art. Piss Boy Supremacy <3

Thank you to my lovely partner for giving me weird names and for listening to me gush about this world I created without complaint. If this story ever becomes a TV series, I want you to play Solveig. (Duh).

To all the wonderful people on Instagram and Threads for hyping me up, for adoring my art, for loving *The Lost Moon* before it even became a real thing. You guys saw that I wanted to write a book about pirates and devoured it right away. Thank you. Ily all so much.

To the musicians in Nightwish and Seven Spires for creating the music that inspired this all. Without you, the world of Syrenis wouldn't exist. Nox Solveig is because of *you,* and while the chances of anyone from either of those bands reading this is next to nothing, I'll thank you regardless.

To Eiichiro Oda, who created the greatest pirates in history, who sparked my love for the high seas and adventure, whose story has changed me for the better. It is an honor to exist at the same time as you and to be able to enjoy everything you make.

Have you guys seen the *cover?!?!* Absolutely amazing. I legit cried when I first saw it. Thank you, Aster, for bringing my story to life.

To Lysandra and Andarna. You guys did absolutely nothing but you're cute so who cares. Also, to my childhood cat Pleo, whom Illie's cat is named after. You were the sweetest little thing and I miss you dearly.

To you, the reader (and to the booksellers and librarians). Out of all the books in the world, you chose mine. Thank you, thank you, thank you.

And to Dani. There isn't a day where I don't miss you. Rest in peace, my love. We'll meet again in the next life.

The search for the lost moon continues in

THE DRAGON KING

About the Author

Emma T. Shannon has been writing since before knowing how to actually write. On the rare occasions where they are not writing, Emma can be found hunched over a drawing, circling the same shelf at the local bookstore, obsessing over 2D men, and singing loud enough to annoy the neighbors.

Emma lives in the dreary PNW with their tiny house tigers Lysandra and Mephisolou, their tiny house dragon Andarna, two cursed dolls, and more tarot cards than they know what to do with.

Instagram @goth.witch.writes

Threads @artem.mxrtis

ko-fi.com/artemmxrtis

Milton Keynes UK
Ingram Content Group UK Ltd.
UKHW031255251024
450245UK00001B/51